D1496703

CANDIDATES FOR THE BACHELOR'S DEGREE—1855
Oliver Lyman Spaulding is in the center of the back row and S. P. Millikan at the extreme right.
(From the original in the Oberlin College Library)

A HISTORY OF OBERLIN COLLEGE

From Its Foundation Through the Civil War

BY

ROBERT SAMUEL FLETCHER

Volume II

OBERLIN COLLEGE
OBERLIN, OHIO
1943

PRINTED IN THE UNITED STATES OF AMERICA
BY R. R. DONNELLEY & SONS COMPANY
CHICAGO, ILLINOIS, AND CRAWFORDSVILLE, INDIANA

TABLE OF CONTENTS

LIST OF ILLUSTRATIONS

Some Abbreviations Used in the Footnotes

T.M.	MS minutes of the Board of Trustees of the Oberlin Collegiate Institute and Oberlin College.
P.C.M.	MS minutes of the Prudential Committee.
F.M.	MS minutes of the Oberlin faculty.
L.B.M.	MS minutes of the Ladies' Board.
A.H.M.S. MSS	Papers of the American Home Missionary Society.
Sec. Off.	Office of the Secretary of Oberlin College.
Treas. Off.	Office of the Treasurer of Oberlin College.
D.A.B.	*The Dictionary of American Biography.*
D.N.B.	*The Dictionary of National Biography.*

See the "Partial List of Sources," page 925 *et seq.*

Book Four

Learning and Labor

"Each student belongs still to the world, not isolated from sympathies and obligations and activities. The ends he pursues are such as appeal to men in general, the reputation he desires is the same that will serve him in the work of life, and the motives to excellence are the natural motives which operate on men at large. . . . The college is a place for education, not merely for the acquisition of learning, . . . The great object is such a discipline as is qualified for service in the world."

JAMES HARRIS FAIRCHILD,
Inaugural Address as President of Oberlin College, August 22, 1866.

"The administration of the college was certainly of a high order; its discipline and control of a thousand students—adolescents of both sexes—I believe to be unequaled in success. Indeed the chief merit of the Oberlin community to my mind is to have evolved such an educational institution, in whose spirit the pupil's participation was itself an education apart from its curriculum of studies. [¶] On the other hand there was weakness in instruction; . . . though it certainly was equal to the average of Western Colleges of that time."

DENTON JAQUES SNIDER
(A. B., 1862), *A Writer of Books* (St. Louis— n. d.), 156–157.

CHAPTER XXXII

THE STUDENTS—PIOUS AND PRUDENT

APPROXIMATELY eleven thousand men and women and boys and girls were enrolled in all branches of the institution from 1833 through 1866.[1] Of these about 6500 were males and a little over 4800, females. Eleven thousand youths thus came under the influence of Finney and Mahan and learned to love religion and the reform causes.

The age of graduation from the Collegiate Department was considerably higher than it is today–about twenty-five years as compared to twenty-two years at present.[2] The trend here evidenced began early, the faculty taking official cognizance of the fact that students were younger and less mature in a report issued in 1855.[3] In the Civil War years graduates averaged about a year younger than in the previous period. There was a great range in ages as a result of the presence, at one extreme, of the youngsters in the Preparatory Department and, at the other, of the family men in the "Shorter Course" and Theological Department. On the roll books for the years 1852 through 1854 the ages of 490 students in all departments are given. Among them were six who were twenty-six years old, two who were twenty-seven, two who were twenty-eight and one, thirty-six. The average of all was nearly nineteen years despite the fact that thirty-nine sixteen-year-olds, thirty-seven fifteen-year-olds, and twenty-four under fifteen were included from the ranks of the Preparatory Department. The total range in this period was from eleven to thirty-six.[4]

[1]Compiled from the *General Catalogue* of Oberlin College (Oberlin–1908).

[2]Of 465 students graduated from the Collegiate Course through 1866 whose ages are known, 168 were 26 years old or older. Ages computed from the *Semi-Centennial Register of Officers and Alumni of Oberlin College* (Chicago–1883).

[3]"Report on Oberlin" from the faculty, in the *Oberlin Evangelist,* Aug. 15, 1855.

[4]MS Roll Book (Misc. Archives).

The students were almost all farmers' sons and daughters with pious intentions, poor preparation and little money. A young man who, in 1836, had just transferred from Yale, found them "coarse & green . . . but noble, good hearted, pious." To him they appeared "far different from those at New Haven, very friendly indeed, rugged & healthy." He was almost disappointed, however, at their dress, for he did "not see that their clothing appears inferior as a general thing to what is ordinarily found in society." "To be sure," he continued, "we have no fops & dandies —nor is it any disgrace to wear coarse & patched clothes. But many dress rich & elegant." The sunburn of manual labor must have lent the men at least the appearance of health and ruggedness. Professor John Morgan wrote his impression of Oberlin to Mark Hopkins in the same year: " . . . The people are genuine Yankees of the best class of plain farmers. . . . The students, though many of them crude, are a fine set of young men. . . ."[5]

That the students were of New England farmer stock appears from a study of their home addresses. Of the 162 enrolled in the Collegiate and Theological courses in 1836, all but ten came from New England, New York or Ohio! New York led with 72; Ohio followed with 44; New England sent 39.[6] Of the ten from elsewhere, one was from Ireland, one from England and one from Alabama. There were 310 students in the entire institution, New York sending 120 to Ohio's 112, Massachusetts' 24, and Vermont's 16. In the following year 92 of the total number of male students came from New York and 66 from Ohio. New England contributed 45.[7] Almost all of these were from rural areas. As Oberlin was founded and led chiefly by New York Yankees it is not surprising to see New Yorkers predominating in the early years. By 1840 Ohio had surpassed New York in the contribution of students to the advanced course, but New York was still unchallenged in second place. In 1850 more states were represented, but the relationship between Ohio, New York and New England remained about the same. Three students from Scotland and one from Ireland appeared; Michigan, Wisconsin and Illi-

[5]George Prudden and Davis Prudden to Peter Prudden, July 18, 1836 (Prudden-Allen MSS), and John Morgan to Mark Hopkins, June 8, 1836 (Morgan-Hopkins MSS).

[6]Computed from the 1836 Catalogue and from manuscript lists in the Misc. Archives.

[7]*Ohio Observer,* June 12, 1837.

HOMES OF STUDENTS IN THE COLLEGIATE AND THEOLOGICAL COURSES IN THE OBERLIN COLLEGIATE INSTITUTE IN 1836

NEW YORK	72	MICHIGAN	3
OHIO	44	PENNSYLVANIA	2
MASSACHUSETTS	15	ILLINOIS	1
VERMONT	10	KENTUCKY	1
CONNECTICUT	8	ALABAMA	1
NEW HAMPSHIRE	5	IRELAND	1
RHODE ISLAND	1	ENGLAND	1

One address in Michigan not located.

(Prepared by Dr. Walter P. Rogers and the author on a United States Department of Agriculture base map.)

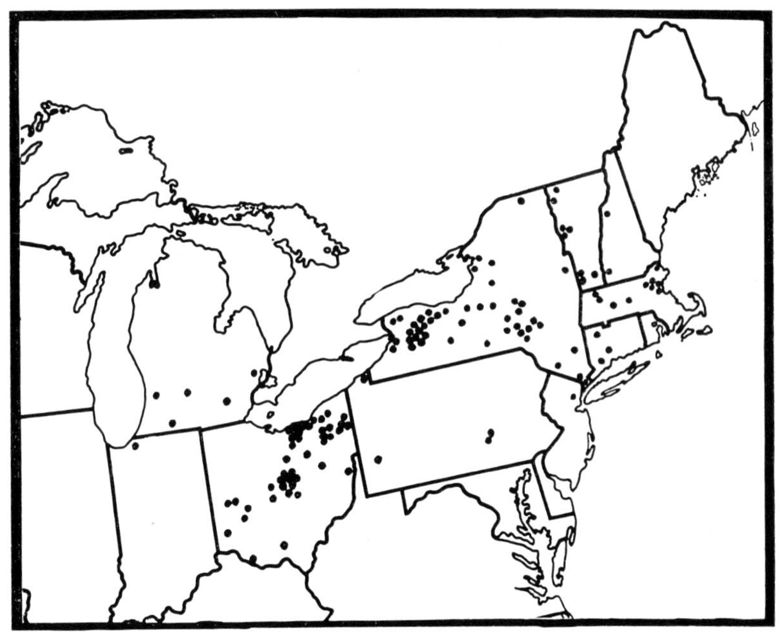

HOMES OF STUDENTS IN THE COLLEGIATE AND THEOLOGICAL COURSES IN THE OBERLIN COLLEGIATE INSTITUTE IN 1840

OHIO	60	MICHIGAN	6
(OBERLIN 15)		PENNSYLVANIA	4
NEW YORK	46	INDIANA	1
MASSACHUSETTS	10	NEW JERSEY	1
VERMONT	8	ALABAMA	1
CONNECTICUT	3	ENGLAND	1
NEW HAMPSHIRE	2	WEST INDIES	2
RHODE ISLAND	1		

One address in each of the states of Ohio, New York and Michigan not located.

(Prepared by Dr. Walter P. Rogers and the author on a United States Department of Agriculture base map.)

nois sent 16 together. By 1860 the Oberlin student body had become more localized on the Western Reserve, as will be seen from the maps. Of the 221 persons registered in the Collegiate and Theological departments, 115 gave an Ohio home address. Only 30 hailed from New York, 14 from Michigan and only 18 from all New England. Of the thirteen hundred students in all departments over nine hundred were Ohioans, mostly from the Western Reserve. Oberlin was becoming more provincial, one of "the Ohio colleges." That this was a long-time trend and not a temporary swing is seen from the fact that in 1866 only about a quarter of all the students and only 48 of the 132 in the Collegiate and Theological departments were from outside Ohio. This change, however, should not obscure the major consideration that, throughout the period, Oberlin students came largely from the area settled by New Englanders and were predominately of Yankee stock.

The hundreds of letters from candidates for admission still preserved in the archives of the College are our best source of information on the ambitions and professed motives of Oberlin students. From them it may be safely inferred that the manual labor system was Oberlin's greatest drawing card. It seemed as if every indigent young man or woman north of Mason and Dixon's Line in search of an education looked to Oberlin as the answer to prayer.

Their poverty was undoubtedly their chief reason for preferring the manual labor system. A typical applicant wrote to President Mahan in 1848: "Hearing of your highly commendible school and that it is sustained by the plan of Manual Labor, where those who have a thirst for the waters of the Pierian Spring and have not the pecuniary means of Satisfying it are . . . Instructed, fed and all their wants suplyed at the christal fount of knowledge by simply performing a few hours labor on the farm belonging to the Institute, I therefore wish to know the particulars in relation to the school." In 1845 a former Oberlin student recommended a friend for admission: "He is desirous of getting an education with a view to the Ministry & greater usefulness. But he is poor having not much else than his mortal body. His friends that *would* help him are also poor. He turns imploringly to you as a 'brother having need,' trusting that you have 'bowels of compassion.'" Mary Lyon applied for a place for a nephew, one of nine children, who had "nothing of his own" and could not expect "anything from his father," but was an "able, skilful laborer on the farm." Charles Livingstone, brother of the explorer, "resolved to go to Oberlin . . . , tho' he [had] nothing beyond his industry to depend upon" because of the attraction of the self-supporting system, and this all the way from Glasgow, too.[8] Everything points to the conclusion that Oberlin was the true "poor man's college," and manual labor, more than anything else, made it that.

One suspects that this financial motive was often basic with those who gave other reasons for selecting Oberlin. A number however, stated that they were attracted by the manual labor system because their health demanded physical exercise.—"Having experienced in some degree the evil effects which result from a close application to studdy without physical exercise I am anxious to obtain a place where Manual Labor is connected with an institution for the benefit of the students." So wrote R. D. Hathaway to President Mahan, and others found it "indispensable" to their health, "to take considerable exercise in the form of manual labor."[9]

Young ladies, too, were often attracted by the prospect of paying at least part of their expenses through their own exertions. When Susan Hooker wrote to the Secretary in 1839, she was careful to state that she was "fond of domestic labor, and," she added, "it agrees with me." There were undoubtedly many, however, who felt as did the sister of an Oberlin student who wrote to him: "I have no desire to cast in my lot at Oberlin yet . . . I do not like to wash, scrub floors, milk &c. &c. for a living, as long as I can get along without it." Nevertheless, this same young woman was in Oberlin within a year washing and scrubbing, if not milking, to help pay for her education. A faculty committee on manual labor reported to the trustees in 1845 its belief that "very few would ever enter the Inst^{n} here if they were not encouraged to expect that labor would be furnished them sufficient to enable them to pay a great part of their expenses."[10]

[8]Charles H. Fairchild to President Mahan, July 27, 1848 (Treas .Off., File H); John S. Lewis to the Faculty of the O. C. Institute [Apr., 1845]; Mary Lyon to J. J. S., July 28, 1834, and H. Drummond to William Dawes, Hamilton, Scotland, Mar. 17, 1840 (File E).

[9]R. D. Hathaway to Asa Mahan, Oct. 27, 1845 (Treas. Off., File N), and David Thurston to Asa Mahan, Nov. 19, 1841 (File I).

[10]Susan A. Hooker to Levi Burnell, Apr. 17, 1839 (Treas. Off., File D); Nancy

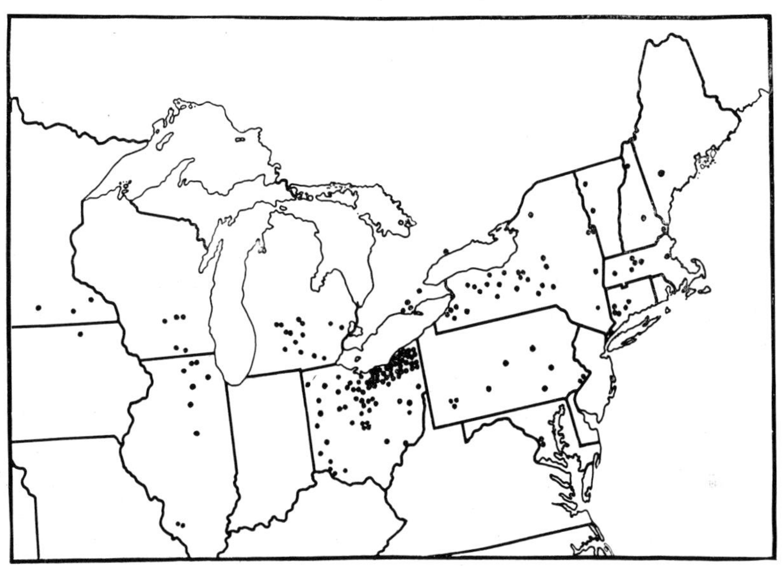

HOMES OF STUDENTS IN THE COLLEGIATE AND THEOLOGICAL COURSES IN OBERLIN COLLEGE IN 1860

Ohio	115	Michigan	14
New York	30	Illinois	10
Massachusetts	6	Pennsylvania	10
Connecticut	5	Wisconsin	5
New Hampshire	4	Minnesota	3
Vermont	2	District of Columbia	2
Maine	1	Iowa	1
North Carolina	1	California	1
Canada	5	England	2
Scotland	2	Germany	1

One address in each of the states of Illinois, New York, New Hampshire and Ohio not located.

(Prepared by Dr. Walter P. Rogers and the author on a United States Department of Agriculture base map)

OBERLIN COLLEGE STUDENTS IN 1851

(From a daguerreotype lent by the late "Ban" Johnson and W. R. Johnson of Coronado, California, and a second copy by Miss Florence N. Jones of Orlando, Florida)

Marcus W. Fay may be taken as typical. In a letter written to Secretary Burnell in 1841 he gave his reasons and qualifications for coming to Oberlin: "First to obtain an education by my own exertions without involving myself in debt, Secondly the religious character of the institution. My object in seeking an education, is a preparation for the gospel ministry. I am poor, but have the blessing of health, I am in my 23 year, and have followed farming as an occupation, except when studying or teaching."[11] Probably the great majority of young men going to college in the early nineteenth century were impelled to do so by religious motives. At a missionary institution like Oberlin this was practically universally the case. Finney's reputation as an evangelist, Mahan's unorthodox advocacy of perfectionism, and the wide circulation of the *Oberlin Evangelist* attracted many zealous young souls who thought themselves called to the ministry or missionary service.

One youth, anxious to enjoy the advantages of "the Oberlin institution," appealed to a local minister for assistance in securing admission: "I feel very anxious to come. My mind is drawn out after ciance. I want to prepare for the ministry. My mind is drawn out some for poor heathen souls. I have no peace of mind when I give up the thoughts of being a minister for Christ. I feel like droping every thing and prepare for the ministry." Doubtless most of the youth who entered Oberlin felt it their "duty to go and proclaim the glad tidings of the gospel unto thousands that sit in darkness and in the region and shadow of Death."[12]

Shipherd had early preached the advantages of preparing for religious work in the West in a western school. Easterners who hoped to take part in the harvest in the Great Valley were apparently often attracted to Oberlin for this reason. In 1836, Elam J. Comings, then a sophomore at the University of Vermont, transferred to Oberlin. Let him give his motives for doing so in his own words:

"My reasons for leaving that institution, and seeking another are simply these. My first and principal reason is—I wish to go

Prudden to Geo. Prudden, Aug. 3, 1836 (Prudden MSS), and "Manual Labor Report adopted August, 1845" (Misc. Archives).

[11]Marcus W. Fay to Levi Burnell, Jan. 25, 1841 (Treas. Off., File C).

[12]John Smith to Rev. Hand, July 30, 1838 (Treas. Off., File I), and John Aiton to Asa Mahan, Apr. 18, 1839 (File A).

where more prominence is given to *religious education*. It is a notorious fact that while the officers of the University are diligent and unsparing in their efforts to thoroughly discipline the intellectual powers, they wofully neglect the *moral training* of their Students. And a second reason has regard to *expense*. It is quite unpopular for Students to labor at all at Burlington, and indeed were it otherwise in this respect, as things are now situated, it would be a difficult matter to obtain work to do. And as a third reason for coming I would say, I have for a long time been anxious to spend my life, after I shall have finished my preparatory course of study, *in the West*: and think that it would, on some accounts, be desirable to finish my studies there. Such as becoming habituated to the climate, acquainted with the people, etc."[13]

The young ladies, too, seem to have been prompted often by pious intentions. Sometime early in 1836, forty-six young ladies, members of the institution, prepared statements, each giving her home address, date of birth, date of entering Oberlin, residence in Oberlin and *future intentions*. Of the forty who included statements with regard to their intentions, seventeen definitely mentioned missionary work as a possible or probable future employment. Cornelia Barnes was studying "to prepare for Foreign Miss. Labor, Teaching, Translating Scriptures etc." Elizabeth Humphrey declared: "Have long contemplated the field of Foreign Missions, & if the 'Lord wills' hope to get to enlist in that glorious cause." Others were less specific. Florella Brown, half-sister of John Brown, later of Harper's Ferry, merely stated that she designed "to prepare herself for usefulness in whatever field the Lord [might] see fit to place her." Several others preferred to limit themselves to similar pious generalizations. Of the seventeen who considered mission work a field of possible "future usefulness," five mentioned teaching as an alternative. Twelve referred to teaching alone. Therefore it would appear that teaching and spreading the Gospel among the heathen were close rivals for popularity among the Oberlin young ladies in the early days. That another ambition was really in many of their minds is certain, but none of them was so bold as to write that she hoped to marry an eligible young minister. Perhaps that is what was meant

[13]Elam J. Comings to Asa Mahan, Jan. 26, 1836 (Treas. Off., File B).

by those who discoursed vaguely about preparing "for laboring more efficiently in the vineyard of Christ."[14]

It was not unusual for a young man and a young lady to come to Oberlin together, enjoy each other's company as much as the rules allowed in this coeducational institution and marry on the completion of their course. A student, Ralph Tyler, wrote to Secretary Burnell in November, 1837:

"You will conclude at once that I am not very formal, & perhaps not formal enough. The object of this letter is to apply for admission in behalf of a lady who has a mind to come to Oberlin with me early in the Spring.

" . . . The Lady is Sarah Ann Lay of Westbrook this state, a plain farmers daughter brought up to the useful employments of domestic life. She became a school teacher at 15 & has taught every summer since & one or two winters. She has had little advantage in select schools. She has been a member of the church for some years. She seems to have gained universal confidence in the different towns where she has taught. She seems very desirous to be prepaired for the greatest usefulness in her Master's cause &, in view of considerations which I presented, she & her parents have concluded that Oberlin is the place for such preparations. We have looked over the catalogue together & conclude she can prepare by spring to enter the middle class.

"This is desirable that she may finish her education at the same time I close mine, for (in confidence) we have concluded after about a years correspondence & an interview of late to become companions & fellow laborers in due time."[15]

As students were not permitted to "form the marriage connection" while members of the Institute, it is probable that courses were often cut short when such conditions obtained. Miss Lay completed her preparation for "greatest usefulness" the very next year and became Mrs. Tyler in 1838. Incidentally, Mr. Tyler's frank description of his fiancée might be taken as a good picture of the typical Oberlin student girl in the early days.

Undoubtedly many young women were attracted to Oberlin merely because there were so few places where girls were admitted at all to the opportunities of an advanced education and because Oberlin was everywhere known to be devoted to the elevation

[14]MSS in Misc. Archives.
[15]Ralph Tyler to Levi Burnell, Nov. 1, 1837 (Treas. Off., File I).

of the "neglected sex." There were some, also, who felt that many female seminaries were too worldly. "I have felt unwilling to go to most of our Seminaries, where the great object is to make mere butterflies of females," wrote Achsah Colburn, who attended from 1837 to 1841. "I wish to go where not only the intellect, but the moral principle will be cultivated, disciplined, and trained for active service in the vineyard of the Lord." It is evidence of the common attitude toward the position of women that a large proportion of the young ladies were modestly presented as candidates for admission by near male relatives rather than venturing brazenly to address the august college officials themselves. Even the feminist Lucy Stone called on her brother to make application for admission for her. When one did dare to write in her own behalf it was, as in the case of Almira Welch, "with no ordinary feelings of embarrassment."[16]

It is probably partly because of this circumstance that the young women appear more commonly to have been "sent" to school, whereas the majority of young men seem to have entered on their own initiative. One father sent his daughter to Oberlin partly to break up an engagement which did not suit the family. Occasional sons were also "sent." Another parent explained: "I wish to have my son educated at Oberlin, as I believe there is a higher stand of piety there than at any other Institution, & the moral influence of the community better than at any other place. I know of no other place where I should feel so safe in sending him."[17] The son, it seems, preferred "some Eastern Institution where he thinks the literary advantages are greater than at Oberlin," but the father felt that there was a better chance of his being converted at the pious new college in the West.

The reasons presented by an ambitious blacksmith for desiring to place his daughter in Oberlin are characteristic: "We are unable to sustain her at any but a Manual Labour Institution. And we also have confidence that there the heart will be cultivated, as well as the mind. And though away from Parents, she will be surrounded by religious influence instead of worldly. And again we sympathize with the Oppressed and those who have no com-

[16]Achsah Colburn to Asa Mahan, Oct. 24, 1836 (Treas. Off., File B); Lucy Stone to W. B. Stone, July 9, 1842 (lent by W. C. MacLaurin, Ware, Mass.), and Almira Welch to Asa Mahan, Nov. 15, 1837 (Treas. Off., File J).

[17]S. H. Dalliber to Mrs. C. G. Finney, Aug. 9, 1836 (Finney MSS), and Wm. A. Thayer to Henry Cowles, Mar. 6, 1840 (Treas. Off., File I).

forter, and we wish our Child to be with those who do so preeminently, manifesting it by their works."[18] Hundreds of Oberlin's best friends were attracted to her support by her stand on the great moral questions of the day, particularly because of her sympathy for the "Oppressed."

One young man expressed "a strong desire to go" to Oberlin because "it possesses an Abolition sentiment of which I am peculiarly fond." An apprentice "in the office of the Alton Observer, edited by Rev. Elijah P. Lovejoy," the Illinois Martyr, planned to enter Oberlin in preference to any other school. Oberlin's abolition principles were so well known that it is doubtful if any would come who did not sympathize with the "downtrodden slaves." The youth who wrote from Hartford shortly after being liberated from jail, in which he was confined "for refusing to violate his conscience" in "performing military duty," doubtless had some inkling of the fact that a Non-Resistance Society was forming in Oberlin, or at least that Oberlin might be expected to favor the pacifist point of view.[19]

Of course, also, there were many applications from colored men and women, because the fact that Oberlin admitted Negroes and that they were well treated had been advertised by the press throughout the English-speaking world. "Having heard however that you the people of Oberlin take a delight in helping to elevate the down trodden of your country I take this opportunity in order to address you in my own behalf," wrote one Negro from Pittsburgh in 1846.[20] In the same year a young, black barber wrote to President Mahan:

"I succeeded in walking out of Slavery on the 22d of April last. I am now in Marion County Ohio where I have worked five months for my board and 3 months Schooling which I am now receiving. I can read a little and write such a hand as you here see.

"Dear sir I understand that you are a lover of liberty not for the white man alone but for all of every Clime and of every Color, and that the literary institution over which you preside is a phil-

18Silas R. Badeau to R. E. Gillett, Feb. 6, 1837 (Treas. Off., File A). Badeau's daughter seems never to have come to Oberlin.

19Lewis Barnes to Asa Mahan, Jan. 25, 1836 (Treas. Off. File A); A. S. Lindsley to C. G. Finney, June 6, 1837 (Cowles-Little MSS); and C. Stearns to Levi Burnell, Feb. 13, 1840 (Treas. Off., File I).

20Alfred Freeman to Henry Cowles, Mar., 1846 (Treas. Off., File M). Freeman was a member of the Preparatory Department during two terms.

anthropic institution seeking to dispense the blessings of knowledge to as many of the human race as possible. And therefore I feel emboldened to address you and to request admission as a student if there is any hope of my getting along there."[21]

These Negroes, were, of course, even more certain to be poor than were the whites, and it is probable that this applicant, like many others, failed to enter because of the slight prospect of his obtaining work sufficient for his support.

Oberlin's reputation as a school where colored students would be received (believed, in fact, by many to be exclusively for Negroes) was so widespread that youths of the darker hue asking for advice as to where they might receive an education, were almost certain to be referred to it. "I doubt not Sir but that you are acquainted with the Hon. Mr. M. M. Clark agent for the Ohio School Institution," wrote another colored man. "He was remarking to me when last in Wheeling that Oberlin would be a very good place for my brother and by the request of my mother I write to you to see If upon what terms they take students. I have a couple of brothers who have been raised, as you may almost term it, in the arms of base and degraded servility with but very little education. It is my wish that they should be well educated if it takes all my labour." In 1855 Lewis Tappan wrote to Oberlin asking if the daughters of "a respectable colored man who lives in the vicinity" and who had "been to California and . . . made money" might be received. Tappan's application in their behalf would, of course, alone have been sufficient to secure a favorable reply. A business firm in Boston wrote early in the sixties to inquire whether "a very intelligent Mulatto" in their employ might obtain an education at Oberlin, and in 1859 William Lloyd Garrison inquired of Professor Monroe whether an opening could be found at Oberlin for "an amiable and worthy colored youth (handsome and but slightly tinctured with African blood, about 19 or 20 years of age), to obtain an education . . . , by paying his way by some sort of manual labor."[22]

[21]Elias Poston to Asa Mahan, Feb. 3, 1846 (Treas. Off., File G).

[22]R. W. G. Anderson to Wm. Cochran, June 12, 1839 (Treas. Off., File A); Lewis Tappan to Hamilton Hill, Jan. 6, 1855 (Tappan Letter Books—Elizabeth Reed and Frances E. Reed of New York, enrolled in the Preparatory Department in 1856–7 and 1857–8 respectively, are undoubtedly the colored girls referred to); Palmer & Bachelder to Pres. Oberlin College, July 28, 1862 (Treas. Off., File S), and W. L. Garrison to James Monroe, Apr. 22, 1859 (Monroe MSS).

Some seemed to think that Oberlin was an asylum for colored undesirables. A slaveholder-by-chance wrote to an Oberlin townsman from Tennessee:

"Dear Sir—The Oberlin Institution being open for the education of all classes, poor ignorant black or white, it is altogether probably that I shall send a black girl now about 14 years of age to it, at the best practical moment. I am married to a southern lady who received the girl, as her servant, from her father. By the law of the State I am regarded as her Master and Proprietor. My wife dislikes her on some futile ground and wishes me to dispose of her. Negroes sell very high at this time. I could get 700 to $800 for her. But I have no notion, thank the Lord, of doing any such thing either to please my wife or for money. . . . She will become free by being carried into Ohio. But she is not fit for freedom without some education. She has many of the defects of the race—Shiftlessness &c—however has as far as can be observed no lewd tendencies. Please inform me of the cost of boarding tuition &c per session and oblige."[23]

During the Civil War, Finney's brother-in-law wrote from Michigan, recommending a freedman for admission to the institution though, he admitted, "he can now barely read a little." Pencilled on the back of his letter is a note: "Wrote that cd not receive the man unless he cd enter the classes & even then we have no fund that cd be appropriated to pay his expenses."[24] Negroes, it is clear, were not to be admitted to Oberlin merely because of the color of their skins any more than they were to be excluded for that reason.

Few applicants, of whatever color, had very high scholastic attainments to present. The faculty could expect little more from new students as a rule than a knowledge of the "three R's." Applicants often frankly admitted their modest attainments. In 1835, Richard Fenn wrote of his daughter, "She has studied but little beyond the branches of a common English education." In 1840 a young man described his previous education as embracing only "a general knowledge of Reading, Arithmetick and English Grammar." "My education is quite limited," wrote another eight years later, "being such as is obtained in the common country district schools of N. Y." Though S. S. Dillman (in

[23]H. E. Ring to J. M. Fitch, [1853] (Cowles-Little MSS).
[24]P. B. Andrews [to C. G. Finney, July, 1863] (Treas. Off., File V).

1850) had made some progress in higher mathematics and read Caesar, four books of Virgil, five of Cicero's orations and part of the Gospels and Xenophon's *Anabasis* in Greek he described his sister's "qualifications" as "about as good as could be attained in second rate, backwoods, common schools; that is, . . . a pretty fair smattering of Geography, Arithmetic, and English Grammar, but not thorough enough to pass either." An applicant of the Civil War years listed all his accomplishments in a few words: "I can read & write, have studied grammar and geography, and arithmetic both mental and practical."[25] There were, of course, a good many, who, like young Mr. Dillman, had more advanced training. Occasional transfers from other colleges and students entering the Theological Course were well grounded in the general cultural subjects. The common school education was, however, much the more usual preparation for entrance to Oberlin.

There were many applications for admission from older men with inadequate preparation. They were doubtless attracted by the "Shorter Course," a three-year academic course designed to prepare such persons of advanced age for entrance into the Theological Department. The 1855 *Catalogue* stated that this course "preparatory to the study of Theology, [might] be pursued, at the discretion of the Faculty, by students of an advanced age ONLY." Let some of these maturer applicants speak for themselves:

1857: "My Education is very inferior, as I have been to School but little, since the age of 10 years. . . . I have seen hard times, to get along—as my health for most part of the time, has been extremely poor, and now at the age of 25 years I cannot boast of a Dollar in this world, but I trust that in the next I have an Heavenly Inheritance."

1839: "I am an ordained Minister, . . . I have a wife & one child & would be glad to rent a house while connected with the Institution."

1837: "I have a family which consists of wife and child about a year old. Could a room be procured sufficiently large to admit

[25]Richard Fenn to J. J. Shipherd, Feb. 9, 1835 (Treas. Off., File G); I. M. McDonald to Pres. of Oberlin College, Aug. 3, 1840 (File F); C. W. Kellogg to Pres. of Oberlin Collegiate Institute, Dec. 18, 1848 (File E); S. S. Dillman to ?, Dec. 12, 1850 (File R), and Zachariah Anderson to C. G. Finney, Oct. 1, 1863 (File V).

COLLEGE SENIORS—1859
(From the 1859 Class Album in the Oberlin College Library)

COLLEGE SENIORS—1859
(From the 1859 Class Album in the Oberlin College Library)

a small cookstove, or with a fireplace that would answer to cook for my small family?"

1837: "At the age of 28 with a wife & 2 sons, one 2½ the other ½ year old, I am, notwithstanding, thinking seriously of leaving my store to commence a course of study preparatory to the Gospel Ministry. . . . Will you be so good as to tell me by return mail or with as little delay as may be whether the preparatory department is filled? whether a *small* house or part of a house with a garden spot connected with it could be rented or purchased at a reasonable price & near the institution?"[26]

Of course the presence of these mature men, some of them with families, almost all dedicated to the ministry, did a great deal to maintain the sober, pious atmosphere which characterized Oberlin especially in the first two decades.

Notable examples of this group of older, married men were David Marks, the Freewill Baptist, and Josiah Willard. Willard came to Oberlin with his wife, Mary Thompson Hill Willard, in 1841. He was enrolled in the Preparatory and Collegiate departments from 1842 to 1845 when an attack of tuberculosis forced him to abandon a sedentary life. Their little daughter, Frances Elizabeth Willard, learned to read in copies of the *Slaves' Friend,* the juvenile anti-slavery periodical, before the family moved on to Wisconsin.[27]

Other letters of application contain revealing statements. A Middlebury student expressed his intention of transferring to Oberlin because, among other things: "I think that the *classical books* which are studyed here have a *bad influence* in forming the *characters* of young men. They have in a great measure an attendency to corrupt the *habits, morals,* and *minds* of those who pursue them, to say nothing of the time which is lost in commiting to memory *ideas* which are of no consequence. The authors read here are very *pure* in style but very *corrupt* in *sentament.*"[28] It is probable that Oberlin's stand against the classics attracted a number of students, either because of their conscientious scruples or

[26]T. B. F. Chamberlain to "Prest. of Oberlin Seminary," Nov. 8, 1857 (Treas. Off., File R); George Needham to Levi Burnell, June 21, 1839 (File G); Richard Hathaway to Levi Burnell, Apr. 7, 1837 (File D), and R. W. Lyman to Levi Burnell, Nov. 30, 1837 (File F).

[27]Frances E. Willard and Minerva Brace Norton, *A Great Mother, Sketch of Madam Willard* (Chicago—1894), 21–25 *et passim.*

[28]Franklin Merrill to Asa Mahan, June 17, 1837 (Treas. Off., File F).

their deficiencies in the dead languages. After the sale of the scholarships in the endowment campaign of the early fifties it is very likely that many came merely because they found themselves in possession of scholarships. One or two letters suggest this rather candidly.

The credentials furnished by friends and acquaintances of the applicants usually, of course, contain references to their mental ability and achievements and just as universally to their pious intentions and moral character. The Oberlin *Catalogue* always made it very clear that "testimonials of good moral character" were necessary. "Certificates of good standing in some evangelical church" were also expected. One young student was described by his sponsor as: "a young man of nobleness of character a pious devoted christian of prudent and economical habits, temperate in all his habits—no tea or coffee, or tobaco in any of its forms. Is willing to endure almost any privation for the sake of obtaining an education. He has heared of the fame of Oberlin and wishes a place."[29] If he lived up to this description he was the model Oberlin student. Sometimes recommendations do not contain one word about scholarship!

One young man inclosed (it is true with some trepidation) a certificate from a phrenologist, prepared after an examination of the bumps on his head. He never came to Oberlin. It may have been that this peculiar type of certificate did him more harm than good as, though much discussed, phrenology was not generally approved in Oberlin.[30]

The Oberlinite of the twentieth century feels a debt of gratitude to the young man, who "in choosing a *Home* that is to become the *Alma-Mater* of five or six the most important years of my life" felt it so important to "make a good selection" that he wrote to President Mahan a list of favorable and unfavorable comments which he had heard on Oberlin and asked the President to reply. Probably Mahan never took the time to do so. The student never came, but the analysis of Oberlin which he made remains as a sample of the common attitude toward Oberlin and of the factors which decided students to come or not to come to the Institute:

"By *report* there are some things that are for, and some against

[29]E. Hosford to Levi Burnell, Dec., 1840 (Treas. Off., File D).
[30]Amasa Skinner to Secretary of O. C. I., Oct. 21, 1844 (File P).

the *Oberlin Institute;* but report is too fallacious to become a criterion of judgement, were I qualified to judge; therefore, though it appear rather indecorous in me, I will mention the principal ones, that I may hear from you directly rellative to them. The first *Con* that I mention is perhaps, all things being considered, of but little importance. It is said that there is an unreserved intercourse of blacks, and whites. I adopt the principles of the anti-Slavery constitution, so far as I am acquainted with them; that is, I advocate the importance of immediate emancipation:—But I have ever lived among whites exclusively, and to be now associated with blacks would be disagreeable, admitting it to be right. Another Con. It is said that the Oberline Scholars are generally *superficial,* in consequence of their being too much *hurried.* I can say nothing relative to this of course. Another and the last Con. It is said, that the no. of Students is too great, for the No. of Teachers. About this I know nothing.

"The first pro. that I mention is one that some consider an objection—viz. The doctrine of Christian Perfection is believed and taught there. I infer from this, that a *good Religious influence* may be enjoyed, and this is what I very much want. Another *Pro.* I infer from the fact that there are a large No. of Students that *good Literary Societies* are sustained, and if so, I could derive benefit from them. Another *Pro.* I am a Grahamite and I understand that the Students feed at a graham-table. Another *Pro.* It is said that those in indigent circumstance, may they chose, *defray their expenses,* or at least *part* of their expenses by *manual labor.* Another and the last Pro. is one at which you may smile, but it is so nevertheless. It is said that males, & females attend the same Institution, and recite in the same room. Such an arrangement, I verily believe, would have a good influence. I suppose there is a preparatory department; of this however I must be certain—for into it, I must first enter; having studied Latin but *eight* or *nine months,* Greek about four, Algebra & Geometry about three."[31]

We smile and wonder if perhaps there were not other young men attracted to the new center of learning in the West, partially,

[31]E. W. Gray to Asa Mahan, Dec. 23, 1843 (Treas. Off., File C).

at least, because "females attend the same Institution, and recite in the same room."[32]

[32]See W. H. Seaman and D. P. Seldon, "The Class of 1934," *Oberlin Alumni Magazine,* June 1931, for a picture of the Oberlin student body in recent years. The contrast is striking. Less than five percent are the children of farmers; over ninety percent come from towns of two thousand or more population. They come to Oberlin because of the influence of some member of the family and because of the College's reputation for scholarly work of high quality. They are notably well-prepared: three-quarters of them from the highest quarter of their high-school graduating classes. But most of them still come from homes in New England, the Middle States and the Old Northwest. Some few students entering in 1931 said that they were influenced toward Oberlin by "the reasonableness of expense, the opportunities for self-support, the lack of fraternities, the fact that the college is cosmopolitan and coeducational." Here are survivals of the old tradition.

CHAPTER XXXIII

THE STUDENTS — THE OPPRESSED RACE

IT WAS the inclusion of young ladies and Negroes which especially differentiated the Oberlin student body from that in other colleges. The mixture of the races in schools was not unheard of but was generally frowned upon in the North as in the South. Joint education of the sexes in a collegiate institution was an entirely new and somewhat shocking departure. The combination of the two made Oberlin odious.[1]

When Oberlin's financial agent in New England received word in 1835 that students were to be admitted irrespective of color, he wrote a strong letter of warning and protest:

"New England will scarcely bear to have young Ladies at the same semy. with young white Gent: this point might be gained, but to place black and white together on precisely the same standing will not most certainly be endured whatever the right may be [in] New England even, and if not here then not in this Country—and in trying to do this you will lose the other object, nay you lose Oberlin. For as soon as your *darkies* begin to come in in any considerable numbers, unless they are completely separated, . . . the whites will begin to leave—and at length your Institute will change colour. Why not have a black Institution, Dyed in the wool—and let Oberlin be? . . . In my humble opinion, if you do not at least keep the blacks entirely separate, so as to *veto* the notion of amalgamation I am persuaded that the Colony & the Institution embracing every interest of this enterprise as I understand it will be blown *sky high* and you will have a black establishment there *thro' out!*"[2]

No large proportion of colored students ever entered Oberlin, but in many localities it was believed to be exclusively, or at least

[1]On Joint Education see above, Chapter XXIV.
[2]Benjamin Woodbury to John J. Shipherd, Mar. 26, 1835 (Treas. Off., File J).

largely, a colored institution, a reputation which, in some quarters, it has not as yet outlived. Artemas Ward undoubtedly scored a great hit with many readers when, in 1865, he wrote that Oberlin was "a very good college," but it was his "onbiassed 'pinion that they go it rather too strong on Ethiopians." "As a faithful historian," he continued, "I must menshun the fack that on rainy dase white people can't find their way threw the streets without the gas is lit, ther bein such a numerosity of cullerd pussons in the town." In 1852 one young lady student found it desirable to reassure her family in Massachusetts: "I received your letter and take this opportunity of answering it so that you can tell anybody that asks that we dont have to kiss the Niggars nor to speak to them without we are a mind to. I dont think that there are six pure Niggars here that go to school. They are almost all part white . . . they dress a great deal better than the rest of the students. You may tell them that ask you that I have not kissed a Niggar yet nor ant a going to nor hant seen any one else . . . ." Many people had a great horror that the association of whites and blacks in such a way would lead to intermarriage—"amalgamation." There is no evidence that this fear was ever realized in Oberlin College, though it is related that one Negro student fell in love with a white girl, and, when she refused his offer of marriage, threatened suicide.[3]

Negro students might room in the boarding house, eat at the boarding house table and attend classes and religious exercises along with the white students. In 1866 the Lady Principal reported with regard to the New Ladies' Hall: "The number of ladies of color in the Hall during the spring was six— the past term eight—and seven names are registered for the coming term. We have as yet rejected no application in that direction, nor would we, if we honorably could, be without a representation of our colored students. These ladies have been seated at different tables by the side of white ladies, and if it so happened opposite white young men." Twenty years earlier a young man wrote to his sisters at home: "About every fifth one at the table is a darky. And the best appearing chap I have seen here is black." "At the Boarding House," wrote Artemas Ward, with characteristic,

[3]*The Complete Works of Artemas Ward* (London, 1900), 59; E. A. Collester to Mrs. John Collester, Apr. 19, 1852, (O. C. Library), and A. S. Blackwell, *Lucy Stone*, 56.

humorous exaggeration, "the cullured people sit at the first table. What they leave is maid into hash for the white people."[4]

In the literary societies and at Commencement the colored youths took their part on the programs. In 1850 Lucy Stanton, a colored girl, was even elected president of the Young Ladies' Association (later Ladies' Literary Society). On the 21st of August Miss Stanton presided "with dignity and honor" at the Annual Exhibition of the society, a formal, public meeting, at which President Mahan offered the invocation. A few days later she graduated from the Ladies' Department. She read her essay along with the rest. The *Oberlin Evangelist* described the event: "One of the graduates was a colored lady. . . . and when her subject was announced, 'A Plea for the Oppressed,' and she stepped into the stand, expectation was raised, and expectation was more than gratified. Her charming voice, modest demeanor, appropriate pronunciation and graceful cadences, riveted attention, while the truthfulness of her pictures controlled the emotions of her hearers." Despite the customary prohibition of applause, there was a burst of clapping after she sat down. Once, five years before, this taboo on applause had been broken when William C. Whitehorne, a colored man from Jamaica, delivered his commencement oration on "Intellectual Conflict," which, the editor of the *Evangelist* observed, "would have done honor to any young man of any complexion in any college in any lands."[5]

There was undoubtedly a tendency among certain persons to overemphasize the virtues and intellectual achievements of colored students and to lionize them socially as part of the anti-slavery propaganda. Delazon Smith declared that, "when the arrival of one of them is announced, there is a great noise, like the rush of many waters, so great is their anxiety to see another of their colored brethren," and "a young lady who is so highly favored, as to obtain a seat at table, by the side of one of these 'southern gentlemen,' especially if he be a fugitive from his master, . . . is then considered a 'sister indeed, in whom there is no

[4]M. P. Dascomb to the trustees of Oberlin College, Aug. 21 1866 [Report of the Female Department for 1865–1866] (Misc. Archives); B. D. Wright to Misses M. & M. Wright, May 1, 1846 (lent by Mrs. H. H. Carter, Oberlin), and Artemas Ward, *Op. Cit.*, 61.

[5]John White Chadwick, *A Life for Liberty, Anti-Slavery and Other Letters of Sallie Holley* (N. Y. & London, 1899), 61; Young Ladies' Association, MS Minutes, July 1, Aug. 21, 1850, and *Oberlin Evangelist,* Sept. 10, 1845, Nov. 6, 1850.

guile.'" This seems to have been more characteristic of the earlier days. Even in 1846 one prep. student, at least, objected to being called "Brother" by a Negro, and in 1866 Mrs. Dascomb admitted that there is "occasionally a manifestation of prejudice against color."[6]

"I wish to know if the colored students associate with the whites on all occasions," wrote a prospective student in 1851, "if they recite in the same class and dine at the same table. There is an opinion prevalent in this community that students are obliged by the rules of the Institute to mingle with the colored population farther than is right with the differences nature has made between the two classes." In replying to this inquiry, the Rev. Henry Cowles stated semi-officially the policy of the College with regard to the association of the two races in the institution:

"The white and colored students associate together in this college very much as they choose. Our doctrine is that *mind* and *heart,* not *color,* make the man and the woman too. We hold that neither men or women are much the better or much the worse for their *skin.* Our great business here is to educate mind and heart, and we should deem ourselves to have small cause to be proud of our success if we should fail to eradicate, in no long time, the notion that nature had made any such difference between the colored and the white classes that it would be wrong for either to associate with the other as beings of common origin and a common nature. We believe in treating men according to their intrinsic merits—not according to distinctions over which they can have no control. If you are a young gentleman of color, you may expect to be treated here according to your real merit; and if white, you need not expect to fare better than this.

"In this college colored and white students of the same sex, walk together when both are agreed to do so—not otherwise. They eat together if both prefer it, or if neither chooses to eat elsewhere. They meet in the same classes for recitations if they happen to be studying the same branches, at the same stage of progress. They worship together before the same common Father—that is, if they both have the heart to worship at all."[7]

This is an accurate statement, except that it should have been

[6]Delazon Smith, *History of Oberlin,* 28, 57; letter of B. D. Wright, May 1, 1846, and M. P. Dascomb, "Rept. of Fem. Dept. for 1865–1866" (Misc. Archives).

[7]*Oberlin Evangelist,* Sept. 10, 1851. Italics are mine.

made clear that there was no special bar to the association of white and colored students of the *opposite* sexes.

The officers of the Institute (and later College) were not anxious, it is clear, to admit an unduly large proportion of Negroes. On the other hand there is no evidence to show that colored applicants, otherwise properly qualified, were ever denied admission. When, in 1852, during the endowment campaign, "the Rev. Saml Cornish . . . made enquiry . . . if the Board [of Trustees of Oberlin College] would be willing & pleased to sell $20,000 of Scholarships to the colored people of Philadelphia, Baltimore & New York," the trustees resolved that they would "be happy to sell $20,000 of $100 Schps to all irrespective of color & also that the Trustees continue to receive Students also irrespective of complexion."[8] It is significant that they were willing to dispose of such a large proportion of the scholarships to Negroes. It is worth noting, however, that they specified $100 scholarships, which would not bring in so many colored students at any given time as would $25 or $50 scholarships.[9] In the 60's the Rev. Charles Avery, of Pittsburgh, gave $6,000, the income of which was to be used for the aid of "indigent and worthy" colored students.[10] The Treasurer, and the principals of the Preparatory and Ladies' departments were constituted a committee to decide "upon the amount of money to be paid to those colored young men & women who shall be recommended either by the Faculty or by the Ladies' Board as suitable objects to be assisted from the proceeds of the Avery Bequest."[11] Many of the abler Negroes were, in later years, given substantial assistance from this fund.

Oberlin never had a colored member on the faculty, despite a petition requesting such an appointment presented to the trustees in 1852.[12] At least one colored college student, however, taught classes in the Preparatory Department.[13]

There were many interesting individuals among the colored

[8]T. M., Feb. 18, 1852.

[9]$100 scholarships were perpetual, $50 ones were for 18 years and $25 were for 6 years, but not more than one student could use a given scholarship at any given time.

[10]The *General Catalogue* of 1908 states that the fund was established in 1864, but the Prudential Committee Minutes contain references to it from 1862 on.

[11]P. C. M., May 23, 1862; June 10, 1863; Aug. 12, 1864; Sept. 26, 1867, etc.

[12]T. M., Feb. 18, 1852.

[13]Fanny M. Jackson. Receipted bills for teaching are in the Misc. Archives.

students who attended school at Oberlin. Frederick Douglass sent his daughter Rosetta to Oberlin in 1854. Several converts of missionaries in Africa and the West Indies were enrolled at one time or another. Tippoo Nunnion, Thomas Tucker, Sarah Rinson, and William Whitehorne were all converts from heathen shores. During the Civil War the Oberlin Company "confiscated" an "intelligent contraband' in West Virginia and sent him back to study.[14] The Oberlinites found him "as white as, and far more intelligent and gentlemanly than the average of the slaveholders." There were others whose stories are worthy of a more detailed narration.

In a surprising number of instances masters sent their own children to Oberlin to school. In 1851 a Mississippi planter sent his colored offspring (two boys) to Oberlin in care of a Cincinnati law firm. From time to time money was provided for their tuition and support. The outbreak of the Civil War naturally terminated the arrangement.[15] In 1855 a slaveholder of Osceola, Missouri, sent his quadroon children and former slaves (a boy and a girl) to Oberlin to be brought up and educated. They were taken into the home of an Oberlin white woman and, after a period of study in the common schools, were enrolled in the Preparatory Department of Oberlin College, the girl living for a while in Ladies' Hall and becoming an accomplished musician.[16] In 1837, through the mediation of Salmon P. Chase, a wealthy white Louisiana planter sent his four colored children, two boys and two girls, to Oberlin and freedom. One of them, Lawrence Minor, eventually became a member of the College Class of 1850 and a leading Negro educator.[17] Southern planters contributed

[14]H. C. Cowles, List of colored students in Oberlin 1835–1862 (Cowles MSS); Thomas Tucker to Gerrit Smith, Sept. 26, 1859 (Gerrit Smith MSS), and *Lorain County News,* Feb. 25, 1863.

[15]A series of letters in the Treasurer's Office (File R) furnish the chief basis for this statement. The boys' names are recorded in the 1908 *General Catalogue,* one for the period 1856–1861 and another for 1859–1860. One of the boys "completed his education" in the State Reform School.—G. E. Howe to H. Hill, Jan. 10, 1862 (Treas. Off., File W).

[16]Mrs. Elisha Gray to G. M. Jones, Nov. 21, 1907 (Alumni Records—Kate Younger file), and Waldo P. Johnson to Henry Cowles, Mar. 20, May 26, 1855 (Cowles MSS).

[17]Shelton H. Minor to A. S. Root, Mar. 11, 1901 (Alumni Records); MS History of the Class of 1850 (O. C. Lib.), and bills for services to the Minor children dated June 1 (two), July 31, Aug. 25, 1837 (Misc. Archives). Further indication of how common this practice was is found in a letter in the Treasurer's Office in which a citizen of Cincinnati inquires about two girls sent from the South to Oberlin for their father the previous year.—E. J. Miller to President of Oberlin College, Mar. 9, 1850 (File F).

quite a bit of money to the support of abolitionist Oberlin!

As a leading agent in the Underground Railway, the Quaker Levi Coffin often had colored children placed in his care for education by their white fathers or relatives. In 1854 a planter of Washington, Kentucky, sent him his daughters to be educated, and Coffin wrote to Oberlin to secure accommodations for them. He wrote of them to Secretary Hill: "Their father lives in Washington, Ky, has kept his daughters at school in Ohio for some years, most of the time. He is a Man of Wealth and White and owns Slaves, but his daughters are nearly White. Their Mother is not living. I feel a deep interest in them. Wilt thou please inform me whether Boarding in a private family can be had, the terms of Board, tuition &c with all the rules & regulations &c &c." There is no definite evidence that these girls came to Oberlin. Possibly they may be identified with the two unnamed Kentucky colored girls referred to by Coleman in his *Slavery Times in Kentucky*. Their master-father, he says, sent them to study at Oberlin. They came back from college to visit him during one vacation and found him dead. In order to settle the estate they were sold from the auction block![18]

In 1860 a member of the Louisiana legislature was much embarrassed to find that he had inherited his cousins, the daughters of his uncle and a light-colored slave. He shipped these girls to Coffin at Cincinnati, with a request that he provide for their education at Oberlin and a draft for five hundred dollars to pay their initial expenses at that institution. Lizzie, Frances and Amelia Cage stayed in Oberlin from June to November of 1860. Coffin sent money and instructions to Secretary Hill from time to time. The youngest sister, Amelia, was never officially registered in the Preparatory Department as were Frances and Lizzie. When the Civil War broke out money ceased to come from their cousin, and Coffin obtained positions for them as household servants. Their relative and legal owner is said to have lost all his property in the war.[19]

In April, 1848, seventy-seven slaves attempted to escape from the city of Washington on the Schooner *Pearl*. Among them were

[18]Levi Coffin to H. Hill, Mar. 10, 1854 (Treas. Off., File R), and J. W. Coleman, *Slavery Times in Kentucky* (Chapel Hill, N. C.—1941), 135–7.

[19]Levi Coffin, *Reminiscences of Levi Coffin, the Reputed President of the Underground Railroad* (Cincinnati—c. 1876), 477–481.

four brothers and two sisters of the name of Edmondson. The schooner was captured and the fugitives brought back to Washington. As a punishment many of them were sold to slave traders. Mary and Emily Edmondson were sold to an Alexandria dealer who took them by sea to the New Orleans market. The brothers were either sold or ransomed, and the sisters were brought back to the Capital with the expectation that their family might be able to raise enough monev to buy their freedom. Their aged father finally went to New York City and appealed to anti-slavery men there for aid in raising the $2,350 demanded for the two girls by the slave traders. The Rev. Henry Ward Beecher took a personal interest in the case, and at a public meeting sponsored by Beecher the money was raised and the two sisters became free.[20]

Harriet Beecher Stowe, the sister of the famous minister, herself already widely known as the author of *Uncle Tom's Cabin,* decided to take these girls under her wing and provide them with an education. She wrote of them to Mrs. Henry Cowles at Oberlin: "They seem to me remarkably amiable and docile as well as intelligent and having come of such an excellent stock, I have great hopes of them." No better place could have been found for them than Oberlin and no better family than the Cowles family of which they became a part. Mrs. Stowe, in the same letter, states her intentions with regard to them:

"I want them to have a thorough solid education calculated to strengthen & develop their reasoning powers & judgment rather than their taste & imagination, which are generally active enough in girls of their class. I want them also to become practically acquainted with household duties. . . .

"One thing with regard to their education I should not forget to mention. They have naturally fine musical abilities and it is very desirable to their success as teachers that they should have a thorough knowledge of vocal music if possible. I consider it one of the most essential things.

"With regard to their religious character I should like to have them imbibe that style of piety of which I have seen many examples from Oberlin, that kind which is pure, peaceful, humble,

[20]Harriet Beecher Stowe, *The Edmondson Family and the Capture of the Schooner Pearl* (Cincinnati—1856), reprinted from the *Key to Uncle Tom's Cabin,* and J. H. Painter, "The Fugitives of the Pearl," *Journal of Negro History,* I, 243–264 (July, 1916).

self denying and willing to spend and be spent anywhere for Christ."[21]

Early in July Mrs. Stowe sent fifty dollars for their support and a little later her husband sent thirty more for her, remarking, "She is using up her 'Uncle Tom' money very fast in charitable deeds to the poor blacks, & as it is all hers, & as it may be the Lord's will that she so use it, I make no objection." In August the "authoress" added twenty dollars and suggested that it, with the thirty last sent, be used to provide two scholarships, "so that when these two have been educated there two others may succeed them. I foresee an opening in this way to accomplish much good. Twenty five dollars of this money was given by the sewing society of the Salem St. Church, Br Edward Beecher minister, & the scholarship may stand in their name."[22]

She took a great interest in the education of the girls as is shown in her letters. "I notice already the improvement in Emily's last letter as to spelling," she wrote. "Tell her to write rather large and form every letter distinctly. Young writers often think that writing a *small* hand makes their writing look better but they are mistaken."[23] Further funds for the support of the girls were raised "by the ladies of Farmington, Conn., at a fair held expressly for this purpose."[24] Altogether Mrs. Stowe sent Mrs. Cowles three hundred and ten dollars—a much larger amount than was available to the average pair of sisters in Oberlin for a year's education.[25]

The little girls of the Cowles household (as undoubtedly many members of the Preparatory Department in which the colored girls were enrolled) found the Edmondson sisters very interesting. Little Mary Louisa Cowles wrote to her aunt in August of 1852: "The Misses Edmondson are living with us this summer. We *like* them both very much to say nothing of *loving* them dearly." Mrs. Cowles seems to have found much "to try" her in Emily. Mrs. Stowe said she was not surprised at this, however,

[21] Harriet Beecher Stowe to Mrs. Henry Cowles, [no place or date—probably June, 1852] (Cowles MSS).

[22] H. B. S. to Mrs. Cowles, July 8, Aug. 4, [1852], and Calvin E. Stowe to Mrs. Cowles, July 20, 1852 (Cowles MSS).

[23] H. B. S. to Mary Edmondson, Oct. 2, 1852 (Cowles MSS), etc.

[24] H. B. S. to Mrs. Cowles, Nov. 13, 1852 (Cowles MSS).

[25] Including $100.00 sent by her agent, John P. Jewett, to pay the expenses of Mary's final sickness. John P. Jewett to Rev. Henry Cowles, June 10, 1853 (Cowles-Little MSS).

adding that Emily had "been through enough to ruin five ordinary girls."[26]

Late in the following winter Mary Edmondson showed alarming symptoms, and soon it became clear that she was a victim of that dread disease which took such a large toll in the Cowles household and in Oberlin in the ante-bellum period. On May 18 she died of "pulmonary consumption." Emily returned to Washington where she entered the family of a lady to "assist in the care of young children, and in return, receive some facilities of education."[27]

Even more famous in his day was Anthony Burns who attended Oberlin from 1855 to 1862 with the exception of one term. A fugitive from slavery in Virginia, he escaped to Boston by sea, but he was followed and arrested May 24, 1854, under the Fugitive Slave Law. Two nights later the friends of the slave gathered in Fanueil Hall at the invitation of Bronson Alcott and Thomas Wentworth Higginson to consider whether a man should be carried back into slavery from the very "cradle of liberty." Heated by the fiery oratory of Wendell Phillips, the crowd became a mob and attacked the jail, only to be repulsed and their leaders arrested. Anthony Burns, guarded by several hundred soldiers, was taken from Boston amid the groans and hisses of a multitude of fifty thousand men who lined the streets and packed the roofs and balconies. It was estimated that this rendition cost the Government at least $40,000. Shortly afterward, however, he was purchased to freedom with funds raised by the members of the Twelfth Baptist Church of Boston.[28]

Later, a Boston woman of anti-slavery tendencies gave him the use of an Oberlin scholarship which she owned. It was a matter of great local interest when Anthony Burns arrived in Oberlin "to prepare himself . . . , by study, for greater usefulness to his oppressed race." In 1856, Charles Emery Stevens published a history of the case entitled *Anthony Burns, A History,* the sale of which helped the young colored man to pay his expenses while studying. He also, at various times, received further

[26]M. L. Cowles to "Dear Aunty," Aug. 9, 1852, and H. B. S. to Mrs. Cowles, Dec. 12, 1853 (Cowles MSS).

[27]*Oberlin Evangelist,* May 25, 1853; H. B. S. to Mrs. Cowles, Dec. 12, 1853, and Emily Edmondson to Mr. and Mrs. Cowles, Jan. 3, 1853 [1854], (Cowles MSS). She later married Larkin Johnson and became the mother of four children.—Painter, *Loc. Cit.,* 264.

[28]Charles Emery Stevens, *Anthony Burns, a History* (Boston—1856), 216 n.

charity from the friends of the slaves. In December of 1860 he wrote in a good flowing hand to Gerrit Smith of Peterboro, acknowledging the receipt of a gift of ten dollars. After leaving Oberlin, Burns became the pastor of the Zion Baptist Church at St. Catharines in Canada. A tall, broad-shouldered Negro of light brown color, he was a good speaker and much loved by his parishioners in the short time that he was with them. He died at St. Catherines in 1862 and is buried there.[29]

The type of the adventuress was not lacking. Oneda Estelle Dubois escaped from her owners in Alabama shortly before the war and came to Ohio. She studied for probably not more than a term at Oberlin, where she was known as Oneda Laco. In 1863 she was lecturing in Washington and attempting to raise money for a Negro college in Haiti.[30] Mary Edmonia Lewis attended Oberlin for four years. She was indicted in 1863 for poisoning two white coeds, but was found not guilty in a sensational trial when defended by J. M. Langston, the Negro lawyer. Three years later she had a studio in Rome (Italy!), where she had made quite a reputation as a sculptress![31]

The first colored student at Oberlin was James Bradley, one of the Lane Rebels, who attended the Sheffield Manual Labor Institute (a branch of Oberlin) in 1836.[32] In 1844 George B. Vashon of Pittsburgh received the A. B. degree, the first to be granted to a colored man at Oberlin. He had a useful career as a lawyer and teacher in Negro schools. William C. Whitehorne, who graduated in the following year, became a merchant and editor in Belize and Panama. William Howard Day graduated in 1847 in the same class with Lucy Stone and Antoinette Brown. He served many years as an editor and lecturer in behalf of his race, in England, Scotland and Ireland as well as the United States. In 1852 he married Lucy Stanton, whose graduation from the Literary Department (Ladies' Course) in 1850 has been previously mentioned. Two Negro men received the bachelor's

[29]Fred Landon, "Anthony Burns in Canada" reprinted from the Ontario Historical Society's *Papers and Records,* Vol. XXII (1925); *Oberlin Evangelist,* July 18, 1855, and Anthony Burns to Gerrit Smith, Dec. 28, 1860 (Gerrit Smith MSS).

[30]*Lorain County News,* Apr. 29, 1863, and list of colored students in Secretary's Office.

[31]J. M. Langston, *From the Virginia Plantation to the National Capitol* (Hartford—1894), 171–180, and *Lorain County News,* Mar. 28, Apr. 4, 1866.

[32]"List of Sheffield Students, June, 1836" (O. C. Lib. Misc. MSS).

degree in 1849: James Monroe Jones (later a gunsmith and engraver) and John Mercer Langston. Langston was probably the most distinguished of Oberlin's Negro graduates of the earlier period. He made a good record as a lawyer at Oberlin. He later became an educator and held various political offices.[33]

Negro men received the A. B. degree in 1850 (Lawrence W. Minor, later President of an Agricultural and Mechanical College at Alta Vista, Texas), in 1856 (John C. Jones, who became principal of various colored schools), in 1857 (William A. Jones, for many years a dentist in British Columbia), in 1858 (John G. Mitchell, later Dean of the Payne Theological Seminary at Wilberforce University), in 1859 (Elias T. Jones, a gold miner in British Columbia for many years), in 1860 (Benjamin K. Sampson, professor at Wilberforce and head of various colored schools), in 1861 (Charles A. Dorsey, who taught in Brooklyn for nearly forty years), in 1862 (James H. Muse, who became a minister in Cleveland, New Haven, and Washington, D. C.), in 1864 (John H. Cook, lawyer and teacher of law in Howard University), in 1865 (George G. Collins, also of Howard, Dr. Thomas L. Harris, a physician, and Thomas De Saliere Tucker, a convert from the Mendi African Mission, who became an editor of various New Orleans' newspapers during Reconstruction and later President of a Negro college in Florida), and in 1866 (James H. Piles, member of the Mississippi legislature and for several years Examiner in the United States Patent Office at Washington).[34]

Lucy Stanton was the first colored girl to graduate from the Ladies' Courses. Her example was followed by others in 1855 (Ann M. Hazle), 1856 (Louisa L. Alexander, Emma J. Gloucester, Sarah K. Wall and Sarah J. Woodson), 1860 (Blanche V. Harris and Susan Elizabeth Reid), 1861 (Maria L. Waring), 1864 (Mary McFarland), and 1865 (Marion I. Lewis). At the Commencement in 1862 Mary Jane Patterson received the A. B. degree, probably the first African Negro woman in the world to attain that distinction. Miss Patterson was born in Raleigh, North Carolina, and was brought to Oberlin in her early youth by her parents, probably fugitive slaves. She studied one year in the Preparatory Department and four years in the College before

[33] J. M. Langston, *Op. Cit.*

[34] This list is based chiefly on information from the Alumni Records in the Secretary's Office.

Oberlin O. Dec 28th /60.

Mr Gerrit Smith.

Highly esteemed Sir.

I avail myself of this Opportunity to say. Your kind letter came to hand in due time. and for the contents of which I truly thank you, It came at a time when, I had just got trust of a Saylor for a Coat. at $10– Being in need of some winter Clothing. but did not know where I should get the money, to pay. On the same day I found your friendly letter in the Office. containing just the amount. This I called a favor from God, through his servant,

Sir I again thank you, Yours truly

In Christ. Anthony Burns.

LETTER FROM ANTHONY BURNS TO GERRIT SMITH
(From the Gerrit Smith MSS in the Library of Syracuse University. Reproduced by permission.)

MARY JANE PATTERSON

First American Colored Woman to be Granted a Bachelor's Degree

(From the photograph in the possession of Mrs. Florence P. Clark, Washington, D.C.)

graduation. Upon receiving her degree she went to Philadelphia where she taught in the "Institute for Colored Youths" for seven years. In 1869 she went to Washington to teach and in 1871 became the first colored principal of the newly-established Preparatory High School for Negroes. She held the position until 1884, except for one year, and did much to build up the institution which now occupies the Dunbar High School building. After the appointment of a Negro man as her successor she continued as a teacher in the school until her death in 1894.[35] The next two colored girls to receive the A. B. degree were Fanny M. Jackson and Frances J. Norris, who graduated in 1865.[36]

In 1860, a Negro, Charles H. Thompson, graduated from the Theological Course. He later served for some time as President of Alcorn University in Mississippi. Many who did not graduate later served as teachers and ministers to their own race. Anthony Burns, already referred to, is a case in point. Samuel Gray, who attended for two years only, became a missionary in Africa under the American Missionary Association. Blanche [*sic*] K. Bruce, Reconstruction Senator from Mississippi from 1875 to 1881 and Register of the Treasury under Garfield and McKinley, claimed education at Oberlin, but the College records contain no mention of his name.[37]

There never was a large proportion of Negroes connected with the Oberlin Institute or College and the majority of these were usually in the Preparatory Department. A list of colored students made out at the request of Father Keep in 1852 shows that there were at that time 44 in all and that all but three of these were either in the Preparatory Department or were taking the Ladies' Course. One was in the Theological Department, two were in College. Seventeen were enrolled in the Ladies' Course and the remaining twenty-four in the Preparatory Department. Thirteen were "Gentlemen" and thirty-one "Ladies." There were over a thousand students listed in the Oberlin *Catalogue* of 1852–

[35]MSS in the Alumni Records, and Mary Church Terrell, "History of the High School for Negroes in Washington," *Journal of Negro History,* III, 252–266 (July, 1917).

[36]On Fanny Jackson see the *Lorain County News,* Jan. 30, 1866, and *Oberlin Review,* VIII, 23 (Oct. 9, 1880).

[37]*Biographical Directory of the American Congress,* 1774–1927, (Washington—1928); G. D. Houston, "A Negro Senator," *Journal of Negro History,* VII, 243–256, and S. D. Smith, *The Negro in Congress, 1870–1901* (Chapel Hill—1940), 25 *et seq.*

1853. Colored students represented less than five percent.[38] Probably there was never a larger proportion than this. In the spring of 1859 only thirty-two Negroes were reported, at a time when the student body numbered 1200 altogether.[39] Of course, there may have been other colored students in the summer and fall terms, but the percentage was probably not so high as that of 1852. An official statement of 1860 placed the proportion of colored students at four percent of the total student body in the year just passed.[40] The Rev. Henry Cowles, editor of the *Oberlin Evangelist,* made a list of colored students in Oberlin from 1835 to 1862. It is known to be incomplete, but is probably as complete as the official list of all students. J. M. Langston, the Negro lawyer, also made a check of colored students; and his list of men contained only two more than Cowles' list. Approximately 8,800 students attended some time at Oberlin before the 1861 Commencement. Professor Cowles lists only 245 Negroes as attending in this same period. This is less than three percent of the total.[41] We seem to be amply justified in concluding that less than one-twentieth of the students attending Oberlin in ante-bellum days were colored.

Yet, though the number educated was small, it was a contribution of vast importance to the civilization of the African race in America—a contribution greater, certainly, than that made by any other educational institution in the same period.

38"A list of names of the colored persons studying in Oberlin, made out at the request of Rev. J. M. Keep by J. E. Green, October 22, 1852" (Keep MSS).

39J. H. Fairchild in *Oberlin Evangelist,* July 16, 1856; "H. W." in the *Independent,* Aug. 7, 1856, and J. H. Fairchild, "Statistics of Oberlin College," June 29, 1859 (Misc. Archives).

40*Oberlin Evangelist,* Feb. 1, 1860.

41Henry Cowles' list of colored students is in the Cowles MSS in the Oberlin College Library. About 30 names of Negroes not on this list have been discovered but the names of hundreds of whites were omitted from the records. A card index of Negroes who attended Oberlin is located in the office of the Secretary.

CHAPTER XXXIV

GOING WEST TO COLLEGE

AS WE have seen, the majority of students in the Collegiate and Theological departments came from New England and New York in the thirties, and a considerable, though declining, percentage continued to represent those sections. In the early years the journey from their homes to Oberlin was an adventure involving many days, occasional hardships and, sometimes, real dangers.

In 1836 when Elam J. Comings started west from his home in Vermont he noted in his journal that it "was fine & pleasant," and he rather enjoyed the ride, "watching the course of the ten thousand little rills tumbling from the snow capt mountains," and "cheered with the songs of birds, bleating of flocks, the life & animation of nature." Nevertheless, at heart, he was sad. "My thoughts were turned inward & were embittered by the sad recollection of friends with whom I had just parted. A painful recollection of Parents, Brothers & Sisters whom I had left in tears now & then rushed upon my mind & started the unbidden tear from its lurking place. O, how severe is it to part with friends. Those tears of affec[tion], those half-uttered blessings, those last parting embraces can never be forgotten."[1] Before the completion of through lines of railroads, the journey from New England to Ohio was not an enterprise to be undertaken lightly.

From the founding of the Institute to 1850 the canal boat, the steamboat and stagecoach were almost the only means of transportation available. In the first generation of its use the Erie Canal was the greatest artery of east-west traffic. The hundreds of blunt-nosed boats, drawn slowly along its course by teams of mules or horses, carried an ever-growing stream of wheat from the West and all sorts of manufactured articles from the East.

[1]Elam J. Comings, MS Journal, May 9 and 10, 1836 (Original in the possession of Mrs. Eliza J. Comings, Kingsville, Ohio). Other references to the experiences of E. J. Comings in this chapter are from this journal.

They also carried thousands of passengers. Students coming to Oberlin from the East usually travelled on the canal. The passenger boats were very much like other canal boats in outward appearance, except that they were perhaps more brightly painted. The inside was divided into three parts: a "forecastle" for the crew of five or six, a ladies' cabin, and the main, gentlemen's cabin. The latter two, separated only by a curtain, were fitted out identically, but the gentlemen's cabin was considerably larger. A fat, squat, iron stove occupied a central position. Near it, at meal-times a table would be constructed by placing planks on trestles. At night wooden shelves furnished the sleeping quarters. These "berths" were in three tiers—one near the floor, one very near the ceiling and one between. At night all doors and windows would be shut tight to keep out the mosquitoes as well as the "deadly night air." As a result the atmosphere in the cabin was certain to become heavy and poisonous, particularly for those "on the top shelf." On hot nights many passengers were forced to climb down and go out on deck, running the risk of insects and fever rather than suffocate. Morning must have been a great relief to the travelling student, when he could douse his head in a pail of water dipped out of the canal and jump to the tow-path and walk for a while. During the day passengers usually spent much of their time on the deck on the roof of the cabin, playing cards (not Oberlin students!), reading, chatting or dozing. The only unpleasant circumstance in fine weather was the occasional passage under very low bridges or a jam at the locks. It was not a bad way to travel if one were patient.

Elam Comings made his journey from Vermont to Oberlin largely by water and as far as possible by canal. His summary of his travelling expenses may serve as an outline of the trip:

Paid for passage Burlington to Whitehall [Lake Champlain]	$1.50
From Whitehall to Troy [Champlain Canal]	1.25
Paid 4 cts for a lemon	
Paid for lodging at Albany	.12½
For ride on rail road from Albany to Schenectady	1.00
For dinner	8
Paid for passage from Schenectady to Buffalo [Erie Canal]	5.00
For breakfast	6

Paid for dinner	.12
For freight [and fare?] from Buffalo to Cleveland	2.50
From Cleveland to Elyria by stage	1.25
For supper & lodging	.75

After crossing Lake Champlain, he "Arrived at Whitehall . . . a town of considerable business but the most ill looking, irregularly layed out & most filthy place that I ever saw. . . . The town in a continual crowd & bustle with ten thousand emigrants. . . . Found it impossible to find a suitable boat. The best I could do was to take one filled with the noisy, intemperate profane trash with a few Americans no better. The wreckless oaths of the whole company (or nearly so), drinking, smoking & . . . the continuous yelling of infants promised a great variety of disagreeables, yea more—of the intolerables. . . . But, however, the ride was not void of interest. The scenery was of a wild romantic character, finely varied by hills & valleys richly clad in the green verdure of spring. The grass starting forth over the hills & valleys . . . formed a pleasing variety for the eye to rest on; and the manners & character of the passengers, though an unpleasing thot, I trust not an unprofitable theme for meditation. . . .

"As night approached . . . the passengers, all aware of their scanty room for sleep, began the strife to see who would have the berths which, resulted in many hard words. . . . But I determined to have nothing to do with it & determined to spend the night on deck rather than camp with 26 or 30 individuals in a little cabin of 12 feet by 10 & according wrapped up in my cloak & camped with naught but the dark & frowning sky for my covering. But the air being warm & sultry was able to sleep some at intervals till 4 o'clock when it began to rain & I was obliged to find shelter in the cabin with my fellow sleepers."

At Albany Comings "for the first time saw a rail car in operation." In fact, as he noted in his itinerary, he rode from Albany to Schenectady on the railroad, returning to a canal boat at that point. His boat was detained at German Flats for three days "by an immense crowd of boats jambed in for 9 miles in length." Comings was much irritated at the ungodliness of the "Canawlers." "To-day several men fell in a contention about whose boats should go through the locks first which resulted in a bloody & shameful fight, such a one as a dog should blush at." And again:

"Have heard little else than the most terrible oaths and blasphemes of the multitude all day. What a complete hell is this!" It was a great joy to the passengers to get started again. The remainder of the haul to Buffalo was comparatively pleasant through the "extended meadows and corn fields" of the Mohawk Valley, past Utica and Rome and through a "long swamp" where only "Now & then the forest was broken & a few log huts erected." Farther west "large fields of wheat stretched themselves on either side & the orchards spread over the hills now full in bloom presented a most lovely appearance." In the vicinity of Rochester the traveller found the country "fertile & delightful" and remarked on the "many very fine fields of wheat the largest & best I ever saw." Of course, he "viewed with some degree of pleasure the locks [at Lockport] & the canal through the rocks for seven miles," but "With pain [he] beheld a great multitude standing about the taverns & groceries & spending the day [Sabbath] in a most wreckless manner."

When Charles Livingstone, younger brother of the explorer, came to Oberlin from Scotland in 1840, he wrote home a long letter describing his journey.[2] From Albany to Buffalo he traveled by canal:

"We reached Albany about 6 next morning . . . where I took canal to Buffalo 363 miles from do [Albany] on the borders of Canada. The canal boats are long & narrow drawn by two horses & very comfortably fitted up to accomodate passengers, cushioned seats & stoves in them. . . . I paid one sovreign & 25 cents, being 36 cents less than the common fare. I told them I came from Scotland & paid a great deal for travelling so they took it. [!] We started from Albany about 11 oclk on Wednesday. In the canal boats all fare alike, there is no distinction between Rich & poor, all have the same privileges. Toward evening I saw a young man looking at a map of Ohio pointing out places to some who were going to the state. I went to look at the map too & asked him if he knew where Lorain County was & did he know what part Oberlin College was. Yes, said he, I am a member of it. I told him then that I had come from Scotland to study there.

[2]Charles Livingstone to Neil Livingstone, May 22 [1840] (O. C. Lib. Misc. MSS). His account of his journey is printed in full in R. S. Fletcher, "Going West to College in the Thirties," Oberlin College Library *Bulletin*, vol. II, No. 1, (Oberlin—1930). See also Sherlock Bristol, *The Pioneer Preacher* (New York—1898), 320–322.

Oh indeed, I wish I had seen you sooner. He then introduced me to a young Lady who was returning to Oberlin. His name is Mr. Sherlock Bristol A. B. from Cheshire Connecticut. Ladys name Miss Ingram. . . . I was then considerably relieved as I could get nobody who knew anything about Oberlin. It rained on Wednesday all day and all night and in the morning we learnt that part of the bank of the canal had been broken down so we had to stop when we got about 15 miles from Albany. We ascertained that it would take eight days to mend it."

The young theological student made the most of the delay. "On Sabbath he [Bristol] preached. There was a great number of boats before us and behind us. Another boat came along side of us. We got a piece of clothe stuck up by 4 poles over his head to protect him from the heat of the sun which was very warm that day. . . . His text was Malachi 3 verse 14 first clause of verse. He had my hymn book and gave out the 75 hymn which 3 or 4 sung accompanied by a flute."

The 1838 *Catalogue* of the Oberlin Collegiate Institute announced that, "None can be received who travel on the Sabbath, on their way to Oberlin." Bristol and Livingstone and the two young ladies, therefore, felt called upon to stop over the next week end at Canastota, though it involved losing the remainder of their fare to Buffalo which had been paid up at Albany. On Monday they resumed their journey. "We passed about 12 miles from the falls of Niagara then came to Buffalo where we left the canal and went on board a steamer on Lake Erie, saw Canada across the Lake. . . . We would have got to Buffalo from N. York in 7 days had the break not happened in the canal. We might have got there sooner by taking the railroad . . . but it is dearer."

The trip by steamboat through Lake Erie to Cleveland was not always too comfortable. Lake Erie was well known for its storms and the little steamers of the day were sometimes badly knocked about. All of the passenger boats in the thirties were of the old side-wheel variety, though usually they possessed a vertical stern wheel also. The first propeller-equipped steamer was put in service in 1841. Explosions, wrecks, and fatal fires, though overpublicized, were all too common. The *Oberlin Evangelist* of August 18, 1841, contains a notice of a "DREADFUL CONFLAGRATION!" in which there were "170 LIVES LOST!"

Deck passage was cheaper and probably not more unpleasant than in the cabins. The Prudden boys from Lockport needed to save money. George, the elder brother, wrote to his parents: " . . . We took deck passage & spent the windy night upon the top of the upper deck, with the clear sky for our bed curtains, alternately engaged in sleeping & vomiting. Had we not been so sick, I think our situation might have been tolerably pleasant. The wind blew hard but as it was directly to our back we did not feel its effects so very much. I understood however the next day that the Passengers in the Boat which was moving the other way, against the wind, were very much frightened at the violence of the storm. Our fare on the lake was two dollars & a half a piece. Freight on our barrel 50 cents. At Cleveland we met with another young man destined for Oberlin who had gone through Lockport but an hour or two before we started, and had come all the way from Buffalo on the same boat. He accompanied us to Oberlin." Few women would care to try the deck passage, as did Lucy Stone, but, at least, she had fair weather.[3]

After reaching the village of Cleveland (1000 people in 1830 and 6000 in 1840), there remained a hard journey by wagon or stagecoach. The famous Concord coach of the type later used in Rocky Mountain staging had come into general use by this time. The great wooden body covered with painted canvas was suspended from the running gear on thoroughbraces made of several layers of leather straps. The nine or more passengers inside (Dickens describes a case when twelve were crowded in.) were thrown against each other and the sides of the coach with great violence whenever the wheels collided with a stone or stump or bounded over baked or frozen ruts. One passenger usually rode on the box with the driver and occasionally others were stowed away with the baggage and other freight on the flat top. Even in the East the roads were abominable, everywhere going up and down steep hills and through fords. They were full of great mudholes that seemed bottomless, and at certain seasons of the year the ruts were so deep and hard that it was almost impossible to turn the coach out of them. Again and again the passengers were

[3]George and Davis Prudden to Peter Prudden, Oberlin, July 18, 1836 (Prudden-Allen MSS), and Alice Stone Blackwell, *Lucy Stone*, 45–46. In the fall of 1841, Samuel Reynolds Eells, a college student from Unadilla, New York, slipped from the gang-plank at Cleveland and was drowned. His tombstone in the Oberlin Westwood Cemetery, erected by his classmates, tells the story.

required to disembark when going up a steep hill or in order to pry the vehicle out of a more than usually boggy spot. It was not an unheard of thing for the coach to be overturned, when all hands were required to right it and help to control and untangle the plunging horses.

In the summer of 1838 the Elyria paper reported an accident. "The Mail coach which left Cleveland for Detroit on Wednesday morning last, on its way to this town, was overturned with a full load of passengers, on the bridge between Dover Furnace and the Stage-house in that place. The editor of this paper, with a young lady under his care, were of the company of eight passengers inside, and there were three outside, two on the top and one with the driver, making in all twelve persons. The coach was turned *bottom upwards* off the bridge *into the creek*. Of those inside *none* were materially injured. One on the outside was *severely hurt*, and one slightly."[4] It is a wonder not that there should have been some such accidents but that there were no more. Charles Livingstone wrote that he rode from Cleveland to Oberlin "over one of the worst roads ever I saw. The carriage was hung on springs drawn by two horses. Such a shaking we got on that road I never got before." The Rev. Jabez Burns, who visited Oberlin in 1847, presumed "that the very worst roads in any part of the civilized world may be found between Cleveland and Oberlin."[5]

A young lady writing to Mr. Finney a few months before the founding of Oberlin portrays the possibilities of staging west of Buffalo in the thirties. She took the stage to Cleveland because she feared to make the trip on the lake in the threatening storm. She found the traveling "most horrible. We rode eight miles upon the lake shore and so near that evry wave dashed upon the coach. It was truly terrifying. We were nearly five hours going Seven miles. But this was not the worst. We had to pass through a swamp nine miles long where it seemed evry minute as if the Stage would upset but the Lord was with us and we were kept from harm. I was in the Stage three days and two nights and stopped at no time only long enough to change horses." Mrs. Dascomb made the trip from Cleveland to Elyria in a stage in 1834. She wrote of it to her parents: "Road very bad—from ruts &

[4]*Ohio Atlas and Elyria Advertiser,* June 20, 1838.

[5]Charles Livingstone, May 22 [1840], and Jabez Burns, *Notes of a Tour in the United States and Canada, in the Summer and Autumn of 1847* (London—1848), 109.

mud—we were in constant danger of overturning. Once when we came to a ditch in the road, the gent. got out & took down the fence so that we cd. turn aside into the adjoining field & *ride around* the obstacle."[6]

Oberlin, in the early days, was not on the main stage line, however. Doctor and Mrs. Dascomb obtained a wagon for the last lap of the way:

" . . . At Elyria we dined and obtained a 2 horse wagon to transport us (& 2 gent. from N. Eng. going to the Institute as students) to *our journey's end.* Found the waggon a very comfortable conveyance, & was in no fear of being turned out into the mud, for the driver assured us it cd. not turn over. You can not conceive of a more miserable road than we had—the last two miles especially—but still I enjoyed the ride & our party was all very cheerful. When passing through the woods, I was so delighted with the black squirrels, the big trees, & above all, the beautiful wild flowers, that at times I quite forgot to look out for the 'scraggy limbs' that every now and then gave us a rude brush—till a warning from Dr. D.—that I wd. *get my eyes torn out,* seconded perhaps by an unceremonious *lash* from a neighboring bough, wd. recall me to the duty of self preservation. Glad were we when an opening in the forest dawned upon us, & Oberlin was seen."

In 1837 Artemas Beebe, the Elyria tavern keeper, ran a stage to Oberlin from Elyria on Tuesdays, Thursdays and Saturdays. In 1839 J. L. Ladd proposed to establish "a two horse stage from . . . [Oberlin] to Elyria, and the mouth of Black River, and back, once a day, stage to leave Oberlin every day at 7 oc. A.M. and return the same evening at 7 oc." There are no records to show whether this service was ever established or not. In the spring of 1840 readers of the *Oberlin Evangelist* were informed that "Mr. Lewis Holtslander will send a team to Cleveland to carry passengers and freight twice each week." In the fall of the same year Mr. Holtslander undertook to "send a carriage to Cleveland to carry passengers and freight three times a week."

[6]Susan Collier to C. G. Finney, Oct. 26, 1833 (Finney MSS), and Marianne Dascomb to Daniel H. Parker, 1834—Postmarked Oberlin, May 30 (O. C. Lib. Misc. MSS). Some students came in on foot. Quincy Bosworth walked from Meigs County, Ohio, to Oberlin in 1845, all "his worldly goods . . . tied up in a bundle and swung over his shoulder."—T. H. Robinson, MS History of the Class of 1850 (O. C. Lib.).

Summer Arrangement of Mail Coaches from Elyria.

DAILY.

The Mail will leave this place, daily, for Detroit and Cleveland, as follows:—
For CLEVELAND, - at 6 o'clock, A. M.
For DETROIT, - - - at 10 o'clock, A. M.

☞Passengers conveyed in Post Coaches

Three Times a Week.

The Mail Stage will leave Elyria—
For OBERLIN, at 1 o'clock, P. M., on TUESDAYS, THURSDAYS, and SATURDAYS.

☞For seats, apply at the *Stage Office*. East end of Broad street.

Extras furnished on short notice, and on reasonable terms.

All baggage at the risk of the owners.

A. BEEBE, Proprietor.

Elyria, May 23, 1837. 48

NOTICE OF THE STAGE COACH SERVICE FROM ELYRIA TO OBERLIN FROM THE *OHIO ATLAS AND ELYRIA ADVERTISER*—1837

(Courtesy of the Western Reserve Historical Society. Photo by Edmondson.)

Carriages left Oberlin on Mondays, Wednesdays and Fridays and departed for Oberlin from the "Cleveland Temperance House" on Tuesdays, Thursdays and Saturdays. In 1841 the same individual began daily service each way. "Good COACHES—good teams—and honest, faithful drivers" were promised. Even before this Henry Cowles wrote to his wife from Oberlin: "There is a daily stage—a real stage coach from Cleveland to this place every day, leaving Cleveland in the morning and carrying through for one dollar. It is the old line of western stages with the addition of an off shoot to Oberlin which leaves Elyria when the stage from Cleveland arrives, and returns from here there in time to fall into the return track."[7] It was only twelve years after the establishment of daily stage service to Oberlin that the railroad reached it.

Before the railroad actually entered Oberlin, however, a line built through Wellington furnished easy connections to Cleveland. In midsummer of 1850 it was triumphantly announced that "the Cleveland, Columbus and Cincinnati Railroad . . . is now complete and in fine running order from Cleveland to Wellington. . . . From the latter place to Oberlin nine miles, carriages are in readiness, so that passengers go through from Cleveland to Oberlin in about three and a half hours, and at the very low price of one dollar, twelve and a half cents."[8] For the next two and a half years this was the usual route of travel to and from Oberlin.

In the spring of 1852 construction was begun on the "Toledo, Norwalk, and Cleveland Rail-Road" which was to bring "to the very doors of our College the facilities of Rail-Road travel." Its progress was watched with the greatest interest and in the autumn the editor of the *Evangelist* proudly recorded: "At this present writing, Oct. 8, the rails are laid a mile or more beyond us and are progressing rapidly. The locomotive now passes our village daily, and we seem to realize that we shall be put in railroad connection with the Eastern and Western world." In the following year one passenger train was running each way every day. In July, 1853, there were three passenger trains each way

[7]*Ohio Atlas and Elyria Advertiser,* Sept. 27, 1832; J. L. Ladd—To the Citizens of Oberlin, July 16, 1839" (Treas. Off., File E); *Oberlin Evangelist,* May 6, Sept. 9, 1840; Aug. 18, 1841, and Henry Cowles to Alice W. Cowles, Oberlin [July] 1840 (Cowles-Little MSS). See the account of mail service below on pages 564-565.

[8]*Oberlin Evangelist,* July 17, Nov. 20, 1850, and Feb. 26, 1851.

"(Sundays always excepted)." For a week in August free rides were offered to all who lived along the line, and one day 1200 people from Oberlin, Grafton and Wakeman took advantage of the opportunity![9] In 1866 three trains stopped in Oberlin going east and four going west. This railroad (later absorbed by the New York Central) originally ran south of Elyria by way of Grafton. The depot was south of the track and east of Main Street at approximately the present location of the freight station. In 1866 the line was changed to connect directly with Elyria. It was at the same time that the present depot was built on a site donated by Oberlin citizens—"the finest of any intermediate station on the road." Oberlinites were so enthusiastic about it that they talked "of an oyster supper and house warming in the most approved style."[10]

Even before the railroad reached Wellington students and others coming to Oberlin found railroad travel opened up for part of their way. Lucy Stone found it possible to ride in "the cars" all the way from Albany to Buffalo even in 1843. It was not nearly such a harrowing experience, she informed her mother, as she had been led to expect. Of course, the trains of those days were nowhere near equal in speed and convenience to those of the twentieth century. One young girl, after arriving in Oberlin, wrote home to her mother in North Blandford, Massachusetts: ". . . Had a very pleasant journey but did not get along so fast as we expected. There was another train ran off the track, one that we was to meet. Wee went so slow that Albert got off and went into an orchard and got some apples and got on agane so wee did not get to Buffelow till most dark."[11]

Most travellers on the early railroads were prone to expatiate on the "wonders of the modern age." Professor Henry Cowles made a flying trip from Oberlin to Newark, N. J., and back in 1852. ". . . The wonderful speed of travel by steam," he wrote, "has almost annihilated distance." On his return journey he

[9] *Oberlin Evangelist,* Oct. 13, 1852; Feb. 16, July 6, 1853, and the *Cleveland Daily True Democrat,* Aug. 15, 1853, quoted in the *Annals of Cleveland.*

[10] *Lorain County News,* Mar. 28, Aug. 8, Sept. 12, Nov. 7, 21, 1866. The contractor who built the road from Oberlin to Elyria absconded, leaving considerable debts, some of them to Oberlin merchants (*Ibid.,* Dec. 20, 1865). An excursion of Oberlin people to Sandusky and Johnson's Island in October, 1866, provided funds to plant 125 shade trees in "Depot Park" (*Ibid.,* May 1, 1867, and W. W. Wright to A. A. Wright, Oct. 11, 1866, in the Wright MSS).

[11] A. S. Blackwell, *Lucy Stone,* 44, and F. A. Collester to Mrs. John F. Collester, Nov. 9, 1851 (O. C. Library).

"chose the route via Erie Rail Road from New York to Dunkirk —a route which never can fail to charm the lover of nature's wild, rugged, and romantic scenery. We were glad to see manifest evidences both of careful supervision and of general prosperity. All along the narrow defiles, we saw sentinels stationed at suitable distances, whose flags gave notice to the flying trains that '*all is right.*' "[12] An English lady visitor to Oberlin, just after the close of the Civil War, rode in a sleeping car. Especially for an English visitor, her comments were flattering:

"Of all modern inventions and appliances for luxury in travel, commend me to the American sleeping cars, in some of which I have enjoyed a better night's rest than at many an inn. The 'cars' on American railways are always long saloon carriages, with an aisle down the center leading to doors at the ends, and down each side a row of seats, each containing two persons, and commanding a separate window. These seats are cleverly made with reversable backs, so that the passengers can sit with either back or face to the engine: Almost all choosing the latter alternative, except when parties of three or four sit facing each other 'sociable' fashion.

"Starting by an evening train, we forthwith secured sleeping berths by payment of an extra dollar, and were initiated into the ingenious plan for their construction. Down came the backs of two opposite seats, which fitted exactly across the space between, and formed a solid couch, on which was laid a good mattress, a brown rug, and some pillows, a curtain separating off the passage-way. My friend and I secured two opposite berths, and, with windows partly open on each side, soon slept the sleep of the just, disturbed only by the conductor's anxiety to shut up our windows, lest we should, as he said, 'freeze to death *and* be burnt up with sparks from the engine!' Having so good a bed, the regular motion on the broad guage was really rather lulling than otherwise."[13]

Such luxuries were not, however, for the vast majority of Oberlin students even after they became available. When John Fraser (a student in the Collegiate Department) reached Cleveland on his way to Oberlin in the same year, he found that "the

[12]*Oberlin Evangelist,* Sept. 1, 1852.

[13]Sophia Jex-Blake, *A Visit to Some American Schools and Colleges* (London—1867), 15 *et seq.*

Toledo train had departed . . . went out prospecting & discovered that there was a freight train going according to various accounts at 4.30, 5., 5.30. & 5.45. Having disposed of our duds we started up Superior St. Saw the city monument &c &c. Went to the Court House and heard some rather amusing things. Left C. at 5.45 on the Freight. Laid over at Grafton nearly an hour. Arrived at Oberlin 9.15. Had the pleasure of jumping off. To add to the sublimity of the occasion, it snowed like everything. Put for Mr. Bardwell's. Found the folks all abed. Succeeded in waking them up. Got something to eat, went to bed." The next day he confided to his diary: "Was quite surprised on waking up this morning to find myself in Oberlin.Went to Latin & Greek—Saw Alphonse & learned that he & C. E. W. came on the express yesterday afternoon. Went in pursuit of my trunk. Found it at the depot (It was left in Cleveland.). Went & got it with a wheelbarrow. Settled my incidentals ($2.00 outrageous). Bot my books. Paid $15.00 on board, was appointed Chief Milker Commanding Dept. Saw Brewer of Farmington Ill. Shook hands with my class mates, wrote home, unpacked by trunk, and did lots of other things, but didn't study any. Feel tremendous blue, almost homesick. What's the use anyhow?"[14]

For periods varying from a few weeks to ten or more years these students were to make their homes in the village of Oberlin under the paternal supervision of the authorities of Oberlin College.

[14]John G. Fraser, MS Diary, Feb. 27, 28, 1865.

CHAPTER XXV

OBERLIN VILLAGE

A LESS attractive natural setting than the flat, glacial plain of Russia Township would be hard to find. The beauty of the present Oberlin is largely man-made. It was partly because of the swampy location that in 1836 James M. Buchanan determined to abandon his position on the faculty after a tenure of only a few weeks. Finney, himself, admitted that the site was "unfortunate, ill-considered, hastily decided upon; and had it not been for the good hand of God in helping us at every step, the institution would have been a failure because of its ill-judged location."[1]

The surroundings must have had a very depressing effect upon the youths who came from homes in the varied and beautiful scenery of New England and New York. One young man whose home was among the splendid hills of Leon, in Cattaraugus County, New York, wrote longingly of "the green woods of my native hills." A young lady student in the early fifties resorted to poetry, lamenting the case of

One whose early years
Among the hills that skirt the east were spent,
Where many a mimic mount its bold front reared,
While from its rugged side cool streams are sent,
Which murmuring o'er their pebbly bottoms go,
To moisten and refresh the vale below.

Who found in Oberlin—

Instead of varied scenery, hill, and dell
With woodland interspersed and flowery lawn,
Where sparkling waters from their fountains well
And dancing, laughing, sing their rippling song,

[1]D. L. Dumond, *Letters of J. G. Birney,* I, 352, and Finney's MS Memoirs, 680.

. . . a level, low and changeless land,
Whose waters sluggish in their channels stand.[2]

Many were the boys who must have longed on a hot day for a decent swimming hole as did one preparatory student who wrote to his brother just before the Civil War:

" . . . I have wished I could have a place to go in swimming, for there is no place nearer than Black River and that is about 4 miles from here. The only stream there is in Oberlin is Plumb Creek, and that is a little larger than the brook which comes into Dayton's pond generally is when it is all dried up.

"But if you were only here so that you could go down and behold the beautiful scenery on its banks, and take a sketch of it you would like it very much, I have no doubt. You would start out, say, just after a rain, when all nature is beautiful. You would stand upon its clayey banks and behold spread out before you in a beautiful landscape, old logs, bits of bone, negroes, old and young, peaces of leather, &c—stumps, rail fences &c. &c. Entranced you would stand taking in, as only such an artist as you are can, the different points of the scene, when attempting to take in a different point your heels fly from under you and in consequence of the attraction of gravitation you paint a full length profile of yourself in Ohio mud. So much for landscape painting in Ohio."[3] Plumb (not Plum) Creek, the only element of natural beauty which Oberlin afforded, appears to have been an object of ridicule from the earliest days.

Not only was the Oberlin region flat and uninteresting, but the stiff, clay soil made life tedious for gardeners and farmers and sometimes almost unendurable for pedestrians. It is a dreary, muddy picture which a daughter of one of the faculty members gives us in a composition written in 1845. The composition is in the form of a letter:

" . . . In compliance with your request I will try to give you something of a description of Oberlin. In the first place it is surrounded by trees. You cannot see more than two miles at the farthest. The soil is very clayey, I should think, for when it rains

[2]T. A. Cheney to F. A. Fitch, Oct. 11, 1848 (in the possession of Mrs. Charles E. Lansing, Albany, N. Y.), and an essay and poem entitled "The First Week in Oberlin," by M. M. Gilbert, who came to Oberlin in 1853 (original now in the possession of Gladys A. Sperling, Pulaski, N. Y.).

[3]Henry Prudden to brother, June 25, 1859 (in the possession of Miss Lillian Prudden, New Haven, Conn.)

THE EARLIEST PHOTOGRAPH OF TAPPAN SQUARE—ABOUT 1860

Note the Chapel on the left and Tappan Hall on the right—also the fence, the Osage Orange hedge, the plank sidewalk, the young evergreens and the bandstand.

(From an original photograph in the Oberlin College Library)

AN OBERLIN HOME OF THE FIFTIES
James H. Fairchild's House on Professor Street, now Fairchild Cottage
(Photograph in the Oberlin College Library)

it is very mudy and there are so few sidewalks that it is very difficult to walk more than a rod without getting a free shoe in mud. Of course [you] are under the nesity of . . . wareing high and thick shouse. The bildings are not very near each other and probelay would look very lonesom to you as you are accostomed to see them surrounded with shade trees and subery while here it is a rare thing to see even [a] rose bush. They have lately built a larg brick meating house, which is surrond by mud and can [only] bee entered by [an] inclined plain made of rough boards."[4]

Henry Howe, who visited Oberlin a year later, of course wished to sell his book. Contrast his description with the foregoing one: "The town is situated on a beautiful and level plain, girted around by the original forest in its primitive majesty. The dwellings at Oberlin are usually two stories in height, built of wood, and painted white, after the manner of the villages of New England, to which this has a striking resemblance."[5] Both of these descriptions were true.—White painted houses, unshaded, stood along rutted streets; the town was surrounded by "majestic"—and swampy—forest.

One young man who came to Oberlin in 1836 declared soon after his arrival: "I was more disappointed in the appearance of the soil, than in any other one thing. It looks almost like a swamp." In 1851 a student wrote to her parents in a postscript to a family letter: "You need not worry about me; the most that I worry about is that I shall get stuck in the mud and cant get out." The next spring a young man wrote to his brother: "You have probably heard of *Ohio Mud* but I never had any *conception* of it untill I saw it with my own eyes and walked in it with my own feet. One good rain here lasting three hours will wet up a mortar bed in the road knee deep. But to balance this, one day's sun will dry it entirely up and leave the roads so that it will be dry walking in the middle of it." Five years later a "prep" apostrophized October in his diary: "Old October, all hail . . . ! You came today open handed, and you poured upon us rain and storm; as a consequence you will leave us *mud!* But nevertheless you are welcome, sit down!" The next day, he added: "Whew,

[4]Composition by Helen M. Cowles, dated Oberlin, March 22, 1845 (Cowles-Little MSS).

[5]Henry Howe, *Historical Collections of Ohio,* (Cincinnati—1848), 315. The description is based on a tour of the State made in 1846. See the frontispiece of volume I of this history.

October! you've did a fine job!" Just as the end of the Civil War period the editor of the local newspaper felt called upon to devote an entire article to "Mud!!" and found that subject "as inexhaustible as the supply," but he was finally forced to stop in order to wash his hands.[6]

Oberlin was never a large town, even comparatively; it was always dependent on education as its chief industry. Writing in January, 1835, Brewster Pelton, the tavern keeper, estimated that there were "thirty dwelling houses within one mile" containing three hundred people including the hundred students then in the Institute. A student wrote to his father in 1837: "I would say . . . that there are 70 or 80 dwelling houses in the collony besides the college buildings. Some are brick & some wood,—besides shops, stores, mills . . . —& this has been done in about 5 years." The Committee on Farms and Gardens reported to the agricultural society in 1842 a population of 1398. By 1847 it had increased to 1736. When Henry Howe visited Oberlin in 1846 he estimated that it contained one hundred and fifty houses. A report made to the agricultural society in 1849 puts the population as only 1570, even including 450 students. The census of 1850 gives the entire population of the township as 1887. A careful enumeration in 1855 revealed a population of over two thousand: 1127 females and 914 males. The incoming student, even in 1859, was not impressed with the size of the community. "When I got off the cars at the Oberlin station," wrote young Henry Prudden to the folks back home, "I looked about to see where the town was, but I could see but 5 houses. What to do I did not know, but I finally asked a young man the way to Prof. Cowles. He said he was going right there so I went with him under his umbrella for it rained very hard."[7] The streets were muddy rivers and the sidewalks were probably not in the best of repair. If it happened to be after dark a guide

[6]Geo. Prudden to Peter Prudden, July 18, 1836 (Prudden-Allen MSS); F. A. Collester to her mother, Nov. 9, 1851, and H. D. Kingsbury to Lewis Kingsbury, May 10, 1852 (O. C. Library); Sprague Upton, MS Diary, Oct. 1, 2, 1857 (in the possession of Prof. W. T. Upton), and *Lorain County News,* Mar. 8, 1865.

[7]Letter from Brewster Pelton, Jan. 7, 1835 (owned by Jeannette Kinney, Willoughby, Ohio); C. Winslow to Zenas Winslow, Sept. 16, 1837 (copy in O. C. Library Misc. MSS); Reports for 1842 and 1847 in Agricultural Society MSS (O. C. Lib.); H. Howe, *Historical Collections of Ohio,* 315; *Oberlin Evangelist,* Oct. 24, 1849; Nov. 21, 1855; *Ohio Observer,* Feb. 1, 1850, and Henry Prudden to his parents, June 3, 1859 (in the possession of Lillian Prudden, New Haven, Conn.).

would be particularly necessary, for there were no gas lights at this date. This reception must have been a partial cause of Henry Prudden's later homesickness. The national census found 2915 residents in Oberlin in 1860 and 3343 in 1870.

After 1850 Oberlin contained the largest percentage of Negroes of any community in the Western Reserve or even northeast of Columbus. In the township Negroes made up nine percent of the total in 1850, 17% in 1860 and 25% in 1870. The percentage in the village itself was somewhat higher: 25% in 1860 and 27% in 1870, separate figures not being available for 1850. Colored persons have made up about a quarter of the population ever since.

In 1835 the plan of Oberlin was merely the intersection of two roads (the present Lorain and Main streets) with a second east-west road (College Street) intersecting the north-south road farther south. In that year Professor Street was laid out north and south in front of the homes of Finney and Mahan, then under construction, and parallel to Main Street.[8] Thus the common, College green, or Tappan (Hall) Square, the present "campus" or park, was bounded on four sides by roads and this has remained the key to the Oberlin town plan ever since. These four streets have been extended and other streets laid out intersecting them at right angles. In 1835–36 a fund contributed by various colonists was used to build "a comfortable passage for carriages to the west line of the Oberlin colony." In the fifties, with the building of the railroad, construction was pushed south along Main Street toward the "Depot." In 1862 Forest Street was opened up west from Professor Street and Mayor and Professor J. M. Ellis' house was built on it.[9] The town plan with the campus at the center is symbolic of the dominant part always played by the College in community life.

Some of the early college buildings were on the square: Tappan Hall near the center, the Chapel just south of it after 1855 and, in the late sixties, French and Society halls at the northwest and southwest corners respectively. South of the square and facing it were (east to west) Oberlin Hall, the New Boarding House

[8]MS Plan of Oberlin—1835 (O. C. Lib. Misc. MSS). Reproduced in W. B. Phillips, *Oberlin Colony,* 21.

[9]Papers dated July 20, 1835, and June 8, 1836 in Misc. Archives, and *Lorain County News,* Dec. 10, 1862.

(Ladies' Hall), and Colonial Hall. Behind these were Walton Hall (on the west side of Main Street) and the Laboratory on the east side of Professor Street. Music Hall was west of Professor Street across from the Laboratory on the present site of Baldwin Cottage. None of these buildings (except, perhaps, the Chapel) was remarkable for beauty. John Morgan wrote truly to Mark Hopkins in 1851: "There is little in the plan or buildings to recommend it—the almost entire attraction is in the living soul."[10]

Probably the best available sources on the appearance of early Oberlin are the papers of the Agricultural and Horticultural Society. Each year a report was made to this society on the condition of door-yards, gardens, streets, etc., as well as on agricultural and industrial production. In 1841 fourteen men were complimented on their excellent gardens, of whom four, including Professor Morgan and Father Shipherd, were selected for special mention. Seventeen were listed as having gardens which were "poorly Managed, Meagre production & a Scandall to Agriculture." In the following year D. B. Kinney was found to have "the best selected fruits of Apples, Plumbs, Cherries & rasberries in this Village," and "Sister Pelton" was declared to have "the best cultivated and arranged Vegetable Garden . . . cultivated by her own hands." In the garden she was often to be seen "with Gentle hands guiding the spade, the shovel, the rake & the how [*sic*] in their appropriate office." It was decided that "Sister Crosby [had] the most beautiful Flower Garden" but to the "Ladies of the Institute" went the palm for second best—"for System in arrangement, due proportion of Mounds, beds, etc." In 1861 Bayard Taylor, after lecturing in Oberlin, commented on the "little evidences of taste and culture everywhere manifest —the vines, flowers, ornamental shrubs, the neat bits of lawn."[11]

Though there were many well kept gardens still there were dooryards which presented quite a different appearance: "Steril Door yards, covered with weeds of every noxious character, pools of stagnant water, piles of Decaying Chips, Shapeless timber, hog pens & hen roosts, the affluvia arising from which finds its way thro. broken windows, to the eating table & sleeping apartments. Add to them the nausea of Drains of the Kitchen and back-house

[10]John Morgan to Mark Hopkins, Nov. 10, 1851 (Morgan-Hopkins MSS).

[11]MS "Reports on Farms and Gardens" to the Oberlin Agricultural and Horticultural Society for 1841 and 1842 (O. C. Lib.), and *Lorain County News*, Nov. 6, 1861.

LADIES' HALL AND COLONIAL HALL ABOUT 1860

Probably taken from a tree on Tappan Square. The road is the present West College Street from Comings' store to Talcott corner. (From a photograph in the possession of Professor W. H. Chapin)

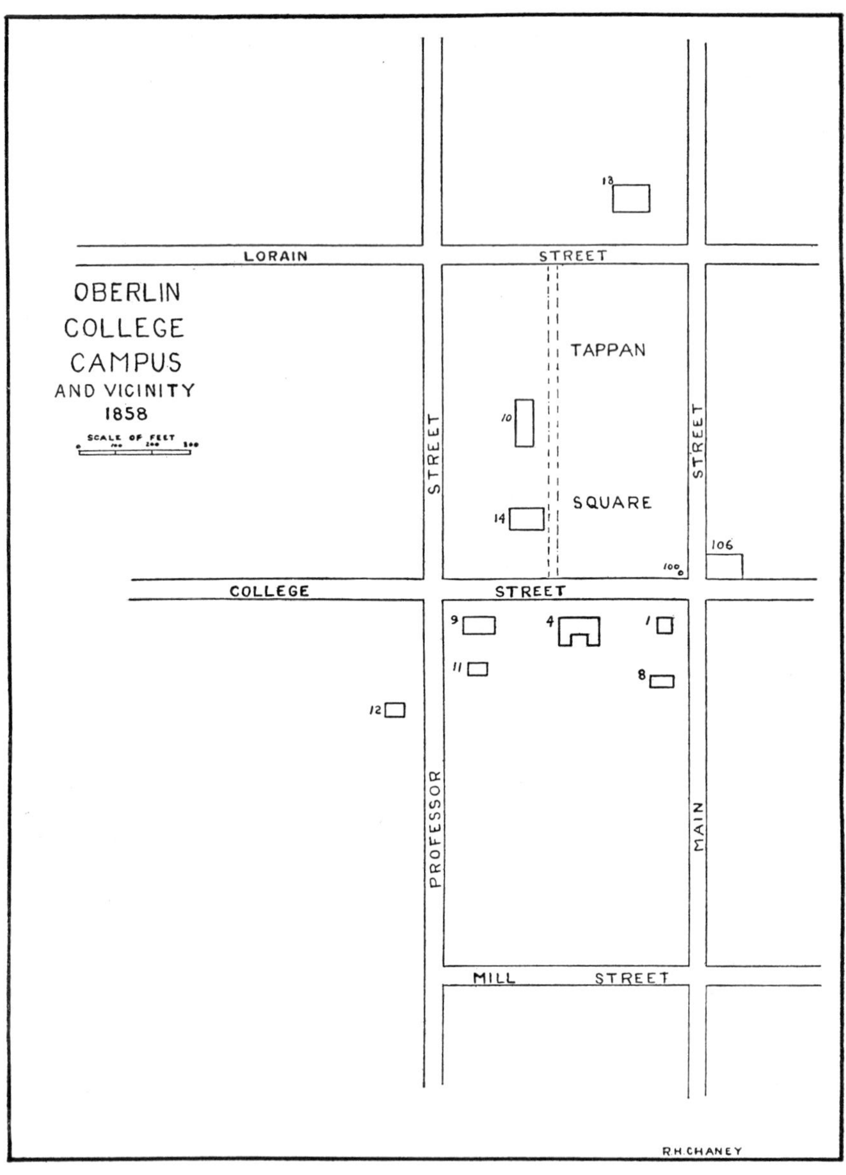

1.	Oberlin Hall	12.	Music Hall
4.	Ladies Hall (First)	13.	First Congregational Church
8.	Walton Hall	14.	College Chapel
9.	Colonial Hall		——
10.	Tappan Hall	100.	Historic Elm
11.	Old Chemical Laboratory	106.	Hotel

OBERLIN COLLEGE CAMPUS AND VICINITY, 1858
(From the 1908 *General Catalogue*)

often pass[ing] in front and in full view, beautified by the Insignia of the house wife with ½ Doz dish cloths, Mops &c—Paraded each side of the Door. . . . Cart wheels, broken sleds &c &c Strewed around."

Everywhere were animals and fowls running at large. In 1841 there were "75 Hogs Turned loose in the beautiful Village of Oberlin—to ravage, waste & discomfort & Destroy the fairest portions of our gardens, vex the peacable Inhabitants, and in particular to war against the most defenceless, *Ladies & children.*" This was despite the fact that as early as 1835 the colonists had voted that hogs should be penned, and in 1839 a special committee had taken up the question of "Hens and Hogs" and reported that "no good Citizen, no sincere Christian will suffer his hogs to run at Large, & that he or she, who does so, violates every good & honest principle. If a citizen suffers his swine to run at Large [he] Should meet & Receive the Marked Contempt of his Neibours—& If a Christian Brother is so neglectful of his duty—Should be kindly admonished, expostulated with and if persists in, The Church should be told of his Offence, &—If no repentance after a suitable Labour is performed his association with the Church Should be Cut Off—and he or she permitted to Continue their association unmolested with the Animals they so Democratically Cherish." As to hens it was decided that they "should be reared in abundance & Suffered to go at Large at all times except in Seed time & Harvest."[12]

Three years later another committee was appointed which prepared a "Report on Street Hogs":

"Your Committee to whom was referred the subject of keeping Hogs, recommends

"1. That those who will keep Hogs, Should keep them inclosed, for the obvious reason that Street Hogs are tresspassers against individuals & the public & as a Hog is not morrally responsible for his actions the owner must of course be morrally responsiable for all trespasses by his Hogs.

"2. Any Hog, Hogs or Pigs found in the Sts. of this Village, Should be reported to the owner if he can be found, & if he neglects to put them up he should be admonished to do so by any member of this Society.

[12]Oberlin Society, MS Minutes, May 9, 1835, and "Report on Hens and Hogs, March 1839," (MSS of Oberlin Agricultural and Horticultural Society).

"3. If any person, after being notified & admonished, Shall refuse to take care of his Hogs, he Should be esteemed as Void of all regard to the rights of his neighbor & the community & as such reported to this Society at its next meeting thereafter."[13]

Hens as well as hogs eventually became somewhat of a problem and in 1847 another committee suggested, "that in case . . . fowls are not restrained by [their] owner . . . it shall be deemed right & not unneibourly, for the person affected to Kill & use such fowls —[and] That all fowls, roosting or laying Eggs shall be deemed as belonging to the Occupier of premises where such fowls roost or lay Eggs."[14]

The village ordinances published in 1848, but adopted soon after the incorporation of the village in 1846, provided for the impounding of hogs and (at certain seasons and hours) of cattle found running at large. Hogs and chickens were not the only trespassers. As late as 1862 the *News* reported that citizens were pestered by vagrant cows: "There must be at least an hundred vagabond animals of this sort which get their entire living in the streets, swarm upon and soil the sidewalks and crowd themselves into whatever door yard is open to their forcible assault. And the worst of the matter is that many of the mischievous beasts belong to people who are abundantly able to give them an honest living, and whose standing in society is such that they should be ashamed of constantly trespassing on the rights of the public. . . . Oh that . . . every nomadic cow and pig might be speedily impounded."[15] The passage of the ordinance had apparently not greatly affected the number of wandering animals.

In the same week that this notice appeared the Prudential Committee voted to "pay some young man to drive the cattle from the Square" and appointed a committee "to see if any alterations can be made to the entrances to Tappan Hall whereby the young cattle may be excluded therefrom." The next week the *News* announced that, "The Students of Tappan Hall inform us that several calves and bovine yearlings will be sold to the highest bidder at half-past eleven o'clock some evening of this week, unless their owner speedily removes them and *keeps them away* from the Square. They vow that the proprieters of said stock will

[13]"Report on Street Hogs," Apr. 1, 1842 (MSS of Agr. and Hort. Soc.).

[14][Report of Committee on Fowls], Sept. 20, 1847 (MSS of Agr. and Hort. Soc.).

[15]*Charter and Ordinances of the Town of Oberlin* (Oberlin—1848), and *Lorain County News*, May 21, 1862.

have to look it up at the meat market unless it is speedily cared for."[16] Photographs taken in the seventies show posts set in the walk at the entrance to the square through the hedges, so we may conclude that by that date the livestock were satisfactorily excluded.

Tappan Square in the early days must have presented a decidedly pastoral appearance: hogs rooting about, chickens scratching for worms (except "in seed time and harvest"), and young cattle endeavoring, for some unknown reason, to get into Tappan Hall. In September of 1843 Professor Henry Cowles recorded in his Day Book: "Put my horse into Tappan Hall square to pasture nights." A dozen years later a student wrote to his sister: "We had quite a novel seen [*sic*] last night in Tappan square as it is called. . . . A man had a horse that he could not ride. It would throw him off. A young man here told him that he would break it for him. . . . When he got it a going it began to jump up and down just as lambs do when they play. He had to hang like a monkey to the horse to keep it from throwing him off but he sucseeded [*sic*] in breaking it so the man could ride it."[17]

There was also considerable agricultural activity on the square. As early as 1836 the Prudential Committee determined to plant mulberry trees there. Many of these trees were still alive in 1841 and 1842, as also some fifteen peach trees. In the latter year it was agreed to rent small tracts of ground on the square to the students to be used for gardens, and very likely the young ladies' flower gardens which received second prize from the Agricultural Society in that season were among those located there. This practice seems to have been kept up for some time; six years later a representative of the town appeared before the trustees to ask the Institute authorities to cover an open "drain running thro the Instu's garden & down the Main St." In 1840 "rooty bagas" were raised on the square and in 1849 a crop of corn. In 1848 President Mahan's oxen and cows got into the corn belonging to the institution and a committee assessed damages of six dollars against him. It is suspected that this corn was also on Tappan Square.[18]

[16]P. C. M., May 23, 1862, and *Lorain County News*, May 28, 1862.

[17]Egbert Smith to Julia Smith, Apr. 3 to May 9, 1855 (Smith MSS).

[18]P. C. M., Nov. 12, 1836; Sept. 14, 1837; May 12, 1841; Feb. 28, Mar. 14, Apr. 14, 1842; May 8, Oct. 16, 23, 1848; Oct. 2, 1849; Apr. 25, 1859; "Inventory of Stock & Farming Implements copied from Book of C. T. Carrier, September 6, 1841" (Misc. Archives), and Receipt for labor done by W. E. Benham, June 23, 1840.

In 1859 the proceeds from the hay cut on the square were appropriated to the preparation of the ground for the setting out of the group of evergreens of which the former "Community Christmas Tree" was a late survivor.

The forest was an enemy and, as in most frontier communities, it does not seem to have occurred to the settlers that it might be desirable to save some trees for shade and ornament. In 1836 a student wrote to his parents: "Oberlin is bounded on all sides by woods. I should think that all that has yet been cleared was not more than 300 acres, but yet they are clearing very fast & in a few years the woods will mostly disappear." It was three years later that the Agricultural Society heard a report from a "committee on *line fences, Ornamental & fruit Trees.*" This committee recommended the "planting of *Mulberry Trees* by the *Sides of the Streets,*" as they were both ornamental and (were expected to be) useful. They also recommended "the *Elm, Sycamore, the Maple & Locust for the Streets—the pair, the plumb, the cherry & the Apple Trees for Door yard.*" They expressed great enthusiasm for fruit trees, especially apple trees, suggesting that they might be planted on "the public common [Tappan Square] at least upon one or more sides . . . if Proper Security could be afforded them from Injury." That these recommendations were not without result is evident from the report of another committee on trees submitted in 1841 which includes an expression of "hope that the *Spirit* of *planting trees,* so laudabley manifested last season, will be revived with the opening of the Spring." Besides the elm, maple, hickory, chestnut and oak this committee suggested the locust and the horse chestnut, particularly for use about buildings. In the middle forties the village ordinances gave special protection to the trees.[19]

The Institute does not seem to have taken a very active part in beautifying its grounds in these early years. Henry Howe's drawing made in 1846 shows only two trees growing on Tappan Square.[20] A year later Mr. Bateham, the editor of the *Ohio Cultivator,* recommended very strongly "the *planting of more trees* about the college buildings, grounds and walks, as in the city of

[19]Davis [and George] Prudden to Peter Prudden, Aug. 5, 1836 (Prudden-Allen MSS); MS "Report of the Com. on line fences, Ornamental & fruit Trees" 1839; "The committee on ornamental Trees report" [1841] (MSS of the Oberlin Agricultural and Horticultural Society), and *Charter and Ordinances . . .* (1848).

[20]*Cf.* frontispiece of Volume I.

elms, where old Yale is located." In 1844 and 1845 the trustees and in 1852 the Prudential Committee issued orders for the setting out of trees around the college buildings and on Tappan Square.[21]

In the spring of 1856 a holiday was allowed the students in order that they might set out trees. A young lady student described the event in her diary: "Wednesday April 23d. Today we students have had a jubilee. The young men are planting or rather transplanting trees into Tappan Hall yard, so because they were thus engaged we have had our jubilee at whatever best pleased us. No recitations at all nothing but evening prayers. Early in the morning the gentlemen met at the new Chapel for assignments. Then they by companies went out into the woods for trees or commenced on the ground digging. The Freshman class passed our house on foot going west earliest of any. Again this afternoon I saw several of them planting in the opposite corner." The group of trees on the northeastern corner of the square is often called "Sophomore Grove" and is said to have been planted by the sophomore class on that "Arbor Day." A clump of evergreens donated by a firm in Rochester was set out on the square in 1859. These trees and many others were set out and cared for by the Arboricultural Association, an organization of college students and faculty members, led and inspired by Professor J. M. Ellis. "On Saturday, April 2, [1859] the gentlemen of the institution turned out in a body to cultivate and set out trees in Tappan Square. The trees already growing were thoroughly mulched and manured, and two hundred more (forest and evergreens) set out. The members of the Senior Preparatory Class planted a grove west of the Chapel, with a view of caring for it during their course. The Freshmen and Sophomores also planted groves. The students generally, assisted by several members of the Faculty, worked heartily and performed a good amount of labor."[22] To these early efforts we owe the larger trees on the present beautiful "Campus."

At a comparatively early date the Square was fenced in, at first by a regular old-fashioned worm fence and later [1854] by "a neat and substantial railing" built jointly by the College and

[21]*Ohio Cultivator,* Sept. 15, 1847; T. M., Aug. 28, 1844; Aug. 18, 1845, and P. C. M. [March 15, 1852].

[22]Mary Cowles, MS Diary, 1856 (Cowles-Little MSS), and *Oberlin Students' Monthly,* I, 142 (Apr., 1859), and 319 (June, 1859).

townsmen. Secretary Hamilton Hill (like a true Englishman) had recommended in 1841 the use of hawthorne hedges, but when in the fifties a hedge was planted around the square, it was not hawthorne but Osage Orange, a very pleasing improvement.[23] Most of the yards of private dwellings were also fenced in. Some of the long-time leases made by the College for building lots prescribed enclosure—"the front being a neat picket or board fence."[24] It was a practical necessity too to put up fences if lawns and gardens were to be protected from the marauding livestock.

The wandering hogs did not help the condition of the streets; the sticky Oberlin clay everywhere made sidewalks very necessary. What was probably the first Oberlin sidewalk was built "of plank from Main Street to Professor Street in front of the Institute buildings." Elsewhere it was described as a "side walk & railing from Collonial Hall to Main Street Constructed at an expense of 140$." In the following year the Institute contributed $25.00 to "a good plank walk 3 feet wide west of the square from Lorain Street to Colonial Hall." At about the same time a board walk was also built across the square from Tappan Hall (where the young men roomed) to the Boarding Hall (Ladies' Hall), largely at the expense of the students who used it so frequently. The first town ordinances included three sections especially devoted to the protection of streets and sidewalks: prohibiting any obstruction of them and providing a fine for "any person [who] shall willfully ride, or drive, or lead any horse or other animal, on any of the said sidewalks."[25]

Before the outbreak of the Civil War a student could be found who would write home to his family that Oberlin was "a very pleasant place with nice sidewalks." Board walks are very slippery, however, when wet. Just after the war a freshman, carrying an armful of books, slipped, fell on the books and broke two ribs! Board walks, too, require constant attention and replacement, which they did not always receive in Oberlin. The local

[23]Josephine C. Bateham, "Ladies' Department" of the *Ohio Cultivator*, Oct. 15, 1854; T. M., Aug. 22, 1853; Ledger 7, page 432 (Treasurer's Office); H. Hill's Report on Hawthorne Hedges, 1841 (MSS of Agricultural and Horticultural Society), and P. C. M., Mar. 19, 1850, and Apr. 6, 1852.

[24]Lease to George N. Allen, 1842 (O. C. Lib. Misc. MSS.)

[25]P. C. M., Dec. 31, 1836; Sept. 14, 1837; May 2, 1842; "The Agent's report, September 5, 1837" (Misc. Archives), and *Charter and Ordinances . . .* (1848).

paper found conditions almost unbearable in the spring of 1861. The editor declared: "One fourth of the walks in our otherwise moral and orthodox village are indecently dangerous. A proper degree of risk is exhilarating, but the amount we daily encounter, is destructive and discouraging. The walk on portions of East and West College streets, Mill street, West Lorain and Main street near the railroad, is suffered to remain, month in and month out, in a state hardly navigable for cats. . . . From the peculiar and workmanlike construction of our walks a few weeks suffice to loosen here and there a plank which are left as so many foot-traps to break the shins of well-meaning pedestrians. Then the nails by which they are fastened, are sure to work up from one to two inches, and so remain, a perpetual terror to wearers of crinoline and a perpetual source of revenue to dry-goods merchants."[26] The editor was not exaggerating the danger to the fair sex as appears from a letter written by a college girl to a former classmate three years later:

"Oh, larful me [She is suddenly reminded of an untoward accident and proceeds to describe it]. I must tell you of a small adventure M. Almira had the other day. Well we were coming from prayers the other night, we came across Tappan, were going to go across lots. You know that path through the grass. Em & I had stepped off from the walk, by the door we used to go into an essay class through, & Mira jumped down. Lo & behold one of the small article's [Almira's] hoops caught upon a nail in the walk & drew out the whole length. Poor M. A. M. was all in a tremble. (You know her). She begged me to 'step on it quick.' As well as I could for laughing I did as I was bidden. She rushed off and drew it from under my feet. I nearly died. What should the little article do but haul out her *penknife to cut the hoop off*. I died then entirely. So did Em. She found it was no go & tried with her trembling fingers to break it, all the while asking Em & I to stand before her so that none of the occupants of Tappan Hall should by some chance see her trouble. Finally I had to get down and break off her hoop for her. We left it in the grass, came past the next day & *it was gone*. We expect she will get it some day in class, probable is it not Sallie Mariar?" Before the crinolines had dis-

[26]Mrs. W. W. Wright to A. A. Wright, Sept. 25, 1866 (Wright MSS), and *Lorain County News*, Mar. 6, 1861.

appeared flagstone walks were being built to supplant the plank ones on the busiest streets and across the square in front of Tappan Hall.[27]

In the sixties the pride of Oberlin was its gas street lamps, first lighted in 1859. The *News* declared: "Nothing in the material convenience of our village strikes visitors with more surprise than our provisions for lighting the town by gas. Our principal streets, depot and all the public buildings are well supplied with it, and it is a rare public convenience."[28] The lights were often life-savers in the days while any of the plank walks remained.

Very little was done to improve the streets, except to grade them occasionally in a rather haphazard fashion. In the early fifties a plank road was built "from the depot to the college," but there was no paving. When Sophia Jex-Blake, the English traveler, heard the shout of "Oberlin" at the door of her railway coach she climbed down to find an omnibus waiting "outside the station, in the midst of roads so like ploughed fields as to make a conveyance very desirable."[29]

In the thirties the Collegiate Institute handled all sorts of merchandise and its account books charge against teachers and colonists: soap, sugar, calico, sheetings, shingle nails and similar necessities. Very early, however, independent stores were established. T. S. Ingersoll was doing business in his general store a few weeks after the founding of the Institute. In 1841 there were three stores, and in 1846 Henry Howe found "3 dry goods and 1 book store."[30]

By 1851 there were two book stores, two shoe shops, two combination drug and grocery stores, two dry goods and grocery stores, one grocery exclusively, a harness shop, and two carriage

[27]Nellie—to Minerva A. Winegar, June 26, 1864 (in possession of Mrs. H. N. Roberts, Wichita, Kansas); *Lorain County News,* May 31, 1865, and P. C. M., Sept. 10, 1868.

[28]*Ibid.,* Jan. 2, 1867. The ordinance providing for gas lighting was adopted Sept. 10, 1858 and then, following a false start, renewed on Oct. 5, 1859.—*Oberlin Evangelist,* Oct. 13, 1858, and *Charter and Ordinances,* 1861, 35–37.

[29]Josephine C. Bateham, *Loc. Cit.; Lorain County News,* May 11, 1864, and Sophia Jex-Blake, *A Visit to Some American Schools and Colleges,* (N. Y.—1867). page 5. Pieces of the old planks were exhumed in 1940 when a new storm sewer was laid in the center of South Main Street.—*Oberlin News-Tribune,* Aug. 2 and 6, 1940.

[30]Warren [and Hannah] Warner to parents, Dec. 24, 1841—Feb. 16, 1842 (O. C. Lib.); and Howe, *Op. Cit.,* 315. There are several orders on Ingersoll's store in the Misc. Archives.

shops besides blacksmiths, carpenters, coopers, and two tailors.[31] James M. Fitch and William H. Plumb were the proprietors of the book stores. Fitch was a leading citizen: printer and publisher of the *Oberlin Evangelist,* superintendent of the union Sunday School and prominent anti-slavery man. Plumb was also, at that time, proprietor of the hotel and a livery stable. It was a great shock to the community when, a little later, he absconded, leaving debts estimated at $20,000.00. Brewster Pelton, the leading merchant of the early days, was the proprietor of one of the general stores. Isaac M. Johnson, who had been converted by Shipherd in Elyria back in 1831–32, came to Oberlin in 1851 and soon superseded Pelton. Hiram Pease's carriage shop was already a landmark on the northeast corner of Mill and Main streets. Edward F. Munson ran a blacksmith shop on the hill south of Plumb Creek and west of Main Street in the interval between his postmasterships.[32]

All of the stores were then on Main Street or on what is now East College Street. The sale of Oberlin Hall in 1854 marked the beginning of the advance of business enterprises along the south side of College Street toward the west. The removal of Ladies' Hall and the laying out of College Place in 1866 put a limit to that advance. The *News* described the business places of the town in 1860: "There are at present three general Mercantile establishments, besides one exclusively devoted to Dry Goods and Clothing, two exclusive Bookstores, four Shoe stores, one Jewelry and Fancy store, three Merchant Tailors, five Family Grocers, a Flour Store, three Meat Markets, one Stove and Tin Shop, Two Steam Flouring Mills, one Saw Mill, one Planing Mill and Sash Factory, two Cabinet Shops, two harness Shops, two Livery Stables, two Hotels, and two Restaurants. Besides these, Lawyers, Brokers, Dentists, Daguerreotypists, Printers, Book-binders and Barbers, in short, all things required to make up a goahead Ohio Village, *excepting a grog shop* is to be found in Oberlin."[33]

Dr. H. A. Bunce, a former student in the College, ran a drug store from 1856 to 1864, when he died of "consumption." H. L.

[31]*A Reference & Statistical Map of Oberlin, Lorain, Co., O.* (Cleveland, O.,–c. 1851).

[32]There is a history of business in early Oberlin in *Camp's Directory of Oberlin, 1873–1874* (Oberlin–1873). On Isaac M. Johnson see A. R. Webber, *Early History of Elyria,* 95–100.

[33]*Lorain County News,* Mar. 28, 1860.

Henry's Drug Store advertised:

CLEAN TEETH
SWEET BREATH!
and sound and
HEALTHY GUMS,
by using
SHART'S TOOTH-SOAP,
PRICE, 10 CENTS

P. R. Tobin sold harnesses "at the sign of the Morgan Horse— 1 door north of the engine house." O. S. B. Wall and David Watson, both colored men and both Rescuers, were partners in the shoe business. John Hancock bought out a shoe shop in 1862 and advertised in the *News:* "Call one and all at the old stand, and have your understanding improved and kept dry."

In the forties David Brokaw came to Oberlin and set up as a portrait painter and daguerreotypist, sharing with a dentist the rooms over the post office on the southeast corner of Main and College.[34] A. C. and Henry M. Platt learned photography in his studio and became Oberlin's leading photographers of the early days. Their advertisements in the *News* offer "Photographs, Ambrotypes, Cartes De Visites." J. M. Fitch sold the photograph albums which now preserve so many of the old pictures taken by them.

In 1833 the mail was brought over from (South) Amherst. When a post office was first established it was called "Russia." A few letters from Oberlin, unstamped and without envelopes, bearing the postmark "Russia, Ohio" are still preserved in the archives of the College. Edward F. Munson, the blacksmith, being the leading local Democrat, was postmaster from 1843 to 1861 except for the Taylor-Fillmore administration when Whigs replaced him. Of course, a Republican triumphantly succeeded him soon after Lincoln was inaugurated. The main mail stage route of the early days went through Elyria, "Whiskeyville," (South) Amherst, Henrietta, etc. Artemas Beebe of Elyria carried the mail in four-horse stagecoaches daily from Cleveland to Fremont over this route. From 1838 to 1840 he sent a man on a horse from Elyria with the Oberlin mail three times a week; in the

[34]Brokaw's lease of a village lot, June 4, 1847 (Misc. Archives).

A. C. PLATT'S
AMBROTYPE & PHOTOGRAPHIC
GALLERY OF ART.

OBERLIN, ... OHIO.

Rooms 3d Floor Daguerrean Building, over E. J. Goodrich's Bookstore, corner of Main and College Streets.

Mr. PLATT has spared no pains or expense in preparing for the production of pictures, In the highest style and finish of the Art, and having the advantage of the

MOST FAVORABLE LIGHT,

And of the

Largest and Best of Cameras,

And being thoroughly and practically acquainted with all the LATE IMPROVEMENTS in PHOTOGRAPHY, with the benefit of the most

UNLIMITED PRACTICE,

. Having taken during the past year

More than 10,000 Pictures,

He is prepared to execute in the best manner and in every variety of style,

Likenesses of all descriptions,

From the smallest miniature to the size of life, at

The Lowest Prices.

This establishment, formerly known as Brokaw & Platt's, has been long and widely known as furnishing pictures surpassed by none.

— *Good Pictures taken for* 25 *cents.* —

IS THIS a GOOD DAY for PICTURES?

Our answer is and always has been,

One day is just as good as another,

For taking Likenesses, but if there be any difference, we prefer, with our large light, an ordinarly coudy day, except for very young children who cannot sit still more than half a second at a time. We hope our patrons will bear this in mind, and not incommode themselves and us by all coming in on bright days.

Call and secure the shadow ere the substance fade 1tf

ADVERTISEMENT FROM THE *LORAIN COUNTY NEWS*

NEW LIVERY STABLE!

The undersigned has opened A NEW LIVERY STABLE in the ELMORE BLOCK,

4 doors east of Palmer's Hotel.

He proposes to keep his stable well supplied with good saddle, draft and carriage horses, and convenient vehicles of every style. He will do teaming of all kinds, will carry transient passengers to neighboring towns, and give

PARTIES TO THE LAKE

a first class outfit. All of which he will do at low rates.

C. T. MARKS.

Oberlin, May 6, 1862. 114tf.

P. R. TOBIN,

Manufacturer of

SADDLES HARNESS and TRUNKS!

One door north of the Engine house, Main St., OBERLIN, O., sign of the big horse. Having on hand a good assortment of Farm-Carriage, Coach and Buggy Harness, and also the

SCOTCH and AMERICAN COLLARS.

Riding Bridles, Halters, Girts, and surcingles, and various small work.

I am prepared to sell any kind of work in my line of business at very low prices for Cash, produce or on Short Credit. All kinds of work made to order: repairing done at all times. Call and examine.

107.

ADVERTISEMENTS IN THE *LORAIN COUNTY NEWS* IN THE SIXTIES

second year a led horse carried the papers once a week—many an *Emancipator* no doubt. From 1840 to 1844 the mail was carried to Oberlin in a two-horse coach three times a week. The Government allowed the contractor three hours to make the journey each way! By 1852 mail was being brought from Elyria by coach six times a week. Then came the railroad.[35]

From pioneer days the corner northeast of the intersection of College and Main streets was occupied by a tavern or hotel. Brewster Pelton played host in 1834 in a log cabin, but built a two-story tavern (30x40 feet) in 1835. As late as 1848 the Agricultural and Horticultural Society held its banquet in the "Oberlin House" kept by "Mr. B. Pelton." The hotel was closed for a time but was opened again in 1850 under the management of W. H. Plumb. Three years later it was officially commended by the *Oberlin Evangelist* as "the home of order and quiet." Wack's Tavern on Main Street was not generally looked upon with so much favor. It was there that the slave catchers stopped at the time of the Rescue. Wack was a Democrat. When W. H. Plumb absconded, the College took over the uptown hotel and leased it to a succession of landlords under whom it was known as the Palmer House and the Monroe House. It was during the war when it was called the Monroe House that a patron blew out the gas and was saved from asphyxiation only when the proprietor broke open the door. In the fall of 1865 the College sold the building; it was burned down in January. Most people agreed that the fire was something of a blessing, the thirty year old hostelry was in such disrepair. Henry Viets built the present brick hotel building, aided by a bounty of $2,500 from the College.[36]

Mr. W. H. Plumb sent a carriage from the hotel to meet all the trains in the early fifties. In 1860 a "NEW and SPLENDID OMNIBUS" was purchased to perform this service. This was probably the very vehicle in which Sophia Jex-Blake, the English

[35]Postmaster General, *Report,* Feb. 21, 1839, 25 Cong., 3 Sess., *Senate Document* 254; "Allowances to Contractors," Mar. 19, 1840, 26 Cong., 1 Sess., *House Document* 149, pages 12–13; "Offers for Carrying the United States Mail," Jan. 5, 1841, 26 Cong., 2 Sess., *House Document* 44, page 168, and *The Western Reserve Register for 1852,* page 95.

[36]Pelton to Mr. and Mrs. Barber, Jan. 7, 1835 (lent by Jeannette Kinney, Willoughby, Ohio); J. H. Fairchild, *Oberlin,* 242; *Ohio Cultivator,* Nov. 1, 1848; *Oberlin Evangelist,* Aug. 28, 1850; Feb. 16, 1853; *A Reference & Statistical Map of Oberlin,* (Cleveland—1851), and *Lorain County News,* Dec. 17, 1862; July 1, 1863; Jan. 27, 1864; Aug. 9, 16, Sept. 27, 1865; Jan. 17, June 27, July 4, 1866.

feminist, rode from the depot to the hotel in 1865. She has left us the most detailed extant description of service at the old "Monroe House":

"Begrimed as we were with our night journey, the national instinct claimed some means of ablution. 'Can we have a room to wash our hands?' A rather wandering gaze, and 'I guess you can,' preluded our introduction to a small room not yet 'red up,' where a basin full of dirty water looked unpromising for our chances. But our host was equal to the emergency,—in a moment the said basin was seized, and its contents flung out of window. I thought of the notice we had seen often at Niagara, 'Stones thrown from above may strike passers below,' but gratefully accepted the goods the gods provided, and washed in peace.

"We then got a good country breakfast of eggs in all forms (being expected to eat the boiled ones American-wise, smashed up in glasses with milk, etc.), with biscuit, and the rather nice pink tea which always puzzled me as to its matériél. By-the-by, with the usual American inversion of words, 'biscuit' means hot rolls, hardly once baked, to say nothing of twice.

"This meal was served in a queer low dining-room, with posts supporting the ceiling and beams running across it, the common eating-room of the house."[37]

From the beginning, the tavern on the corner was under conservative, moral, and temperate management. A visitor in 1848 commented: "I put up at the hotel, and found no swearing, no drinking or smoking, no noise and confusion. When called to partake of our meals, the blessing of our common Father was asked to rest upon the fruits of his bounty, and all seemed with a willing heart to say, the presence of the lord is here! May God's choicest blessings rest upon those who conduct that and similar houses." Fourteen years later the *Evangelist* announced: "An excellent public house is now kept at the centre of the village. . . . Visitors will find it a quiet Christian *Home,* free from the nuisance of tobacco and of whatsoever doth intoxicate. Of his own accord, the lease under which he holds the house binds him to 'keep it on strictly temperance principles, neither keeping for sale nor selling anything that can or will intoxicate, including under this, ale, strong drink, hard cider, tobacco and cigars.' "[38]

[37]*Lorain County News,* Sept. 12, 1860, and S. J. Blake, *Op. Cit.,* 6–7.
[38]*Oberlin Evangelist,* Aug. 30, 1848; Dec. 17, 1862.

In the sixties there were various refreshment stands. The year before the war a "NEW ICE CREAM SALOON" was opened on the east side of (South) Main Street. Dr. Bunce, the apothecary, advertised that he sold "The most Delicate Flavored Soda Water in the Village." Burnett's Restaurant offered beef steak, pork steak, broiled chicken, fish, game, oysters, tea, coffee, and toast. You could buy candy of John Watson, a colored man and one of the Rescuers. It is recorded that when "Watson's horse died and he could not raise money to buy another he gave up draying and kept a confectionery store."[39]

Down to 1856 liquor might be sold in Oberlin by license, but in that year a village ordinance was passed entirely prohibiting the sale of intoxicating liquors, especially defined as including "every species of spirituous liquors, including cider, ginger wine, ale, porter and strong beer." By 1865, however, a citizens' committee, including Dr. Dascomb, Professor Fairchild and others, reported that liquor was sold in two drug stores and in Samuel Munson's saloon. They reported that Munson had no respect for "the sentiments that prevail generally in this Community." (He was one of the Democrat Munsons, of course.) A month later he was fined $25.00 and costs for liquor selling.[40]

Besides the college publications (the *Evangelist,* the *Quarterly Review,* and the *Students' Monthly*) two newspapers were printed and published in Oberlin. The first was the short-lived *Oberlin Times and Students' Literary Journal* attempted by J. M. Fitch in 1853. The second was the *Lorain County News* which has had a continuous life, under different names, from 1860 to the present day. It was printed by V. A. Shankland and J. F. Harmon and ably edited by Professor H. E. Peck, L. L. Rice, and J. B. T. Marsh in succession. It is the most important single source of information on life in the village in the later years.

There was some manufacturing in Oberlin from the building of the community steam mill in 1833–34. Run by the Institute for the first two years, it was leased in 1836 and later sold. It burned in 1844. In the late fifties and the sixties there was a considerable boom in local enterprise. In August, 1860, the *News* editorially

[39]Advertisements in *Lorain County News,* Sept. 12, 1860; June 17, 1863; Mar. 13, 1864; Mar. 13, 1867, and *passim,* and *Camp's Directory of Oberlin, 1833–34,* 13.
[40]*Charter and Ordinances,* 1856, 25–26, and *Lorain County News,* Oct. 25, Nov. 29, 1865.

called attention to the advantages (?) of Oberlin's location and bragged: "We make the best lumber, the best flour, the best of sash and blinds, the best of photographs, the best of harness, the best of boots and shoes, the best of gas (notice politicians who need the article) and *do the best of printing*."

Local industry was distributed along Plumb Creek (though certainly no power was secured from it) from Water (Park) Street on the east nearly to Professor Street at the west. Lumber and saw mills were in the Water Street area, while the blacksmith shops, wagon shops, sash-and-blind and cabinet shops, machine shops, and a carding mill were grouped around the intersection of Main and Mill (Vine) streets. In addition James Bailey made military saddles for the army; C. C. Hudson & Co. concocted Hudson's Tooth Paste put up in "neat, opaque, glass bottles," and the local tombstone-maker also produced "elegant marble mantles and sideboards." In 1866 the enterprising Samuel Plumb even incorporated the Oberlin Woolen Manufacturing Company. Every American town in those days hoped to be the Lowell or Pittsburgh of tomorrow.[41]

As the buildings were, with few exceptions, of very frail wood construction there was always much danger from fire. Some provision had been made for fire fighting in 1836, and as early as 1837 two voluntary fire companies were organized and were considering the purchase of an engine. Just ten years later the Prudential Committee appropriated fifty dollars to help in buying one, and in 1850 the Oberlin Society voted to give the northwest "basement room of the church for an Engine House." It would appear, however, that engines were not actually secured until 1852. From 1852 to 1858 fire drills were held on the meeting-house grounds. These engines were, of course, of the old hand-pump type and evidently not the only reliance in time of need, for on the back page of the *Charter and Ordinances* for 1856 is printed in large letters:

ON THE OCCURRENCE of FIRES,
Let every man
TAKE WITH HIM A PAIL,
and also
WATER, IF PRACTICABLE.

[41]Besides *Camp's Directory* see the *Lorain County News,* Aug. 29, 1860; Oct. 10, 1866, and two articles on "Our Manufactures" in *Ibid.,* Nov. 11, Dec. 2, 1863.

Later in the fifties a very elaborate ritual was provided for the fire department. "At all fires the Mayor and Councilmen shall severally bear a staff with a gilded flame at the top, . . ." The Chief Engineer was to "wear a leather cap painted white, with gilded front and the words 'Chief Engineer' painted thereon in black," and other officials were to be similarly designated.[42] All this must have greatly increased the temptation to turn in a false alarm!

The two years 1865 and 1866 constituted a climactic period in the history of Oberlin fire fighting. The old Empire Hook and Ladder Company of pre-war days was reorganized and re-invigorated—almost all of its members now being ex-soldiers. In July, 1865, the Whitney livery stables on Main Street were burned, with considerable loss of harnesses, buffalo robes, hay and grain. Early in 1866 there was a fire in the Union School. Little damage was done except to the schoolbooks, which were all thrown out the windows! Then the hotel burned down as the whole town watched—burned to the ground despite the fact that students working at the pumps were furnished free stimulants from one of the drugstores! The sight of inebriated college students was more of a shock to most than the prospect of the burning tavern.[43]

There was a great to-do about the inadequacy of equipment and the freezing up of one hand engine when it was borrowed to flood the skating pond. (Two members of the Excelsior Skating Club were arrested while on their way to church on a Sabbath morning.) In the fall of 1866 a steam fire engine was purchased and at a public demonstration threw a stream of water over the College Chapel.[44]

But fighting fires was hardly more than a secondary activity for the volunteer fire companies. Firemen's conventions were much more important. In 1860 the Oberlin hook and ladder company rode to Sandusky with the Oberlin Citizens' Brass Band in their gorgeous new band wagon and came home with the silver trumpet. "They ran eighty rods, planted a ladder, and had a man on the top of it in one minute and fifteen seconds." In

[42]Levi Burnell to H. D. Hatch, Sept. 28, 1837 (O. C. Lib. Misc. MSS); P. C. M., Feb. 8, 1847; Nov. 12, 1852; Oberlin Society, MS Minutes, Aug. 16, 1850; J. H. Fairchild, Op. Cit., 239, and *Charter and Ordinances,* 1861, 40–41.

[43]*Lorain County News,* July 5, 12, 1865; Jan. 17, 1866, and Mrs. W. W. Wright to A. A. Wright, Jan. 16, 1866 (Wright MSS).

[44]*Lorain County News,* Jan. 3, 1866, and Nov. 28, 1866

1865 and 1866 the revived "Empire" company appeared at all the tournaments in northern Ohio wearing red pants, white shirts and red ties.[45]

Commencements, rescues and fires did not furnish the only interruptions to the rural quiet of the village streets. There were occasional runaways past the rigs hitched before the stores, as in 1860 when a driverless team dashed down Main Street and smashed an expensive carriage against the railing of the Plumb Creek bridge. Fourth-of-July was a nerve-wracking day for dogs, horses and old ladies, begun at dawn with the firing of the "Baby Waker" cannon on the square.[46] Tuesday evenings in the sixties the Citizens' Brass Band played patriotic music on the bandstand near Tappan Hall.

Places of business stayed open until eight o'clock most evenings and much later on Saturday. On Saturday nights the country people drove into town to do their weekly shopping, and knots and crowds of men and boys gathered on the board walks at the corner of Main and College streets and before the more popular stores. There was an increasing amount of rowdiness in the war years. Crowds of riotous boys disturbed home-stayers with their shouts and cat-calls and even severed the traces of the teams and removed the wheels of carriages during services at the church. Storms of hand-clapping and stamping often preceded public lectures. Disturbances accompanied the arrival and departure of trains at the depot.[47] There were a few burglaries. In 1858 two stores were broken into, and in 1865 four thousand dollars worth of government bonds were stolen from the home of a pious deacon while he was at church.

After Dr. Dascomb gave up his practice and began to devote himself wholly to his college duties Dr. Alexander Steele was invited to Oberlin to take his place.[48] By 1851 Oberlin had a dentist and four physicians: one homeopathic, one autopathic and two orthodox. Dr. Jennings practiced autopathic or orthopathic

[45]*Ibid.,* June 20, Sept. 12, 1860, and Empire Hook and Ladder Company, MS Minutes, 1865–1874.

[46]See Mayor Samuel Hendry's Fourth-of-July Proclamation in the *Lorain County News,* July 3, 1861.

[47]On rowdiness see the *News,* June 27, 1860; July 23, 1862; Oct. 21, 1863, and Mar. 7, 1866. In 1858 the Oberlin Society (First Church) ordered Dr. Dascomb to ask the mayor for special police to preserve order about the church "during the times of public worship."—Minutes, June 7, 1858.

[48]Dr. Steele bought a lot from the College on June 20, 1836 (Copy of deed in Misc. Archives).

medicine. Dr. Keys was the homeopathist. In 1855 a student wrote to her sister: "I am taking medicine yet, it is Homeopathy and very pleasant to take, I will send you one pill. I have seven of them to take at once." Homer Johnson, the other "regular" doctor, had come to Oberlin in the forties and was to have a long period of service.[49] In the sixties anyone who thought he needed psychiatry could go to William Smith or Gillanders, phrenologists. "Those who are doubtful as to what is in their heads," advised the *News,* "will do well to call and be 'examined.'"

There were no lawyers or banks in Oberlin until the fifties. Anson P. Dayton and the colored man, John M. Langston, hung out their shingles in the middle of the decade. Ralph and Samuel Plumb followed them a few years later. The Plumbs soon gained high rank among Oberlin's leading citizens.[50]

Ralph Plumb stuck mainly to the law and Samuel Plumb became a business man and banker. It was Samuel Plumb who built the gas works in 1859. By 1861, at least, he was engaged in private banking, having set up his office on the present site of Comings' bookstore next to the old Ladies' Hall. Less than two months after the National Banking Act of 1863 was passed he opened the stock subscription list for the First National Bank of Oberlin and put his own name down for $20,000.00. Other large subscribers were President Finney, Professor Cowles, Professor Peck, John Keep, I. M. Johnson, Ralph Plumb and Henry Viets. In June, Plumb was elected president and business began in September. By February, 1864, the bank was doing so well that Plumb was authorized to buy new furniture worth nearly thirty dollars; a stove, a table, six chairs, a wash stand, "etc.," and a duster. In August the First National Bank was advertising government bonds for sale.[51]

Thus in the war years Oberlin's economic organization was brought to normal maturity. Who remembered the dreams of Christian communism?

[49]Pamela Smith to Julia Smith, Sept. 25, 1855 (Smith MSS), and Homer Johnson to Samuel Johnson, Mar. 17, 1846 (Copy in office of Assistant to the President). *Cf.* G. C. Jameson, "Historical Sketch of Medicine in Oberlin," *Ohio State Medical Journal,* XXXIII, No. 3 (Mar. 1937).

[50]On the Plumbs see above pages 394–395.

[51]Directors of First National Bank of Oberlin, MS Minutes, 1863–. On the location of the building see *Lorain County News,* Apr. 18, 1866.

CHAPTER XXXVI

VILLAGE SOCIETY

IN AUSTERE and shocked dignity, its back turned toward the institution of which it was once so essential a part, the old meeting house stands across from the northeastern corner of the square, the only building now surviving from the Finney era. It is appropriate that it should be the last survivor, for the church which it housed was the most powerful factor in the life of the Oberlin community, excepting only the College itself.

It was in August of 1834 that the "Brethren & Sisters of Oberlin assembled at the school room—Br. J. J. Shipherd in the chair" and "Resolved that a church be formed" to be styled "The Congregational Church of Christ at Oberlin."[1] At first services were held in "the school room" in Oberlin Hall. In 1836, however, Colonial Hall, built jointly by the Institute and the colonists, was available, with a much larger auditorium. As both school and town grew, this, in its turn, became too small. In the spring of 1842 a young lady student wrote to her mother: "The congregations are still growing larger [under the stimulus of Finney's preaching]. The Laboratory and Chapel in Colonial Hall are crowded every Sabbath." Later in the summer the big tent which was used for Commencement was put up every week-end in order that the congregation might be united.[2]

Over a year before, it had been decided to "proceed forthwith to take measures for building a meeting house."[3] A committee was appointed to take charge of construction, fortunately including Thomas P. Turner, an experienced house carpenter, formerly of Thetford, Vermont. Plans were donated by Willard Sears, of Boston, a friend of Finney's. They were apparently the work of

[1]Oberlin Church, MS Minutes, Aug. 19, 1834.

[2]Elizabeth Maxwell to Mrs. Rebecca Maxwell, May 5, 1842 (in the possession of Mrs. Emma Monroe Fitch), and *Oberlin Evangelist,* June 22, 1842.

[3]Oberlin Church, MS Minutes, Feb. 10, 1841.

THE MEETING HOUSE (FIRST CHURCH) AS IT APPEARS TODAY
(From a photograph by A. L. Princehorn)

THE INTERIOR OF THE MEETING HOUSE AS IT APPEARS TODAY

The chief recent changes in the part shown in this picture were the raising of the backs of the pews, the removal of the pew doors and the substitution of the iron posts under the gallery for the original, large wooden columns.

(From a photograph by A. L. Princehorn)

an architect named Lodge. Turner was given direct charge of the work of construction, though under the surveillance of the committee.[4] On June 17, 1842, the corner stone was laid. Professor Finney led in prayer and a special hymn was sung:

God of Israel! lend thine ear,
Listen to our humble prayer;
Let our praise ascend on high,
Hear, Oh hear our fervent cry.
As we lay the corner stone,
For thy worship, Lord, alone.

May the presence of thy love
Rest upon us from above;
May thy glory and thy grace
Shadow o'er this holy place;
Shield us by thy power divine
O thou God of Oberlin.[5]

The Oberlin people taxed themselves to the limit to provide for the construction of the building, and appeals for financial aid were sent out through the columns of the *Oberlin Evangelist*. From time to time acknowledgements were made of receipts: a hundred dollars, fifty dollars, one dollar, a hat, "12 lbs. nails," a cheese, four bushels of apples, "2¾ yds. fulled cloth," "1 horse waggon" and even two cows from two residents of Medina. As late as June of 1843 the appeal was renewed. The meeting house was progressing slowly due to the lack of funds. "Donations in money, provisions, goods, or materials . . . [would be] thankfully received." Not until late in 1844 was the building ready for occupancy.[6] "A large brick meating house, which is sur-

[4]Oberlin Society, MS Minutes, Jan. 26, Mar. 14, 18, 1842. The original design is preserved in the Finney MSS in the Oberlin College Library. Finney wrote Henry Cowles, Dec. 23, 1841, from Boston:
"Tell Br. Whipple that Br. Sears has paid 50 dollars for a draft of the new church. It is so definite that the shape size & length of all the timbers are marked. The plan will be sent by the first opportunity." This letter is in the Cowles MSS.

[5]Oberlin Society MS Minutes, June 17, 1842.

[6]*Oberlin Evangelist,* June 22, July 6, 1842; Mar. 1, June 7, July 5, 1843. It was always intended that the tower should contain a clock, an intention unfortunately not carried out. In 1852 an effort was made to procure the money for a clock and a promise was given that a bell would be donated. The tower remains today blank and dumb.—P. C. M., Jan. 12, 1852.

rounded by mud and can only be entered by an inclined plain made of rough boards."[7]

The relation of the church to the Institute and College was always very close. When the original confession of faith and covenant were adopted the faculty of the Institute took an official part in their preparation. Often in the making of an important decision the advice of the faculty was asked. The preaching was done by professors from the Institute. After the pastorate of Shipherd, Professor Cowles and Professor Morgan filled the pulpit temporarily. Then Professor Finney became pastor and Professor Morgan was associated with him. At first the pastor's salary was entirely furnished by the Board of Trustees of the Institute, the colonists of course contributing to his support through their contributions to the Institute. No change was made in this relation even though the trustees appealed to the colonists in 1842 to make some direct contribution to the support of the pastor.[8] Some money, however, was raised by the church members to pay a small salary to Professor Morgan for his assistance during the extended absence of Professor Finney. The singing was furnished by a choir which was practically identical with the Musical Association in the Institute and, therefore, made up mostly of students. Professor Allen directed this choir, receiving a stipend of a hundred dollars a year for his services. As the students were required to attend church services as a part of their training, the gallery was usually filled at all services. The church was as closely bound up with the Institute and College as it was with the community.

To understand the great importance of the church in Oberlin it must be borne in mind that the prominent characteristic of the community, as well as the College, was piety. The Sabbath was devoted, without reservation, to the worship of the Lord. "Is there a place in the wide world which has such Sabbaths as we have?" James Fairchild wrote to Mary Kellogg from Oberlin. "In Palmyra last winter, even while we were at meeting, the railroad cars would go rumbling by as if in mockery of the truth which we had met to acknowledge but here there is no such contradiction. No sound is heard but the voice of prayer and praise

[7] *Cf. supra* page 551.

[8] F. M., Mar. 16, 1836, and "Report of Committee on mutual sharing of Salary of Pastor of 1st Church by Colonists and College," 1842 (Misc. Archives).

and there is no gathering place except the house of God."[9]

A visitor to Oberlin from New England in the early fifties has left us a revealing description of Oberlin of a Sunday:

"The Sabbath was Peace from beginning to end, for there is probably not a community in the world more pervaded by religion than that of Oberlin. Religion is the very atmosphere of the place, so that not unfrequently impenitent young men and women as they are traveling thither for the first time to commence study, are brought under deep conviction by the fact that they are going to Oberlin, where such multitudes have been converted. . . . The church edifice is very large and will seat twenty-five hundred persons. This immense house was perfectly full from top to bottom . . . and in the deep galleries running entirely round the house, were seated a *thousand* young men and ladies, students in the institution from fifteen to twenty-five years of age. A more interesting sight we never beheld, and it brought the tears instantly to our eyes. Among them, here and there, might be seen neatly dressed colored persons, sitting with bright intelligent faces, and with no apparent consciousness that they belonged to a proscribed race. . . . The choir was composed of about one hundred and twenty choice singers, seated directly behind the pulpit, and accompanied by several instrumental performers, and the music was as nearly perfect in its general character and effect for church music as could well be conceived. I noticed five colored persons in the choir. Mr. Finney preached in the forenoon from the text 'My grace is sufficient for thee,' and to those who have heard him in his best moods, on so spiritual a theme, we need scarcely say it was a rich treat. Ministers do not often hear preaching, but one such discourse would last us a year. . . .

"As usual Oberlin is enjoying a revival, though without the use of any special services. . . . The afternoon was occupied with the reception of members and the administration of the Lord's Supper. At six o'clock there was an inquiry meeting, at which there were eighty present, though there had been scarcely a word addressed to the impenitent during the day. Some twenty or thirty neighborhood prayer meetings were held during the evening."[10]

[9]James H. Fairchild Letters, *Oberlin Alumni Magazine,* June, 1905, page 247.
[10]*Oberlin Evangelist,* July 20, 1853.

In the last analysis the Oberlin pulpit meant the preaching of Finney. To Lucy Stone he was merely "the crossest looking man I ever saw,"[11] but to most students, townsmen and visitors his glittering eyes, shaggy brows, beak-like nose and expressive mouth represented the very center and symbol of Oberlin and the Oberlin idea. To go to Oberlin was to hear Finney, the great actor of the American pulpit. His preaching was always live, emotional, spontaneous, and dramatic as well as logical—qualified particularly to appeal to younger people. He never wrote out his sermons, using only a brief skeleton or outline, itself referred to seldom or not at all. His sermons were essentially extemporaneous, though, of course, thought out carefully before hand.

Often he would begin one of his sermons in the morning and then continue it in the afternoon, as in July of 1855 when he preached all day on "Faith" and in 1857 when two sermons were required for his exposition of the text: "Whoso covereth his sins shall not prosper: but who confesseth and forsaketh them shall have mercy."[12] Though Finney sometimes preached on worldly matters such as the assassination of President Lincoln, he dealt for the most part with the great central theme of sin and salvation. "Robbing God," "A Sinner a Nuisance," "Joined to Idols," "Turn or Die," "Blood the Condition of Pardon," "Sinners Condemned," "Your Sins Will Find You Out" were typical sermon subjects. He was probably most effective in dealing with the terrible scenes of judgment, redemption and damnation. Here was a real opportunity for the full use of his descriptive powers. One of his most famous sermons was on "The Wages of Sin." Others of similar tenor were: "Guilt and Doom of Sinners," "Plowing of the Wicked, Sin," "Wicked Turned into Hell," and "The Devil Seeks to Devour." The latter part of his skeleton for the sermon having the last named title (as preached in 1863) runs:

> "4. Suppose you *must* cross a *desert swarming with lions.*
> 5. Lions seek *their prey* in *darkness.*
> 6. So the *devil carries off* his victims in the *night.*
> 7. He prowls *about* you in the *night peculiarly.*

[11]A. S. Blackwell, *Lucy Stone,* 47.

[12]Smith Norton, MS. "Notes on Pres. Finney's sermons, 1855" (in O. C. Lib.) and MS diary of Sprague Upton, Sept. 13, 1857 (lent by Prof. W. T. Upton).

FINNEY IN OLD AGE
(Oberlin College Library)

α 63

Acts 16:30. What shall I do to be saved.
I. What salvation is. 1. Deliverence from sin.
2. Do. From its consequences. 3. Eternal life.
II. What you can not do. 1. Can't be saved by your
own good works. 2. Nor in sin. 3. Nor without Ch.
4. Nor without being fitted for heaven.
III. What you need not do. 1. Wait to make yourself
worthy. 2. Nor try to make any amends to God
3. Nor wait to feel deeply. 4. Nor for greater sense of sin.
5. Nor for God's time. 6. Need not pray & wait for new heart
7. Nor to use means with God.
IV. What you must not do. 1. Not be dishonest with your
self. 2. Nor with any one else. 3. Not think you
have nothing to do. 4. Nor expect God to do what
he requires you to do. 5. Not procrastinate.
6. Not wait passively to be convicted. 7. Must
not forget what salvation is. 8. Not think to trust
for pardon, while you don't give up all sin.
9. Not adjourn the question obedience till you are safe.
10. Must not cover sin. 11. Nor try to compromise.
12. Nor spend your time in trying to feel.
11. Not wait to get better. 12. Not be ashamed to
own yourself a sinner. 13. Nor to stand up
for Jesus. 14. Not wait for others.

V. What you must do. 1. You must believe in Ch.
This involves. 1. Conviction of who & what he is.
2. Do. of his relations to & claims upon you.
3. Do. of your condition & dependence on him.
4. Your personal committal to obedience

ONE OF FINNEY'S SERMON "SKELETONS"
(From the Finney MSS)

8. If *this doctrine* were *really believed* it would beget *general sobriety, vigilance,* & *anxiety.*
9. The *skepticism* that *prevails* is as the *devil* would have it.
10. Many a *soul* has been *carried captive because* of *unbelief.*
11. What would you *think* of one *crossing* the *desert swarming* with *lions* as careless as *you are.*
"You *would expect him* to be *devoured.*"

The final portion of his outline of the sermon on The Wages of Sin is of a similar nature:

"10. *Hell* has its *use.*
11. *Hell the less of two evils.*
12. The *best use* that God can *make of sinners.*
13. They *shall glorify God.*
14. But *can you endure it?* Have *you considered* the *import* of the figures. Heaven—*City of Gold, Robes, Harps,* Eternal Joy, *Songs, Shouts,*—not overdone. Hell—*Lake of Fire, Chains, Darkness, Furnace, Smoke, Wages, Death, How Long-Eternally, Cruel* to *conceal this.*
15. *Christ interfered* to *save from this.*"[13]

But it was Finney's striking manner of delivery, his importunate personal appeal to each individual hearer that made these sermons most effective. Few who had heard that sermon on The Wages of Sin could ever forget it.

"Indeed, it almost makes one shudder, even after the lapse of years," wrote the Rev. Charles Bush in 1876, "to recall some of them [Finney's Sermons]—that especially from the text, 'The Wages of sin is death'! The preacher's imagination was as vivid as his logic was inexorable. . . . How he rung the changes on that word 'wages' as he described the condition of the lost soul: 'You will get your "wages"; just what you have earned, your due; nothing more, nothing less; and as the smoke of your torment, like a thick cloud, ascends forever and ever, you will see written upon its curling folds, in great staring letters of light, the awful word, *wages, Wages, WAGES*'!

"As the preacher uttered this sentence, he stood at full height, tall and majestic—stood as if transfixed, gazing and pointing toward the emblazoned cloud, as it seemed to roll up before him: his clear shrill voice rising to its highest pitch, and pene-

[13]Skeletons in Finney MSS.

trating every nook and corner of the vast assembly. People held their breath. Every heart stood still."[14]

No wonder students dreamed of the Last Judgment as Mary Gilbert did in 1853.[15] Young people carried away with them from Oberlin the memory of these terrible sermons, if of nothing else.

Finney's prayers were also impressive but of quite a different character. His prayers before the largest congregation were as intimate as if he were in his own closet. Supplications took the place of warning, tears the place of sweeping, stabbing gestures. The great orator-preacher became mild and simple as a little child. These prayers were evidently never prepared but were the spontaneous gushings of a highly emotional and impetuous spirit wrought up to its highest point of pious zeal. He prayed for the poor and sick of the community, for the students; he prayed for rain and accepted ensuing showers gratefully as the answer of an anxious, listening Deity. More than once he noticed the choir in his petitions, "Telling the Lord how he could not hear the words of the first pieces we sang, but heard the second etc." One Sabbath in the summer of 1864 he prayed about the ladies' long dresses. Sometimes his phrasing in prayers as in sermons was more forceful than elegant, as at the Thanksgiving Service in November, 1848, when he prayed "that the southern aristocrats might *spit* in the dough faces of the north until they provoked them to put an end to Slavery, [and] that the dinner of the ungrateful might not *choke them* to death."[16]

Sometimes Finney would direct a part of his discourse especially to the student-filled gallery, as in 1859 when one of the young ladies noted in her diary: "He addressed a portion of his sermon to the seniors, a large class. Also the Senior ladies' class. Mentioned the cases of two individuals . . . who . . . had come all this way through College and were not yet converted. Said he had spoken with one or two of the class about this. . . . He appealed strongly to them, fearing the blood of their souls would be on their skirts. I saw a member who was deeply affected and put his handkerchief to his face." Of course, every effort was

[14]Rev. Charles P. Bush, "Mr. Finney in Rochester and Western New York" in *Reminiscenses of Rev. Charles G. Finney* (Oberlin—1876), 12.

[15]Mary Minerva Gilbert, MS Diary, June 12, 1853.

[16]Mary L. Cowles, MS Diary, May 28, 1859; W. W. Wright to A. A. Wright, July 17, 1864 (Wright MSS), and Charles Penfield to Helen Cowles, Nov. 21 to 24, 1848 (Cowles-Little MSS). On Finney's prayers in general see G. F. Wright, *Charles Grandison Finney* (Boston and New York—1893), 274–279.

made to convert the students, this being Finney's first aim in Oberlin. At the conclusion of many sermons the evangelist-professor issued the call for sinners to come forward and acknowledge Jesus Christ as Lord. Large numbers of students went forward on many such occasions and later joined the church by hundreds.[17]

The perennial revivals were, of course, community as well as college affairs and kept the religious zeal of the village at a high pitch. The whole town would be given over to prayer meetings, experience meetings and song service. Class meetings in College, faculty meetings, sessions of the agricultural society, social gatherings were turned to the dominant religious questions of the hour.[18]

But it was not only at times of revival or on the Sabbath that the inhabitants of Oberlin turned to religion. To most of them religion was life, and life itself was only significant as it seemed to reveal to them the Deity and His will. "I believed I sinned in taking a small piece of pie after I had finished my meal," confided the wife of a professor to her diary. "It would have benefited others, & did not, but perhaps injured me. The great law of love was violated. I came into my room immediately to kneel before my Savior, & *repent,* that I had grieved His infinite heart of love." When drought burned down the crops and threatened famine a "Day of Humiliation and Prayer for Rain" was set aside. Such a day was August 28, 1854. The practice was fully justified by the *Evangelist,* though it was recognized that: "God has higher and better ends in view than large harvests and uncounted stores, so that He will measure out to us of the latter, only as He sees he can do so, the higher and better good not being imperiled thereby," and also that it was perhaps for the *moral* good of the country that it should be so scourged.[19]

The church was the chief arbiter of morals in the community. The Institute sometimes entered this field, as when in 1848 the Prudential Committee refused the application of a certain Mr. Lake for the lease of a lot. The committee concluded "that said

[17]Mary L. Cowles, MS Diary, June 25, 1859; Sprague Upton, MS Diary, Sept. 20, 1857; Elizabeth Hanmer to mother, July 24, 1852 (lent by Mildred Durbin, Columbus), and *Lorain County News,* Jan. 3, 1866.

[18]See the account of such a revival in the *Lorain County News,* Jan. 3, 1866.

[19]Alice Welch Cowles, MS Diary, July 14, 1838 (Cowles-Little MSS), and *Oberlin Evangelist,* Sept. 13, 1854.

Lake is not a man that the Com[mitte]e can satisfactorily lease a Lot of land to, he being upon his own confession given to swearing." Earlier, when a lot on Main Street "South of the Creek on which the steam mills stand" was leased by the trustees it was specifically provided that "in no case are the premises to be occupied by females except as members of a family having a married head and in all cases to be subject to the general regulations of the Institution." When Professor George Allen leased the lot on which he built his house south of the Music Hall he agreed to "occupy and use the said premises in all respects in accordance with the principles and precepts of the Christian religion," and "in conformity to the 'Oberlin Covenant' so-called."[20]

Of course, almost every Christian man in the community considered himself to be his "brother's keeper" and the same was true among the students. The students were, likewise, subject to a separate system of disciplinary administration to be examined later. Most of the cases brought before the local Justice-of-the-Peace were for the recovery of money due. In 1838, for example, Bela Hall claimed payment from Nathaniel Gerrish "on a note of hand . . . of three Dollars and sixty-eight cents."[21] The names of church members do not appear often in these suits.

The church itself was a court which heard all sorts of cases, civil and criminal as well as questions of doctrine. In 1838 one "sister" brought the charge against another sister that she was guilty of "Unchristian conduct" on four points:

"1. Busy body in other persons' matters
2. Tattling
3. Slander
4. Falsehood."

Such cases were tried before the body of members of the church assembled in regular or special business meetings. The case named lasted through several meetings. In the previous autumn another church member had been indicted for continuing the use of tea in violation of the Oberlin Covenant. There were cases of Sabbath breaking to be considered. In 1839 a young man confessed to the charge of having worked as steward on a lake

20P. C. M., Nov. 20, 1848; leases to Martin Fitch, Mar. 1, 1836 (Misc. Archives), and to George Allen, May 28, 1842 (O. C. Lib. Misc. MSS).

21Justice of the Peace of Russia Township, MS Records, 1838 (O. C. Lib.).

boat on the Sabbath. Three years previous a colonist was charged with having "violated the Sanctity of the Sabbath by travelling and driving a loaded team from Ridgeville to Oberlin on that holy day." In 1851 Henry Bates was charged with a long list of crimes, not only Sabbath breaking but also disobedience and disrespect to parents, dancing and card playing. W. H. Plumb, who was in charge of the boarding house for a time and thus brought in close relation with the young ladies of the Institute, confessed that he had in the case of one of them "trampled upon her affections and . . . permitted her to be exposed to the sneers and ridicule of others." One man was brought before the church for breaking a fence. In the early fifties a political conflict between two candidates for the postmastership was aired in the church, the case running over a period of more than four years.[22]

Of course, there were trials for heresy. Delazon Smith, a student, was excommunicated for his acknowledged atheism. In the thirties a citizen was indicted for:

"1. The neglect of reading the Holy Scriptures and prayer in his family.

2. The neglect of meeting with God's people on the sabbath and on other days to worship.

3. The neglecting the Ordinances of God's house."

Purely business matters were also dealt with. The tavern keeper and his wife were excommunicated for absconding in order to escape payment of debts. One particularly complicated case involved the charge that a man had kept property out of his father's estate in order to defraud his father's creditors. Another case arose out of the delivery of ten barrels of poor flour. Not the least interesting cases were those involving the relation between husband and wife.[23]

There is a pleasanter side to the picture. The church was also a charitable institution and its beneficences were large for that day. The poor fund of the church was usually between one and two hundred dollars. This was distributed to the "Widow Smith," "Clark's family," "funeral Expenses [of] Miss ____," for "Half load of wood for Mrs. Butts," etc. Fifty-one

[22]Oberlin Church, MS Minutes, Oct. 24, 27, 1837; Apr. 28, 30, May 1, 3, 1838, and Oberlin Church MSS (O. C. Lib.).

[23]Oberlin Church MSS, and MS Church Minutes, *passim*.

dollars was appropriated in 1856 "for a colored woman to aid in the purchase of her Daughter." Several hundred dollars was usually raised annually for the use of various benevolent societies. In 1859, when the poor fund was $115.88, there was also raised and expended for the American Missionary Association, $160.83; for the Oberlin Bible Society, $59.35; for the Congregational Church in Nebraska, $41.11; for the Home for the Friendless, $27.36; for the Seaman's Friend Society, $75.14; for the American Board of Commissioners for Foreign Missions, $3.38 (not popular in Oberlin because considered pro-slavery); for the Home Missionary Society, $25.63; and for the Rescuers' Fund (this being the year of the Oberlin-Wellington Rescue), $185.81.[24]

The Town of Russia was left to care for some of the poor. In 1856 the records show that a meeting of the township trustees was held, "the object of the meeting . . . [being] to dispose of the town poor." "Mr. Charles Woodman was put up, and it being found that Isaac Hill offered to keep him at the rate of $1.30 per year—no one biding less, the trustees then declared that Mr. Hill have the keeping of him."[25] It is doubted whether any Oberlin colonist was ever taken care of by the town.

The sick were nursed by neighbors and acquaintances. A family in which there was sickness could expect the aid and comfort of most of the community, especially, of course, fellow church members. When Professor James Monroe was ill in 1850, Mrs. Monroe wrote to her parents: "He has not been able to sit up except to have his bed made & is very weak & much prostrated. . . . He has had the very best of care. I think I never saw a sick person receive such attention, five or six individuals take turns in watching nights & they did take care of him through the day until the last week. We have not wanted for anything that friends could do for us. Mrs. Prof. Hudson has the babies."[26] The students followed the same practice: taking turns in "watching" with any of their number who might be ill.

Before the war the meeting house had become entirely too

[24]Oberlin Church, "The Treasurer's Ann. Report, 1855–56," and "The Treasurer's Ann. Report, 1858–59" (Oberlin Church MSS).

[25]Russia Township, MS Records, Feb. 23, 1856.

[26]E. M. Monroe to her parents, Oberlin, Dec. 25, 1850 (in the possession of Mrs. Emma M. Fitch).

small for the number of persons who desired to attend the services. So in 1860 the congregation "swarmed," and the Second-Congregational Church was organized, including in its membership many prominent citizens: J. M. Fitch, J. M. Ellis, Samuel Plumb, Henry Cowles, G. N. Allen, the Fairchild brothers, Elisha Gray (co-inventor of the telephone), John Keep, Henry E. Peck, Giles Shurtleff, and W. W. Wright among others. Services were held in the College Chapel during the war years; the Rev. Minor W. Fairfield, a graduate of the Collegiate and Theological departments and brother-in-law of Professor Fairchild, was the pastor. There never were any differences between the two churches. The great Sunday School, which had had a continuous history since 1833, remained united for some years longer. Its six or seven hundred attendants met in the Chapel at nine o'clock on Sunday mornings under the superintendency of J. M. Fitch, as they had been accustomed to do since 1855. When, after the war, a building was constructed for the Second Church the members of the old church contributed over five thousand dollars.[27]

But other organizations had divided the community. In the decade of the fifties the Episcopalians organized the opposition to "Oberlinism" and the college administration which existed among some groups of townsmen. Their effort was to combat in its very lair what they called Oberlin's "wild ultraisms," "indecent dogmatism" and "politico-religious teaching." They wished to provide a place where Oberlinites could enjoy "Christian *worship* in which their devotional feelings shall not be chilled by the crude & often disgusting puerilities of the 'College Chapel' & its head Prof. F." This enterprise seems to have been chiefly the work of the Rev. Francis Granger, an Episcopalian missionary having his headquarters at Elyria. He had the backing of a Cleveland Rector and of the Rt. Rev. Charles P. McIlvaine, Bishop of Ohio, of President Lorin Andrews of Kenyon College and of certain churchmen in the East. Apparently Episcopalian services were held in Oberlin as early as 1851. Christ

[27]*Lorain County News,* May 9, 1860, and Second Congregational Church of Oberlin, MS Minutes, May 5, June 3, 1860; Aug. 4, 1861. On the Sunday School see Fitch's account in the *Oberlin-Evangelist,* July 6, 1853, and Chauncey N. Pond, "Ohio Sunday-School History," Ohio Church History Society, *Papers,* III, 1–20 (Oberlin—1892).—On March 31, 1867, there were 711 teachers and pupils in attendance.—*Lorain County News,* Apr. 3, 1867.

Church Parish was organized in 1855. The first name among the subscribers is that of Attorney Anson P. Dayton who was soon to be known as chief informer in the Rescue Case! Democratic Postmaster E. F. Munson was another charter member. The College and the Congregational church did not welcome the invasion![28]

Apparently it was the Episcopalians who introduced into Oberlin the celebration of Christmas. As late as 1863 most Oberlinites looked upon it as "a sort of heathen institution" and treated December 25 exactly like any other day. In 1866, however, Christmas services were held at Christ Church, and the merchants rejoiced in much buying of presents.[29]

After the Episcopalians the Methodists were the next to organize, and were holding religious services and "sociables" in Union Hall in 1861. By 1864 they had been granted the use of a room in old Colonial Hall. In the mid-sixties there were also small congregations of Wesleyan Methodists and Baptists. The views of the Methodists and Wesleyans being not so very much in conflict with the dominant Oberlin attitude, they were apparently more hospitably received than the conservative Episcopalians and the Calvinist Baptists.[30]

Secret societies had always been opposed in Oberlin, and the establishment of a local Lodge of Free Masons in 1867 stirred up a great storm. Professor Finney preached three sermons against them and, with the support of Dr. Dascomb, attempted to secure their exclusion and expulsion from membership in the First Church. President Fairchild spoke, of course, in favor of compromise, caution and tolerance. Masonry triumphed. In the spring of 1868 a grand Masonic convention was scheduled for the old meeting house on condition that those opposed should be allowed to express their views. The convention was held and, amid a scene of considerable confusion and disorder, all non-Masons who attempted to speak were ruled out-of-order.

[28]The chief sources are in the Christ Episcopal Church MSS, especially R. B. Claxton to W. Welsh, Oct. 21, 1854; John Springer to Francis Granger, Aug. 12, 1854, Lorin Andrews to H. C. Safford, Apr. 30, 1856, and Articles of Association dated Apr. 18, 1855.

[29]Mollie Clark to A. A. Wright, Dec. 29, 1863 (Wright MSS), and *Lorain County News*, Dec. 26, 1866.

[30]*Lorain County News*, Feb. 27, Apr. 10, 1861; May 5, July 6, 1864, and Mrs. L. E. Rowe, "History of First Baptist Church, Oberlin," in Lorain County Baptist Association, *Minutes*, 1903, pages 21–24.

But Professor Finney continued his one-man campaign in the press and from the pulpit.[31]

The lives of the mothers of Oberlin did not differ greatly from those of other women of their day. In the ten years from 1834 to 1844 the number of children per family averaged a little over three. If they took student boarders, as most of them did, their cares were further increased. With no plumbing, no sewers, no modern conveniences of any sort, fretful days must have been the rule in many families. The church furnished the chief relaxation from a home life of drudgery. There were, however, other social diversions. In the very first year a sewing circle was established.

At the beginning of 1835 the Maternal Association of Oberlin was founded. Mrs. Shipherd was the first superintendent and Mrs. Stewart the first corresponding secretary. "Deeply impressed with the great importance of bringing up our children in the nurture and admonition of the Lord," began the constitution, "we the subscribers, agree to associate for the purpose of devising and adopting such measures as may be best calculated to assist us in the right performance of this duty." Meetings were to be at least once a month and to be devoted largely to the problems involved in the training of their children. Among other items it was provided that, "It shall be the indispensable duty of every member to qualify herself by prayer, by reading and by all other appropriate means, for performing the arduous duties of a christian mother, and to suggest to her sister members, such hints as her own experience may furnish or circumstances render necessary." There was also for a while a "Paternal Association" but it seems to have been short-lived and inactive.[32]

The regular meetings were, of course, occasions for social intercourse. There is much to be read between the lines of a resolution passed at the annual meeting in 1836 to the effect, "that the knitting for benevolent objects be excluded, unless individuals bring it from home, and make no remarks upon it, that our at-

[31]Various letters in the Wright MSS (Oct. 13, 15, Dec. 8, 1867, and Mar. 2, 1868), *Lorain County News*, Apr. 3, 1867, W. H. Phillips, *Oberlin Colony*, 116–117; the suppressed chapter on Masonry in Finney's MS Memoirs, and C. G. Finney, *The Character, Claims, and Practical Workings of Freemasonry* (Cincinnati—c. 1869).

[32]Oberlin Maternal Association, MS Minutes, May 10, 1843; Jan. 1, 1845; July 1, 1857, and Constitution and Annual Report for 1844.

tention may not be diverted from the object of the meeting." Later in the same year a whole afternoon was spent in discussing "the advantages and disadvantages arising from afternoon visits." Some felt that such visits "had a tendency to dissipate the mind, to induce scandal ie. tale bearing." The conclusions finally reached were: "That all invitations for large parties & even small ones should be discouraged, but when we could visit our friends without injury to our children or disarranging our domestic regulations, and do it for the glory of God, we were at liberty to do so, and yet, no one should expect us to return that visit, unless perfectly consistent with other duties."[33] Thus was one social problem settled directly and effectively.

It was generally the Oberlin view that no child was too young to be converted. At an early meeting of the Maternal Association discussion centered on a boy of "4 years who seemed anxious to please God in every thing he did. Would often ask if God would like such & such a thing. Even the manner in which he should take his food was matter of inquiry that he might not sin." The assembled ladies concluded that the evidence seemed to show that this "child had been born of the Spirit." At a previous meeting one mother gave "an account of the hopeful conversion of her little son, aged 4 years 4 months, a few weeks before his death." Even in the middle sixties the Pastor of the Second Church stated that he believed that at least a hundred children had been converted within a short time.[34] Of course the Sabbath School was a numerous body and an important influence in the lives of the pious children.

The Oberlin Sabbath, it is clear, was the Puritan Sabbath transplanted into the forests of northern Ohio, and it must have been rather tiresome for the younger children. It was undoubtedly not without reason that the Maternal Association devoted an entire meeting to the discussion of the question, "How can we make our children happy on the Sabbath & yet prevent their desecrating that holy day?" Among other ideas brought out, "It was remarked that all play things which the child was allowed during the week should be put away Saturday night &

[33]MS Minutes, Jan. 6, Nov. 9, 1836.

[34]*Ibid.*, Dec. 7, 1836; Mar. 5, 1835, and J. M. Fitch to James Monroe, Oberlin, Apr. 11, 1864 (Monroe MSS). See Sandford Fleming, *Children & Puritanism* (New Haven—1933).

AN OBERLIN FAMILY OF THE FIFTIES

The Cowles-Penfield Family, front row left to right: Charles Penfield (a member of the College faculty), Mrs. Minerva Dayton Penfield Cowles, Rev. Henry Cowles, Josephine Penfield Cushman Bateham; and back row left to right: Smith Penfield (musician), Sarah Cowles, J. G. W. Cowles (a student), Thornton Bigelow Penfield (later a missionary to India), and Mary Louisa Cowles (student and diarist).

(From a daguerreotype owned by the Misses Alice and Elizabeth Little, Oberlin, retouched by Arthur E. Princehorn)

THE OBERLIN ELM AND TAPPAN SQUARE IN THE SEVENTIES
See the hay scales at the extreme left.
(From a stereoscopic photograph in the Oberlin College Library)

books proper for the Sabbath brought forward, . . . Singing hymns was mentioned as adding to the interest to be awakened on the Sabbath." One is not surprised to read that Mrs. Mary Willard got her ideas for bringing up Frances E. Willard from meetings of this association.[35]

There is abundant evidence that Oberlin youngsters even in the early days took delightful rambles through the woods, played games, had simple parties and picnics and enjoyed themselves in a mild way as children in a rural town were accustomed to do. Mary Cowles, the daughter of the editor of the *Evangelist*, records in the diary kept in her twelfth and thirteenth years that on various days she: "Played ball . . . with johny kendall," "went to see adelia hall . . . went out to the barn and hunted hen's eggs," "went with smith [her half brother] after the cows. Went into the woods with him and got a large bunch of flowers," etc.[36] The religious and moral values and dangers in all such activities were carefully weighed, however.

The Maternal Association, at one time or another, considered most of the important phases of child management in Oberlin. The problem of what amusements should and should not be encouraged was often discussed. Among the amusements which could be listed as "harmless" were placed: "Dolls & Tea sets for little girls . . . also raising broods of chickens, pet kittens &c. Family picnics including the members of several neighboring families, a ride &c." It was decided that "Games in the form of marbles or checkers" need not be discouraged "when amusement simply was the object." "Children's parties were spoken of as of doubtful utility" and many even "deprecated the effect of the intense excitement which would be likely to attend"—"the approaching Exhibition of the Union School." As for the Fourth-of-July, most mothers "objected to the use of powder in any of its forms. The practice of having Sabbath School Celebrations on that day was by some thought a good one. Some spoke of picnics as not objectionable provided parents accompany their children & join with them in their sports." Some children were,

[35]Oberlin Maternal Association, MS Minutes, June 3, 1840, and F. E. Willard and M. B. Norton, *A Great Mother, Sketch of Madam Willard* (Chicago—1894), 144–145.

[36]R. S. Fletcher, "Oberlin in the Fifties as recorded by Twelve-Year Old Mary Louisa Cowles," *Oberlin Alumni Magazine*, May 1, 1931.

of course, without the pale with their parents among the "publicans and sinners." Mary Cowles noted one day in her diary: "While we were going down . . . as we passed Mr. Wacks tavern we saw one man who was gray headed, lame, bent over pitching quoits with a man about as old as father. . . . As we came back as we passed mr wacks we saw not old men but eddy and helen wack, quite small children, engaged in the same business. . . . How much this exercise of chance and skill must be loved."[37] The little bigot did not explain just why quoits was so much worse than other games. Probably whatever a non-church-goer and a Democrat did seemed wrong.

Thrift combined with benevolence was in Oberlin a major virtue and instilled into the children as early as possible. One Oberlin mother told her sisters that when her children seemed "disposed to spend a penny foolishly she always reminded them that one penny alone would purchase fifteen pages of tract." In the children's column of the *Oberlin Evangelist* a story appeared of a little girl who "lay upon her death bed, parched with a fever." A visitor asked her if she would like an orange, and, receiving a reply in the affirmative, gave her a penny. But the little girl resolved at once to give up the orange, and send the penny to the heathen. An accompanying poem repeats the story, beginning:

Upon her bed of death, she lay,
That gentle child and young;
And the slow moments passed away,
By fevered anguish wrung.

At last

. . . she passed in weakness on,
Through death's dark gate of pain,
To taste the living fruits, nor know
Faintness or thirst again.[38]

Oberlin children were well prepared for later benevolence to missionary societies, anti-slavery societies, moral reform societies and church work in general.

[37]Oberlin Maternal Association, MS Minutes, Dec., 1848; Feb. 6, 1856; July 1, 1857; Apr. 5, June 4, 1859, and R. S. Fletcher, "Oberlin in the Fifties. . . ," *Loc. Cit.* Helen Wack later married Senator Stephen Dorsey.

[38]Maternal Association, MS Minutes, June, 1846, and *Oberlin Evangelist,* Mar. 31, 1847.

The provisions for common-school education were certainly no better than in other Ohio towns of the same size in these early years, this despite, or perhaps because of, the existence of the Institute and College. The original plan quite definitely did not envisage public schools apart from the Institute. Children of colonists were to be educated in the Institute from the Infant School through as far as they could, or wanted to, go. After 1834, however, the elementary school in the Institute was abandoned and the tuition charged in other branches later was a barrier to some older children. So a system of free schools was needed, though not always enthusiastically supported.[39]

At first the Oberlin public schools were merely ungraded one-room affairs administered by Russia Township School District No. 5 (later 3) and supervised by the Russia Township school manager. The schools were kept in rented rooms: in President Mahan's house (!), in George Fletcher's shop, in Tappan Hall, in the meeting house, etc. and the teachers (usually college students) were hired at low rates of pay, $20.00 a month without board or $1.50 or $2.50 a week boarding round.

A small schoolhouse was built on the parsonage lot (in front of the site of the present James Brand House) in 1836, but it provided room for only one of the two or more schools which had to be maintained. As in most schools of that day, the children studied Sanders' *Spelling Book,* Colburn's and Adams' *Arithmetics*. Woodbridge's *Geography,* and the *Eclectic Readers*. Conditions in the schools were apparently sometimes quite unsatisfactory. In 1842 the Russia Township school manager (or superintendent) visited a school kept in a room in Tappan Hall and reported "a manifest deficiency in the government." There was much "noise of moving the feet, crowding through the seats, moving of chairs, whispering and talking aloud." "When a recess was allowed," he continued, "the boys went out disorderly making much noise. When they came in . . . instead of hanging their hats or laying them in their places some were flung half way up the house."

[39]The important sources on Oberlin public schools are: "History of Oberlin Public Schools," *Historical Sketches of Public Schools . . . of Ohio* (1876); Oberlin Union School, *Manual* [1867]; State Commissioner of Public Schools of Ohio, *Sixth Annual Report, 1859* (Columbus—1860), 88; Board of Education of Russia Township, MS Minutes, 1842–71, and School District 5 (later 3), Russia Township, MS Minutes, 1834–51.

As early as 1838 it was recognized that a large schoolhouse was needed, but not until 1851 was the brick Union School built on a lot donated by the College just north of President Mahan's house on Professor Street. The dedication ceremonies attracted so many citizens that it was necessary to adjourn to the College Chapel where addresses were delivered and songs sung by a "select choir" including among other pieces:

"The old-fashioned Bible, the dear, precious Bible,
The family Bible, that lay on the stand."[40]

In this building was established Oberlin's first graded school. In 1860 a high school course was added and the first board of education elected with the colored lawyer John M. Langston as secretary. The school was literally and figuratively under the shadow of Oberlin College, its first superintendents and teachers being all members or graduates of the College.

Perhaps the reason that the Paternal Association did not prosper as the Maternal Association did was that the interest of the men was already largely taken up with the Oberlin Agricultural and Horticultural Society. This society was in existence as early as 1837, probably founded a year or two before. Several professors were charter members, undoubtedly including Professor Henry Cowles and Dr. Dascomb, who were always leaders in agricultural activities.[41] The period of the greatest prosperity of the organization seems to have been the forties, though at the very end of our period, in 1865 and 1866, numerous meetings are reported in the local paper. At the annual meetings reports on various agricultural problems were presented and discussed. There were usually, as we have noted, a "Report on Farms and Gardens" and reports on hens and hogs, on ornamental trees, line fences, bees, silk, alternate cropping, horses, plowing, manufactories and statistics of Oberlin. Father Shipherd, himself, made the report on alternate cropping in 1841. The report on statistics constituted a sort of agricultural census. In 1842 the record listed: 113 horses, 271 cows, 54 oxen and 217 sheep in the Oberlin Colony. The harvest of the preceding year

[40]*Oberlin Evangelist*, Dec. 3, 1851.

[41]Davis Prudden wrote to his brother, ". . . An agricultural society has been formed, at the head of which stands some of our Professors . . ." Davis Prudden to George Prudden, May 23, 1837 (Prudden MSS). *Cf.* also D. B. Kinney in the *People's Press* (Oberlin), Oct., 1845.

had produced 1390 bushels of wheat, 4725 bushels of corn and rye, 2450 bushels of oats and peas, 14,250 bushels of potatoes and 355 tons of hay. Several acres of sugar beets, rutabagas and carrots were also reported. Similar censuses were taken in 1839, 1847 and 1849. It seems probable that it was not done every year, though some of the reports may have been lost.

The annual meeting of 1847 seems to have been particularly successful. A meeting in the chapel of Colonial Hall was scheduled for nine o'clock, to be "opened by prayer." The "Plowing, Ex.[hibition] of Cattle, Horses, Sheep, Hogs, etc." was at ten o'clock. The plowing took place on the square. The dinner was at twelve-thirty and after that the procession "will be formed and repair to the Church under the direction of the Marshals." The address, by Professor Thome, came at the afternoon meeting. The several reports on hogs, horses, plowing, etc. were heard in the evening preceded by prayer, followed by a benediction and interspersed with music by the choir. The line-up for the great noon procession included in order:

"Pres. of the Society and orator of the day
Executive Committee
Pres. and Officers of County Society
Farmer wives generally
Farmers "
Farmers Daughters
Farmers Sons
Mechanics
Banner born[e] by two young men
Inst. Music
Faculty of College & Prof.[essional] men generally
Young Ladies of Inst.[itute]
Young Gents. of Inst.[itute]"

Evidently everybody was in the procession. The banner carried bore a device showing "a beautiful Farm house & farm, tastefully laid out & embellished with shrubbery & ornamental trees" and the motto, "Liberty and Labor," which was also the title of Professor Thome's lecture.[42]

In this year, as in some others, the society sponsored a fair. Horses and cattle were displayed in an open lot near Colonial

[42]Oberlin Agricultural and Horticultural Society MSS, *passim; Elyria Courier*, Oct. 12, 1847, and the *Ohio Cultivator*, Oct. 18, 1847.

Hall, sheep and hogs in the Institute barn, and fruit, flowers, vegetables and "manufactories" in the Music Hall. The display of beets, cabbages, carrots, etc., was said to be gratifying. Many were awed by the sugar beet which weighed over thirty pounds. There were also, of course, "rich boquets of flowers and specimens of fancy work, and of the fine arts." The "manufactories" included a black buggy, two bird cages, a case of dental instruments, "two selfsupplying or Phonographic Penns," an "atmospheric churn," books printed by J. M. Fitch, lasts and boots, and "some Paintings by Misses March possessing both the beauties of art & nature, being the representation of Birds with the feathers attached." Similarly ambitious anniversaries were held in the two following years.

The meetings of the agricultural society also furnished, in the words of the editor of the *Ohio Cultivator,* "a rich *intellectual feast.*" The address, usually on some subject related to agriculture, was the central feature. Most of the professors discoursed one year or another. In 1847, as we have seen, it was Professor Thome. In 1844 the orator was Professor Fairchild, in 1848, Professor Hudson, and the next year, Professor Cowles. Professor Cowles spoke on "Science and Agriculture." The *Cultivator* editor commended the "sly wit with which he discoursed on weeds" and "the poignant humor with which he touched on the farmer's neglect of drainage." His only criticism was that the address was too short.[43] In 1845 Dr. J. P. Kirtland, outstanding physician and naturalist of Cleveland, was the speaker. No wonder that the organization was considered so important that on one occasion, at least, the "Faculty adjourned without transacting any business for the purpose of attending an agricultural meeting."[44]

The history of the society through the fifties and early sixties is obscure, but the *Lorain County News* contains brief notices of occasional meetings. There seems to have been a revival of interest in 1865, but certainly after the forties it did not again occupy such an important place in the community. The Oberlin society had a direct influence in the organization of the Lorain County Agriculture Society in 1846. Several of the char-

[43] *Oberlin Evangelist,* Nov. 20, 1844, and *Ohio Cultivator,* Nov. 1, 1848; Oct. 15, 1849.

[44] *People's Press,* Oct., 1845, and F. M., May 6, 1841.

ter members of the county association were Oberlin men. At the first fall meeting H. C. Taylor won the premium for subsoil plowing and D. B. Kinney for the best cultivated farm. In 1847 the organization sponsored a series of lectures to farmers. The lecturers were Dr. Norton S. Townshend of Elyria, Professor Dascomb and Professor Fairchild.[45]

Oberlin was an agricultural community; cows, horses, hogs and chickens roamed at large. Corn and rutabagas grew on the college green. In 1850, 121 agricultural and horticultural papers were received at the post office. Students and faculty members, as well as townsmen, milked cows, raked hay and hoed potatoes. In 1846 Professor Henry Cowles recorded in his journal: "Week ending July 18, did all the rest of my haying, viz. four good loads from S. lot—12 from middle parsonage lot; 7 from N. village lot . . . in all . . . 31 for the season." The year previous, the Professor of Sacred Music, then on a tour in the border states, received a letter from his wife with regard to affairs at home. "Our potatoes I am sorry to say," she wrote, "are diseased. . . . We have spread ours on the barn floor. . . . The new cow is very troublesome in bucking down the fence." D. B. Kinney, an Oberlin farmer, testified in an address before the Agricultural Society: "Often have I stood beside the President [Mahan] in the logging field, and he lifted well. . . . The Professors . . . are truly agriculturalists . . . and I am free to say that they are neither afraid nor ashamed to engage in the preparation and application of the various manures with their own hands."[46]

The Oberlin Collegiate Institute was established in a setting of rural piety. The Reverend professors hoed their corn and tended their cows; and the male students, preparing for the ministry, left their Moral Philosophy and rhetoricals to spread manure and work in the hayfield in the afternoons.

[45]*Lorain County News,* Jan. 25, Feb. 1, Dec. 13, 1865; Jan. 10, 1866, and *Ohio Cultivator,* May 15, Dec. 1, 1846, Mar. 1, Nov. 1, 1847.

[46]"Statistics of Oberlin, 1850" (Agr. and Hort. Society MSS); Henry Cowles' MS garden journal, 1846–48 (Cowles-Little MSS); Wife to Geo. N. Allen, Oct. 22, 1845 (Allen MSS), and *Peoples' Press,* Oct., 1845.

CHAPTER XXXVII

"PLAIN & HOLESOME"

"O thou boarding house! place of all on earth most happy, looked upon by all as the abode of the most lovely and the most learned ladies. Many look upon thee with deep and intense interest for the sake of thy occupants. Many come into thy halls at morning, at noon, at evening, where they are bountifully supplied with all necessary food. Many a youth has come tremblingly to thy door, with determination strong, yet fearing. Many have been joined in the holy bonds of wedlock which man is not to put asunder. Joy and mirth have there dwelt. Thou hast had trials also, fire has been a devouring enemy of thine, then were there anxious looks. . . .

"Sure thou are not surrounded by the most beautiful nor art thou of a very lovely appearance outwardly, yet thou hast a gardin like unto the gardin of Eden. There thou displayest thy treasures, which have been compaired to the most beautiful flowers. There are certain laws which govern thy inmates are there not? are these laws ever broken or is the authority of those in office ever disregarded? Some for this self same fa[u]lt have been told to depart to return no more, have they not? There have [been] meetings and partings at thy gate, have there not? There friends have bid adue to friends never to meet again on earth. There have sisters met brothers who come laden with the love and hearty good wishes of those at home. Thy life has been an eventful one though short."

—From a composition written by HELEN COWLES, July 29, 1846 (Cowles-Little MSS).

LADIES' HALL, commonly known as the Boarding House, was the center of the social life of Oberlin Institute. Oberlin Hall, the first frame building, was the first boarding house but gave up its common name and its purpose to Ladies' Hall when that building was completed in the summer of 1835. A considerable number of the young lady students roomed in the building and many of the young men came in for their meals. In 1845 it was seriously damaged by fire, but it was repaired and continued to be used for twenty more years.[1] It is this building which is usually spoken of as the first dormitory for college girls in the United States. It was torn down in 1865 when the second Ladies' Hall was nearing completion.

The agitation for a new boarding hall began in the fifties. In 1853 a special committee was appointed to gather funds, including Mrs. Finney, the Dascombs, Mr. and Mrs. Cowles and the Pecks. The need was advertised in 1855 through the *Oberlin Evangelist.* Mrs. Finney secured promises of large donations from W. C. Chapin of Providence, her husband's friend and special patron, and from Lewis Tappan of New York. In 1860 the Prudential Committee "Voted that J. H. Fairchild be a Com[mittee] to visit the Ladies Seminaries at College Hill, Cincinnati, at Oxford & any other in his way, with a view to obtain the best information & most improved plans & other details having reference to our contemplated Building."[2] On May 22, 1861, the corner stone of the new hall was laid and dedicated, Father Keep leading in the consecrating prayer and Professors Monroe and Fairchild delivering addresses on joint education and its significance. The raising of funds went forward slowly because of war conditions, and construction had to be stopped after the foundation walls had been finished.[3] Not until early in 1866 did the "varnish brush and carpet hammer" give "the last touches to the New Ladies' Boarding Hall." The new building contained 47 rooms for about twice that number of young ladies, and on the first floor was an office, reception room and parlor for the Lady Principal, a large room for "General Exercises," a parlor where young gentlemen might be entertained until eight o'clock in the evening, a common sitting room, an office for the Steward, a room for the ladies' literary societies and the large dining room.[4]

Tappan Hall, located in the center of the square, was the main men's dormitory and also contained recitation rooms and the men's society rooms. In the later thirties a high cupola was

[1]P. C. M., Jan. 10, 1845.

[2]P. C. M., Sept. 12, 1853 and Sept. 4, 1860; T. M., Aug. 22, 1853; *Oberlin Evangelist,* Aug. 15, 1855, and Lewis Tappan to Mr. and Mrs. Finney, Oct. 9, 1856 (Lewis Tappan letter books).

[3]*Oberlin Evangelist,* June 5, 1861, and Jan. 15, 1862.

[4]*Lorain County News,* Feb. 14, 1866.

erected on the long barracks-like, four-storied, brick structure. It was expected that eventually it would be provided with a clock, but, as in the case of the meeting-house tower, the clock was never obtained. In fact, in 1841 the tower was cut down as it was feared that it might otherwise be blown over. The whole building swayed perceptibly in a strong west wind and there was always some fear that it might collapse. In 1851 braces and studs were put in to further strengthen its frame.[5] A student wrote home in the late fifties: " . . . Some of the people here [are] scared for fear that Tapan Hall will blow over. . . . It has always been considered insecure, when there is considerable wind it rocks perceptably. Hull was thinking of rooming there next term but he has given up that idea now."[6] As the old Ladies' Hall gave way to the new Ladies' Hall, so, eventually (after our period), Council Hall took the place of Tappan as the chief men's dormitory, inheriting its reputation for instability on the upper floors.

The rooms in Tappan Hall were all single ones without closets, with a ventilator opening over each door into the large central hall. At first they were furnished by the institution with a bedstead, a table, three chairs and a stove. The stove was a small open one, a Stewart invention.[7] Charles Winslow engaged a room furnished in this way in 1837, and Charles Livingstone arrived just in time to secure a room provided with "a table desk, stove & bedstead."[8] That very year the trustees decided to dispose of all movable furniture in the men's dormitories except the stoves, and from that time on the young men furnished their own rooms. Students were requested to paper and paint their rooms neatly if they hoped to retain them for their entire course of study. Occasionally they were allowed to sell improvements to successors.[9]

[5]T. M., Feb. 11, 1836, and P. C. M., Aug. 3, 1841, and Apr. 21, 1851.

[6]Henry Prudden to parents, June 3, 1859 (in the possession of Lillian Prudden, New Haven, Conn.).

[7]P. C. M., July 28, 1835; T. M., Sept. 22, 1835, and Feb. 11, 1836; F. M., July 28, 1836. Cf. also the 1836 *Catalogue,* 26, and "The Stewart Stove" in the *Oberlin Evangelist,* Mar. 28, 1860. In 1845 more than one student was prohibited from occupying an individual room, F. M., Feb. 5, 1845.

[8]Charles Livingstone to Parents, Oberlin, May 22 [1840], and C. Winslow to Zenas Winslow, Sept. 16, 1837 (O. C. Lib. Misc. MSS).

[9]T. M., Aug. 31, 1840, and P. C. M., Apr. 9, 1850 and June 5, 1852. Beginning in 1845 it was announced in the catalogue that, "Each room is furnished with a stove only."

TAPPAN HALL IN THE SEVENTIES
(From a photograph in the Oberlin College Library)

We may well be grateful to the student, who, in 1860, realizing that many had seen nothing of Tappan Hall rooms but the occasional glimpse of "a pair of boot-heels looking calmly down upon them from a fourth story window," wrote a realistic description of the interior of such a room:

"Enter then. On your right is a clothes-press, minus shelves and front, within which are suspended some old clothes, a hat and a towel; in one corner a broom; in the other a backless chair, on which stands a bucket of water, flanked by a bar of yellow soap, part of which seems to have suffered decomposition in the water during the morning ablutions, from which it came dripping and so softened that it is perfectly secure in its attachment to the stool. With end jutting up to the outline of a clothes-press is an article of furniture. Two boards six feet long and six inches wide, two boards two feet long at the ends—this quadrangle supported by posts one foot high; short boards laid across; a narrow straw tick; sheets and covers, tumbled together, and not overly clean; this is the bed. At the head of the bed a box, with an old coat on it as a cushion—this is the study chair. Before the box is a red table, rickety, and old, on which is a slate and an Algebra. Arranged against the wall at the back of the table, are books on Phrenology, 'Constitution of Man,' &c. At one end of the table is a discolored plaster model of a head, full of bumps, well-developed and labeled. This is one side of the room.

"All there is to be seen on the other side is a little rusty stove, with a shoe-brush and an open box of blacking upon it, a pair of old boots, a wood-saw, an old trunk, three square inches of mirror, and two sticks of wood."[10]

The rooms in Ladies' Hall were somewhat more completely, if not necessarily better, furnished. In 1835, when the hall was new, Delia Fenn found it "done off quite handsome." The double rooms (occupied by four girls in the boom period) were provided with closets and equipped with a stove, bedsteads, tables and chairs. Some, undoubtedly, supplemented this furniture, as did Lucy Stone, who bought "a fine big rocking chair, with one arm-shelf" costing four dollars, an expense which she felt would be counterbalanced by her increased comfort gen-

[10]"Ukollyandi" in the *Oberlin Students' Monthly,* III, 86–87, Jan., 1860.

erally and "rest for my headaches."[11] Mrs. Emily P. Burke, Lady Principal in 1849–1850, carried on a campaign to have the young ladies' rooms supplied with bureaus and rag carpets, but evidently without great success, as none of the *Catalogues* for the years immediately following list any such furnishings. She did succeed in having the rooms papered.[12]

Mrs. Burke also won the hearts of the young lady students by her war on the bed bugs which seem also to have been a regular part of the equipment. During the winter vacation "she had the hall vacated . . . ," wrote a faculty wife. "No one remaining but herself and one young lady for a room mate—so . . . she had a nice time to freeze out the bed bugs . . . she had all the pillow ticks emptied and washed thoroughly, every bedstead in the hall taken down and thoroughly scalded and then frozen."[13] Despite this thorough cleaning, three years later the plague was back again. When one college girl arrived in Oberlin in July, of 1854, she "went to bed tired, liked to have been eaten up by the bugs, got up and killed about a hundred, went to bed and could not sleep much." After having scalded her bedstead a few days later it is reported that she found more comfort.[14]

When the new Ladies' Hall was completed each room was "furnished with neat new furniture to the extent of a stove, table, wash-stand, curtains, chair, bedstead and straw bed." A few rooms were furnished with carpets, but for these an extra charge was made. In 1868 a large majority of the rooms were provided with a carpet—looking glass—wash bowl and pitcher—chamber and a soap dish, besides the furniture already in said room."[15] "All other articles of bedding [besides the straw mattress] will be furnished by the occupants; also, table napkins."[16] Some uncarpeted rooms, however, were still available at reduced rates.

Early college bills (1835) carry charges not only for board but

[11]Delia Fenn to Richard Fenn, Oberlin, Aug. 21, 1835 (O. C. Lib.), *Catalogue*, 1850–51, page 32, and A. S. Blackwell, *Lucy Stone*, 55.

[12]Mrs. C. H. Churchill to brother, Jan. 27, 1850 (in possession of Mrs. Azariel Smith of Whittier, California).

[13]*Ibid.*—On June 5, 1850, a young lady student read a paper on "Natural History of the Bed Bug" before the young Ladies' Literary Society (MS Minutes).

[14]Mary Minerva Gilbert, MS Diary, July 10, 17, 1854.

[15]*Lorain County News*, Feb. 14, 1866, and P. C. M., Jan. 19, 1866, Jan. 10, and Feb. 5, 1868.

[16]*Catalogue*, 1868–69, page 64.

THE SECOND "LADIES' HALL"
On the site of the present Talcott Hall
(From a photograph taken about the time of its completion and now in the Oberlin College Library)

also, as rooms were free at that time, extra items such as candles, wood, washing, "Damage on broken Furniture," "2 Sheets @ 56¢.," "2 Pillow cases @20¢.," "Use of Bedding" and "Use of bowl & Pitcher." Wood for use in the little stoves was, of course, a necessity, but it was available in unlimited quantities. "Wood is only 1.00 a cord," wrote one young man to his parents in 1837, "cut, dried and delivered at the door, first rate wood, maple, beach, hickory & black walnut—or free of expense if we cut it & get it up ourselves." Each dormitory usually had its ugly wood house, adding to the generally unsightly appearance of the surroundings.[17] Though candles were the usual source of artificial light, oil began to be used in the fifties. In 1858 Miss Abbie Summers, of Livonia, N. Y., "obtained special leave to sit up late in her room to get her lessons; had protracted her studies until 2 A. M. when having occasion to replenish her lamp of burning fluid, she attempted to fill it while it was burning. An explosion of the vapor set fire to her clothes, and before she arrested the flames she was fatally injured, surviving only some 6¾ hours."[18] It is not doubted that the Lady Principal used this instance as an argument against the granting of future light cuts.

The new Ladies' Hall was not only provided with an assembly room, a parlor and a sitting room, but the attic was floored and provided with a sky light "for rainy day promenades and exercise." The old Ladies' Hall had had an assembly room (used by Theodore Weld for his anti-slavery lectures in 1835), and in 1856 the Prudential Committee set aside a reading room, but were rather shocked when it was reported to them "that the young ladies were expecting to have the room furnished with a carpet, etc., etc." The dumb waiter provided in the new hall for carrying up trunks and the ubiquitous fire wood must have

[17]Bills in the Misc. Archives, Charles Winslow to Zenas Winslow, Sept. 16, 1837 (O. C. Lib. Misc. MSS), and T. M., Feb. 11, 1836.

[18]*Oberlin Evangelist,* Dec. 8, 1858. Abbie Summers is buried in Livonia, New York. Her tombstone reads:

> "Abbie, daughter of Munson and Jemima Summers, Born March 13, 1841, died at Oberlin, Ohio, Dec. 4, 1858.
>
> "Heroes have been lauded;
> And victors have been praised,
> But on the crown that Abbie wears,
> This world has never gazed."
>
> —Information from Mrs.
> T. H. Alvord, Livonia, N. Y.

been a welcome relief to those already overtired with much climbing of stairs.[19]

Stimulated by Dr. Dascomb, the faculty and trustees took an unusually advanced stand on the subject of student health and sanitation. In 1836 the faculty "Appointed J. Dascomb & H. Lyman a Board of health on the part of the institution." In 1854 the trustees provided for paying the expenses of students during sickness, though it was also determined that "repayment of such expenses should be asked from the friends of such sick Students." At the very same meeting, on the recommendation of Dr. Dascomb, it was voted to install a water filter in the new College Chapel then under construction.[20] Nevertheless, the amateur nursing of fellow students and faculty wives and the practice of excluding fresh air from the sick room rather reduced the chances of a student's recovery. A young lady student wrote in 1842 to her parents: "One of the young ladies had a touch of the ague last Sabbath and I don't know as she is over it yet. Last Sabbath morning I went into her room and was there about five minutes when I became very sick and went out as quick as I could. I was hardly able to speak when I got to my room, and Mary said I was white as ashes. I suppose it was caused by the bad air although there were several in the room that had been in some time without affecting them!"[21] Deaths from diseases such as typhoid and dysentery as well as tuberculosis were all too common. Minerva Gilbert reported that there was a death from dysentery and cholera almost every day in the summer of 1854.[22] It is obvious that the sanitary conditions were not too good.

Evidences of poor sanitation are not hard to find. An open sewer flowed through the square. The outdoor toilets connected with all dormitories were noisome nuisances. The minutes of the Prudential Committee contain repeated references to the problem involved in caring for them. The new Ladies' Hall erected in 1866 included a running water system: "two large water tanks on the third floor with a capacity of nearly 100 barrels each, and

[19] *Lorain County News,* Feb. 14, 1866, and P. C. M., Apr. 17 and June 5, 1856.

[20] F. M., July 16, 1836, and T. M., Aug. 22, 1854.

[21] Elizabeth Maxwell to Parents, Oberlin, Apr. 1, 1842 (in the possession of Mrs. Emma Monroe Fitch).

[22] Mary Minerva Gilbert, MS Diary.

from them pipes . . . to convenient faucets on each floor."[23]

The By-Laws of 1834 contain various rules regarding the dormitories. There were three rules for the prevention of fires:

"1st. Fire shall not be removed from one place to another except in a close firepan one of which shall be kept for the use of every story in each building.

"2d. Combustible matter shall not be left more exposed to fire than the floor nearest the fire; and the doors and dampers of stoves shall always be closed by Students when they leave their Rooms or retire to rest.

"3d. Monitors appointed by the Faculty shall visit all the Rooms assigned to them & see that every fire is secured and every light extinguished at 10 o'clock P. M.—Sickness excepted."

There is no evidence to show whether fire monitors were actually appointed in the thirties, but in 1840 the Prudential Committee were "instructed to appoint a vigilence fire Committee consisting of a number sufficient to furnish one person for each floor of all the College Buildings, whose duty it shall be to examine each stove or fire place every week & report the state of the same to the Prud. Committee to see that such report be duly made & generally to see that the laws adopted by the Trustees respecting fire be duly executed." In the following year such student "committees" were appointed, and some of their reports are still preserved in the archives of the College. Sporadic efforts were made to check the fire danger at later dates as in 1858 when the Prudential Committee voted a fine of fifty cents to be levied on any student who changed the location of his stove.[24]

The By-Laws also provided that "The Rooms shall be kept in a neat and cleanly manner, and well aired." Occasional inspections were made by members of the faculty. In 1841 a regular committee, made up of Professor Morgan and Secretary Burnell, was chosen for that purpose. The Lady Principal was supposed to inspect the young ladies' rooms. When Mary Ann Adams was Principal it is said that she always looked under the beds. Lucy Stone remembered that Miss Adams once complimented her on the fact that her room was always clean. To this Lucy replied, "I always know when you have been there, Miss Adams, for you always leave the hem of the vallance of my bed

[23]*Lorain County News,* Feb. 14, 1866.

[24]T. M., Aug. 20, 1842, and P. C. M., Sept. 6, 1841, and Jan. 19, 1858.

turned up." There were also inspectors who appraised the damage done to furniture and saw that the cost of repairs was put on the offending student's bill.[25]

The rules also provided that no student should "enter another's room without his permission, nor do that in his own room which shall disturb his neighbor." All students were required to be in their rooms by 10 o'clock and "refrain from loud talking, singing, or any other noise that might disturb the repose of others" after 9 o'clock. Young ladies were required to go to their rooms at 7:30 in winter and 8 o'clock in summer. Passers-by and innocent bystanders were protected by the regulation prohibiting any student from throwing "water, dirt, or anything offensive or dangerous, from the windows of any building of the Institution." The sweepers were expected to sweep the hallways between 5:30 and 7 A. M. on week days and also after 4 P. M. on Saturday "preparatory to the Sabbath." Taking it for granted that all students would desire to sweep their rooms out every week-day, the faculty ordered that: "No student is permitted to sweep the dust out of his room into the passage or entry, at any time after the hall has been swept, till nine o'clock P. M. On Saturday dust shall not be swept from the rooms into the hall, after four o'clock P. M., nor on the Sabbath at all."[26]

The earliest rules provided that "The ladies shall not receive at their rooms the visits of Gentlemen." This simple regulation was later expanded to read: "Students are prohibited, on pain of expulsion, from visiting those of the other sex, at their rooms, or receiving visits from them at their own, except by special permission from the President, or the Principal of the Female Department, in a case of serious illness." This regulation is repeated in the special rules issued for the government of the Female Department.[27] It was a very important regulation because of the experiment in joint education in general, but particularly because young ladies and young gentlemen sometimes roomed

[25]F. M., Mar. 1, 1837, Feb. 18, 1841, and MS Reminiscences of Lucy Stone to her sister, Mrs. Sarah Stone Lawrence, Aug. 11, 1898 (lent by Miss Alice Stone Blackwell).

[26]MS By-Laws of 1834; *Laws and Regulations of the Oberlin Collegiate Institute*, 1840, 1842, and 1853, and *Laws and Regulations of the Female Department of the Oberlin College*, 1852.

[27]MS By-Laws of 1834, Chapter 7, No. 5; *Laws and Regulations*, 1840, and *Laws and Regulations of the Female Department*, 1852.

in the same buildings. When Ladies' Hall was completed in 1835 the faculty voted that "after a sufficient number [of rooms] is selected for the . . . Young Ladies, the highest class have the right to choose, then the next highest and so in order to the lowest." One of the young lady occupants of the hall wrote in August of the same year: "This building is designed for the ladies and when other buildings are erected sufficient to accomodate the gentlemen this is to be occupied alone by them." Early in the following year a number of students petitioned the faculty "that the partition in the hall between the Ladies' & Gentlemen's apartments be made more secure."[28]

There is no evidence to show that this coeducational rooming continued in the dormitories after 1835. The great majority of students in later years, however, lived in private homes, and many of these homes kept students of both sexes. The propriety of such an arrangement depended entirely on the character of the family heads. In 1852 facts came to the attention of the Ladies' Board showing that, in some families, there had been "carelessness . . . in placing [young ladies] in rooms loosely connected with rooms occupied by gentlemen." The members of the Board decided to make an inspection. In the following year they found it necessary to inform one "matron" that because of certain "improprieties which have occurred in her hall," she would not, henceforth, be allowed "to *room both* gentlemen & ladies."[29]

While the number of students was quadrupled in the period from 1836 to the middle fifties, no new dormitories were completed until after the War, so that a larger and larger proportion found it necessary to live in private houses. Whereas only 12 out of the 70 students in the Collegiate Department lived with private families in 1839, 61 of the 107 male college students whose rooms are given in 1856 lived out of dormitories. In 1865, after Oberlin Hall and Walton Hall had been sold, three-fourths of the young men in College (67 out of 88) did not live in dormitories.[30]

Rooms in private homes were far from luxurious as a rule.

28F. M., Feb. 12, 1835, Jan. 27, 1836, and Delia Fenn to Richard Fenn, Aug. 21, 1835 (O. C. Lib.).

29L. B. M., May 10, 1852, and May 15, 1853.

30*Catalogues,* 1839–40, 1856–57 and 1865–66.

"My room is about a quarter of a mile from the institute," wrote George Prudden in 1836, "in a garret— (quite a poetical place). The place is such that when the house is finished &, that is, is plastered there will be two very convenient rooms here. But now it is so near open to the rooms below that we can hear all the noise in those rooms & consequently are much disturbed. Near the house is a steam saw mill, which keeps a constant noise all the day." Nor were the rooms of a later period much more comfortable. Twenty years afterward his son attending Oberlin also lived in a garret.[31]

Girls, too, sometimes lived in "small and unplastered" rooms. Delia Fenn described to her sister in a letter written from Oberlin in the thirties the accommodations she might expect if she came to Oberlin and lived with Mr. and Mrs. Asahel Munger: "Wood Mrs. Munger said would always be close by and, as they have a boy with them, it would, a part of the time at least, be brought in. They have a good stone trough for water from which they will expect you to get water though I have no doubt but they will assist at any time if you do not feel able to get it. Water for rinsing clothes she said would be brought. They now live in a log house. Before it is their framed house into which they will move before long. You will have the log house to wash in. I shall be so near you that if at any time you are not well or for any other reason want assistance I can help you."[32]

Of course, the Lady Principal and the Ladies' Board supervised the administration of the private rooming houses as well as of the regular dormitories. In 1852 the Ladies' Board passed on a request to allow one young lady to room in one house and board in another. Ten years later they ruled, "That no young lady shall board in any but a regularly organized family, where one at least of the heads of the family presides at table and family worship." In the early sixties "Matron's meetings for those who have young ladies of the Inst. in their families" were regularly held under the supervision of Mrs. Marianne Dascomb, the

[31]George Prudden to Peter Prudden, Oberlin, July 18, 1836 (Prudden-Allen MSS), and Henry Prudden to Parents, June 3, 1859 (lent by Lillian Prudden, New Haven, Conn.).

[32][Davis and] Nancy Prudden to George P. Prudden, Apr. [8] and 13, 1837 (Prudden MSS), and Delia Fenn to Sister, Oberlin, Apr. 11, [? 30's] (O. C. Lib.).

Lady Principal. There were over a hundred such matrons in 1862.[33]

Relations between students and the families in which they boarded were not always of the pleasantest. "One sister remarked [to the Maternal Association] that she had her faith, and patience, sorely tried every day by the conduct of those boarding in her family." The Lady Principal did what she could to improve the attitude of roomers but her efforts were not always successful. Mrs. Cowles occasionally gave talks to her charges on their duties toward the families in which they boarded. She especially advised them to cultivate good manners, correct language, good pronunciation, neatness, and love of children, all qualities, which, she pointed out, were also necessary in a good minister's wife. "Identify yourselves with the interests of the family," she exhorted the young ladies. They were warned against selfishness, tattling, "busy curiosity," slander and gossiping. Mrs. Cowles kept roomers and boarders, herself, and understood clearly the problems involved.[34]

Each rooming house, whether owned by the College or not, tended, of course, to become a social unit. It was generally felt by Oberlin mothers that young lady roomers and boarders (also often employed as servants) should be furnished the same "privileges and . . . means of moral and mental improvement . . . as we would have furnished to our own daughters were they left to the mercy of a cold world." The matrons felt called upon also to "exercise over all those connected with our family circle, as boarders, a maternal care, and watchfulness by trying to make the home circle pleasant and attractive, not only to our own sons, but to those Lads, who may be with us as boarders."[35] In many instances, of course, such a homey atmosphere was successfully created. The girls who stayed at the Crockers' in the thirties always spoke "of going home to grandpa's" when referring to their return to their rooming house. Not all young ladies were pleased with the idea of close association with Negroes in the dormitories, but none was ever excluded on account of her color. Neither were roommates always the most desirable. Mary

[33]L. B. M., May 24, 1852; Jan. 20, 1862, and Report of M. P. Dascomb to the Trustees, Aug. 25, 1862 (Trustees' MSS, Misc. Archives).

[34]Maternal Association, MS Minutes, Dec. 4, 1851, and Mrs. Cowles' lecture notes (Cowles-Little MSS).

[35]Maternal Association, MS Minutes, Oct. 6, 1852, and Jan. 5, 1853.

Barnes was troubled by the fact that her roommate was "impenitent and a careless sort of person." Another "female student" wrote home that she had been "put in with a real old maid, wears spectacles, gray hair." "I am watching for an opportunity to escape," she admitted. This same young lady gave a very favorable picture of life in the Ladies' Hall in general, however. "They are like a family," she wrote to her mother. "One young lady goes to the post office every day and brings in letters to those to whom they are sent. She does not read them as I told you [!]."[36]

"Board shall be of a plain & holesome [*sic*] kind; only one dish with its accompaniments shall be eaten at one meal." So read the first rules with regard to the Steward's Department. "Tea & Coffee, high seasoned meats, rich pastries & all unwholesome & expensive food shall be excluded from the Commons table; & yet the steward shall always make the diet as palitable as consistent with these rules. . . . The students shall be furnished with only 3 meals a day." It was also provided that, "Students who choose their board without meat may be gratified, and the price charged accordingly, provided there is enough of this kind to fill a table, and they do not change without the consent of the Steward." From the facilities for sleeping and eating provided it is quite clear that students coming to Oberlin must be "disposed to deny themselves the 'lusts of the flesh and the pride of life.' "[37]

The period from 1835 to 1841 is the period of experimentation both in diet and in management in the boarding department. A vegetable table was installed alongside the regular diet in the summer of 1835. A young lady student wrote to her father in August: "All must sit at the meat or vegetable table. I of course go to the latter. At this table they live well, have puddings 2 or 3 times a week and frequently boiled rice. They also have garden sauce such as berries, potatoes, squashes, beets,

[36][Davis and] Nancy Prudden to George P. Prudden, Apr. [8] and 13, 1837 (Prudden MSS); Report of M. P. Dascomb to the Trustees, Aug. 21, 1866 (Misc. Archives); Mary A. Barnes *et al.* to Laura Branch, Mar. 23—Apr. 23, 1843 O. C. Lib. Misc. MSS), and Elizabeth Hanmer to her family, July 7, and May, 1852 (lent by Mildred Durbin, Columbus, Ohio).

[37]"By-Laws of 1834," and John J. Shipherd in the *New York Evangelist,* Apr. 11, 1835.

onions, &c and frequently baked apple."[38] In 1835 and 1836 the students seemed to be engaged in a contest, as Delazon Smith later wrote, to see *"who can live the longest,* and eat the *least amount of wholesome food."* In the spring of 1835 about twenty of the sixty or seventy eating at the commons ate only bread and drank only water. "Probably you think this would be hard living," wrote one of them, "but I assure you it is better than you or I think it is."[39]

Bread was the chief, sometimes the only, solid basis of diet. Bread with water, bread with salt, bread with milk, bread with gruel, bread with gravy made from flour and water mixed with "pot liquor," and occasionally bread with butter too ancient to tempt the most ravenous appetite were the commonest menus. George Prudden found that there was "no intention . . . of pampering mens' appetites, and making them slaves to their stomachs." "Cold water, milk & wheat will make the sum almost entirely of our articles of food. . . . We have not had what you could call a meal of meat since we have been here. Twice we had a few mutton bones—just enough to set the appetite, once we had a little fish, & a little dried beef several times—We frequently have what is called Graham pudding made of wheat just cracked, & boiled a few minutes in water. Boiled Indian puddings sometimes, & Johnecakes—This makes the sum total of our living—a splendid variety—I assure you. . . . If I only could have a little coffee & a mouthful of meat now & then, with a pretty respectable room in which to deposit my body, I should consider myself well provided for, as to temporal wants."[40]

And such bread! It was soggy, sour and indigestible and said to contain the crusts discarded at previous meals. In December of 1835 the faculty had found it necessary to vote "that the Agent be directed to secure *sweet bread* for the commons' table." In 1836 the almost bankrupt state of the Institute treasury added a very practical reason to the theoretical motives for providing a "plain & holesome" diet. The plain fact of the matter seems to have been that money was not forthcoming with which to pur-

[38]Delia Fenn to Richard Fenn, Aug. 21, 1835 (O. C. Lib.), and P. C. M., Aug. 15, 1835.

[39]Delazon Smith, *The History of Oberlin,* 20, and James and E. Henry Fairchild to Joseph B. Clark, Apr. 2, 1835 (lent by Miss Edith M. Clark, Oberlin).

[40]Davis and George Prudden to Peter Prudden, Aug. 3–5, 1936 (Prudden-Allen MSS).

chase meat, except "a few mutton bones." In September the bill of fare was reduced to bread and salt![41]

Mr. and Mrs. Stewart, who were in charge of the dining hall during these first years, were enthusiastic supporters of dietetic reform but not particularly skilled in business management. By the middle of September the boarding department and the Institute were practically bankrupt. Many students had failed to pay their board bills, and gratuities from outside were not coming in. The situation was critical. Finally the trustees proposed to the students that they take over entirely the management and financial responsibility for the boarding department.[42] A mass meeting of students and teachers was held to consider the proposition. One of the students who attended wrote home:

" . . . The faculty last evening called together those students who board in the Hall & stated to them that the students were owing the Institution about $1,000, that there was not one dollar in the treasury nor no provisions in the pantry. This was owing partly to students not paying their bills & partly in the negligence of the Agent in requiring those students who will not pay to leave the hall. A resolution of the trustees was brought Proposing to the students to take the charge of the boarding establishment upon themselves which was rejected. A motion to adjourn was made untill the next evening. But one of the Professors arose & said we do not know as we can live untill another day, we cannot live without eating, no money in the treasury, no food in the larder, therefore if we adjourned the meeting we also must adjourn eating. I assure you we were in desperate circumstances & the students showed it, for necessity put eloquence on their tongues unrestrained till the hour of midnight."[43]

There seemed to be no alternative. The students organized a "boarding department" independent of the Institute and chose Professors John P. and Henry Cowles, Mrs. Henry Cowles, George Whipple, and a student, W. L. Parsons, a committee to manage it. Mrs. Cowles became the matron. The students

[41]F. M., Dec. 22, 1835; P. C. M., June 16, 1836, and Davis [and George] Prudden to Peter Prudden, Sept. 20, and Nov. 12—Dec. 12, 1836 (Prudden-Allen MSS).

[42]N. P. Fletcher, MS Critical Letters, No. 8 (1837) (Misc. Archives), and T. M., Sept. 13, 1836.

[43]Davis [and George] Prudden to Peter Prudden, Sept. 20, 1836 (Prudden-Allen MSS).

(through this committee) paid to the Institute $300.00 rent *per annum* for the use of the dining hall and kitchen, purchased food, collected bills and ran the establishment generally on an entirely independent basis.[44]

By the spring of 1837 the board had considerably improved if we may believe a young lady student, who wrote to her brother: " . . . Our fare here is generally *very good,* as good as I could wish. We have meat as often as four or five days in a week, and crust coffee almost every morning, which I like very much, and not unfrequently a graham pudding with maple sugar or molasses, besides every Sabbath we have either pie or cake for dinner. We had once some of those large apple pies, that Brother Buchanan spoke of last fall. You can better imagine, than describe my surprise when on entering the dining hall one day, I saw something that looked like a pie, in a sheet iron platter about two feet long, and one wide, and three inches deep, these were in fact, *monstrous pies,* the upper crust was about an inch thick, the lower, half an inch, and the rest was filled with apples, —they were very nice however."[45]

That pie must have been a sight for sore eyes after the long, lean months of bread and salt of the preceding year. During the winter of 1838 and 1839 the control of the dining room began to slip back into the hands of the officials of the Institute, whether because of mismanagement by the independent department or because of a desire on the part of some to enforce stricter Grahamism it is hard to determine. The diet during that period was certainly less satisfying, some meals consisting only of rutabagas and potatoes, beets, bread and salt. In the spring the Prudential Committee offered the stewardship to W. H. Plumb, the hotel keeper, but he refused.[46]

In 1840 David Cambell of Boston, the former editor of the *Graham Journal,* was secured to come with his wife and assume the duties of steward. He served in this capacity from the spring of 1840 to the spring of 1841. Unfortunately there are no descriptions of meals during the Cambell regime, but Charles Living-

[44]P. C. M., June 26, 1837; J. P. Cowles in the *Cleveland Observer,* Nov. 27, 1839, and R. E. Gillett MS "Report on Farm and other Improvements" (Misc. Archives).

[45]Nancy [and Davis] Prudden to George P. Prudden, Apr. 8–13, 1837 (Prudden MSS).

[46]J. P. Cowles in the *Cleveland Observer,* Nov. 27, 1839, and P. C. M., May 20, and Aug. 21, 1839.

stone described the diet as it was just before, when the Graham system was supposedly being followed. "Mother will be anxious to know what we get to eat," he wrote home to Scotland. "Well at breakfast we have wheat bread & Milk with corn bread that they call engine [*sic*] corn. It grows very high and thick. There is no oat meal. We crumble the bread in the milk and sop it. Sometimes [we have] apples beat up with sugar made from mapletree. . . . Sometimes at dinner . . . we have eggs beat together & potatoes beat to the eggs with apples. . . . Sometimes cheese just resembling squeezed curds [*cottage cheese?*]. Supper bread and milk. Our living is very plain you see but excellent. It is named the Graham system by one of that name in N. York living in that manner upon vegetable diet. Some of the students in the hall will have meat, others live in this way."[47]

Cambell, as a leading Grahamite, could "not conscientiously furnish flesh meat" and, therefore, for a time, at least, the meat table was abandoned. There was opposition to his administration from the first by the "confirmed flesh eaters." In the winter the father of one of the students wrote to Professor Finney that his son was "absolutely hungry a good part of the time" and raised the question whether perhaps "animal food was [not] intended by our Creator as congenial to our health." In March a mass meeting of colonists was called to meet in the chapel to protest against the continuation of the Graham diet, "which is inadequate to the demands of the human System as at present developed." The Prudential Committee and faculty took up the question, and in mid-April Mr. Cambell resigned upon the request of the Prudential Committee.[48] This seems to have been the end of experimentation in diet in the Oberlin Boarding House.

This does not mean, however, that the food served to Oberlin students ceased to be "plain & holesome" and economical. When Lucy Stone ate at the boarding house table in 1846 she had "meat once a day, bread and milk for supper, pudding and milk, thin cakes, etc. for breakfast." At no time during the early days

[47]Charles Livingstone to Parents, May 22 [1840] (O. C. Lib. Misc. MSS).

Lib., [Framed]); James Sperry to C. G. Finney, Dec. 26, 1840 (Finney MSS);
[48]P. C. M., May 23, 1840; Levi Burnell to William Dawes, June 26, 1840 (O. C. MS call for the meeting in O. C. Lib. Misc. MSS, dated Oberlin, Mar. 20, 1841, and signed by fifteen citizens, including J. Fairchild, T. P. Turner, N. P. Fletcher, Brewster Pelton and L. Holtslander; F. M., Apr. 2, 1841; P. C. M., May 23, 1840, Mar 31, and Apr. 14, 1841. On Cambell see above, pages 323–326.

do the meals approach those served at Franklin College in Georgia, for example, where breakfast included bacon or beef, corn or wheat bread with butter, coffee and tea; and dinner (at noon) consisted of corn bread, bacon, vegetables, beef, lamb mutton, and shoat or poultry![49] Take, for example, a student's description of board in 1852:

"For dinner today we had brown bread and nice white bread too, butter, cheese, apple pie, Stewed apples and cold water. Our dinners are better on other days; I will tell you what we had through the week for dinner . . . one day fish & potatoes, another fresh meat, potatoes and dressing with good gravy, another day—rice with raisins in, a very few in it, and potatoes and sallet green. Sometimes we have warm pancakes, wheat flour ones with sugar and cream on them. Breakfast is indeed very spare but our dinners on week days are warm and good. Supper is like breakfast—rather down-hill—I call it."[50] Economy rather than principle seems to have been the chief reason dictating the plainness of the food served in these later days.

Against this background it is easy to understand the enthusiasm with which a former student later wrote of the "bowls of luscious milk with blackberries, and the warm biscuits and delicious honey" occasionally enjoyed by some lucky ones at the home of a neighboring farmer.[51]

After 1841 the boarding house and the farm (so long as it was maintained by the college) were rented to stewards who agreed to board the students, taking upon themselves the financial and managerial responsibility. Grandison Fairchild, W. W. Wright, Henry Viets, Hamilton Hill, W. H. Plumb, and Deacon Follett held this position at various times. They bought the equipment: linen, plates, knives, forks, spoons, etc. as well as the cows and pigs which were part of the establishment, and when they departed sold this material to their successors.[52] The

[49]A. S. Blackwell, *Lucy Stone,* 46, and E. Merton Coulter, *College Life in the Old South* (New York—1928), 71.

[50]Elizabeth Hanmer to mother, [Oberlin] May, 1852 (lent by Mildred Durbin, Columbus, Ohio).

[51]T. H. Robinson, MS History of the Class of 1850.

[52]"An account of Manual labor furnished to Students by those who occupy the College lands & who hold leases from the College etc, etc." (O. C. Lib.), and P. C. M., Oct. 11, 1841, and Mar. 10, 1847. In 1868, however, the college bought "two cows for the use of the Boarding Dept.—Ladies' Hall."—P. C. M., May 28, 1868.

Steward always agreed to employ students in the establishment. It should, of course, be noted that where the stewards were married it was their wives who were really in charge and did much of the work.

The Oberlin commons must have looked strange to those familiar with the commons at Yale or others of the old colleges in the East. Here and there sat a Negro, and usually at least every third person was a "female." The sexes were intermingled for practical as well as (or rather than) social reasons. "At meals the ladies set around among the gentlemen to wait on the table, get milk, bread, etc. when wanted," wrote a young man in 1836. This common table at the boarding house was an important element in Oberlin joint education. "I tell you what it is," one youngster confided to his brother in the late forties, "it seemed quere enough when I came here too get up at five oc[lock] and then at six go out into the dining hall and take Breakefast with so many by Candle light. Oh! fudge Charlie you think there aint any body worth looking at but Harriet Smith. I wish you could see some of our girls out here; especially a couple that set opposite me at the table. I tell you they are about X."[53] It was here, if ever, that the young ladies must exercise their "civilizing influence" upon the young gentlemen.

For the first twelve years the students sat at the long tables on backless benches or "forms," but in 1847, as the result of a petition from the young lady boarders, the Prudential Committee agreed that "as far as the *female* portion of the Boarders be concerned, a chair at abt. 50 cts be substituted for benches." Not until 1854 were chairs secured for the young men also, hence the custom of seating the young men on one side and the fair sex on the other, as, obviously, if men sat on benches and women on chairs they could not well be seated together. Elizabeth Hanmer, a student in 1852, wrote to her mother from the Oberlin Boarding House: "The gentlemen take their meals here in the dining room, ladies on one side of the table and gentlemen on the other, the dining hall itself is longer than our house, three rows of tables, and while they are eating it is constant laughing and talking a merry time enough. I have not learned to talk as

[53]Davis Prudden to Peter Prudden, July 18, 1836 (Prudden-Allen MSS), and "Brother" to Charles Wright, Jan. 27, 1847 (lent by the late Mrs. H. H. Carter, Oberlin).

THE COMMON DINING ROOM OF THE NEW "LADIES' HALL"
(From a stereoscopic photograph probably taken in the seventies, in the Oberlin College Library)

fast as some yet." Each young man had his tablemate who sat opposite him and, it is said, cared for his napkin between meals.[54] One's luck in tablemates might well make or mar a whole term. Lucien Warner, of corset fame, benefactor of Oberlin, boarding at the hall for a time in the early sixties, was lucky. "I sit at one of the best tables," he bragged, "and have for a table mate one of the finest and smartest ladies in the Hall. I never before knew a person whose conversation was so interesting and profitable as hers. She has travelled considerable, and can converse on any subject."[55]

The dining room in the new Ladies' Hall, completed just at the end of the Civil War, seemed almost luxurious with its "twelve long tables, each seating eighteen persons–giving ample accomodation for 216 boarders," its "gas chandelier over each" table, and the 600 silver-plated forks and spoons stamped "Ladies' Hall." A photograph taken in this room in the early seventies shows round tables instead of long tables, but the gas chandeliers are still in evidence–gas flares, without mantles. Again "the ladies set around among the gentlemen," but gentlemen in white coats do the serving. It is the beginning of a new epoch.[56]

Many students ate at private boarding houses, at the hotel and elsewhere. Some boarded themselves. "I buy bread at the boarding hall," Warren Warner informed his sister in 1841. "I can buy butter & meat and etc. etc. and bake potatoes on the stove and live rich enough for two thirds of the expense that it would be to me to board in the hall." In 1854 another boy wrote: "I have not had any boarding place since I came back from looking after a school, but have lived on a few crackers and tea cakes. I went down to the Grocery this morning to get something

[54]P. C. M., Dec. 13, 1847, Feb. 20, 1854, and Elizabeth Hanmer to mother, May –, 1852. Zephaniah Congden wrote to his sister from Oberlin, June 1, 1853: "They have two tables in [the] hall about fifty feet long, which are filled. The girls sit on one side of the table and the boys on the other, each having his table mate as it is called." (O. C. Lib.) "Our dining Hall–it is a curious place, isn't it?" wrote James H. Fairchild to Mary Kellogg. "What strange recollections we shall have of that some twenty years hence if we live. . . . Many who have been there are now mingling with the busy world. . . . I wonder if they will not now & then look back to that as a place full of interest around which their most pleasant associations will cluster?" (J. H. F. to M. K., Nov. 22, 1839, Fairchild MSS).

[55]Lucien Warner, *The Story of My Life* (New York–1914), 37.

[56]*Lorain County News,* Feb. 14, 1866.

for my breakfast, but behold when I handed them my money, they said it was not good. It made me feel rather bad seen [*sic*] it was the only two dollars that I had."[57] Married students sometimes rented or built houses and, of course, ate at home.

In 1836 the trustees provided that young men might club together and build rooming and boarding houses on leased Institute land. Lucien Warner boarded part of the time at a club of fourteen young gentlemen. He missed that peculiar "civilizing influence." "The society of such a collection of boarders," he wrote in a letter, "is just what could be expected from a lot of young men living secluded from ladies. Some would like to have everything carried on in the best of order, but others only wish to swallow their food and run. Without the restraining and refining influence of ladies, it is found impossible to maintain decorum, and instead of our meals being a place to cultivate refinement and to refresh our minds from our studies, it is only a place for satisfying hunger."[58] There were evidently no such remarkable conversationalists among the young men as the tablemate who so inspired him at Ladies' Hall.

[57]Warren W. Warner to sister, Dec. 28, 1841 (O. C. Lib.), and Geo. W. Smith to J. A. Smith, Nov. 17, 1854 (Smith MSS).

[58]T. M., Mar. 9, 1836, and Lucien Warner, *Op. Cit.*, 37.

CHAPTER XXXVIII

THE STUDENT BUDGET

ECONOMY was a basic principle at Oberlin. If the Institute was to be of real service to the sons and daughters of poor Yankee farmers it was essential that the expense be as low as possible. Tuition at first was from $10.00 to $14.00 a year; in 1834–35, $12.00 in the Preparatory Department and $18.00 in the Collegiate Department.[1] This was cheap in comparison to the charge in eastern colleges: $72.00 at Harvard, $40.00 at Yale, $40.00 at Princeton, $57.00 at Union, $36.00 at Bowdoin, and even $27.00 at Dartmouth, the "poor man's college." Tuition at western schools like Granville (later Denison), Illinois College and Western Reserve was roughly the same, however. The poverty of the frontier made these low rates necessary; beneficences from the East made them possible.[2]

In 1835 Oberlin executed a great *coup* when the tuition was made free in the Theological and Collegiate courses. This was done at the suggestion of the Oberlin Professorship Association in New York, that group of philanthropists who constituted themselves a living endowment of the Oberlin faculty. The fees in the Preparatory Department were to be $15.00 a year for men and $12.00 for young ladies. As a special concession to the colonists, however, and, it would seem, as an encouragement to large families, the trustees "*Voted,* That families residing in Oberlin, and sustaining the principles of the Oberlin Covenant be allowed to send all their children of suitable age to the Institution, and that two students only from each family be charged with tuition."[3] To all the world it was advertised that higher education at Oberlin was free.

[1]*The First Annual Report* [and Catalogue] *of the Oberlin Collegiate Institute, November, 1834,* and the MS By-Laws of 1834.

[2]The author has been greatly aided in his study of comparative costs by a paper prepared for his seminar in 1930 by Mr. Donald Eldred of the Class of 1931.

[3]P. C. M., Aug. 15, 1835; *Catalogue* for 1835–36, and T. M., Feb. 19, 1840 and Aug. 24, 1842.

The income from the Professorship Association was very much curtailed within a short time after its establishment, due to the financial depression which swept the country in the next few years. The Institute was in a very difficult position financially, being unable to pay its teaching staff in full at any time. It was natural that there should be a movement to reestablish tuition charges in order to augment the income of the institution. In 1836 and, again, early in 1842 the faculty voted against such a measure, despite the fact that they would gain personally by its adoption. The trustees at their annual meeting in August, 1842, however, voted to charge tuition in the College beginning with 1843. A fee of $10.00 was assessed for the spring term of 1843. This decision was affirmed at the next annual meeting, and it was decided that the Preparatory Department rates ($15.00 for men and $12.00 for ladies) should be charged to students in the College. The Board, however, assured "those Students who are pennyless of their deep & abiding sympathies, referring them to the example of the Indians for encouragement [?!] & that their necessities when made known to the Board of Education shall receive prompt attention & every practicable judicious measure be adopted to meet them." Furthermore, it was determined to order the Prudential Committee to admit to the Collegiate Department "free of all charge for tuition such pious & indigent youth as in the opinion of the Faculty give satisfactory evidence of proper intellectual & christian character & of their intention to enter the gospel ministry or some approved field of Christian effort, on condition however that if anyone having received such tuition free afterwards shall fail to carry out such intention he shall become indebted to & bound to pay the Institution the full amount of such tuition with interest." Pious young ladies in the fourth year of the Ladies' Course might expect a similar exemption.[4] Tuition in the Theological Course continued to be free.

The charge of $15.00 for men and $12.00 for young ladies was not changed until 1860 when the tuition for the latter was raised to $13.00. Though, as we have already seen, this was much less than the amount charged in most other colleges, there was

[4]F. M., Aug. 17, 1836, Mar. 10, 1842; T. M., Aug. 25, 1842, Aug. 22, 1843, and *Catalogue*, 1843-44.

some complaint among the students and some were very tardy in their payments. Professor Henry Cowles was delegated to make a study of the situation in 1845 and reported that those who did not pay their bills were not deserving, for the most part, and that there seemed to be no reason for reducing tuition. At any rate, tuition was not changed. In the fifties and sixties the cost of tuition was really much less than the nominal charge. This was true because the scholarships sold in the endowment campaign were transferable and were rented out at low rates. Zephaniah Congden paid out only $6.00 a year scholarship rent in lieu of tuition in 1853.[5] The College *Catalogue* of 1866 in its estimate of student expenses includes scholarship rental of $8.25 to $9.00 instead of tuition charges. The tuition charges at Brown in 1866 were $50.00 and at Western Reserve, $30.00.[6] Oberlin tuition costs were, throughout this period, very reasonable.

Room rent at first was from three to six dollars *a year*. It was provided free to members of the Theological and Collegiate departments in 1835 and 1836 and to all ladies in the boarding house from 1837 to 1842. Otherwise it was usually $4.00 (in a double room) or $6.00 (in a single room). In 1842 young ladies were assessed $2.50 per term of 40 weeks for rooms in Ladies' Hall. A few years later they were paying from seven to ten cents a week. The young men also sometimes paid by the week: in 1853, 15 cents a week in Tappan Hall, a shilling (12½ cents) a week in Walton Hall and 10 cents a week in other college dormitories. In the late fifties and in the sixties rent advanced somewhat. Rooms in Ladies' Hall went up to $4.50 to $6.00 in 1857; and $6.00 to $12.00 was assessed in the new Ladies' Hall when it was first opened, extra charges being made for the carpeted rooms. Rooms in Tappan Hall cost $7.80 per year at the same time.[7] Room rent in private houses was also low. Davis Prudden and his brother paid a shilling and a half a week (18¾¢) for two attic rooms in 1836. In 1836 Henry Cowles was renting rooms for 75¢, $1.00, and $1.25 a month, and house-

[5]*Catalogues* (The figures *$16.00* instead of *$15.00* in the 1844–1845 *Catalogue* are probably a misprint.); Henry Cowles' Report on "Rates & terms of Tuition," 1845 (Trustees' MSS, Misc. Archives), and Zephaniah Congden to sister, June 1, 1853 (lent by Eulala Smith, Exeter, Nebraska).

[6]At the University of Michigan, however, in the fifties the only charge was an admission fee of $10.00.

[7]P. C. M., July 14, Aug. 15, 1835; Feb. 14, Sept. 15, 1842; Feb. 5, 1868; T. M., Mar. 10, 1836; Aug. 24, 1853, and *Catalogues*.

keeping apartments for $1.50 a month and 50 cents a week. In 1842 and 1843 he was charging 16 and 20 cents a week for rooms. Henry Prudden, living at the Cowles home in 1859, paid 25 cents a week room rent.[8]

Board at the Oberlin Institute Boarding House (Ladies' Hall) was at first from 80 cents to $1.00 a week; the second year it was from 75 cents to $1.00. When in 1835 the vegetable table was introduced young gentlemen paid only seven shillings (87½ cents) for it. There is one record of a man paying only 50 cents. Board at the meat table continued to be a dollar, and ladies were charged 75 cents. In 1836 the charge was raised to $1.00 to $1.25 for young men and $.75 to $1.00 for young ladies.[9] In 1837 board was fixed at one dollar a week for all, a price which remained unchanged for sixteen years. In 1846 a rumor reached the trustees that board at some other institutions was cheaper and, with praiseworthy jealousy, they ordered the Prudential Committee to make an investigation and see if "the present price can be diminished."[10] The rumor seems to have been unfounded, for at this time board was $2.25 per week at Harvard, $1.50 to $1.75 at Brown and from $1.00 to $2.00 at Amherst. Even in the West at Hudson (Western Reserve) and Denison board was $1.25. Whether or not the committee had these facts before them, no change was made in the charge. Of course, their prices must be considered in relation to the money standards of a day when students received from 2¾ to 10 cents an hour for work, and oats and potatoes were 25 cents a bushel. Nor, as we have seen, was the board furnished at these prices of a very elaborate or varied character. Board at private houses was little, if any, cheaper. Mr. and Mrs. Cowles were furnishing board to students at one dollar a week in 1842 and 1843.[11]

Beginning with 1853 the price of board steadily advanced. Students coming to Oberlin in the summer of that year were discouraged by the increasing costs. One young man wrote to

[8]Davis Prudden to Peter Prudden, July 18, 1836 (Prudden-Allen MSS); Henry Cowles' Day Book, 115, 123, 125, 131, 147–148 (Cowles MSS); and Henry Prudden to Parents, n.d., [1859] (lent by Lillian Prudden, New Haven, Conn.).

[9]*The First Annual Report* (1834), and 1835 and 1836 *Catalogues,* and T. M., Nov. 25, 1835.

[10]*Cleveland Observer,* Nov. 9, 1837; *Catalogues,* 1838–53, and T. M., Aug. 24, 1846.

[11]Henry Cowles' Day Book, 115, 123, 131 (Cowles MSS).

his sister: "Board costs more than we expected—it is 9 shillings at the boarding-hall, in some places it is ten and at the hotel they ask twelve." There were a few who kept to the old low rates, he found. "There is a widow lady living in the next house from the one that we room in that boards for six shillings per week. I am acquainted with a young man that boards there and he says they have first-rate board. She might have several hundred boarders at that rate, but her number is limited to ten and when one leaves a vacancy the rest choose out of the students one that shall fill it." In 1855 the college boarding rates were advanced to $1.25 and $1.50 and two years later were listed at $1.50 to $1.75. Mrs. Cowles received $1.50 per week in 1859. Of course, the appearance of war prices meant a further rise. In 1864 board was $1.75 to $2.50 a week and three and four dollars in town. In 1866 board cost Oberlin students from $2.50 to $3.50 a week.[12]

There were, of course, other minor expenses. A regular incidental fee was charged, beginning with 1835 when the Prudential Committee "Resolved, That each Schollar shall be charged fifty cents at the close of the quarter for Bell ringing & warming, Cleaning & Lighting Resitation Rooms." In the following year this was raised to $2.00 for gentlemen and $1.00 for ladies and in 1857 to $2.25 for all students and in 1865 to $6.00. Many students cut their own wood from the forest for their little heating stoves. Up to 1850 it could always be purchased at $1.00 per cord. After that it went up to $1.25 and $1.50. Sometimes it was furnished by the week. In the winter of 1864–65 wood was provided for 60 cents a week and in the spring for 50 cents. Washing was three shillings (37½¢) a dozen in the early days, 50 cents a dozen in the late fifties and sixties. This was not a very large expense, however, if, like one young man in 1853, you wore only one shirt and one collar a week and washed your own socks![13]

Then there were such items as lighting, repairing clothes, making clothes, soap, charity, doctor bills, travel, books, etc. Elam Comings included in his incidental expenses in 1836: a

[12]Zephaniah Congden to sister, June 1, 1853 (lent by Eulala Smith, Exeter, Nebraska); *Catalogues,* and Henry Prudden to parents, n.d. [1859] (lent by Lillian Prudden, New Haven, Conn.).

[13]P. C. M., Nov. 25, 1835; Oct. 28, 1864; Feb. 10, 1865; *Catalogues;* T. M., Aug. 24, 1857, and Zephaniah Congden, *Op. Cit.* Also student bills in Misc. Archives.

Hebrew Grammar—1.37½; an ax—1.50; "for Missions—.50"; soap—.04; shoes—2.00; "for trimmings for pantaloons"—.31, and "for fruit—.12." This gives some evidence of the character of the dissipations of the early days also! Besides tuition, traveling expenses, board and room, Frances Hubbard, who attended in the middle fifties, purchased an umbrella, a penknife, "scissors," ambrotypes, soap and soap jar, candles and lighting fluid, blacking and brush, apples, pencils and rubber, "Post Office stamps," a "Moreno dress and trimmings," garters, "Gum Elastic shoes" (overshoes or rubbers), bonnet lining and trimming, "Morocco bootes," a sun bonnet, mitts, "ivory birds" (?), and "velvet and flowers for bonnet." She also expended some money for collections: "for Seamen," "for Missionary," "for Colored woman," "for Burrett" (Elihu Burritt, peace advocate), "for Kansas," etc. On one occasion she even paid out 37½ cents for a "present for teacher." The list of miscellaneous expenses grew as time went on, students had more money, and Oberlin shops offered more temptations. Items in the expense account kept by a young man in 1865–66 have somewhat of a modern sound: neckties, peaches, concert, two tickets to Theodore Weld's lecture at 25 cents each, paper collars (!), photographs (no longer "ambrotypes"), shoe heel, "6 stub pens," "Nov. 27—By one tooth filled—.25"; "Dec. 23—Tooth pulled—.50," maple sugar, lemonade, music lessons, expenses of Jr. Ex. (Junior Exhibition), and broken glass. This young man subscribed to the *Lorain County News* of Oberlin and *Harper's Weekly*. He paid a quarter for getting his trunk up from the depot, spent ten cents "treating Bedient" and 16 cents for "Laughing Gas." Oberlin interests at this time are reflected by his contribution to the freedmen and 25 cents to a "Colored Soldier."[14]

In 1834 it was officially estimated that "a study year of forty weeks" would cost from $58.00 to $89.00. In 1839 necessary expenses, including board, room, incidental charge, tuition (free) and lights, were placed at only $50.00. The total annual expense of an economical student at Oberlin was officially esti-

[14]E. J. Comings' MSS (lent by Eliza J. Comings, Kingsville, Ohio); Frances M. Hubbard's MS Account Book (lent by Fred P. Bemis, Santa Monica, California), and John G. Fraser's MS Journal, 1865–66 (lent by Mrs. G. F. Waugh, Mentor, Ohio).

mated at $75.00 in 1846 and $85.00 in 1851. In 1857 Professor Timothy B. Hudson stated in an article in the *Independent* that the cost of a year's study at Oberlin need not exceed two hundred dollars. The *Catalogue* published in 1866 gave an expense estimate of from $150.00 to $225.00, scholarship rent, incidental charges, board, room, lights, washing, books and fuel being included.[15] The earlier estimates are undoubtedly too low, taking into account, as they do, only part of the actual necessities of student life. Books were often a large item; and all must spend something for clothes. The later estimates seem to be more nearly accurate, though many undoubtedly spent more.

The Oberlin estimate of $58.00 to $89.00 must have looked attractive to many poor but ambitious young men at a time when Princeton, Harvard and Yale essentials cost from $160 to $200. Even at Amherst the expense of a school year was placed at over $100.00. Alexander H. Stephens' expenses at Franklin College in Georgia were about $200.00 a year, and Charles Sumner spent about the same amount at Yale. Both have been praised for their economy. Average expenses at Western Reserve for the academic year 1834–35 were estimated to be about $147.00. Board, room and tuition at Illinois College cost about a hundred dollars in 1836. In the thirties expenses at Oberlin were undoubtedly as low as anywhere in the country. Considering the general rise in prices, costs in the 60's were also low, though not so markedly so. The cheapness of tuition or "scholarship rent" was a major factor. The average expenses reported by 32 young men in the Collegiate and Theological departments in the fifties or early sixties was $188.90 a year. Of course, as Professor Cowles wisely said in reporting this investigation, "What it costs young men to obtain an education at College, turns not merely on his bills for board, tuition, room, fuel, & books; but is largely affected also by the style of dress which general usage demands, or is thought to demand; . . ."[16] In early Oberlin a young man or woman might wear patched clothing, and public opinion was always kind to those forced to be economical. There is little doubt, however, that expenses demanded by "general usage" increased considerably in the

[15]*First Annual Report,* 1834, page 8; *Catalogue,* 1839–40; 1866–67; *Oberlin Evangelist,* Mar. 4, 1846, Dec. 3, 1851, and *The Independent,* Jan. 29, 1857.

[16][Henry Cowles] "The Finances of Education at Oberlin" (Misc. Archives).

50's and 60's. In the final analysis, however, it is not possible to gain a very good idea of the comparative cost of education at different schools except by the comparison of such items as tuition, room, and board, other expenses being so much dependent on the individual. Some could live cheaply at Harvard, their budget limited only by the high tuition charges. Some spent a good deal at Oberlin despite the low official costs.

The Institute at first furnished most supplies and services and charged them to students. In 1834 even books and other students' supplies were dispensed in this way. A typical early bill runs:

W. P. Cushman to O. C. Institute		Dr.
May 29—To 1 Latin Reader	–	$0.83
June 5—To 1 Greek Reader	–	1.15
July 14—To 1 Doz. Quills	–	.24
		$2.22

Oberlin, July 23, 1834.

After a few years books were purchased from individual book stores but other items foreign to term bills of the twentieth century continue to appear on students' statements.[17] A typical bill is that made out to a Miss Foote in 1835:

Miss P. Foote Dr. to board 12 weeks at 6/	$9.00
to Washing 10 pieces	.15
to Candles	.37½
to Wood	.63
Incidental charges	7
	$10.22½
Credit by labor 260½ at 3 cts per hour	7.82

Dec. 31, 1835. P. P. Stewart, Steward.

On other bills appear such items as: "2 Sheets @ 56¢," "Cloth for Curtins—9 yds. @ 14," "1 Mattras," "Use of Bowl & Pitcher —8," and "1 Axe-helve." One girl's bill included not only "8 weeks board @ 4/," "eleven weeks at 6 Shillings, candles and washing," but also "Expense in Sickness—.50." This was in 1835. In a statement to the Institute made in May, 1835, Dr. Dascomb

[17]The Secretary's Office possesses thousands of students' bills. The book store was sold in 1837.—"The Agent's report, Sept. 5, 1837" (Misc. Archives).

Mr. L. D. Weeks has boarded 1½ weeks @ 6/- 7/ $8.75
has had 26 pieces washed @ 3/ pr doz .81
$9.56
Mending Pantaloons .12½
Nov 27 1835. $9.68½
P. P. Stewart,
Steward.

Mr. E. S. Grumley has boarded 5 weeks & 5 days @ 6/- 5.02
" 4 " @ 7/ 3.50
has had 2½ doz. pieces washed @ 3/ .87½
Knitting .06¼
Making 1 Tow Frock .25
Dec. 28 1835. P. P. Stewart $9.70¾
Steward.
Entered Jany 1
3/2 Decr 28th

EARLY BILLS FOR BOARD AND MISCELLANEOUS SERVICE, 1835
(From the original in the Miscellaneous Archives)

Miss Mary Williams has boarded 6 weeks & 3 days @ 4/ – 3.21
15 " & 4 days @ 6/ 11.67
Candles —— 1.44
Washing —— .18¾
Use of Bedding —— .88
" Bowl & Pitcher 8
17.46¾

Miss W. has laboured 497 hours @ 2¾ c $13.66
Dec 9 1835 P. P. Stewart
Steward

AN EARLY BILL FOR BOARD AND INCIDENTALS
Note the signature of P. P. Stewart as Steward.
(From the original in the Miscellaneous Archives)

includes charges against several students. Fortunately the cost of medical service was very low. The Doctor Professor charged one student 12½¢ for a dose of calomel, another, 25¢ for an emetic and cathartic, a young lady, 12½¢ for a dose of Rhubarb, another, the same for a dose of castor oil. It cost only ten cents to get a blister plaster, and the same for "salts & senna." Dr. Dascomb pulled teeth for a shilling apiece.[18] The furnishing of medical service like the handling of books was, for the most part, discontinued after the first few years. Even in 1836, however, there appear in students' statements, in exceptional cases, such items as "One hat," "½ quire of paper @ 12½ cents," "8 catalogues—50 [cents]," "one steel pen," and "1 Botany."

Much more common are other charges, at first sight, equally odd. Washing at 3/ (37½ cents) a dozen appears as regularly as board. In 1835: Mr. Grumley was charged 6¼ cents for knitting and 25 cents for "Making Tow Frock"; Mr. Butts paid 37½ cents for "Making Collars"; another young man was charged a shilling by the Oberlin Collegiate Institute for "mending Pantaloons"; a colored boy paid 13 cents for "Hemming 2 pocket h'kf"; and E. B. Sherwood, besides being indebted to the Institute for board and washing, was also required to pay 78 cents for "Making a Vest, etc." In 1836: William Sheffield paid 6 cents for "Mending Cloak" and sixty cents for "Making Apron"; James H. Fairchild paid 15 cents for "Washing 5/12 doz . . . @ 3/"; another young man paid 75 cents for "Making one pantaloons," and another 38 cents for "footing 1 pair stockings." The Institute hired the "coeds" to do the washing, ironing and sewing and put the charges on the young men's bills.

There is more than sufficient evidence that the bills incurred by students were not always promptly paid. The spirit of philanthropy was, we may perhaps fairly say, only slightly tempered by business acumen, and the result was that students let their bills run on, and the College authorities, conniving in this laxity, lost considerable sums of money which were rightly due. In 1834 to 1836, under the management of Shipherd and Stewart, it would seem that a majority of the students became indebted to the Institute. The trustees decided finally that the time had come

[18]"O. C. Institute in Acct. with J. Dascomb, May 12th 1835" (Misc. Archives), and James Dascomb's MS Account Book (O. C. Lib.).

to balance the budget by requiring prompt payment of delinquent charges. A formal notice was read to the students at the boarding house table, therefore, declaring, "that by the rules which govern the Faculty and Trustees No Student indebted to this Institution at commencement of next term can be admitted to recitations or a seat at commons. But until such indebtedness is adjusted," the announcement continued, "must be regarded as standing in the attitude of a new applicant, irrespective of their previous connexion with the Institute—and no persons after the first of March next will be expected to avail themselves of the privileges of the boarding department until they have presented the Steward with a certificate from the office that the above regulations are complied with."[19] In June of the same year a more rigid regulation was announced, providing that full payment would be required of every student on the first days of September, December, March and June respectively, and also at the close of each term.[20]

It was as a result of the financial collapse of the Steward's Department at this time that the management of the commons table was turned over to a student organization. At the same time the students were also notified that they were "expected to render at the office of the Treasurer a copy of their account current monthly as near the first day of the month as may be, and that the same is required to be in business form." Hundreds of these monthly statements made out by the students furnish to us our best source on student finance.

In the *Laws and Regulations* of 1840 it was provided that "Every student [is] required to settle his bills with the Treasurer, before the expiration of two weeks after the commencement of each term." For the stricter enforcement of this rule it was further provided that, "No student shall be permitted to recite, after that time has elapsed, till he shall have obtained the Treasurer's certificate that he has complied with this regulation." Professor Finney preached a sermon from Romans 13:8: "Owe no man any thing," in which he held that it was a sin to be in debt.[21] But many students continued to be delinquent. For this situation

[19]"Notice to Students read at table previous to March 1, 1836" (Misc. Archives). The financial condition of the boarding house which resulted is shown in Ledger No. 1 (1834–36), page 333 (Treas. Off.).

[20]"Notice to Students, June 16, 1836 re Tuition Bills" (Misc. Archives).

[21]*Oberlin Evangelist*, July 31, 1839.

they cannot be exclusively blamed: first, the public was allowed to believe that students at Oberlin could pay most of their expenses by manual labor and would, therefore, need little money; second, Shipherd's doubtfully ethical "scholarships" did not include tuition, though many of their purchasers believed that they did; and, lastly, money was very scarce, at the time, anyway, and most of the students came to Oberlin because they were impecunious. As late as 1845 Professor Cowles and a committee prepared a report on the problem in which they stated "that the evils of nonpayment of debts here are becoming enormous & seriously threaten the very existence of the Institution." As the school was subject to a considerable annual deficit at this time the situation was truly a serious one. The committee recommended that "a culpable negligence in any student to pay honest dues whether to the Institute or for board, be treated by the Faculty as a moral offense, & made a matter of discipline, & that a special law be introduced into our code to this effect." No new rules were added to the *Laws and Regulations,* but the findings of the committee are significant to us as evidence of the late continuance of the debt problem.[22]

Americans of the twentieth century have little conception of the scarcity of currency, especially sound currency, a hundred years ago. As a result of this scarcity business was often carried on by barter, or some commodity was used as a medium of exchange. On the outer frontier it was fur or whiskey; on farms farther east, usually grain. Farmers often would not see more than a few dollars of cash for a year at a time. Now Oberlin students were (as we have seen) the sons and daughters of poor farmers, and it was with difficulty that they could scrape together enough cash to pay their traveling expenses to college. They were attracted to Oberlin particularly by the manual labor system, whereby they might barter their wages for tuition, board and room. The institution itself was impecunious also, so accounts were kept in such a way as to obviate as far as possible the handling of cash. On one side of the monthly or quarterly statements was an account of charges accrued against the student for board, room, tuition, etc. On the other was an account of wages due to the student for manual labor performed. The

[22]Henry Cowles, "Report on rates & terms of tuition" (Misc. Archives).

balance either to credit or debit was carried over to the next month or quarter. Faculty, and even colonists at first, as well as students, kept accounts on the Institute books, thus making it possible to do business without much actual cash. Those having such accounts would write orders on the Institute to the credit of other individuals. These orders were comparable to bank checks and circulated more or less as currency. The Institute usually paid students their surplus earnings, if any, in such orders.[23] A student wrote to his family in 1843: "The greatest trouble we have is want of money. There is but little in the place. I tried hard to borrow enough to pay for a pair of shoes, this afternoon but found it impossible. I have had but two dollars in money of my last years wages. What I shall do I know not. My boarding is paid by my teaching, but there is no money to be had." The shortage of money at this time may be partly explained by the expenditure of all the cash the community could collect for the meeting house. It is not surprising that the institution orders sometimes spoken of as "Treasury Script" should have depreciated, especially as the Steward required part payment in cash in the middle forties.[24]

Many students were helped out of their financial difficulties by charitably minded friends of Oberlin. It was a difficult problem to do enough manual labor to pay any considerable portion of expenses, and study and attend classes at the same time. The Female Principal wrote to her husband in 1838 of what must have been a common experience: "One dear, promising young lady was in my room last night. Pay day had come, and she had enough for this time, but said—now, I must study less or not pay next month. The tears were in her eyes. She said she labored now so as to hinder study some, she thought. O how precious the boon from Mrs. Chapin and others for the benefit of such ladies appeared to me."[25]

For some time several students at Oberlin were beneficiaries of the American Society for Educating Pious Youth for the Gospel Ministry, receiving small stipends to make up the difference

[23]A bill made out in the name of Amos B. Adams, in Jan., 1837, shows that he was paid $5.00 in "Treasury Script." Many of these "orders" are still preserved in the Miscellaneous Archives.

[24]J. B. Trew to Andrew Trew, May 29, 1843 (lent by Mary Ewalt, Lakewood, Ohio), and A. S. Blackwell, *Lucy Stone*, 54-55.

[25]A. W. Cowles to Henry Cowles, Jan. 2, 1838 (Cowles-Little MSS).

between the returns from their manual labor and their expenses. Oberlin's "peculiarities" were too much, however, for the orthodox directors of the American Education Society, as it was usually called, and in 1838 all further receipts from this source were cut off.[26] An independent "Oberlin Board of Education" was forthwith organized, and early in July the *Evangelist* published an appeal for aid for indigent students in Oberlin. Special agents were named to receive funds in New York, Boston, Providence, Rochester, Detroit, Cleveland and other smaller towns. By August 14 it was possible to report gifts of over $170.00 in money besides "two shirts, three prs. pantaloons, two coats, one vest" from "Ladies in Franklin, O." Receipts did not equal the sums previously supplied by the American Education Society, and in the autumn the members of the Oberlin Board of Education issued a second plea. "Those who love Oberlin" were reminded that "the wants of a large number of indigent young men, pursuing their studies here for the gospel ministry, are peculiarly pressing." These appeals were renewed from time to time in the next few years. "Dear brethren and sisters in the Lord," ran one of them, "think of your brethren here who have given themselves to Christ in his precious gospel. They cheerfully forego all the lucrative employments of life: they give up their time to study for the gospel ministry, or to benevolent labor for the destitute, and now may they not ask your aid in bearing some of their unavoidable burdens?"[27]

At first the receipts were in currency for the most part, but, in that time of money scarcity, it was much easier to secure donations in goods. Oberlin agents, appreciating this fact, emphasized the need for warm clothing. In 1840 one list of acknowledgments was concluded with a plea for winter wearing apparel: "It is hoped the friends of our young men will remember, as winter approaches, that the wants of many cannot be supplied by parents, that some of them are sons of widows; and, that substantial materials for clothing, suited to the season, warm woolen socks, &c., as have heretofore been received and acknowledged, will be very acceptable, and greatly encourage them in their laudable undertaking of preparing for the gospel ministry."[28]

[26]See pages 434–436.
[27]*Oberlin Evangelist,* July 3, Aug. 14, Sept. 25, 1839, and Mar. 30, 1842.
[28]*Ibid.,* Oct. 7, 1840.

Some of the gifts were of the particularly useful kind desired: "3 pair woolen socks," "1 vest," "1 pair linen pillow cases," "1 bosom," "2 flannel aprons," "1 towell," "1 pair drawers," and "1 pair mittens." "Miss Conkling" of Rensellaerville, N. Y. contributed "1 printed calico coverlid, 6½ yds. bleached cotton, 10 yds. unbleached sheeting." Some gave candles ("4 lb. stearin candles"); some, soap ("5 gallons [!]"); one man presented "10 lbs. feathers" to rest the study-weary heads; another gave razors, and another, a buffalo robe. Food was, of course, gladly received: butter, pork, cheese, dried apples, "1 heifer," "1 sheep," onions, dried pumpkins, and corn. Some donations were not so directly useful to the indigent students: for example, a "two-horse lumber waggon" given by a Cleveland friend, a churn, a hundred acres of land, and a quarter of a ton of hay! Professor Finney was overwhelmed with benevolence and self-abnegation one Sabbath in the very midst of a prayer. He there and then consecrated to the Lord (to be used by pious and poor students) "1 Spring cushion Mahogany Sofa, 6 Cane-Seated Curled Maple Parlor Chairs, 1 Blue Broad Cloth Cloak, 1 Goat's Hair Camblet Wrapper." These he kept at his home awaiting purchasers, but, as no one appeared to buy his household goods and personal clothing, he settled with God for $70.00.[29]

Individual patrons often helped notably in the support of worthy students. Gerrit Smith must always be included among the best friends of Oberlin and Oberlin students in the early years. At the request of Professor Morgan he sent $15.00 to aid James Monroe (later professor at Oberlin, Congressman and Consul to Rio de Janeiro) in the completion of his course.[30] In the same year George Thompson (of Missouri prison fame) wrote to the New York philanthropist:

" . . . I should be exceedingly glad of some help to prosecute my *Studies,* in preparation to preach the gospel to the suffering Poor—*the colored Race*—in this country—or Africa if the Lord permit.

"Myself, & dear wife feel strongly bound to the Slave & Colored race—to live & die for the present, & eternal good—

[29]*Ibid.,* May 20, Oct. 7, 1840; Dec. 20, 1843, and Jan. 3, 1844. Also statement of gifts of $70.00 in lieu of these articles in Finney's own hand, dated Sept. 23, 1840 (Misc. Archives).

[30]John Morgan to Gerrit Smith, Mar. 2, 1846, and James Monroe to Gerrit Smith, Mar. 20, 1846 (Gerrit Smith MSS).

"My house rent here is 30 dollars a year—besides our Provisions & clothing—

"I have my Books to buy—but with what shall I buy them? I have just come from Prison—Tho *I* may not be able to recompense you here you shall be . . . recompensed at the Resurrection of the Just—& he that giveth to the Poor, *lendeth to the Lord* &c. &c. Inasmuch as ye did it unto one of the least of these My brethren—ye have done it unto Me &c. &c.— . . .

"I will not *plead*—I will not prescribe—Nor will I murmur, should you feel unable to aid me at all—The Lord direct you & give me that which is good—

"I shall wait with some anxiety to hear from you—that I may know whether I must travel & beg this winter"[31]

It seems scarcely possible that this plea was entirely without result. Sallie Holley was especially aided by Smith. In 1850 he helped pay for the education at Oberlin of the famous fugitive, Anthony Burns.[32]

Oberlin students, however, were always encouraged to support themselves as far as possible. The two chief means of self-support were manual labor (in the boarding house for the young ladies and in the forest and on the farm for the young men) and teaching.

The preparatory students (as we have seen, representing the larger part of the total) were taught almost exclusively by the more advanced students in the Theological and Collegiate departments. In 1836, when 37½ cents a dozen was charged for washing, young men received 18 cents an hour for teaching. Three years later James H. Fairchild was paid 15 cents an hour for teaching Geography and Arithmetic and 18 cents for teaching Latin. His brother was earning 15 cents an hour for teaching Arithmetic and 10 cents for teaching Grammar. Sallie Holley made a shilling an hour teaching a composition class in 1850. In the following year Jacob Dolson Cox received 18¾ cents an hour for 179 hours of Algebra classes, and C. H. Churchill received the same pay for 24 classes in "Geog. of Heavens." At the commencement of the war Judson Smith was paid 25 cents an hour as a student teacher, and at the end of the war Lucien Warner was

[31]George Thompson to Gerrit Smith, Oct. 31, 1846 (Gerrit Smith MSS).

[32]Sallie Holley to G. S., June 21, 1848, and other dates, and Anthony Burns to G. S., Dec. 28, 1860 (Gerrit Smith MSS).

paid at the same rate.[33] Some students, unable to obtain teaching appointments, gave independent lessons in drawing, music, or languages. Antoinette Brown (the first ordained woman minister) supported herself while studying theology in this way. Frances Hubbard made over fifty dollars teaching drawing and painting in 1856.[34]

During the three-months vacation in the winter most Oberlin students scattered to the country schools of all the Northern and some of the Southern States "with shawls strapped to full valises, and hopes clinging to lean wallets."[35] Their first aim was to get money which would make possible the continuance of their college studies. Teachers in Ohio in 1840 might expect between $13.00 and $14.00 a month on the average. Men averaged about $16.00 but young ladies only $10.00. In 1837 one Oberlin student hired out for $17.00 a month. Five years later another was promised $20.00 a month in lumber or bank notes. He preferred lumber as not being "quite as precarious property . . . as bank notes." Sometimes there were additional gratuities if a teacher happened to be popular. Lucy Stone received for teaching a school in Wellington, besides her regular pay, "a great lump of maple sugar," some apples, and "a good new broom."[36] A young man teaching a subscription school in Tennessee in 1849 collected from $1.50 to $2.00 a day. He considered this unusually profitable.[37] Sixteen years later John G. Fraser was offered $40.00 a month without board at one place and $100.00 for three months with board, at another.[38] Teachers' wages were fortunately advancing as were costs of an education.

The experience was a valuable part of their education, bringing them in contact with all sorts of people, and placing them in a position of responsibility requiring tact and initiative. It was often extremely difficult work with many hostile pupils, suspicious parents, unwilling tax-payers, and the Oberlin reputa-

[33]Bills for instruction preserved in the Misc. Archives.

[34]Reminiscences of Antoinette Brown Blackwell to Alice Stone Blackwell (lent by A. S. B., Boston), and Frances M. Hubbard's MS Account Book.

[35]*Lorain County News,* Oct. 25, 1865.

[36]*American Almanac,* 1841, page 234; *1840 Catalogue,* 24; W. S. Curtis to Henry Cowles, Mar. 10, 1837 (Cowles-Little MSS); Thomas Homes to H. Hill, Mar. 15, 1842 (Treas. Off., File N), and A. S. Blackwell, *Lucy Stone,* 54.

[37]A. A. Gates, Mar. 8, 1849 (Treas. Off., File M).

[38]John G. Fraser, MS Diary, Dec. 15, 1865 (lent by Mrs. Grace F. Waugh, Mentor, O.).

tion to live down. The number of pupils might be ten or twelve or it might be seventy. There were sure to be all ages up into the twenties and all grades and classes. Not only did they teach Reading, Writing, Arithmetic, Geography, Grammar and Spelling but when called upon to do so instructed the more advanced in Latin, Greek, Chemistry, Philosophy, Rhetoric, Geography of the Heavens, etc. Mary P. Fairchild, teacher in Michigan in 1843, found that, "There are so many different books and such a variety of scholars, that it is quite easy to spend six or seven hours in hearing recitations." For a while she divided the grades with a companion teacher, part of them being taken into a separate room. This very desirable arrangement had to be given up, however, after a short time "when the gentleman of whom we borrowed a part of our stove pipe needed it." The school room must have been conducive to study with *two* teachers carrying on classes at the same time! An Oberlin man who taught in a district school in the winter vacation of 1865–66 near Rolling Prairie, Indiana, heard thirty-seven recitations in a six hour school day, even though he usually had but twenty scholars in attendance.[39]

Of course there were serious disciplinary problems in these one-room, rural schools. In 1839 Welcome Benham bragged that he managed the boys in an obscure district without a single whipping, but twenty years later William H. Long, a freshman, was struck on the head with a heavy iron fire poker by one of the pupils in his school and deprived "of reason for several weeks thereafter." George Smith, a prep student, had a school at nearby Camden in the winter of 1854–55. He boarded 'round in the log cabins of the local farmers and found the food rather poor because of the scanty crops of the previous season.—"But I have had the pleasure of having some wild turkey and venison to eat." "I have not had occasion to punish any very severely yet," he wrote to his sister, "and am in hopes that I shant. There is 30 scholars that come to me now, some of which, are larger than I am. . . . I have four scholars in the a b abs, Ten in arithmetic, and two in grammar. The others study reading, spelling, and

[39][Warren and] Hannah Warner to parents, Dec. 24, 1841, to Feb. 16, 1842 (O. C. Lib.); Mary P. Fairchild to Cyrus Baldwin, Nov. 25, 1843, and Jan. 18, 1844 (lent by Dr. C. G. Baldwin, Palo Alto, Calif.), and J. G. Fraser, MS Diary, Dec. 24, 1865.

writing."[40] The young teacher at Rolling Prairie after the war had to resort to all sorts of disciplinary measures in order to persuade a certain six-footer to speak a piece.[41] Nor did the teachers' duties stop with the schoolroom. He was expected to run a spelling school, sometimes a singing school. He usually felt it to be his duty to attend prayer meetings and other church services and take an active part, often, in fact, to preach.

In 1860 the Ohio State Commissioner of Common Schools reported that a large percentage of Ohio teachers were undergraduates on vacation from the local colleges. "This is especially true of Oberlin College . . . ," he continued. "I am informed that there are now from five to seven hundred of the Oberlin students, male and female, engaged in teaching in this state; . . ."[42]

Many of these teachers were poorly prepared, it is certain. Many took schools after only a term or two in the Preparatory Department. At first they went without special preparation in teaching methods and without certification. From 1846 a special Teachers' Course was maintained in the Institute and those who chose this department supposedly received some professional training. In later years special lectures to teachers were delivered in the autumn just before the beginning of the long winter vacation. In most of the states a system of certification by examination for prospective teachers was established. All were expected to be able to answer such questions as: "Why are there twice as many degrees of longitude as latitude?" (To which one hopeful answered, "Becas the circumferance is greater than the diamiter."), "If I sell 2/3 of a farm for what 3/4 of it cost what per cent do I gain?" "How wide must a man make a door-way 7 ft. high so that a circular saw 8 ft. in diam. may pass through?" and "Describe the liver, its location and office."[43]

There was other vacation work for those who preferred it or failed to obtain a school. One young man tried lecturing on

[40]W. E. Benham to Levi Burnell, Dec. 22, 1839 (Treas. Off., File A); *Oberlin Students' Monthly* I, 243 (Apr., 1859), and George Smith to Julia Smith, Dec. 21, 1854 (Smith MSS).

[41]J. G. Fraser, MS Diary, Jan. 18–20, 1866.

[42]Ohio State Commissioner of Common Schools, *Seventeenth Annual Report*, 1859–60 (Columbus, 1861), 58.

[43]Henry Prudden to parents [1859?] (lent by Miss Lillian Prudden, New Haven, Conn.); *Lorain County News*, Oct. 23, 1861, and John G. Fraser, MS Diary, Dec. 24, 1865.

Phrenology. In 1840–41 James Fairchild took a pastorate for the three months in Palmyra, Michigan. His duties were the usual ones of a pastor: "to preach on the Sabbath, attend prayer meetings during the week, visit families, stand by the bedside of the sick and dying and direct the fearful soul to Him who tasted death for every man." Another tried lecturing on the wonders of nature. He wrote of his enterprise to Secretary Hill: "Shortly after leaving Oberlin in November I entered into partnership with a Mr. Rider; went to Cincinnati and purchased a large and beautiful assortment of Philosophical Apparatus, which cost about $500; I have been lecturing, on the subjects enumerated in the enclosed bills [what they were we can only guess], from county to county during the winter and have been so far fortunate as to meet with considerable success."[44] One preparatory student went too far in his efforts to make money and was apprehended as a counterfeiter![45]

It was officially estimated that of approximately $11,400.00 earned by male students in the academic year 1841–42, $5,400.00 or nearly half, came from school teaching. Unfortunately, over $800.00 of this amount was lost in bank failures. The remaining $6,000.00 represented receipts from manual labor.[46]

[44]Mary P. Fairchild to Cyrus Baldwin, Nov. 25, 1843; James H. Fairchild to Mary Kellogg, Nov. 22, 1840, *Oberlin Alumni Magazine,* I, 6 (March, 1905), 151, and James I. Fraser to Hamilton Hill, Mar. 10, 1849 (Treas. Off., File M).

[45]*Cleveland Leader,* Mar. 19, 1859, quoted in *Annals of Cleveland.*

[46]*Catalogue,* 1842–43, page 32. It was reported that the young ladies earned a total of $1,540.57 in teaching and domestic labor.

CHAPTER XXXIX

MANUAL AND DOMESTIC LABOR

THE manual labor system was basic in the scheme of the Oberlin Collegiate Institute. Shipherd announced in the first official presentation of the plan in the autumn of 1833 that, "The Manual Labor Department will receive unusual attention, being not (as is too common), regarded as an unimportant appendage to the literary department; but systematized and incorporated with it. A variety of agricultural and mechanical labors will be performed by the students under circumstances most conducive to their health and support. *All will be required to labor* probably four hours daily." "All its Students, rich and poor, male and female," declared the *Circular* of the following March, "are required to labor four hours daily; little children, peculiar cases and providences excepted." All of the other early reports and notices refer to the manual labor department as a characteristic feature.[1] In 1844 the Founder declared that if the departments of "Biblical Instruction & Physiology, including Manual Labor . . . wane, the life current will flow out, & the heart of Oberlin die." We have already seen that a large proportion of the students were attracted to Oberlin by the prospect of self-support. As late as 1845 a select "Committee on Manual Labor in the O. C. I." reported that "the success of the institution . . . depends upon the continuance of this system."[2]

The first rules of the Institute provided that, "The Students shall be classed in convenient numbers, under suitable monitors, who shall keep an accurate record of their classes with a daily account of the hours & minutes which each one shall labor, the degree of diligence, & efect with which they labour, and an ac-

[1] *Ohio Atlas and Elyria Advertiser,* Oct. 17, 1833; *New York Evangelist,* Sept. 7, 1833, Sept. 1, 1836, and Shipherd in the *Ohio Observer,* July 13, 1834.

[2] J. J. S. to H. Hill, Aug. 17, 1844 (Treas. Off., File O), and "Manual Labor Report adopted August 1845" (Misc. Archives).

July 20th 1835

Date.	Mon	Tues	Wed	Thu	Frid	Sat	Total
J. C	$4\frac{3}{4}$	4	$1\frac{1}{2}$	4	4	$3\frac{1}{2}$	$21\frac{3}{4}$
C. C	$5\frac{1}{2}$	$4\frac{1}{4}$	$\frac{1}{4}$	2	4	$3\frac{1}{2}$	20
C. S	4	4	4	4	4	—	20
D. H. [illegible]			$3\frac{1}{2}$		2		$5\frac{1}{2}$
G. H. L	4	$3\frac{3}{4}$	$4\frac{1}{4}$	2	4	2	20
O. Z. S					2	2	4

Gilbert H. Littjohn Monitor.

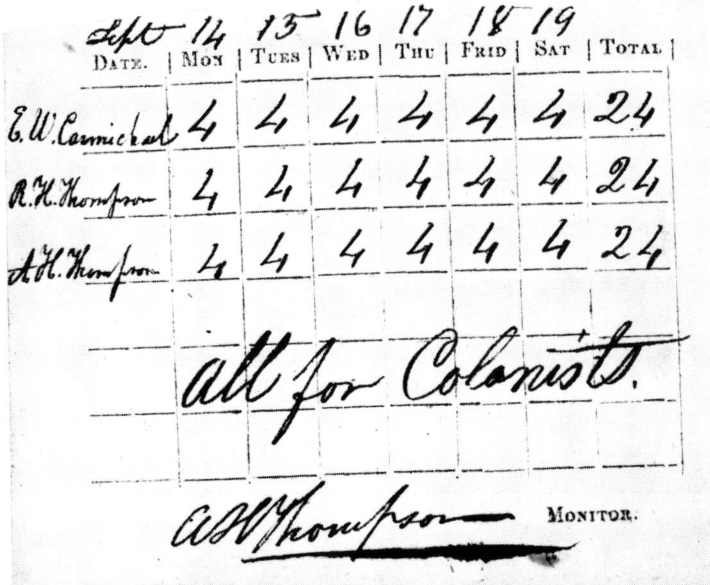

Date. Sept	Mon 14	Tues 15	Wed 16	Thu 17	Frid 18	Sat 19	Total
E. W. Carmichael	4	4	4	4	4	4	24
R. H. Thompson	4	4	4	4	4	4	24
A. H. Thompson	4	4	4	4	4	4	24

All for Colonists.

A. H. Thompson Monitor.

MANUAL LABOR BILLS OF 1835—FIRST PRINTED REPORT FORM
(From the originals in the Miscellaneous Archives)

REPORT OF LABOR,

FOR THE WEEK ENDING June 10th 1837.

	TIME.	KIND OF LABOR.	PRICE.	AMOUNT.
Monday,	3	Fencing, Diging, Picking	a 6	$0.18
Tuesday,	3	Harrowing - -	a 6	0,18
Wednesday,			a	
Thursday,			a	
Friday,	2½	moving Lumber	a 6	0.15
Saturday,	3¾	Plowing - -	a 7	0.25
				0,76

Oberlin, June 10th 1837.

P.R. Skinner Farmer Wm S Curtiss

Monitor.

REPORT OF LABOR,

FOR THE WEEK ENDING Fr July 17th 1837.

	TIME.	KIND OF LABOR.	PRICE.	AMOUNT.
Monday,	2h 30m	To Planting seeds	a 11 [illegible]	,20 cts
Tuesday,	3h 00m	To Diging - -	an hour 8cts	,24 cts
Wednesday,	3h 15m	Do do do	an hour 8cts	,26 cts
Thursday,	3h 00	do do do	an hour 8	,24 cts
Friday,	3 hrs	Do and Plowing	a 8	24 cts
Saturday,	3 hours	Plowing	a 8	24 cts
				1,42

Oberlin, July 10th 1837.

P.R. Skinner Farmer H. Whittlesey

Monitor Self

MANUAL LABOR REPORTS—1837
(From originals in the Miscellaneous Archives)

count of their deportment in general; and report the same to the general Agent on Saturday of each week; and no account shall be passed to the credit of the Students for Manual Labor by the hour, or by the Job, unless sanctioned by some monitor or agent of the Institute weekly."[3] The next year the trustees ruled that "an account of the labor performed by each Student who labors for, or boards in the Institute, shall be handed into the Office of the Institute on Saturday of each week by a Monitor when he has one, if not by the individual himself. This is to be done whether work has been performed for the Institute, or for individuals by the job or by the hour. Every Student who boards in the Institution is required to labor for the Institution, unless permission be granted by the Agent to labor elsewhere."[4]

Thousands of the reports handed in to meet this requirement still exist and constitute one of our best sources of information about the manual labor system at Oberlin. In November, 1835, T. P. Turner, Oberlin's carpenter and builder, reported that "Henry Fairchild has labored for O. C. Institute 284 hours at 7 cents per hour . . . getting out 70 floor boards . . . planing 237 feet board." In the next year Edward Grumley's account of labor includes: "milking and tending cows," "cutting wood at boarding house," "putting bedsteads in ladies Hall," and "digging potatoes." In August, 1838, another young man reported:

"2 Hours burning Stumps
3 " building walk for Prof. Finney
3 " hanging Gate etc.
4½ " preparing . . . sewer for Prof. Finney"

Printed forms were provided for these reports during part of the early period, and were almost always used in 1837 and 1838.[5]

The authorities insisted that all students should put in the minimum amount of labor. George Prudden wrote in the late summer of 1836: " . . . we are *compelled* to work three hours. My time is from 3 to 6 o'clock in the afternoon." The faculty required "that the unmarried students who do not work for the Institute shall labour the same number of hours as those who

[3]By-Laws of 1834, chapter 5.
[4]Frederick Hamlin, "Terms of Admission to the O. C. Institute, 1835" (Misc. Archives).
[5]*Cf.* illustrations on opposite page.

do, and work regularly." A certain Mr. Baldwin felt called upon to report: "Labored 24 [hours] last week but not for O. C. I." In 1835 the hours of labor required were reduced to three instead of four and this was officially announced in the catalogue published in that year.[6]

The students were organized in divisions: "Preparatory students to constitute the first division and labor from 7 to 10 A. M. —the Freshman class to constitute the second division and labor from 9 to 12 A. M.—The Sophomore & Junior classes to constitute the third division and labour from 1 to 4 P. M.—The Theological classes to constitute the fourth division and labour from 3 to 6 P. M." At first tools were charged to the student laborers when taken and credited to them when returned.[7] The earliest day-books in the Treasurer's Office give lists of tools lent to students: axes, wedges, etc. It was determined a little later, however, "that the circumstances of the Institution render it Impracticable to Lend its tools and any person who shall take them, shall be charged and required to pay for same." A fine of a shilling was imposed on any student who took tools belonging to another.[8] Manual labor was given an academic flavor by the rules and directions adopted and by the organization of the workers into classes. Samuel Cochran reported in August of 1836: "The classes organized, & I set to labor in E. J. Wilcox's class at Rolling logs—8 cts per hour." Father Shipherd, himself, prepared a set of "Rules for cutting cordwood *on the Institution Farm*." These rules provided in part that: "The wood shall be four feet long; & split as small as four inches in its greatest diameter. No round wood over four inches in diameter will be received. Limbs must be trimmed close. . . . The wood must be closely piled on poles which shall raise it a little from the ground."[9]

Wages for "the best Class of Mechanical Labourers" were at first set at 7 cents an hour and "the Standard price for the first class of Labourers on the farm" at 6¼ cents and a little later at 5 cents an hour.[10] As a matter of fact the wages paid were some-

[6]Geo. Prudden to mother, Aug. 16, 1836 (Prudden-Allen MSS), F. M., June 14, 1836, and T. M., July 1, 1835.

[7]F. M., June 14, 1836; By-Laws of 1834, and T. M., July 1, 1835. A short-lived schedule was also adopted on Feb. 26, 1836.

[8]P. C. M., July 31, 1835.

[9]Misc. Archives.

[10]P. C. M., July 24 and July 28, 1835 and T. M., Nov. 25, 1835.

what higher. Labor reports show that in 1836, 8 cents was paid for "loging," 7 cents for "chopping," 6 cents for hoeing potatoes, and 10 cents for harvesting, though one boy received only 5 cents an hour for "thrashing wheat." Eight cents an hour seems to have been the regular wage in the following year for binding wheat and carting manure. One cent less was paid for milking, picking up sticks, and "Plowing the Green." In 1838 a student received 8 cents for sledding timber, cleaning oats and "shoveling manure." But another was paid only 6 cents an hour for planting corn and another 5 cents for "Planting Beens." There is a lack of uniformity in the wages paid for the same kind of work which leads us to believe that they varied somewhat with the energy and ability of the laborer.

There was work enough and to spare in the first few years. The forest must be cut away and the stumps grubbed out. There were roads and buildings to be constructed. The General Agent (R. E. Gillett) reported for the season of 1835:

> "There has been 25 acres Land cleared this season & sown to wheat.
>
> "There has been on the Home Farm 30 acres chop^{d} & 37 acres ½ chop^{d}. . . .
>
> "There has been chop^{d} 50 acres one Mile off on the east farm.
>
> "There has been for Mill 350 cords wood cut & sold to Mill Company & 250 more is to be furnished."[11]

It seems clear enough that Delazon Smith was entirely justified when he wrote in 1837 that, "Nearly all the labor since this Institution was first established, has been chopping, logging and burning brush; and this too, a great portion of the year, *ankle deep in mud and water!*" Such work, though necessary, was certainly not very profitable to the Institute nor yet, perhaps, appropriate for students. The critic continued: "How beneficial *such* labor must be to a student, and how pleasurable the transition from log-heaps and burning brush to books, is better imagined than described."[12]

The mechanical work performed by students was mostly in the erection and repairing of the Institute buildings. Preference

[11]"The Agent's Report, Feby. 9, 1836" (Misc. Archives).
[12]Delazon Smith, *History of Oberlin,* 15–16.

was always given to contractors who would use student labor.[13] Thomas P. Turner, who was in charge of much of the construction, used students regularly. Under his direction students in 1835 worked at: "laying flour [*sic*]," "putting up 7 bedsteads," putting up a pump, "staining bookcase shelves," "tending board-kiln," and tending mason. In the late thirties reports of labor contain such items as: "putting up stove pipe," "carrying brick," "sawing laths & carrying them into the Office," "mixing & carrying mortar," "making steps," "hanging gate," and "filing & setting saw." Of course, after the first few years, work on construction ran out, but repair work was always necessary. Even in the sixties we find Lucien Warner, as a student, doing the necessary repairing on the college buildings.[14]

In the ideal manual labor system mechanical work, more profitable and perhaps more educational than logging and farming, played a large part. The steam engine purchased to saw lumber for the colonists was also intended as a part of the manual labor establishment. The *First Annual Report* (1834) states that the manual labor department "is also furnished with a steam engine of twenty-five horse power, which now propels a saw mill, grist mill, shingle and lath saw, and turning lathe, to which will be added other machinery, as experience shall prove expedient. One work shop is now erected and supplied with tools. Others are to be added as necessity requires, & funds allow." Students were warned, however, that the "agricultural system is much more extensive than the mechanical" and that "a large majority can work in mechanism to but little pecuniary profit."

There is no evidence to show that any considerable amount of shop work was ever done by Oberlin students. At first the shop was under the direct control of the Institute but was transferred after a few years to a group of students who constituted themselves the "Oberlin Mechanics Steam Engine Company." This organization became deeply involved financially and the shop was therefore sold off to individuals. The Institute lent $200.00 to J. M. Eells, a student, to enable him to buy a quarter interest in the shop with the understanding that he would "fur-

[13]T. M., Feb. 11, 1836. In the same year the Agent reported: "The building & all Mechanical Work has been transfered from the Institution to T. P. Turner, D. S. Ingraham & others."—"Agent's Report, July 5, 1836" (Misc. Archives).

[14]Lucien Warner, *Story of My Life,* 36.

nish students in the Institution with manual labor at the chair making business to as great an extend as his means will allow." The arrangement with Eells lasted less than one year, at the end of which time the whole shop was taken over by "Jennings, Wilder & Co." a corporation organized by Oberlin citizens "desirous of increasing [their] power of doing good, supporting [their] families, and advancing the cause of righteousness, especially in the education of pious young men in Oberlin."[15] There are no known records of the students (if any) who worked for this company. Of course, students were engaged in mechanical labor for individual mechanics in later years. Charles Livingstone, for example, worked in the printing office. In 1849 students ventured into broom making. Twenty-two acres of broom corn was raised, and sufficient material produced for the manufacture of 600 dozen brooms. Over 175 dozen had already been made by the last of October.[16]

Some men were employed at ringing the bell as a signal for rising, meals, classes and public meetings. Others were engaged in sweeping the halls and sawing wood. A few were employed as amanuenses in the college office, copying records and writing letters. In short they would do any kind of work to help pay for their education from teaching classes to skinning a cow. One student reported on the same sheet: "Instructing in Biblical Ant[iquities] and History" and "Chopping wood." The vast majority of work, however (after the forest had been cleared and the buildings constructed), was that done by the men on the college farm: hoeing potatoes, watching cows, feeding pigs, "planting rooty bagas," haying, plowing, moving the barn, "sewing grass seed," cutting peas, milking, spreading manure, threshing beans, cultivating "corn & pumions," and planting and hoeing mulberry trees,—and by the young women in the dormitory and in village homes: washing, ironing, scrubbing, mending, waiting on table, and "doing the dishes."

The *Catalogue* of 1835 announced that the young ladies "perform the labor of the Steward's Department, together with the washing, ironing, and much of the sewing for the students."

[15]P. C. M., Jan. 15, July 21, Sept. 23, 1840, and Agreement of Isaac Jennings, William Wilder, Seth B. Ellis and James H. Green, dated at Oberlin, July 1, 1841 (Misc. Archives).

[16]*Oberlin Evangelist*, Oct. 24, 1849.

The economic relation between the sexes in the thirties was much the same as that in any well-regulated family. While the male students worked in the fields and in the shop, the female students prepared their meals, washed their dishes, cleaned their rooms, washed their socks and linen, mended their trousers and made shirts for them. The Steward received from the young men clothing to be washed and mended and distributed it to the ladies. The ladies were, in turn, paid by the Institute for this labor, and the men paid the Institute by the piece for washing and sewing done. One of the major reasons why joint education was supported in Oberlin was that this mutual economic dependence of the sexes made it possible to cheapen the cost for both.[17]

It was claimed that this system made for sound bodies and clear minds among the young ladies, that through it they learned something of domestic science, and, of course, that it was a great aid to the female students financially. In a letter written by Miss Mary Ann Adams in behalf of the Oberlin young ladies to John Keep, Oberlin's agent in England, the ladies are made to say:

" . . . Our manual labor system . . . we all consent in saying is the very thing we need. After having our minds absorbed in some abstract subject until we become weary with intense thought, we repair to some household duty & the mind & body becoming relaxed, we return to the page we left & grasp the thoughts with avidity, & instead of the pale face which too often belongs to the student we see a continual freshness & glow. There are other benefits resulting from this system. While the majority of well educated ladies are ignorant of domestic affairs, here the two are blended, here domestic economy which it is true should be inculcated by the mother is carried on to still greater perfection, here knowledge of domestic affairs, high intellectual culture & even refinement of manners are considered as consistent with each other."[18]

Fortunately the "Hints and instructions for the benefits of those connected with the domestic department of Oberlin Collegiate Institute" prepared by the Principal of the Female Department in 1838 are preserved.[19] Here we have the essentials of

[17]Anon. letter, Oberlin, Sept. 1, 1836, in *New York Evangelist,* Oct. 1, 1836.

[18]Mary Ann Adams and others to John Keep, Oberlin, July 10, 1837 (Keep MSS).

[19]Alice Welch Cowles (Cowles-Little MSS).

the simple system of domestic economy taught. There was a special list of

"INSTRUCTIONS FOR THOSE WHO PREPARE FOOD.

1. Begin in season.
2. Assist in cooking and placing the different articles of food on to table. Bread butter & etc & etc.
3. Arrange the food tastefully.
4. Temper the seasoning; so as to make the dish healthy, palatable and economical.
5. After meals. Gather the food from each table.
6. Carefully preserve it all.
7. Put that which is eatable in its proper place.
8. Such as is fit for soap grease into a barrel of lye down cellar.
9. Put such as is unfit for either of the above places, into the slop barrel.
10. Leave the pantry in as good order as it is found."

On the first day of January, 1839, a young lady student wrote to her parents: "I have just come from the kitchen where I have been scouring knives. Every day immediately after breakfast and dinner, you may imagine me in the kitchen, engaged with several young ladies in scouring or washing knives and forks."[20] This washing of the knives must have been quite a ceremony for it required eight rules:

"1. Commence when the bell rings for leaving the table.
2. Gather the knives and forks from the table.
3. Place them on the north end of the table, at the east side of the kitchen.
4. Wash them clean.
5. Wipe them dry.
6. Avoid wetting the handles.
7. Place the knives and forks in separate departments in knife box.
8. Place those of a kind in the same department."

There were eleven rules for mopping:

"1. Never use a dirty mop.
2. Always have clean suds or clear water.
3. Change the water often, when necessary.

[20]Sarah Ingersoll to David Ingersoll, Dec. 31, 1838–Jan. 1, 1839 (lent by Mrs. Friedrich Lehman, Oberlin).

4. Never touch the mopboards with a dirty mop.
5. When washing a specified portion of the floor, wash against the mop boards first.
6. Use the mop when first wrung to wipe near the mop boards, while the water and mop are clean.
7. When wiping the floor do not mop across the boards.
8. Wipe the floor dry.
9. Always leave the mop and pail clean.
10. Never leave dirt on the mop boards.
11. Never leave the corners of a room dirty."

Elizabeth Maxwell found Monday "the hardest day of all the week" next to the Sabbath. She explained: "Monday is our wash day. We have no lessons but generally a longer lesson for Tuesday. We are always so glad to get to bed that we never think of our straw beds and sleep more soundly than if it was down."[21] It was partly because of the necessity of washing that Monday morning was set aside as a half holiday and not interrupted by classes for a period of over eighty years, long after the domestic system of manual labor had been forgotten. A few suggestions entered by Mrs. Cowles, the Lady Principal, in her notebook in 1836 give some small notion of the washing and ironing work:

"WASHING DEPARTMENT.

Never carry your own articles into the wash room until the gentlemen's are finished.
Perfect punctuality.
Improvement of every moment.
Wed. & Fri. ladies wash their colored clothes.
Ironing room vacated by 7 o'clock."[22]

The "gentlemen's" washing came first! Evidently Monday was not the only wash day either. The "Resolution passed by the young ladies as regulations of the boarding house" in 1838, dealt with ironing, washing, and sewing.

Retire at 10 o'clock.
Rise at 5 o'clock.
Ironing room vacated Sat. 7 o'clock.
Ironing sheets left by each young lady in a suitable condition for ironing.

[21]Elizabeth Maxwell to parents, Mar. 31, 1842 (lent by Mrs. Emma Monroe Fitch).

[22]Alice Welch Cowles, MS Notebook, Nov. 1, 1836 (Cowles-Little MSS).

Each young lady can put 10 articles of clothing a week into the wash if she pleases, but is not to exceed that number.

No clothes washed except they are marked the whole name and a bill pinned on to the bundle.

Clothes to be brought as early as 7 o'clock. Wed. Eve.

The young ladies can wash their dresses, dark clothing and woollens at such times on Tues. and Thurs. as will not interefere with the general washing, and any time on Wednesday provided a class of three or more can be formed.

No washing specified in the preceding regulations done after Thurs.

"SEWING

No sewing carried from the sewing room unless a given piece is placed under the special supervision of a young lady, and the superintendent permits her to take it away from the rest of the work."[23]

The returns from domestic labor were small but, at least in 1835 and 1836, played a considerable part in enabling the "co-eds" to pay their expenses. From three to five cents an hour was promised for domestic labor. In the winter of 1834 and 1835 Sarah Capen worked 547 hours at 3 cents per hour and Fanny Fletcher 359 hours at 3¼ cents per hour, but another young lady received only 2½ cents an hour for a hundred hours of domestic labor. In the later months of 1835 young ladies received from 2½ to 3 cents an hour. In statements rendered on December 31, 1835, P. P. Stewart, Steward, credited Miss M. F. Kellogg (later the wife of Professor and President Fairchild) with 68½ hours of labor at 2½ cents an hour; Miss Elizabeth Prall (one of the three first female recipients of the A. B. in 1841) with 563 hours at 2¾ cents, and Delia Fenn with 611 hours at 3 cents. During the summer and fall of 1836, however, Zeruiah Porter (the first graduate from the Ladies' Course) received regularly three or four cents an hour. In March, Florella Brown (half-sister of John Brown of Harper's Ferry) worked in the boarding house for 3 cents an hour; Catherine More was paid 4 cents.[24]

[23]Alice Welch Cowles, "Hints and instructions . . . ," 1838 (Cowles-Little MSS).

[24]*1838 Catalogue,* 31; E. C. Stewart (Mrs. P. P.), Steward's Report, Mar. 4, 1835 (Misc. Archives), and MS reports in the Misc. Archives.

In 1836 the *Catalogue* announced encouragingly that "nearly all the young ladies . . . paid their board by their manual labor." This estimate is easily checked because double entry statements of student finances were prepared in that year, credit from manual labor being listed on one side and indebtedness for board, washing, tuition and other expense on the other.[25] From these it appears that at this time a considerable number of the young ladies did receive enough from manual labor to pay for their board at least. In 69 accounts taken at random from those rendered in 1836 receipts from domestic labor were over 60% of total expenses, including washing, tuition, lights, etc. as well as board. As far as the students were concerned the system appears to have been financially successful at that time.

Labor in the domestic department was considered so important that applicants for admission were required to certify "their ability and disposition to perform domestic labor" as well as their character and present educational advancement. All were at first required to labor four hours a day, but this requirement was soon reduced to three and then to two hours. In April of 1836 two young ladies were dismissed from the boarding house "simply because their health [was] not sufficient to enable them to perform the manual labor required."[26] It was not logical, however, that the students should go on forever literally supporting themselves by taking in each others' washings. Beginning with 1840 the *Catalogue* becomes less encouraging. Prospective students in the Young Ladies' Department are told that "many have paid their board by manual labor, but they were those . . . who had some responsible situation in the domestic department." The young ladies are warned that, "It is found that [their] highest good . . . , physical and mental, is best promoted, by not attempting more than three hours' daily labor *besides her own work.*" In the 1855 *Catalogue,* and for several years following, female students are advised not "to do more than defray about half the expense of their board." Of course many of them continued to do some work around the boarding house and others worked as "hired girls" in homes in town. In the middle forties Lucy Stone worked in the kitchen of the boarding hall, keeping her Greek grammar, it is said, propped up before her

[25]*Cf.* typical statement reproduced on opposite page.
[26]*1835 Catalogue,* 25, and F. M., Apr. 13, 1836.

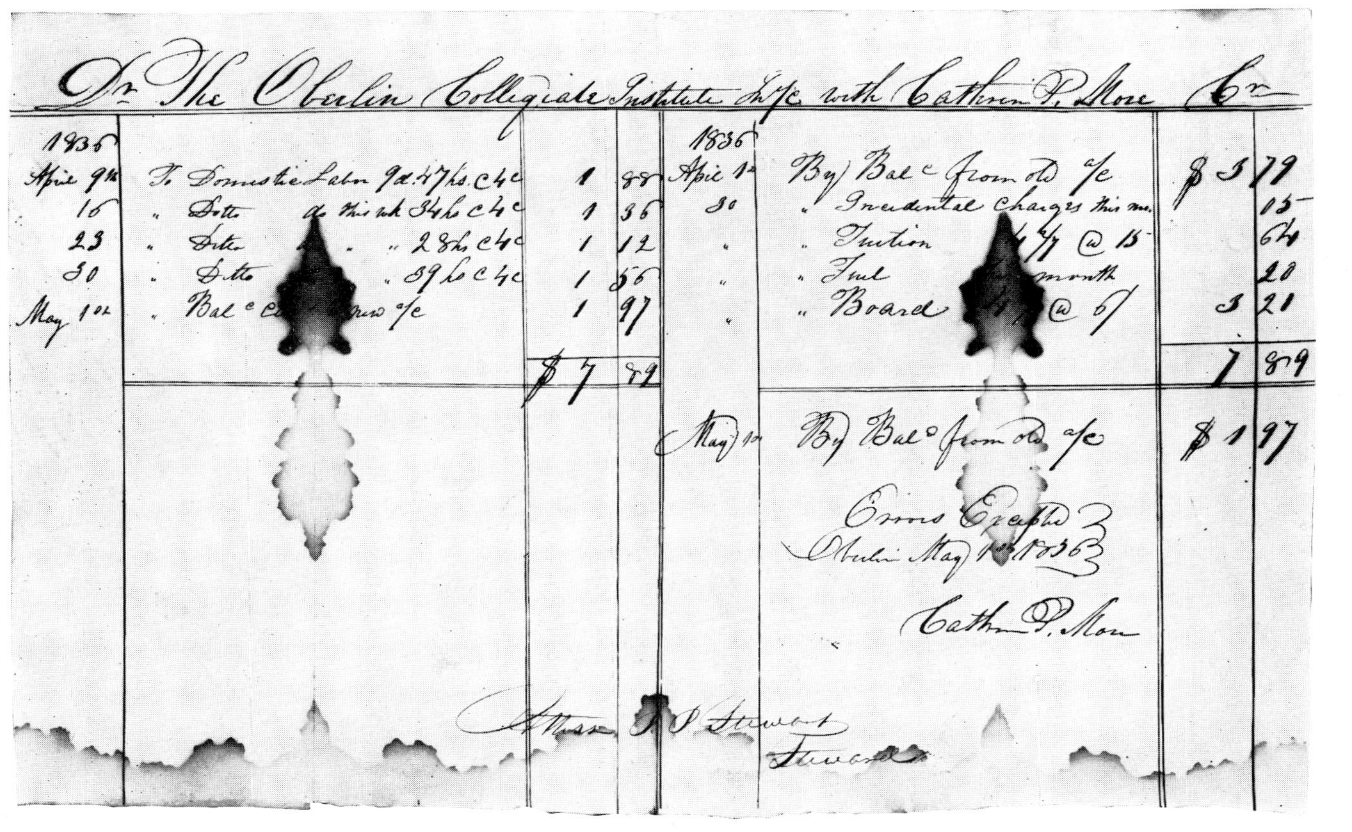

Dr The Oberlin Collegiate Institute in a/c with Cathrin P. More Cr

1836				1836			
April 9th	To Domestic Labor 9d. 47 hs. @ 4c	1	88	April 1st	By Balc from old a/c	$ 3	79
16	" Ditto do this wk 34 hs @ 4c	1	36	30	" Incidental Charges this mo.		15
23	" Ditto [illegible] " 28 hs @ 4c	1	12	"	" Tuition [illegible] @ 15		64
30	" Ditto [illegible] " 39 hs @ 4c	1	56	"	" Fuel [illegible] month		20
May 1st	" Balc [illegible] new a/c	1	97	"	" Board [illegible] @ 6/	3	21
		$ 7	89			7	89
				May 1st	By Bal. from old a/c	$ 1	97

Errors Excepted
Oberlin May 1st 1836

Cathrin P. More

Attest P. P. Stewart
Steward

A YOUNG LADY STUDENT'S ACCOUNT FOR APRIL, 1836
(From the original in the Miscellaneous Archives)

so that she could read as she wiped the dishes. In the late fifties one student wrote to her mother as a matter of course: "It is Monday and the rest of the Boarders are washing."[27] Throughout the sixties the *Catalogue* carried the statement that, "Young ladies, in the Ladies' Hall, have the privilege of defraying a part of their expenses by domestic labor." In the 70's, however, as we have previously seen, young men appear as waiters in the hall. Various odd jobs and teaching in the Preparatory Department were open to women as well as men. In 1858 Miss L. M. Stiffler received "one dollar seventy-eight cents for taking care of the reception rooms thirteen weeks." Nine years later girls were earning money by "ringing Hall bell during the Spring term" or by "carrying the Hall mail." Housework was, nevertheless, the usual type of manual labor for young ladies.

Young men often worked cutting and carrying cord wood for the hall. There were even, occasionally, one or two in the Steward's Department. In 1835 and 1836 E. B. Sherwood did the baking in the boarding house and was, therefore, "properly intitled to $1.50 per week for his service."[28] In the fifties, when Lucy Stone was washing dishes, Jacob Dolson Cox (later General, Governor and Secretary of the Interior) baked the bread. For the most part, however, the men were employed outdoors on the college farm.

27A. S. Blackwell, *Lucy Stone,* 49, and Adelia Whipple to mother, May 19, 1858 (lent by Miss Jessie Wright, Wellington, Ohio).

28Undated statement of P. P. Stewart (Misc. Archives).

CHAPTER XL

THE COLLEGE FARM

THE lands belonging to the institution furnished opportunity for much student labor. The "college farm" was, in fact, the mainstay of the manual labor system for men, as the boarding house furnished most of the labor for the young ladies. The General Agent was put in charge of "the manual labor of the male Students & all the farming operations, together with the Mills and erecting of buildings," by order of the trustees early in 1835. Frederick Hamlin, of Wellington, was at first appointed to this important post but, due to his unwillingness or inability to handle the agricultural part of his duties, a practical farmer had to be employed in addition. In 1835 Jonathan T. Baldwin held this position. In the following year Robbins Burrell and Perez Otis took his place, Burrell at Sheffield and Otis at Oberlin.[1] R. E. Gillett succeeded Hamlin as agent in 1836. His reports for that and the next years, list buildings completed, land cleared and manual labor performed. P. R. Skinner became practical farmer in the spring of 1837; his signature succeeds that of Gillett in manual labor reports the last of May. In 1838 the office of General Agent was discontinued and the new farmer, C. T. Carrier, who succeeded Skinner in the spring of the year, took complete charge of the farm and of agricultural manual labor for the next four seasons.[2]

Of course, the farm had to be stocked and equipped. It has been impossible to discover what became of "Scrawney," "Scrawney's Mate" and the other cows that Shipherd bought in the autumn of 1833, but three years later it was necessary for the students to raise funds to purchase "9 cows @ 25$ each . . . or

[1]T. M., Apr. 7, 1835; Feb. 11, 1836; P. C. M., July 24, 1835; June 16, 1836, and N. P. Fletcher, MS Critical Letters, 1837, No. 3 (Misc. Archives).

[2]P. C. M., Apr. 23, 1838; Skinner to Gillett, Mar. 28, 1837, and to Burnell, Aug. 10, 1838 (Treas. Off., File I), and "Suspense Book," 1836–40 (Misc. Archives).

starve," says N. P. Fletcher. In 1837 seven members of the faculty subscribed ten dollars each to buy a yoke of oxen, and the next year Carrier reported 11 cows ("2 lost!"), 4 oxen, 1 bull, and 2 horses. In 1841 there were 24 cows, 4 oxen, 2 bulls, 13 calves and heifers, 34 sheep, and 5 hogs. The institution had by this date accumulated many tools and other equipment: cradles, sickles, scythes, rakes, hay forks, hoes, wedges, beetles, a fanning mill for winnowing, "a X cut saw," axes, spade, "1 Grub How & 1 Mattock," etc. In addition there was a wagon, a cart, "Whippletrees & Neck Yoke," "One large water trough at Barn," and the "relics of the Threshing Machine." Wheat was the chief crop raised: there were about 45 acres of it in 1838, which produced, however, only a little over 10 bushels to the acre. Considerable land was put into pasture, and oats, potatoes, peas, beans, buckwheat, rye and corn were raised in the later years. Some fruit trees were set out: apple trees, and peach trees on Tappan Square. Of the fruit trees set out only about one out of ten lived.[3]

The students milked the cows, mended the fences, hoed the potatoes and threshed the grain at from six to ten cents an hour. But "Labour on the Farm," as Agent Gillett reported, was "unproffitable," to the Institute at least. In the period from June 1, 1836, to August 31, 1837, expenditures on the farm amounted to $2,996.47 and receipts to only $974.77. To balance the account the Treasurer charged $2,021.70 to "stock," but value of stock on hand, it is clear, had increased by no such amount. The Treasurer's books show that the farm was "in the red" to the extent of $2,664.67 on January 1, 1841. A report to the trustees later in the same year states that, "Recent very thorough investigation by a com. appointed for that purpose shows that for the last 3 years the farm has drawn upon the treasury of the Institution for its support about $474.57 or 158.19 pr year—over and above all it has done and produced. The same com. also ascertained that but for the milk which was furnished by the farmer to the boarding house at from 2 to 4 cts per quart the farm would have sunk some 3 or 4 fold that sum." Though it is not easy to reconcile these figures with the accounts in the Treasurer's books, it is clear enough that the farm was a finan-

[3]"Agent Gillett, Report, Sept. 1836"; N. P. Fletcher, MS Critical Letters (1837), No. 4; C. T. Carrier, Farmer's Report, Sept. 3, 1838; "Inventory of Stock & Farming Implements copied from Book of C. T. Carrier, Sept. 6, 1841," and Trustees' MSS, 1841 (all in Misc. Archives).

cial liability. Considering the fact that the number of students thus employed averaged only about twenty, we are entirely justified in concluding that the farm was a failure from every point of view.[4]

Figuring largely in this failure was the ill-advised silk-culture experiment. Throughout American history sporadic and ineffectual efforts have been made from time to time, usually encouraged by governmental agencies, to establish the culture of mulberries and the silk worm. During one period only, however, did the interest in the industry become widespread among the people and seem to hold any considerable prospect of success. This was in the second quarter of the nineteenth century, and Connecticut was the center from which the movement spread. In February of 1828 certain citizens of Wyndham and Tolland counties petitioned Congress for aid "in the Cultivation of the Mulberry Tree and of Silk."[5] Already the House of Representatives had adopted a resolution directing the preparation of a manual on methods of silk culture, and in the same month published, as a government document, De Haggi's, *Treatise on the Culture of Silk in Germany*.[6] In 1831 the legislature of Massachusetts appropriated $600.00 for the compilation and printing of "a concise Manual, to contain the best information respecting the growth of the Mulberry tree, with suitable directions for the culture of silk." J. H. Cobb's *Manual Containing Information Respecting the Growth of the Mulberry Tree,* published in Boston in 1831, was the result. A year or two later Congress ordered 2000 copies of this little booklet for free distribution, and it was therefore reprinted in 1833.

Cobb's *Manual* stimulated great interest. Production boomed in Connecticut, and in 1833 four tons of silk cocoons were said to have been produced in Wyndham County.[7] In 1835 the Hart-

[4]"Agent Gillett, Report, Sept., 1836," and Trustees' MSS, 1841 (Misc. Archives), Ledger No. 2 (1836–1837), pages 123–127, and Ledger No. 4 (1839–1843), pages 42-43 (Treas. Off.).

[5]*Memorial of Sundry Inhabitants of the Counties of Wyndham and Tolland, State of Connecticut, Praying for the Aid of Government in the Cultivation of the Mulberry Tree and of Silk,* (Washington—1828), 20 Cong., 1 sess., *House Doc.,* No. 159.

[6]20 Cong., 1 sess., *House Doc.,* No. 226.

[7]J. H. Cobb, *A Manual Containing Information Respecting the Growth of the Mulberry Tree, with Suitable Directions for the Cultivation of Silk.* (Boston—1833), and L. O. Howard, "The United States Department of Agriculture and Silk Culture," in the *Yearbook of the United States Department of Agriculture, 1903,* (Washington—1904), 137–138.

ford County Silk Society began the publication of the *Silk Culturist,* which became the organ of the movement as the boom advanced. The object was stated to be "to introduce and extend the knowledge and practise of cultivating and raising mulberry trees, feeding and managing silk worms, and reeling silk from cocoons, in the most approved method."[8]

The culture of silk was urged with the same fanatic zeal which characterized the anti-slavery, temperance, and moral reform movements of the period. Not only was it urged that silk culture would be profitable but it was insisted that there was "in the whole range of man's varied manual labor pursuits none, . . . so innocent, moral and healthy." " . . . Women, children, cripples, and indigent paupers can be useful in this fascinating occupation [tending silk worms]," wrote one enthusiast. "The refined intellect can here scrutinize the ingenuity of a most wonderful insect." The silk industry was recommended as particularly appropriate for the employment of persons in the penitentiaries. Silk societies similar to the Hartford society were formed in nearly every county in Connecticut and in most of the northern states. Indeed a map of these societies would cover much the same area as a map of anti-slavery or temperance or other reform societies. The state governments joined the crusade. Bounties for silk production were provided by Massachusetts (1835), Vermont (1835), Pennsylvania (1836), Maryland (1836), Georgia (1838), and New Jersey (1838). So great was popular enthusiasm that the editor of the *Silk Culturist* felt called upon to warn people against buying cabbage seeds from itinerant peddlers of "mulberry tree seeds." *Morus multicaulis* was the most popular mulberry tree, and interest in *Morus multicaulis* assumed the proportions of a craze. Thousands of these trees were planted all over the country; eighteen advertisements for mulberry trees appeared in one issue of the *Silk Culturist.* Already in August of 1835 the editor announced that, "Silk must eventually become one of the staple productions of the United States."[9]

Ohio, so closely linked with Connecticut and New England in general, would not be expected to escape the epidemic. In the summer of 1835 the *Cleveland Whig* reprinted at least two arti-

[8]*Silk Culturist and Farmer's Manual,* Apr., 1835.
[9]*Ibid.,* Aug. 1835; Apr., Oct., 1836; July, 1837; Apr., 1838, and *passim.*

cles on silk. Early the following year the editor of a Hudson paper reported the receipt of "130 skeins of sewing Silk, manufactured by M. E. Patchen, of Newbury, Geauga County." Others were recommended to follow this example. In 1837 Cyrus Ford of Massillon advertised 100,000 *Morus Multicaulis,* and A. S. Chen of Columbus announced that he had on hand for sale "100,000 plants and cuttings of genuine *Morus Multicaulis.*" John Boyden of Cleveland was also ready to supply the silk grower with mulberry trees of the favorite varieties.[10] In his annual message to the legislature in December, 1836, the Governor of Ohio declared: "The soil and climate [of Ohio], so well adapted to the growth of the Mulberry, may place Silk manufactories in a favorable position; and the adaptation of our soil to the Sugar Beet, may bring that article into successful competition with the sugar cane of the South." (The interest in beet sugar was contemporaneous but not so widespread. The *Silk Culturist* espoused its cause as well as that of silk.) Numbers of persons were engaged in cultivating mulberries near Canton, Dayton, Columbus, and Xenia. Ohio rapidly rose to the first place among western states in silk production. In 1839 when Connecticut was credited with 17,500 pounds of silk cocoons out of a total of 61,500 pounds produced in the United States, Pennsylvania came second with 7,260 pounds and Ohio third with 4,300 pounds. Every state in the Union reported some silk made.[11]

Northern Ohio seems to have been the favorite western habitat of the *Morus.* A silk grower writing from Geauga County early in 1837 declared that, "Whoever has visited Ohio, especially the northern part of the State, will readily perceive the adaptation of the soil, more particularly that situated on the route of the great ridge road, for the rearing and cultivating the mulberry." In 1839 almost exactly three quarters of the silk reeled in Ohio came from the northwestern part of the State,

[10]*Cleveland Whig,* July 8, Aug. 5, 1835; *Ohio Observer,* Feb. 11, 1836; and *Silk Culturist,* Nov. and Dec., 1837.

[11]*Reports, Including Messages, and other Communications, Made to the Thirty-Fifth General Assembly of the State of Ohio,* (Columbus—1836), 24; *Silk Culturist,* Dec., 1836, and June, 1837, and *Compendium of the . . . Sixth Census* (Washington—1841), 358–359. See also Robert Price, "Morus Multicaulis, or Silk Worms Must Eat," *Ohio Archaeological and Historical Quarterly,* XLV, 265–272 (July, 1836), and L. H. Bailey, *Sketch of the Evolution of Our Native Fruits* (New York —1898), 151 *et seq.*

nearly one quarter from Huron County alone.[12] It is clear enough, therefore, that the Oberlin silk experiment was no freak but part of a widespread campaign for silk production.

The original germ of the Oberlin scheme came, however, from New York, the State in which so much of early Oberlin originated. Eliphalet B. Coleman was a minister of Pembroke, N. Y., and a friend of Father Keep. His heart, it seems, had "long been pained for destitute young females, who possessed an ardent desire to obtain an education."[13] He determined to set up a female or, more likely, a coeducational institute on the manual labor plan, silk culture to furnish the labor for both sexes. Silk culture seemed to him ideal work for self-supporting female students. "The labor in rearing the Silk Worm," he wrote, "is not only very light and simple, but more productive than any other that has ever yet been undertaken at such an institution; and in every point of view, peculiarly adapted to that object." The young ladies could earn, he believed, instead of the pittance of 3 cents an hour received at Oberlin "with perfect ease, . . . more than one shilling per hour, and with industry twice that much."[14]

In February of 1836 he wrote to a friend in Oberlin describing his scheme and suggesting its advantages for Oberlin Institute. "My present plan," he wrote, "is to set out the coming spring 50,000 trees on 50 acres of land, which in three years will, I calculate, defray all the expense of 200 students. I mean, Cloaths, Board, Books, Tuition and everything. This will be easily done by their devoting three months in the Summer exclusively to this object; and then attending to their studies the other nine months of the year." This letter was turned over to the Oberlin Board of Trustees and the plan so enthusiastically received that on March 10, 1836, they appointed Shipherd and Burnell "a committee to correspond with Rev. E. B. Coleman with a view to preparing the way for uniting his enterprise in the cultivation of Silk with this Institution."[15] Burnell wrote immediately to

[12]*Silk Culturist*, June, 1837 (Jesse Pike, Perry, Ohio), and *Compendium of the . . . Sixth Census*, 276.

[13]Eliphalet B. Coleman to Levi Burnell, Mar. 30, 1836 (Treas. Off., File B). Both Coleman and Goodrich were graduates of Williams College.—Calvin Durfee, *Williams Biographical Annals*, 227, and 273–274.

[14]Coleman to Rev. Caleb Pitkin of Oberlin, Feb. 24, 1836, and to Burnell, Apr. 4, 1836 (Treas. Off., File B).

[15]To Pitkin, Feb. 24, 1836, and T. M., Mar. 10, 1836.

Coleman, suggesting that he visit Oberlin to discuss preliminaries of a merger and look over the local situation.

Coleman had agreed to take 50,000 White Italian Mulberry trees at $30.00 a thousand of Elizur Goodrich, President of the Hartford County (Connecticut) Silk Society and a leading figure in the silk movement.[16] Being unable to find land for his trees he agreed to give up his own scheme for one season at least and "bring the 50,000 trees on to you as soon as they can be got there . . . provided you will furnish me with the means of defraying the expense, and allow me eight dollars per week for my services." The Prudential Committee seized upon the proposition with avidity, immediately authorizing the payment of $8.00 a week to Coleman, $100.00 for the transportation of the trees and $1,500.00 for the trees.[17] The treasury of the Oberlin Collegiate Institute could hardly bear such a drain, but it was evident that new charities were depended upon. A representative of the Prudential Committee immediately wrote to Mr. Goodrich at Hartford, informing him that it had been decided that Oberlin should go into the silk industry and that a large number of mulberry trees was needed for that purpose: ". . . Knowing that you, sir, have a large nursery in N. Y. State, they wish to lay the claims [of] this infant, but great & rising institution before you, having strong hope that your benevolence, & wish to promote christian education in this way, may induce you to permit a quantity of your trees to be removed to this place, & receive as a reward, the pleasing conscienceness of having done an essential service to multitudes who are now preparing or who may hereafter prepare themselves for usefulness in the world." In June, apparently as an afterthought, the Committee, with doubtful benevolence, appointed the Rev. Mr. Coleman an "Agent of the Oberlin Collegiate Institute in soliciting funds" to help pay for the mulberry trees which he had been instrumental in selling them.[18]

In the middle of May Coleman started the mulberries for Oberlin. The actual number shipped was 39,105, no more being available. They were put on board a schooner at Sacket's Har-

[16]For Goodrich see the *Silk Culturist,* Apr., 1835, and Apr., 1836.

[17]Coleman to Burnell, Mar. 30, 1836, Apr. 4, 1836 (Treas. Off., File B), and P. C. M., Apr. 12, 1836.

[18]Copy of a letter from E. P. Ingersoll to Elizur Goodrich, Apr. 14, 1836 (Misc. Archives), and P. C. M., June 7, 1836.

bour and sent by way of the Welland Canal to Cleveland. Arriving in Cleveland early in June they were transferred to another schooner which landed them at the mouth of the Black River (Lorain). Packed in twenty boxes, 6 feet long, 3 feet wide and 3½ feet high, it required ten teams to bring them overland to Oberlin. The expenses for packing and transportation alone were over two hundred dollars.[19]

Great expectations were held with regard to the silk venture. Coleman wrote to Burnell: "I calculate that 100 acres of trees will, in 4 years, sustain 400 students, that is, 4 to the acre. And then you can go to any extent desirable, that your means will admit of. Those 50,000 trees the first or present summer will sustain from 500,000 to 1,000,000 worms, & if 50,000 more should be added in the fall they would probably yield the next Summer $2,000, and then increase at the rate of two or three thousand Dollars a year for ten years; and by the calculations of some of the best judges (or those who ought to be such) four or six times as fast as that."[20] Shipherd, in New York, trying to raise money for an already almost bankrupt Oberlin, approved. "All my reading & conversation since I left home," he wrote, "confirms my opinion that there is no branch of Manual labor that can be carried on half so profitable as the culture of silk." He was, however, not sure of the fitness of Oberlin soil for mulberry growing and therefore doubted "the propriety of planting 50 A. altho' I like grand movements." He also called attention to the fact that the Chinese Mulberry, or *Morus multicaulis,* was said to be much better than the Italian White Mulberry, or *Morus alba,* which had been purchased for Oberlin.[21] Certainly, in this case, Shipherd was not the rash one, though it should not be supposed that he was in any way, opposed to the enterprise.

Coleman wrote detailed instructions for preparing the land and planting the mulberries. Whether or not the managers of the enterprise in Oberlin had any other directions for setting the trees and cultivating them is unknown. A copy of Cobb's *Manual . . . Respecting the Growth of the Mulberry Tree* . . . (Boston–1833) was in the possession of the Institute at

19Coleman to Burnell, May 18, June 2, 1836 (Treas. Off., File B), and P. C. M., June 7, 1836.

20East Bethany, N. Y., Apr. 4, 1836 (Treas. Off., File B).

21J. J. Shipherd to Levi Burnell, May 6, 1836 (Treas Off., File H).

least as early as the forties but whether at this time or not is uncertain.

Anyway, shortly after the arrival of the shipment of trees, work was begun on planting. E. S. Grumley reported in his labor bill for June 1836: "setting out mulberries—11 hours—.08—88," "plowing drains in mulberry lot—5 hours—.10—.50," and "harrowing for mulberries—8½ hours—.6—.53." Lewis Cowles was at work as early as June 5 "planting *mulberries*" at 6 cents an hour. O. D. Botsford reported "21½ hours [!] work at *Mulberrys*" on the 11th also at 6 cents per hour. On June 13 another young man spent "11½ hours planting Mulberry trees at 6d." On June 10 the last of 21,585 trees was planted at Oberlin; the remaining 17,520 being set out on Robbins Burrell's farm at the "Sheffield Manual Labor Institute." More were secured and transplanted in the autumn; altogether 55,000 were set out in 1836: 30,000 at Oberlin and 25,000 at Sheffield. In the next spring still more were planted on Tappan Square where some of them still stood five years later.[22]

The process of cultivation began immediately. In the middle of July, Davis Prudden wrote to his father: "I expect to pay for my board & tuition by labor, but I suppose it is rather uncertain. They give the students 33 cents for hoeing a row of mulberries. Some hoe a row in 2½ hours, others 3, 4 & 5 hours. At log[g]ing they give them 8 cents per hour." His brother, George, wrote the same day: "I began to-day to labour on the farm. My employment was to hoe mulberry trees, & such hard hoeing I scarcely ever saw. I worked at it about an hour & a half & got completely tired out. I think I shall try to obtain some other lighter employment. Davis's work for a time is to watch the cows. He has five cents an hour & scarcely nothing to do. I suppose he will tell you more about the matter himself."[23] Both Davis' and George's labor bills for July, 1836, are preserved in the College archives. George is credited with "hoeing 1 row of mulberry trees" on July 18 and 19, but he turned to other occupations for the rest of the month; "moving barn—3 hours—8c per hour" and "Hoeing Potatoes." Davis' bill shows that he earned

[22]"Suspense Book," 1836; and "Agent Gillett's Report," 1836 (Misc. Archives); P. C. M., May 30, June 16, Nov. 12, 1836; Sept. 14, 1837; May 12, 1841; Mar. 7, Apr. 14, 1842, and Coleman to Burnell, June 2, 1836 (Treas. Off., File B).

[23]Davis Prudden to Peter Prudden, July 18, 1836, and George to Peter Prudden, July 18, 1836 (Prudden-Allen MSS).

15 cents on July 18 "watching Cows—5^d—3 hours." During the rest of the month, however, he hoed mulberries, making $1.75 at this occupation in the course of July.

The Oberlin leaders were morally certain "of maintaining the Female Department from [this] promising plantation." But the management was bad and very few worms were ever procured to feed upon the mulberry leaves. The heavy clay of Russia Township was not well suited for mulberries and the trees lacked intelligent care. It is even said that the cattle were let into the patches where the trees were planted and the new shoots were broused down. The summer of 1836, to cap the climax, was very dry and the chances of the trees surviving thus farther reduced. Thousands of them were dead by the next spring.[24]

The "Silk Department" account for 1836–37 shows a deficit of $1564.69, of which $1,373.15 was the cost of the trees, and most of the remainder chargeable to student labor. The credit side of the silk account was $2.50! This did not discourage from further planting, however, and in the spring of 1837 the young men were as active setting out *Morus multicaulis* (or Chinese Mulberries) as they had been in setting out the *Morus alba* the year before. The labor reports of 1837 contain not only frequent references to planting and cultivating mulberries, but also list many hours of work at pruning trees. There are no reports of pruning in the droughty season of 1836, which must partially account for the large loss of trees in that year. Writing in 1837, P. P. Stewart was still advising the maintenance of a mulberry plantation as a means of encouraging female education.[25] Work on the mulberries practically ceased in 1838. One report referring to setting trees in June and another including a charge for "wartering trees" in September are the only evidences in the records that the trees still existed.

There are a few reports which contain statements of labor spent in planting or cultivating beets, which implies that the sugar beet craze was also touching Oberlin. This is not surprising, for the arguments presented by advocates of that cause were the

[24]J. P. Cowles in the *Cleveland Observer*, Jan. 1, 1840; N. P. Fletcher, MS Critical Letters, No. 5 (Misc. Archives), and E. B. Coleman to Burnell, Dec. 8, 1836; Mar. 15, 1837 (Treas. Off., File B).

[25]O. C. Institute MS Ledger, 1836, page 35; P. C. M., Apr. 14, 1842, and P. P. Stewart to Burnell, Apr. 10, 1837 (Treas. Off., File I).

kind to which Oberlinites were particularly susceptible. One of them wrote to Mahan in 1836: "Now, it has suggested itself to me, that you may connect the cultivation of this most valuable root, for the purpose of manufacturing *sugar,* with the cultivation of silk, and thus serve the double object, yes; quadruple,—aye—and still more—e. g. a healthful and agreeable kind of manual labor,—a profitable kind of employment for the students,—and last that I can mention, *introduce* the cultivation of that which, if I mistake not, is to be the barley loaf to roll down against the tents of Slavery and crush them."[26] Beet sugar would be a great comfort to those whose consciences pricked them when they purchased or consumed slave products.

But Oberlin was not to be allowed to forget the mulberries. In 1839 a "friend" in Lockport, N. Y., wrote to Secretary Burnell that he was "satisfied that rearing Silk worms & the Chinese Mulberry would be more profitable to your institution than any thing you can do." In the following year another friend wrote from Michigan to state that he had "about 10,000 trees and some of the most approved kinds of silk worm eggs" and wished to remove with them to Oberlin, providing the attractions offered were sufficient. In the previous spring a Quaker, interested in the Institute, collected donations of *Morus multicaulis* trees and shipped them (1250 in all) to Oberlin. In 1841 an Elyria man offered a gift of trees to the Institute, as he was not "able to dispose of them in any manner." The trees in the Square furnished ever-present reminders and eventually aided the manual labor system further when students were hired to dig them out. Elizur Goodrich of Hartford, whom they still owed for the 40,000 *Morus alba* of 1836, sent them occasional notices by mail. In 1844 the Institute was still negotiating with him in an attempt to persuade him to take land in lieu of cash.[27]

The failure in Oberlin was typical. Silk culture declined rapidly and "the very name became a byword." Production of silk cocoons in the United States dropped from 61,552 pounds in 1839 to 10,843 pounds in 1849. Production in Connecticut declined from 17,538 pounds in the former year to the negligible

[26]T. M. Hopkins to Asa Mahan, Oct. 7, 1836 (Treas. Off., File D).

[27]L. A. Spalding to Burnell, July 25, 1839 (Treas. Off., File I); A. C. Holt to H. C. Taylor, Nov. 23, 1840 (File D); J. R. King to Burnell, Apr. 15, 1840 File E); W. N. Mussey to Burnell, Apr. 14, 1841 (File F); Goodrich to Burnell, June 5, 1837 (File C), and Goodrich to Hamilton Hill, Dec. 10, 1844 (File M).

Dr. The O. C. Institute in acct with J. H. Fairchild Cr.

1836		$	1836		$
June 10	To work at Mulberries 20 hours	1 60	June 20	By 1 Botany @ 12/	1 50
" 15	" work for Burnell	30	July 1	" Board 4 2/7 weeks @ 8/	4 29
	" Balance acct	3 99		" Incidental expenses	10
		5 89			5 89

July 1. due O. C. Institute 3 99

REPORT OF LABOR,

FOR THE WEEK ENDING July 1st 1837

	TIME.	KIND OF LABOR.	PRICE.	AMOUNT.
Monday, June			a .80	
Tuesday, 28th	1 3/4	O. Hoeing mulberry trees	a .80	.14
Wednesday, 29th	3	" "	a .80	.24
Thursday, 30th	3	" "	a "	.24
Friday,			a "	
Saturday, July 1st	2	Raising the boarding house	a "	.16
				[illegible]

Oberlin, July 3d 1837

P. R. Skinner Farmer — Joseph S. Edwards, Monitor.

BILLS FOR WORK DONE BY STUDENTS ON THE MULBERRIES
(Miscellaneous Archives)

amount of 328 pounds in the latter. The Ohio output decreased about 75 percent.[28]

A "cocoonery" was established in Oberlin on East College Street. In 1838 a certain Hezakiah Brooks rendered a bill "for feeding silk worms."[29] There is no evidence, however, of any silk ever having been produced in Oberlin.

Much had been expected of the manual labor system and in proportion to the expectations were the disappointments. At the request of the American Education Society it was officially announced on behalf of the Oberlin faculty that young men expecting to come to Oberlin should be disabused of the "impression that without any other resources than the daily labour of three hours, they can fully support themselves." All of the students did not work the required minimum period each day. Some, said an observer, were "left to the Fostering Liberality of their Friends and permitted to roam at Large in Indolence, and effeminacy." The General Agent reported officially that the "average of Students' Labour through the winter or from the first of Dec. [1835] to first Feby. [1836]–[was] 2¼ Hours per Day."[30]

The *Catalogue of* 1836 was the last to state that students were *required* to work three hours a day. The next to be published (in 1838) merely gives the information that: "At present no pledge can be given that the Institution will furnish labor to all the students: but hitherto nearly all have been able to obtain employment from either the Institute or colonists." Increasingly cautious statements appear in most of the later *Catalogues*. The rule on manual labor in the first printed *Laws and Regulations* (1840) required only two hours of labor per student daily, and included provisions for excusing students from even that amount, "for good and sufficient reasons."

At the opening of the fifth decade in the century there came a crisis in the history of manual labor at Oberlin. The trustees

[28] L. O. Howard, "The United States Department of Agriculture and Silk Culture," in the *Yearbook of the United States Department of Agriculture, 1903*, page 138, and *The Seventh Census of the United States: 1850* (Washington—1853), LXXXIII.

[29] Bill in Misc. Archives, Feb. 12, 1838, and Camp's *Oberlin Directory*, 1873-74, page 25.

[30] John Morgan in the *New York Evangelist*, Apr. 28, 1837; N. P. Fletcher, MS Critical Letters (1837), No. 8, and "The Agents Report, Feby. 9, 1836" (Misc. Archives).

voted at a meeting early in 1840 "that the Faculty be requested to co-operate with the Prudential Committee & Farmer, either by delivering frequent lectures to the students or otherwise for creating in the Institution a healthful public Sentiment in favor of not less than three hours daily manual labor; and so far as practicable see that no student fail of his appropriate Physical exercise, whether he makes that labor available at the highest price or not." The students seem to have been stirred up on the question, to a certain extent, at least, for one of their literary societies debated the question: "Does the interest of this Institution demand a law requiring students to labor?" A member of the Board of Trustees resigned, partially because "of the manifest failure to fulfill the so often made, and reiterated pledge to sustain the manual labor department of the Institution—allowing as a substitute, profitless and hurtful recreations."[31]

Due to the financial failure, the office of practical farmer was discontinued, the farm rented out, and the independent agricultural venture given up. A "Manual Labor Department" was organized in the school with Horace C. Taylor as Superintendent of Manual Labor. The trustees still regarded manual labor "in this Institution as an essential & indispensable part of its arrangement." In August of 1841 Taylor made his first report as head of the new department. Manual labor in Oberlin, however, was not to be revived at this time. In the following winter one student wrote to his father: " . . . Work is very scarce except choping. I can get but very little except choping cord wood which is most too hard work for me, and I can earn but little. I have to go about a half a mile to the woods and get three shillings per cord." A year later the faculty "Voted to omit calling for reports of Manual Labor until more labor can be provided for students."[32] Thus low had the system fallen.

Most of the farm was rented to Grandison Fairchild, who took charge of the boarding house at the same time. He also purchased or "borrowed" the larger part of the stock, tools and produce on hand. "The home farm," as it was called, which was rented to Fairchild, consisted of about 80 acres south of College

[31]T. M., Feb. 19, 1840; Dialectic Association, MS Minutes, Mar. 10, 24, 1841, and William Dawes, Letter of resignation, Aug. 20, 1840 (Misc. Archives).

[32]P. C. M., Mar. 10, 31, Apr. 28, and May 5, 1841; T. M., Aug. 21, 23, 1841; F. M., Apr. 19, 1843, and Warren Warner to parents, Oberlin, Dec. 24, 1841—Feb. 16, 1842 (O. C. Lib.).

and west of Professor streets. The rent was $100.00 per year, better certainly than the losses under Institute management. Other smaller tracts were rented out for smaller sums, the rents from the former "farm" amounting to over $200.00 altogether in 1842. Twelve acres west of the present Finney Chapel and Peters Hall were rented to President Mahan at a nominal rate. By sale of stock, equipment and rentals, etc., the debt on the farm had been reduced by over a thousand dollars before January, 1844. In 1846 or 1847 W. W. Wright succeeded Grandison Fairchild both in charge of the boarding hall and as tenant on the farm. Wright agreed to furnish labor to students in the Institute to the amount of at least $700.00 a year.[33]

For part of this period the lands were divided up among the students in small lots in a sort of a manorial system, the Institute taking the part of landlord and the students of villeins. The students were subject to the forfeiture of their holdings if they failed to take good care of the crops growing on them. The Institute reserved to itself "the privilege of purchasing any or all crops in the fall by paying for the same a fair market price in Oberlin." The General Agent reported in 1837 that, "The Tillable ground has been parcelled out & rented to students in quarter acre lots at the rate of six dollars per acre after the land was fitted for seeding." In the forties gardens on Tappan Square were rented to the students, male and female, Lots were let to agriculturally inclined youth—"such Students as may wish it for purposes of gardening"—as late as 1860.[34]

In the late forties there was a renewed effort to revive the system. A committee reporting in 1845 recognized that "the Manual Labour department [was] declining and falling into disrepute with the students," but insisted that all students, especially those indebted to the Institute, be required to work, and reaffirmed its belief that the manual labor system was essential to the success of the institution. The very next winter Professor Henry Cowles found it possible to write a glowing letter

[33]T. M., Aug. 21, 1841; P. C. M., Oct. 11, Dec. 20, 1841; Nov. 3, 1845; "Report of Prudential Committee, Supplementing their official action for the year, especially covering lands, buildings & repairs, etc. [1842]" (Misc. Archives); Ledger, No. 4 (1839–43), pages 42–43 (Treas. Off.), and "An account of Manual Labor furnished to Students by those who occupy the College lands & who hold leases from the College, etc., etc." (O. C. Lib.).

[34]"The Agents Report, Sept. 5, 1837" (Misc. Archives), and P. C. M., May 27, 1837; Feb. 28, 1842; Apr. 2, 1860, and T. M., Aug. 20, 1860.

to the *New York Tribune* describing the remarkable success of the system (?!), a letter which Greeley called "of more real worth to mankind than all the Presidents' and Governors' Messages, Kings' speeches and Diplomatic despatches of the last ten years." In June of 1847 a college literary society again debated the advantages of labor with study.[35] In August the trustees "Resolved, that the P. Come [Prudential Committee] be requested to take the most prompt & efficient possible measures to resusitate [*sic*] & carry forward the manual labor department & they are hereby authorized to make such appropriations & make such use of the Institutes land as may be deemed needful & proper to give the greatest usefulness to the department," and, "Resolved that the hearty cooperation of the Faculty & the Colonists be solicited to encourage & stimulate the Students to engage in systematic manual labor & to afford them all the possible facilities for procuring employment."[36]

In the spring of 1848 Richmond Hathaway was appointed "superintendent of the Manual Labor department" to manage agricultural activities on the portion of the lands not rented out, to "see to & superintend, . . . the repairs made about the Instn.," and "do all that can be done towards obtaining employ other than by the Instn for all the students that require labor." Two plows were donated by a friend to education. A yoke of oxen, horses, a cart and a wagon were purchased.[37] The college farm was revived. For the two following seasons Hathaway continued his administration. In the first year most of the work was expended in cultivating summer fallow, clearing land, re-laying rails and cutting wood. Thirty tons of hay were produced, however, and ten acres of corn planted, cultivated and harvested. In 1849, besides corn, there were fields of potatoes, beans, wheat and broom corn. The wheat crop was small because of a visitation of the rust. It was estimated that the male students earned about $3000.00 in manual labor in 1848; and in 1849, $2160.38 was reported paid out for labor by the Institute alone. Hathaway's report is enthusiastic and optimistic, but there was a "big nigger in the woodpile." He wrote: " . . . Although there

[35]"Manual Labor Report adopted Aug. 1845" (Misc. Archives); *Oberlin Evangelist,* Mar. 4, 1846, and Young Men's Lyceum, MS Minutes, June 8, 1847.
[36]T. M., Aug. 27, 1847.
[37]P. C. M., Mar. 27, Apr. 27, and May 8, 1848.

are some pecuniary disadvantages that attend in the employment of Students these can never counter-balance the moral, intellectual and physical advantages that he derives from manual labor. [¶] There is no other system of education that is so perfectly adapted to his nature, it develops in beautiful harmony all his powers, and is well pleasing in the sight of God, as it tends in an eminent degree to preserve the student in his fear. The Manual L. Dept. should therefore receive the prayers, the warmest sympathy, the fostering care, and the hearty cooperation of the Board of Trustees." Unfortunately, Oberlin was not in a position to bear the burden of those *"pecuniary disadvantages."* In the autumn of 1849 farming was again abandoned to independent farmers.[38]

In the fifties the College began to lease its lands for ninety-nine years, "renewable forever," on condition that lessees would furnish labor to college students. A grant in fee simple could not be made because of restrictions in the original deed to the Institute, but the permanent lease amounted to much the same thing. In 1853 W. W. Wright bought the largest tract of land, previously rented by him, for a little over $2,000.00 and agreed "Yearly, . . . to employ Students of said College, in some department of Manual Labor, (when applied for,) and pay them for their labor the current market price, to an amount each year of at least Two Dollars for each Acre of Land hereby demised." The Board of Trustees, on its part, agreed to use the funds received for the "sustaining of said Literary Manual Labor Institution."[39] By 1866 all of the college farming lands had been thus leased.[40]

Student self-support by manual labor did not come to a sudden end but declined more or less steadily. Even after the College gave up an institutional farm the young men often engaged in agricultural labor. In 1855 a student wrote to his sister: "O I forgot to tell you that I am to work for my board now. I have a cow to milk, a horse to curry and feed, two pigs to feed, and one

[38]"Manual Labor Department of the O. C. Institute, Statistics & Remarks"—1848, and "Manual labor Report—1849," (Misc. Archives); Ledger No. 6, 1847–50 (Treas. Off.); P. C. M., Sept. 4, Oct. 2, 1849, and T. M., Aug. 23, 1849. The abandonment is implied in these citations.

[39]Deed lent by the late Mrs. A. A. Wright, Oberlin, Ohio. Even as it was, the heirs of Street & Hughes tried to recover the title.—R. B. W. Hughes to T. B. Hudson, Sept. 21, 1852, and Jan. 24, 1853 (Treas. Off., File N).

[40]*Lorain County News,* June 13, 1866.

of the prettiest little dogs to take care of that you ever did see."[41]

Nor did the authorities cease to give lip-service to the manual labor idea. The official endowment appeal, issued in 1851, placed first among Oberlin's claims to public support the system of manual labor. A few months later in a reply to a letter criticizing manual labor schools published in the *New York Tribune,* Professor Cowles declared: "Oberlin has never thought of giving up manual labor. She has no temptation or occasion to do so. On the contrary, her Trustees and Faculty are monthly making new arrangements to provide labor for the students, and have in their experience a growing testimony in favor of the manifold utility of the system." A faculty report published three years later declared that, "Full as much manual labor is performed absolutely, yet, less relatively, than in the early years of the College. It still appears that more than half of those who have the ministry in view, depend solely on themselves for their means of education."[42]

Doubtless the official spokesmen of the college could not see, as we can, how steadily and surely the system was declining. The sale of the college farm lands made this outcome inevitable! In 1859 one student wrote to his parents: "I have not found any work to do steadily. I doubt whether I shall. Mr. Cowles says he does not know of any regular work. He will supply me with some now and then. I am going to do some for him this afternoon."[43] From 1856 through the sixties the College *Catalogue* announced modestly: "The Institution does not pledge itself to furnish labor for the students; but arrangements have been made with those who have the land of the College, to furnish employment, to a certain extent. The College also gives employment to a few around the buildings. Diligent and faithful young men can usually obtain sufficient employment from the inhabitants of the village. . . . Many, by daily labor, have been able to pay their board."

Labor furnished by private persons could not be depended upon to a certainty. The employment "around the buildings" naturally became the chief reliance of laboring students in the

[41]George W. Smith to Julia Smith, Aug. 19, 1855 (Smith MSS).

[42]*Oberlin Evangelist,* Dec. 3, 1851; May 26, 1852, and Aug. 15, 1855.

[43]Henry Prudden to parents, June 3, 1859 (lent by Miss Lillian Prudden, New Haven, Conn.).

Oberlin College Dr.

11 mo. 1855.	To Opening, warming and Sweeping church for Thursday lecture during fall term 1855.	6	87½

James R Raley.

Oberlin Coll. May 22d 1858

Mr. Hill Treas. O.C.

Dr. for fixing side-walks $0, 50.

" for sweeping music Hall, building fires &c. $6, 50.

" for seeing to the rooms Spring Term $6, 00

13. —

E. H. Baker.

Treasurer Hill,

Will you please pay Charles Dean twenty-five cents for blacking the stove in the front Reception Room at the Ladies Hall

Mrs. R. Rayl

Oberlin

LATER MANUAL LABOR BILLS
(Miscellaneous Archives)

Oberlin Apr. 22nd 1861.
Oberlin College Dr. to L. C. Warner for sawing five cords of wood at Tappan Hall [illegible] 3.75

[illegible]

Aug 30 1861
Oberlin College Dr. to L. C. Warner for mopping and cleaning $1.75

E. H. Fairchild,

Received L. C. Warner

Mr. Kinney;
Please pay to Miss Mathews, for Miss Worcester, $2.50 for carrying the Hall mail a part of the Spring Term.

M. E. Martin

May 21/67

LATER MANUAL LABOR BILLS
(Miscellaneous Archives)

later years. Labor bills of 1855 include such items as: "sweeping music hall," "fixing sidewalk," "piling up the wood at the Chapel," "cleaning up the yard," and "warming and sweeping church for Thursday lecture." A few years later a student received "twenty-five cents for blacking the stove in the front Reception Room of the Ladies Hall." Lucien Warner earned $1.75 "mopping and cleaning" in 1861. William Harris earned one dollar "blowing [the organ] for commencement exercises 2 days" in the same year. There was almost an endless quantity of wood to saw, for which the college paid 6 shillings a cord after 1864.[44] In 1866 O. G. Morgan earned money lighting lamps, sweeping Tappan Hall and cleaning stove pipes and chimneys. Another student made four dollars in the same year "taking up & putting down carpets in Ladies Hall." No large-scale manual labor system could, of course, depend on such odd jobs, nor were there any great educational values in such labor. The editor of the *Lorain County News* interpreted correctly the significance of the sale of the last of the college farm lands when he wrote in June of 1866: "The College has disposed of its last farm property, and *Finis* is written on the lingering relics of the manual labor school that occupied such a goodly place in Father Shipherd's scheme."[45]

The manual labor system was financially almost fatal to the Oberlin Institute and College. The loss from the mulberries was a heavy burden assumed at a crucial moment in Oberlin's financial history. Most of the labor performed by the young men was largely unproductive; clearing the forest in the early years and sweeping the halls in the later. From the point of view of the students the system was, financially at least, more nearly successful, though the earliest expectations were never realized. In the thirties and forties manual labor was undoubtedly the chief means of support of a majority of students.[46] Sixty-two bills of young men students in 1836, taken at random, averaged $7.37 due to the Institute, as against $4.21 earned by manual labor. In eleven of these accounts the wages for manual labor actually exceeded expenses. This, of course, does not take into account money earned by school teaching during the winter vacation, a

44P. C. M. Sept. 17, 1864.

45*Lorain County News,* June 13, 1866.

46"Schedule of those Students in the Oberlin Collegiate Institute who have either entirely or chiefly sustained themselves in their education," 1836 (Misc. Archives), and labor reports.

source of earnings probably almost as important as manual labor. Sixty-nine bills of young lady students taken at random in the same year show an average expense of $5.12 as against $3.15 earned by manual labor. As late as 1851 it was officially declared that "four fifths of all the students who have graduated at Oberlin the last twelve years have mainly supported themselves during their entire course of study."[47] But, as time went on, it became more and more necessary to have other means of support.

The effect on the main end of education and on the students' lives in general we have no means of measuring. The modern critic would be likely to conclude that such labor was not generally conducive to the best results in scholarship. One of the earliest students, writing some years later, corroborated this estimate. In a letter to Professor Fairchild, Amzi D. Barber wrote: "I labored during my entire course of study both from principle & choice. I do the same now. I supported myself by the blessing of God & so far I may be regarded as successful, but as it respects the acquiring of a good sound education I regard myself as having been very *unsuccessful*."[48]

It is clear enough, however, that many poor young men and women attended Oberlin who could never have afforded an advanced education without the labor system. In view of this fact and the apparently generally good effect on student health and morale it seems unfair and untrue to call the manual labor system, without reservation, a failure. With better management, under the early frontier conditions, the system might have been really successful.

[47]*Oberlin Evangelist*, Dec. 3, 1851.
[48]A. D. Barber to Prof. Fairchild, Oct. 4, 1847 (Treas. Off., File K).

CHAPTER XLI

IN LOCO PARENTIS

THE Board of Trustees was the corporate body legally responsible for the Institute and College. As originally constituted it included among its members the founders and their associates: Shipherd, Stewart, Redington (the Amherst postmaster), Burrell (Shipherd's pupil), Pease (the first settler), prominent local citizens like Judge Henry Brown, and Addison Tracy of Elyria (a convert of Shipherd's revival of 1831); and nearby ministers of the Gospel—Joel Talcott of Wellington (Yale—1824) and John Keys of Dover. Within the year after the granting of the charter these were joined by the Rev. John Keep (Yale—1802) of Ohio City, Nathan P. Fletcher, an Oberlin colonist, and Judge Frederick Hamlin, postmaster at Wellington. The bickerings and financial difficulties of the first years did not make for long terms of service, and by 1840 only three of the charter members remained: Shipherd, Pease and Burrell. After Shipherd's death in 1844 only Pease was left. Peter Pindar Pease, a comparatively uneducated and exceedingly "modest and diffident" farmer, continued officially on the board until 1861. Father Keep, who missed being a charter member by a few months only, was long the dean of trustees, winning his paternal title by thirty-six years of intelligent and conscientious service. The Oberlin trustees were all pious but of varying ability. Probably Owen Brown, the stuttering tanner of Hudson, father of John of Ossawatomie, who served as trustee from 1835 to 1844, was not much more of an intellectual or a business executive than Peter Pindar Pease. Dr. Isaac Jennings, the reform physician, and an active member for many years, was a man of some education and experience. Amasa Walker's term was only three years; he was a man of broad interests, probably the most scholarly of them all, America's outstanding economist. Dr. Norton S. Townshend of Elyria, primarily a veterinarian, was a trustee from 1845 to 1857. An able and well-educated scientist and abolition politician, he was chiefly interested in agricultural education.[1]

Francis D. Parish, a Sandusky lawyer, gave long and valuable service; he was a trustee from 1839 to 1878. Parish was a New York Yankee who had studied two years at Hamilton College before beginning his legal career at Sandusky in 1822. Being also an active church worker and a reformer, he was naturally drawn to Oberlin. In 1834 he had joined with two others to ask the American Home Missionary Society to send a pastor to his frontier community. In 1843 he became the first president of the Oberlin-sponsored Western Evangelical Missionary Association, and was, for a while, vice-president of the American Missionary Association. He was a notorious agent of the underground railroad and in 1845 was arrested for protecting two fugitives from arrest. The three trials that followed lasted until 1849, when he was subjected to a fine of $500.00 for his infraction of the old Fugitive Slave Law of 1793. He was a leader in Ohio in the early days of the Free Soil Movement.[2]

Samuel D. Porter of Rochester (trustee, 1844–1876), a devoted friend of the "oppressed," was one of Finney's early converts. Willard Sears, of Boston, served on the board from 1845 to 1862. He was another Finney man. John M. Sterling (Yale—1820), the Cleveland lawyer and leader in all reforms at whose office Weld had held his anti-slavery seminar, was a trustee in the forties. William Dawes of Hudson, Ohio (1839–1851), was a loyal fiscal agent and a pious promoter of the founder's ideals. Of course, Mahan was an *ex-officio* member during his presidency. Finney was elected in 1846 and continued ex-officio after succeeding to the presidency in 1851. The Rev. James Barr Walker had been editor of religious papers published at Cincinnati and Chicago and during his trusteeship (1851–1863) was preaching at Mansfield and Sandusky. He was an active anti-slavery man (a convert of Theodore Weld), and a believer in Oberlin "Sanctification."

[1] *Cf.* pages 356–360 and 388 on Townshend, and on Pease "Testimony of A. Mahan at G—— divorce trial in 1850" (Church MSS).

[2] Rush R. Sloane, "The Underground Railroad of the Firelands," *Firelands Pioneer,* n.s., vol. V, 28–59 (July, 1888); H. L. Peeke, *A Standard History of Erie County, Ohio* (Chicago—1916), I, 427–8; Hamilton College, *Complete Alumni Register* (Clinton—[1922]), 25; W. S. Siebert, *Underground Rail-Road,* 277; F. D. Parish to A. Peters, Sept. 22, 1834 (A.H.M.S. MSS); *Oberlin Evangelist,* July 5, 1843, and Leo Alilunas, "Fugitive Slave Cases in Ohio Prior to 1850," *Ohio Archaeological and Historical Quarterly,* XLIX, 182–184 (Apr.–June, 1940).

FRANCIS D. PARISH, TRUSTEE
(From a painting in the Secretary's Office)

He founded a colony and school in Michigan on the Oberlin plan and called it Benzonia.[3] The Rev. Henry Cowles (formerly of the teaching staff and editor of the *Evangelist* for many years), Rev. James Thome (a Lane Rebel and leading preacher in Cleveland), and Rev. Michael Strieby, Secretary of the American Missionary Association after 1864 (a member from 1845 to 1899), were other ministerial trustees. The trustees were lawyers, physicians, ministers—notably not merchants or bankers. None of the chief benefactors—the Tappans, Gerrit Smith, W. C. Chapin of Providence, Aristarchus Champion or George Avery of Rochester, etc.—except Willard Sears were among their number.[4]

The Board dealt largely with matters of grand strategy: educational policy, the appointment of teachers, the erection of buildings and financial matters generally, the latter being usually exceedingly urgent. As the Board usually met only once or twice a year it was necessary to appoint a group of local residents to deal with finance in the intervals between such meetings.[5] The first Prudential Committee was chosen in October of 1834: Shipherd, Stewart, Pease, and two others. The committee was not expected to dispose of property or determine important policies but only to transact "such business as becomes ordinarily requisite to carry on the daily operations of the Institution."[6] Its minutes are filled with resolutions providing for the purchase of cows, tools, and equipment in general, orders for the repairing of buildings and construction of sidewalks, decisions on the rates of payment of student teachers, prices of room and board and the like.

To the faculty under the chairmanship of the President was left the internal administration of the College. The first By-Laws provide that: "The executive authority shall be vested in the Faculty. Consisting of the President, Professor, Tutors & General Agents. It shall be their duty as far as practicable to advance the Students in their several departments of moral, mental & physical education, and faithfully execute the laws established by the Trustees." They were required to: "hold stated meet-

[3]See the sketch in the *D. A. B.*

[4]Alexander Seymour, a Finney convert from Utica, a banker in Cleveland, was a trustee for a year.—Citations in the *Annals of Cleveland*.

[5]The trustees met oftener in the earlier years.

[6]T. M., Oct. 30, 1834, and Aug. 26, 1852.

ings once in two weeks to promote the general interest of the Institute," "keep a legible & accurate record of their proceedings," "register in a permanent book the names, ages, and residences of all the Students with the address of their parents or guardians and of their benefactors, with their subscriptions & payments, the time of their entering & leaving the Institute, their attainments in knowledge at the time of entering, their conduct & progress in the different departments, and whatever may present a fair view of their present & prospective characters, and annually report so much of the same as they shall deem expedient to the Benefactors whose scholarship they may enjoy," and "report the state of the Institute to the trustees at their annual meeting." Unfortunately for history the personal record was never kept in the detailed form provided.

Discipline was exclusively under the control of the faculty. "The Faculty," read the 1834 By-Laws, "may make & enforce such rules as they may judge expedient, provided they do not infringe upon the laws and general principles of the Institute." The Prudential Committee, it was provided, might sit with the faculty "in such cases of discipline . . . in which the Faculty shall need counsel," upon the invitation of the latter body.[7] To make sure that the faculty should always be independent in this sphere, Professor Finney required as a condition of his coming to Oberlin that the trustees promise never to interfere in the "internal control" of the institution. This promise was made in a resolution of February 10, 1835.[8]

The first By-Laws, so-called, included a few disciplinary rules. In the chapter headed "Deportment of Students" are the following regulations: "1st. It [their deportment] is to be that of Gentlemen & Ladies according to the known rules of propriety & virtue. 2d. All vulgar & profain words, writings, & actions with all gambling or playing at games of chance, use of intoxicating Liquor for drink, riot quarrelling or insubordinations and contempts of Institutional Authorities are expressly forbidden. 3d. No Students shall use fire arms, or burn Gun Powder in any way without permission from the president or Principal of his department."

[7]T. M., Oct. 30, 1834.

[8]*Cf.* above, Chapter XIV, and Maynard M. Metcalf, "Oberlin as a Model of College Administration," *School and Society* (Apr. 29, 1916), III, 635–638.

These prohibitions were undoubtedly copied from the codes of Eastern colleges. They may be duplicated in the laws of English colleges at Cambridge and Oxford and of Harvard and Yale in the colonial period. Students were also prohibited from doing anything "on the Sabbath or the evening preceding the Sabbath which may be inconsistent with their own religious duties or the religious privileges of others." Students must not create disturbances in the dormitories and the "Ladies" must "not receive at their rooms the visits of *Gentlemen*." The faculty was fully empowered to "dismiss any students, who, after fair trial, in Scholarship, moral, or manual labor shall appear too delinquent for continuance, or whose deportment in other respects may render him unworthy of the privileges in the Institute."

These laws of 1834 seem never to have been published and were intended by the trustees merely for the guidance of the faculty. The original idea was that the students would be expected to follow the common rules of decent etiquette and morality and obey the dictates of Christian charity. Delinquencies would be dealt with when they arose according to the particular exigencies. As late as 1837 the faculty definitely voted against the preparation of any formal code of student laws. Not until 1840 was the first set of *Laws and Regulations* approved and printed.[9] It contained thirty-eight paragraphs of rules, but the introduction addressed to "Dear Pupils" and signed by President Mahan emphasized the fact that it is not "a complete code," that "oral rules" might be added from time to time and, in addition, "the ordinary laws of Christian morality" were "to be considered as binding on every pupil." The "Dear Pupils" were further reminded that the "regulations are made for the good of the students themselves" and that, "Every student should feel that the law is his helper and support, that its spirit is the spirit of benevolence, and its mandate the voice of love."

The great majority of the rules dealt with the payment of bills, absence from classes and prayers, the library, student preaching and teaching, rooms and board, manual labor, literary societies and the procedure of discipline. Students were supposed to be allowed only two weeks grace at the beginning of the term to settle with the Treasurer. Absences from literary or religious

[9]F. M., Mar. 15, 1837, and *Laws and Regulations of the Oberlin Collegiate Institute* (Oberlin: Printed by James Steele—1840).

exercises must be excused by some member of the faculty, and previous permission must be secured for leaving town. Library hours and fines for books over-due and payments for books damaged were provided. There were only a few rules dealing with matters of deportment in the restricted sense. The traditional prohibition against using firearms or burning gunpowder reappeared. The drinking of intoxicating beverages and the use of tobacco in any way continued, of course, to be listed among the taboos. The rule against gambling and "games of chance" was made more specific, the latter being explicitly defined as "cards, checkers, chess, or any other game of chance or skill." It was definitely ordered that, "No student shall travel on the Sabbath." (The trustees had formally resolved at a meeting in July of 1836 that "journeying on the Sabbath" was "an infraction of the Moral Law."[10]) Also, students must not visit those of the other sex in their rooms, and the marriage of a student would automatically lead to his dismissal.

Revised codes were issued every few years, but not many important changes were made in them. Provisions with regard to the hours of "athletic exercises and sport" were added in 1847. In the same revision there appeared for the first time the "peculiar" Oberlin rule against secret societies. "No student," it runs, "is permitted to join any secret society, or military company." In Civil War days the "or military company" was naturally dropped. The rules for manual labor were omitted after 1842. In 1853 and thereafter students were "prohibited from unnecessarily frequenting groceries, taverns, and similar places of public resort." In 1859 this was extended to include the railroad stations. In 1867 the adjective "sedentary" was introduced to describe the "games of chance" prohibited to Oberlin students, thus somewhat liberalizing the literal meaning of this regulation.[11]

Of course, Oberlin's peculiar and chief disciplinary problem grew out of the experiment in the "joint education of the sexes." The basic Oberlin rule was that which prohibited students from

[10]T. M., July 6, 1836. The faculty later "voted that no student shall be received as a member of this Institution who is known to have travelled on the Sabbath day on his way hither." F. M., Aug. 3, 1836.

[11]A number of editions of the *Laws and Regulations* are not now available. The statements with regard to the time of first inclusions of rules, etc. might be changed somewhat if these editions could be consulted.

visiting those of the opposite sex in their rooms. It appeared, as we have seen, in the "By-Laws of 1834" and in more elaborate detail in the printed laws of 1840 and later. On March 4, 1836, the faculty resolved to "recommend to the Board of Trustees to pass a law prohibiting students from forming the marriage connection while members of the Institution." Five days later the trustees ratified this action (though just why it needed their ratification is not clear) and it has remained a rule of Oberlin Institute and College ever since.[12] "Any student entering into the marriage relation," read the first printed rules, "shall be considered as permanently debarring himself from the privileges of the Institution."

At least as early as 1852 it was found desirable to issue a separate set of regulations for the young ladies. In the general laws for all departments issued in the following year "Young men are required, in all their associations with ladies of the Institution to respect the regulations of the Female Department, and are not allowed to protract a call so as to interfere with study hours." The rules for ladies repeat some of the rules and all of the preface of the general laws and regulations. The rules against traveling on the Sabbath and against visiting or receiving visits of those of the opposite sex in private rooms are among the repetitions. Young ladies were required to study from eight until twelve in the morning, from two until five (four in the fall term) in the afternoon and after seven-thirty in the evening (eight in the fall term). They were required to remain in their rooms after the beginning of the evening study hours, except when attending literary societies, choir practice or evening religious services. All must retire at ten o'clock. A formidable list of prohibitions were laid upon these early "coeds." Their walking was especially restricted: They were not allowed to walk in the streets for recreation on the Sabbath. They were not allowed "to walk for recreation with gentlemen" on any day of the week except by special permission. Those who did not live with their parents could not even "walk in the fields or woods without special permission from the Principal." They must have special permission to go to the railroad station. None could ride horseback at any time. Finally, to make doubly sure that they never

[12]F.M., Mar. 4, 1836; Recommendation to Trustees, Mar. 9, 1836 (Misc. Archives), and T. M., Mar. 9, 1836.

had an hour of unsupervised freedom, it was provided that no young lady shall "leave her boarding place for any *length of time,* excepting for her regular exercises in the Institution, without previous consultation with the matron of the family." After 1865 "Gentlemen and ladies" were not supposed "to accompany each other to or from religious meetings."[13] This last regulation survived into the twentieth century.

Disciplinary cases were tried before the faculty in full session, or (in most cases when young ladies solely were involved) before the Ladies' Board, a body made up of the Lady Principal and several wives of professors. All students were held to be on probation for the first six months of their connection with the school and might be dismissed summarily at any time during that period if any undesirable traits of character appeared. At the end of this term the faculty voted those who had sustained a good character and made satisfactory progress in their studies into the full status of students in the institution. The names of those thus formally received were read at evening prayers.[14] This practice was helpful in keeping down the percentage of dismissals, for technically those dropped during probation never had been members of the institution. The control of the faculty over the conduct of students did not stop at the termination of probation, but the procedure of trial and dismissal became somewhat more elaborate.

Members of the teaching staff, special monitors or students were supposed to report breaches of the rules. The accused would be brought personally before the faculty and grilled. Other students were required to testify at such a hearing and were liable to expulsion themselves if they refused. Often a committee would be appointed to investigate a particular charge, "labor with" the accused, and report to a later meeting. If found guilty, the culprit might be only privately admonished, *privately* dismissed or expelled or, in the worst cases, *publicly* dismissed or expelled. Public dismissal meant that the decision of the faculty was announced at prayers before the full student body.[15]

It was truly hard, however, for the Christian faculty to wash their hands of these souls, and even after a student was dismissed

[13] *Laws and Regulations of the Female Department,* 1852, 1859, 1865.
[14] F. M., Mar. 16, 1843, and July 30, 1846.
[15] *Laws and Regulations,* 1840.

some of them usually went again to "labor with" him to make a confession and, perhaps, thereafter be received again into the school. In 1841 three students were tried for having "held a mock [revival] meeting in the woods" where one of them "acted the part of an exhorter." They were found guilty and it was ordered that two of them be "sent away, and that the reason be stated publicly." All were readmitted, the prime disturber "on the profession of repentance before God, having publicly confessed his sin."[16]

Confession would usually lead to reinstatement though sometimes only to a mitigation of punishment. "If he makes full confession," the professors provided in one case, "he is to be privately dismissed, otherwise publicly." In another case it was determined that a guilty student should "make a public confession dictated by the Faculty & receive a public admonition, and at the same time be advised privately to leave the Institution, if he refuses to make this confession, that he be publicly expelled."[17] The confession drawn up by Professor Henry Cowles and signed by the student in this case is still preserved, as are a number of others.

The scene in chapel on the occasion of such a public confession must have been impressive and singularly reminiscent of old Puritan New England. The students and faculty members being assembled, there was a strained silence and every eye was turned toward the culprit who walked slowly with bowed head to the front of the room and, in a faltering voice, read his statement:

"I, W—— W————, do hereby confess before the Faculty & students of this Institution that I have rashly transgressed one of its most sacred laws by entering the apartment of a young lady not only without permission but after permission had been twice refused me. Though my conduct in this matter may admit of a slight extenuation in the fact that the young lady was confined by sickness, yet it has no apology; & I do now confess that the act was precipitate, unjustifiable, & adapted to break down the wholesome & needful regulations of the Institute, & bring disgrace upon its character before the public. For this offence I ask forgiveness of my fellow students, of the Faculty, & of my God; I solemnly promise hereafter to yield implicit obedience to the

[16] F. M., June 1, 2; July 15, 1841.
[17] F. M., Dec. 14, 1835, and Feb. 26, 1836.

laws of the institution & study in all things to promote its honor & welfare."[18]

We are unfortunately left in the dark as to the nature of the admonition but it certainly was pious and, must have been, under the circumstances, terrible—something like John Wilson's excommunication of Anne Hutchinson two hundred years before. Despite the implication of the last sentence this young man was not readmitted.

Dismissal, especially under such circumstances, was a bitter thing for the students and their parents to swallow. A dismissed student, who seems not to have profited much more intellectually than morally by his attendance, agonized as follows in a letter to the treasurer in 1849: "O, I would give this World . . . if I had never met with Such Misfortune . . . I want you Gents in the Name of God to reseve me back and Try me, and See if I dont Due right." "I have basely neglected the high privileges you have extended to me," wrote another. "With fools I have prostituted myself at the shrine of vanity. I have madly squandered immortal treasure . . . I wish to come back like the prodigal. I will be a servant. I will live for the good of the whole world. I will improve the benefits you afford me. As I love the course of truth I will love the interest of this *Inst.* I do not wish to have you decide that I am worthy to be received. . . . I am *unworthy*. Let me have the crumbs that fall from your table. I do not know of another *Inst.* so well adopted to my circumstances. . . . I ask to be restored to the privileges I have *again & again* forfeited."[19]

Parents were variously affected. Some were merely disappointed in their children; some were irate. "Your very kind letter was duly received, communicating very painfull intelligence of the conduct of my Son," wrote one father in 1848. "I am under many obligations for the kind and frank manner you have manifested for my Sons and his parents interest. Permit me dear Sir to apologize for his rudeness. I am sure when he reflects [upon] his position [he] will regret his conduct, as much as I can do, and I assure you I have had many troubles and disappointments in my life, this one is more severe than any that has happened to

[18]Original in the Oberlin College Library.

[19]Letters dated June 14, 1849 (Treas. Off., File O), and Mar. 15, 1836 (Oberlin College Library).

me or my family." A less well educated parent was equally depressed under similar circumstances: "Dear Brother in Christ," he wrote to Secretary Burnell. "I must tell you that I right this line with great pain in hart [to] think that Nathanil conducts himself so that he have to leve the school." Some, it was to be expected, took the part of their children. A mother objected to the expulsion of her son because it was her impression "that it was the invariable practice of all Colleges to reprimand twice—and the third time for the same offence *expel*." A father expressed himself as "Much disappointed in the course of the faculty." They "injured me in a most injust manner," he declared, "in the expulsion of my Son without cause . . . & that without giving me the least intimation of what [they] was about to do."[20]

Besides being dismissed from college, students guilty of gross misconduct might, if, as was often the case, they were members of the church, be tried before their fellow members and excommunicated. Delazon Smith, who led the atheist group of students in the late thirties, was never formally expelled but his excommunication from the church amounted to the same thing. A college freshman was called before the church to answer charges of "irregularities as a student, leaving town without permission etc. . . . intercourse with females of questionable reputation . . . night carousals & improper company." In the very same month a church committee found two preparatory students guilty of an immoral relationship.[21]

Outside of those arising from the close relation of students of the two sexes disciplinary cases were generally of a decidedly petty nature from the point of view of the twentieth century. They were petty also as compared to the misdemeanors dealt with in contemporary colleges like the University of Georgia, where students stabbed each other, staged wholesale riots and assaulted members of the faculty.[22] Perhaps the presence of students of the gentler sex accounted for this also. Punishments were meted out, however, for petty thefts, for lying, for breaking the Sabbath, for profane swearing and blasphemy, for card-playing, for fighting, for indulgence in tobacco, for absences from exercises, and for visits out of town without permission.

[20]Letters dated Oct. 21, 1848 (Treas. Off., File O), Feb. 19, 1840 (File F), Feb. 4, 1842 (Cowles-Little MSS), and May 19, 1841 (Treas. Off., File F).

[21]MS Church Minutes, Feb. 24, Mar. 3, 1837; July 1, 18, 1845.

[22]E. M. Coulter, *College Life in the Old South*, 77–115.

One of the earliest cases was that of a young lady student charged with petty pilfering. Others were found guilty of "stealing from fellow students," "deliberate lying in numerous instances," and "stealing sundry articles from citizens and students." In 1861 a young woman from Cincinnati was "charged with theft, falsehood, & general unwillingness to submit to the authority of the Principal." She confessed and was allowed to remain, on condition that she restore the stolen articles and "make an acknowledgment of her guilt before the ladies of the Boarding Hall." Two years later "a colored girl from Indiana" was "found guilty of *lying & forgery*," and summarily dismissed.[23]

Blasphemy, breaking the Sabbath and general impiety were not likely to be tolerated in pious Oberlin. One young man was expelled for "irreverent & blasphemous expressions with regard to the deity & for gross insolence of [to] the Faculty." Another was publicly dismissed on being convicted "of profanity, mockery of religion, blasphemy, prevarication, neglect of study & concealing those guilty of other crimes." A young fellow who came from Elyria to Oberlin on the Sabbath because he had no money to pay for his keep in the former town was "admonished and required to make a public confession."[24] Antoinette Brown believed that some who were expelled for other reasons nominally, were thus harshly dealt with in reality because they were not Christians.[25]

Though the rules required students to abstain from the use of tobacco the faculty was evidently not prepared to punish those who occasionally indulged. They did, however, appoint a committee "to inquire into the facts relative to the use of tobacco in the institution," on another occasion requested President Mahan "to make a communication to the students on the use of Tobacco," and, again, ordered the monitors in Tappan Hall and other dormitories to "take cognizance of any use of tobacco which comes within their knowledge." When students were reported to be in the habit of using tobacco, faculty committees

[23]F. M., May 13, 14, 1835; Nov. 1, 1836; Oct. 17, 1838; Mar. 7, 1842; H——— K———'s confession (O. C. Lib.), and L. B. M., Oct. 8, 9, 1851, and Oct. 4, 1853.

[24]F. M., Jan. 24, Feb. 21, 22, and July 7, 1837.

[25]Antoinette L. Brown Blackwell's reminiscences noted down by Alice Stone Blackwell on Aug. 19, 1903.

were appointed to "converse with" them.[26] No records survive of any instance when the use of the "filthy weed" was the sole cause of discipline. Probably the pressure of public opinion was ordinarily sufficient to enforce the prohibition against it.

There were a few instances of physical encounters being punished—evidently in no case anything particularly desperate. In 1835 two roommates "had a contention between themselves which was proved to have been a most unchristian affair." In the mid-forties two young men were admonished publicly "for engaging in angry contention and blows."[27]

The want of faculty minutes for the period from 1846 to 1866 renders our picture of discipline necessarily incomplete. Certainly many other kinds of misdemeanors must have been dealt with. There are isolated instances in the existing records. One student was expelled for setting fire to the outbuildings. Another was dismissed for "having in his possession a Pack of *Gamesters Cards*." It was rumored that a young lady was dropped "in consequence of her wearing Corsets."[28]

Absences from classes and other exercises and unauthorized journeys out of town required some attention. On one occasion a special committee was appointed to "labor with" a student "for absenting himself from recitation." Similar cases among the young ladies were usually dealt with by the Ladies' Board. One young lady was threatened with suspension because she had "taken a trip to Toledo with a bridal party" without permission. Two others were, on another occasion, reprimanded for "protracting their vacation two or three days after the close of the regular vacation." In 1840 seven young men who attended a circus in Elyria without permission were summarily dismissed, despite the fact that some of them had permission to go out of town.[29]

Since the Middle Ages students in many institutions were required to put their money in the hands of tutors. The Oberlin faculty recommended that parents and guardians of minor

[26]F. M., Feb. 28, 1844; Feb. 12, Mar. 26, Apr. 3, 17, 1845.

[27]"Records of the proceedings of the Faculty of Oberlin Inst. December, 1835" (O. C. Lib.), and F. M., May 1, 1844.

[28]F. M., Oct. 4, 1839; Sophia T. Matson to the Faculty, Feb. 4, 1842 (Cowles-Little MSS), and N. P. Fletcher to Levi Burnell, Oct. 20, 1840 (Treas. Off., File C).

[29]F. M., July 23, 30, Aug. 6, 1840; Apr. 16, 1846, and L. B. M., July 16, 1852; Mar. 4, 11, 1854.

students at Oberlin "secure the services of someone of the teachers in the Institution," to whom their funds might be committed. The necessity of drafting "a rule respecting trafficking with and by such students as are minors" was discussed.[30] Some parents were glad to have the teaching or administrative staff check up on their children's finances. "I wish my son to be very prudent & careful in making bills," wrote one father to the principal of the Prep Department. "I intend to pay all charges against me, if they be any way reasonable." "What is William doing now?" another anxious parent inquired of the Secretary of the Institute. "He never writes me excepting he wants money and he is then very brief. . . . Will you please say (in confidence) what his general course has been for the last year—and what his standing is as a scholar & a Christian? Also in what state that debt for the Buggy & Horses is, and whether you know him to be much in debt."[31] Of course, this paternal supervision was probably necessary in the case of many younger preparatory students.

The responsible head of the Female Department was the Lady Principal, and upon her devolved some of the most difficult problems of administration and discipline. The first woman to assume these duties was Mrs. Eliza C. Stewart, the wife of P. P. Stewart. She was not only matron of the boarding hall and in charge of domestic labor, but also did the work of a principal of the Female Department, though she never had the title. She served over a year from the spring of 1834 to the late summer of 1835. Then she was succeeded by Mrs. Marianne Parker Dascomb, wife of Professor James Dascomb. Mrs. Dascomb had studied under Zilpah Grant and Mary Lyon at Ipswich Female Seminary, Ipswich, Massachusetts, and was, in the opinion of her charges, "well fitted in heart, mind and manners for the responsible station." She also served about a year, retiring to give way to Alice Welch Cowles in the following summer.[32]

Mrs. Cowles was the wife of Professor Henry Cowles and a woman of more than ordinary attainment and piety. She was a

[30]F. M., Mar. 27, 1844, and Feb. 26, 1846.

[31]Richard Valentine & W. W. Wright, July 10, 1845, and J. P. Williston to H. Hill, Nov. 6, 1847 (Treas. Off., File Q).

[32]Mary Ann Adams *et al.* to John Keep and William Dawes, July 10, 1839 (Keep MSS); P. C. M., Sept. 1, 1835; T. M., July 6, 1836, and Levi Burnell to Mrs. Cowles, July 7, 1836 (Cowles MSS).

close friend and relative of Zilpah Grant with whom, and Mary Lyon, she studied in Joseph Emerson's school at Byfield. Mrs. Cowles was an enthusiastic moral reformer, an active leader in that movement. She resigned in 1839 on account of ill-health, the beginning of the tubercular attacks which were eventually to cause her death.[33]

In 1837 there had been some talk of securing Angelina Grimké to assist Mrs. Cowles. "Mrs. Cowles is good, uncommonly good; fills her place admirably, I know of no one that would do better," wrote Mrs. Mahan (the wife of the President) to Theodore Weld. "But as she must have assistance, would it not be for the interest of our Institution to have Mrs. [*sic*] Grimké here?" Nothing ever came of the proposal. In 1840 considerable pressure was exerted to secure Sarah Towne Smith, the "editress" of the *Advocate of Moral Reform,* as Mrs. Cowles' successor. Miss Smith considered the proposal seriously, but finally turned it down. In 1839 Mary Ann Adams, a young Oberlin graduate, became Assistant Principal of the Ladies' Department and, in fact, Acting Principal.[34] In 1842 she was made Principal, holding the position until 1849. Though she is described by one student as "the prettiest and sweetest young lady here," she was generally quite unpopular and considered unnecessarily strict. In the late forties she lost the confidence of her associates on the Ladies' Board with the exception of President Mahan's wife. She was requested to resign in 1849.[35]

The search for "someone better fitted to mould & influence the numerous pupils coming under her direction" was not, however, an easy one. Mrs. Emily Pillsbury Burke was appointed Principal in the summer of 1849. She had had some experience in a seminary in Georgia, and seems to have been very popular at first with teachers, townsmen, and students. Her popularity increased in the following winter when she

[33]A. W. Cowles to President Mahan, Aug. 12, 1839, and A. W. C. to Henry Cowles, July 19, 1840 (Cowles-Little MSS).

[34]M. H. Mahan to Theodore Weld, Feb. 21, 1836 [1837] (Weld MSS), and T. M., Sept. 4, 1839. On Miss Smith see the *D. A. B.,* "Sarah Towne (Smith) Martyn."

[35]Elizabeth Maxwell to parents, Mar. 31, 1842 (lent by Mrs. Emma Monroe Fitch); Helen Jones to Helen Cowles, Dec. 14, 1848 (Cowles-Little MSS); Emily S. Bartlett to Mrs. Finney, Apr. 27, 1846 (Finney MSS), and petition of Ladies' Board to the Trustees asking for her removal, signed M. P. Dascomb, Anna Hill, and A. A. Thome (Misc. Archives).

made a great effort to renovate and repair the Ladies' Hall. Her downfall came suddenly and soon. She was so unwise as to kiss one of the male students. He reported it to the Ladies' Board! Despite the petitions of half the students and population, she was dismissed. Mrs. Mary Sumner Hopkins served from 1850 to 1852. She finally resigned when the trustees overruled her decision on the admission of a young lady student.[36] The trustees retracted their decision, but evidently to no purpose.

In 1852 Marianne Dascomb was recalled and served for the next eighteen years. Mrs. Dascomb was a pious product of the pious Ipswich school. We, today, would consider her extremely "strait-laced," but her Irish wit seems to have saved her from unpopularity. She completely identified herself with the College; she was to the Female Department what Finney was to the College in general and Keep to the Board of Trustees. "Mrs. Dascomb, the principal just came in to invite me to a meeting," a young lady recently admitted to the college wrote her mother in 1852, "she is the lady I wrote to, and we all love her." She resigned in 1858, but was persuaded to reconsider by the insistence of the students and the trustees.[37] She continued as Principal until 1870 and served on the Ladies' Board until her death in 1879.

The Principal and Ladies' Board were by no means entirely dependent on negation. "Moral suasion" was supposed to be a major factor in student government in Oberlin. Often new regulations were submitted to the young ladies for comment and acceptance before being promulgated. The Principal was, in the earlier years, aided by some of the older and "more advanced young ladies" who acted as assistants. Students were urged to correct each others faults in a kindly and sympathetic manner. At first the young ladies were gathered together to report to the Principal every afternoon. In later years they were required to attend "General Exercises" every Tuesday. At these exercises all must report their own "failures" (infringements of the rules). A record of such infringements was read before the faculty and Ladies' Board at the end of the term. "General

[36]On Mrs. Burke see above, pages 480–482. On Mrs. Hopkins see T. M., Feb. 18, 1852; Ladies' Board to M. P. Dascomb, Feb. 12, 1852, and M. P. Dascomb to Prudential Committee, Feb. 23, 1852 (Misc. Archives).

[37]Elizabeth Hanmer to mother, May 1852 (lent by Miss Mildred Durbin, Columbus, Ohio); T. M., Aug. 24, 1858; and letters in the Trustees' MSS., 1858.

MARIANNE PARKER DASCOMB
About 1853
(From the original ambrotype in the Oberlin College Library)

MARIANNE PARKER DASCOMB
About 1860
(From a photograph in the Oberlin College Library)

Exercises" also furnished the occasion for lectures to the lady students by the Principal on morals, manners, religion and hygiene. A committee of young ladies wrote to the financial agents in England in 1839:

"We have also each week a lecture from our beloved principal in which she embodies much important instruction. She holds up before us the great laws of life & health, teaches us that we are fearfully & wonderfully made and not guiltless if we trample upon these laws. Again we listen to her kind voice pointing out some defect in character, habits, manners &c and the remedy suggested. But the center around which all her feelings circle is the cross of Jesus, and here she leads her young charges. And to sit where Mary did is held up as of more importance than any other attainment."[38]

Mrs. Cowles gave her charges all sorts of advice: "Be accurate in everything," "Be scrupulously honest in very little things," "Cultivate a cheerful countenance," "Make short calls," "Never wear dark skirts under light skirts or dresses," "Never wear dress and cape of different colors." She gave talks on "Benevolence," on "Learning," on "Marriage," on "Politeness," on "Conversation" and on "Woman's Duties." She discussed "Elevation of Character," "A Complete Finish," "Personal Cleanliness," important qualities for a minister's wife, and "Rules for gaining knowledge and improvement." In her talk on cleanliness she advised a general bath frequently.

As rules for conversation she suggested the following, among others:

"Never attempt to speak when you have nothing to say.
Never slander.
Never attempt to shine.
Avoid egotism, boasting, indelicacy, etc.
Learn the meaning of words and phrases in common use among good speakers and writers.
Use clean and *chaste* language.
Learn to listen to others."

There are college students of both sexes in the present century

[38]Mary Ann Adams *et al.* to John Keep and William Dawes, July 10, 1839 (Keep MSS); Mary Gorham to Rosetta Mann, Oct. 20, 1853 (lent by Miss Esther A. Close); *Laws and Regulations of the Female Department,* 1852 and 1859.

who ought to be offered some such advice. She also presented certain pertinent aids to "gaining knowledge":

"Learn your own ignorance.
Investigate thoroughly.
Guard against dogmatism.
Learn to retract willingly.
Never trifle with sacred things.
Indulge not in ridicule.
Be humble."

Of course, she gave many talks on the relations between the sexes. "The connection between the caress, the pressure of the hand, lounging on each others shoulders & laps, and the increase of the human species is exceedingly intimate," she told them. "If young ladies knew how intimate they would not *laugh* and say it was old-maidish and old-womanish to disapprove of these things."[39] She found the moral reform movement a helpful auxiliary in maintaining chaste and decent relations between students of the opposite sexes.

Sometimes similar talks were given to men, but they were not regular. In 1838 Professor Henry Cowles gave some wholesome advice that sounds as if it may have been influenced by his wife's ideas. He made "a few remarks on punctuality" and cautioned them "with respect to singing and praying loud" in their rooms. He also listed the main requisites for successful study—four in all. The first requisite he declared to be "a heart at peace with God"; the second, the avoidance of "excitement of every kind"; third, "the absence of all corroding care"; and finally, "a wise and careful control of the youthful feelings and affections." Undue "anxiety with respect to future connection" and long engagements he believed to be especially hurtful. Some betrothed couples, he believed, should stop school and get married, even though this might mean "farewell to their high hopes of usefulness and farewell to the presence of Christ."[40]

The enforcement of the rules of the Female Department and the punishment of delinquencies of all sorts among the female students was left to the Ladies' Board under the chairmanship of the departmental Principal. "The Female Board of Managers

[39]Lecture notes in Cowles-Little MSS.

[40]James Fairchild to Mary Kellogg, Aug. 28, 1838, in the *Oberlin Alumni Magazine* (Nov., 1904), I, 31. On March 27, 1844 the faculty voted "to recommence the lectures to the male students."

in the Oberlin Collegiate Institute" was established by vote of the trustees early in 1836 "with power to regulate & control the internal affairs of the female department of this institute." Though created by the trustees it seems generally to have been looked upon as subordinate to the faculty, who committed special powers to it, such as the right to admit and exclude young ladies applying for membership in the school, and sometimes, as in 1840, ordered it "to institute inquiries relative to the character and promise of the young ladies of the Institution." This board was made up of the wives of faculty members, who left their babies, their bread, and their dusting to pass upon the moral character of young women of the student body. "I have but just 10 minutes in which to write, as I have a meeting of the Ladies' Board to attend this afternoon, besides various household duties to perform." So wrote the second Mrs. Henry Cowles to her step-daughter in 1849. "My cares have never been greater I think than at present, but I have strength equal to my day," she added. "I think, however, that I was not quite wise in attempting to take care of a family of seventeen [!] without the aid of a hired girl."[41] One must always think of these administrative and disciplinary officers as stealing a moment only amidst other pressing and often burdensome duties.

The Ladies' Board not only considered cases of improper conduct but propounded supplementary regulations when they seemed to be called for. In 1852 they ruled that young ladies who wished to visit the cupola of Tappan Hall to enjoy the view must obtain permission from Mrs. Dascomb. A little later in the same year the Prudential Committee aided in handling this particular problem by having "a lock & key put upon the door leading to the cupola upon Tappan Hall & that sd key be kept at [the Treasurer's] office."[42]

The ladies were called upon to deal with all sorts of petty disciplinary cases. In the early fifties five young colored ladies were tried on the charge of "general inattention to their studies, great laxness in observance of the rules of the department & disrespectful treatment of their teachers." The Board prayed with them

[41]T. M., Feb. 11, 1836; F. M., Aug. 6, 1840; Sept. 25, 1845, and [T. B. P., Henry Cowles and] M. D. P. Cowles to Helen Cowles, Dec. 29, 1849 (Cowles-Little MSS).

[42]L. B. M., May 10, 1852, and P. C. M., Dec. 24, 1852.

and put them on special probation for three months. Later in the same summer a sub-committee was appointed to decide on the case of a young lady who had "been impudent to her teachers & very troublesome to her classmates by the various little tricks which she practiced upon them." The supervising ladies, at another time, took cognizance of certain female students who "had been seen standing on the fence near the public highway" and "sitting on the steps [of their boarding place] in an unbecoming manner." Young ladies whose behavior at public meetings was not exemplary were liable to receive attention. One young lady was convicted "of having studied her lessons at the Thursday lecture," and two others "admitted the charge of improper conduct in whispering & writing during the sermon" but were given a second chance.[43]

The rule that young ladies must be in their rooms by eight o'clock or half past seven in winter was one of those most often violated, therefore it was a rule which the Board enforced jealously and zealously.[44] When the ladies studying "Geography of the Heavens" asked "the privilege of being out to study the constellations after eight o'clock in the evening" it was decided that they might be out in the yards of their boarding houses until ten, if the teacher considered it essential. When, however, a certain Miss White requested permission to spend one evening a week at Mrs. Finney's practicing singing in preparation for a literary society anniversary, the ladies of the Board, though they "regretted much to disoblige Mrs. Finney . . . decided not best to grant the request." Every now and then a young lady who had stayed out after hours was hailed before the female court of justice charged with: "keeping late hours with gentlemen," "prolonging her visits with gentlemen much beyond the usual hour, & . . . at least in two instances [having] been out to walk with gentlemen after nine o'clock," being "out on a pleasure ride and detained beyond the usual study hour at eve," or even "violating the rules of the school in remaining in company with a gentleman till after ten o'clock."[45] Necessary as it undoubtedly

[43]L. B. M., Aug. 21, Sept. 2, 1851; Apr. 22, 29, July 15, Aug. 5, 1854.

[44]". . . Our requirement," wrote Elizabeth Hanmer, "is to be in our rooms at half past seven o'clock. True it is violated, but that does not detract from the propriety of the rule." E. H. to "Mr. Gilmore," Sept. 26, 1853 (lent by Miss Mildred Durbin, Columbus, Ohio).

[45]L. B. M., June 2, 1851; June 21, 28, 1852; June 16, 1853; Apr. 29, 1854, and Mar. 23, 1855.

FEMALE DEPARTMENT.

LADIES' BOARD OF MANAGERS.

Mrs. M. P. DASCOMB,
Mrs. A. HILL,
Mrs. M. D. P. COWLES,
Mrs. E. M. L. MORGAN,
Mrs. E. A. FINNEY,
Mrs. B. B. HUDSON,
Mrs. C. M. ALLEN.

Mrs. MARIANNE P. DASCOMB, Principal;
Miss C. AMELIA DICKSON, Assistant Principal.

LADIES' HALL.

A PAGE FROM THE *CATALOGUE*, 1854–55

was to maintain this rule during the experimental stage of "joint education," it is not surprising that it was unpopular. It seemed to these "pre-historic coeds" that the rules for men and women ought to be the same. In 1861 one of the young ladies' literary societies debated the issue: "Resolved that the young gentlemen of the Inst. ought to be subject to the eight o'clock rule."[46] The affirmative must certainly have won an easy victory.

The question of the relation of the sexes in the institution was the most serious and peculiar of all the disciplinary problems. Girls were sometimes dismissed by the Ladies' Board "for unwise & improper intimacy with several lads" and the faculty occasionally disciplined some male student for "spending too much time with the young ladies."[47] Most such cases were handled by the faculty as involving male students and being of a particularly serious nature. It was the faculty which authorized Professor Cowles to write to a certain probationer in 1841:

"Dear Brother: It is made my duty by the Faculty to appraise you that you cannot be received into our Institution, & that in our judgment it is desirable for you to *leave* the *place* as *soon* as it can conveniently be *done*. . . . Bro. Sterry & Mr. Graham satisfy us *most fully* that your habits of associating with young *ladies* are not such as will sustain the character of this Institution or the honor of the Christian name. We have good reason to fear the presence of young men whose conduct indicates an *unchaste* mind. They may do less mischief elsewhere—here their example & influence cannot fail to be most pernicious!

"*We* shall be *happy* to *avoid* a *public* investigation & expose of the matter above referred to. We think the best course for *yourself* & for the Institution is for you to withdraw *silently* & immediately. . . .

"In behalf of the Faculty
Henry Cowles"[48]

Great emphasis was placed upon the rule prohibiting students from visiting those of the opposite sex in their rooms. On the successful enforcement of this rule the whole experiment of joint education of the sexes must stand or fall. It was by far the most important of all rules in Oberlin and it was enforced with

46Young Ladies Lyceum, MS Minutes, Apr. 8, 1861.
47L. B. M., Jan. 28, 1853, and F. M., Aug. 1, 8, 1838.
48H. Cowles to Mr. E———, June 30, 1841 (Cowles-Little MSS).

the greatest strictness—at least after the first two or three years. In 1836 a student was dismissed because he had "broken one of the fundamental laws of the institution, which is, that no male student shall go into the chamber of the young ladies on any occasion, without a special permission from the principal of that department." After this case was settled it was voted that any male student visiting a female student in her room should be punished by expulsion.[49]

Probably the most famous disciplinary case in the history of early Oberlin was that of two college sophomores, Walter Smith and Jonathan E. Ingersoll, who visited a young lady student while the latter was lying ill in her room. The young men had carried a trunk to the floor where she was lying sick and were told by young lady students who were nursing her that they might go in. But the law was the law, and the faculty, after seven meetings on the question, expelled them. "It proved a tremendous excitement . . . ," wrote a coed to her family. "The students, all or nearly so petitioned the Faculty to permit them to return . . . No one thought they had any immoral motive in view but it was a thoughtless thing, they did not think of the consequences. We expect it will produce quite an excitement abroad. Please write in your next if you have heard the report."[50] The students were re-admitted.

The furore created is certainly not exaggerated in this letter. The petitions from the students are still preserved: one signed unanimously by the twenty-five seniors, one subscribed to by seventeen juniors, one signed by twenty-four sophomore classmates, another by a majority of the theological students, and a fifth by their fellow boarders. The students were sufficiently respectful and subservient in their approach to the august faculty, but insistent nevertheless. "We recognize the Law violated," agreed the sophomore, "and also its penalty, to be just. We fully acknowledge the propriety of the proceedings of the faculty in inflicting this penalty upon those of our number who had violated this Law. But considering the general character of the in-

[49]E. P. Ingersoll's first draft of Faculty Minutes, Jan. 16, 1836 (O. C. Lib.), and F. M., Feb. 26, 1836.

[50]J. B. Trew to Andrew Trew, May 29, 1843 (lent by Miss Mary Ewalt, Lakewood, Ohio). An almost exactly parallel account of the episode is given by Mary Barnes in a letter to Laura Branch, Mar. 23 to Apr. 23, 1843 (O. C. Lib. Misc. MSS).

dividuals expelled, that their usual conduct has hitherto been irreproachable, and remembering that the individuals have already suffered much for their offence, and remembering that the impression is fully made upon the minds of the Students generally, that this Law cannot be violated with impunity, we cannot but indulge the hope that a consideration of all the circumstances in the case will lead you Honorable Body to decide, that these individuals may again be restored to our number, and the object contemplated by the violated Law secured."[51]

It is not doubted that the punishment had been sufficient and that Oberlin students and the public generally had been impressed by the fact that improper intimacies would not be permitted among Oberlin students.

[51]Petitions in O. C. Lib. (Charles Livingstone was among the sophomores signing these petitions.); F. M., Apr. 21, 1843 *et seq.*

CHAPTER XLII

THE COLLEGIATE DEPARTMENT

ASA MAHAN and Charles G. Finney, the two Presidents, were the dominant leaders and most popular teachers. But Henry Cowles, John Morgan and James Dascomb were the wheel horses, patient, hard working, discreet, well balanced, highly esteemed and respected and possessed of sound judgment. It was they who gave solid stability to College and community and offset the heat and freaks of Mahan and Finney.[1] These five together gave Oberlin over a hundred and seventy years of loyal service, an average of thirty-four years apiece.[2] These five men were the guardians of the inner temple, who kept the fire burning at Oberlin through stressful years and, in the meantime, trained others to take their places when their watch should be up.

Asa Mahan was, all agree, an aggressive and effective speaker, a stimulating teacher who stirred his pupils in College and in the Theological Course to a high pitch of enthusiasm for the subjects which he taught. There were always some, however, among the students as well as among the members of the faculty, who resented his overbearing and intolerant manner and his rash and dogmatic utterances. Finney did little teaching in the Collegiate Department but his fiery sermons on the Sabbath constituted the lodestone which drew many a student to Oberlin. Though a man of "deep piety and boundless genius," he was probably at no time so much attached to Oberlin and its interests as were his associates. His long absences, running into months and years, stirred repeated rumors of resignation, and kept the other members of the faculty almost constantly on the "anxious seat." James Dascomb, whose science classes included pupils from all the departments but the theological, was an excellent

[1]Paraphrased from Leonard-Fairchild MS, I, 43–44.

[2]Counting in Henry Cowles' service as editor of the *Evangelist* from 1848 to 1862 after he had left active teaching.

CHARLES G. FINNEY

JOHN MORGAN

HENRY E. WHIPPLE

JAMES H. FAIRCHILD

JAMES MONROE

HENRY E. PECK

FACULTY MEMBERS ABOUT 1853
(From a composite daguerreotype in the Oberlin College Library)

FACULTY MEMBERS ABOUT 1853
(From a composite daguerreotype in the Oberlin College Library)

teacher, deeply immersed in his subject, though his achievements were sharply limited by the lack of good laboratory facilities. Henry Cowles, who first taught languages in the College and later "Ecclesiastical History and Pastoral Theology" and the "Literature of the Old Testament" in the Theological Department, was a "studious, mild, careful, kind & lovely" man. He was however generally a poor teacher and "not much as a preacher," his greatest work being done as an author and as editor of the *Evangelist*. The genial Irishman John Morgan was Professor of New Testament Literature from 1835 to 1880, and the most influential conservative in Oberlin. Mahan and Finney were the sails which swept the ship along before the wind; Morgan was the sturdy anchor which held it safe in dangerous shallow waters. Venerating Luther and Calvin and the New England church fathers, he was, in theology and other matters, cautious almost to the point of timidity, always ready to compromise, to qualify, to limit and state more exactly. Finney once said to him, "Unbelief is one of your principles of interpretation." He was a thorough scholar but not a particularly successful teacher except with a few of the brightest and most studious who did not require the sparkling presentation which he could not give.[3] Finney never attended college. Mahan graduated from Hamilton College and Andover Theological Seminary, Henry Cowles from Yale, Dr. Dascomb from the Dartmouth Medical School, and John Morgan from Williams.

The second generation of Oberlin professors were all Oberlin trained, thoroughly steeped in the spirit and purpose of Oberlin. Two of them were Lane Rebels of the famous Theological Class of 1836. James Armstrong Thome, the son of a Kentucky slaveholder, converted to abolitionism by Theodore Weld, was Professor of Rhetoric and Belles Lettres from 1838 to 1848. He was a friend of equality between the sexes as well as between races. George Whipple stepped from the principalship of the Preparatory Department in 1838 to the professorship of Mathematics and Natural Philosophy. During many years he kept the

[3]Leonard-Fairchild MS, I, 36, and 42–43; Sherlock Bristol to Henry Cowles, Dec. 26, 1844 (Cowles-Little MSS), and P. H. Irwin to Levi Burnell, Mar. 6, 1840 (Treas. Off., File D). The career of John P. Cowles at Oberlin is treated on pages 432–434. Edwin S. Williams wrote of John Morgan: ". . . Him of the old Scotch-plaid shawl, the loving eye, the white hair, the sunny heart, and the Irish humor."—A. T. Swing, *James Harris Fairchild* (New York—c. 1907), 156.

minutes of meetings of the faculty and served as a member of the Prudential Committee. In 1847 he resigned to become secretary of the American Missionary Association.

In 1840 a former student wrote to Levi Burnell that he did not intend to return, "Because Oberlin has deviated from the original intentions of its founders," "Because you have an expelled sophomore student [T. J. Keep] for a Principal of the preparatory department," and "Because you have a sophomore student for a linguist." The last statement referred to Timothy Hudson, who left Western Reserve in 1835, when in his second year, to become Tutor in Latin at Oberlin, and Professor of Latin and Greek from 1838 to 1841 and, after an interval as an antislavery lecturer, again from 1847 to his death in 1858. He did not receive his bachelor's degree at Oberlin until 1847, though all agree that he was a man of high attainments in his chosen field of ancient languages. He was remembered in Oberlin as intellectual rather than pious, but as a stern exponent of morality, a "specimen of the ancient Puritan of the type of Milton and Vane." (He had been one of the "lynchers" of Norton in 1840.) It was a great shock to Oberlin when he was killed on the railroad at North Olmsted in 1858.[4]

William Cochran was a student at Oberlin from 1835 to 1842, a tutor from 1839 to 1842, and Professor of Logic and Associate Professor of Intellectual and Moral Philosophy from 1842 to 1846. His colleague, James Monroe, wrote of him: "Prof. Cochran was a most successful teacher. Many will remember forever the vivid and indelible impressions which his accuracy, his thoroughness, and his tireless vivacity made on their minds. He had the rare power of making the dryest formulas of logic interesting, and inspiring his class with constant enthusiasm."[5] He was associated with President Mahan in the development of the Oberlin theology and in the editorship of the *Oberlin Quarterly Review*. In interests, in ability, in character and temperament there was much in common between him and the President. He died in 1847 at the age of thirty-three shortly after resigning his

[4]P. H. Irwin to Burnell, Mar. 6, 1840; *Oberlin Evangelist*, Apr. 14, 1858, and J. H. Fairchild, *Oberlin: the Colony and the College*, chapter XI. This last chapter is very useful on all of these teachers. On Hudson see *Professor T. B. Hudson, the Casualty, Biographical Sketch, the Funeral, the Coroner's Inquest*, etc., an undated pamphlet.

[5]*Oberlin Evangelist*, Sept. 1, 1847.

post on the faculty. Unlike Hudson, he was one of those most zealous for the saving of the students' souls.

James Monroe was politician, financial agent and professor rolled in one. He succeeded Thome as Professor of Rhetoric and Belles Lettres in 1849, serving in that capacity until 1862. Already in 1847, when he was still a tutor, Professor Morgan described him as "a fine scholar and one of the most splendid orators I ever heard speak" and "as pure and noble as his talents are extraordinary." James Harris Fairchild– "altogether a noble man, of a sound head, an equally sound heart, accurate scholarship, too much modesty for so much merit"[6]–came to Oberlin as a student in 1835 and finished his course in 1841. From 1839 to 1842 he was a tutor; from 1842 to 1847 he took Hudson's place as Professor of Latin and Greek; then for twelve years he was Professor of Mathematics and Natural Philosophy, becoming Associate Professor of Theology and Moral Philosophy in 1859. George Nelson Allen, a pious, hard-working, sensitive soul, was also an all-round handy man. Coming from Western Reserve in 1835, like Timothy Hudson, he served at various times as Professor of Music, Principal of the Preparatory Department, Professor of Geology and Natural History and Secretary and Treasurer.[7]

Four of the youngest were Charles H. Penfield, Henry Everard Peck, John M. Ellis and Charles Henry Churchill. Penfield, a stepson of Henry Cowles, graduated from the College in 1847. He taught Latin and Greek with moderate success from 1848 to 1870 when he resigned to take a position in the Central High School at Cleveland. Henry Peck, son of Everard Peck of Rochester, studied at the Oneida Institute and then graduated at Bowdoin. He graduated from the Theological Course at Oberlin in 1845. He was Professor of Sacred Rhetoric and Mental and Moral Philosophy from 1851 to 1865. A radical and something of an eccentric, he was not always in perfect agreement with the more conservative members of the faculty. As a thorough abolitionist, he teamed up well with Professors James Monroe and John M. Ellis. He died in Haiti in 1867 where he had been serving as Minister from the United States since the close of the War. His

[6]John Morgan to Mark Hopkins, Dec. 15, 1847 and Aug. 28, 1849 (Morgan-Hopkins MSS). On Monroe's political career see page 390.

[7]On Allen see pages 784 *et seq.*

chief claim to fame was his part in the "Rescue Case."[8]

John Millott Ellis, a graduate in the Class of 1851 with General J. D. Cox, Professor J. A. R. Rogers of Berea, Charles G. Finney, Jr., and L. F. Parker of the University of Iowa, recaptured the spirit of the founders perhaps more completely than did any of the other younger men. A moral exemplar, he was deeply pious; Oberlin granted to him her first D.D. He was popular as a teacher, respected as a leader in the community (Mayor of the village in 1861–62 and chairman of the volunteer committee throughout the war), active in the Musical Union, and deferred to by older heads in the Prudential Committee for his business acumen. Like James Fairchild and Churchill, however, his greatest work was done in the post-war period. Charles Henry Churchill was a native of Vermont and a graduate of Dartmouth in the Class of 1845. After teaching for a while in Cleveland he came to Oberlin to study theology, completing his course in 1853. For five years he taught Latin and Music at Hillsdale College in Michigan. In 1858 he came back to Oberlin as Professor of Mathematics (including Astronomy and Physics). He was always interested in music, having played the organ in chapel during his last year at Dartmouth. In Oberlin he ranked next to Allen as a teacher of music and leader in the Musical Union. He was always a popular teacher, particularly of the scientific subjects.[9]

College students often objected to the use of recent graduates and even undergraduates in college classes. It was their feeling that these youngsters assumed too grand a manner and lorded it over them with unnecessary dignity. The use of theological students and even collegiate undergraduates to teach elementary college classes was a common, but certainly unfortunate, practice. In 1844–45 fifty dollars was expended for the hiring of student teachers in the Collegiate Department. In 1840 an undergraduate declared that one of the chief faults of the institution was the practice of the professors "of leaving their classes in the

[8]On Peck see Rochester Historical Society, *Publications*, I (1892), 106, and J. A. Padgett, "Diplomats to Haiti and their Diplomacy," *Journal of Negro History*, XXV, 265–330 (July, 1940).

[9]J. H. Fairchild, *Oberlin: the Colony and the College*, 298–299; *A Tribute to the Memory of John Millott Ellis, D.D., Professor of Philosophy in Oberlin College* (Oberlin—1894), and Archer H. Shaw, "Charles Henry Churchill" (MS in O. C. Lib.). See the comments on Oberlin teachers in Denton J. Snider's *A Writer of Books* (St. Louis—n.d.), 157 *et passim.*

PROFESSOR
CHARLES H. CHURCHILL
(From the 1859 Class Album in the Oberlin College Library)

PROFESSOR
J. M. ELLIS
(From the 1859 Class Album in the Oberlin College Library)

charge of senior students." In 1851 Charles C. Starbuck, a college senior, received twenty-five cents a recitation for teaching freshman Greek for thirty-two recitations. In 1864 a student in the Theological Department was paid fifty cents an hour for teaching freshmen.[10]

The sole justification of such a practice was to be found, of course, in the tremendously heavy teaching schedule of the regular instructors. In 1849 John Morgan wrote to Mark Hopkins that for his "meagre and ill paid salary" he was required to take charge of five classes daily.[11] When James H. Fairchild was a senior in the Theological Course but also already a tutor in the College he wrote to his fiancee, describing a typical day with a young Oberlin student-teacher:

"Let me tell you how I have spent the day. Commencing with 6 o'clock A.M. The first half hour I officiated at the morning devotions in the chapel. The next half hour at breakfast. From 7 to 8 I was engaged in preparing two lessons in Hebrew. From 9 to 10 listened to a lecture from Professor Cowles on Church History. From 10 to 11 heard a lecture from Prof. Morgan on the 'Epistle to the Hebrews'; from 11 to 12 is my hour for manual labor; from 12 to 1 I was occupied with dinner and a bit of Theological discussion with Samuel Cochran, Professor Hudson and some other young men who board at our house; from 1 to 2 heard the senior college class in Hebrew; from 2 to 3 spent in my room, studied a little; from 3 to 4 spent in our little singing circle; from 4 to 6 (nearly) at the Thursday lecture of President Mahan; from 6 to 7 at supper and playing with George Thompson, who makes sport for us all; from 7 to now in the Faculty meeting which occurs every Thursday evening. So the day is finished. . . .

"Here are fifteen compositions which must be criticized before next Monday. Some of them are quite long."[12]

Recitations, chapel, "Thursday Lecture," faculty meeting, manual labor, papers to grade—it was a full day. Many teachers found it necessary, in addition, to preach or engage in other bread-

[10]C. G. Finney, Jr. to C. G. F., July 9, 1850 (Finney MSS); "Amount of Institution Expences of Teaching, Aug. 1845," and various bills in the Misc. Archives, and P. H. Irwin to Levi Burnell, *Loc. Cit.*

[11]John Morgan to Hopkins, Aug. 28, 1849 (Morgan-Hopkins MSS). See also "Reports on Instruction & On Preparatory Department adopted Aug. 1845" (Misc. Archives).

[12]James H. Fairchild to Mary Kellogg, Mar. 17, 1841, in *Oberlin Alumni Magazine,* I, 179 (Apr., 1905).

winning activities in vacation and in term time in order to make both ends meet financially. The teaching burden was greatly increased by the sale of the endowment scholarships in the 50's. At the same time the advance in salaries lagged considerably behind the rise in the cost of living. The Oberlin teaching staff was kept together only by the repeated appeal "to the principle of self-denial and self-sacrifice for a great object."[13] This was one reason why Oberlin graduates received all the new appointments; men of equal ability from other institutions would not have stayed on similar terms.

Besides the regular faculty and the student teachers there were at least three visiting lecturers: Edward Wade, Professor of Law from 1838 to 1848, Amasa Walker, Professor of Political Economy and History, 1842–50, and James Barr Walker "Lecturer on Harmony of Science and Revealed Religion," 1856–66. Though these men gave only short courses of lectures, they were not uninfluential among faculty and students. Both of the Walkers were also members of the Board of Trustees. Wade and Amasa Walker will be further dealt with in this chapter.

The standard American college curriculum of the middle third of the nineteenth century consisted of liberal doses of Greek, Latin and Mathematics in the freshman and sophomore years (the classics predominating in both years but Mathematics occupying more time in the second), courses in science in the junior and senior years (Mathematics and Classics being continued, but much less time being devoted to them), and Mental and Moral Philosophy in the senior year. Rhetoric was usually studied and practiced at least throughout the last three years. Weak courses in Political Science, Political Economy, and History were sometimes included, usually in the later years. Less often there were classes (sometimes optional) in French. In general, however, we may say that the first year was the year of Classics, the second the year of Mathematics, the third the year of Science, and the fourth the year of Philosophy.

Of course, all took the same subjects; electives (or "optional courses") were almost unheard of, except at Harvard where the parents or guardians of undergraduates might choose between a certain few alternative courses. A writer in the *New Englander*

[13] *Oberlin Evangelist,* Sept. 12, 1855, and Oct. 8, 1862.

in 1851 even defined a college as "a collection of students who from beginning to end pursue together an appointed course of study."[14]

In Oberlin's early years, as we have seen, the Institute reduced considerably the amount of Greek and Latin classics studied and substituted Hebrew, English Literature and other subjects instead. Orthodox college teachers and scholars all over the United States heaped opprobrium on Oberlin therefore, and an unhappy dissension broke out within the ranks of teachers and students. Gradually the amount and character of Latin and Greek studied in the regular course was restored to something approximating that required in other colleges, and Hebrew was dropped.

The Oberlin freshman studied Cicero (*De Senectute* and *De Amicitia* or in later years, Cicero's *Epistles)* and Livy and, in the sixties, Latin Prose Composition. In Greek he read the Acts of the Apostles and Xenophon's *Cyropaedia,* to which was later added the *Odyssey* and Greek Prose Composition. Freshman "Math" included Algebra, Geometry and Trigonometry. First year men (and women) of the Collegiate Course attended the lectures on Physiology with students from the other departments.

The second year student read Cicero (*De Officiis*), Tacitus and Latin poetry. The poetry was Buchanan's *Psalms* at first, but eventually became a course in Horace. The Greek included Xenophon's *Memorabilia* and Aeschines and (or) Demosthenes *On the Crown*. Courses in "Greek Tragedy" and "Greek Composition" appear in the later years. Geometry and Trigonometry were continued and Conic Sections begun.[15] All sophomores were protected against atheism and deism and prepared for conversion by a course in the "Evidences of Christianity," in which the classical work of William Paley was the text. An introductory science course (Botany or Geology) prepared the student for the emphasis on that field which came in the following year.

In the early days "Cowper's Poems" and General History

[14]Harvard *Catalogue,* 1846, and "Reform in the Collegiate Education" in the *New Englander,* IX, 129 (Feb., 1851).

[15]In the sixties Conic Sections was studied in the first and Calculus in the second year.

(Alexander Fraser Tytler, *Elements of General History, Ancient and Modern*) were studied throughout the freshman and sophomore years. These courses were, however, dropped in order to make way for classical studies and make the curriculum more orthodox. All college students were required to attend a weekly class in the English Bible and take part in extempore discussions or declamatory exercises throughout their course.

The work in Latin and Greek seems to have consisted mainly of drill in grammar and vocabulary and as a rule students did not find it very stimulating. Just when blackboards were introduced in Oberlin for use in classes in Mathematics is not clear but they were certainly in use in the late fifties. A college student of 1859 described an Algebra class in her diary:

"This A. M. in Algebra had a sad time. Mr. Parmenter asked me to do an example which I could not do and so failed. Then he called on me for another example which I failed on. And then after another lapse of time wished me to go to the board and put on an example in elimination. I told him I could not, he said he would help me and tell me what to do, and I was obliged to go, but I can assure [you] I felt as though I would rather be anywhere else. We got part way through the example when the bell rung and we left it. I felt like a little fool upon the board expressing my infant ignorance, before the whole class. Well I mean never to do the like again."[16]

The chief object of Mathematics was felt to be the training in mental discipline, and efforts to make the subject interesting or practical were, therefore, likely to be frowned upon. The texts used at Oberlin were the standard ones of the time: the *Algebra* by Professor Day of Yale, the *Geometry* adapted from the French text by Prof. Charles Davies of West Point, Bridge's *Conic Sections,* and later the various mathematical texts by Prof. Elias Loomis, for some time of Western Reserve College. Day's text was rather elementary but clear and logical and well adapted for college use in this period when preparatory work in Mathematics was so much neglected. Davies' books were well arranged and not too difficult for the ordinary student. Loomis' textbooks were written in a clear, simple style and well adapted for class use. They were popular with the students because so compact

[16]Mary Louisa Cowles, MS Journal, July 13, 1859.

and because of the unusual emphasis placed upon practical application rather than theory.[17]

Against the comparatively drab background of these courses the lectures in Anatomy and Physiology stood by contrast as by far the most interesting and practical course of the freshman and sophomore years. "We have lectures dayly on Physiology & Anatomy from Proff. Dascomb," wrote a student in 1837. "An extremely interesting study, but no less interesting than important. But alas! its importance is not realized by the great mass of men. How many live from 10, 20, 50, 70 years & know nothing at all about the house they inhabit! How many diseases might be prevented if men only understood this science. Proff. Dascomb estimates them at 9/10—truly appalling." The local interest in "physiological reform" and Dascomb's unusual ability as a teacher probably furnish the chief explanation of the extraordinary popularity of this course.[18]

The junior year was mainly devoted to scientific studies: Natural Philosophy, Astronomy, Chemistry and an advanced course in Anatomy and Physiology. No Mathematics and little or no Latin was included. The study of Demosthenes and Aeschines *On the Crown* was continued and the Epistles of the New Testament were read in the original Greek. The third year curriculum also included Whately's *Logic* and *Rhetoric* and Stewart's or Mahan's *Intellectual Philosophy*.[19]

James Dascomb, as Oberlin's scientist, was the presiding genius of the junior year. Generally well-founded in his field by his study under Dr. Mussey at Dartmouth, he kept up with developments by reading scientific journals, engaging, in so far as his duties as a teacher allowed, in practical investigations and visit-

17Florian Cajori, "The Teaching and History of Mathematics in the United States," U. S. Bureau of Education *Circular of Information,* No. 3, 1890 (Washington—1890); *Oberlin Students' Monthly,* III, 57–58 (Dec., 1860), and especially Walter P. Rogers, "College Education One Hundred Years Ago" (MS Thesis in O. C. Library).

18Davis [and Nancy] Prudden to George P. Prudden, Apr. 8[–13], 1837 (Prudden MSS). In a letter written by Elizabeth Hanmer to her mother (Sept. 26, 1853—lent by Mildred Durbin of Columbus) she expresses enthusiasm for Dascomb's courses and refers to his announced intention to "present a human being in a complete state of preservation to the class, requesting young ladies that think they cannot endure it to remain at home." For early faculty action on this course see F. M., Feb. 29, 1836.

19Hebrew Grammar, Plato's *Phaedo,* Cousin's *Psychology,* "Leslie on Deism" and Milton's poems were studied in the Junior year in the earliest period only.

ing courses at other institutions. Dascomb taught the Chemistry. Natural Philosophy, now known as Physics, was taught by the successive professors of Mathematics, none of whom was a specialist in science.

The text in Natural Philosophy (Physics) was the standard one by Denison Olmsted of Yale, which contained chapters on the basic principles and laws of Physics and on Projectiles and Gunnery, Machinery, Hydrostatics, Hydraulics, Pneumatics, Atmosphere, Mechanical Agencies of Air and Steam, Acoustics, Electricity, Magnetism, and Optics. Olmsted defined natural Philosophy as "the science which treats of the laws of the material world." An Oberlin student's notes contain a similar definition: "What is natural philosophy? It is [the] science which investigates the reasons of the various phenomena which occur in the material world."[20] In general the fundamental principles presented by Olmsted would be recognized as valid today, though in the field of electricity, of course, this is not true. Olmsted is little beyond Benjamin Franklin and defines electricity as a "peculiar fluid" the velocity of which is apparently "instantaneous."

Students' notes on Natural Philosophy and Chemistry contain much that is illuminating, although, in some instances, they may be misquoting the lecturer: "What is meant by Hydrostoticks? It is that branch of natural Philosophy which explains the nature, gravity, pressure and motions of fluids. Hydrolicks considers & explains particularly the law and operations of fluids in motion whether comprehensible or incomprehensible." "Chymistry," scribbled a student at the first lecture in 1842–1843, "is science which investigates the properties of all bodies and determines the laws by which its action is regulated." The approximately fifty lectures in Chemistry followed roughly the order of discussion used in J. L. Comstock's *Elements of Chemistry* (which later supplanted Graham's *Chemistry* as the textbook) from "Calorick" through fermentation. The course was so brief, however, that not all topics were covered. There appears to have been no mention of analytical chemistry, for example. The emphasis on fermentation (two lectures at the

[20]Notes by Fanny Fletcher taken in 1834 or 1835 lent by Miss Eliza J. Comings of Kingsville, Ohio.

DR. DASCOMB'S CHEMISTRY LABORATORY
(From a photograph in the Oberlin College Library)

end of the course) may very likely have been associated with Oberlin's position on temperance.[21]

In both Natural Philosophy and Chemistry the equipment and apparatus was entirely inadequate. But this was the normal state of things even in the eastern colleges, and it was never intended nor allowed that students should themselves do experiments. In the winter of 1836–37 Dr. Dascomb went to New York and New Haven where he heard lectures by Professor Silliman of Yale, the "Father of College Chemistry Teaching," and secured some apparatus and also plans for a laboratory building. The laboratory was completed in 1838, a one story masonry building approximately fifty by thirty feet, containing a lecture room copied after Silliman's at Yale—with raised seats, arched ceiling, etc. In the same year the Prudential Committee expressed their willingness that the Doctor should expend $400.00 for further apparatus provided he would personally take the field as financial agent and raise the money.[22] The equipment continued unsatisfactory and incomplete throughout our period. As late as 1864 we find Professor Churchill writing a pitiful note to the Treasurer:

"Oberlin, July 29, 1864

"Treas. Hill,

Dear Bro.

If the College can afford one of these little Hygrometers I wish very much you would purchase one for the Philosoph. Department, price $3.50.

Truly yours,

C. H. Churchill."[23]

Though the apparatus was poor and inadequate and though the demonstration lecture method seems to have been used exclusively, there were probably no more popular courses than

[21] *Id.*, and W. A. Westervelt's MS Notes on Political Economy, Chemistry and Pastoral Theology, 1842–1843 (O. C. Lib.).

[22] Davis Prudden to George Prudden, Mar. 3 [–5], 1837 (Prudden MSS); P. C. M., Mar. 16, May 27, 1837, and Dec. 20, 1838. See also W. C. Chapin, "Dr. Dascomb's Old Laboratory and the Beginnings of the Chemistry Department," *Oberlin Alumni Magazine*, XXVI, 205 (Apr., 1930); F. F. Jewett and F. G. Jewett, "The Chemistry Department," *Loc. Cit.*, XVIII, (July, 1922), and S. R. Williams, "A History of Physics in Oberlin College," *Loc. Cit.*, XI, 50–56 (Nov., 1914). Professor Dascomb wrote to A. A. Wright, Jan. 20, 1875, that he had subscribed to the *American Journal of Science and Arts* (Silliman's Journal) from the time he began his work in Oberlin up to "2 or 3 years ago."—(Wright MSS).

[23] Misc. Archives.

those in Natural Philosophy, Chemistry and Physiology. The students always found the demonstrations entertaining if not universally enlightening. "I've just come home from Chemistry," wrote Elizabeth Maxwell to a friend in the early forties. "We have had some beautiful experiments and a very interesting Lecture. But had to run home in the rain as fast as we could." It must have warmed the good Doctor's heart after over thirty years of teaching at Oberlin to be singled out by his students for special recognition. In 1865 the "Senior Class and Fourth Year Ladies" expressed their appreciation of Professor Dascomb's teaching by presenting to him an "elegant" and "beautiful copy of Irving's Sketch Book, costing twenty dollars."[24]

As the keynote of the third year was physical law, that of the final year was mental, moral, human, and divine law. Neither Latin nor Mathematics was studied and there was only one class in Greek.[25] Hebrew was studied in the senior year until that language dropped entirely out of the college curriculum in the fifties. There was one course in Science, usually Geology. All seniors were supposed to attend lectures on Law or Political Economy, or "Social and Political Science." But the characteristic studies of the fourth year were Butler's *Analogy,* Kames' *Elements of Criticism,* Intellectual and Moral Philosophy and, for a time, "Mahan On the Will."

Moral Philosophy was the mother of all of these subjects. Except for the course in Greek, the entire fourth year was devoted to it or to its offspring. Moral Philosophy, as taught by Aristotle, was studied in the universities of Europe in the Middle Ages. With very little change it was taken over by the Scottish and English universities of later years and passed on to Harvard, Yale, and Princeton in America. Other American colleges copied it from them. Even in the eighteenth and early nineteenth centuries it included almost every topic under the sun: ethics, religion, psychology, logic, aesthetics, politics, law, and political economy. Excursions were even sometimes made by the lecturer into the field of natural science.

During the first third of the century of Oberlin's existence the

[24]Elizabeth Maxwell to "Kate" [1842?] (lent by Mrs. E. M. Fitch), and *Lorain County News,* June 7, 1865.

[25]Aeschylus was usually included in the senior year. In the thirties there were two classes in Greek: Sophocles and Aeschylus together and the Epistles of Greek Testament.

course was beginning to disintegrate. Separate courses in the social sciences were appearing, for example, though social questions were still discussed in "Moral Philosophy." In later years "Psychology" and "Philosophy" sloughed off and left only the "Senior Bible" of the twentieth century. Two things held the course together: the moral purpose which characterized the treatment of all topics discussed and the personality of President Mahan (the subject being everywhere, almost invariably, taught by the head of the college).[26]

Mahan's course in Mental and Moral Philosophy at Oberlin, though fundamentally like similar courses in other colleges, was exceptional in that the President was a student of German Idealism. He acknowledged his debt to Cousin, to Coleridge, and to Kant and the name of the last appears on many pages of his printed lectures. His associates believed him most indebted to Cousin. A contemporary reviewer wrote: "Mr. Mahan is an ecclectic, being more decidedly a follower and imitator of Cousin. His ecclecticism degenerates sometimes into the merely aggressive, and he delights occasionally in strange and incongruous combinations of Kant, Coleridge, Cousin and himself, but showing here and there great vigor and acuteness, and very considerable philosophical ability." It is a tribute to Mahan that years after his departure "metaphysical investigations" should still have been considered Oberlin's strongest point scholastically. It is a greater tribute that he should have had as a pupil a James Harris Fairchild who in turn should be the teacher of a Henry Churchill King. At the time of Mahan's death in 1889 Fairchild wrote: "His work here as a teacher can never be forgotten by his pupils, and the impulse which he gave to the study of philosophy in the College is not yet exhausted."[27] Nor was it to be for many more years.

The study of this subject had a two-fold object: the establishment of sound moral character and conversion to Christianity. Something was done by way of preparing the students' minds in

[26]See the excellent account in George P. Schmidt, *The Old Time College President* (New York—1930), 108–145.

[27]Asa Mahan, *Abstract of a Course of Lectures on Mental & Moral Philosophy* (Oberlin—1840), and *A System of Intellectual Philosophy* (New York—1845); "Recent Works on Psychology," *New Englander,* XIII, 129 (Feb., 1855); Schmidt, *Op. Cit.,* 123; *Oberlin Students' Monthly,* III, 57–58 (Dec., 1860), and *Oberlin Review,* Apr. 30, 1889.

the second and third years when Paley's *Evidences of Christianity* and Whately's *Logic* were ordinarily read. In the late thirties Cousin's *Psychology*, Stewart's *Elements of Intellectual Philosophy* and "Leslie on Deism" were studied in the third year. The inclusion of "Leslie on Deism" indicates another aim of the study which was to combat the rationalism which had so completely dominated thought in the late eighteenth century. For a while *The Elements of Moral Science* by President Wayland of Brown was used as a text, but this gave way to Mahan's own writings, when published. Bishop Joseph Butler's *Analogy of Religion, Natural and Revealed* was assigned throughout the period and into the eighties. When its use was discontinued, an "Alumnus" (probably an old one) wrote to the *Oberlin Review* protesting. It was a "hard" book he admitted, but should be retained for this reason if for no other—as a source of mental discipline. Besides, he declared, "no other work can pretend to rival the *Analogy*, in presenting the foundation arguments for both natural religion and revelation. None of us are too secure in our religious belief. Butler's argument appeals to the true basis of all belief, the reason; and by convincing it, gives us a firm foundation on which to build." Lord Kames' *Elements of Criticism* contains eight hundred pages devoted to aesthetics and particularly to literary criticism. Probably at Oberlin as elsewhere, however, it was used as the springboard from which to dive into religious and moral disquisitions.[28]

Our best source on "Mental & Moral Philosophy" as taught at Oberlin is, of course, the abstract of Mahan's lectures printed in 1840. "Mental Philosophy," declared the President, "is the science of mind." "Moral Philosophy . . . is the science which defines the rules of moral conduct, and the reason or ground of moral obligation, or the reasons why moral agents are bound to act in conformity with such rules."[29] Over a hundred lectures were included dealing with such topics as: "Idea of Right and Wrong," "Consciousness," "Sense," "Association," "Imagination and Fancy," "Reason" (several lectures), "The Soul," "God," "The Will," "Love," these all under Mental Philosophy, and under Moral Philosophy: "Intentions," "Moral Obligation" (several lectures), "Rewards and Punishments," "Govern-

[28]*Oberlin Review,* Jan. 10, 1885, and Schmidt, *Op. Cit.,* 136–137.
[29]Mahan, *Abstract,* 9 and 189.

ment," "Prayer," "Temperance and Dress," "Contrasts," "Integrity of Character," "Duties arising as members of Civil Society." In such a course naturally Mahan found many opportunities of instilling into his pupils the peculiar Oberlin point of view. "The individual that will stop his ear at the cry of the needy and perishing and lay out the Lord's treasures of which he is the appointed steward, for the gratification of vanity, or pride, or ambition, will, in the great day of final reckoning, be regarded and treated as a robber," he told them. Mahan, the moral reformer, denounced "dress so arranged as to excite lust" and declared that seduction should be made a crime punishable by death. As between man and wife he believed, however, that ultimate authority always rested with the husband. It was the duty of all citizens he said, "To regard the law of right or the will of God as of supreme authority above all human enactments." Here is the "Higher Law" ten years before the Fugitive Slave Act was passed. Slavery, he described, as "the perfection of tyranny." In his lectures before the seniors Mahan trained himself and his hearers for those remarkable series of debates on come-outerism and war.[30] The chief link between the Oberlin curriculum and the real world of reform societies and fugitive slaves was through "Mental and Moral Philosophy."

When Mahan resigned in 1850 Finney succeeded him as President and as lecturer in this course. He was absent so much, however, that it was eventually determined to appoint an assistant to take his place in teaching Theology and Moral Philosophy. James H. Fairchild was therefore "promoted" in 1859 from the professorship of Mathematics and Natural Philosophy to be Associate Professor of Theology and Moral Philosophy. Fairchild taught the latter subject for over thirty years, carrying on the tradition of Mahan and making noteworthy contributions of his own. In the very first year of this new work he made a great impression on his students. "I have always thought," wrote one of them in later years, "there was never anything better."[31] In 1869 Fairchild published these lectures as a text-book, *Moral Philosophy, or the Science of Obligation,* later revised and renamed *Moral Science, or the Philosophy of Obligation.*

Geology, as then taught, fitted beautifully into the scheme of

[30]*Ibid.*, 269, 300, 299, 305, and 234.
[31]A. T. Swing, *James Harris Fairchild* (New York—c. 1907), 184–189.

studies of the senior year, for it amounted essentially to another course in the evidences of religion. One of the chief objects of this course was to show the students that the facts of Geology and the story of Creation as given in *Genesis* were in perfect agreement and that science generally supported revealed religion. Professor George Nelson Allen, who taught Geology in Oberlin from 1848 to 1871, explained that the word "day" as used in the Mosaic narrative did not mean twenty-four hours but merely a certain epoch of unknown length. He took up the account of Creation in class, verse by verse, and analyzed it "scientifically." It is significant that in his lectures to a Bible Class ten years later Charles Penfield covered the same subject in much the same way.[32]

Illustrative material was felt to be absolutely essential to proper instruction in Geology. Hence the emphasis placed in all institutions upon the collection of specimens in "cabinets." The students formed a "Natural History Society" in 1839 and commenced collecting minerals, etc. The cabinet thus begun was housed in Tappan Hall. It was evidently small, however, and not very satisfactory for instructional purposes. In 1846 the faculty decided that regular courses in Geology should be introduced and George Allen, two years later, began teaching the subject. Immediately he set to work collecting more "rocks," shells, minerals, insects, etc. In 1849 the old Music Hall was divided to furnish a place for exhibiting this material. From time to time the trustees made special grants to enable Allen to visit other cabinets and buy more specimens. In the seventies the former Union School building was purchased and renamed Cabinet Hall in honor of the collection which was then moved into it.[33] Undoubtedly some of the specimens now in the possession of the College date back to this early period. At an early date

[32]George Allen, MS Lecture Notes on Geology and Physical Geography (Allen MSS), and Theodore Wilder, "Index Rerum" [MS notebook, 1860, O. C. Library]. Walter Rogers' study of this material has been very useful to me (*Op. Cit.*, 63–70). Prof. Edward Hitchcock's *Elementary Geology* (Amherst—1850), used as a text in Oberlin at least from 1850, also deals with the relation of religion and science in a similar fashion (Pages 264 *et seq.*). See Conrad Wright, "The Religion of Geology," *New England Quarterly*, XIV, 335–358 (June, 1941).

[33]Julia M. Read to Helen Cowles, Oct. 10, 1841 (Cowles MSS); George Allen, *Circular Presenting the Claims of the Cabinet of Natural History in Oberlin College* (n.d.—n.p.); F. M., June 26, 1839; Oct. 22, 1846; P. C. M., Oct. 9, 31, 1849; Dec. 15, 1865; T. M., Aug. 20, 1860; Aug. 22, 1865, and "Geological Notes" in *Oberlin Students' Monthly* I, 52 (Dec., 1858).

there were "field trips." A student wrote in 1859: "We have been studying Geology this term which is a very interesting study. Next Monday we are intending to take a trip to the lake and thereabouts for the purpose of putting our knowledge in practical use by making attacks upon Rocks & investigating the forces at work in forming deposits. We have engaged teams to take the ladies and all, a good time is anticipated."[34]

The political and social sciences, as we have seen, were just in the process of separating off from Moral Philosophy. Political Economy (Economics) appeared first as an independent study at Harvard in 1820, at Yale in 1824, at Dartmouth in 1828 and at Princeton in 1830. Francis Wayland's *Elements of Political Economy,* first published in 1837, was the standard text, though the French economist Jean B. Say's earlier work was also sometimes used. Courses in Political Science were usually devoted to the study of international or American constitutional law. One course in social science was included in the curriculum for the final year throughout the early history of Oberlin. It is not at all certain, however, that the course was always actually given.

It seemed to be rather difficult to secure a satisfactory man to give the lectures in this field. In 1835 James G. Birney, the famous anti-slavery leader, was elected "Professor of Law, Oratory and Belles Lettres," but he did not accept the appointment. A short time afterward the Hon. Zebulon R. Shipherd, the father of the Founder, was approached, but also declined. The next year, successive, unsuccessful efforts were made to obtain the services of Alvan Stewart, another anti-slavery lawyer, of Utica, New York, and of the Reverend Theodore Spencer. (The reader will recognize all three as Finneyite lawyers from New York.) At last, in 1838, Edward Wade of Cleveland, brother of Congressman Ben Wade, accepted the position of Professor of Law. But, though his name appears with the faculty in the three succeeding catalogues, he never gave but one course of lectures at Oberlin. The young men who attended cross-questioned him so mercilessly that he concluded that his preparation was, for the time at least, inadequate. In 1840 and again in 1850 efforts were made to get Finney to lecture on the "Great Principles of Law." "Law" was finally dropped from the curriculum in 1856, after having

[34]E. C. Barnard to J. D. Fowler, Nov. 5, 1859 (Fowler MSS).

actually been taught during only one term. Of course, these lectures were never intended to train professional lawyers, but merely to give the students a general knowledge of government and to prepare them for Finney's legal theology.[35]

In 1842 Amasa Walker became "Professor of Political Economy and General History." Walker was a former wholesale shoe merchant of Boston who had retired to his family home at North Brookfield, Massachusetts, when only forty-one years of age on account of ill health. Living on the moderate fortune which he had accumulated he devoted himself to reform, politics and the study of Political Economy. He was an advocate of the immediate emancipation of the slaves, Elihu Burritt's first lieutenant in the peace crusade, an active proponent of free trade, a leading promoter of the Lyceum movement, a one-time president of the Boston Temperance Society, and a friend to every other reform. It was natural that he should be attracted to Oberlin and that Oberlin should be attracted to him.[36]

"He is a self-made man," wrote Mr. Finney in December of 1841 when his appointment was being discussed. "Of a very philosophical turn of mind. A pretty good English scholar. Has read considerable Latin. . . . His views of political economy are certainly unlike anything ever taught in any school so far as I know. He maintains with us that true political economy must consist in national and individual obedience to the law of God. . . . He has been unable to attend meeting much for some time. He regrets this much & so do I. I have told him that we do not want him there unless he has the spirit of doing good & that should he go without that spirit he will be very unhappy

[35]T. M., May 29, 1835, Mar. 8, 1836, Sept. 5, 1838; Sept. 23, 1856; P. C. M., July 14, 1835, Oct. 5, 1836, June 5, 1856; F. M., Sept. 11, 1844; T. Spencer to C. G. Finney, Sept. 16, 1836 (Finney MSS); John Morgan to C. G. Finney, Aug. 31, 1850 (Finney MSS); Leonard-Fairchild MS I, 7, and James H. Fairchild, "The Professorship of Law in Oberlin College" in the *Oberlin Review*, Nov. 8, 1884. There is a sketch of Wade in the *Biographical Directory of the American Congress*. In January, 1835, before coming to Oberlin, Mahan wrote that he would insist on the inclusion of Political Science and Political Economy in the Curriculum.—Mahan to Birney, Jan. 12, 1835, Dumond, *Letters of James Gillespie Birney*, I, 168–9. The author furnished information on this course to Anna Haddow for her *Political Science in American Colleges and Universities, 1636–1900* (New York—c. 1939), but it was not referred to, apparently because it was called "Law" and not "Political Science." See page 208 in *Ibid.*

[36]James S. Loring, *The Hundred Boston Orators* (Cleveland—1852), 508–513; *National Cyclopedia of American Biography*, XI, 438–439, and the *Dictionary of American Biography*.

there as well as useless. He knows fully what we expect of him if he goes there. He calculates & wishes to conform to Oberlin habits of living. To sell his furniture & get it made there, etc., etc. His business talent is said to be peculiar. His piety will I trust improve." On January 17, 1842, Walker wrote to Hamilton Hill accepting the appointment to teach Political Economy but not History. "Such are now the indications of Providence," he wrote, "that I have concluded to accept the appointment and come to Oberlin as soon as the weather & travelling will admit, which I understand will be about the last of May or first of June. . . . After having made a fair experiment, should it appear that I am useful, and that I am clearly in the path of duty, and in a station which I am qualified to fill, I trust that I shall unite my heart and interests as fully with the dear Institution as those who are now so devoted to its welfare."[37]

Fortunately one set of notes taken by a student on the forty-seven lectures delivered to the seniors and theologs in 1842–43 is still preserved. Though very rough and sketchy they give us a generally good idea of the character and content of Political Economy, "the science of national wealth," as taught by Walker that year. Twenty of these lectures were devoted to banking and currency, showing the practical nature of the presentation. Banking was a pertinent question in that period of depression, and Walker, as a former Boston bank official, was especially qualified to speak on the subject. Nine lectures were devoted to the tariff. Six dealt with capital ("the accumulated productions of labor which is employed in the production of wealth") and labor ("any sort of action performed by man or beast or machinery which produces wealth"). There were three lectures on trade and three on taxation. Less than two hours were devoted to the theories of value ("just what an article will fetch") and cost ("the amount of labor which it costs to produce" an article). The two final lectures dealt with credit and interest. Credit, Walker defined as "the use of property without paying for it immediately." He continued: "It enables those who cannot use property to assist others. . . . It is a stimulus to industry." He recognized, how-

[37]C. G. Finney to Henry Cowles, Dec. 23, 1841 (Cowles MSS), and Walker to Hill, Jan. 17, 1842 (Treas. Off., File J). Walker arrived in Oberlin in July (*Oberlin Evangelist,* July 20, 1842), and took a ten-year lease on a lot on Sept. 19, 1842 (Lease in Misc. Archives).

ever, its dangers: "The idle can rob the frugal. It holds out temptations to be too expensive. Farmers' credit is sometimes injurious. It many times induces men to enter into speculation. It operates as a tax. Merchants must charge more for [because of] bad debts."[38]

While in Oberlin, Walker contributed in other ways. He charged nothing for his services. He stimulated interest in the peace movement. He served actively on the Prudential Committee and Board of Trustees. In 1843, he went to London as Oberlin's representative at the Peace Convention. The evidence is not clear as to how many and what years Walker taught in Oberlin. Certainly he did not give the course in 1843–44, but he was back again the next year.[39] His name continued to be listed with the faculty in the catalog until 1850 when he formally resigned. In later years, though much involved in politics, he gave a considerable part of his time to Political Economy. He lectured on that subject for a number of years at Amherst College. In 1850 he spoke before the session of the American Institute of Instruction at Northampton on "Political Economy as a Study for Common Schools." His text book, *The Science of Wealth,* was first published in 1866 and early in 1867 he donated a copy to the Oberlin College Library.[40]

Henry Peck taught Political Economy in 1855, but who, if anyone, conducted the courses in Law, Political Economy, and "Political and Social Sciences" in other years is unknown. It may fairly be said, however, that Walker, together with Mahan and Finney, established the tradition of the Social Sciences in Oberlin.

[38]W. A. Westervelt's MS notes on Political Economy, Chemistry and Pastoral Theology, 1842–1843 (O. C. Lib.).

[39]F. M., Apr. 3, 1844; *Schedule of Examination,* 1845. However, in a statement written by Professor Walker at some unknown date and kindly furnished to the author by his grandson, Francis Walker of Washington, D. C., he declared:

> "I gave lectures each year at Oberlin (I think) till 1848 when in the fall of that year I was elected to the Legislature of Massachusetts and resigned my professorship.
>
> "The engagement at Oberlin kept my mind connected with the subject of Political Economy and made me feel the great want of a suitable text-book. There was not one which I could full approve, not one that to my apprehension taught the right principles in regard to the great question of the currency."
>
> —Francis Walker to the author, Jan. 11, 1933.

[40]T. M., Apr. 20, 1850; *Lectures delivered before the American Institute of Instruction . . ., 1850* (Boston—1851), and P. C. M., Mar. 28, 1867.

AMASA WALKER

(Reproduced from James P. Munroe, *A Life of Francis Amasa Walker* [New York—1923] by special permission of Henry Holt and Company)

The study and practice of rhetoric and oratory constituted almost the entire work in English in the American colleges in the middle of the nineteenth century. Oberlin departed from the usual rule in the early years by introducing the study of English Literature in the College Course (Milton, Cowper's Poems, "English Poetry"), but soon abandoned it and conformed to the normal practice.[41] Richard Whately's *Rhetoric* and *Logic* were studied throughout our period, at first in the sophomore and later in the junior year. From 1858 to 1863 "Practical Lectures on Rhetoric" were given in the first term of the freshman year. All students were required to attend weekly classes in composition throughout the period of their attendance. The emphasis on rhetoric in literary societies and in the curriculum was the strong point in the college training of those days.

[41]Some of these courses were continued in the "Scientific Course" and the "Teachers' Course.'

CHAPTER XLIII

FROM PREP TO THEOLOG

WHEN the name Oberlin Collegiate Institute was officially changed to Oberlin College in 1850 there were some who thought it inappropriate. The College proper was after all, they pointed out, only a part of the institution. In 1850 only 69 out of over 500 students were in the College: in 1852, 64 out of 1,020, in 1860, 199 out of 1,311. Not until 1875 was this number surpassed. The great majority of the students were, at all times, in the Preparatory and the Female departments; in 1853 these two departments enrolled 1,182 out of the total of 1,305! The Theological Department (not "Seminary") climbed from 35 in 1835 to 64 in 1840 and then declined more or less steadily to 32 in 1844, 22 in 1849, 20 in 1852, and 16 in 1857. After a recovery, which brought its enrollment up to 36 in 1859, it declined again almost to the point of extinction in 1867 when it contained only eleven students. Small numbers were enrolled in the Teacher's Course and in the Scientific Course, never more than thirty at any one time in our period. Besides, there were the associated schools and independent private classes: the Winter School (or schools), the Ohio Agricultural College (one year), the Department of Music (and later Conservatory), the Commercial Institute, the French School, the German classes, writing classes, elocution classes and drawing classes. It should be understood that Oberlin College, after 1850, was the official designation of this whole conglomerate of departments and not of the "Collegiate Department" alone.

Yet the "departments" were not water tight compartments. As a matter of fact the institution offered a single series of classes ranging from Arithmetic, English Grammar, Algebra, Geometry and introductory Latin Grammar, to Conic Sections, Natural Philosophy, Chemistry, Hebrew, advanced Greek and Latin, and Intellectual and Moral Philosophy, etc. Young men in the

Preparatory Department took one combination of courses; preparatory students in the Young Ladies' Department took another. The same was true of the other departments except for Theology which required a special group of courses. In 1851, for example, the freshmen in the Classical and Scientific Courses in the Collegiate Department and in the Teacher's Course, the men in the second year of the "Shorter Course . . . preparatory to the study of Theology," and the third year students in the Young Ladies' Department, all attended the lectures on Physiology and Hygiene together. The *second year* young ladies and the freshmen in the Scientific Course and Teacher's Course pursued "Conchology" together. Those enrolled in the "Shorter" and Classical courses (sad to relate!) did not pursue it at all. "Classical" freshmen were required to read Xenophon's *Cyropaedia* and *Cicero de Amicitia et de Senectute* in the first term, but it was optional with members of the Scientific Course, while the students in the Teacher's Course read "Cicero's Four Orations vs. Catiline" and the young ladies read no Latin or Greek at all. Some of these courses called for three years of study, some for four.[1] The time spent in the Preparatory Course depended, naturally, entirely upon age and achievement.

The first requirement for admission to the Oberlin Institute was that the candidate should be of unimpeachable morals. "Conditions of admission to the Institute shall be trustworthy testimonials of good intellectual & moral character, ability to labor 4 hours daily, freedom from debts, total abstinence from ardent spirits as an article of drink or refreshment & Tobacco except as a medicine," and the use of a "scholarship." Such was the rule in 1834 and 1835.[2] The word "intellectual" was interlined! Perhaps it was an afterthought.

The "intellectual" prerequisite was somewhat elaborated in the 1835 *Catalogue,* which required that applicants provide "evidence by personal examination and by certificate of possessing such mental qualifications as will enable them to improve the facilities afforded here for a thorough education." In the following year youths considering entering Oberlin were warned

[1]*Catalogues.*

[2]1834 By Laws and First Annual Report (1834). Only a slight change in wording was made in 1835 (Cf. "Terms of admission to the O. C. Institute, 1835" in the Misc. Archives).

that they might "be subjected to an examination as to their character, talents, and literary attainments." After 1836 male students appear to have been received into the Preparatory Department regardless of scholastic attainments. Young ladies, however, must always "make previous applications in writing, certifying their age, state of health, character, present attainments, and the time they propose to continue here." The six months period of probation took the place of scholastic admission requirements to a certain extent, those who failed utterly in their studies being dropped summarily during that period or sent back to a more elementary department or class.

Chief emphasis, however, was laid upon the piety and morality of applicants. The requirement of "testimonals of good moral character" was never dropped. None would be admitted who travelled on the Sabbath. In 1835 a young lady student wrote to her sister: "I have just been over to Mr. Shipherd's to inquire if I can have a sister received here next winter. He said if I had a sister who was a pious person and whose object was to be useful in the world . . . he thought likely they would receive her." In 1853 a young lady was refused admission because her parents were not legally married. A few years later there was an incredible rumor among the students that one young man was not received because he "was seen drinking a glass of root beer."[3] The existence of the rumor, however, indicates the general understanding of the strictness of the moral prerequisites. There is nothing surprising in this in view of the declared preëminence of the training of the "moral sensibilities" and the instillation of true Christian piety in the Oberlin scheme of education.

After the discontinuance of the short-lived "Infant School" (1834) no students were received under eight years of age; those entering the Collegiate Department must be not younger than fourteen. After 1850 females "from abroad" must be at least sixteen, and beginning in 1855 it was required that all students from out of town should be sixteen or older "unless committed to the special care of some approved resident of the place"; nor should any be "under fourteen except by special arrangement

[3]Delia Fenn to Richard Fenn and family, Aug. 21, 1835 (O. C. Lib.); L. B. M., Mar. 4, 1853, and Henry Prudden to parents, June 3, 1859 (lent by Miss Lillian Prudden, New Haven, Connecticut).

with the Faculty or Principal of the Female Department."[4]

Young men with little or no schooling but otherwise admissible were placed in the Preparatory Department. This department was a real necessity in the early days of Oberlin when academies and other secondary schools preparing for college were exceedingly rare in the West. Geography, Mathematics, elementary Latin and Greek, English, History and Religion were the fields taught.[5]

W. C. Woodbridge's *Geography* was the first one used, supplanted by S. Augustus Mitchell's in 1843 and by the geographies of Colton and Fitch in 1857. From 1856 to 1867 the text was supplemented by the *Key to Pelton's Hemispheres,* the famous rhymed geography. The scientific information in this book was not only presented in metrical form but set to music. It was suggested, for example, that the verses on the "States and Territories" be sung to the tune of *Auld Lang Syne:*

1.

"Our Country, the United States, shall now engage our rhyme,
And Washington is capital of this most favor'd clime;
Now every individual State in order we repeat;
New England, or the Eastern States, our notice first shall meet.

* * *

5.

"Now to the Middle States we come;—of these New York stands first,
And Legislative wisdom there in Albany is nursed:
New Jersey is the next we name, a fruit-producing State,
At Trenton, its Metropolis, the Hessians met their fate.

* * *

14.

"Ohio, pride of Western plains, where grain and pork abound,
Columbus is thy capital, and fertile is thy ground;
New Michigan invites our lay, among the lakes it lies,
A growing town, 'tis Lansing called, a capitol supplies."

And much more on the same order.

At first Mathematics included only Arithmetic, but Algebra was added later. The arithmetic textbook used in the early years

[4]*Catalogues.*
[5]Physiology and a little Natural Philosophy came in in later years.

was the famous text by Dr. Daniel Adams "in which the principles of operating by numbers are analytically explained, and synthetically applied; thus combining the advantages to be desired both from the inductive and synthetic mode of instructing" etc., etc. The book begins with simple numeration and notation and carries through to cube root and arithmetical and geometrical progression. From it pupils might learn apothecaries weight, how to deal in "Federal Money" and English money,

"Thirty days hath September
April, June and November, . . ."

as well as that remarkable verse:

"At Dover Dwells George Brown, Esquire,
Good Carlos Finch and David Fryer,"

by which one was supposed to be aided in determining the day of the week of the first of the month. In the middle fifties Adams' gave way to Stoddard's and Ray's *Arithmetic.*

The trend toward classical studies in Oberlin generally, which was the reverse phase of the decline of Hebrew, appeared in the Preparatory Course, the reading in Latin and Greek becoming much more difficult and extensive. For those, however, who were not preparing for college a special English curriculum was provided to train them for teaching or serve as preparation for the Teacher's or "Scientific" Course.

The work in English included grammar, rhetorical reading, compositions and exercises in declamation. The "immortal" McGuffey's *Rhetorical Guide* was used in the forties but was superseded by Henry Mandeville's abstruse *Elements of Reading and Oratory*. The study of oral English through the latter text involved the mastery of a remarkable technical vocabulary, according to which one sentence of Brutus' oration at the death of Caesar was described as a "compound declarative single compact of the second form" and another as a "compound indefinite interrogative close"! Bullion's *English Grammar* was used for many years.

"Grimshaw's Goldsmith's Histories of Greece, Rome and England" were prescribed in the thirties and early forties along with Noah Webster's *History of the United States, to which is prefixed a Brief Historical Account of our English Ancestors, from the Dispersion at Babel, to their Migration to America and of the Conquest of South America, by the Spaniards!* These gave way to "Taylor's *General History*" and later to the universally popular *Outlines of Universal History* translated from the *Lehrbuch der Weltgeschichte* of Dr. Georg Weber of Heidelberg. In addition to the study of the Bible, preparatory students of the first few years also read Josiah Hopkins' *Christian's Instructer* and Nevin's *Biblical Antiquities.*

The curriculum for young ladies in the preparatory course of their department was considerably lighter and more elementary. It included, for example, no History, no Greek, and no Latin, until the fifties when Latin Grammar was added. The preparatory work of the young ladies before 1850 was really not secondary education at all.

The regular Young Ladies' Course, entered by those who had "passed" the ladies' preparatory course, was itself partly secondary. The course covered three years at first but was later extended to four years. Many classes were attended with the male preparatory students; English Grammar, History (Grimshaw and Webster and later Weber), Geography, Bible, etc.

The young ladies were given an especially heavy dose of religion. Long after the young men in the "prep" course had ceased to study Hopkins' *"Instructer"* it was assigned for the ladies; Nevin's *Biblical Antiquities,* included in the Ladies' Course in 1836, was still listed thirty years later! Josiah Hopkins, the teacher of John J. Shipherd, was the author of the *Christian's Instructer, Containing a Summary Explanation and Defence of the Doctrines and Duties of the Christian Religion.* This little book, the second edition of which was published in 1833 with a recommendation by Charles G. Finney, was a sort of a layman's guide to theology and contained chapters on "Truth of Revelation," "Atonement," "Regeneration," "Natural Ability," "Perseverance of the Saints," and "Future Punishment." It certainly must have been an aid in understanding Finney's "double-header" sermons which all students were required to attend on the Sabbath. John W. Nevin's *A Summary of Biblical Antiquities; for the use of Schools, Bible-Classes and Families* was an elaborate aid to the study and understanding of the Bible. It contained an account of the Jewish religion and data on the geography, vegetation, climate, buildings, furniture, agriculture, social customs, etc. of the Holy Land. Its study should have been good preparation for prospective Sunday School teachers, missionaries, and ministers' wives.

In the early forties, in addition to these two books studied in the first year, William Paley's *Evidences of Christianity* was read in the second year, Marsh's *Ecclesiastical History* and Jahn's *Biblical Archaeology* in the third year, and Joseph Butler's *Analogy of Religion, Natural and Revealed* along with "Lectures on Intellectual and Moral Philosophy; Principles of Sacred Interpretation; [and] Lectures on Theology" in the fourth year! Paley's *Evidences* was the best known apology for Christianity of that period and a textbook in many English and American schools and colleges. John Marsh's *Epitome of General Ecclesiastical History* was highly recommended by Rev. Joseph Emerson, the patron saint of higher education for women, and was a sort of abridged and revised "Book of Martyrs," illustrations and all. Jahn's *Archaeology* served the same purpose as Nevin's *Biblical Antiquities* and repeated much of the material. It was probably considerably more difficult and must have been rather confusing to the young ladies because of the many Hebrew and Greek quotations. Butler's *Analogy* was another much-used defense of Christianity, a masterpiece of logical argument, "a compact of profound thought." A student in the Young Ladies' Course wrote an essay on the *Analogy* in 1849. "Butler's argument," she wrote, "was addressed to that class of persons who believe in God as the author of nature, but not as the author of the Bible. His object is to show that from analogy we might expect a revelation and such a one as is contained in the Bible, for there is nothing against the truths taught by it in natural religion but much in favor of them."[6] In later years the young ladies also read Mahan *"On the Will"* and his *Mental and Moral Philosophy*.

The feminine mind, though dragged through this morass of theological profundity, was not considered strong enough to conquer the difficulties of Latin and Greek. No classical languages were included in the course until 1858 when Cicero's *Orations* were introduced. In 1859 Virgil's *Aeneid* and Sallust

[6] H. M. Cowles, "Some of the Arguments I have learned from Butler's Analogy," a MS Essay dated Oct. 2, 1849, and now in the Cowles-Little MSS.

YOUNG LADY GRADUATES—1855

Mrs. Dascomb, with the bonnet and lace mitts, and Mrs. Finney, also with a bonnet, are in the front row.

(From a daguerreotype in the Oberlin College Library)

were added. Cicero and Virgil and several other classes were shared by the young ladies in the first year of the regular course with the young men of the senior preparatory class. At no time in our period were any ancient languages included in the other years of the Ladies' Course. Except for Hebrew, Latin and Greek, however, the young ladies attended practically all the classes of the Collegiate Course: Geometry, Trigonometry, Conic Sections, Botany, Natural Philosophy, Chemistry, Astronomy, Geology, Physiology, Mental and Moral Philosophy, Political Economy, and Kames' *Elements of Criticism.* To make up for the classics omitted, after 1850 the ladies studied French, Zoology, Elijah H. Burritt's *Geography of the Heavens,* Conchology and Mineralogy, "Watts on the Mind," Guizot's *History of Civilization,* Marcius Willson's *American History* (in the early fifties), Constitution of the United States, "Linear Drawing," and English Literature.[7] Burritt's *Geography of the Heavens* is half an elementary scientific astronomy and half a literary guide to stargazing. With each account of a star or constellation there is associated an account of the mythological name and pertinent quotations from classical literature. Conchology was very much in vogue as a study in seminaries and colleges at the time. It was the study of the form and structure of shells and their arrangement in systematic order. The first year young ladies studied Webster's *United States* and Grimshaw's Goldsmith's *History of England and France,* through the forties. In 1850 these were dropped for Guizot and Willson. Guizot's *History of the Civilization of Europe* was probably the best general survey of world history then available. Willson's *American History* is a solid volume of nearly seven hundred pages which treats not only the United States but Canada, Mexico and, appropriately at that date, the history of Texas and the late Mexican War. The young men in all departments wrote compositions, delivered declamations and engaged in discussions regularly throughout their course. The "misjudged sex" only wrote compositions.

To make the curriculum comparable to those of the leading female seminaries French, Poetry, Modern Literature, and Linear Drawing were added. These were subjects supposed to

[7]In the thirties and forties the general relations of the departments were the same though the subjects studied differed somewhat.

be peculiarly appropriate to the feminine mind. Drawing was the only one of the so-called "ornamental branches" taught at Oberlin, embroidery, wax work, the making of hair ornaments, etc., found in the curriculum of some "finishing schools" being noticeably absent.[8] Antoinette Brown had a private drawing class in the late forties. In 1852–53 Miss L. D. Fuller taught the regular drawing classes for a shilling and a half an hour. A few years later Frances M. Hubbard, a student in the Ladies' Course, taught Linear Drawing and also "Oriental" and "Grecian Painting." Anna M. Wyett began her 32 years of service as teacher of drawing in Oberlin in 1855. A private studio for teaching drawing and painting was opened in 1860 "over Mr. Fitch's bookstore" by a Professor Couch.[9] Young ladies also often studied piano or voice in the "Music Department" or later in the "Conservatory."

But it was never intended "to send out into the world a company of Butterflies, to glitter a while, and then vanish, but to send out a set of *pious, well educated* and genteel (not fashionable) young Ladies prepared to be useful in any circumstances." The more serious and "useful" subjects received the chief emphasis. "Our course of study embraces five years [with the preparatory work], the works which we investigate are such as are calculated to furnish discipline of mind and a supply of rich thought," wrote Mary Ann Adams in 1839. "Indeed so far as we know, no female seminary in our country is more thorough. We are taught not only to fully appreciate the worth of an author but to *think* for ourselves upon the various subjects brought before us, and we do feel that this knowledge after which we are searching is of more value than the diamond which sparkles in the sands of India and the pearl in its ocean bed." Except for the ancient languages, young ladies were admitted to a course exactly like that of their brothers in the Collegiate Department. Indeed, they attended the very same classes! This made a great impression. "Our advantages here are *great, very great,*" wrote another student. "I heard one of the young Ladies remark that when she first came here, at almost every recitation her heart

[8]In 1853 two young ladies applied to teach embroidery and "ornamental branches."—L.B.M., Mar. 1, 1853.

[9]L. B. M., May 10, 1852; Bill for services, May 25, 1853 (Misc. Archives); MS Account Book of Frances M. Hubbard (lent by Fred P. Bemis, Santa Monica, California), and *Oberlin Students' Monthly,* XI, 317 (Aug., 1860).

was so melted down in view of her great privileges that she could hardly keep from weeping."[10]

The teaching in the Preparatory Department was done by a principal or principals sometimes aided by a tutor and by a number of college and theological students who were paid by the hour. In the Ladies' Course there were one or two principals and several student teachers. Taking the year 1844–45 as an example: George N. Allen and W. W. Wright received $600.00 together for their salaries as Principal and Assistant Principal in the Preparatory Department. Nelson W. Hodge, the genial punster, received $400.00 as tutor. $350.00 was distributed among seven student teachers. James Monroe received eighteen cents an hour for teaching languages and Henry E. Whipple a shilling for Arithmetic and fifteen cents for Elocution. The two Lady Principals, Mary Ann Adams and Lorinda Moore, received only $350.00 together, and $150.00 was paid to the student teachers. Lucy Stone was paid a shilling an hour for teaching Arithmetic and Lucretia Smith the same for Grammar but Sarah J. Curtis received only ten cents for teaching Arithmetic.[11]

Pay for student teachers varied all the way from ten cents up to twenty-five cents an hour, the latter wage sometimes being paid in the middle sixties, when the currency was depreciated and general prices high. In 1838 George W. Bancroft taught Latin and Greek at a shilling and a half an hour; in the following year another student was paid fifteen cents an hour for taking charge of a class in Roman History. In 1840 William B. Brown, later the distinguished pastor of the First Congregational Church of Newark, New Jersey, secretary of the American Congregational Union, and a trustee of Oberlin College for over twenty years, taught Arithmetic and Grammar classes for fifteen cents an hour.[12] Other student teachers received 18¾ cents an hour

[10][Davis and] Nancy Prudden to George P. Prudden, Apr. [8 and] 13, 1837 (Prudden MSS); and Mary Ann Adams *et al.* to John Keep, July 10, 1839 (Keep MSS).

[11]"Account of Institution Expenses of Teaching, Aug. 1845" (Misc. Archives). This account gives $700.00 for the salary of Allen and Wright but the Trustees, at their meeting on Aug. 18, granted only $600.00 (T. M., Aug. 18, 1845). On Hodge see J. H. Fairchild to M. F. Kellogg, Mar. 17, 1841 (Fairchild MSS). The "Female Department" was an administrative unit and the "Ladies' Course," a curricular unit, but the terms were often confused.

[12]On Brown see: "Obituary Record of Alumni of Oberlin College for the Year 1912–1913," *Bulletin* of Oberlin College, New Series, No. 6.

for teaching Geometry and Nevin's *Biblical Antiquities* in the same year. Edward H. Fairchild, later Principal of the department and then President of Berea College, was paid 15 cents for teaching Arithmetic and 18¾ cents for Bible and "Retoric" in 1841. In 1850 Sallie Holley, anti-slavery speaker and daughter of the reformer and sponsor of the Erie Canal, received only a shilling an hour for instruction in composition. At the same time two young men were credited at the rate of 15 cents an hour for teaching Marsh's *Ecclesiastical History* and Burritt's *Geography of the Heavens*. In the spring of 1861, Jacob R. Shipherd, one of the Oberlin-Wellington Rescuers was teaching for a shilling and a half; W. W. Parmenter, who died in a Confederate prison a few months later, received the same. A. A. Wright, later one of the most distinguished members of the Oberlin faculty, obtained twenty-five cents an hour in 1864, but Frederick D. Allen, who became a Leipzig Ph.D. in 1870 and was Professor of Classical Philology at Harvard from 1880 to 1897, received only 18¾ cents. Sometimes also the wives of professors taught classes by the hour or corrected compositions at 31 cents a week.[13]

The cost of instruction in these classes was evidently very low and as a result the Preparatory and Female departments were always profitable, in contrast to the Collegiate and Theological departments where most of the instruction was given by salaried professors. No doubt some of the teaching of such brilliant youngsters as Frederick Allen, A. A. Wright, W. W. Brown, Sallie Holley and Lucy Stone was excellent, but the great majority must have been poorly equipped both in knowledge of content and method. The use of these student teachers could hardly be justified on any grounds but those of economy. By the end of our period the many disadvantages of the practice were being recognized and the trustees were being urged to supply more permanent, salaried tutors for the elementary classes.[14] The senior preparatory class was taught by the Principal and other regular teachers when the available staff made this possible.

Even the Principals of the Preparatory Department (with one

[13]MS Bills for instruction in the Misc. Archives. Mrs. Hudson, Mrs. Allen and Mrs. Monroe (Elizabeth Maxwell) sometimes did this.

[14]John Morgan to C. G. Finney, May 7, 1850 (Finney MSS), and MS Report of E. N. Bartlett, Acting Principal, Aug. 23, 1867 (Misc. Archives).

PRINCIPAL E. HENRY FAIRCHILD
(From the 1859 Class Album in the Oberlin College Library)

or two exceptions) seem not to have been men of particular fitness for their work. Daniel Branch and E. P. Ingersoll (also Professor of Sacred Music) held the position for only a year apiece. George Whipple, a Lane Rebel and later secretary of the American Missionary Association, was an able executive and may have been a successful teacher. He was in charge from 1836 to 1839. Theodore J. Keep, who succeeded him, was not a college graduate, having left Yale in his sophomore year. George Nelson Allen, Principal from 1842 to 1846,[15] was scandalously underpaid and overworked and much more interested in his music than in "prep" teaching. Little is known of the work of Henry E. Whipple (1846–1853), but as a teacher later at Hillsdale College he was successful and popular. E. Henry Fairchild was the most outstanding, both for the length of his term of service (sixten years) and for the reputation which he made as a teacher and administrator. Doubtless the duties of the Principals of the Preparatory and Female departments were unusually laborious; certainly the salaries paid were small. In view of these considerations it is perhaps surprising that it was possible to secure persons as able as Marianne Dascomb, Alice Welch Cowles and E. H. Fairchild.[16]

Evidently the prep students were no more universally sober and industrious than high school students of today. "Attended recitations as usual," wrote a young lady in 1849, "and between them our class engaged in lively play, for exercise, a few minutes. When the Professor entered, I rather feared he was displeased, but do not know." As to composition class, one girl confessed: "My pieces are generally picked up in a few minutes and I assure you correspond with the time employed in writing. I cannot take time to do justice to a piece of writing and unless we are naturally smart a good composition would . . . look too much like borrowed greatness." Another admitted to her mother that she was so busy that she "took an old composition." In 1854 a young lady "read in her composition class as her own an article which her teacher afterward found in a periodical." She was, of course, disciplined. A few months earlier another student soliloquized in her diary: "The bell has just told [*sic*] 9 and with a feeling akin to satisfaction I have shut myself in my little room

[15]On the date when Allen succeeded Keep, see F. M., Feb. 9, 1842.
[16]On the Lady Principals see pages 678–680.

having just returned from the Ladies lyseum. But whence this feeling of satisfaction? Does it arise from a sense of duties well performed? Let me see, my latin lessons only half looked out for tomorrow, which should have been all done, and then my subject for declamation is not yet found whereas it should be partly learned. But then I have done what I could, and why not be satisfied." Ten years later another wrote to a former classmate: "Do you know that you took *my old Algebra* home instead of yours? I have wanted it lots. I wish we could exchange. I want the answers to the examples in it."[17]

For students on the college level who did not care to attempt the study of advanced Latin and Greek, alternate courses were offered from which the classics were largely or entirely omitted. This was the scheme which had been tried at Amherst in 1827 and 1828, but which failed and was abandoned. The University of Virginia was securing the same result by allowing students to choose between the various "schools" within the university. These were first steps toward the development of the modern "elective" system.

A student at Oberlin might, after 1846, enroll in the Teachers' Department (or Course) or, after 1850, in the "Scientific Course." The former course, as the *Catalogue* announced, embraced "most of the studies pursued in the Collegiate Course, except the [ancient] languages, with such additions as are necessary to adapt it to its purposes." The students in this course attended some classes with the college students and others with the young ladies. There is a marked similarity between the Teachers' Course and the course of studies pursued in the Young Ladies' Department, though the young men in the former completed their work in three years whereas the Young Ladies' Course covered four years. A diploma but no degree was granted to graduates of these courses. On the other hand the regular A.B. degree was granted to those who completed the four-year "Scientific Course." In the latter course, offered from 1850 to 1858 only, and especially intended for "such students as have not the ministry in view or may have little taste or ability for the study

[17]Helen Cowles, *Grace Victorious*, 160–161 (Nov. 13, 1849); Elizabeth Hanmer to Mr. Glin, Sept. 26, 1853 (lent by Miss Mildred Durbin, Columbus, Ohio); Sarah Cowles to Mrs. Cowles, Jan. 11, 1853 (Cowles-Little MSS); L. B. M., May 20, 27, 1854; M. M. Gilbert, MS Diary, Jan. 7, 1854, and "Classmate" to M. A. Winegar, June 26, 1864 (lent by Mrs. H. N. Roberts, Wichita, Kansas).

of the languages,"[18] the Latin and Greek was omitted as in the Teachers' Course, but additional work in Mathematics and Science was given to replace it and fill out the full four years. Some confusion has resulted with regard to these courses for two reasons: First, the Teachers' Course was placed under the supervision of the Principal of the Preparatory Department and hence the students pursuing it came to be classified (even in the official *General Catalogue* of 1908) as preparatory students, even though they were pursuing much work of college grade. Second, there has been confusion because, in 1864, several years after the four-year scientific course was abolished, the designation of the Teachers' Course was changed to "Scientific Course," though the content was in no way altered, no degree being granted and only three years required for completion. The important fact remains that, from 1846, a student might enroll in a course which included no Greek or Latin but did include all of the other subjects usually pursued in collegiate institutions, though for eight years only were degrees granted for the completion of such a course.

In 1833 when Shipherd announced his plans for the Institute he had declared that special provisions would "be made for those who are more advanced in life when they commence their studise." This promise was fulfilled when the "Shorter Course" was established in 1836. Only "students of advanced age" were admitted to this course and then only by special vote of the faculty. It was a three-year course including some of the subjects studied in the regular Preparatory Course and some of those studied in College. There was no Latin, but Greek and Hebrew were both included. This practice was continued throughout our period but the number enrolled was always small. Those who successfully completed the course were received into the Theological Department but granted no degree.

Down to 1850 no modern foreign languages were taught in any department of the Institute. In that year, French was introduced in the second year of the Scientific Course, the second year of the Young Ladies' Course and, optionally, in the first year of the Teachers' Course. In the late forties, however, there seems to have been something resembling a stampede to enter independ-

[18]John Morgan to C. G. Finney, Aug. 31, 1850 (Finney MSS), and T. M., Aug. 28, 1850, and Aug. 22, 1854.

ent French classes. There were private classes at least as early as 1844. "I have just commenced studying French," wrote a young lady student to a classmate four years later."There seems to be a general panic among the people here, and strange to tell large classes in French have been formed." In the same year (1848) Charles Penfield was learning both Italian and French. In the spring of 1850 a student applied to the Prudential Committee "for the use of one of the recitation rooms in Tappan Hall to have a class in French one hour in the afternoon daily." The request was granted and he was charged 12½ cents an hour without wood or 25 cents with wood. In the autumn the regular instruction in French began.[19]

There never seems to have been quite so much interest in German as in French, though private instruction in German is known to have been given as early as 1854, and a native German appeared on the scene to conduct a class in 1860. In 1854 some 78 college and "prep" students petitioned the trustees to make German or French an alternative to Hebrew.[20] Hebrew was dropped from the curriculum, but the modern languages were not added, nor for many years were they, despite student agitation and discussion, to become a part of the regular classical college course.

Though he was not the first teacher of French in Oberlin, nor in the Institute, Joseph Albert De La Forêt may rightly be called the Father of the Oberlin French Department. It is said that De La Forêt left France with his father because of political differences with Louis Napoleon Bonaparte.[21] He turned naturally to French teaching as a means of making a living in America. De La Forêt arrived in Oberlin in 1860 and remained approximately six years, until the autumn of 1866. At first he organized a French Boarding School (something like the present Maison Française) in a house on North Main Street above the First Church. In 1864, however, he moved into a classroom in Tappan Hall where he taught his private classes and also the

[19]"Martha" to Hannah Warner, Dec. 25, 1844 (O. C. Lib.); Charles Penfield to Helen Cowles, Nov. 21–24, 1848, and Helen Jones to H. C., Dec. 14, 1848 (Cowles-Little MSS), and P. C. M., Mar. 8, 1850.

[20]Mary Minerva Gilbert, MS Diary; *Lorain County News,* Nov. 21, 1860; Feb. 27, 1861; *Oberlin Students' Monthly,* III, 94 (Jan., 1861); MS Petitions in Trustees' MSS, 1854 (Misc. Archives), and T. M., Aug. 22, 1854.

[21]Statement of his grandson, Mr. Roy De La Forêt. Note the anti-Napoleonic bias of De La Forêt's letter to the *Oberlin Evangelist,* Feb. 13, 1861.

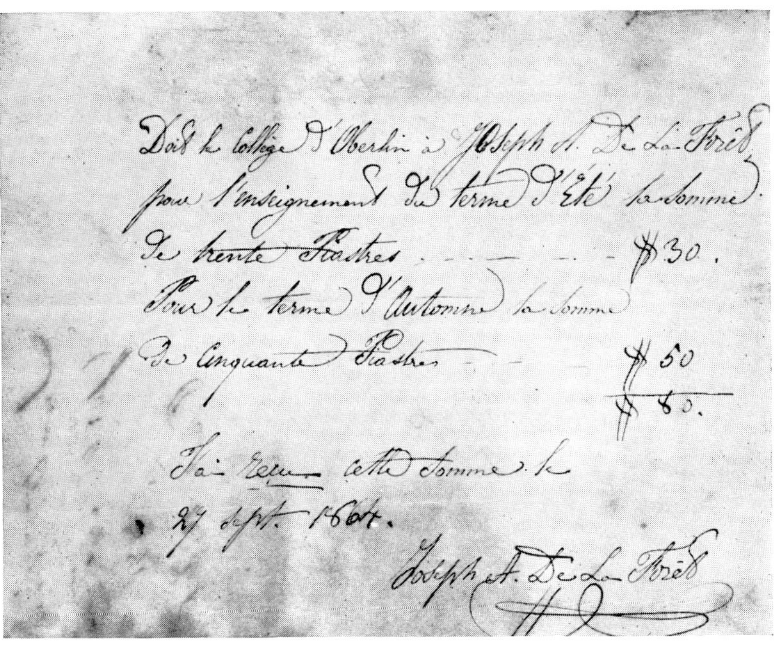

Doit le Collège d'Oberlin à Joseph A. De La Forêt
pour l'enseignement du terme d'Été la somme
de trente Piastres . . . . . . $30.
Pour le terme d'Automne la somme
de Cinquante Piastres $50
$80.

J'ai reçu cette somme le
27 sept. 1864.

Joseph A. De La Forêt

DE LA FORÊT'S BILL FOR TEACHING FRENCH—1864
(Miscellaneous Archives)

classes in the Ladies' Department of the Institute at salaries varying from $30.00 to $75.00 a semester.[22]

Never a master of the English language De La Forêt amused the students with his faulty grammar and strong continental accent. "Prof. De La Forêt" wrote one of his pupils in 1863, "expresses himself as comically as ever. The other day he was greatly excited about the conspiracies in Ohio, & in his indignation declared the copperheads ought to have the head cut immediately." He appears, nevertheless, to have been an able and stimulating teacher and his classes became steadily more popular, and, in 1865, the Prudential Committee consenting, he found it desirable to enlarge his Tappan Hall classroom at his own expense.[23] As a means of advertising his classes and recognizing those who took a full course in the language, a French Commencement was usually held, at which students received special diplomas and read French essays or delivered orations in French:

"Le Changement, Madam Tibbits, d'Oberlin.
L'armure du Chrétien, Sarah E. Furnas, de Troy.
Les Trois Mondes, Mary C. Raymond, de Bowling Green. . . .
Le Temple Inconnu, Amelia Chapman, de Kingsville . . ."

In 1866 De La Forêt left for Cleveland where he continued his profession as a teacher of his native language.[24]

The Theological Department was the crown of the Oberlin Institute. The complete Oberlinite passed from the Preparatory Department through the Collegiate Department and graduated finally from the Theological Department. Such men were thoroughly impregnated with Oberlinism. The ablest minds and the choicest spirits were all urged to go on through the full course in order to prepare themselves for greatest usefulness. The Theological Department set the tone of the whole Institute.

22*Lorain County News,* Dec. 5, 1860; May 22, 1861; *Oberlin Students' Monthly,* III, 94 (Jan., 1861); P. C. M., Sept. 17, 1864; Dec. 29, 1865; MS Bills in Misc. Archives, and *Catalogues.*

23Louisa Fitch [and Mary Dascomb] to James Monroe, Nov. 12 & 16, 1863 (Monroe MSS); P. C. M., Apr. 21, 1865, and *Lorain County News,* Feb. 15, and May 31, 1865.

24*Lorain County News,* Aug. 26, 1863; Aug. 24, 1864, and Aug. 30, 1865. About the time he went to Cleveland, De La Forêt published a textbook called *The Method of Learning and Teaching French* (*Cleveland Leader,* Feb. 7, 1866, in *Annals of Cleveland*). He sold his house on North Main Street in the spring of 1867 (*Lorain County News,* Apr. 3, 1867), and died in Toledo in 1891 (Death Certificate on file at Toledo). He and his wife were members of the First Church (Oberlin Church, MS Minutes, Apr. 2, 1865).

The professors in that department were the leaders of the faculty: Finney, Mahan, Morgan, Henry Cowles, and, later, Henry E. Peck and James H. Fairchild. It was never forgotten that it was the founding of the Theological Department that brought the first three of these and the Lane Rebels to Oberlin and refounded the institution when it was on the verge of collapse. The students of Theology were, especially in the thirties and forties and only to a lesser degree in later years, looked up to as the leaders of the student body. In all religious and many secular activities they took the prominent part. Theological students regularly taught classes in the Preparatory Department and sometimes in the College. They instructed the great Oberlin Sabbath School and did a large part of the teaching in the missionary Sabbath Schools in surrounding districts. Occasionally they engaged in personal conferences with other students on the state of their souls. In the work of maintaining the high standard of piety for which Oberlin was famous the inspirational preaching of Finney was ably supported by the precepts and example of other professors and of the theological students.[25]

Unlike the College curriculum the course of study in the Theological Department remained practically unchanged throughout the period. The conditions of admission were "hopeful piety and a liberal education at some college, unless the candidate has otherwise qualified himself for pursuing with advantage the prescribed course of study" as in the Oberlin "Shorter Course," and a "certificate of good standing in some evangelical church." In the first or "junior" year the course included "Evidences of Divine Revelation, Sacred Canon, Introduction to the Study of the Old and New Testaments; Biblical Archaeology; Principles of Interpretation; Greek and Hebrew Exegesis; Mental and Moral Philosophy; Compositions and Extemporaneous Discussion." "Biblical Geography" was added to the studies of the junior year in the 50's. In the second or "middle" year the subjects studied were "Didactic and Polemic Theology; History of Theological Opinions; Greek and Hebrew Exegesis; Composition and Exposition Discussion." The only changes made in the work of this year was the transfer of "History of Theological Opinions" to the third year and the addition of

[25]See especially the *Oberlin Evangelist,* Nov. 19, 1862.

"Biblical Theology" and "Homiletics." In the third or senior year the courses were "Pastoral Theology; Sacred Rhetoric; Composition of Sermons; Sacred and Ecclesiastical History (including the History of Theological Opinions); Exegesis continued; Church Government; Extemporaneous Discussion." It is notable that introductory Hebrew was not included, students being expected to have studied that language in their college course.

Though there were other effective teachers in the old Theological Department, it was for forty years after its founding essentially a one-man institution. The Lane Rebels came in 1835 on condition that Charles G. Finney should be their teacher, and later students were attracted mainly by the prospect of studying under him.[26] Professors J. H. Fairchild and H. E. Peck ably substituted for and supplemented him, but nobody ever took his place or supplanted him. When Finney was away, as so often happened, the attendance fell off; when he returned, it climbed again.

Finney, as was natural for a self-educated man, believed that most formal education was too theoretical and cold. In his inaugural address as Professor of Theology in 1835 he attacked the usual education of ministers. "Their physical education was defective. It rendered them soft and effeminate. Their mental education was defective. Their studies, for the most part, consisted in efforts of memory, while it should consist in the disciplining of the mind and invigorating of the understanding —in teaching students to reason consecutively,—*to think on their legs*—to draw illustrations living from nature around them—and understand the law of God. . . . Their moral education was defective. They pursued such studies that the more they studied the more cold their religious affections must become, because their minds were employed upon topics that alienate them from God.[27] In view of Finney's interest in "practical" training for the pastorate, of his dominant position in the seminary, and of his personal eccentricities, it was to be expected that his lectures on Pastoral Theology given in the senior year would constitute one of the most distinctive and characteristic courses in Oberlin's theological curriculum.

[26]Morgan to Finney, Mar. 15, 1852 (Finney MSS).
[27]*Ohio Observer,* July 9, 1835.

Three different sets of students' notes on these lectures survive: One set taken in 1837, one in 1843 and one in 1857. Three of Finney's own manuscript lecture outlines for Pastoral Theology are in the Oberlin library. One is undated, but apparently belongs to the period of the forties and fifties. The other two are dated 1872 and 1875 respectively.[28] The outline for 1875 is in script nearly an inch high, legible even to the failing eyes of an old man. Our sources then span most of the forty-one years history of the course. In 1837 it apparently consisted of only six lectures which were almost entirely devoted to manners and the relations of ministers with the opposite sex. It is understandable that Finney, the gentleman from New York City, should have been troubled by the uncouth manners of the farmer boys who attended Oberlin in that early period. Undoubtedly the talks on etiquette were called for. By 1843 the course had expanded to about twenty lectures and to include study habits, business habits, hints on the preparation and delivery of sermons and suggestions regarding pastoral visits. There appear to have been no major changes in content or treatment after 1843.

At the beginning Finney told his students that pastoral theology embraced "the whole field of the Pastoral Office," and he differentiated sharply between the tasks of the evangelist and the pastor. It was the province of the former, he declared, to "win souls to Christ & gather a flock" and of the latter to *"feed, lead,* superintend, & *watch over* it." General theology, he defined as treating of "God, His attributes & relations," while pastoral theology was the practical study of the pastor's relations with his flock.

The pastor and his flock had reciprocal duties, according to Finney. The Pastor must "demean himself [so] as to deserve the confidence of the People," "give himself wholly to the work" and "avoid every irrelevant engagement," "feed the flock with truth well digested," "warn them publicly and privately," "pray for & with them," and "bring everything into the light of the

[28]E. J. Comings' MS Notes, 1837 (lent by Miss Eliza J. Comings of Kingsville, Ohio); William A. Westervelt, MS Notebook—notes on Political Economy, Chemistry and Pastoral Lectures, 1842–1843 (O. C. Lib.), and Smith Norton, MS Notebook—"Notes on sermons & lectures, 1857, also notes on Pres. Finney's Lectures on pastoral theology (O. C. Lib.)." See the reference to this course in W. L. Holman, "Diary of the Rev. James-Hanmer Francis, 1837–1838," *Ohio State Archaeological and Historical Quarterly,* LI, 46 (Jan.—Mar.—1942).

law of God." On the other hand, it was the duty of the people of his flock "to relieve him as far as possible from all that . . . is not his proper work," "to receive him as one called and sent of God as an ambassador from the court of heaven," "to attend his appointments," "to receive and obey the truth," "to cordially & boldly coöperate with him in forming & controlling publick sentiment in respect to every branch of morals," and "to illustrate the Gospel in their lives."

He submitted a list of qualifications for the ministry: "A *living, ardent* piety—not last year's piety—but living now." ("A deeply pious man," he said, "will do good though he have not good talents"),"age and manhood," sound education, "aptness to teach," ordination and "the call." Also he should have "an amiable temper," a "body not deformed," "a spirit of self-sacrifice," a "gift of personal conversation, moral courage, patience and perseverance, independence," "a mellow sensibility," strong faith, "deep spiritual discernment," and "common sense." His education should provide him with an understanding of logic, "a sound mental philosophy," "at least so much knowledge of language as to be accurate & perspicuous," "an outline at least of natural science," and a thorough grounding "in the fundamentals of both natural & revealed theology." He should possess "dignity of Character" not as shown in "studied reserve," "anti-social carriage," "affected sanctity," or in officious "airs & manners," but demonstrated in "such serious purity of conversation as to forbid all trifling in [his] presence," and "such a compassionate earnestness of piety as shall force the impression that [he is] a serious & a holy man."

It was very important, he felt, that a minister should be married to a good wife. "Marriage [is] the right of women & no man for slight cause should defraud them." "An unmarried minister is a peculiar temptation to the other sex." "Ministers need a wife more than other men." "When a man is tied up to a bad wife and cannot be divorced he had better get out of the ministry." In one lecture he suggested ten "Indispensable or important qualifications in a [minister's] wife:"

" 1. Good health.
2. A thorough and extensive education.
3. Prepossessing appearance.
4. Conversational powers.

5. Discretion.
6. She should be a leader of her sex.
7. Gifted in prayer.
8. A good house keeper.
9. A good judgment in the qualities of articles to be bought.
10. Economy."

A minister's wife ought to have, said Finney, the "ability to keep a secret," a "spirit opposed to caste and aristocracy," an "unambitious temper," a body not weakened "by tight lacing," and a "willingness to be poor." She must avoid "getting mixed up with neighborhood scandal," and "indulgence in dress," and "every appearance of fondness for the society of the gentlemen."

He opposed early engagements for various reasons, especially because they distracted the attention from study and from prayer and other religious exercises. As a young man approached his ordination, however, he should look about him for a suitable mate, gauging the available young women by the standard previously submitted. The neophyte was warned that after entering the ministry, whether married or not, he must be particularly careful about his relations with women. Gallantry must be avoided. "Show me a minister that is a Gallant among ladies & I will show you one who is doing little good." "Suffer not yourself to trifle with young ladies in conversation nor in any way." *"Beware how you write ladies; what is written is written."* Finney recognized, however, that the minister must be at ease in the company of the opposite sex and not live as a recluse. It was one of the arguments in favor of coeducation that the prospective pastor was thus prepared to take his place in the mixed society of his parish.

Apparently Mr. Finney did not object to the attendance of young lady visitors at these lectures. In 1840, James H. Fairchild, later President of Oberlin, but then a young "theolog," wrote to his future wife: "Mr. F.[inney] has just closed his pastoral Lectures. He gave us a *half* dozen or more on the subject of marriage & the qualifications necessary in the wife of a pastor, probably both for the benefit of those young men who have yet a choice to make & for the young ladies who were present at the lectures. . . . He spoke at some length on early engagements etc., said much that is true & some things that are not so true."[29]

Finney's advice with regard to manners throws some light on the practices of the time and the region, as well as on his own attitude and on the status of the Oberlin theological students. Ministers, he said, should always avoid levity and "all winking and roguishness," should be grave but not morose, dignified but not sanctimonious. "Where ministers hold out the idea that they are the great ones of the earth they create a false impression of religion." A minister should be polite and considerate, should "observe unusual personal kindness." In 1843 he told his students: "True politeness is nothing else than the practice of true benevolence," and, in 1857: "Good manners [are] benevolence acted out, bad manners, selfishness acted out." Ministers, of all people, he insisted, must avoid slovenliness, affectation, effeminacy, coarseness and vulgarity, selfishness, impertinence, and a spirit of contradiction. They should beware of "band box manners" and of anything "foppish." They should not wear ruffles, rings, breast pins, beards and whiskers (This was in 1843, before he took to wearing them himself.), and they should not carry "gaudy pocket handkershiefs." Evidently much more needed and occupying much more time in his talks were warnings against vulgarity and coarseness. They should not blow their noses with their fingers; they should not use a dirty handkerchief; they must not spit on the carpet; they must not put their feet and muddy boots on the sofa or on the door jambs, nor pull off their stockings before a family! He related the story of a young clergyman who "called on some ladies after walking some distance, took off his boots & hung his socks on the andirons the first thing," and told of another ministerial acquaintance who "put his feet up in a window in a lady's parlor to enjoy the cool air!" He advised the embryo preachers to keep their nails cleaned and pared and their teeth clean. It was disgusting, he said, "in anxious meetings to be obliged to smell the breath of a filthy mouth." At table, he reminded them, they were not supposed to cut their meat with their pocket knives nor wipe their mouths on the table cloth!

The minister, declared the teacher, must be the true shepherd of his flock. He ought to be the leader in his community in sec-

[29]James H. Fairchild to Mary Kellogg, Aug. 25, 1840 (Fairchild MSS).

ular as well as ecclesiastical matters, and "He is not to admit for a moment that he is going out of his sphere" when he takes such leadership. "The legitimate field of Pastoral influence," said Finney, "is as extensive as the field of moral obligations & responsibility." It was desirable, of course, for the minister to be "acquainted with the principles of reform," though he ought not to be an "ultraist" fanatic. "The minister must have a natural adaptation to be a leader—he is to marshall the host of God's elect." He should visit his parishioners often and deal with them directly and frankly. He should not "go to get a dinner" but to transact the business of the Lord and rebuke them for their transgressions. Though the pastor ought to be straightforward, he ought, when possible, also to be tactful. "Be careful to find your people when they are not out of humour," Finney advised. "Never get all the family together when you want to talk to them. The devil often makes children cry, etc." "If possible visit the sick in the morning. Ask what kind of medicine they have been using so that you may not be deceived." "Don't assume that God is visiting them with judgments." "Don't appear unfeeling." "Always have respect for the state of the nervous system . . ." In their business affairs they were recommended to set a good example for others: "Be punctual in all business transactions." "Avoid trading horses." "Do not throw too much business upon your wife." "If you have a garden attend to it. If the weeds grow in it they will grow in your heart."

He gave detailed advice as to the conduct of religious services. The invocation should be solemn and short. The Scriptures should be read slowly, emphatically and "with unction." The Bible should be handled reverently. In announcing the hymns "name the place twice," "notice whether you are understood," and in reading the hymns be careful to "avoid nasal tones." His own prayers were likely to be long and emotional, and he advised the theologs: "Pray in the Spirit"; "If the Lord draws you near to Himself don't be too short"; "Be honest, *earnest,* childlike," but "Don't be tedious."

He urged careful preparation of all sermons. A minister should not study more than three or four hours a day, preferably in the morning after a light breakfast. The subjects should be timely and suited to the congregation. Illustrations should be drawn "from familiar circumstances and not from ancient history and monarchs." Though sermons need not be written out, an outline or skeleton was suggested. This was Finney's own practice. He opposed the reading of sermons and favored preaching from notes, because, he said, it was more easily understood, more interesting, more instructive and more easily remembered. This was the Oberlin style of preaching throughout the early years. In delivery he advised that they be "animated but never vociferous" and "avoid studied gesticulations" and all stiff formality. Finally, they must put their whole soul into it. "Men are not cabbage heads," he told them. "You may [be] the most learned—yet you have God as one of your hearers. Preach so as to please God, for He is taking notes."

The course quite clearly was fresh, realistic and stimulating, and must have contributed greatly to the effectiveness of the many young ministers who went out from Oberlin in those early days.

When he was in Oberlin Finney also taught the course in General or Systematic Theology (Didactic and Polemic Theology). As originally taught it dealt in a broad way with God and His attributes and with divine law. As time passed, however, a larger and larger emphasis was placed upon the development of the peculiar Oberlin views. Freedom of the Will and "human ability" were defended and the related doctrine of Sanctification or perfectionism was elaborated. In the theological classes as in all classes the meetings were opened with prayer; Finney had introduced the practice in Oberlin. With him it was far from a matter of form; often the keynote of the hour's discussion would be struck in the prayer. Sometimes, even, his deep, personal piety led him on and on until a large part or the whole of the recitation period had been consumed in divine supplication. Professor Finney did not usually lecture in this course, but led the discussion. One great theological theme after another would be taken up and pounded out in informal debate and sometimes the facts and reasoning presented would lead the evangelist-teacher to change his own point of view. In the days of the Lane Rebels it was not necessary to use artificial methods to stimulate discussion, but in later years he sometimes drew names out of a hat and called on the persons whose names were drawn to speak. The tone of Finney's classes was always lively though always also fundamentally serious. He, himself, joined in the laughter which followed really witty thrusts by the debaters, though he always frowned upon any mere smartness or lightness.[30]

Finney was fundamentally, however, the ideal, the inspirer and the figurehead of the institution. He was so often absent that the best a student could hope was that sometime during the three years of the Theological Course Finney would be on the job, and then, perhaps for a semester, he would be privileged to sit under him. The everyday routine work of running the department and of teaching most of the courses was in the hands of Morgan, Mahan, Cowles, Peck and Fairchild. It was John Morgan especially who kept it going and substituted in the pulpit during the only too frequent and too much extended absences of Finney.

* * *

From the beginning the long vacation had been placed in the winter instead of the summer in order to give the students an opportunity to teach in rural schools. This vacation lasted for twelve weeks—after 1847, from the fourth Wednesday in November to the fourth Wednesday in February. Up to 1850 there were two terms of school only: one, the short term, beginning at Commencement in August or September and the other, the long term, after vacation in February. In the early years there was also a short vacation in early July conforming with the season of heavy work on the farm. In 1850 the two-term plan gave way to a scheme of three terms, each twelve weeks in length. The First or Fall Term lasted from the fourth Wednesday in August (Commencement) to the fourth Wednesday in November (the beginning of vacation). The Second or Spring Term was from the fourth Wednesday in February to the fourth Wednesday in May, and the Third or Summer Term from the latter date to Commencement.[31] The nearness of the

[30]The sources on Finney's course in General Theology are his *Skeletons of a Course of Theological Lectures* (Oberlin—1840), and *Lectures on Systematic Theology,* 3 vols., (Oberlin—1846–47), especially the prefaces; MS Reminiscences of Antoinette Brown Blackwell noted down by Alice Stone Blackwell in 1903 (lent by A. S. Blackwell), and J. H. Fairchild in *Reminiscences of Rev. Charles G. Finney* (Oberlin—1876), 87–88. On Finney's prayers in class see E. B. Sherwood, *Fifty Years on the Skirmish Line* (Chicago—c. 1893), 37–38.

[31]For the first two years the Preparatory Department did not participate in the winter vacation except for a short two weeks. The practice of commencing and ending terms and vacations on Wednesday, probably in order to accommodate students who obeyed the Sunday travel rule, continued until recent years.

beginning of the winter vacation to Thanksgiving Day and of the end to Washington's Birthday had much to do with the tradition of festivity long associated with those holidays in Oberlin.

What Summer School is to students of the present generation, Winter School was to the students of the mid-nineteenth century. There were many, particularly among the residents in town, who had no teaching appointments and preferred to continue their studies throughout the winter. Winter School gave the student a chance to make up entrance requirements or other deficiencies and catch up with his class. The Winter School or "Winter Term" as it was sometimes called was not an integral part of the school year. All responsibilities, including the financial ones, were assumed by the little group of teachers who chose to take charge of it. Sometimes the managers were charged for the use of classrooms, etc. The 1851 scholarships did not apply to this term. The usual rules were in effect, however; some manual labor was usually available, and full credit was given for the courses taken. At first there were separate schools for young men and young ladies but these were later united under one management.

In the forties only the elementary subjects were given but, later, various college classes were also included. In 1864–65 for example there were advanced classes in Greek, Latin and Mathematics. The usual facilities for studying music, drawing, and French were also usually available during the winter. "During the vacation a Winter school is held here, using the recitation rooms and apparatus of the College," a student wrote to the *University Quarterly* in 1861. "This is conducted by two members of the Faculty and several Tutors. Its excellent advantages are availed of by about two hundred and fifty preparatory Students, and a sprinkling of College men bringing up classical arrears. A few, too, who wish to get more French and German than they find in the regular curriculum, or who wish to secure some culture of a miscellaneous character, hybernate beneath the wings of Alma Mater." Among the available sources of "miscellaneous culture" there were usually a lecture course, informal literary societies and singing schools. Throughout the fifties and sixties the number of students in attendance ran slightly over 250 on the average. In 1864–65 only 34 of the total of 261 were doing work of college grade. The tuition varied from $3.25 to $7.00.[32]

Nevertheless, Oberlin in the winter must have almost equalled in dullness Oberlin in the summer at the present day. The older and more experienced professors usually did not teach in Winter School; all of the "theologs" and most of the college students went out teaching and preaching or back to their homes. The fourth Wednesday in February when the students returned from their winter adventures was a day of great excitement. "The winter has been a very pleasant one on the whole," wrote a college girl on Thursday, February 28, 1856. "But there have been some flaws in the picture as there always must be. . . . Yesterday the term commenced. We had a happy time at the Chapel that morning shaking hands with old friends, I assure you. Today is fast day." A year later the same young lady commented in her diary: "The term opened yesterday morning. A pleasant day and many pleasant meetings with old acquaintances. Today is fast day, and no classes therefore until tomorrow. I am in a quandary about mine. Two classes which I wanted to join come at the same hour. What a poor body can do or had best do in such a case I don't know. Probably I shall give up Livy and study the Freshman Greek instead. I don't like to a bit, it will be bad every way almost."[33] Evidently even before the coming of the elective system one could have conflicts.

Monday was set aside for Rhetorical Exercises.[34] Bible classes, which also met only once a week, were held on Saturday. Other classes met on Tuesday, Wednesday, Thursday and Friday or on five days including Saturday also. There were no classes in the afternoon, which was reserved for exercise, manual labor, study and special meetings. It seems clear that students were not graded at all on their work in early years. Later, however, grades expressed in digits from 0 to 6 were given for daily recitations

[32]*University Quarterly,* III, 178–179 (Jan., 1861). On the Winter School in general: P. C. M., Nov. 19, 1855; *Oberlin Evangelist,* Oct. 23, 1839; Jan. 2, 1856; Mar. 18, 1857; *Oberlin Student Monthly,* I, 40 (Nov., 1858), and I, 79 (Dec., 1858); *Lorain County News,* Nov. 21, 1866; *Catalogue of the Oberlin Winter School, Taught During the College Vacation, 1864–5* (Oberlin—1865); Davis Prudden to George P. Prudden, Dec. 10, 12, 13, 1836 (Prudden MSS).

[33]Mary Louisa Cowles, MS Diary, Feb. 28, 1856; Feb. 26, 1857 (Cowles-Little MSS).

[34]Saturday in the earliest days.—Aaron Penfield to A. Craig, Mar. 4, 1837 (Office of the Assistant to the President).

and oral examinations. Professor Churchill's classbook for the period from 1858 through 1862 shows that he, at least, had a strong partiality for 6, which was, of course, the highest grade obtainable.[35] Course grades do not appear to have been recorded; students merely being reported as passing or failing. The giving of prizes or honors was frowned upon; there were no valedictorians or salutatorians, no *cum laudes* nor ranking of any sort. "At the close of each term," a committee of young ladies wrote to John Keep in 1839, "we are thoroughly examined in each study by our teachers, and our progress recorded only by their sweet smiles and a sweet consciousness of having performed our duties."[36] The Oberlin faculty did not believe in the appeal to emulation.

Though there are evidences of occasional outline maps, blackboards and some "philosophical apparatus," teachers were generally poorly provided with the mechanical aids to instruction. The classrooms themselves were poor, often badly ventilated and overcrowded. In 1843 we find the senior prep class making representations to the Prudential Committee regarding "the crowded state of the Recitation Room in Oberlin Hall" and requesting that it should be enlarged "by moving the partition between it and the adjoining room." Students sometimes contributed to the furnishing or repairing of the classrooms which they used. In 1844 the theologs helped fit up the classroom under the choir in the new meeting house which was assigned to their use. In 1850 Professor Timothy Hudson "presented a request to the . . . effect that as the class under his charge are about to paper the walls & carpet the floor of the Southwest recitation room . . . the woodwork should be painted by the Inst. & that they should have the sole use of it for their recitations."[37]

Apparently there was much that was sophomoric in the attitude of the students (even those of college grade) in the latter years. One student diarist noted at various times in 1865: "The Sophs. got 'high' and received two lectures, one from Prof. P—d, and the other from Prof. E—s"; "Attend Bible class at 8. Having waited 10 minutes for Prof. P—d, the class (according

[35]This classbook is in the Oberlin College Library.

[36]Mary Ann Adams *et al.* to John Keep, July 10, 1839 (Keep MSS).

[37]P. C. M., Apr. 5, 1843; Aug. 19, 1844, and Mar. 8, 1850.—On ventilation see P. C. M., May 1859.

to his command previously given) adjourned. While in the act a man loomed up in the distance. We were not certain as to who it was. . . . Don't know whether it was right, but I can't see anything really wrong about it, as Prof. has instructed us so to do." "Had a small excitement Sat. J. G. Hamilton on his own private hook (Prof. Churchill being sick) went and got a teacher in Evidence. Several of the class bolted (among them I). A good many of the class were a good deal disgusted. A set of resolutions was drawn up (mei auctoris), censuring him, but on account of mitigating circumstances & some slight explanation, they were not publicly presented."[38]

There were some lecture courses like Dascomb's Chemistry, Mahan's Mental and Moral Philosophy and Walker's Political Economy in which students took notes on lectures (verbatim if possible) and memorized them. In general, however, classes were conducted on the recitation or "question-and-answer" method which was the rule in all American schools at the time, in which the intention was not to elicit discussion but to drill the students in memorizing rote answers. It is enlightening that as late as the middle sixties the literary societies should debate such questions as: "Resolved that reciting from books is more beneficial than reciting from notes" and "Resolved that we ought not to confine ourselves to textbooks in our course of study."[39] Certainly there was little or no required library reading.

All students in all years of all courses were required to attend and participate in weekly classes in practical composition. The young men engaged in writing and speaking ("Compositions, and either Extempore Discussions or Declamations weekly throughout the whole course; and also public original declamations monthly") but the young ladies practiced writing only (". . . Compositions, weekly, throughout the course").

"Let me see," wrote Tutor James H. Fairchild to his betrothed. "You would be glad to know how I officiate at the composition class? Well, the exercise is opened by prayer, as usual. Then I call the roll and take my seat in front and listen with the most profound interest and attention while the young ladies bring forth out of their treasure, things new and old—

[38] J. G. Fraser, MS Diary, Mar. 4, 21, and July 25, 1865.

[39] Aelioian, MS Minutes, May 2, 1865, and the Young Ladies' Literary Society, May 11, 1864.

dreams, visions, tales, descriptions, and metaphysics—(I mean no burlesque). This done I gather up the compositions and we disperse. At my room I proceed to examine these same compositions more *critically,* making a point here and a note or interrogation there, putting in one word and taking out another and on the margin and blank page making certain notes and remarks and suggestions. The employment is interesting and profitable for me, but I do not feel fit for it."[40] Of course, the subjects dealt with were legion: "dreams, visions, tales, descriptions, and metaphysics."

Class or interclass, public rhetoricals were held once a month. The young ladies took considerable vicarious satisfaction in attending these public performances. A college girl recorded in her diary in 1856: "This P. M. Composition class, and a composition, and then I went to John's [rhetorical exercises], senior's. He had a declamation; he is an orator; it was terrible but grand." In later years the ladies in the Collegiate Department themselves took part, but intermediately their essays were read for them. On October 26, 1857, Sprague Upton, a "prep": "Attended Rhetorical in A. M. and extemporized on a political question. In the P. M. went to the Chapel and had the honor of listening to what is called the Monthly Rhetorical. Three Freshmen, two Sophomores, and two Seniors were the combatants for the honors. A lady's essay was also read by Prof. Monroe. The exercises were good. Weather: very windy and cold."[41] The program was often interspersed with music, and occasionally there was a special feature. Of a Latin Dialogue at a "Monthly" in 1863 the local paper said: "The characters were stated to be Coppercaput (a copperhead) and Conjunctionis Miles (a Union Soldier). The Latin was spoken unhesitatingly and well pronounced. The performance reflected great credit upon the two gentlemen representing the characters. Altogether the exercises were good, and well pleased the large audience present."

[40]J. H. F. to Mary Kellogg, Mar. 17, 1841, printed in the *Oberlin Alumni Magazine,* I, 179 (Apr., 1905). In 1855 a boy wrote to his sister from Oberlin: "There has nothing happened unusual to day. The restations come and go as usual. Today is Monday a day that we all dread for we have retorical exercises from 9 o'clock till 12. This exercise is considered of the most consequence. It consists of writing essays and declemations and discussions."—Egbert Smith to Julia Smith, Apr. 3 to May 9, 1855 (Smith MSS).

[41]Mary Cowles' MS Journal, Mar. 24, 1856 (Cowles-Little MSS), and Sprague Upton's Diary (MS lent by Prof. W. T. Upton).

It was the tradition in most of the colleges of the time for the juniors to put on a special, public program of speaking shortly before Commencement. The Junior Exhibition, as it was called, did not appear in Oberlin until 1860, but was a regular institution for many years thereafter. Usually there was a Latin Oration, a Greek Oration, a discussion, English orations by the young men and essays read by young ladies.[42] At literary society meetings, private and public rhetoricals, Junior Exhibition, and Commencement, the Oberlin student had many opportunities to practice public speaking.

Students might withdraw books from the library if they paid a special fee but they were not encouraged to do so. The original laws of 1834 provided: "No student shall draw more than one volume from the Library at a time, nor shall books be drawn, except at the times appropriate to this purpose, which shall be fixed by the Faculty." After the spring of 1837 students might draw two books at a time, but in the next year the librarian was granted the power to censor the students' reading by giving out or withholding books at his discretion. In 1843 the faculty voted further to guard the books from the students by "so arranging the library that hereafter students making applications for books shall be waited on at the door."[43]

Professor Dascomb served as librarian from 1834 to 1873, except in the years 1846 to 1853 when Henry E. Whipple was in charge. Of course, his other onerous duties left him little time and energy to devote to this particular chore.[44]

The original library was small and of irregular quality. Early in 1835 Dr. Dascomb valued the whole collection at a little over a hundred dollars. At the end of 1836 it consisted of less than eight hundred volumes, mostly donations from members of the faculty and relatives and friends of Shipherd and of Finney. In the field of *belles lettres* there were the works of Southey, Milton, Dryden, Cowper, Burns, Goldsmith, Pascal's *Letters* and Irving's *Bracebridge Hall.* History and biography were

[42]*Lorain County News,* May 23, 1860; July 29, 1863; and *Oberlin Evangelist,* June 4, 1862.

[43]F. M., Apr. 1, 1837; Mar. 14, 1838, and Apr. 19, 1843.

[44]The *Catalogues* do not mention Dascomb's service as librarian before 1853. He was appointed at the first reported meeting of the faculty.—F. M., Nov. 21, 1834. His "Librarian, Physician & Lecturer's Report" dated Feb. 13, 1835, is in the Miscellaneous Archives.

represented by Rollin's *Ancient History,* Scott's *Napoleon,* "Life of Jackson," "Life of Pinkney," "Henry Clay," Gibbons' *Roman Empire,* and Jefferson's *Notes on Virginia.* Of these, Goldsmith, *Bracebridge Hall* (as near the novel as they dared to go) and Scott's *Napoleon* were particularly popular with the readers. The number of times that "Spurzheim on Education" and Fowler's *Phrenology* were withdrawn bespeaks the popular interest in the science of bumps on the head. The frequency with which the three copies of "Wesley on Christian Perfection" were charged out suggests that the Methodist doctrine may have been directly instrumental in the development of Oberlin perfectionism.[45]

The list of books also includes many titles of interest to the students of Mental and Moral Philosophy: "Cousin's Introduction to Philosophy," "Rush on the Mind," "Brown on Cause and Effect," "Cunningham on Infidelity," "Zimmerman on Solitude," and the works of John Locke. All of these were repeatedly borrowed in the first four years of the library's existence. Also often referred to was Brown's *History of Missions,* in two volumes. The first volumes listed in the catalogue were the *Annals of Education* for 1831, 1832 and 1833, the gift of the Founder. They are still in the library, the second volume bearing Shipherd's autograph in pencil on the fly-leaf. Of course there were copies of Samuel Read Hall's *Lectures on School-Keeping* and *Lectures to Female Teachers* as well as the "Memoirs of Oberlin."

There were a few volumes on scientific subjects: "Dictionary of Chemistry," "Kirby's History of Animals," Malte Brun's famous *Geography* translated from the French, several volumes of *Silliman's Journal* and a number of textbooks. Characteristic was the inclusion of works on music: Porter's *Musical Cyclopedia,* "Dissertation on Musical Taste," and Callcott's *Musical Grammar.* Serials included *Blackwood's,* the *Biblical Repository,* the *American Quarterly Observer,* and six volumes of the *Spirit of the Pilgrims.* Naturally there were many volumes on religion: Fox's *Book of Martyrs,* "Campbell on Miracles," "Salvation made Sure," and the sermons of Lyman Beecher as well as of Charles G. Finney. An inventory of January, 1836,

[45]MS "Catalogue of Books in the Oberlin Coll. Institute Library," 1834–36, and Record of Books Withdrawn, 1834–38, in the Oberlin College Library.

listed altogether over 120 volumes of "Theological Books."[46]

The reform spirit of the institution was reflected in the number of titles on slavery and "physiological reform." Among these were "Right and Wrong in Boston," A. A. Phelps, *Lectures on Slavery and Its Remedy;* Lydia Maria Child, *An Appeal in Favor of That Class of Americans Called Africans,* William Jay, *Inquiry into the Character and Tendency of the American Colonization and American Anti-slavery Societies,* and the *Anti-slavery Record.* In the latter field were Hitchcock's *Dyspepsy Forestalled & Resisted,* George Combe's *Constitution of Man,* and "Physical Culture of the Finns."

Naturally the library included such reference works as the *Encyclopedia Americana,* the *Library of Entire Knowledge,* and "Lardner's Cabinet Cyclopedia." There was a copy of Aesop's Fables and two volumes of Blackstone. There were many volumes of Greek, Latin and Hebrew classics and at least two books in French, but no other foreign language was represented. All and all, those students who got access to the library may well have profited by the opportunity.

The library grew slowly. In 1837 a thousand dollars was appropriated for new books. In 1840 Keep and Dawes purchased over four hundred dollars' worth in London and secured gifts of approximately two thousand volumes besides, bringing the library up to 3,700 volumes in that year. There must have been further additions in the forties because in 1848 "H. E. Whipple presented a request [to the Prudential Committee] that there may be an extra shelf put up in the library." In 1852, however, accessions had been so few that some of the students felt called upon to petition the same body "to do what they can to improve the Library by an infusion of some modern works," and five years later Professor Hudson reported that the library was entirely inadequate and that some new books constituted one of the greatest needs of the College. When first reported in the *Catalogue* the number of books in the college library was estimated at 5,500 and the number in the literary society libraries at 2,500. In 1862 these figures were raised to 6,000 and 3,000 respectively and in 1863 to 6,500 and 4,000. A plea for donations of printed works always followed.[47]

[46]R. E. Gillett to Henry Cowles, Jan. 20, 1836 (Cowles-Little MSS).

[47]Ledger No. 1, 1834–1836, page 393 (Treas. Office); MS "Minutes & Documents

Throughout most of our period examinations were oral and public. Those at the end of the Summer Term occupied a whole week immediately preceding Commencement and may be considered as having been practically a part of those exercises; the anniversaries of literary societies and other special rhetorical exhibitions were usually scheduled for the late afternoons after the examinations.

Each instructor took charge of the examination of his own classes, either asking questions orally or passing out cards on which the questions were written. Students were expected to stand before their classmates and visitors and answer clearly and accurately. Other members of the faculty and distinguished guests were encouraged to ask additional questions. John Monteith, principal of the Elyria High School, visited the examinations on at least two occasions. The entire Board of Trustees adjourned one of their regular sessions in August of 1840 in order to attend the examination of President Mahan's class in Moral Philosophy. James A. Garfield, then of the Eclectic Institute at Hiram, planned to visit the Oberlin examinations in 1853. A professor from Williams College was in the audience in 1859.[48] Room-mates of other classes, ambitious "preps," and giggling younger brothers and sisters attended to gloat over their friends' discomfiture. Parents came to see if it was really worth while to continue their children in school.

Of course, as one young lady student wrote home to her parents, they "felt it a duty to make all the preparation they reasonably could & then resign all into the hands of him who guideth all things right." In 1838 James Fairchild wrote to a fellow student: "If you wish to see us in trouble come in on Monday at half-past ten a.m.—examination in Natural Philosophy, Olmsted's . . . I reviewed one volume of this work yesterday, 300 pages, besides 35 of Dr. Dascomb's lectures on

—Connected with Annual Meeting of the Board of Trustees—1841" (Trustees' MSS, Misc. Archives); P. C. M. [1848]; Mar. 22, 1852, and T. B. H. in the *Independent* (New York), Jan. 29, 1857. The library was in Room 11, Colonial Hall, in 1836 (Room Assignment Book, Sec. Off.), in Oberlin Hall in 1852 (J. H. Laird, "College Surroundings Twenty-Four Years Ago," *Oberlin Review,* III, 49–50 [Apr. 19, 1876]), in the Chapel Building after 1855 and in Society Hall after 1868 (*General Catalogue,* 1908, Int. 78 and 82).

48Henry Prudden to parents, Aug. 20, 1859 (lent by Lillian Prudden, New Haven, Conn.); T. M., Aug. 27, 1840; J. A. Garfield to H. Hill, July 29, 1853 (Treas. Off., File M), and *Oberlin Students' Monthly,* I, 471 (Oct., 1859).

Astronomy, and 10 of President Mahan's on Moral Philosophy —how thoroughly you can imagine."[49]

Most any student of the twentieth century might write home as did a freshman in the Young Ladies' Course in 1862: "Another thing that I know will please you is that in both my examinations I got *6.* Trigonometry and History. We were examined in Mineralogy some time ago, and in that also I received a 6, and I had had nothing else in that all the term. We are not to be examined in Botany until next term I have had nothing but 6 so far. In every thing but Trigonometry I have done better this term than ever before, and in that my marks are better than I feared." More exclusively characteristic of its period is the entry in the diary of a "coed" of 1854: "Have been examined in Botany, Conic Sections, and History of Civilization. All done satisfactorily. But O my wicked heart. We had several spectators in the last class, and I performed my own part satisfactorily and was called on to recite for two others which the Lord helped me to do, and do it well, and now I keep feeling sensations of pride, because my performances were approved. O my Father help me to drive this evil far from me, help me to overcome it entirely and may the place which it fills in my heart be filled with gratitude."[50]

One suspects that these examinations were not particularly difficult, as they were looked upon not only as a test of individual students but also of the institution and the teacher. As a result the instructor was as anxious as were the students that they should answer satisfactorily. Occasionally visitors wrote commendatory letters for publication. In 1839 one anonymous observer wrote to the editor of the *Evangelist:* "I have witnessed the examinations in different colleges and seminaries, yet I never recollect to have attended one where the classes manifested a more thorough acquaintance with the respective branches."[51]

In 1862 written examinations were introduced in some of the

[49][Warren and] Hannah Warner to parents, Dec. 24, 1841—Feb. 16, 1842 (O. C. Lib.), and James Fairchild to Mary Kellogg, Aug. 28, 1838, in the *Oberlin Alumni Magazine,* I, 31 (Nov., 1904).

[50]Maude [Little Macy] to mother, May 29, 1862 (O. C. Lib.), and M. M. Gilbert, MS Diary, Aug. 15, 1854.

[51]*Oberlin Evangelist,* Sept. 11, 1839; Sept. 15, 1841, and *Ohio Atlas and Elyria Advertiser,* Oct. 27, 1840.

college subjects.[52] It was plain enough that such examinations were found more satisfactory as tests of the students' achievement but, of course, they lacked entirely the advertising value of the public, oral examinations.

52*Lorain County News,* May 28, 1862.

CHAPTER XLIV

EARLY TO BED

THE Oberlin student led a busy life. Numerous classes, study hours, daily periods of manual labor, religious exercises and meals occupied most of the time. Davis Prudden wrote to his brother in 1837: "For this week I have been obliged to spend 24 hours in the recitation room, debate twice, read and write a composition. Besides working 3 hours daily, spending 3 hours more daily in public prayers & other necessary duties. But there is one consolation in regard to it, that it learns the habit of hard study when I do study."[1]

His sister, Nancy Prudden, gave a detailed account of a typical day in the life of a young lady in the Preparatory Department of the Oberlin Institute in the same year. "Perhaps you will wonder how my time is occupied so that I can spare no more of it to write," she explained to the folks at home. "I will give you a description of my duties through the day. At five o'clock in the morning we are awakened from our slumbers by the ringing of the large Institution bell which is the signal for rising, fifteen minutes from this time the small bell is rung for one of the young Ladies to leave her room, that the other young Lady may have half an hour alone to spend in devotion, at the close of this half hour the first young Lady returns to her room while the second leaves it. Thus each young Lady can enjoy the privilege of private devotion. After that, breakfast, then work, at nine, either lecture, or recitation, from ten to eleven recitation in History, from eleven to twelve study—dinner fifteen minutes after twelve. At one meet Mrs. Cowles in the sitting room, then work again, recitation in Arithmetic at 3, from 4 to five study, at 5 practice Calisthenics, entering and leaving the room courtesying etc. Fifteen minutes before 6 prayers, then supper, then work, study hours at eight. At half past nine the bell

[1]Davis [and Nancy] Prudden to George Prudden, Apr. 8–13, 1837 (Prudden MSS).

rings for the young Ladies to retire, and thus ends the day."[2]

The rules of the Boarding House adopted by vote of the young ladies provided that all should rise at five in the morning and retire at ten in the evening. Among the "Duties to be performed" listed by the Female Principal in her notebook were: "Devote half hour in the morning to private devotion"; "Present at table, morning Noon, Night"; "Room in order at eight o'clock"; "Punctual at labor"; "No calling in study hours"; "Not going to the pantry or bakeroom without a reasonable excuse."[3] Mrs. Cowles was the Principal at the time and the meeting with her after dinner was the occasion for reporting and explaining "failures"—infractions of the rules.

The routine had changed very little when described by another young lady student nearly two years later: "I have just come from the kitchen where I have been scouring knives. Every day immediately after breakfast and dinner, you may imagine me in the kitchen, engaged with several young ladies in scouring, or washing knives and forks. This is all the work I have. At nine o'clock we all have recitation in the Bible. . . . From 10 to 12 I am generally engaged in studying. After dinner we all meet Mrs. Henry Cowles in the sitting room, where we spend about half an hour, then we work until nearly two o'clock. From that time until 4 I am employed with my book, or at work for myself. From 4 to 5 I recite in Geography. From 5 to 6 all the students both male and female are assembled in the dining hall for evening worship, after which we take our supper, which generally consists of bread and butter or milk, or for a rarity we have *jonny cake* and milk and sometimes *hulled* corn and milk, and it is all very good. After supper I study, or work again, till 7. From 7 to 8 I recite in Arithmetic. As this recitation is in the evening I cannot attend any evening meetings, or singing school, which renders it very unpleasant. We hope, however, to have the hour changed in a few days. So you see that every hour in the day is taken up. I think the winter will pass away pleasantly, and I hope profitably."[4]

[2]Nancy in *Ibid.*

[3]A. W. Cowles, "Hints and instructions for the benefit of those connected with the domestic department of Oberlin Collegiate Institute" (Cowles-Little MSS).

[4]Sarah P. Ingersoll to David Ingersoll, Dec. 31, 1838—Jan. 1, 1839 (lent by Mrs. Friedrich Lehman, Oberlin).

Writing in 1842 Elizabeth Maxwell lamented her tardiness: "Saturday morning I did not get up till 5 o'clock and it took me until half past six to dress, sweep the Assembly room and attend to devotion, then 'twas breakfast time and at seven I commenced work which kept me till half past eight, then came up to my room & studyed till 12, 3 hours & a half to get 3 lessons, at 12 went to dinner, half past to the sitting room as usual to 1 o'clock, then a recitation in Greek in the Chapel, at two Arithmetic at Tappan Hall, at 3 Composition class in the Assembly room, at 4 writing class in Oberlin Hall, at 5 History of Rome which we are reviewing for examinations in the Ass[embly] room. At 6 prayers, half past supper, 7 work half an hour, and then I was almost tired out."[5]

Lucy Stone took naturally to the full schedule, which she described to her parents: "I want to tell you how I spend my time, so that you can think of me, and know each hour of the day what I am doing. I rise at five o'clock, and am busy until six taking care of my room and my person. At six we go to breakfast, which, with family worship, lasts until seven. Then I go and recite Latin until eight; from eight to nine recite Greek; from nine till ten, study algebra; from ten till eleven, hear a class recite Arithmetic; from eleven to twelve recite algebra; from twelve to one, dinner, and an exercise in the sitting room which all the ladies are required to attend. From one to two, hear a class recite arithmetic; from two to five I study; five to six we have prayers in the chapel, and then supper. We study in the evening. These are the duties of every day except Monday, which is washing day. In the afternoon of Monday, from three to four, I attend composition class. In addition to what is done during the other days, we have, every Tuesday, to go to the Music Hall and hear a lecture from some of the Ladies' Board of Managers—this from three to four o'clock. Every Thursday there is a prayer meeting which we are all required to attend."[6] The Tuesday afternoon lecture gave an opportunity for the Female Principal and others of the Ladies' Board to discourse to the young ladies on morals, manners, and domestic science.

The original laws of the Institute provided that the "Hours of Labor, Study, Food, and Devotion shall be arranged by the

[5]Elizabeth Maxwell to parents, Aug. 25, 1842 (lent by Mrs. Emma M. Fitch).
[6]A. S. Blackwell, *Lucy Stone,* 53–54.

Faculty to meet the change of Seasons, provided that the Students are required to labor 4 hours daily, Study 8 hours except the time be employed in religious Services, Keep their beds from 10 o'clock P.M. to 5 o'clock A.M. & are permitted to retire at 9 o'clock P.M. & rest till 5 A.M. if they please, & have allowed them at least a half hour in the morning and as much in the evening for devotion."[7] The routine for male students varied in detail from that of the young ladies. There was, of course, no meeting with Mrs. Cowles for them. In the early years they met together for prayers in the chapel at six in the morning in addition to private devotions and prayers (or chapel) again in the afternoon. The teaching force was so pressed for time that classes were held not only in the evening but, in one instance at least, at five o'clock in the morning.[8]

Charles Livingstone, the explorer's brother, gives an excellent summary of the male student's day in a letter written in the spring of 1840: "We rise in the morning some at 4, mostly all up at 5. Then you may hear the voice of prayer in every room. At 6 o'clock we assemble in the chapel for prayers; a chapter is read by someone of the professors; a hymn sung by the choir. . . . Then, when we come out of the chapel, Breakfast bell tolls. This is about half past six. There is a large hall capable of seating upwards of 200 students at meals. I don't board in the hall but at Mr. Burnells. Then my recitation of arithmetic at 7, Geography at 8, & Grammar at 11, all large classes. Dinner bell at ten minutes past 12. Go to work at two till six when we all assemble in the chapel for evening prayers. Half past six supper bell tolls. After supper Mr. Benham [his room mate] and I read a chapter and pray to our Heavenly Father. Then we study till 9 or ten, then go to bed. You will be taking a laugh at my expense I think at rising so soon when Janet recollects so much trouble she had to get me up to be at the warehouse at 8."[9] Young Livingstone was still in the Preparatory Department at this time.

Students of the fifties also led busy lives and arose before the birds. One student wrote to her mother in 1852: "I have learned to get up early. Monday morning I was up at three and washing." "Time spent here," she wrote to a friend the next year, "is filled

[7]MS By-Laws of 1834.
[8]George Prudden to parents, Aug. 16, 1836 (Prudden-Allen MSS).
[9]Charles Livingstone to parents, May 22, [1840] (O. C. Lib. Misc. MSS).

up with a great variety of exercises. Indeed I know no leisure after Monday morning until the following Saturday evening. It is certainly harder work than teaching can possibly be. But there is a reward up in life's future years, well deserving our energies here."[10]

Church on Sunday, washing on Monday, General Exercises on Tuesday and Thursday Lecture were the outstanding events of the week for the girls of this period. Mary Gorham was a special music student. "You probably would like to know something about what I am doing," she wrote to a former classmate "Well! I will give you my regular week's business: I have to go to church twice on Sunday and hear the *longest dullest sermon* you ever heard. Monday I wash, read Composition, and rehearse pieces. Tuesday my lessons begin. I practice music from seven to eight, have a recitation from eight till nine, one from eleven till twelve, practice from one till *two,* then four go to General Exercises, to Prayers at five. Wednesday the same excepting General Exercises. Most always have a lecture on something that hour. Thursday the same, with the exception of Thursday lectures. Friday we have no lecture. Saturday a bible class at ten."[11]

John G. Fraser had budgeted his time. He noted in his dairy in 1865:

"*Thursday*. As Prof. gave us a scheme to time ourselves by, I have concluded to get up an opposition trusting to the comparative merits of the two and the impartial judgment of mankind—

	Prof. Penfield	*My Plan*
Get up . . .	5.00	6.20
Dress . . .	5.00–5.30	6.20–6.30
Milking . . .		6.30–7.00
Breakfast . . .	6.00–7.00	7.00–7.50
Study . . .	7.00–9.50	
Recitations . .	9.00–12.00	8.00–11.00
Study . . .		11.00–12.00
Dinner . . .	12.00–1.00	12.00–1.00
Exercise . . .	1.00–3.00	1.00–2.00
Study . . .	3.00–5.00	2.00–4.30

[10]Elizabeth Hanmer to parents, July 7, 1852 and to Mr. Gilmore, Sept. 19, 1853 (lent by Mildred Durbin, Columbus, Ohio).

[11]Mary Gorham to Rosa Mann, Mar. 16, 1854 (lent by Esther A. Close, Oberlin).

Milk . . .		4.30–5.00
Miscellaneous . .	5.00–6.00	5.00–6.00
Supper . . .	6.00–7.00	6.00–7.00
Study . . .	7.00–9.00	
Cut up . . .		7.00–9.00
Retire . . .	9.30	9.15"

For the most part he followed his schedule fairly closely, studying, attending classes and milking "as yewzhuaul," but now and then there were days when he didn't "feel very studious," as in July of the same season: "Scrabbled around and kinder got my lessons this morning. Got all-one of the Ex.s in Calc. and was not called on once. Got tired of studying this P.M. and went up to C. E. W.'s and persuaded him to go down to the Depot; then to p.o. then to library (drew two books by proxy, Easy way. You don't have the trouble of reading them), thence back to the house with the milk, thence to supper, thence to Society, thence back again, and at the present time (10.10) I am engaged in writing in this Journal. Have spent a respectable kind of day, though I don't feel as though I had done much. Don't feel very studious. Bad. bad."[12]

It is perhaps characteristic of students to be proud of being busy and to desire to impress their parents and friends with their long hours and heavy duties. This seemed to be the purpose of one youngster who wrote home in 1867: "My recitations were changed yesterday and now I recite Grammar at 8 P.M., Elecution [*sic*] at 1 P.M., attend Law Lecture (in the commercial) from 2 P.M. until 3 P.M., and from 3 P.M. until 4 P.M. Arithmetic, from 4 till 5 Musical Union (free), and lastly, from five till 6, prayers in College Chapel. Then I go and get my crackers and strong butter. It keeps me humping to get my lessons you better believe. I usually get up about half past four or five and study until called for *hash* and *slop* called Coffee and then start for class."[13]

Allowing for the tendency to exaggeration it is safe to conclude that the Oberlin student's time was pretty fully occupied even after required manual labor had been discontinued.

[12]John G. Fraser, MS Diary, Mar. 23, and July 11, 1865 (lent by Mrs. Grace Waugh, Mentor, Ohio).

[13]Dan Babst to Mr. and Mrs. Daniel Babst, Sept. 9, 1867 (lent by Mrs. D. Babst, Toledo, Ohio).

As religion played a large part in the thought of students and teachers, religious services occupied a considerable portion of the busy weekly program. Attendance at chapel was required of all. The By Laws of 1834 provided that: "There shall be daily public prayers in the Institution Morning & Evening under the direction of the Faculty, at which all the Students shall regularly attend, except those who for sufficient reasons may be excused by the Faculty, and those exercises shall be attended by the reading of the Holy Scriptures."

Morning chapel was an asceticism practiced only in the early years. The faculty voted to allow the young ladies to have morning devotions in the Boarding House as early as 1836. Public morning prayers were entirely discontinued in the early forties.[14] Prayers consisted of reading from the Bible by a professor and the singing of a hymn. The faculty members officiated "in the Chapel in alphabetical order—the first each morning during one week,—the second each evening during the same week, thus going through the list." This did not mean that all of the teaching staff attended all services. It was looked upon as an innovation when in 1860 "the Faculty took upon themselves the duty of attending the daily college prayers in a body." Though there was certainly nothing of irreverence there must have been some informality in the chapel meetings of the early years, for Charles Livingstone wrote to his parents in 1840: "Some come to chapel without their coat and napkin. Others have a thin linen jacket. Some stand up when they get tired sitting."[15] Morning chapel, in particular, must have been somewhat characterized by that general sleepiness and preoccupation with secular matters so prevalent in college chapel exercises of a later era.

As we have seen, opportunity was afforded to all for private devotions in their rooms. Morning religious service in the boarding hall was substituted for public chapel. Every meal was first

[14]The Faculty voted on Feb. 4, 1841 "that morning prayers be for the present conducted in the dining hall" (F.M.). However the *Laws and Regulations of the Oberlin Collegiate Institute* for 1842 still refer to "morning and evening prayers in the Chapel." The *Laws and Regulations* of 1847 refer only to "prayers at the Chapel in the evening"; "in the morning at their respective boarding places."

[15]F. M., May 28, 1835; Mar. 1, 1836; J. H. Fairchild, "Report to the Trustees, of the operations of the Institution for the year ending August, 1860" (Trustees' MSS, 1860, Misc. Archives), and Charles Livingstone to parents, Oberlin, May 22, 1840 (O. C. Lib. Misc. MSS).

consecrated by a prayer. Classes were opened with prayer and sometimes with the singing of a hymn. A special young peoples' prayer meeting was usually held on Monday evening, and class prayer meetings were held on Tuesday or Sunday. A religious lecture was delivered on Thursday afternoon. Then there were two church services on the Sabbath.

The Monday evening meetings were the center of active religious life for the more pious students. These meetings seem not to have been under supervision but depended on the spontaneous religious interest of the student body. "This evening," wrote one pious young girl in the mid-fifties, "Young Peoples Meeting was peculiarly interesting. God was there and our souls received much good. I enjoy these meetings so *very, very* much, I told them tonight of God's goodness to me. I love to speak. I feel so much at home." A little later she commented: "Monday in the evening was Mon. prayer meeting. I enjoy and value it more than any other meeting in all the week. Mr. Barber says this is because of its social nature. He, Mr. Barber, and I walked together from meeting to the corner."[16] Mr. Barber was certainly quite right, for religious gatherings of this type furnished, as they often have, much-needed social recreation.

Class prayer meetings do not seem to have been held continuously nor under uniform arrangements. In the forties the faculty sponsored prayer meetings "on Sabbath evening for each department of the Institution." In 1852 a number of "Ladies who are members of the school" petitioned the Ladies' Board to be allowed "to meet in circles Sabbath evenings for religious conversation and prayer." The Board agreed that they should be "permitted to do so but are recommended to return to their homes before 8 o'clock." In the following year each of the rhetorical classes was expected to meet once on the Sabbath for Bible study in addition to the Bible-study classes during the week. In 1859 a prep student wrote in his journal: "I have been to our class prayer meeting this evening. It is probably the last one we shall have. I wish I could have my heart as warm at all times as it is at these meetings, but my studies seem to drive out the thought of religion and it is very often hard to get my thoughts back again to it." The following year in a period of normal but

[16]P. C. M., Mar. 17, 1856, and Mary L. Cowles, MS Diary, Apr. 28, May 12, 1856.

not unusual religious interest, Professor Fairchild reported to the trustees: "Weekly prayer meetings have been maintained in all the classes, attended by some member of the Faculty, or by the teachers of the classes. In the Theological Department a daily prayer meeting is maintained for several weeks during a portion of the spring term, with considerable interest."[17]

From 1852 until 1864 there were fairly regular meetings of the Students' Missionary Society of Oberlin College. An address or addresses on missions and the taking up of a missionary collection were the essential features of such meetings. Returned missionaries furnished most of the speakers. S. G. Wright and Alonzo Barnard told of their experiences with the northwestern Indians; J. M. Fitch, Loren Thompson and Bigelow Penfield described conditions in Jamaica; George Thompson and Albert Bushnell reported on Africa; other speakers contributed inspiring accounts of mission work from Siam, India, the Sandwich Islands, Kentucky and Kansas. In 1859, "Rev. R. G. Wilder, who has spent twelve years as a missionary in India, entertained a large audience for an hour and a half by giving a description of some of the horid [*sic*] customs of the Hindoos." The collections taken up were usually devoted to the work of the American Missionary Association, of which the Students' Society was an auxiliary. These collections were sometimes comparatively small, on one occasion in 1862 being only $3.03 "together with a lead pencil from Father Keep which he promises at some time to redeem." At another meeting, however, between sixty and seventy dollars was raised.[18]

Thursday Lecture (a week day sermon) was a survival from Puritan days. The College and the church cooperated in paying the expenses of the meeting and there was considerable disappointment if the attendance of townsmen as well as students was not large. In 1843 the Prudential Committee urged the Oberlin business men to close their stores during the period of this service (3–4 P.M.). Usually members of the faculty were the preachers, but occasionally outsiders appeared, as when in 1856 Horace Bushnell preached an anti-slavery sermon. Many of the

[17]T. M., Sept. 11, 1844; L. B. M., May 31, 1852; Zephania Congdon to sister, June 1, 1853, (lent by Eulala Smith, Exeter, Nebraska), Henry Prudden, MS Diary, Nov. 8, 1859 (lent by Miss Lillian Prudden, New Haven, Conn.), and J. H. Fairchild, "Report to the Trustees . . . , 1860" (Loc. Cit.).

[18]MS Minutes of the society, *passim*.

lectures must have been deadly, leaving little or no impression on the students' minds. "I went over to Thursday lecture," Mary Cowles wrote in her diary. "Mr. Patton and Sarah went with me; there not the sermon but my own thoughts did me good. I listened little to the former, but much to the latter."[19]

Nor were all activities at Thursday Lecture on the program. In the middle sixties a sprightly young coed wrote to a former classmate: "I read your letter in Thursday lecture. (We have to go to the church yet. Is it not mean?) . . . I giggled audibly & showed it to Beck, who did likewise. I glanced across the room and caught W's eye. It had a sort of amused, *enquiring* look in it that tickled me more than ever." There was even more going on on another Thursday.—"You know that side seat," wrote the same young minx, "all along the church next to the wall? Nell, Em, Frank S., Louise Clark, Miss Clary, Lot Blackney & ever so many of us sat on that seat, as it was the only one vacant. Just across from Lot, sat Miss Brigham. (Mira's classmate) We were all laughing and whispering. . . . What should Miss B. do but write a little note to *Ladies* & hand it to Lot? It was a request *to stop whispering* as it disturbed her so she could not hear the lecture. Lot passed it clear up & down that seat—nearly the whole length of the church. When it came to me I, not knowing who wrote it & supposing it was Louise, wrote on the paper, 'We follow your example.' I soon found who wrote it, but before I could help myself they had handed it back to her, not before they had written lots more on it. Miss B. felt dreadfully, cried ever so much. Said she only meant it for Lot & the girl next her, begged pardon E. F. & I, &c, &c. She is going to report those girls."[20]

All students were required by the rules to attend "the weekly religious lecture." Students were also required to attend church services *twice* (sometimes there were three sermons) on the Sabbath. The rule adopted in 1834 was never changed in any vital way in our period. It provided that, "The officers & Students of the Institution will attend worship on the Sabbath with

[19]P. C. M., Feb. 18, 1843; Mar. 17, 1856; F. M., Feb. 18, 1841; Oberlin Church, MS Minutes, Feb. 1, 1843, and Mary L. Cowles, MS Diary, Mar. 27; July 3, 1856.

[20]Classmate to M. A. Winegar, June 26, 1864 and [?] 1865 (lent by Mrs. H. N. Roberts, Wichita, Kansas). Excerpts from the two letters are combined in the first quotation.

the Congregational Society in Oberlin. Any student of a different religious denomination from the Congregational Society in Oberlin, if of age, on his own request, and if under age, at request of his parent or guardian, may attend worship on the Sabbath with any other religious denomination by leave of the Faculty, provided his attendance with such other denominations shall be regular."[21] As for some years no other religious denomination was represented in Oberlin all of the students must necessarily attend the Congregational services. Even after the establishment of the Episcopal church and other religious societies the great body of young people continued to do so.

Attendance at divine services was certainly not an onerous duty for most students. Many had come to Oberlin because of its reputation for piety and others found it convenient to conform to majority opinion. The meeting house was the finest building in Oberlin, one of the finest in the region. There was always a large crowd present and the singing of the choir was impressive. To the farmers' sons and daughters all of these things were very wonderful. "It is the largest church that I ever saw, and it is crowded full every Sabbath," wrote one. A young lady explained enthusiastically to her mother: "Now, about our church, there is but one, and we all go twice on sunday. It is a rather splendid affair, will seat about three thousand persons they tell me. If you could hear the singing you would call it sweet music. Today there were about seventy in the choir. There were two base [*sic*] viols and some other music besides and several negroes too."[22]

A boy from New York State saw surprising resemblances between Oberlin and New York City: "Every hour when the bell rings the streets every way are thronged and remind me of Broadway. At church yesterday I should think there were over twenty five hundred people and still the house was not full. There are more people attend here every sabbath than there are at Broadway Tabernacle & this Church will seat nearly as many as that. The Choir numbers over a hundred choice singers for no one can enter it without going before a committee chosen for the

[21]*Laws and regulations of the Oberlin Collegiate Institute* (Oberlin, 1842) and MS By-Laws of 1834.

[22]Zephania Congdon to sister, June 1, 1853; Elizabeth Hanmer to mother, May, 1852 (lent by Miss Mildred Durbin, Columbus, Ohio).

purpose, and showing himself to be *independent alone*. The Professor of Music in the College leads the choir and their singing is very fine. Then add to all this, Finney in the pulpit and Oberlin is a very attractive place on the Sabbath. . . . Every Sabbath he winds up with an appeal to the feelings & then invites the *anxious* ones forward. Yesterday after preaching he had the front seats cleared & about two hundred came forward, but the excitement was not so high as it was a week ago & Finney has commenced lashing the Church to pay for it."[23]

No academic year was really successful which was not marked by a special season of revival among the students. The Christianizing of students having been long recognized as a chief purpose of the American College, the Day of Prayer for Colleges was instituted in the 1820's as a season of fasting and special prayer, "that God will pour out his Spirit on the colleges of our country." It was hoped that these "Concerts of prayer" would stimulate student revivals, and such was often their effect. As early as 1839, if not previously, the practice was copied in Oberlin and February 28 was set aside as a day of special supplication for American colleges. The opening of the spring term was believed to be a time peculiarly propitious for stimulating a revival. The exercises of the day usually consisted of a general meeting for prayer and conference in the morning and preaching in the afternoon and evening.[24] President Finney often delivered the sermons, calling the students' attention to the need of a new consecration of all schools and colleges to the missionary and evangelistic cause. "The young should *renounce worldly ambition* and *follow Christ* in *this work*," he told them one year. "College *students* should *organize* to *keep up this spirit*."[25] As college work was opened after vacation by the Day of Prayer so it was closed in the autumn by the special Thanksgiving services, when gratitude was expressed to God for His grace during the past year and intercession made for the protection of the students while at their tasks as teachers during the coming winter.

Revivals among the students were almost yearly and sometimes seem to have grown out of the Day of Prayer. Often classes

[23]H. D. Kingsbury to brother, May 10, 1852 (O. C. Lib.).

[24]W. S. Tyler, *Prayer for Colleges* (Boston—1877), 149–150; J. H. Fairchild to Mary Kellogg, Feb. 28, 1829 (Fairchild MSS); F. M., Feb. 4, 1840; T. M., Feb. 17, 1840, and *Oberlin Evangelist*, Feb. 29, 1860.

[25]Skeleton of a sermon for the Day of Prayer, 1867 (Finney MSS).

would be suspended and all time devoted to prayer meetings, experience meetings and occasional sermons. The revival of February, 1840, was the result of the second known Day of Prayer in Oberlin. The revival of July of 1841 grew out of a period of prayer for rain. Neither Finney nor Mahan were present and the movement began more or less spontaneously among the students. Prof. James Thome wrote to Theodore Weld:

"A more powerful work of grace has perhaps never been witnessed in O. It broke out about a week ago in the preparatory dept. & is extending through all the departments. The theological brethren have been much blessed.

"The work still goes on with deep power. Bros. Finney & Mahan are both absent, attending the convention at Rochester, still the revival makes a mighty headway. In many cases the recitations are suspended, & the hours of recitation are devoted to prayer. Prayer meetings are held day & night in several different places. The voice of prayer & the song of praise may be heard of evenings through the entire place.

"Praise the Lord for his wonderful goodness to usward. To day the sisters have a fast and general prayer meeting."[26]

At about the same time a student wrote enthusiastically to his father: "The Lord is doing a mighty work in this place. The class to which I belong have a prayer meeting together every sabbath evening. Last Sab. evening the Spirit of the Lord was poured out in a powerful manner & the whole class prostrated before God. . . . Our class have spent the week in meetings & self examination. . . . The work has spread from one class to another until the whole place seems to be solemn on account of the presence of God."[27]

Professor Morgan declared, "I never in my life I think, witnessed such proofs in the simplicity, earnestness, and confidence of prayer, of the presence and power of God's spirit." Weeks after the beginning of the movement the editor of the *Evangelist* declared: "At the time of writing this the interest is deepening and extending. All feel it to be a work of God. Brethren, pray for us." During much of the time scholarly activity was suspended. There were undoubtedly many, who, like James H.

[26] J. A. T. to T. D. W., July 7, 1841 (Weld MSS). Not in Barnes and Dumond.

[27] J. B. Trew to father, July 2, 1841 (lent by Miss Mary F. Ewalt, Lakewood, Ohio).

Fairchild, raised the question: "Is this sustaining the literary character of the Institution?" but answered that question, as he did: "If there be such a thing as the reality of religion . . . all other things are and must be subordinate to it."[28] Oberlin was always ready to recognize the subordination of all other things to piety. Certainly the students were not likely to be less pious because revivals sometimes resulted in the omission of classes.

[28]John Morgan to Mark Hopkins, July 13, 1841 (Morgan–Hopkins MSS); *Oberlin Evangelist,* July 21, 1841, and J. H. Fairchild to Mary Kellogg, Feb. 11, 1840 (Fairchild MSS).

CHAPTER XLV

LITERARY SOCIETIES

THE nineteenth century was the great age of popular oratory, and no college or academy was complete unless it had two rival literary or debating societies. Oberlin, being coeducational, usually had at least four —two for each sex. The Oberlin societies differed from similar societies in other institutions in that no element of secrecy was involved. Oberlin men and women believed that secret societies were undemocratic and endangered republican institutions. At least from as early as 1847 students were explicitly prohibited from joining secret organizations.

Two men's literary societies destined to a long history of friendly rivalry were organized in 1839.[1] The one was first known as the Dialectic Society. When finally chartered in 1844 by the state legislature, after much opposition from the Democratic pro-slavery element in that body, it was arbitrarily given the title of the Young Men's Lyceum. This continued to be its name until 1859 when it adopted the Greek letters Phi Kappa Pi. The rival organization was first known as the Philomathesian Society and was made up at first mostly of freshmen, whereas the Dialectic was recruited exclusively from the upper classes. In 1841 an unsuccessful attempt was made to form a third society. The members of this abortive organization joined the Philomathesian and the new name of Union Society was adopted. In 1854 the Union Society became the Phi Delta.[2]

These societies met at first in various recitation rooms in

[1]The two men's societies in 1834, the Oberlin Lyceum and the Philo Lyceum, were apparently short lived. There is a reference to them in the Treasurer's Ledger, No. 1 (1834–1836), page 204, and an account of a meeting of one of them in a letter from Davis Prudden to Peter Prudden, Oct. 7, 1836, in the Prudden MSS.

[2]*University Quarterly,* II, 374–376 (Oct., 1860); Young Men's Lyceum, MS Minutes, July 5, 1859, Union Society, MS Minutes, Sept. 16, 1854.

Oberlin and Tappan Hall. In 1841, however, they joined with the Musical Association to build the Music Hall. The hall was a very plain building with one large room used for the regular music classes, for the meetings of the choir and of the men's literary societies. Professor George N. Allen collected the funds for its construction on his own responsibility. He persuaded the Prudential Committee to contribute about $100 in the form of the proceeds of the sale of the old mill—if he could collect it. The two men's literary societies contributed about $200 together. About the same amount was solicited and collected from colonists. The Musical Association raised another hundred from the sale of tickets to concerts. Professor Allen contributed largely from his own pocket. In 1847 the Musical Association moved to the choir of the church. Three years later the literary societies gave up their claim to the Music Hall and received a room in Tappan Hall again, instead. When the new College Chapel was built in the late fifties the society room was transferred to this new building.[3]

To the Ladies' Literary Society belongs the honor of having the longest continuous history, though at various times its existence hung by a thread. It was founded in July of 1835 at a meeting in Cincinnati Hall (a men's dormitory!), declared to be devoted to "the promotion of literature and religion" and first christened "The Young Ladies' Association of the Oberlin Collegiate Institute."[4] In a formal statement prepared especially for the attention of British philanthropists in 1839, a committee of young ladies reported the purpose and activities of this association:

"We have connected with our Seminary, a Literary & Religious association, in which capacity we meet frequently and each one in turn, according to appointment, writes and communicates to us her thoughts on some important and interesting subject. We hold correspondence with many distinguished & pious ladies of our own and other lands and with some who have left for

[3]Dialectic Society, MS Minutes, June 15, 16, 1841; Young Men's Lyceum, MS Minutes, Aug. 10, 1847, and Aug. 24, 1848; G. N. Allen to the "Prudential Board," May 28, 1842 (Treas. Off., File K); Oberlin Musical Association, MS Minutes, Apr. 9, 1841, and June 18, 1847, and P. C. M., Apr. 2, 1860.

[4]Mrs. Emilie Royce Comings and Francis J. Hosford, "The Story of L. L. S., The First Woman's Club of America," *Oberlin Alumni Magazine,* XXIII, No. 6, page 10 (Mar. 1927).

pagan shores, by this means we collect much valuable information and often have our spirits refreshed."[5]

The Young Ladies' Association of the Oberlin Collegiate Institute received a new lease on life from Lucy Stone and Sallie Holley in the middle forties. (It is, of course, untrue that Lucy Stone founded it, the society having been in existence for eight years when she came to Oberlin.) The name was officially changed to the Young Ladies' Literary Society in 1850,[6] and in 1867 it became the Ladies' Literary Society or L. L. S. There were periods when this organization was almost defunct. It reached a particularly low state in 1848 after the graduation of Lucy Stone. There were other years when the scantiness and dullness of the minutes lead us to conclude that the society was in a state of more or less suspended animation. In many meetings a large part of the program was omitted due to the absence of the performers. The period of the sixties was one of reviving interest and energy. In 1852 or 1853 a second ladies' society was organized, named the Young Ladies' Lyceum, and by 1856 was an active and ambitious rival of its sister society. In 1861 this society adopted the name Aelioian.[7]

The ladies' society met in the early years in the attic of Ladies' Hall, an unfinished room with long backless benches like those used in the dining room. The young men presented the society with a stove, and later a carpet and chairs were obtained. In 1865 the two ladies' societies moved into a fine new room in the New Ladies' Hall.[8]

There were other minor, shorter-lived societies. As the regular societies did not ordinarily admit prep students, young men in this department sometimes had their own organizations and argued and orated to their hearts' content in imitation of their elders. In 1844 the students and faculty of the Theological Department formed a literary society and regularly elected Professor John Morgan president, at least through 1851. Founded

[5]Mary Ann Adams *et al.* to John Keep, July 10, 1839 (Keep MSS).

[6]MS Minutes and constitution as adopted Apr. 10, 1850. This name of Ladies Literary Society is sometimes used in newspaper articles before 1850, but the records make the date of the official change quite clear. The constitution adopted May 6, 1846, for example, still retains the title, "Young Ladies Association, etc."

[7]Minutes, July 30, 1861; Nov. 6, 1867, and Helen [Jones] to Helen Cowles, Dec. 14, 1848 (Cowles-Little MSS).

[8]Comings and Hosford, "The Story of L. L. S.," *Loc. Cit.*, and Y. L. L. S., MS Minutes, July 12, 1865.

as the Theological Literary Society the second adjective in the title was dropped after 1857. H. E. Peck and C. H. Churchill were active members, and J. Mercer Langston, the negro lawyer and politician, was secretary for one year. Other secretaries were G. F. Wright, the scientist-theologian, and W. E. Lincoln, one of the Rescuers. During the winter vacation of 1849 the stay-at-home faculty formed a literary society. "Your father and I," wrote Mrs. Henry Cowles to her step-daughter, "are attending this winter the weekly meetings of a Literary Club, composed of the following individuals—Professors Morgan, Hudson, Dascomb, Fairchild, Messrs. Hill, Cowles, Tutors Hodge & Whipple and their Ladies, Tutor Penfield, Miss Tenney & Miss Wyett. We meet at the several houses of these individuals by rotation, and occasionally by invitation go early and take supper. Two hours are usually occupied with compositions and declamations and the remainder of the evening with general conversation. I think them profitable and pleasant."[9]

College literary societies of the nineteenth century always prided themselves on their libraries and many a college library of today (including that of Oberlin College) owes much to the contributions from the literary societies. The Union Society became active in book-collecting in the early fifties, managing to wheedle a number of volumes, probably government documents, out of both William H. Seward and Salmon P. Chase. In 1853 Professor Peck promised the Young Ladies' Literary Society twenty dollars worth of books if each member would read one book during the ensuing year. In 1854 and 1855 the Phi Delta Society took the initiative in forming the College Literary Societies' Library Association. In 1857 the library established by this organization, supported by the joint efforts of the Phi Delta and the Young Men's Lyceum, was made a regular depository for United States Government documents. In the following year it could report over eight hundred volumes: 185 volumes of history, 223 of poetry and general literature, 143 volumes dealing with the arts and sciences, 67 volumes of theological works, and 179 volumes on "Jurisprudence," the last mostly government documents. Lectures were sponsored by the association as a means of raising money, but, though these lectures may

[9]Theological [Literary] Society, MS Minutes, 1844–1851; 1857–1864, and M. D. P. Cowles to Helen Cowles, Jan. 23, 1849 (Cowles-Little MSS).

have enriched life for the listeners, the financial results were not satisfactory. In 1860, 1200 volumes were reported. Only about three hundred volumes were added in the next three years.[10]

In 1859 the two ladies' societies resolved, following the example of the men's societies, to form the Ladies' Society Library Association. The book committee immediately proceeded to Fitch's book store and bought Motley's *Dutch Republic,* Tennyson's works in two volumes, and Irving's *Washington.* Mr. Fitch contributed a discount of $5.00 on the total purchase price of $13.75. On a purchase of $26.00 worth of books at Goodrich's they received a discount of $10.00. It might have paid the men's association to hire a committee of young ladies to make their purchases. In about a year and a half they had assembled between three and four hundred volumes.[11] Eventually the College Societies' Library Association and the Ladies' Society Library Association were merged in the Union Library Association and their libraries united. Later their combined collection was absorbed in the College library.

The literary societies engaged in another joint activity, the publication of a college magazine. As early as 1846 the Young Ladies' Association had planned a publication to be known as the Oberlin Ladies' Banner. A committee was appointed to obtain the consent of the Ladies' Board and the faculty, but returned at the next meeting to report that "the measures of the society respecting the publishing of a paper were totally disapproved." It was in the autumn of 1858 that the Phi Delta Society proposed the publication of a monthly magazine through the joint efforts of the four college societies—"to be of 40 pgs. same size and style as the Atlantic." Early in October an agreement was reached and the first number of the *Oberlin Students' Monthly* was issued under the date of November, 1858. For the next two and a half years this ambitious periodical made its appearance regularly every month, each number containing from thirty-five to forty pages of essays, stories, editorial com-

[10]Union Society, MS Minutes, Apr. 27, 1853; Apr. 19, 1854; Y. L. L. S., MS Minutes, Aug. 3, 1853; Phi Delta Society, MS Minutes, Oct. 28, 1854; *Oberlin Evangelist,* Jan. 20, 1858; *University Quarterly,* II, 375 (Oct., 1860), and *Lorain County News,* Sept 2, 1863.

[11]*University Quarterly,* II, 375; Young Ladies' Lyceum, MS Minutes, Apr. 12, 1859, and accounts of the Book Committee of the Ladies' Society Literary Association, 1859–1869.

ment, Oberlin news, book notices, poetry and musical compositions. "In general," commented the *Evangelist* in 1859, "it fairly represents the ability and energy and aims of the students of the college—their habit of thinking upon whatever concerns mankind and of saying what they think—usually with earnestness, often wisely and well."[12]

Its contents certainly, in general, compare very favorably with student magazines produced in Oberlin in more recent years. It roused strong criticism from the *Yale Literary Magazine,* however, whose editors took offense at an unfavorable comment on their periodical in the columns of the *Monthly.* After all, the Yale editors declared in a leading article, the Oberlin publication was not strictly a student enterprise as it contained articles by graduates and faculty. They were also inclined to be rather supercilious about the *Monthly's* preoccupation with religion, morals and politics, the inclusion, for example, of "long editorials on the 'Dred Scott Decision,' 'Popular Sovereignty,' and 'Stephen A. Douglas'—a rehash of what has been in the country papers for the past year or two."[13] But one can hardly imagine an Oberlin publication of this era not being concerned with slavery and reform.

The *Students' Monthly* was brought to a sudden end by the outbreak of the war. In one of the last issues a poem appeared entitled "The First Gun," commemorating the firing on the *Star of the West.* Another bombardment in Charleston Bay in the next month brought on real civil war and in Oberlin spelled the end of the gymnasium and of the *Student's Monthly.* The last number issued is dated April, 1861.

During this same pre-war period the Oberlin literary societies joined with the societies of other colleges in the publication of an intercollegiate magazine: *The University Quarterly: Conducted by an Association of Collegiate and Professional Students, in the United States and Europe.* The periodical, published at New Haven from January, 1860, through October, 1861, contained news and essays from students in thirty-odd colleges and universities in the United States, Germany and England. Ober-

[12]Young Ladies' Association, MS Minutes, June 16, 23, 1846; Phi Delta Society, MS Minutes, Sept. 22; Oct. 6, 1858; John Cowles to Henry Cowles, Sept. 27, 1858 (Cowles-Little MSS), and *Oberlin Evangelist,* Oct. 13, 1858, and Aug. 17, 1859.

[13]"College Magazines" in the *Yale Literary Magazine,* XXIV, 333–340 (July, 1859).

lin items are in a prominent place. The only other western schools represented at first were Antioch and Beloit. Later the names of Marietta and the University of Michigan appeared.

Meetings of the literary societies were limited to Wednesday evenings by an order of the faculty passed in 1839, but when two societies used the same room, one of them had to meet on Tuesday evening. Meetings began all the way from 5:30 to 7 P.M. Those who were tardy or absent were fined 6¼ cents, 5 cents, or sometimes 10 cents. The faculty at first recommended that meetings should close at or before 9:00 P.M., but in later years the regular closing hour was 9:45 or 10 P.M. Ordinarily the societies met every week. For a short time, however, the Young Ladies' Association, at the request of Mrs. E. P. Burke (the Lady Principal) and Mrs. Dascomb, who felt that "the young ladies were very much pressed with study . . . and needed . . . more time or less duties," voted to meet only every other week.[14]

All meetings began with roll call and prayer and sometimes with the singing of a hymn. The literary program would include essays, orations or declamations and usually a discussion. The critic gave the criticism of the program immediately after or at a subsequent meeting. Regular and miscellaneous business (or as one secretary spelled it: "messalanious bussiness") took up a great deal of time, sometimes, in fact, to the entire exclusion of the literary program. In the men's societies there seemed to be a more argumentative spirit. Sometimes even the motion to adjourn would be debated, amended, laid on the table, and taken up again before the meeting could be brought to an end. Discussion played a much more important part than it did in the women's societies, the young ladies favoring set essays, poems, and declamations. One of the commonest subjects for discussion in the ladies' societies was: "Is discussion worth while?" In 1852 it was moved at a meeting of the Young Ladies' Literary Society that discussion should henceforth be omitted from the regular exercises. After a long debate the motion was voted down.[15]

The most important item of regular business was undoubt-

[14]F. M., March to June, 1839; *Laws and Regulations of the Oberlin Collegiate Institute,* 1840, and minutes of various societies, *passim,* especially of the Y. L. A., Sept. 19, 1849.

[15]Minutes, Mar. 31, 1852.

edly the election of officers. This took place in most cases every month, and so, as there were a goodly number of offices, everybody stood a good chance of being elected to something at least once a year. These officers practically always included a president, vice-president, recording secretary, corresponding secretary, treasurer and critic. The president was required to give an inaugural address and sometimes an "exaugural," so succeeding presidents filled a considerable part of the total program. In the Young Ladies' Literary Society in the fifties it was one of the duties of the vice-president "to prepare the room for the meetings of the society." This would seem to be an excellent solution to the great question, "What should the duties of a vice-president be?" In the Union Literary Society, however, the office of sexton (whose duty it was "to ring the bell, light the lamps, keep them in order, make the fires and attend to the general comfort and neatness of her Room") was auctioned off to the lowest bidder. In 1843–44 this appointment went at the low figure of $3.75, which may explain why at a later meeting of the same year "the Sexton . . . neglected to build a fire" and a volunteer had to perform the service gratuitously.[16]

All applicants for membership were voted on and occasionally the decision was in the negative. Members of the men's societies were required to be enrolled in the Collegiate Department. At first "any young lady" could become a member of the Young Ladies' Association by subscribing to the constitution, but later both of the ladies' societies limited their membership to young ladies in the College, the Ladies' Course, or the Senior Preparatory Class. Colored students seem always to have been welcome. Lucy Stanton and Fanny Jackson were active in the ladies' societies; George B. Vashon, the first Negro graduate, W. C. Whitehorn and J. M. Langston were prominent in the men's societies. Elizabeth Maxwell, who attended a meeting of one of the men's societies in 1842 reported that "a colored man read an original poem *exquisitely grand*."[17]

Another important matter of business was the grand question of badges. The Young Men's Lyceum in 1850 considered a "blue satin ribbon one inch in width & three fourths of a yd. in length."

[16]Society minutes are the source unless otherwise indicated.

[17]Elizabeth Maxwell to Mrs. Rebecca Maxwell, May 5, 1842 (lent by Mrs. Emma M. Fitch).

Four years later a gold key was recommended as more suitable. The Phi Delta adopted a pin with "a delta crossed by a phi and . . . engraved [with] the date of organization and also of incorporation." The members of the Young Ladies' Literary Society appeared at the 1857 anniversary exercises wearing "blue and white rosettes . . . in front of the left shoulder."

There were many matters to be settled with regard to the equipment and care of the society rooms. In 1843 the Union Society appointed a committee "to see that there be no more holes made in music hall." Nearly two years later a motion "to cover the opening in ceiling with glass was lost!" Resolutions which called for the expenditure of money were likely to be defeated. A motion "to purchase a box to serve as a wood box for the Soc. Room" introduced at a meeting of the Lyceum "was lost by a majority of *one.*" When, at a March meeting of the same society, the attention of the members was called to the fact "that it was a cold day & wood was needed . . . & also that seven panes of glass were needed for the windows," it was moved that the sexton be empowered to purchase the required wood and glass. The motion was laid on the table, however, and the shivering but economical members proceeded calmly to debate the question whether inmates of penitentiaries should be paid for their labor! Then there was the great problem of lights. In 1854 the Ladies' Literary voted to instruct the treasurer to procure a supply of candles. Two years later the ladies' society room was equipped with lamps and an agreement reached between the two societies whereby each society "would pay for one of the two lamps and each furnish one half of the fluid." At an even earlier date the president of the Union Literary Society "appointed a committy to enquire the price of two young *Chamdoliers.*" The men's societies also had joint problems with regard to their meeting place. Consultation between them seemed to be required for: "obtaining a border for the walls of the room," "getting two drawers put into the desk," "procuring a sweeper or duster," removing the clock, and making "a more suitable disposition of the Bust of Chase (S.P.)." The painting of "Demosthenes on the Sea Shore," presented by the artist A. H. Pease to the Union Society in 1842, must have complicated the question of the location of this "Bust of Chase (S.P.)." At a meeting of the Lyceum in 1858, "It was moved and seconded that the Board of Directors be instructed to purchase Worcester's Dictionary in conjunction with the Phi Delta Soc. It was moved to amend this motion by inserting, 'and two spitoons' after the word 'dictionary.' The amendment was lost." Undoubtedly the amendment was considered funny, as Oberlin students did not smoke or chew, at least on so public an occasion as a literary society meeting. At a meeting of the Aelioian in 1863 it "was moved & carried that the young ladies come together on Saturday, June 13th at 1 of the clock and mend the carpet."

There were often applications for excuses from taking part in the exercises or from attendance "on account of pressure of study," "because he had to milk," or "on account of domestic duties. At one meeting of the Union Society so many members asked for excuses that one young man "moved an adjournment *sine die.*" The pessimist was voted down. Occasionally some one asked for an honorable dismission, which was also occasionally, though not often, refused. Graduating members were regularly dismissed and usually made honorary members. Taxes of a few cents were now and then levied to meet small expenses. Fines were the usual method of punishment, because of their financial advantage to the society. It required a special vote of the Union Society "to refund 6¼ cts. to Mr. Weed, having been fined by mistake." More drastic disciplinary measures were sometimes used, however. In 1848 Sallie Holley was expelled from the Young Ladies' Association because she "had not fulfilled her duties faithfully as a member of the society." She was later readmitted.

Resolutions of sympathy and sorrow were drawn up and adopted on the occasion of the death of a member. The Lyceum "lost one of its most valuable members and the cause of truth an earnest advocate." The Young Ladies' Literary Society took "pleasure in remembering the lovely example & christian character of the one 'not lost but gone before.' "

Except for a short-lived coeducational society which met in the winter terms of 1859–60 and 1860–61, the men's and the ladies' literary societies were always separate. In the early years guests of the opposite sex were allowed to visit meetings, but later this privilege was limited to the occasions of special public exercises.

The debates of all the societies, often dealt with the "woman question," the advisability of coeducation, and marriage problems. When in 1855 the Young Men's Lyceum debated whether "the sexes ought to be educated under the same course of study," the secretary reported that "a fiery discussion ensued." There must have been an equally warm debate when the same society considered the resolution, "That no college student until the senior year should dabble in matrimonial affairs" and when at an earlier date the members of the Dialectic discussed the question: "Should students form matrimonial engagements while persuing their studies?" The young ladies, too, entered the field. In the fifties questions for debate included: "Is married life more conducive to a woman's happiness than single?" whether "the marriage relation is essential to the happiness of mankind," and whether "it is proper for ladies to make proposals of marriage." The ladies' societies naturally spent more time in discussing women's rights than did the men's societies. Woman suffrage was before the ladies repeatedly. It is unfortunate that the two sexes could not have joined in some of the debates; they would have been undoubtedly less one-sided: "Resolved that the intellectual ability of ladies equal that of gentlemen," "Resolved that ladies have a right to debate and declaim in public," "Resolved that women should enter the medical profession." The ladies voted in the affirmative on the last and would probably have done so on the others had a ballot been taken. The men also occasionally discussed similar subjects: "Res[d], That for equal labor, the wages of women should be the same as those of men . . ." and "Resolved that it is right for women to attend as delegates the great conventions on Temperance, Anti-slavery, Religion, etc." The tendency on the part of some of both sexes to ridicule feminism is apparent in the burlesque subjects debated in the Young Ladies' Literary Society: "Resolved that Betty the cook's discoveries are of more advantage to society than the discoveries of Sir Isaac Newton," and "Resolved that women should be allowed to sing bass!"

The literary program often included essays, poems and orations as well as a debate. The ladies sometimes omitted the debate and the young men in later years often devoted the whole evening to it. Usually some subject was presented for general discussion once a month or occasionally.

That there was a tendency for the young disciples of Demosthenes to soar is clear enough from the titles of some of the essays and orations: "Life More Solemn Than Death," "Sublimity of Nature," "What Needs the Soul in Affliction," "Whither Are We Tending?" and "Instability of Earthly Pleasure." Perhaps some of these were trial balloons for commencement essays. Of course the subjects were infinite in variety: "The Secret of Success," "The Asylum for Idiots at Columbus," "The Willow and Dewdrop," "Boil Your Peas," "Is Art a Perfect Medium?" "A Trouting Excursion to Plumb Creek." In 1856 George W. Andrews read an essay before the Young Men's Lyceum on "Whiskers." Extempore speeches were often inspired by immediate surroundings: "Our Clock" and "The Bust of Chase."

Student interest in the stirring current events of the periods is clearly shown in some of the debate subjects:

1840—"Resolved that the U. S. Bank should be immediately rechartered."

1842—"Ought the United States to render assistance to Texas under existing circumstances?"

1849—"Has the War with Mexico resulted in any good to the United States?"

1849—"The recent discovery of Gold in California a curse (or a blessing) to our Country."

1850—"Resolved that the extension of territory is beneficial to this nation."

1850—"Ought Christians to obey the new Fugitive law?"

1850—"Ought Webster to be hung?" [After the Fourth-of-March speech.]

1850—"Resolved that the United States government ought to provide a homestead for every man who does not now possess one."

1852—"Resolved that the recent publication of Mrs. Stowe will be productive of more good than the efforts of Anti-Slavery lecturers."

1852—"Resolved; That it is the duty of anti-slavery men to separate themselves from the old parties (Whig and Dem.) and vote with a third party."

1854—"Resolved that the question of slavery extension should be left to the inhabitants of the territories."

1854—"Resolved that the people of Massachusetts would have been justified in resisting the forces of the United States and detaining the Slave Burns in freedom by violence."

1855—"Resolved, that Utah should be admitted into the Union with a constitution allowing poligamy."

1855—"Resolved that the avowed principles of the Know Nothing Society are consistent with the principles of the American Government."

1855—"That the Friends of progress have reason to rejoice in the success of the *Allies* at Sevastopol."

1858—"Resolved, That the citizens of Kansas should resist the Lecompton Constitution."

1858—"Resolved, that it would be expedient for the people of the U. S. to support Stephen A. Douglass for Pres. in the next Pres. Campaign."

1859—"Resolved that it is the duty of citizens of Oberlin to forcibly resist the Fugitive Slave Law, henceforth and forever." (The Rescue Case was on at this time.)

1860—"Resolved, That Jno Brown should have the sympathy of true friends of freedom."

The ballot taken on the last question resulted in 14 ayes and 12 noes.

Of course the slavery question took up much of the Oberlin students' attention. The popularity of this issue is evident from the subjects just listed. Topics which were definitely propagandist in nature were also debated. In 1840 the Dialectic Association debated the question: "Would it be practicable to extend the right of suffrage to the colored men of this nation, were they all emancipated?" A discussion as to whether "the Constitution of the United States [was] a pro-slavery document" was "engaged in with considerable animation" at a meeting of the Young Men's Lyceum in 1849. The young women of the Young Ladies' Literary Society debated a few years later whether a slaveholder could be a Christian. Just before the outbreak of the war one of the men's societies took up the problem of inter-marriage between the races: "Res, That the amalgamation of the white and black races in this country is feasible, proper, and should be encouraged." This was a dangerous subject, even in Oberlin.

As early as 1836 the Young Ladies' Association put on a dialogue on slavery, and one young lady representing a slave blackened "her face, neck & hands with smoked cork," and "took cold on account of having her neck exposed." Mrs. Alice Welch Cowles opposed such a demonstration because she believed it was contrary to "good taste for young ladies to appear in any coloring, except what nature had given them." She was overruled by the majority of the Ladies' Board, however, despite the fact that she had the support of the Lady Principal, Mrs. Dascomb, and the "colored" girl participated in the dialogue.[18] In later years there were enough members of Negro extraction to make such resorts to artifice unnecessary.

Other reforms came in for occasional consideration also. There was "a some what lively discussion" when the desirability of maintaining a standing army in time of peace was considered. Discussions of the peace question seem usually to lead to conflict. Prohibition was a practical issue in the fifties. In 1852 and 1853 both the Young Men's Lyceum and the Young Ladies' Literary Society debated the advisability of adopting the Maine Liquor Law in Ohio. Socialism and communism had made little impression on Oberlin students so far, but one of the men's societies in 1851 considered the question: "Resolved, That a general and equal distribution of property would tend to benefit mankind." Of the various issues involved in the moral reform movement the question of the theater and the reading of fiction attracted the most interest: "Is the reading of fictitious works injurious to the mind?" "That the inherent tendency of the drama is to vice," and "Resolved that Theatres might be made agencies in moral reform." The works of Byron caused considerable worry. "Is the reading of Byron & Shakespeare beneficial to a student preparing for the Christian Ministry?" This was the difficult problem thrashed out at a meeting of the Dialectic in 1843. At a later date somebody presented a copy of Byron's works to the library of the Ladies' Literary Society Library Association. The men of the Phi Delta were disturbed about the influence that such reading might have upon their "sisters" and raised the question whether "the works of Lord Byron ought to be excluded from the Ladies' Library."

Religion furnished an almost unlimited mine of subjects for debate, especially suitable because never settled: "That the light of nature is sufficient to prove the existence of the Deity," "Is an inebriate accountable to God for the crimes he commits while intoxicated?" "Resolved that inferior animals have a fu-

[18] A. W. Cowles to H. Cowles and Zilpah Grant, Jan. 16, 1836 (Cowles MSS).

ture existence," "Resolved that the Noachian Deluge was universal." The new revelations and "isms" of the period contributed excellent and timely programs: "Res., That the General Government ought to suppress by force the Institution of Mormonism in Utah," and "Resolved, That the Rappings [near Rochester] are worthy of confidence as revelations from the Spirit World." The Catholic question was much in the public eye and Oberlin students discussed such matters as: "Ought the government of the United States to adopt any measures to prevent the increase of papacy in the Country," and "Res., that catholics should receive their share of public money [for schools]." George W. Andrews, uncle of the late Oberlin organist, and S. P. Millikan, father of the scientist, took part in the debate on the latter issue.

Scientific and pseudo-scientific subjects were settled off-hand in an hour or two of perhaps eloquent but usually totally uninformed debate. In 1859 the Phi Kappa Pi Society "went into committee of the whole to discuss the ques. of the plurality of worlds. After an animated discussion the chairman . . . reported that the Com. had discussed the question without coming to any conclusion." The next year the same society spent an evening debating the question: "Resolved that the undulatory theory is the true theory of light." The rival society conceded one session to the consideration of the nebular hypothesis. The young ladies of Aelioian were attacking an equally difficult though more mundane problem when they debated whether "Roosters crow in the morning from observation [or] instinct."

The young ladies' societies discussed some subjects of peculiar interest to their sex and seldom, and never formally, debated by their brothers: "Resolved: it is a good thing to have lady clerks in dry-good-stores," "Resolved that domestic happiness is enhanced by housekeeping," and "The comparative merits of sweeping, cleaning, baking, and dusting." Many sessions were devoted to the always-enthralling subject of feminine attire: "That a frequent change of the fashions is a benefit to the world," "That ladies do not sufficiently cultivate taste in dress," "That laced stays are beneficial," "That large Sunbonnets are a nuisance," "That Hooped Skirts are a nuisance," "Would it be for the advantage of our Country to have a National Costume established by law?" Bloomers were discussed in the Young

Ladies' Literary Society at no less than four separate meetings. A few Oberlin girls actually wore bloomers but to the vast majority it never became a practical problem.

The college life around them contributed many "discussable" propositions. "Resolved that the Natural Sciences should be substituted in the regular college course for the Dead Languages" aroused much partisanship. There were other live questions of a similar nature: "Is it advisable that the faculty of Oberlin College should introduce the study of the Modern Languages into the College Course?" "Ought Hebrew to be left out of the collegiate course?" "Resolved that reciting from books is more beneficial than reciting from notes," and "Resolved that mathematical studies are of more practical benefit than linguistic studies." They even dared occasionally to discuss matters of administration: "Resolved: That the long vacation of this Institution should occur in the summer," and "Resolved that the young gentlemen of the Inst. ought to be subject to the eight o'clock rule." It was onc of the young ladies' societies that offered the latter suggestion!

Considering the avowed literary nature of the societies it is surprising that so few debates dealt with truly literary matters. There were some, however: "Resolved that the influence of the writer is greater than that of the orator," "Resolved that the popularity of a literary work is an evidence of its real merit," "Resolved that there are greater causes for producing literature now than there were in the reign of Queen Elisabeth," "Is Criticism on the whole beneficial to Literature?" "Whether the times of ancient Greece and Rome were more favorable to the production of poetry than the present," "The comparative merits of the Dictionary of Webster and the Dictionary of Worcester." In the latter debate Webster's carried off the palm.

There were also a good many entirely unclassifiable topics, concocted by the youthful imagination to meet the unlimited demand for subjects for debate. It was the Young Men's Lyceum which took up the question whether or not dogs ought to be taxed, but it took the ladies of the Aelioian to spend an evening arguing the pros and cons of whether "a cow is better than a dog." The ladies' programs also included: "Resolved that yesterday is past and can never return," "Resolved that two little trunks are preferable to one large one," and "Resolved that it is never best to indulge in the *Blues*." The cosmopolitan character of the Oberlin student body made it possible for two young Scotchmen (Livingstone was one.) to debate with two Yankees the question: "Does *Scotland* furnish more interesting associations than *New England*?" There was enough of the strutting patriotism of the time in Oberlin to suggest "that America is more than a match for Old England in everything," but undoubtedly some of the British students came valiantly to the defense of Britannia. In the sixties the young men of Phi Kappa Pi considered (we hope with candor) the problem: "Is the increase of education favorable to the growth of eloquence."

From 1861 to the end of our period the Civil War furnished a large proportion of the problems debated:

March 19, 1861

"Resolved that the sentiment, 'The Union must and shall be preserved' embodies the policy that should be pursued in the present crisis."

July 16, 1861

"Resolved that dissolution without Slavery is preferable to union with Slavery."

November 12, 1861

"Resolved that the Administration did right in deposing John C. Fremont." (A vote taken on this question resulted in a tie.)

March 11, 1862

"Resolved that the rebellious States if they shall be subjugated should be reduced to the condition of territories."

March 25, 1862

"Resolved that Gen. McClellan ought to be relieved from his command of the Army of the Potomac."

April 7, 1863

"That persons uttering disloyal sentiments ought to be dealt with as traitors." (Negative decision.)

November 11, 1863

"Resolved that our government does right in removing Generals." (This from the ladies!)

March 1, 1864

"Res'd that Abraham Lincoln should be renominated for the Presidency."

April 4, 1865

"Should the Government furnish men and means to educate the freedmen?"

May 2, 1865

"Resolved that the Military leaders of the Rebellion, who will take the oaths of allegiance, ought to be allowed to remain in this country unmolested."

All of the societies adopted resolutions of "sorrow and grief" upon the assassination of Lincoln, whom one of them described as "an Honest man, a Representative man, the Emancipator of Millions, the Preserver of the Union, and a Leader whose virtue, wisdom and administrative acts place him side by side with the *Father* of his *Country*." In June the Phi Kappa Pi held a mock trial of Jefferson Davis and found him guilty of high treason.

As a rule the society minutes are dry and sterile, particularly those of the ladies' societies. Occasionally, however, the wit of a secretary broke through the formalities, and the reader gains a glimpse of the actualities of society meetings and of the genius of the recorder. In 1843 J. H. McClelland referred to "a season of small talk and altercation as usual," but at the next meeting this "offensive portion [of the minute] was voted to be expunged." It is, nevertheless, still legible! Such was too likely to be the fate of frankness. One very informal meeting of the Young Men's Lyceum was recorded in informal style and the minutes allowed to stand. There must have been other meetings of a similar character.

"Owing to the Term being so far advanced the house was small.

"The season was late and the attention of the Pres. was called to the fact of the extreme looseness of the ventilator over northwest door in Soc. room. A suggestion was acquiesced in to come down from the presidential chair and take a seat by the stove.

"Thus arranged the remains of the 'Young Men's Lyceum,' its true friends, those who 'stuck to it to the last,' proceeded to the transaction of business. First, the calling of the roll was omitted. The Sec. was unable to find minutes of the last meeting which in the hurry of the occasion had been neglected by the absconding Sec. It was understood to be the evening for general discussion but the Soc. had no disposition to engage in discussing the question before the house. It was thrown overboard and then followed motion after motion which is not our purpose to transcribe. Soc. became loquacious. Every one talked but the Sec.

"The only remarkable thing which was done was to adjourn which some member was happy enough to move."[19]

Descriptions of society meetings by visitors are rare but, of course, generally more enlightening than official minutes. Mary Dascomb described an interesting meeting of the Theological Society in a letter to Professor Monroe in 1863: "I attended an interesting exercise in the Theol. Society Wed. night. After an animated discussion of the 'Wine' question, in wh. all took the right side [!], and gave their reasons, an extempore exercise took place, highly beneficial I shld. imagine. A topic and name were given by each member, and when the Pres. drew a name, the owner thereof had to come forward, take a topic from the mass, and speak on it *five* minutes *immediately*: 'Who was Melchisidec,' 'Was the Flood universal,' 'Nature or Art, which is ahead,' 'Unity of the Human species,' 'Matrimony &c,' were well treated."[20] Similar extemporaneous programs were not unusual in the other societies. One of the societies, however, debated the question whether "the habit of extemporaneous discussion is an evil one."

Seldom did the secretary have the temerity to comment on performance as in the middle forties when the minutes of one meeting of the Union Society state that "The Exercises opened up with a superlative richness, which did honor to those who performed a part, as well as to the Soc." It was the duty of the critic to do this, and the critic has performed a service of great value to posterity in giving us an unusual insight into the actualities of society meetings. One critic "complained that the gentlemen did not *pour themselves out* sufficiently," and another commented on a debate of the middle sixties: "Mr. N.'s remarks were evidently written out and committed—they certainly were well written. They deserved a little more *vim* and naturalness in delivery. . . . Mr. Pond's arm movements had too

19MS Minutes, Nov. 14, 1854.

20Mary Dascomb and Louisa Fitch to James Monroe, Nov. 12, 16, 1863 (Monroe MSS).

much of a slashing character to be graceful . . . Mr. Jeakin's eyes were cast down too much of the time. Every speaker needs the magnetic fire which he draws from the eyes of his audience."[21]

Whispering and other irregularities were not uncommon. At a meeting in 1860 "the chairman reported a good discussion with some disorder." The personal encounter which took place between two members in the Mock House of Representatives held by the two men's societies in 1861 was probably due to emulation of the real body at Washington. Of a regular meeting of the Phi Kappa Pi in 1866, however, the critic reported: "In general we feel compelled to say that there is an abundant lack of good order in our society. The attitudes assumed by some members of the society—e.g. a full length extension on a sofa—are probably very comfortable, perhaps very striking, but positively very unbecoming. If a man is sleepy he had best go to bed and pay his fine." He noted a "Senior asleep on the back seat" and a "Junior located as follows, head in one chair, feet in another, corporal frame in a state of suspension between, toothpick in mouth engaged in reading; highly respectful both to the Society and the speaker." In commenting on another meeting the critic wrote: "Those of us who have taught school have doubtless been annoyed by the oft-repeated query by the youthful idea 'please may I gowout?' Thirteen youths were seen to leave the society last week. We would suggest to the president that he apply the old rule 'only one to be out at a time.'" At a meeting of the Theological Literary Society in 1845 the secretary reported that, "some slipped out before the exercises were through and others stood a long time with hats in hands, as if very impatient, all which tended to create an uneasiness among all the members of the society present and almost render it impossible for a good effect to be produced."[22]

Neither is it to be supposed that programs were always carried out according to schedule. Very often some, or even occasionally all, of the speakers and debaters were absent or had failed to prepare. The Young Men's Lyceum adopted the policy of bluffing the orators into action. In 1849 they author-

[21]John G. Fraser, MS Critique, Mar. 27 [1866?] (lent by Mrs. Grace F. Waugh of Mentor, Ohio).

[22]John G. Fraser, "Critique on the exercises of the Phi Kappa Pi for April 10th, 1866," and "Critique on the Exercises of Phi Kappa Pi for May 7th, 1867" (lent by Mrs. Grace F. Waugh, Mentor, Ohio).

ized a certain Mr. Parker "to appoint members to take part in the colloquy, and to enforce them in the name of the Lyceum to commit their parts & to rehearse them a sufficient number of times to render them able to perform their parts with credit two weeks from this night." Two years later a "motion [was] made to *sternly command* the speakers at the Anniversary to have their pieces prepared for rehearsal in one week from that time." Often members who failed to fill their allotted appointments were fined. In 1847 the Theological Literary Society voted that "those who are delinquent . . . shall be marked by the president, and reported by the chairman of the committee of assignments, to the treasurer, as obnoxious to a fine." The same rule was adopted in Phi Delta, but one of the members of that society "preferred to pay to the treasurer of Soc. twenty-five cents than to bore it (the Society)."

The period of the sixties saw the men's societies attacked by an epidemic of mock meetings of various types. In 1860 came a Mock Republican Convention, in 1861 a session of a Mock House of Representatives, in 1862 a Mock Cabinet Meeting, and in 1865 a mock trial of Jefferson Davis. The Mock Convention is significant because it served as a precedent for a long line of illustrious succeeding conventions. Though it lasted two days it seems to have been a comparatively unpretentious affair, held entirely under the auspices of the Phi Delta Society. There seems to be no record even of who the nominee was. The final minutes read: " . . . The society went into Committee of the whole to nominate a President & Vice-President of the U.S., since which time it has not been heard of." The Mock House of Representatives which convened under the joint auspices of the Phi Delta and Phi Kappa Pi was a much more ambitious and elaborate project. The session lasted through six nonsuccessive days. Representatives were selected for the various states roughly according to population; the House was organized with A. B. Nettleton as speaker (to represent the Hon. Frank P. Blair, the choice of the Oberlin boys), twelve standing committees were appointed and considerable business taken up. The President's message was received and discussed; a compromise between the North and the South was debated but voted down by 18 ayes to 24 noes, and a motion to recognize the Southern Confederacy was tabled and then taken up and negatived. The Mock Cabinet

Meeting held at a meeting of Phi Kappa Pi in 1862 was evidently a minor event. The mock trial of President Davis, however, was described by the *News* as "spirited and ably-conducted." There was a large audience in attendance at each of the sessions. The paper continued: "Much skill and ability, and no little amusement, were manifested in the conduct of the trial, which resulted of course, in the conviction of the arch traitor for treason. The unexpected and exciting mock-tragedy, at the close of the trial, in which a band of desperadoes rushed in to rescue their doomed chief, was well carried out, and the whole affair was pronounced a decided success."[23]

The societies, singly or jointly, invited outside speakers to appear before them in public meetings during the year or at Commencement. They uniformly selected the most distinguished names: John Greenleaf Whittier, Horace Greeley, Mark Hopkins, S. P. Chase; and these gentlemen almost as uniformly declined the invitations. A member of the faculty would finally be called upon; Monroe would speak on some phase of the slavery question or Penfield would deliver his address on "The Latin Language and Literature." There were exceptions, as when in 1852 C. C. Burleigh, the radical abolitionist, addressed the societies jointly. In 1861 the two men's societies inadvertently invited two men for the same Commencement, and, as luck would have it, they both accepted. In the end both James A. Garfield (then at the Western Reserve Ecclectic Institute and a member of the Ohio Legislature) and the Reverend Edward Beecher (the former president of Illinois College and then a pastor at Galesburg) were heard, though on different evenings.

Each society usually held one special meeting or "exhibition" each year known as the "Anniversary." The Anniversary differed from other meetings in that the program was longer, interspersed with special music ("Mr. Pease and Sister," ran the minutes of one annual meeting of the Y. L. L. S., "relieved the audience with a Song, 'The Old Oak Tree.' "), open to the public and the pieces more carefully prepared. These meetings were held in the Music Hall, the Chapel, or the Church and were looked upon as among the really important events of the college year.

[23]*Lorain County News,* June 21, 1865, and MS Minutes of Phi Kappa Pi, June 6, 13, 1865.

Preparation for the Anniversary involved not only many hours of worry for the performers but the joyous labor of decorating the place of meeting. James H. Fairchild wrote of a semi-annual meeting of the Y. L. A. in 1859: "The Chapel seemed like a grove of evergreens. The orchestra was occupied by the singers (young ladies) so concealed among the pine trees as to be almost invisible."[24] The "ladies and gentlemen" usually joined in the work of decoration, making of it a social event in itself. "Spent some time to-day," one student confided to her journal, "with a number of young ladies and gentlemen, wreathing flowers and evergreens to decorate the chapel [in Colonial Hall], for the Anniversary of the Lyceum."[25] It was the music and the decorations which gave to these anniversaries their special flavor.

At first, Anniversaries were held at most any time, in March, in June, in September and in August. Eventually the faculty insisted, however, on confining them to commencement or examination week. The societies were not easily reconciled to this arrangement, and when in 1853 the Musical Association was allowed to hold a public meeting in term time the men's societies were stirred almost to rebellion. The Young Men's Lyceum passed resolutions denouncing such favoritism, and the Union Society went so far as to vote to "withhold patronage from the concert" to be sponsored by the Musical Association. A committee of the faculty came down to a later meeting of the society, however, and overawed them into expunging the resolution.

In the late fifties and sixties the two college men's societies would sometimes join in Union Exhibitions and often united in plentiful "collations." In 1860 the Young Ladies' Literary Society proposed to hold a collation after their anniversary but this proposal was negatived by Mrs. Dascomb. For the men, however, such feasts were the order of the day. In 1858 the members of the Lyceum and some invited guests enjoyed "a sumptuous oyster supper" followed by "sentiments and speeches." The Phi Delta and Phi Kappa Pi held a joint collation in 1859 which a reporter called "The Great Event of the nineteenth century." "After a feast of fat things, (oysters et cetera,) [continues the account in the *Monthly*] in the getting

[24]J. H. F. to Mary Kellogg, Oct. 29, 1839 (Fairchild MSS).
[25]Helen Cowles, *Grace Victorious* (Oberlin—1856), 137.

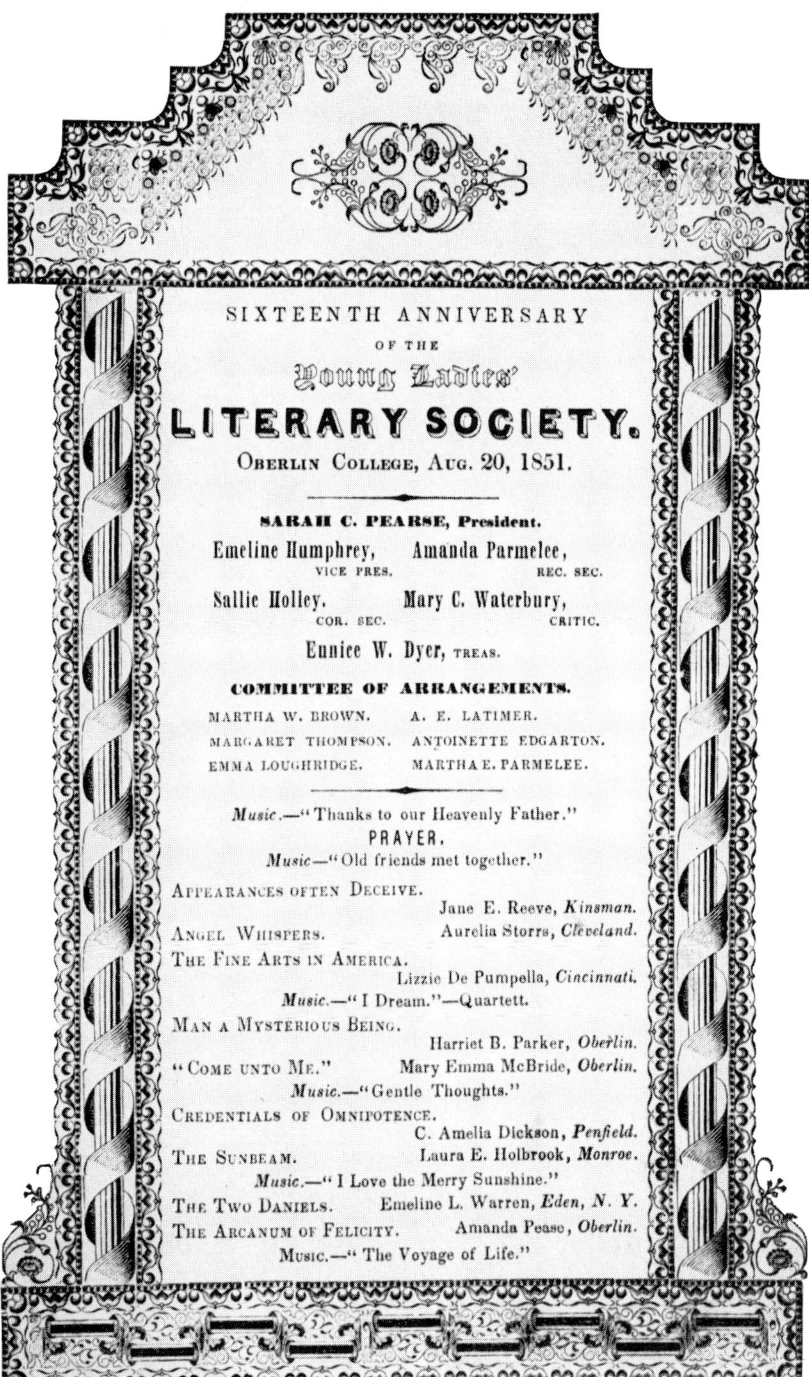

SIXTEENTH ANNIVERSARY
OF THE
Young Ladies'
LITERARY SOCIETY.
OBERLIN COLLEGE, AUG. 20, 1851.

SARAH C. PEARSE, President.

Emeline Humphrey, VICE PRES.
Amanda Parmelee, REC. SEC.
Sallie Holley, COR. SEC.
Mary C. Waterbury, CRITIC.
Eunice W. Dyer, TREAS.

COMMITTEE OF ARRANGEMENTS.

MARTHA W. BROWN.
A. E. LATIMER.
MARGARET THOMPSON.
ANTOINETTE EDGARTON.
EMMA LOUGHRIDGE.
MARTHA E. PARMELEE.

Music.—"Thanks to our Heavenly Father."
PRAYER.
Music—"Old friends met together."

APPEARANCES OFTEN DECEIVE. Jane E. Reeve, *Kinsman.*
ANGEL WHISPERS. Aurelia Storrs, *Cleveland.*
THE FINE ARTS IN AMERICA. Lizzie De Pumpella, *Cincinnati.*
Music.—"I Dream."—Quartett.
MAN A MYSTERIOUS BEING. Harriet B. Parker, *Oberlin.*
"COME UNTO ME." Mary Emma McBride, *Oberlin.*
Music.—"Gentle Thoughts."
CREDENTIALS OF OMNIPOTENCE. C. Amelia Dickson, *Penfield.*
THE SUNBEAM. Laura E. Holbrook, *Monroe.*
Music.—"I Love the Merry Sunshine."
THE TWO DANIELS. Emeline L. Warren, *Eden, N. Y.*
THE ARCANUM OF FELICITY. Amanda Pease, *Oberlin.*
MUSIC.—"The Voyage of Life."

PROGRAM OF A YOUNG LADIES' LITERARY SOCIETY ANNIVERSARY

up of which the committee manifested exquisite taste, and in the getting *down* of which all manifested very exquisite appetites; the company was regaled with another feast—of sentiment, toasts, poetry, music and eloquence." The toasts included: Music, The Legal Profession, The Republican Party, The Students' Monthly, The Sophomore Class, Oberlin, John Brown, and the Ladies' Literary. The toast to the Sophomore Class was: "A band of 'United Brethren'—first in play—first in study—and first in the hearts of the ladies." And to "Oberlin: Born on the soil of poverty, rocked in the cradle of persecution, now enjoying a glorious triumph over all; her College the home of the poor, the patron of Progress, the fortress of Truth: its students—the gentlemen, beaux-ideal of true manhood; the ladies, belles-*real* of all that is lovely."[26]

At a joint meeting in 1862: "The Committee on lemonade through its chairman Mr. Day assisted by the other members of the committee brought in a report of well-prepared lemonade which by general consent was temporarily *laid on the table*."

Such convivial meetings often closed with singing, if not "Auld Lang Syne," then, a society song:

For the Truth and our banner, we are ready to die
Right and true is the heart of the Phi Kappa Pi.[27]

[26] *Oberlin Student's Monthly,* II, 58–59 (Dec., 1859).
[27] Anniversary program of Phi Kappa Pi, Aug. 26, 1861.

CHAPTER XLVI

MUSIC IN OBERLIN

TO George Nelson Allen more than to any other man belongs the credit of giving music the place it had, and has, in Oberlin. He was a student and apostle of Lowell Mason of Boston.

Mason was not only a teacher and a teacher of teachers, but a compiler of song books and a composer and arranger of hymn tunes, and is remembered by many people more for the music for "Nearer, My God, to Thee," "My Faith Looks up to Thee," and "Greenland's Icy Mountains" than for his work as an educational reformer. Over a million copies of Mason's song books were sold. This combination of music teacher, song-book compiler and hymn-tune composer was repeated in each of that group of men more or less directly associated with Mason in this period and usually known as the New England School of hymn writers. Among these, and all later influential in one way or another in Oberlin, were: Thomas Hastings, Finney's friend from Utica, who wrote the music for "Rock of Ages," compiled several important collections of songs, directed music at the Broadway Tabernacle, and was later associated with Mason in a school for training music teachers in New York; George James Webb, Mason's partner in Boston and author of the music of "Stand Up, Stand Up for Jesus"; William B. Bradbury, composer of Sunday School songs and disciple of Mason; Benjamin Franklin Baker, Mason's successor as teacher of music in the Boston schools and compiler of the *Haydn Collection of Church Music,* and the mild and pious Isaac B. Woodbury, one of the most popular of the composers of his day and the compiler of widely used collections of choruses, especially the *Cythara* and *Dulcimer.*[1]

George N. Allen was a true disciple of Lowell Mason. For over a generation he taught music in the Oberlin Institute and

[1]John Tasker Howard, *Our American Music* (New York—1931), 142–158.

College and, like his better-known associates, compiled a song book, *The Social and Sabbath School Hymn Book,* first published in Oberlin in 1844, and composed several hymn tunes, the best known of which is *Maitland,* the tune usually sung with the words of "Must Jesus Bear the Cross Alone." Like his prototypes, too, he was renowned for his piety.

Allen, however, was not the first teacher of music in Oberlin. The honor of having been the first Professor of Music in an American college belongs to Elihu Parsons Ingersoll, who was born at Stockbridge, Massachusetts, and graduated from Yale College in 1832. After studying a year at the Auburn Theological Seminary in central New York he returned to Yale, graduating from the Yale Seminary in 1835. By 1833 he had become one of Finney's satellites, which probably accounts for his appointment in 1835 as "Professor of Sacred Music" in the Oberlin Collegiate Institute at the time of Finney's coming to Oberlin in 1835. He served in that position one year, resigning in the summer of 1836 to become associated with Father Shipherd in the ill-fated Grand River Seminary in Michigan.[2] The next year the faculty instructed Professor Morgan to write to a certain Lewis Bradley with regard to his accepting the professorship. It was also determined to make indirect "inquiries regarding Bradley's piety." His appointment was later recommended but Mr. Bradley never came.[3] Professor Finney was always intensely interested in church music and was somewhat of a musician and singer, himself. It will be remembered that as a young lawyer he was directing the church choir at Adams at the time of his conversion. Probably he deserves considerable credit for the introduction of the teaching of music in Oberlin.

It was during the academic year of 1836–37 that George Nelson Allen, of Boston, transferred from Western Reserve College to Oberlin. This transfer seems to have been the result of the clash between Allen's liberal opinions on reform and religion and the views held by the college authorities in Hudson. Allen had taught a singing school in the same town. One of his pupils wrote him early in 1836: "There are many who deplore

[2]T. M., July 5, 1836; Edward E. Salisbury *Biographical Memoranda Respecting All Who Ever Were Members of the Class of 1832 in Yale College* (New Haven—1880), 165; Auburn Seminary, *General Biographical Catalogue,* 1818–1918, page 60, and Ingersoll to Finney, Apr. 27, 1833 (Finney MSS).

[3]F. M., Feb. 10, Mar. 1, 1837.

the unhappy circumstances that make it necessary to take this step. [The closing of his singing school by the college officials?] We feel as if the spirit again called forth, was the same that banished Mr. Green, and the lamented Storrs [reform members of the faculty], and though we do not know how to be reconciled to the loss of every choice spirit that is raised up, yet we know Hudson is not worthy of them, and it is better to go where their worth can be *appreciated*. You may be assured that the members of your singing class, are grateful for your faithful instructions, and very much regret that they can enjoy them no longer." The next year when "The students . . . requested advice in regard to employing G. N. Allen, who had applied to teach a Singing School in Coll[ege]," the faculty of Western Reserve "Resolved that they be not advised to employ him."[4]

Allen was enrolled in the Collegiate Department at Oberlin for one year and in the Theological Department for two years. In 1837 while still a student he became the "Teacher of Sacred Music" in the Institute, at a salary of one hundred dollars.[5] He served the Institute and College for thirty-three years: as Teacher of Music from 1837 to 1841 and Professor of Music from 1841 to 1856 and again from 1858 to 1864 and as Professor of Geology and Natural History (1848 to 1871) and Secretary and Treasurer (1863 to 1865). In addition to his other duties he was also Principal of the Preparatory Department from 1842 to 1846.

Young George Allen, living in Boston before coming to Western Reserve College, may very likely have attended the Boston Academy of Music and certainly would have come under the influence of Lowell Mason. Whatever the course of Allen's earliest musical training we know that in the winter vacation of 1838–39 he attended one of the conventions for music teachers which Mason had inaugurated in 1836. While he was away Enoch Noyes Bartlett, a student in the Theological Department, substituted for him, teaching music at a shilling and a half an hour. In February of 1839, Allen wrote from Boston: "I have, during my stay here this winter, been taking lessons on the Piano-Forte and violin and attending other instruction in music under Professors Mason and Webb,—with a view to

[4]Anon. letter to G. N. Allen, Jan. 16, 1836 (Allen MSS), and Western Reserve College Faculty, MS Minutes, Oct. 4, 1837.

[5]F. M., Feb. 24, 1838.

preparing myself to be more useful in this department."[6] Allen introduced Mason's method, ideas and singing books at Oberlin. After his return from Boston the classes in vocal music became increasingly popular. The 1839–40 *Catalogue* stated: "Instruction in sacred music is free to all. Not far from one hundred have attended the regular classes in this department." The next annual *Catalogue* gives the number of music pupils at 250 and the year after it was announced that, "Systematic instruction [in Sacred Music] has been given to upwards of four hundred pupils, including a large class composed of children of the citizens of the village." Allen also often led singing school during the winter vacation and was for many years the guiding spirit and first chorister of the Oberlin Musical Association, later the Musical Union.

The regular instruction was supplemented by occasional conventions. In October of 1851 Professor Mason, himself, took charge of a musical convention in the meeting house. Particular attention was given in this convention to "the manner of correctly performing the different styles of Church Music." In the summer of 1855 a convention was held during commencement week under the direction of Professor I. B. Woodbury. Those who took part were expected to aid in the regular commencement concert, also directed by Woodbury.[7] Of the other musical leaders mentioned, Hastings and Baker also later visited Oberlin, the one as a guest, the other as a concert director.

There was a tendency among the pious to frown upon most instrumental music. About the only instrumental music heard in Oberlin in the early years was the accompaniment to the choir and other choruses—a bass viol alone, or with violins, cellos, and sometimes a parlor organ called a "seraphine." Allen had written from Boston, while studying there under Mason, suggesting the purchase of a piano: "Is it not desirable that there should be a Piano-Forte connected with the Institution? Can you encourage me any in making the purchase? Will the Institution be able to appropriate money for that object within two years say—a part if not a whole? Or will the Institution so

[6]Bill from Bartlett, June 8, 1839 (Misc. Archives), and G. N. Allen to Levi Burnell, Feb. 1, 1839 (Treas. Off., File A).

[7]*Oberlin Evangelist,* Sept. 10, 1851, and printed invitation to the Musical Convention dated July 20, 1855 and signed by Allen and four others (O. C. Lib.).

favor me with respect to my support in consideration of my services as teacher of music, that I can assume the responsibility myself? My own opinion is that there ought to be a piano connected with the Institution." A piano is said to have been established in one of the buildings of the Institute a year or two later, but whether purchased by Allen or with funds furnished by the school is not certain. Considerable opposition was aroused by what was looked upon by some as the worldly character of such music. At a meeting of the trustees in 1841 a resolution was actually passed "that it is not expedient to introduce *Piano Music* as a branch of Instruction in the Institution." Five years later William Dawes offered his resignation from the Board of Trustees partly because "a vast amount of time, and money [had] been expended for fashionable amusements and accomplishments, such as *Piano Music,* Dress, etc., etc."[8]

In the early forties the trustees generally kept a close watch for fear that worldly music would supplant the pious and moral variety. In 1841, when Allen was appointed "Professor of Sacred Music" it was also "Resolved that it is the sense of the trustees in the appointment of Mr. Allen that the style of Sacred Music taught in this Institution be in accordance with what is understood to be the style of the Manhattan Collection or of Thos. Hastings." The following year a committee including Amasa Walker, President Mahan and Father Keep was appointed "to wait upon George N. Allen to confer with him respecting the pieces as well as the style of music generally adopted by him."[9]

Beginning with 1849–50 there appears in the *Catalogue* the announcement that, "Instruction in Instrumental Music can also be had at moderate charges." The 1853–54 *Catalogue* carefully explains, however, that "Instruction in Instrumental Music forms no part of the course of this Institution," this despite the fact that the Ladies' Board had in the previous year appointed "a committee to confer with the Faculty on the propriety of having Piano Music under the control of the officers of the school." This *Catalogue* last cited continues, nevertheless, to announce that, "ample facilities are here afforded, WITH EXTRA CHARGE, to those who wish instruction in instrumental

[8]G. N. Allen to Levi Burnell, Feb. 1, 1839; T. M., Aug. 20, 1841, and William Dawes, MS Letter of Resignation, Aug. 20, 1846 (Misc. Archives).

[9]T. M., Aug. 27, 1841, and Aug. 22, 1842.

music. In this department special pains have been taken during the past year to provide suitable instruments for practice, and to procure thoroughly competent teachers, while at the same time the terms are as moderate as can possibly be afforded." The tuition for instruction in piano was placed at $8.00 a quarter. It is quite clear that the "Department of Instrumental Music" was under the general administration of Oberlin College even though such instruction may have formed "no part of the course." The expansion in the catalogue announcement corresponds with a parallel expansion in the work offered. Writing in 1855, George Allen refers to a committee which was named by the faculty "to establish or inaugurate the Dept. of Instrumental Music" and which appointed him "superintendent to provide instruments and teachers."[10]

A disagreement between Allen and other teachers and members of the administrative staff, largely over the question of finances, led to his resignation. Professor C. H. Churchill took his place both as Professor of Sacred Music and as Superintendent of the Department of Instrumental Music in 1856–57. The arrangement made with Professor Churchill is given at length in the minutes of the Board of Trustees and gives an excellent idea of the work expected of the Professor of Sacred Music in Oberlin College:

" . . . In the department of Music he is expected to teach the vocal classes as they have been taught heretofore by the professor in that department: he is with the concurrence of the Church and the Oberlin Society to take charge of the Choir and the arrangement of the music for the Sabbath and give one or more public concerts of music annually under the direction of the faculty and will have charge also of the instrumental music, the avails of which last services is to be his own. In the department of mathematics he is to teach an amount equivalent to one recitation per day. Of his compensation, $200 is to be drawn from the Professorship fund; $100 is expected to be paid by the Oberlin Society for his services in the choir on the Sabbath as well as for the teaching given to the children of the Society in vocal music in connection with the students, which amount is by agreement to be paid to the trustees of this College for this

[10]L. B. M., May 10, 1852; George N. Allen to Mary C. R. Allen, Nov., 1855, and G. N. Allen to the Oberlin Church [1855] (Allen MSS).

purpose; and $300 it is expected will be raised by one or more public concerts the avails of which are to go to the said trustees to be by them paid towards his salary."[11]

The "Professor of Sacred Music" was clearly more than a mere college professor; he was a community official. In 1857–58 the position was vacant despite the offer made to Professor Babcock of Boston. In 1858 Allen resumed his teaching of music in addition to his professorship in Natural History, and was granted a regular salary of $600 by the College.[12]

A great impetus to appreciation of and interest in instrumental music was given by the building of the organ in the Oberlin meeting house. The first public performance on this organ was given on March 6, 1855. The editor of the *Oberlin Evangelist* was ready some months later to give it official approbation: "We are now prepared to say that we regard this organ in its place, and used judiciously, as a valuable auxiliary to religious worship. It has great compass, admits a wide range of modulation, and holds all its immense resources subject to the will of one man. In this latter respect it has a great advantage over a large band of performers on small instruments. The melody of its tone is unrivalled. Indeed, it seems to us, in this respect, to leave nothing more to be desired. No instrument can have the power of expression which God has given to the human voice; but so far as mere melody of sound is concerned, the organ seems to have come as near perfection as it is given mortals to attain." It is probable that there were some who were never quite satisfied with the use of the organ in meeting and there must have been even more who were occasionally reminded of Mr. E. M. Foote's remark that after a solemn sermon the organ should never seem to say, "Hurrah boys, meetin's out."[13]

That there was already a demand for musical instruction of a higher order in the West is certain. In 1848 a young lady wrote from Kentucky asking to be admitted as "a member of the ensuing term, for the purpose of studying *Music*." Two years later

[11]T. M., Sept. 22, 1856. In 1851 when Churchill taught music as assistant to Allen he received 75 cents a week and $15 for "Conducting Commencement Music."—Receipt in Misc. Archives.

[12]T. M., Aug. 26, 1857, and Aug. 21, 1858.

[13]*Oberlin Evangelist,* Mar. 14, June 6, 1855, and [Mary Dascomb and] Louise Fitch to James Monroe, Nov. [12 and] 16, 1860 (Monroe MSS). The organ was built by A. Andrews of Utica, N. Y. The author has found no clear contemporary evidence of the existence of any earlier pipe organ in Oberlin.

Mathias Day wrote from Mansfield, Ohio: "*Forty Pianos* are heard groaning and sputtering all over town. And quite frequently as I pass up and down the streets I see through an open window some doomed little prodigy turning her eyes impatiently towards outdoors and wishing her lesson was over. Now to the question." The upshot of his letter was that he desired to secure a music teacher from Oberlin who could give private piano lessons and in addition play the church organ for a salary of seventy-five or a hundred dollars. It seems that the church didn't have an organ as yet but the members were "almost persuaded" as one was offered to them "on very favorable terms which is said to be a very good one and the owner of it says that if we won't buy it *he will put it up and let us play on it at any rate*— quite liberal! The next question is who will play it? We have no one in our congregation who can murder music quite scientifically enough to manage the machine so that it [would] do us about as much good as a one horse cart." Soon there were many ambitious young musicians in Oberlin, though many of them doubtless philosophized as did Mary Gorham in 1853: "It is very dull to thump upon a piano for an hour at a time and play no tune, but if I keep athumping perhaps I will do something some day."[14] Already in the 1850's the way was being prepared for the Oberlin Conservatory of Music.

The center of Oberlin's musical life was the Oberlin Musical Association which changed its official name to the Oberlin Choir in 1856, and to the Oberlin Musical Union in 1860, under which name it continues at the present date.[15] This organization is one of the oldest musical societies in the West, dating as it does from 1837.

In February of that year seven young men petitioned their "Beloved Instructors," the faculty of the Institute, " . . . in behalf of a number of students, who feel deeply interested in the cause of *Sacred Music,*

"1st. That a Society may be formed whose object shall be to elevate the standard, and improve the style of church music in this Institution.

[14]Mary R. Smith to Hamilton Hill, July 3, 1848 (Treas. Off., File P); Mathias Day to H. Hill, June 9, 1850 (File R), and Mary Gorham to Rosetta Mann, Oberlin, Oct. 20, 1853 (in the possession of Miss Esther A. Close).

[15]Oberlin Musical Association, etc., MS Minutes, May 9, 1856 and May 5, 1860.

"2nd. That a committee of three may be appointed by the faculty to examine individuals, and to recommend those, who possess the necessary qualifications, as worthy of membership; and that no one unless thus recommended, be permitted to belong to the Society—

"3rd. We feel that without the hearty approval and cooperation of the faculty, we cannot, we wish not to do anything. If, therefore, they can recommend the formation of a Soc. as above requested, and sustain it when formed, we further ask that they would manifest the same publicly to the students, that nothing may appear to be done clandestinely."[16]

The petition was favorably received, and George Allen and two other students (signers of the petition) were appointed a committee to examine candidates. The successful applicants for membership met in the chapel in Colonial Hall, March 15, 1837, and adopted the constitution presented by Allen. The constitution stated that the object of the Oberlin Musical Association thus established was "to advance its members theoretically and practically in the knowledge of musical science, with special reference to correctness, facility and taste in church Psalmody." Meetings were to be once a week. New members might be admitted if recommended by the committee of examination and "accepted by a vote of the members present at any regular meeting." Choristers, a secretary, a treasurer and a librarian were to be elected. By 1846 there were 72 members; in 1855, 136, and in 1860, 179.[17]

The organization was distinctly a religious association. The original by-laws provided that, "No person shall be admitted to membership . . . except such as can give testimonials of Christian character." This is to be expected considering the Oberlin environment and the well-known piety of George Allen. In 1845 Mrs. Allen wrote to her husband, then in Boston: "I was struck with a remark of Anna Hill last week. She said, 'Abby, is it not a pity that I can't join the choir?' 'Why don't you?' 'Oh, because I am so wicked!' " In the next year a special committee was appointed "to report on the propriety of admitting those who are not professors of religion to take part in the singing on

[16]The petition, dated Feb. 27, 1837, is in the College Library.

[17]MS Minutes, Mar. 15, 1837; F. M., Mar. 1, 1837; MS Report to O. M. A., Aug. 28, 1846, and Minutes, Aug. 30, 1853, and Mar. 24, 1860.

GEORGE NELSON ALLEN
(From a photograph in the 1859 Class Album in the Oberlin College Library)

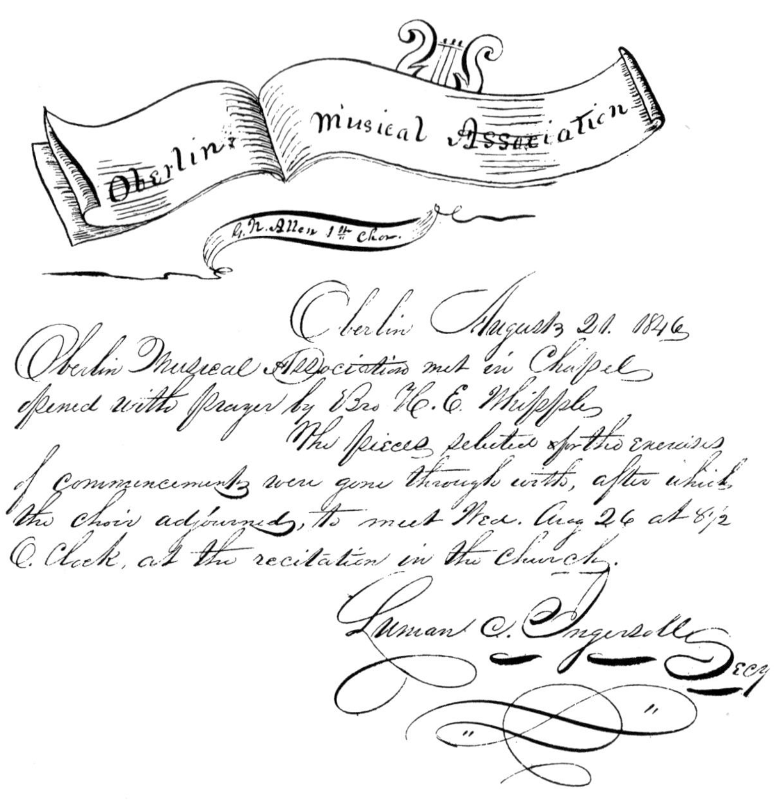

Oberlin Musical Association

G. N. Allen 1st Chor.

Oberlin August 21. 1846

Oberlin Musical Association met in Chapel
opened with prayer by Bro H. E. Whipple
The pieces selected for the exercises
of commencement were gone through with, after which
the choir adjourned, to meet Wed. Aug 26 at 8½
O.Clock, at the recitation in the church.

Luman C. Ingersoll Secy

FROM THE MINUTE BOOK
(Original in the Oberlin College Library)

the Sabbath." The songs sung at regular meetings as well as at church services were, almost all, religious in theme. Meetings were always opened with prayer. The rules adopted in 1847 provided that, "Any member convicted of immoral conduct that would be a disqualification in a candidate for membership, shall be debarred from the exercises of the Society."[18]

George Nelson Allen served as first chorister and was the leading spirit in the organization from its founding in 1837 to the late fifties. Professor C. H. Churchill took his place; John P. Morgan and George Steele led after the founding of the Conservatory. Allen was paid entirely by the Institute at first, but in 1847 the church undertook to provide a hundred dollars of his salary in view of his services as leader at religious meetings.[19]

One of the most outstanding events in the early history of the association was the visit of Thomas Hastings in 1845. The secretary was stimulated to unusual literary efforts: "Sat. July 19, *1845*.

"Thomas Hastings being in town the news ran like wild fire —the choir were gathered at a moment's warning—Mr. Hastings appeared and by request took charge of the choir for the evening. His valuable instructions were most gratefully Recd.—His grave and venerable appearance produced profound respect—His mildness and gentleness were most winning—The smile on his countenance bespoke a soul at peace and filled with most heavenly music—and as it flowed from his lips it charmed to the most exquisite pleasure. The house was nearly filled with listeners, who gazed entranced."

Hastings' song books as well as those of Woodbury, Webb and Mason were used by the association. Mason's books seem to have been the most popular, which is to be expected in view of Allen's training under him. All of these men, but particularly Hastings, were noted for their piety, and thought of music primarily as a mode of worship. Probably the supereminent piety of Hastings explains the trustees' preference for his music as expressed in their official resolution.[20] The very first song books purchased for the use of the association in 1837 were Mason's

[18]Mrs. G. N. Allen to G. N. Allen, Oct. 22, 1845 (Allen MSS), and MS Minutes, Apr. 23, 1846, and May 28, 1847.

[19]Geo. Allen to the Oberlin Church [1855] (Copy in Allen MSS).

[20]T. M., Aug. 27, 1841, and see above, page 788.

Boston Academy Collection of Church Music, published in the preceding year. Three years later a dozen copies of Mason's *Lyra Sacra* (1837) and two dozen copies of the *Boston Academy's Collection of Choruses* (1839), probably also by Mason, were ordered purchased. In 1847, when there were nearly two-hundred volumes in the library of the Oberlin Musical Association, there were still 19 copies of the *Collection of Choruses.* Of other song books by Mason, there were 20 copies of the first volume and 30 copies of the second volume of the *Sacred Harp: or Beauties of Church Music* (coyprighted in 1841), and 30 copies of the *Psaltery,* prepared by Mason and Webb in 1845. The library also included 31 copies of Hastings' *Manhattan Collection* and 30 of his *Psalmodist* and 7 copies of the *Sacred Lyre,* also by Hastings. There were a few copies of three books of secular songs: Webb's *The American Glee Book, The Liberty Minstrel,* and *Freedom's Lyre.* These last anti-slavery song books would be expected in an Oberlin collection. In the fifties the *Dulcimer* (125,000 of which were reported by the publishers sold in one season) and the *Cythara,* both compilations by Isaac B. Woodbury, were exceedingly popular. The association passed a special resolution of commendation of the *Cythara* in 1854.[21]

Meetings of the musical association constituted, for the students, a popular extracurricular activity, rivalling the meetings of the literary societies. Most meetings it is true were largely taken up with singing like the one written up by a poetical secretary in 1851:

"At the early toll of bell
Choir met in the *Chapelle;*
Nearly all the members there—
G. N. Allen in the chair:
Choir spent an hour or two
Singing as they always do.
Business none: at least 'twas such
It did not amount to much.
Several pieces were rehearsed
For Commencement. Choir dispersed."[22]

[21]Oberlin Musical Association, MS Minutes, Apr. 14, 1837; Sept. 11, 1840; May 7, 1852; Sept. 15, 1854, and "List of Books in Library of Oberlin Musical Association, Oberlin, September 3, 1847" (loose sheet in the Minutes of the Association).

[22]MS Minutes, May 25, 1861.

There was, however, occasionally some business to be done. A long list of officers must be elected each year. Now and then there must have been considerable rivalry as at a meeting when 52 votes were cast for candidates for treasurer though only 40 members were present. Of course there was the even more important question of seating to be argued—always a matter of hot dispute in choirs. Now and then members were expelled by general vote because of delinquency or failure to abide by the rules. Taxes must be levied to pay for new music and other equipment. Light was very necessary when meetings were held in the evening. At one of the very first meetings the treasurer was instructed "to procure six lamps for the use of the Society of cheap quality." Throughout the months of May and June, 1845, meetings had to be given up because "there was no oil for lighting the house." It took some such emergency to prevent a meeting, though one rehearsal was adjourned in 1846 to make way for the debate between President Mahan and the Fosters on "Come-Outerism," and the meeting of December 2, 1859, was "postponed on account of the 'John Brown' meeting in the Chapel."

Strict rules of discipline were necessary to keep the singers in order and assure their presence. A young lady student wrote in her diary in the fifties: "Choir meeting. Went over with Sarah. . . . When we arrived there were very few present. No ladies. Presently when the five minutes allowed for the tolling of the bell had expired S. and I went over to the front seat and Sarah took a pencil from her pocket and marked the names of those on the front seat who were then absent, which were all but herself. I had half a mind to open the melodeon and commence playing, thinking it well to improve the time but did not. Mr. Thompson came down and tuned his bass viol. Then it was very lonely up in my old seat without Lilly. The evening passed but without raising me to that state of happiness which it sometimes does. Although I enjoyed the music very, very much, still it made me sorrowful." And: "This evening was choir meeting. Went again with Lilly. We were the first ladies present. Others came in however in course of time . . . Then we did have such a fine sing, such beautiful music. Friday nights are *so, so* very delightful, the best in the week . . . Several new members joined and consequently some seats changed."[23]

[23]Mary L. Cowles, MS Diary, June 2, 1856 (Cowles-Little MSS).

The musical society had one great social advantage over the literary societies: both sexes were members. "Choir practice" was the chief coeducational activity. We even hear of a wedding being solemnized at one meeting in 1842. In January, 1863, Deacon W. W. Wright wrote from Oberlin to his son: "Very cold today 4 deg. below zero this Morning yesterday morning o. . . . Freddy froze his toe last evening waiting on a young lady from quire meeting." "Freddy" was Frederick De Forest Allen, later Professor of Classics for many years at Harvard.[24]

The great musical occasion of the year was the grand concert or concerts at Commencement in August. The activities of each season pointed up to Commencement. In the first Commencements after its organization (1837 and 1838) the association assisted with incidental music, one piece in 1838 holding the audience, as said one reporter, "chained in breathless and painful suspense." In 1837 William L. Parsons delivered an "Oration on Sacred Music" as the official representative of the Musical Association at the exercises. The independent musical concert first appeared in 1840. At the 1841 commencement exercises when the association gave a concert of sacred music in the chapel, "The house was crowded, the audience appeared well satisfied, amount of money received about $150." From that time on concerts of vocal music by the Musical Association were a regular part of Commencement.[25] The association also continued to sing numbers between the student orations.

The climax of the history of the association under the leadership of Professor Allen was the performance of the Oratorio of Absalom in 1852. This oratorio was originally arranged by Professor Woodbury and published in his *Dulcimer.* It contained music taken from the works of Beethoven, Rossini, Händel, Hummel, Haydn, Romberg and Mine, as well as original compositions by Woodbury. As expanded for the Oberlin presentation it contained also an *aria* and *recitative* by Professor Allen. The people of Oberlin showed much curiosity about this, to them, new form of vocal concert. The church was well filled each night; over $500 was taken in at 25 cents per

[24]Minutes, July 1, 1842, and W. W. Wright to A. A. Wright, Jan. 18, 1863 (Wright MSS).

[25]*Cleveland Observer,* Sept. 13, 1838; 1837 Commencement program; MS Minutes, Aug. 26, 1841; Aug. 28, 1844; Aug. 27, 1845, and *Oberlin Evangelist,* Sept. 9, 1840, Sept. 1, 1841.

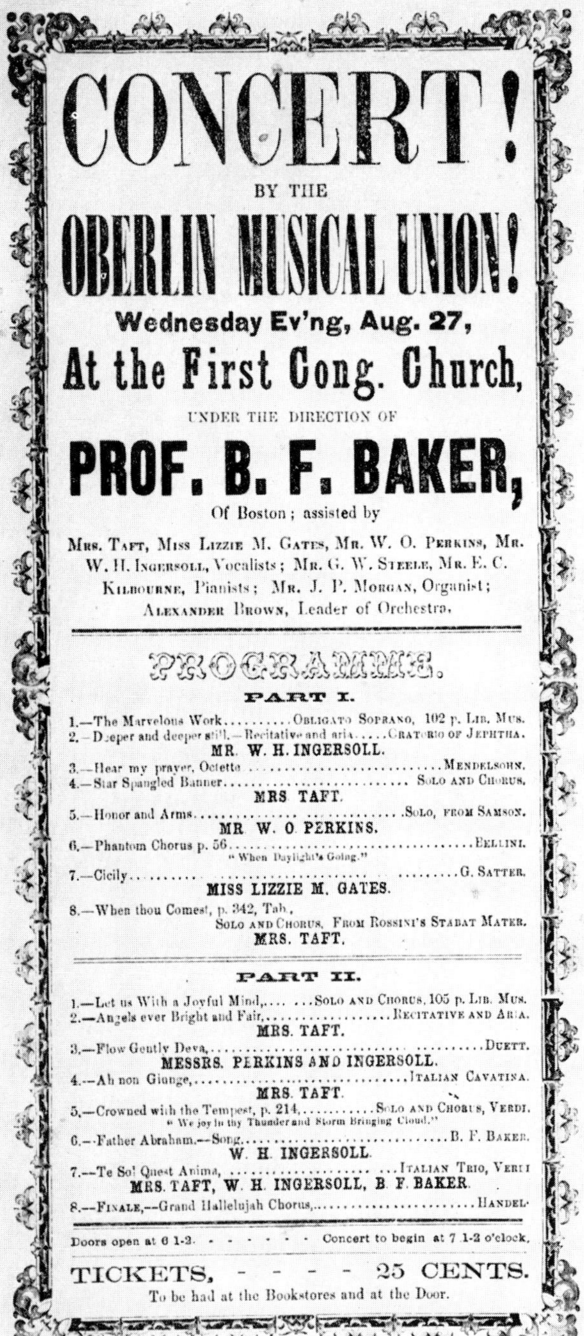
CONCERT!

BY THE

OBERLIN MUSICAL UNION!

Wednesday Ev'ng, Aug. 27,

At the First Cong. Church,

UNDER THE DIRECTION OF

PROF. B. F. BAKER,

Of Boston; assisted by

MRS. TAFT, MISS LIZZIE M. GATES, MR. W. O. PERKINS, MR. W. H. INGERSOLL, Vocalists; MR. G. W. STEELE, MR. E. C. KILBOURNE, Pianists; MR. J. P. MORGAN, Organist; ALEXANDER BROWN, Leader of Orchestra.

PROGRAMME.

PART I.

1.—The Marvelous Work..........OBLIGATO SOPRANO, 102 p. LIB. MUS.
2.—Deeper and deeper still.—Recitative and aria.....ORATORIO OF JEPHTHA.
MR. W. H. INGERSOLL.
3.—Hear my prayer, Octette..........................MENDELSOHN.
4.—Star Spangled Banner.......................... SOLO AND CHORUS.
MRS TAFT.
5.—Honor and Arms............................SOLO, FROM SAMSON.
MR W. O PERKINS.
6.—Phantom Chorus p. 56..................................BELLINI.
"When Daylight's Going."
7.—Cicily...G. SATTER.
MISS LIZZIE M. GATES.
8.—When thou Comest, p. 342, Tab.,
SOLO AND CHORUS, FROM ROSSINI'S STABAT MATER.
MRS. TAFT.

PART II.

1.—Let us With a Joyful Mind,.... ...SOLO AND CHORUS, 105 p. LIB. MUS.
2.—Angels ever Bright and Fair,..................RECITATIVE AND ARIA.
MRS. TAFT.
3.—Flow Gently Deva,.......................................DUETT.
MESSRS. PERKINS AND INGERSOLL.
4.—Ah non Giunge,..............................ITALIAN CAVATINA.
MRS. TAFT.
5.—Crowned with the Tempest, p. 214,...........SOLO AND CHORUS, VERDI.
"We joy in thy Thunder and Storm Bringing Cloud."
6.—Father Abraham.—Song............................B. F. BAKER.
W. H. INGERSOLL.
7.—Te Sol Quest Anima, ...ITALIAN TRIO, VERDI
MRS. TAFT, W. H. INGERSOLL, B. F. BAKER.
8.—FINALE,—Grand Hallelujah Chorus,........................HANDEL.

Doors open at 6 1-2. - - - - - - Concert to begin at 7 1-2 o'clock.

TICKETS, - - - - 25 CENTS.

To be had at the Bookstores and at the Door.

PROGRAM OF A CONCERT OF THE MUSICAL UNION, 1862
(Oberlin College Library)

person. The crowd was further swelled by the holders of the complimentary tickets, which were distributed to all singers. Oberlin's first oratorio, first music on a grand scale, created a sensation. "It is rare," declared the editor of the *Evangelist*, "that the plains of the great West have rung to the echoes of music so varied, so chaste, and so charming. But the Genius of musical culture is on her way westward, and we hail her coming."[26]

With the middle fifties the practice began of hiring a director from outside to train the chorus in the last few weeks before Commencement and take charge of the actual concert. No less a person than Professor Woodbury, himself, trained and directed the singers for the 1855 Commencement. Though not an impressive looking man, "below medium stature, with black hair and whiskers," his reputation as a composer, editor and director of sacred music set him apart, in the eyes of Oberlin people, from ordinary men. Of the directors who came to Oberlin each year through 1863, Professor Woodbury and Professor E. M. Foote, of Ypsilanti, Michigan, were probably the most popular.[27] In 1857 Professor Cowles reported to his wife then on a visit: "Professor Babcock [another outside director] . . . , is leading the choir every evening till nine, and they sing *loud*. I fear some of them will suffer for these late hours and violent exercises of voice." In 1858 and 1861 the Cantata of Esther was presented, and in 1859 the Oratorio of David, as arranged by Webb, was sung. On the latter occasion Foote was aided by three soloists brought from Cleveland. The concert of 1860 was of an unusually popular and secular nature. The program included

[26]Minutes, Aug. 23, 24, 25, Sept. 3, 1852; the *Oberlin Evangelist*, Aug. 18, and Sept. 1, 1852, and the programs distributed at the concert.

[27]The directors were:

1855—Professor I. B. Woodbury
1856—Professor E. M. Foote
1857—Professor Babcock
1858—Professor Foote
1859—Professors Foote and Churchill
1860—Professor Foote
1861—Professor J. G. Barnett of Hartford, Conn.
1862—Professor B. F. Baker of Boston
1863—Professor Foote

"Death of Prof. Isaac B. Woodbury" in the *Oberlin Students' Monthly* (Dec., 1858), I, 84; Minutes, Aug. 27, 1856; Aug. 26, 27, 1857; Aug. 20, 23, 24, 1860; Mar. 28, Aug. 26, 1862; July 3, and Aug. 7, 10, 1863; *Oberlin Evangelist*, Sept. 1, 1858, Sept. 11, 1861. The description of Woodbury is from the MS Diary of Mary L. Cowles, Aug. 1, 1859.

not only the Hallelujah Chorus, but also the "Anvil Chorus, Marseillaise, various opera choruses, ballads, waltzes, and all sorts of quartettes and solos, with organ, piano and orchestral accompaniments." This concert proved so very attractive that three performances were given within a week. Most Oberlinites evidently liked this sort of thing, though there was some criticism. The editor of the *Evangelist* commented favorably on the omission in 1861 of "those exceptionable pieces which are sometimes introduced for popular amusement, of low taste and of doubtful or bad social or moral influence." Undoubtedly, opera choruses were somewhat out of place in the Oberlin meeting house. One is a little surprised, however, to find on the highly commended 1861 program, not only "Moses in Egypt," "The Transient and the Eternal," but also a quartette, "Charge of the Light Brigade, music by Professor Barnett," and solo, "God Bless Our Volunteers" also with music by the director.[28]

John P. Morgan of the newly-founded Conservatory of Music directed the concert for the first Commencement after the War. The secretary of the Union recorded his "unbiased" opinion of it in the minutes: "*Second* and *final* concert was grand! . . . Choruses more effective. Audience—quite large (!) Some appreciated and were delighted; others were *stupified*; and still others went away (only a *few,* be it said, for the honor of the people at large) at the close of the first part, saying they had got their *fifty cents worth* already." The *News* reported that the "house was densely packed, and ten o'clock dismissed a weary audience." In the opinion of the editor the program (an Oratorio) was too long. It may be guessed that he was one of those who concluded that the first part was worth the full fifty cents. George Steele, also of the Conservatory, took charge in 1864 and 1866. The programme given in 1866 was another of the popular variety and the editor of the *News* expressed his opinion "that the concerts of the Union would be still more popular were there more interspersions of the simple style of song and ballad music."[29] There was no one to speak up in defense of the

[28]H. C. Cowles to wife, Aug. 14, 1857 (Cowles-Little MSS); *Oberlin Evangelist,* Sept. 1, 1858; Sept. 11, 1861; MS Minutes, May 17, 1861; Sept. 3, 1858; Aug. 12, 22, 24, 1859, and *University Quarterly* (Oct., 1860), II, 376–377.

[29]MS Minutes, Aug. 24, 1865, *Lorain County News,* Aug. 24, 1864; Aug. 30, 1865; Aug. 22, 1866, and MS Minutes, July 25, Aug. 17, 22, 1866.

CHORUS OF THE "OBERLIN CHOIR" WHICH PRESENTED THE ORATORIO OF DAVID IN 1859
Taken in the Meeting House. Those on the platform are probably Professor Foote and the soloists. Professor Churchill appears in a white coat.

(Photograph in Oberlin College Library)

THE OBERLIN STRING BAND
WHICH ACCOMPANIED THE PERFORMANCE OF THE ORATORIO OF DAVID IN 1859
Directed by Alexander Beethoven Brown, a student.
(From a photograph taken in the "First Church," now in the Oberlin College Library)

old standard religious music, the *Evangelist* having ceased publication.

In the earliest days the sombre notes of the bass viol, which was always looked upon by New Englanders, for some reason, as the least worldly musical instrument, formed the usual accompaniment to the chorus. The first of these instruments owned by the association is said to have been built by the Scotch theological student, Lane Rebel, and cabinet maker Alexander McKellar under the direction of George Allen. Anyway, in the autumn of 1840 the society was paying the last installment on "the double Bass Viol." Six years later some money had to be provided to repair it. In 1850, "the committee on double Bass Viol reported that they found the instrument in a sad state and [that it] ought to be sent abroad for recovery." On motion of J. D. Cox, $12 was appropriated for the purpose. The condition of this venerable and sober instrument was very likely due, in part at least, to an accident of three years previous, described by one of its would-be torturers in a letter of January, 1847: "I have had the Double Bass in My room on till [*sic*] within a few days, got so I could play on it considerable, and was agoing to play on it in Singing School but I let an other fellow take it to His room and He let it fall and split the back of it, so I am up stump there, and shall not play on it this winter." Ten years later, the instrument having outlasted its usefulness, was presented by the association to Professor Allen. Rivals soon appeared. A piano, a seraphine, and a flute occasionally joined in. In 1851 a firm in Buffalo presented a melodeon to the association. The organization formally thanked the manufacturers and donors and agreed "to recommend their instruments to purchasers."[30]

Very early in the forties (or possibly in the late thirties) an Oberlin Band was organized and affiliated with the Musical Association. The enterprise was a financial (if not an artistic) failure, and in 1842 and 1845 the instruments, including a cornet, bugle and bass trombone, were taken over by the Musical Association in lieu of a debt owed by the Band. This apparently spelled the end of the latter organization. At the performance of the Oratorio of Absalom in 1852, instrumental accompani-

30MS Minutes, Sept. 11, 1840; Mar. 20, 1846; May 24, 1850; Apr. 20, 1859; Nov. 3, 1851, and "Brother" to Charles Wright, Oberlin, Jan. 27, 1847 (lent by Mrs. H. H. Carter, Oberlin).

ment was furnished by an orchestra including a piano, a melodeon (the gift of the previous year?), two flutes, two violins, a violoncello, a violone [?], a horn and a drum. After 1855 the Department of Instrumental Music stimulated interest and furnished trained musicians. At the 1859 Commencement music was furnished by the Choir and the Oberlin String Band alternately. In the following year the Union was assisted by an orchestra, containing five violins, a viola, two flutes, two horns, two violoncellos and a violon[e], and also by the Citizen's Brass Band of nineteen pieces.[31] These, together with the chorus, should have furnished sound enough for one evening. Occasionally this brass band performed independently from a band stand on Tappan Square. It seems to have become defunct in the war period, but in 1866 a new band was organized by George Steele as another musical expression of the new conservatory.[32]

Oberlin became famous for its chorus. Visitors at Commencement and on the Sabbath commented on the singing in superlatives. Hastings is said to have declared that Oberlin had the finest sacred music in the land.[33] At great celebrations like that on the return of the Wellington Rescuers from the Cleveland jail in 1859 the choral music always played a large and widely heralded part. There were three things which made the greatest impression on new students: Finney, the meeting house and the choir. The association was also a financial asset. With funds raised at concerts chandeliers were purchased for the meeting house in 1844, gas fixtures in 1860, and the chapel bell in 1859. Alonzo Pease was hired to paint the portraits of Finney, Fairchild, Dascomb, and Mahan in 1860, and the choir paid him $50 apiece. All of these generally excellent paintings now hang in the College library. Part of the receipts were used to pay the salaries of visiting directors and in 1857 of the regular Professor of Music. Much of the cost of the church organ was met from the same source.[34] Most important of all, the Musical Association educated the musical taste of Oberlin students and townsmen.

[31]MS Minutes, Apr. 8, 15, May 6, 20, 23, June 3, 1842; Mar. 14, 1845; Aug. 24, 1852; Aug. 24, 1859, and Aug. 20, 1860.

[32]*Lorain County News,* June 20, 1866. See the bandstand in the illustration opposite page 553.

[33]Asa Mahan, *Autobiography* (London—1882), page 263.

[34]Minutes, Aug. 9, 1844; Feb. 18, Aug. 31, Sept. 7, 1860; P. C. M., July 13, 1859; *Oberlin Students' Monthly* (Dec., 1860) III, 62–63.

There was and is a tendency to think of the Oberlin Musical Association (–Choir–Union) as merely a church choir, but its history as just outlined shows that it was much more than that. Yet its contribution to the Sabbath services, in which it always took part, was a very great one. It was one of the unique features of early Oberlin.

The return of John Paul Morgan, son of Professor John Morgan, from the Leipzig Conservatory of Music in the summer of 1865 was a sensation and an event of the first importance in the history of music in Oberlin. He not only took charge of the regular commencement concert but gave a Grand Organ Concert, himself. The people of Oberlin in general "were on the 'qui vive' in anticipation of the rich treat" and when the concert actually took place some selections "elicited rapturous applause." Many listeners, like the editor of the local news sheet, however, "were unable to fully appreciate . . . some of the . . . inexplicable German productions" but heartily enjoyed "the beautiful execution of the overture to 'William Tell' and variations on 'The Last Rose of Summer.' "[35]

After having studied for some years under Allen and Churchill in the Department of Instrumental Music, Morgan had begun private teaching in 1861. For nearly two years thereafter he gave piano lessons in Oberlin and Cleveland, leaving for Germany in the spring of 1863. That fall Professor Churchill and another Oberlin boy, George W. Steele, son of Dr. Alexander Steele, announced that they would give instruction at Oberlin in "Cultivation of the voice, Musical elocution, Elementary Principles of Notation, Harmony, Thorough Bass, Piano and Organ."[36]

George N. Allen had given up his musical activities in 1864 and in 1864–65 Professor Churchill again took temporary charge of musical instruction in the College at a dollar a lesson. The way seemed to be open for a more elaborate program of musical instruction in Oberlin. John P. Morgan and George W. Steele joined forces and in September, 1865, opened the Oberlin Conservatory of Music, at the same time assuming the work

[35]*Lorain County News*, July 5 and Aug. 2, 1865.

[36]*Ibid.*, Aug. 28, 1861; Apr. 15, Nov. 11, 1863, and Mrs. W. W. Wright to A. A. Wright, Feb. 15, 1863 (Wright MSS).

of teaching vocal music in the College for a remuneration of $250 a year. This arrangement continued through 1866.

The Leipzig Conservatory had been founded in 1843 by Felix Mendelssohn and quickly established its reputation as the leading center of musical education in Germany. The three founders of the Oberlin Conservatory—Morgan, Steele, and Rice—all studied there. John P. Morgan and George Steele had gained their interest and early training in the Oberlin Department of Music while students in the Preparatory Course. Oberlin's musical tradition and the history of musical instruction is continuous from Ingersoll and Allen (1835 and 1837) to Morrison and Shaw in the present generation. The tradition of the Oberlin Conservatory of Music thus stems from Mendelssohn's Leipzig Conservatory and from Lowell Mason through George Allen and the Oberlin Department of Music of earlier days.[37]

This dual background was recognized in the division of the Conservatory in the earliest days into a school of church music "including instruction on the organ, solo and choral singing, directing, etc." and a school of secular music "including the study of the piano-forte, violin, viola, violoncello, and other orchestral instruments; solo and chorus singing, solo playing with accompaniment and *ensemble* playing." Instruction was to be given in classes of three or four pupils each in all departments.—"In the 'Conservatory' (what a name) they teach in classes altogether," wrote an Oberlin woman to her son shortly after the opening, "and it doesn't seem to me to be a very good way for one who is so nearly a 'new beginner.' " Tuition was $100 per year for those not connected with the College and twelve dollars per term for college students.[38]

A really ambitious program was immediately undertaken. Early in the autumn of 1865 the Oberlin paper boasted: "The Conservatory of Music have added to their teaching force a fine instructor on Brass instruments and the violin. Mr. Steele assures us of his efficiency. They expect to secure, in the Spring, another teacher of vocal music, who has a fine reputation. We hope the growing popularity of the Conservatory may keep all of them busy." The announcement for 1866 states that: "The

[37]On Leipzig see *Oberlin Review,* I, 17–18 (Apr. 29, 1874).

[38]P. C. M., Dec. 15, 1865; receipts dated May 16, Aug. 10, Nov. 15, 1866 (Misc. Archives), and Mrs. W. W. Wright to A. A. Wright, Nov. 19, 1865 (Wright MSS).

piano-forte instruction is given on the principle adopted at all the conservatories of Europe, the working of which has been tested and approved by the most eminent pianists. At the weekly rehearsals only works of acknowledged excellence are produced, the constant performance and hearing of which must contribute greatly to the cultivation of a correct and elevated taste in the pupils." The announcement continues: "The organ is taught in the most thorough manner, the system used combining the excellencies of the Leipzig school and that of A. G. Ritter, of Magdeburg. A weekly organ recitation is held, in which the pupils have constant opportunity to hear the compositions of the masters for that instrument, and organ pupils who are competent are allowed to perform." The organ in the church was used by teachers and students. For those studying the piano-forte there were "ten or fifteen brass instruments and a Chickering Grand Piano for . . . evening rehearsals." Instruction in violin and voice was also offered. The announcement for 1867 lists under "Authors Studied": Piano—Czerny, Heller, Plaidy, Bertini, Clementi, Moscheles, Cramer, and Bach; Organ—Ritter, Schneider, Bach, Rinck and Händel; Voice—Duprez, Danzi, Bassini, Bagioli, Vaccai, Concone, Zolner and Brambilla. In choral singing it was planned to take for practice in the advanced classes Mendelssohn's oratoria "St. Paul," and Handel's oratoria, "The Messiah."[39] By 1867 over one hundred students were enrolled for these courses.

In 1866 Morgan left Oberlin to continue his musical activities in New York. Steele carried on the work, but concluded that he needed training abroad. In 1867 he left for Leipzig, the College taking over the Conservatory and appointing Steele Professor of Music (note that the adjective "Sacred" is definitely dropped) at a regular salary, payment of which was to begin on his return to Oberlin. The College hired teachers to carry on the instruction in the interim: John C. Fillmore, Cyrus A. Bentley and A. L. Barber.[40]

John Comfort Fillmore was another Oberlin product who

[39]*Lorain County News,* Nov. 29, 1865, and *Oberlin Conservatory of Music* [Announcement, 1866].

[40]MS Annual Reports of President James H. Fairchild, Aug., 1867, and Aug., 1868 (Sec. Off.); Oberlin College, *Catalogue,* 1868–1869, and P. C. M., Sept. 26, 1867.

also studied at Leipzig. In a long letter written from Germany in 1866 to his classmate, A. A. Wright, he described the reactions of an Oberlinite at the fount of musical culture: "The classes here are wonderfully different from those to which you and I were accustomed at Alma Mater. No roll is called, we go when we please and I know a New Yorker who hasn't been in his Harmony classes for months. I happen to know also (for he told me himself) that he spends his nights drinking and wh–ing, . . . Sunday too, is a very different day here from the Oberlin Sunday. The churches are usually full in the morning, and in the afternoon the congregations may be found enjoying social chats in the Beer Gardens, dancing in the various dancing Halls, rowing on the river, or walking in the parks." Fillmore described his routine of hours of practice, attendance at orchestra rehearsals and at Opera performances. "Every Friday evening we have general exerises in solo playing, a sort of musical Rhetorical Exercise where the best of the pupils perform Piano and Violin Solos, Quartettes, Trios, Etc. Etc." Here was a tradition to be handed on to Oberlin. Fillmore stayed only the one year as teacher at Oberlin, going on to spread the Oberlin-Leipzig musical influence at Beloit, Milwaukee and Pomona colleges. He is perhaps best remembered for his work with Alice Fletcher on Amerian Indian music.[41]

In 1868 the Prudential Committee took sufficient interest in this new department to vote to "favor the proposal to exchange a gold watch belonging to the College for a piano for the use of the Conservatory." The Conservatory was to be, quite definitely, a part of the College. The trustees voted that, "All pupils receiving instruction in music, whether vocal or instrumental, shall be subject to the rules and regulations of the College, it being understood that the professor of Music and his pupils sustain the same relation to the faculty in respect to government as the Principal and students of the Preparatory Department or Ladies' Department." This was a much-needed reform according to at least one Oberlin mother and landlady. "I can assure you," wrote Mrs. W. W. Wright to her son, "It makes a great buzzing here among the girls—but it was high time for something to be done. Now they must go to church, observe the study

[41]Fillmore to A. A. Wright, Sept. 2, 1866 (Wright MSS), and sketch in the *D. A. B.*

hours, go to prayers, & render their reports to the Principal. . . . Hitherto they have been the most careless members of our schools. Indeed they have had no laws. Now they will not be all the time running over our students in their study hours or tempting our young men to visit till ten o'clk when they ought to be at their Latin & Greek." Besides being under the rules of the College, the students in the Conservatory were declared to "be entitled at their graduation to official testimonials from the College to that effect." The arrangement seemed to be satisfactory all around. Though in 1867–68 expenses were barely paid, in 1868–69 there was a profit of $260 and no charge whatever was made upon the College treasury for the free vocal instruction still given to all college students.[42]

Professor Steele returned from Germany late in the autumn of 1868, which fact may very likely have accounted for the better financial returns of the latter year. In the summer of 1869 Mr. and Mrs. Fenelon B. Rice, also just returned from study in Germany, came to Oberlin to assist in the commencement concert. Steele persuaded them to stay as teachers in the Conservatory. Rice was a Freewill Baptist, educated at Hillsdale College and the Boston Music School (under Benjamin F. Baker and others) as well as in Leipzig. As early as 1864 he had visited Oberlin when he appeared as a soloist on a program conducted by Steele . In the following year (1869–70) the staff was made up of Steeles and Rices: George W. Steele and Lottie M. Steele, and Fenelon B. Rice and Helen M. Rice. Besides these regular instructors, Judson Smith, Chas. H. Churchill and Stephen C. Leonard taught respectively "Art and Science," "Laws of Sound," and "History and Aesthetics of Music."[43] One hundred and forty-seven pupils are listed in the special Conservatory of Music *Catalogue* issued for that year.

Beginning in 1869 the arrangement with the College was somewhat changed. As President Fairchild stated it in his "An-

[42]P. C. M., June 18, 1868; Mrs. W. W. Wright to A. A. Wright, Sept. 15, 1869 (Wright MSS); T. M., Aug. 26, 1867, and MS Annual Report of President J. H. Fairchild, Aug., 1869 (Sec. Off.).

[43]*Biographical Record of the Counties of Huron and Lima, Ohio* (Chicago—1894), 680–682; Jennie H. Porter, *Hannah Johnson and Polly Palmer with Some of Their Kinsfolk* (Kansas City—1930); *Lorain County News,* Aug. 24, 1864; Helen M. Rice, MS "Musical Reminiscences of Oberlin," Sept. 7, 1908 (Office of the Director of the Conservatory of Music); Conservatory of Music, *Announcement,* Oberlin College, 1869–70, and sketch in the *D. A. B.*

nual Report" for 1869–70, Professors Steele and Rice took "the pecuniary responsibility of the department, teaching without charge the classes in vocal music which the College has heretofore provided for and leading the singing daily at prayers and providing the music for the monthly Rhetorical Exercises and for Commencement, and receiving in return the use of the Conservatory room and of the chapel when necessary and the advantages of the position (as part of the College), thus saving the College from any outlay for the music." This understanding remained in effect until 1885 with no notable alteration.

In 1871 disagreements between Steele and Rice came to a head. Steele withdrew from all connection with the College but established a conservatory of his own in the village, for which he secured articles of incorporation dated January 15, 1872. The corporation was to have a total capital of $1000, all shares (of $200 each) being held by members of the Steele family.[44] The corporate name was "The Oberlin Conservatory of Music." So Oberlin found itself with two conservatories of the same name, for Rice continued with the College as Professor of Music and also taught with Mrs. Rice the courses in his own conservatory. Steele issued an announcement for 1872 containing the names of two new teachers and notably omitting the names of the Rices. Quarters were taken up "on College Street, fronting the Square."[45]

Professor Rice reported the work of the other Oberlin Conservatory (the one associated with the College) in August of 1872: "At the beginning of the year we were thrown into some embarrassment by the unexpected resignation of Prof. Steele just at the opening of the Fall Term, and the organization by him of an opposition school. We succeeded in securing the services of Miss L. C. Wattles, a graduate of the Leipzig Conservatory of Music, and with the very unanimous cooperation of the College authorities and citizens generally we have been able to keep the Conservatory in about its former condition with only a slight falling off in the number of pupils. The increased expenses of the Conservatory by this, and the results arising from our pupils being under rules while Prof. Steele publicly advertised that his were

44The charter is in the Office of the Director.
45Oberlin Conservatory of Music, *Announcement* (1872).

not—these and various other annoyances, made it seem better—when he made an offer last Spring to sell his entire interest here—to accept it."[46]

It was undoubtedly advisable to combine the schools. In April, Rice and an associate purchased the equipment, the charter and the good will of Steele's "Oberlin Conservatory of Music": "1 Organ, 1 Piano, 3 Stoves with pipes and zincs belonging with them, 108 Chairs, 2 Busts and Brackets, 1 wash stand and the furniture belonging thereto, 2 signs, All the small signs, 3 Music Stands, 1 Blackboard, 2 Wood boxes, Shovel, 7 tongs, and 1 Ash bucket, All except the Piano being in and upon the premises leased by the said Steele of Samuel Royce in said Village of Oberlin, and now used by the Oberlin Conservatory of Music." And further Professor Steele agreed that he would "never in any way engage in the business of teaching music in any of its branches in the said Village, or be in any way whatever connected or interested with any other person or persons in such business in said Village."[47]

This fiasco, which gave Rice a financial interest in the Conservatory as a corporation, put it on a somewhat more independent footing, though the agreement of 1869 still remained in force and the Conservatory can never be said to have been entirely separate from the College. The Conservatory *Catalogues* of 1872–73 and following years, for example, carry at the head of the list of the faculty the names of "Rev. James H. Fairchild, President," and "Mrs. A. A. F. Johnston, Principal of the Ladies' Department." Both, of course, held the same position in the College. Except for the few months of the schism under Steele the students in the Conservatory were always subject (after 1867) to the disciplinary rules and administration of Oberlin College. The number of music students taking special work in the school increased to nearly 350 in 1874 and approached 500, ten years later. In that latter year Warner Hall, the present main music building, was completed. In 1885 the financial administration was partly merged with that of Oberlin College, "it being under-

[46]F. B. Rice, MS "Report from the Conservatory of Music to the Honorable Board of Trustees of Oberlin College, August 3, 1872" (Misc. Archives).

[47]MS Deed dated April 13, 1872 (in the Office of the Director of the Conservatory).

stood that all the receipts of the Conservatory will be devoted to its uses and the Conservatory will be self sustaining."[48]

The establishment of the Conservatory made certain that music, originally introduced in Oberlin as a means of grace and reformation, would come more and more to be appreciated for its own intrinsic value and be assured of a permanent place in the life of the College and community, despite changing conditions and viewpoints.

[48]T. M., June 29, 1885. Of great value in connection with the story is a sworn statement made by Fenelon B. Rice on Aug. 27, 1900, and now in the Office of the Director of the Conservatory.

CHAPTER XLVII

"DIVERTING INFLUENCES"[1]

THE serious-mindedness of early Oberlin is appalling. The consciousness of a wicked world and an approaching day of atonement clouded the spirits of students and teachers. Life was a serious business and death was momentarily awaited. Anything which diverted the attention from religion was sinful. Religious gatherings were considered by most as more important than study; literary society meetings and rehearsals of the musical association furnished the only other regular form of recreation, unless manual labor (!) and mealtimes at the boarding hall be included under that head. Finney believed that "glee, fun, hilarious mirth, games, charades, and pleasure seeking grieve the Holy Spirit, destroy [the] spirit of prayer, offend [the] conscience, harden [the] heart, darken [the] mind . . . and break up . . . fellowship with the Father, and His Son Jesus Christ."[2]

In the forties there were a few lectures and other evening entertainments. They became steadily more numerous and more popular in the fifties, and a regular part of college life in the next decade. The old timers were right when they accused Oberlin of having forsaken its pristine puritanism. In 1843 a series of lectures were delivered on Phrenology and Phreno-magnetism.[3] Two years later a Greek, who had been captured by the Turks, delivered two lectures. The wife of one of the professors wrote of the event to her absent husband:

"We have been very much interested in attending two lectures from a *Greek*. He was formerly a slave taken in the capture of Scio by the Turks in 1826. He gave us a correct idea of Grecian costume & habits & together with a description of the massacre.

[1]The term applied by Finney to all outside activities in 1860.

[2]Charles G. Finney, "Innocent Amusements," MS dated Jan. 16, 1873 (Finney MSS).

[3]Musical Association, MS Minutes, Jan. 27, and Feb. 3, 1843.

He was dressed (during the lectures) in the war habiliment. It consisted of crimson velvet tunic white *chemise* beneath—breeches—sandalls—red sash—brace of pistols—& another weapon resembling a large carving knife sheathed. . . . The sword he asserted was the same which Lord Byron 'that benefactor of Greece' inherited & brought to them. He was quite a learned man & came with recommendations from Yale College, &c. He married an American lady—has been in the country but a few years. His recitation of Greek war songs & the like was peculiarly interesting. . . . A number of specimens of curiosities was exhibited. The turkish pipe was singular . . . He was very graceful in all his movements. Spoke with a brogue of course."[4]

In 1850 the famous and popular Alleghenians sang in Oberlin. Their repertory was not at all pious, though generally considered very moral, containing such "simple but touching" pieces as:

"The farmer sat in his easy chair
Smoking his pipe of clay,
While his hale old wife with busy care,
Was clearing the dinner away—
A sweet little girl with fine blue eyes,
On her Grandpa's knee was catching flies."

It is very possible that the audience was pleased, but the *Evangelist* assumed a critical tone. The editor found that there was not enough of soul in the music and that the dress of the one lady member was "offensive to modesty and genuine good taste."[5]

In the spring of 1853 Bayard Taylor lectured in Oberlin on "the Arabs, their character, customs, literature, etc." An evidently realistic and impressive portion of his address was that in which he described in detail his experience while under the influence of hashish. A young lady student confided to her diary: "'Twas on the whole so interesting hated to have it close. Evening very pleasant. Company, Mr. Smalley." Two years later Horace Mann delivered two public lectures.[6]

There were, of course, many reform lecturers and they were

[4]Mrs. G. N. Allen to G. N. A. White Cottage, Oct. 22, 1845 (lent by Miss Mary Cochran, Cincinnati).

[5]*Daily Cleveland Plain Dealer,* May 16, 1850, and *Oberlin Evangelist,* May 22, 1850.

[6]Mary Minerva Gilbert, MS Diary, May 3, 1854, and "Book of Accounts for the Directors of the College Societies Library Association, Oberlin, 1855."

generally more welcome than those who merely strove to entertain. Temperance lecturers, woman's rights advocates and peace propagandists were occasionally heard. Anti-slavery speakers were always on the program: the Fosters, Garrison, William Goodell, C. C. Burleigh, Frederick Douglass. Returned missionaries and Kansas emigrants spoke now and then in the church. Joshua H. Giddings gave formal addresses in 1856, 1859, and 1860. In 1859 he was reported to have held the audience "in breathless attention for more than an hour and a half." In 1856, however, a young lady student, unaffected by the considerations which influence a journalist to mercy, wrote in her diary: "Friday evening went to a lecture by the Hon. J. R. Giddings. In our seat with Sarah. The lecture [was] 'fierce'; Put that in quotation marks—another fierce for myself."[7]

Of course the theatre was anathema at Oberlin. The greatest concession ever made to this tool of Satan was when, in 1856, the dramatic version of *Uncle Tom's Cabin* was read by a Mrs. Webb of Philadelphia at a gathering in the Chapel. Several "panoramas" were exhibited at Oberlin in the fifties. In 1853 the use of the church building was granted for a Panorama of Niagara Falls, which presented this "world-famed Cataract . . . to every point of view, in every variety of phase, by sun-light and moon-light, and in every season of the year," thus saving the expense of several trips and much climbing. In the middle fifties the Rev. Mr. Cowles took his whole family to a panorama on a complimentary ticket.[8]

Soon after its formation the College Societies Library Association sponsored a series of public lectures, including the reading of a poem by Rev. James Barr Walker entitled "Ten Scenes in the Life of a Lady of Fashion," said to be a graphic presentation of the "emptiness and vanity of such a life."[9] These long poems must have been popular. In 1861 the Rev. John Pierpont, the poet-reformer and grandfather of J. P. Morgan, read his poem "The Golden Calf" as one of the numbers of the same associa-

[7]*Oberlin Evangelist,* Oct. 26, 1859; *Oberlin Students' Monthly* II, 33 (Nov., 1859); II, 255–256 (June 1860), and Mary L. Cowles, MS Diary, June 17, 1856 (Cowles-Little MSS).

[8]*Oberlin Evangelist,* Mar. 12, 1856; Oberlin Society, MS Minutes, Sept. 2, 1853; *Oberlin Students' Monthly,* I, 242 (Apr., 1859), and Mary L. Cowles, MS Diary, Mar. 1, 1856.

[9]*Oberlin Evangelist,* Feb. 13, 1856. Walker was a trustee and regular lecturer on Theology at Oberlin.

tion's course of lectures, and the *Evangelist* accounted "it a rich treat to hear such a poem delivered." Though Prof. Youmans' lecture on the "Chemistry of the Sunbeam" was sponsored by the Oberlin Fire Fraternity it was given in the Chapel and favorably reported in the *Students' Monthly*.[10]

Horace Greeley appeared in 1859 on his way to the Colorado gold fields and again on his return in the spring of 1860, on both occasions speaking on "Western North America." A "prep" student reported: "He had the old drab coat on, but not the white hat. I went down to the depot the next morning on purpose to see how he looked, and I never saw a man who looked more as if he did not know any thing than he did." Carl Schurz spoke on "France since 1848" and "American Civilization" in consecutive years. Though some Oberlinites were under the impression that he was a "Russian by birth" Schurz seems to have been appreciated. Besides Schurz, the lecture courses of 1861 included John G. Saxe, Bayard Taylor and Dr. J. G. Holland, co-editor of the *Springfield Republican* and later first editor of the *Century Magazine*.[11]

The faculty had always frowned upon evening meetings. In 1837 the hour for such meetings was set at 5:30. Ten years later the Musical Association was persuaded (temporarily) to give up its meetings after supper and hold its rehearsals at four in the afternoon. The rage for lectures and other evening gatherings was an evidence of corrupting influences. In 1860 a committee of trustees and faculty members wrote to Professor Finney: "Public lectures and other public evening entertainments are a growing pest. Wc deplore them: have labored hard to exclude almost every application." Finney believed that only drastic measures could bring Oberlin back to the early standards. He was opposed to all social gatherings and even considered the desirability of discontinuing Commencement and literary society anniversaries![12]

[10]*Ibid.*, Feb. 27, 1861; *Lorain County News*, Feb. 20, 1861, and *Oberlin Students' Monthly*, I, 77 (Dec., 1858).

[11]Henry Prudden to mother, Feb. 6, 1859; *Lorain County News*, Apr. 25, 1860; Feb. 20, 1861; *Oberlin Students' Monthly*, II, 219–220 (May 1860), 155–156 (Mar. 1860; III, 127 (Feb., 1861). On Dr. Holland see the *Dictionary of American Biography*.

[12]F. M., May, 1837; Oberlin Musical Ass'n, MS Minutes, Mar. 5 and 12, 1847, and John Keep, John Morgan, Henry Cowles, E. H. Fairchild, "In behalf of all the Faculty & resident Trustees" to C. G. Finney, July 21, 1860 (Finney MSS).

Needless to say, Finney and the conservative members of the faculty were fighting a losing battle. Lectures and evening entertainments continued to be popular and came to be accepted by the pious as well as the worldly as at least not positively sinful. In 1863, though a notice of it was refused a reading in the church services, the lecture of J. G. Holland on "Fashion" seems to have been quite successful. In the same year Mrs. Helen Markham Wheeler delivered a series of five lectures for ladies only on Anatomy and Physiology. These lectures were illustrated with "the celebrated French 'Modelle de Femme' or artificial female figure." The proceeds above expenses were donated for the building of Ladies' Hall. It was during the same season that what was probably the first humorous lecture in Oberlin was delivered by "Artemas Ward." Not even the *News* could find a good word to say for him, but found him "funny often, witty rarely, vulgar occasionally, seriously earnest never." Ward got revenge in an essay on Oberlin written some two years later, an essay which shows more insight than his Oberlin critics were willing to allow him.[13] In 1865 President Fairfield of Hillsdale gave a series of three addresses. "In the evening," noted a student in his diary, "I attended Prof. Fairfield's second lecture, subject, 'Tent-life in Palestine.' I think I can say with truth that it was the most interesting lecture to which I ever listened. At its close I went and saw a stone from the Pyramid of Cheops, another from the old wall of Jerusalem, some Olive wood from the Mount of Olives &c &c. I also saw a bottle of Dead Sea water and tasted of it. It was intensely salt with a somewhat sickish taste. That will do to tell of to my posterity or in other words to future Frasers."[14] In the following year came Theodore Tilton, "six feet and some inches in his boots . . . seemingly more of a nineteenth-century Puritan than he is," and Ben Butler "with his drooping eye-lid, twisting of the mouth, short neck, shambling gait and hesitancy of speech," both denouncing President Johnson and demanding equal suffrage for the Negroes. Early in the same year Ralph Waldo Emerson spoke on "Social Manners" but left his audience

[13]*Lorain County News,* Feb. 11, Apr. 22, Sept. 23, 1863; Artemas Ward, *Complete Works* (London—1910), 59–61. Frances D. Gage and Grace Greenwood were other lady lecturers.—*Lorain County News,* Mar. 9, 1864, and *Cleveland Leader,* Mar. 20, 1860, quoted in *Annals of Cleveland.*

[14]John G. Fraser, MS Diary, Mar. 10, 11, 1865.

as cold as himself. They found in his lecture "nothing new or striking whatever in thought," just "the old, old art of 'putting things.' "[15]

Even in the early period there were occasional happy, but informal, social gatherings. If so many youths of both sexes are brought together the joy of their very youth and vigor will find some way to express itself, no matter how sober the atmosphere about them. Even in 1837 when Davis Prudden's young sister, Nancy, arrived in Oberlin from Lockport it was the signal for the gathering of many Western New Yorkers in what must have been suspiciously like a party. Davis wrote of it to their brother:

"But the pleasure of her company . . . has made me feel so well that I have hardly contained myself since, like a wild colt let loose from confinement which expresses its delight by its antic movements & caperings. . . . The evening on which she arrived those who came from Lockport & its vicinity assembled in the sitting room, quite a large company, 14 in number. We spent the evening in bringing fresh to our minds things that occurred in times past by & gone & refreshing ourselves with the fond associations which cluster around the word home. How pleasant when one is far away from this magnet of our earthly happyness to meet with those who were formerly conversant with those friends who surround this hallowed spot. It seems as if Providence had not only provided this means of happyness to guilty & fallen man, but has set his own seal of approbation upon it & invited us all to come & drink deep of its sweets."[16]

Such reunions must have occurred often, and no one thought of reprimanding those who took part in them. When the students returned from the long winter vacation to attend the opening service of the new term there was much hand-shaking, some embraces and caresses, and many social chats. As in September in the twentieth century so in February three-quarters of a century earlier the whole body of students were in gala spirits, which mood wore off only when tales of vacation experiences had been twice-told and the renewed glamour of college life had become tarnished with familiarity.

Though the terms "stag party" and "bull session" are undoubtedly of modern origin, the practice must go back into

[15]*Lorain County News,* Jan. 17, Oct. 3, Dec. 5, 1866.
[16]Davis to George Prudden, March 3–5, 1837 (Prudden MSS).

antiquity. As early as 1840 James H. Fairchild wrote to his sweetheart: "Hudson & Hodge & Henry [his brother] have been in my room & hindered me one hour. That hour I would have spent in finishing this scrawl but it is gone now. We had a fine [chat?] & some finer apples.—My head aches a little & I must sleep."[17] How many, many students since have spent just such Sundays as that described in a student diary of 1857: "After breakfast went into Mr. Marshall's room where I got into a debate with Mr. Hayden and which was continued by him and Mr. M. and Mr. Walker. Problem, on the subject of Demonstration in Metaphysics. As they were all against me, I necessarily had a savage time. Discussed with them until meeting time. Attended church all day. Finney preached. In P. M. strolled with Chester. Weather very pleasant all day." Late in the season the same student noted more mysteriously: "In eve. Chester, Morey, Crall, Ferril and Humphrey were in my room. Had a glorious kick up and enjoyed ourselves at the expense of the institution."[18] At the very end of our period (1865) another young man confided to his journal: "In the afternoon Cassius and Alphonse were at my room. I didn't study much, but 'cut up.'" And a little later: "Spent the evening very pleasantly with A. W. We discussed the following, 'Resolved, is the moon made of green cheese.'"[19]

In the more worldly period of the fifties and sixties, sweets of one sort or another furnished a cheap and comparatively harmless form of amusement. Of course, such orgies would hardly have been tolerated in David Cambell's day. One young man, reporting his activities to a classmate gone to war, confessed that he "went to Dewey's room & with him, Bostwick, Dan & Royal indulged in a musk-melon & fixins till eleven." Another admitted that he "Was foolish enough to go in for some lemonade (10 cents), of which I drank 6 or 8 glasses," but this could be excused on the ground that it was Independence Day.[20] Maple sugar parties have always been popular on account of the abund-

[17]J. H. Fairchild to Mary Kellogg, Feb. 11, 1840 (Fairchild MSS).

[18]Sprague Upton, MS Diary, Oct. 11 and Nov. 9, 1857 (lent by Prof. W. T. Upton).

[19]John G. Fraser, MS Diary, Mar. 11 and Apr. 13, 1865 (lent by Mrs. Grace F. Waugh, Mentor, Ohio).

[20]Will[iam N. Hudson] to Charles Fairchild, Sept. 17, 1861 (lent by the recipient), and John G. Fraser, MS Diary, July 4, 1865.

ance of the wherewithal. The daughter of the editor of the *Evangelist* attended a sugaring off in 1856: "Wednesday our folks and some others . . . went out by invitation to Mr. Roserter's sugar bush and spent the afternoon. We had a very pleasant time indeed. I enjoyed it exceedingly. It is always pleasant in the woods even if the branches are bare. It was a very pleasant relaxation and pleasant every way."[21] In 1861 the senior class, never having given a party before, concluded unanimously that it would be desirable to have a maple sugar pull. The faculty seems to have been particularly anxious during this year to maintain the Oberlin reputation for sobriety and earnestness, and to restrain "the overplus of animal feeling in the young." Permission for the party was refused.[22]

Sleigh riding in the winter time was a splendid and exhilarating sport as well as a social diversion. It seems never to have been expressly forbidden but was supposed to be closely supervised. In January of 1836 a disciplinary case regarding a sleigh ride came to the faculty. The minutes state: "Several students having recently taken a sleigh-ride to Elyria without permission of the faculty; it was ordered that, although a repentance and proper feeling seems to be manifested on the part of those students, still the good of the institution requires that public expression of the feeling of the faculty be made respecting the case. Which is to be done this evening." An almost exactly parallel case arose in Western Reserve College two years later.[23] College students everywhere were kept firmly in hand by the faculty. Of course, sleigh riding was even more narrowly limited by the weather than by man-made restrictions. Many a gay party has been ruined by an untimely thaw. A little note written in the late forties tells its own story:

"Sister Mary Jane,

"I am sorry to say that on account of the weather, and the state of the roads, we have concluded it best not to go on that sleigh-ride we proposed last evening. I hope you will excuse me for the

[21]Mary Louisa Cowles, MS Diary, Apr. 11, 1856.

[22]*Oberlin Students' Monthly*, III, 187–188 (April 1861).

[23]This is from E. P. Ingersoll's original Faculty Minutes (Jan. 27, 1836), now in the College Library. Prof. Dascomb copied the gist of them into the official minute book in slightly different form.—Faculty of Western Reserve College, MS Minutes, Feb. 28, 1838.

disappointment, if such it has been. And as 'we know not what a day may bring forth,' we may have one yet.

Yours respectfully,

Thursday morn. Kenyon Cox."[24]

Almost any unexpected event will furnish a pleasant feeling of excitement to a group of students tied down by studies and college rules. Every town has fires. The smell of smoke and the lurid glow of a house in flames, not to mention the uniforms and insignia of the firemen running with the fire engine, furnished a show that no puritanical regulations could ban. It was not entirely with sadness that a young lady student reported two fires of 1859 in her diary: "This A.M. there was a fire. We girls were in our room when we heard a man hollering, we thought he said fire, but then thought not until he repeated the cry, which was issued from many mouths. The fire was west from here, and proved to be Mr. Edward Smith's new brick house. A lot of us girls went up stairs into the garret and looked out to the fire. Hundreds of men kept running by our house on their way to Mr. S's. The house was not burnt down fortunately." The last sentence appears to have been an afterthought, tacked on by a pricking conscience. The second fire was at night: "I had hardly gone to sleep when the alarm was given. All men were of course up and out. The girls most of them came into our room as it was not visible from their rooms. The fire proved to be a house belonging to Mr. Kush over on Main street north of the church. The sight was perfectly grand and sublime yet awful in its sublimity. The house we saw smoking then it burst into flames but they were subdued and the house saved. We saw the timber fall in and such a *beautiful* sight."[25]

Occasionally, of course, the heavens themselves put on pageants of a grander and sublimer nature than anything possible to puny man. "Eclipse of the sun between 4 and 6 P.M. Quite a sensible difference in the intensity of the light during the eclipse. It seemed mellow like moonlight." This from a girl student's diary in 1853.[26] There was another eclipse six years later and

[24]Lent by Mrs. A. A. Drew of Chicago. Kenyon Cox, who was enrolled from 1846 to 1849, was a brother of J. D. Cox. It will be remembered that it was the practice for the young gentlemen and ladies to call each other "brother" and "sister" in this period.

[25]Mary L. Cowles, MS Diary, Apr. 17, and June 23, 1859.

[26]Mary Minerva Gilbert, MS Diary, May 25, 1853.

"we girls" enjoyed it almost as much as the fire: "The sun was eclipsed this afternoon. . . . We girls were all out on the front walk and steps most of the time. . . . We took our Latin books and intended to study, but I did very little studying, only looked at one word and that I knew before was a common noun in Plato. . . . We had a very pleasant time of it with each other, our smoked glasses and the great sun, which at first shone very brightly as if in defiance of its coming shame. . . . The eclipse was not *quite* completed [?] here, but farther north no doubt it was. At its height the moon left only a small half circle on our man as we called it, in view. They say there will be another eclipse in '66, fifteen years, where shall I be then? When the eclipse was waning we left the place and went into the house, many of us with smutty faces from the glasses we had used."[27]

After all, there were many kinds of recreation that were strictly within the law. Here and there groups of "young ladies and gentlemen" would gather for a social hour of singing about a piano or melodeon. Especially if the songs sung were religious, there was no one to object. One young lady indulged in "unloading hay with some other girls for the fun of it." Hannah Warner was invited by "a sister classmate . . . to take a ride of ten miles with her & spend a day & night with some friends of hers." She "accepted the invitation with pleasure, for I [she wrote to her parents] had been in a wagon but once since I left home & I had but one ride on runners." Seventeen years later ten fellows ("Quite a jolly crew," said one of them.) rode to Elyria in a lumber wagon to attend the County Fair and hear a political speech. They "had an excellent time" and felt "well repaid for [their] labor, and [their] money."[28]

In the springtime nature beckoned as enticingly as it does today even in Russia township. "Spring is getting ready to arrive," a college man reported on March 15, "I heard a killdeer and a slew of frogs today making observations to that effect." A young lady student wrote as early as 1842: "Pleasant weather continues and we have some pleasant walks in the evening after

[27]Mary L. Cowles, MS Diary, May 26, 1859.

[28]*Ibid., passim;* Diary of Mary M. Gilbert, Aug. 8, July 13, 1853; Warren and Hannah Warner to parents, Dec. 24, 1841 to Feb. 16, 1842 (O. C. Library); and Sprague Upton, MS Diary, Oct. 8, 1857.

supper and sometimes in the morning before breakfast."[29] Eleven years later another noted with unconscious humor: "After tea took a walk to the graveyard, very pleasant." Another in 1856: "We had a pleasant moonlight walk coming home," and a year later: "Bro. Wheeler . . . wanted to know if I had got to study, and asked me to walk down that way. So we walked to the end of the sidewalk up north and back, and he escorted me to the gate at home."[30] Each of these quotations was written in spring.

But one might err even in a springtime stroll. Young ladies were prohibited from walking "in the street for recreation on the Sabbath." They were not "allowed to walk for recreation with gentlemen" at any time without the permission of "the Principal or the lady with whom they board." In May, 1859, a young lady's diary informs us, a group of girls "went to the woods behind Dr. Dascomb's new place."[31] It is to be feared that they thus became subject to disciplinary measures, for the *Laws and Regulations of the Female Department of Oberlin College* revised and republished in that very year provided that, "Young ladies, who do not reside with their parents, are not allowed to walk in the fields or woods, excepting the grove assigned for this purpose." Ladies' Grove furnished one sylvan retreat where the student nymph might wander. As the miscalled "Arboretum" it continues to furnish Oberlin its one romantic spot. In 1854 the Ladies' Board even concluded that "the practice (which prevails so extensively) of ladies and Gentlemen engaging promiscuously in playing in the yards of their boarding house" was improper and should be discouraged.[32] These rules against promiscuous playing and walking were probably never strictly enforced, certainly not in the fifties and sixties when youthful zest and vigor began to wash away the dikes of stiff repression. If one walked "with a gentleman" on the Sabbath it was of course never "for recreation," but though the journey might be ever so necessary that did not prevent the production of a certain amount of pleasantly guilty satisfaction being developed as a by-product!

[29]John G. Fraser, MS Diary, Mar. 15, 1865, and Elizabeth Maxwell to parents, Mar. 31, 1842 (lent by Mrs. Emma M. Fitch).

[30]Diaries of M. M. Gilbert, May 20, 1854, and Mary L. Cowles, Mar. 26, 1856, and May 26, 1857.

[31]*Laws and Regulations of the Female Department of Oberlin College* (Oberlin 1852), and Mary L. Cowles, MS Diary, May 22, 1859.

[32]L. B. M., May 27, 1854.

It has long been an open secret that breaking rules is itself a most attractive form of student recreation. Professor Coulter concludes that "the college student of the Old South was a happy creature: [because] he had so many rules to disobey."[33] Though the pious and moral spirit of Oberlin was too strong to tolerate anything like the savage roisterings and open flouting of the laws which were characteristic of the University of Georgia, there were still some among the students who took pleasure in doing that which was forbidden. Students were prohibited from playing "cards, checkers, chess, or any similar game of chance or skill." Professor Fairchild even condemned "Authors," quoting the text, "If meat make my brother to offend, etc." Very early in the history of the Institute a student was dismissed for "having in his possession a Pack of *Gamesters* Cards." It was proved that this young man "for diversion . . . did play himself and entice others to play with him."[34] A dismissed student "peached" on a classmate in a letter to the Secretary: "My class can tell you that Mr. H. was anxious to learn to play at cards and carried a pack to the room of Mr. Weed . . . for instructions in the game." In the sixties a group of "young men who met on Tappan Hall Cupola . . . for a casual (?) game of cards" forgot that someone in the town might have a telescope![35] There is no known instance of students being punished for playing checkers or chess. The playing of these games was probably not uncommon, though prohibited throughout the whole period covered in this volume. In 1839, however, the faculty of Western Reserve College ordered Tutor Clark to admonish some students who had "been engaged in playing checkers" on the Sabbath.[36] The puritanical attitude was evidently not confined to Oberlin. Smoking and drinking always hold a special charm for young men attending schools where they are forbidden. Less than six years after the founding of the Institute two young men were brought before the faculty "charged with having gone to Gibb's tavern in Carlisle on the 4th July, without

[33]E. M. Coulter, *College Life in the Old South* (New York—1928) 115.

[34]*Laws and Regulations, 1840;* John G. Fraser, MS Diary, July 16, 1865, and Sophia T. Matson to Faculty of the Oberlin Institute, Feb. 4, 1842 (Cowles-Little MSS).

[35]P. H. Irwin to Levi Burnell, Mar. 6, 1840 (Treas. Off., File D), and *Lorain County News,* Apr. 29, 1863.

[36]Faculty of Western Reserve College, MS Minutes, Apr. 3, 1839.

leave, with there having smoked segars." In the sixties two students were dismissed for going to Elyria, becoming intoxicated and annoying "a sleighing party of young ladies and teachers."[37] A great deal of satisfaction was always to be had out of staying out after hours, particularly in mixed company.

Mixed parties and picnics were unheard of in the early years. George Prudden complained in 1836 that it was "next to impossible for one to see or become acquainted with more than two or three of the ladies." The stiff, puritan face slowly relaxed. A young lady writing to a former classmate in 1846 shows a phase of student thought that letters to parents give no hint of: "I board at the Hall and there is some good folks here, and some slick *fellers* too, one in particular, a Mr. Cox [Jacob Dolson Cox!] from New York city—*O Now that makes me think of something, but don't let it get back here what I have told you.* Timothy H's girl has *mittened* him & it has almost *killed* him." The boarding house table, mixed classes, and choir practice, etc. were fully taken advantage of by those who sought the society of the other sex. In the letters and diaries of the pious it appears as a significant fact that they were often more interested in the souls of those of the opposite sex than of those of the same sex. The ways of the world seem to have been creeping in. William Dawes, in 1846, complained that the faculty was allowing "profitless and hurtful recreations."[38]

The most rapid transition in the trend toward a generally more liberal attitude came in the fifties, particularly the later fifties. This is characteristically notable in the matter of feminine attire. One young lady was reported to have been dismissed from the Institute for "wearing corsets" in 1840.[39] The young ladies in the picture of the graduating classes of 1854 and 1855 are all dressed in black silk with long sleeves and high necks ornamented only with lace or linen collars and cuffs. Their hair is tied up smoothly and simply. The ladies in the graduating classes of 1857 and later appear in their class picture wearing dresses of various colors, some with short sleeves, occasional low

[37]F. M., July 10, 1839, and *Lorain County News,* Jan. 31, 1866.

[38]George P. [and Davis] Prudden to Peter Prudden, Oberlin, Aug. 3, 1836 (Prudden-Allen MSS); M. A. Broadner to Julia Clark, Oct. 4, 1846 (lent by Mr. Herbert Clough), and William Dawes to the Trustees, Aug. 20, 1846 (Misc. Archives).

[39]N. P. Fletcher to Levi Burnell, Oct. 20, 1840 (Treas. Off., File C).

necks and elaborate coiffures.[40] In 1862 the Young Ladies' Literary Society debated the question: "Resolved, that the primitive style of dress in Oberlin was more conducive to study than the present" and the rival society, in 1865, considered the issue, "Resolved, that laced stays are beneficial."[41]

Beginning with the late fifties there is sufficient evidence of the popularity of "promiscuous" parties and picnics. Earlier, with the exception of family picnics, and informal gatherings in boarding house parlors, they seem to have been entirely lacking. In 1859 a junior and senior "pic-nic" was held "in D. B. Kinney's orchard." There was "toasting and speechmaking."[42] In 1860 the boarders at Ladies' Hall (gentlemen as well as ladies) "held a picnic in the woods known as 'De Forests' Grove,' situated one mile and a half northeast from town. The committee had the ground neatly prepared with seats, tables and speakers' stand. The company assembled in the highest spirits, and after passing some time in playing games, etc. proceeded to the intellectual part of the entertainment. The program consisted of orations, poems, political speeches, toasts and responses, music and cheering. Everything in this part of the programme was spicy and taking; the music especially was well executed, and in the open air produced the happiest effect. Substantials followed, and by the way, the feast did credit to the getters-up. Among the other good things was a box of layer raisins donated by the gentlemanly clerks in the store of Kinney and Reamer. After the disposition of the edibles, charades came in,—then games—'Pizen' predominating. It was rather amusing to see venerable Seniors and Theologues performing impromptu, classical revolutions among the russet leaves, and dancing metaphysical jigs about the 'pizen' centre.

"After spending the time thus from three o'clock until seven, the jolly company of one hundred and fifty dispersed, pronouncing the affair an entire success."[43]

The *News* contains other notices of the students' social activities. In 1861 it reported that, "Pic-nicking, parties, visits, &c., have been the order among the students for the last six days.

[40]See pictures opposite page 716.
[41]Y. L. L. S., MS Minutes, July 9, 1862, and Aelioian, July 18, 1865.
[42]H[enry] C[owles] to Mrs. Cowles, 1859 (Cowles-Little MSS).
[43]*Lorain County News*, May 16, 1860.

The weather has been very favorable, and all affirm that they 'have enjoyed themselves first-rate.' "The next month it was noted that, " 'Ye young men and maidens' held a strawberry Festival at the Ladies' Hall on Saturday evening, and crowded a great deal of enjoyment into a couple of hours. New chairs for the sitting room are to be one of the practical results of the gathering." Two years later: "The Oberlin and Wellington band wagons, crowded with jubilant Sophomores, drove out of town on Monday, bound for the lake. The Sophs. report that the 'Elephant went round.' "[44]

A letter written in the summer of 1864 introduces us fully into the modern era. It is addressed by a young lady to her former classmate:

"Would you like to know how that ride came off to Clarkes' [?] I'll proceed forthwith to tell you. The P.M. after you left about one, had you been looking from the window, as were all the tribe here, you might have seen Mr. P. K. assisting your humble servant into the carriage in which was Miss Merwin, his coz, a pretty girl, black hair & eyes, something like Jule Tucker in style, & Mira in size. We started off & just behind us in a real stylish double carriage, two nice ponies, came Frank and Henry, Lem & Anna. Had a gay ride. The boys raced till I was nearly frightened to death. We went to Elyria to a cave there. It was gay, something like *Tinkers* Falls, but not quite so nice. Then we went to his home. It is a real nice little place, the yard very much like Mr. Morrisons. . . . We had one of the gayest suppers this side of Jordans strand. Had everything I could think of & much more. We finished our tea at just *ten minutes past seven,* & we were only *nine miles from home.* [All ladies were required to be in by eight o'clock!] Well we played hide & coop & blind man's buff a few moments & then at half past 7 the boys started for the horses, & at quar. of 8—we were on our way home. Gay wasn't it? It was also gay when C. proposed that Miss M. should drive, which she was very glad to do. She sat on that little seat in the middle or rather *out of the middle* & his majesty sat mighty close to me, nearer than I had any desire for, even me, & you know my desires are not small. Well, to make a long story short, & not to go in to too many particulars, I will only

[44]*Ibid.,* May 29, and June 26, 1861; July 8, 1863.

say—that I do not wish *truly* & *honestly* to have another *kiss* from Perkins K. Clarke to the longest day I live."[45]

It is clear enough that many in the student body did not trouble themselves over the question whether "glee, fun, hilarious mirth, games, charades and pleasure seeking" might harden the heart or destroy the spirit of prayer.

There is no evidence of anything that could be called athletic sport in the period of the thirties. There was no time for it. In the forties, however, the crude and irregular game of football of those days, in which no uniform was used and almost any large number might play on a side, was sometimes played on Tappan Square. In 1847, however, the regulations provided that, "Athletic exercise or sports must be confined to the hours between 12 M. and 2 P.M. and between 6 P.M. and 7½ P.M." In 1850 even the trustees took notice of sports, voting that "the Prudential Com. be authorized & directed to prohibit all games of play by persons not connected with the College on Tappan Hall Square."[46]

In 1859 and 1860 there was a rage for cricket. A preparatory student wrote to his brother in June of the former year: "Instead of wicket they have Cricket here for a play. There are 8 or 10 companies belonging to the college; the green [Tappan Square] is all marked up with alleys. I am going to join the Junior Prep club if I can get a chance. Every noon after dinner those who do not have recitations have an hour to play ball in."[47] Townsmen as well as students became interested in this sport; the *Monthly* stated that it was becoming "alarmingly popular." It was a seven days' wonder, however; after the craze of 1859 and 1860 little more is heard of it in Oberlin.[48]

Skating was the prime sport of the war period. In February of 1862 it had become popular enough to call for a discussion by the Maternal Association. The secretary reported that: "The propriety of allowing boys and girls to skate together in the eve-

[45]Classmate to Minerva A. Winegar, Oberlin, June 26, 1864 (lent by Mrs. H. N. Roberts, Wichita, Kansas).

[46]"Brother" to Charles Wright, Jan. 27, 1847 (lent by Mrs. H. H. Carter, Oberlin); *Laws and Regulations, 1847,* No. 18, and T. M., Feb. 18, 1850.

[47]Henry Prudden to brother, June 25, 1859 (lent by Lillian Prudden, New Haven, Conn.).

[48]*Oberlin Students' Monthly,* I, 361 (July, 1859), and *Lorain County News,* May 9, 1860.

Excelsior Skating Club.

Chas Hall

Is hereby constituted a Member of the Excelsior Skating Club, for the Winter of 1865-6.

E. H. FAIRCHILD, Jr., } Board of
A. B. FITCH, } Manage't.

Oberlin, O., Dec 14 1865

M C H Hall

Is entitled to the privileges of WRIGHT'S SKATING PARK for the Winter of 1866—7.

H. H. WRIGHT.

Oberlin, Dec 10 1866.

SKATING CLUB MEMBERSHIP CARDS
(Oberlin College Library)

ning was introduced. Many, indeed most, objected to this; one elderly sister who represented the views of our mothers upon such subjects remarked, that skating for girls was a new idea & she could not give her opinion; when she was a girl there was work enough to be done to furnish all the exercise they needed & if girls were out after dark mothers might have reason to feel anxious."[49] A place was provided for the sport by damming up a tiny creek so as to make a pond in the hollow behind the present Lord Cottage. It was a sad thing when, one night, the muskrats bored a hole through the dam and let the water out. In the winter of 1862 and 1863 the Burnside Skating Club (the General must have been popular at Oberlin), and in later years the Excelsior Skating Club, rented the pond, membership fees being collected from those who cared to skate. When the ice was sufficiently firm a streamer was raised on a pole so that all could know that there was "Skating Today," when there was "a general rally to improve the precious opportunity."[50]

Various simple ball games like "three o'cat" were undoubtedly played very early. Henry Prudden wrote to his brother in 1859 that he had "played base more times than he ever said scat to an owl."[51] The organized game of baseball in something like its modern form was played in the East in the fifties. In the war it was a popular sport in the army and directly afterwards was being taught to the local boys by returned soldiers in every town and hamlet in the country. In 1866 the game became tremendously popular, and early in May ball players were very much in evidence on the college grounds.[52] The *News* reported later in the year: "Base ball rages. The fever is running down to the youngsters and the eight-year olds have their 'clubs' and match games, and talk glibly about 'crack' players, fly catches, home runs, &c. All right, boys.—Base ball won't sting you, as some other B's might—such as betting, brandy, billiards, &c."[53] The moral appeal was, of course, the right one for Oberlin.

[49]Oberlin Maternal Association, MS Minutes, Feb. 5, 1862.

[50]*Lorain County News,* Jan. 7, 22, 1863; Nov. 16, Dec. 14, 1864; Dec. 20, 1865, and H. H. Wright to A. A. Wright, Jan. 2, 1863 (A. A. Wright MSS). The pond was on the W. W. Wright farm, the Wright home being on the Lord Cottage site.

[51]Henry Prudden to brother, Oberlin, June 3, 1859 (lent by Lillian Prudden, New Haven, Conn.).

[52]*Lorain County News,* May 9, 1866.

[53]*Ibid.,* Nov. 14, 1866.

Soon after the surrender at Appomattox the Penfield Base Ball Club was organized at Oberlin and in October, 1865, defeated the Forest City Club of Cleveland by the score of 67 to 28! It was quite a game: one Oberlin player was hit in the face by a batted ball and a Cleveland boy had two teeth knocked out. It was the first game played by a Cleveland ball club with an outside organization. The Penfields played two games with Cleveland teams in 1866, one being lost 14 to 48 and the other won to the tune of 64 to 21 runs. In 1869 the Forest City Club beat the Oberlin "Resolutes" 17 to 2; two years later this Cleveland team was playing the Cincinnati "Red Stockings" and the Philadelphia Athletics.[54]

Of course the very "live" ball used in these games accounts for the large scores. They certainly furnished sufficient exercise! Home games were played on the diamond on Tappan Square. Even in the late sixties, however, many students seldom or never engaged in games of any kind. Lucien Warner, who graduated in 1865, remembered taking part in only one game of baseball while in Oberlin. Even in the great baseball year of 1866 the editor of the *News* admitted that "the saw and hoe have more friends yet, in the Oberlin Catalogue, than the shot gun or ball club."[55]

The comings and goings which have always been so characteristic of American college life meant that there would naturally be seasonal periods of special social activity. New students must be welcomed and old friends greeted at the beginning of a term or end of a vacation. In November and August came the temporary or, often (unexpectedly perhaps), permanent partings. The secretary of the Young Men's Lyceum put his own feelings in the minutes of the last meeting before winter vacation in 1853. He recorded that; "the Fraternity was dissolved peacefully and quietly, but withal in Sorrow and Sadness of heart, with the hope of meeting again at the appointed time to strengthen the bonds of friendship and pursue the flowery paths of Science." After the building of the railroad it was a ceremony

[54]*Lorain County News,* Oct. 25, 1865; *Cleveland Leader,* Oct. 21, 1865; Oct. 11, 1869; July 13, 24, 1871, quoted in *Annals of Cleveland,* and W. C. Cochran, "Base Ball in Old Times," *Oberlin Review,* XII, 44–46, 54–56 (Nov. 8, 22, 1884).

[55]Lucien Warner, *Story of My Life,* 38, and *Lorain County News,* June 13, July 11, Oct. 3, 1865.

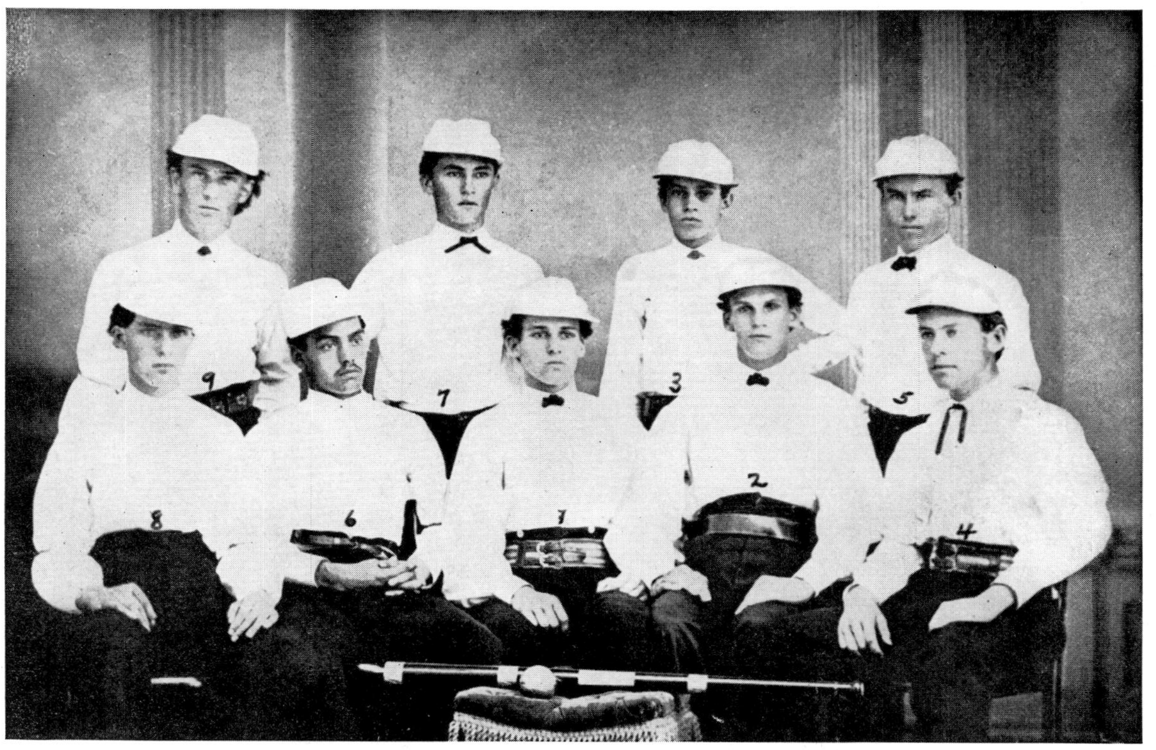

THE OBERLIN "RESOLUTES" BASE BALL CLUB—1868
(Oberlin College Library)

TAPPAN SQUARE IN THE SEVENTIES SHOWING THE BASEBALL DIAMOND
(Oberlin College Library)

to visit the depot at the opening or closing of school and bid farewell to departing friends or welcome the new arrivals. "This morning," [Henry Prudden wrote to his parents in 1859], "all our lady boarders went away, I went down to the depot to see them off & got wet through before I got back. Our recitations are all through with except Rhetorical." The reunion after the winter vacation was a time of special rejoicing.[56] But Commencement was, of course, the greatest social event of the year, as it marked not only the end of one academic year but also the beginning of another.

[56]Young Men's Lyceum, MS Minutes, Nov. 8, 1853; Henry Prudden to parents, Nov. 14–19, 1859 (lent by Miss Lillian E. Prudden, New Haven, Conn.), and *Oberlin Students' Monthly,* II, 157 (Mar., 1860).

CHAPTER XLVIII

COMMENCEMENT

AFTER examinations came the great event of the year, the time when village and college were placed on formal exhibition before the world, an opportunity for reunions of former students, a big show for the country people, a feast of oratory for all.

"Commencement! The week of all the fifty-two. 'Busses roll to and from the trains loaded with passengers. Portly Trustees take an annual look after 'Institution' interests. Alumni in white cravats shake hands and introduce the alumni-in-law of Alma Mater. Ushers bustle about with their blue badges. Melons, sweet cider and gingerbread are hawked and consumed on every corner. The graduates-to-be saunter about with quiet, conscious dignity. Busy cooks muster their resources in the way of pastries and substantials. Country couples of either sex walk up and down the street or sit in some quiet corner of the big church in the very fullness of enjoyment. The essays are read or orations spoken. Fathers from the farm, the shop, or study, mothers from 'home' listen with beating hearts, justly glad—justly proud perhaps. The 'Praeses' cuts, with the kindly diploma, the web of training which has been six years weaving. Great week! Memorable to the Freshman just bending to the work; memorable to those to whom the pleasant associations of hall and recitation room, the kindly relations of class and societies are to be hereafter—memories."[1] There were many who deprecated this carnival spirit at the anniversaries. Finney, in 1860, even advocated their discontinuance as being undesirable worldly celebrations.[2] In the earlier years Commencements partook more of the character of revival camp meetings.

Not until 1836 were there diplomas to be granted, and then only to Theological Department graduates. The first college

[1]*Lorain County News,* Aug. 28, 1861.

[2]John Keep *et al.* to Finney, July 21, 1860 (Finney MSS).

degrees were conferred in 1837. In both 1834 and 1835, however, public exhibitions were held in lieu of regular commencement exercises. The first of these exhibitions, which took place on October 29, 1834, included the reading of compositions, the speaking of pieces, "an ingenious dialogue, and sacred music." The "Anniversary" of 1835 was marked by the inauguration of President Mahan, Professor Finney and Professor Morgan and the installation of Shipherd as pastor of the church.[3]

The exercises of 1835 and later years, until the meeting house was available in 1843, were (when the weather permitted) held in the Big Tent or "Tabernacle," which had been presented to Finney by admirers upon his coming to Oberlin. A woman who had attended the Commencement in 1837 wrote shortly after to a friend: "The first thing that attracted our attention after we entered the Village was Mr. Finney's Tent which will hold three thousand people, a flag on the top with the inscription, 'Holiness unto the Lord.' It is indeed a beautiful sight."[4] Four years later another commencement visitor waxed even more enthusiastic. "I shall not easily forget," she wrote, "the emotions that filled my mind, as on the morning of the 24th of August I caught a view of the majestic tent, stretching its whitened canvas to the breeze beneath the glowing canopy of heaven, like a hilloc of snow on an islet of green. From the top staff its banner of blue, on which was inscribed, 'HOLINESS TO THE LORD,' while the stillness of the scene, the freshness of the air, and the serenity of surrounding nature, combined to render it one of the most interesting objects, on which I had ever looked. . . . Methought the object before me was a fit emblem of those, under whose direction it had been raised, laboring on the one hand to preserve the purity and sanctity of that law, first promulgated in thunder on Sinai, and on the other, striving 'by pureness, by knowledge, by long suffering, by kindness, by the Holy Ghost, by love unfeigned, by honor and dishonor, by evil report and good report,' to bring forward the latter day glory of the church, when she shall be presented 'holy and without blemish' to Him who hath redeemed her by his blood."[5]

[3]*Ohio Atlas and Elyria Advertiser,* Nov. 13, 1834, and *Ohio Observer,* June 11, 1835.

[4]Elizabeth Hall to Hannah Breck, Sept. 11, 1837 (O. C. Lib.).

[5]M. A. S. in *Oberlin Evangelist,* Nov. 24, 1841.

In the forties the meeting house was easily the finest church building in the Reserve, and the commencement exercises lost nothing in impressiveness when transferred to that structure. Every inch of sitting and standing room was usually occupied on such occasions. The regular carpets were usually taken up to save the unusual wear on them and sawdust procured and dumped in the aisles to deaden the sound of leather heels upon the wooden floor. This was very important because there was always a steady stream of people coming and going during the program. The general preparations were in the hands of the juniors but the sophomores were given the special task of procuring the sawdust. They made a gala event out of it, each young man "dressing up" in some fantastic costume and securing some rawboned nag to ride. Each would then secure a bag of sawdust and the whole number would ride solemnly to the meeting house, each rider bearing a sack on the saddle before him. The sawdust had to be taken out at the expense of the institution, however. In 1863 cheap, rough carpets were furnished in lieu of the sawdust and perforce the interesting custom was abandoned.[6] Sawdust or carpets, the gatherings at commencement time in the Oberlin meeting house were great occasions.

The week before Commencement was occupied with examinations, the "Exhibition" of the senior class of the Preparatory Department and the anniversaries of the various literary societies. On Sunday a special sermon was usually addressed to the graduates. The official graduating exercises were usually on Tuesday, Wednesday, and sometimes Thursday. The exercises for the graduates from the Ladies' Course took place almost invariably on Tuesday afternoon. The graduating exercises of the Collegiate and Theological departments were usually on Wednesday but were shifted from one time to another. The meeting of the alumni and the musical concert, the latter usually in the evening, were other high points on the commencement program.

The greatest Commencement of the Theological Department was the first one, which took place in September of 1836. Despite unfavorable weather, about two thousand persons as-

[6]P. C. M., Aug. 7, 1863; *Lorain County News*, June 17, 1863; A. L. Shumway and C. DeW. Brower, *Oberliniana* (Cleveland–[1883]) 44–46, and bill for commencement expenses, 1859 (Misc. Archives).

THE BIG TENT ON TAPPAN SQUARE

President Mahan's house, Tappan Hall [with the wrong number of windows and a disproportionately large cupola], and Professor Finney's house are in the background. Note the rail fence.

(From a pen sketch by Professor Churchill in the Oberlin College Library)

TO THE

REVEREND **ASA MAHAN**, PRESIDENT,

TO THE

RESPECTED FACULTY,

TO THE

HONORED TRUSTEES,

TO OUR

ASSEMBLED FRIENDS,

AND THE

PATRONS OF LETTERS GENERALLY,

this

SCHEDULE

OF THE

COMMENCEMENT EXERCISES

OF THE

SENIOR CLASSES OF THE LADIES', COLLEGIATE, AND THEOLOGICAL DEPARTMENTS

of

O. C. I.

IS HUMBLY DEDICATED BY

THE GRADUATING CLASSES.

Ladies.

Mary Atkins,
Mary Ann Barnes,
Laura Gulianna Branch,
Prudence Jane Everett,
Angeline Fisher,
Susan Irvine,
Almira Kilbourn,
Mary Newton Makepeace,
Minerva S. Mc Conoughey,
Electa Maria Pixley,
Phebe Sterling Pratt,

Collegiate.

Edwin Thompson Branch.
Thomas Corlett,
Danforth Leander Eaton,
John Chandler Grannis,
John Hopkins Gurney,
Ithiel Burt Ingersoll,
Jonathan E. Ingersoll,
Charles Livingston,
John Low,
James Newberry,
Charles Henry Peirce,
Ebenezer Smith,
Isaac Cushing White,
W. Cuthbert Whitehorne,
Joseph Clinton Whitney,
Harry Edwin Woodcock,
Sarah Blachley,
Lucia Jennison,
Mary Abigail Platt,
Jane Baxter Trew,
Laurette Lydia Turner,
Hannah Maria Warner.

Theological.

John Adams Allen,
Horace Roscoe Grannis,
Moses Maynard Longley,
Andrew Jones Drake,
Jeremiah Butler,
Henry Everard Peck.

OBERLIN:

MDCCCXLV.

FIRST PAGE OF THE COMMENCEMENT PROGRAM—1845

Note the similarity in form to the dedications of the thesis sheets of colonial colleges.

(Oberlin College Library)

sembled under the "impressive awnings" of the Tabernacle to hear orations on "New Measures," "Power of the Heart," "Signs of the Times," "The True Standard of Human Action," and similar weighty topics. James Watson Alvord's piece on "New Measures," which was, in essence, a defense of the revival methods of Finney, was printed in full in the *Ohio Observer*. Friends and visitors were very flattering in their comments on the performance. But never again did the "Theologs" hold the limelight, being forced from this time on to yield the center of the stage to the graduates of the Collegiate and Ladies' courses.[7]

The first graduate from the Ladies' Course was Zeruiah Porter who finished in 1838. In the next year there were five young lady graduates (including Florella Brown, John Brown's half-sister) and in 1840, four. In none of these years, however, were graduation exercises held for them. In 1841, however, in connection with the Anniversary of the Young Ladies' Association (or Literary Society) "testimonials" were distributed to seven young ladies who at that time had completed the regular Ladies' Course. Delia Fenn read an essay entitled "The Royal Road to Excellence"; Catherine Snow's essay was on "Contrasting Spectacles"; another discoursed on "The Importance of Cultivating a Literary Taste."[8] President Mahan then addressed them briefly and, we may be sure, appropriately.

The young ladies attracted special attention because of the talk about joint education and the rarity of educated women. There was considerable comment on the exercises of 1845, partly because as many as eleven young ladies were included in this graduating class. The reporter for the *Cleveland Herald* wrote: "Each young Lady read her own production, and the entire performances were exceedingly creditable to the pupils and teachers. The compositions evinced a thorough course of instruction, cultivated taste and talents, and a moral force and beauty, the bright sun-light of woman's mind. The exercises, even to the music, which was sweet as the carol of birds and in fine keeping with the melodious voices of the speakers—were

[7]*Ohio Observer,* Sept. 29; Oct. 20, 1836, and John Keep to Gerrit Smith, Oct. 14, 1836 (Gerrit Smith MSS).

[8]*Oberlin Evangelist,* Sept. 1, 1841. It was also in 1841 that the first certificates were granted.—T. M. Aug. 20, 1841.

conducted by Ladies. At the close, Diplomas were presented to the members of the class by President Mahan . . ."[9]

Somewhat more realistic is the description of the exercises written by a girl in the Preparatory Department as part of a composition: "In the afternoon at 2 o'clock I went to the new church which is a large brick building opposit Mr. Gillet's house; you remember the place. The church was almost full, especialley the gallery. The order of exercises were distributed —one sheet served for both days. The exercises commenced with music by several of the young ladies, accompanied by a Seraphena—prayer by the President. Music again—10 young ladies read composions [*sic*], some of which were very good. . . . The Ladies Board of Managers sat in the pulpit and the young ladies of the Institution sat in the archestry. It was with great difficulty that the ladies were heard the house was so large and full. After the Diplomas were Presented we were dimissed with Benediction and I presume to say that the ladies were glad enough."[10]

The young lady graduates and attending lady students invariably dressed in white with blue sashes. The procession of "young ladies of the Institution, dressed in white muslin with the inevitable blue sashes," wrote a local journalist of the exercises in 1861, was "a goodly, fair sight to see." Four years later one of the young ladies wrote to a classmate: "Commencement is approaching rapidly. We are beginning to talk of white dresses, partners for marching, etc."[11]

In 1860 the *Lorain County News* became lyric in describing the exercises:

"At an early hour yesterday morning visitors began to assemble from all directions. The streets were lined with teams and the morning trains from the east and west came in heavily loaded. By noon the village was alive with strangers from the rural districts and neighboring cities, and the prospect for a sublime

[9]Quoted in the *Oberlin Evangelist,* Sept. 10, 1845.

[10]Helen Cowles' composition in the form of a letter, addressed to "Dear Louisa" and dated Sept. 10, 1845 (Cowles-Little MSS).

[11]*Lorain County News,* Aug. 28, 1861; Classmate to Minerva A. Winegar [1865] (lent by Mrs. H. N. Roberts, Wichita, Kansas); Adelia Whipple to mother, May 31, 1858 (lent by Jessie Wright, Wellington), and *Independent* (New York), Sept. 11, 1856. At least as early as 1850 the lady students dressed in white for the commencement exercises.—*Oberlin Evangelist,* Nov. 6, 1850.

jam at the church in the afternoon was painfully flattering. Long before two o'clock the mammoth church edifice was crowded to its utmost capacity. Every available inch of sitting and standing room was eagerly appropriated by those who had 'come to the Commencement.'

"At a quarter before two the young ladies of the Institution, numbering nearly four hundred, marched in procession from the Chapel across Tappan Square to the church, where they were seated together at the west end of the gallery.

"This feature of yesterday's entertainment was one of the finest sights we have ever witnessed. The young ladies were dressed in uniform snow-white, with blue flowing sashes, and uncovered heads. The airiness of their dress and their personal beauty made the effect half enchanting, and hundreds who had never witnessed the spectacle before were perfectly enthusiastic in their compliments—rapidly exhausting their fund of exclamation points and double superlatives.

"When the exercises commenced hundreds were remaining outside in the shaded yard that surrounds the church, being unable to obtain a respectable peep within. Those inside the building must have numbered from three to four thousand, yet remarkably good order was preserved though out.

"After a brief and eloquent prayer by Rev. Mr. Whipple of Boston, the reading of essays began, and continued with frequent intermissions of music, until 5 o'clock. When the last one had been read, the whole class of twenty-nine took their positions in double rank upon the stand to sing the 'class song,' and receive from Dr. Morgan their diplomas.

"The sight was a beautiful one, and produced a fine effect. When the class had sung the first verse of the song the ladies of the Institute rose, at the same instant, and joined in singing the chorus, which was a reply to their sisters that were going out. The air of spontaneity and absence of all stiffness that characterized the whole proceeding, added much to the effect.

"Pausing in the middle of the song, the young ladies remained standing while the venerable Dr. Morgan addressed the graduating class and presented the diplomas. We would like much to reproduce the remarks made by the Professor. They were certainly the most touching and appropriate that we have ever listened to on a similar occasion.

"The diplomas being presented, the song was concluded, all joining in the chorus:

"Then Farewell, Farewell dear sisters,
And may each one's motto be,
All through life's uneven pathway,
Lo! 'The world hath need of thee.'

"This closed the exercises of the afternoon, and the numerous congregation that had spent nearly four hours on a warm day in a crowded house, quietly dispersed expressing themselves richly repaid for all their trouble and inconvenience."[12]

Some of the young ladies' essays really seem to have made quite an impression. In 1846 Louisa Jane Lovell read an anti-slavery and anti-war essay entitled "True Valuation of Human Interests." She declared, in conclusion, "the brightest omen is the spirit of reform, which everywhere breathes throughout our land, *every branch* of which has for its ultimate aim the promotion of human interests." Michael Bateham, editor of the *Ohio Cultivator* of Columbus, was in attendance. The impression made on him was so great "as subsequently to induce him to seek her acquaintance and love." They were married the next year; she died the year following; and two years later he married another Oberlin wife, the step-daughter of Professor Cowles.[13] We do not know whether he selected her on the basis of her graduation essay or not.

But the essays of the young ladies read on Tuesday—"rich in thought—correct in sentiment, chaste in language," as they were said to be—were only the appetizers which prepared the intellectual palate for the strong meat offered by the college and theological graduates on Wednesday. The young men's orations dealt with all sorts of weighty matters in the fields of social problems, ethics, philosophy and theology. Such subjects as: "Right the Basis of Law," "The Political Economy of Slavery," "National Responsibility," "Moral Heroism" (by James Monroe), "Position of the American Christian on the Moral Battle-field," "The Influence of Philosophy in Forming the Character

[12]*Lorain County News,* Aug. 22, 1860. The song is given complete in the *News* of Aug. 15, 1860.

[13]A. L. Demaree, *The American Agricultural Press, 1819–1860* (New York—1941), 162–3, and *Oberlin Evangelist,* Sept. 30, 1846.

SENIORS IN THE LADIES' COURSE—1857
(From daguerreotypes in the Oberlin College Library)

of an Age," and "The Dawn of Mental Freedom" were characteristic. A visitor in 1855 heard "little . . . of 'Demosthenes and Cicero,' of Parnasus and Olympus, but much of our relations to our Country and the race, of our duties to man and to God."

The Oberlin gospel of reform was continually cropping out and the orations were invariably characterized by seriousness of purpose. In 1848 a man who attended the exercises at Western Reserve College at Hudson as well as at Oberlin compared the two. He found that: "At Hudson the reasoning powers were cultivated more than the imagination and sensibilities. At Oberlin the order was reversed. At Hudson they manifested great reverence for the church and her institutions as they now exist; at Oberlin the church was often criminated. At Hudson we had the bright side of the picture—all was well; at Oberlin this was pronounced a 'degenerate age,' 'a faithless generation,' and 'reform' was demanded. At Hudson marked attention was shown to the Faculty; at Oberlin very little. . . . At Hudson there was an inexcusable hesitancy; at Oberlin the pieces were thoroughly committed. At Hudson the speakers seemed to have learned elocution more from *precept* than from *example*; at Oberlin more from example than from precept."[14]

Four young men received the bachelor's degree in 1837 and twenty in 1838, including George N. Allen and the Fairchild brothers, James and Henry. This number was not greatly exceeded until 1861 and 1862, in both of which years degrees were granted to twenty-eight men and women.

The first degrees were granted to women in 1841, to Mary Caroline Rudd, Mary Hosford and Elizabeth Prall. One would like to have heard Professor Morgan read Mary Hosford's essay: "A Lady's Apology"—supposedly for aspiring to the bachelor's degree. A visitor found the young ladies' essays good and deserving "to be spoken with all the spirit and life which the feeling of maternity could not have failed to produce, instead of being condemned to an indifferent reading by a Professor who had nothing to do with the composition." Not until 1858 was a young lady allowed to read her own essay on the Wednesday program. Though prohibited from speaking, these

[14]*Oberlin Evangelist,* Sept. 13, 1848; Sept. 12, 1855, and accounts of other Commencements.

first female bachelors "received the diplomas to which they were entitled, on the stage, in the same manner as the young gentlemen, same degree, to wit, that of Bachelor of Arts."[15]

Music always played a large part in the exercises, especially choral music. There were usually occasional intervals of singing interspersed in the program between the orations and essays and, after 1840, a special commencement concert. In 1839 James Fairchild found the singing "divine" and declared that: "The audience could hardly contain themselves.—There were many shed tears that do not often weep."[16] At the end of each program the graduates usually sang a "parting song," sometimes as in 1851, written by a member of the class:

> Friends, fare ye well!
> The parting hour is nigh,
> And we must leave each soul-embalmed spot,
> Where we have met
> In the sweet years gone by—
> Sweet years!—whose joys can never be forgot!
> What our full heart
> Feels, none can tell;
> But as we part,
> Farewell, farewell!
>
> * * *
>
> This side the tomb
> We may not meet again!
> One of our number now lies in the grave!
> Briefly he beamed
> A mental star, and then
> Sunk as a meteor 'neath the midnight wave!
> We too shall soon
> Sleep, and the knell
> Ring for our last
> Mournful farewell!
>
> Teachers, farewell!
> Our hearts must always feel
> For you, whose kindness made our pathway bright,
> Affection deep:

[15] *Ohio Atlas and Elyria Advertiser,* Sept. 1, 1841.
[16] J. H. F. to Mary Kellogg, Aug. 24, 1839 (Fairchild MSS).

We go to draw the steel
Of truth, whose power ye taught us, for the right!
For your kind care,
Our bosoms swell
With gratitude!
Farewell, farewell.

The alumni association was formed in 1839 as the Association of Alumni of the Oberlin Collegiate Institute, and its purpose declared to be "to cultivate & strengthen friendly feeling among its members—to perpetuate the purity and prosperity of the Institution from which they have graduated—& to secure mutual aid and sympathy in carrying forward efficiently & successfully the great objects of our being." Membership was limited to graduates of the Collegiate Department and provision was made for the expulsion of those who should become "decidedly immoral."[17] Young lady recipients of a degree were included from the beginning, it being voted on August 26, 1841, "that we consider the ladies of the present graduating class as included in the motion of reception."

The association met annually during commencement week, listened to an address by one of their number and elected an orator for the following year. In 1847 John Todd, the founder of Tabor, discoursed on "The American Clergy & the Times"; in 1862 Professor J. M. Ellis spoke on "Weakness & Strength of the Republic"; Professor Robert C. Kedzie of the Michigan Agricultural College delivered an address on "Wind and Water" in 1864, and J. M. Langston spoke on "Ethical Reconstruction" in 1866. A banquet was often featured. In 1842 the trustees of the Institute paid the steward twenty-five dollars to prepare a dinner for two hundred.[18] The reunion of 1856 was especially successful. One hundred and seventy out of two hundred and twenty-two living graduates were present—probably an all-time record. James H. Fairchild delivered an oration on the history of Oberlin. There was a grand "collation" and "after the material repast came the feast of reason and the flow of soul"; sixteen responses to toasts—each (fortunately!) limited to five minutes.

[17]Oberlin Alumni Association, MS Minutes, in the office of the secretary of the association. In 1854 a resolution to admit graduates of all departments was voted down.

[18]T. M., Aug. 19, 1847.

Among them were: "Oberlin and her children—well met again" by Father Keep, "The Faculty—Tried and found Faithful" by Professor Morgan, "The glorious good fellows of Lane Seminary —May their shadows never be less" by Rev. George Clark, "Our graduates, the Ladies—Much learning hath not made them mad, but with womanly grace they sustain their honors and duties" by Rev. James A. Thome, and "The Presidential Campaign—The Sons and Daughters of our Alma Mater are always among the tried friends of Freedom" by C. B. Darwin of Iowa. A ten-thousand-dollar fund for the college library was inaugurated and four thousand dollars pledged on the spot.[19]

Another great Commencement was that of 1858. President Hitchcock of Western Reserve College spoke on Monday night and his audience went directly from the church to prevent the capture of a fugitive slave. The governors of both Ohio and Michigan were present on Wednesday and addressed the assembly at the close of the regular exercises. "I suppose you have heard the commencement exercises all talked over long before this," a junior man wrote to his coed fiancee. "I need not notice them. All there is to say is, that all the lions duly roared according to order, from the two governors down to the stupidest sen —alumnus,—no *senior,* for they were seniors then. They had not yet graduated into nonentities. The choir did its roaring in the evening. I was there—made a desperate dash through the crowd at the imminent risk of my bones and my lady's—crinoline —secured a third rate seat and a first rate head ache—sat there for three mortal hours, except such part of them as I spent in the delightful recreation of standing up (which part was about two thirds)."[20] A gentleman from Elyria had his horse and buggy stolen while he was attending the exercises.[21]

In 1849 the usual ceremonies were dispensed with on account of the cholera epidemic, it being "understood that large gatherings of people, protracted excitement, and mental and physical exhaustion" encouraged the spread of the much-feared plague. Professor Morgan, however, delivered an address to the graduates, their families and friends, other students and the

[19]*Oberlin Evangelist,* Sept. 10, 1856.

[20]*Ibid.,* Sept. 1, 1858, and "Frank" to Mary Cowles, Aug. 26, 1858 (Cowles-Little MSS).

[21]*Cleveland Leader,* Sept. 2, 1858, cited in *Annals of Cleveland.*

townspeople on the customary day. In 1850 during the program on Wednesday the alarm of fire was given and a panic averted only by the presence of mind of a student who announced to the audience that it was a false alarm. As a matter of fact a fire had broken out in a student's room in Colonial Hall. The exercises were adjourned until the flames had been subdued, when the audience and orators returned to the regular business of Commencement, the more enthusiastic, undoubtedly, for the intermission.[22]

Directly after the conclusion of the exercises came the weddings of the new alumni and alumnae. Then, fortified by the advice of President Finney and Mrs. Dascomb on successful matrimony and, in at least one year, by the gift of a patent stove from Philo P. Stewart, they sallied out to make over the world.[23]

The undergraduates and preparatory students reopened their textbooks and elected new officers for their literary societies. "It is the day after Commencement," wrote one of these undergraduates. "The students are hurrying up & down the hall in all the bustle of choosing rooms for the year. I can hear them now, through my closed door—questioning, disputing, knocking at the doors, & discussing the relative worth of the rooms as if the fate of the kingdom depended on a correct decision. Through the early morning the two weddings seemed to be *the* topic. Now they are over with and, for the moment, half-forgotten in this new excitement."[24]

[22]*Oberlin Evangelist,* Aug. 1, 29, 1849; T. M., Aug. 28, 1850; P. C. M., Sept. 13, 1850, and T. M. Haskell to Henry Cowles, Nov. 21, 1851 (Cowles-Little MSS).

[23]There is a list of weddings in the *Oberlin Evangelist,* Sept. 1, 1841. In 1860, Mr. Stewart offered stoves to married seniors who commenced the study of theology.—*Lorain County News,* July 4, 1860.

[24]"Frank" to Mary Cowles, Aug. 26, 1858 (Cowles-Little MSS).

Book Five

War and Transition

"In this collision the cause of the slave is that of humanity, of liberty, of civilization, of Christianity. It is the cause of God against Satan, & woe to the power that attempts to longer crush labor under the heel of capital."

CHARLES GRANDISON FINNEY (In a letter to Barlow, February 13, 1863—O. C. Library).

"Oberlin commenst this war. Oberlin wuz the prime cause uv all the trubble. What wuz the beginnin uv it? Our Suthrin brethrin wantid the territories — Oberlin objectid. They wantid Kansas fer ther blessid instooshn — Oberlin again objecks. They sent colonies with muskits and sich, to hold the terrytory — Oberlin sent 2 thowsand armed with Bibles and Sharp's rifles — two instooshns Dimokrasy cood never never stand afore — and druv em out. They wantid Brechinridge fer President. Oberlin refused, and elektid Linkin. . . .

"Oberlin won't submit. We might 2-day hev peese ef Oberlin wood say to Linkin, 'Resine!' and to Geff Davis, 'Come up higher!' When I say Oberlin understand it ez figgerative fer the entire ablishn party, uv wich Oberlin is the fountin-hed. There's wher the trubble is. Our Suthern brethren wuz reasonable. So long az the Dimokrasy controld things, and they got all they wanted, they wur peeceable. Oberlin ariz—the Dimokrasy wuz beet down, and they riz up agin it."

PETROLEUM V. NASBY [David Ross Locke], *The Struggles (Social, Financial and Political) of Petroleum V. Nasby* (Boston—c. 1872), 44–46.

CHAPTER XLIX

COMPANY C

LINCOLN and the majority of Northern men may have fought the war for the Union, but Oberlinites were interested only in the slavery issue. There was no tremendous enthusiasm for Lincoln in the election of 1860, though a noisy ratification meeting was held when news was received of the nomination. Oberlin considered Lincoln's "ground on the score of humanity towards the oppressed race" altogether too low and was much irritated at his promise to enforce the fugitive slave law. Editorially the *Evangelist* wished the Republicans had chosen a better man, but agreed to support him as certainly better than any Democratic candidate. Deploring the weakness of the Republican position, Oberlin men must strive to elevate the "moral tone" of the party and "bring it more fully into sympathy with freedom and righteousness." There was considerable local political activity. Cassius M. Clay of Kentucky spoke to a capacity crowd in the meeting house; the Lincoln Glee Club furnished the music. Stephen A. Douglas' campaign train stopped at the depot. The Little Giant, said the *News,* "drew himself up one inch above his usual height, so as to attain the dizzy altitude of five feet two," and made a brief speech. There was not much applause. The election of Lincoln was celebrated with a grand torch-light procession and a bonfire on Tappan Square.[1]

Immediately they went to work to exert pressure to make sure that there would be no compromise to save the Union at the expense of the slaves. In March, Ralph Plumb, Rescuer and ambitious local political leader, wrote to James Monroe, then a member of the Ohio Senate, expressing his preference for peaceable separation rather than any effort to patch up the Union with slavery. He agreed that it might "be the best thing

[1]*Lorain County News,* May 23, Aug. 8, Sept. 25, 1860, and *Oberlin Evangelist,* May 23, Sept. 12, 1860.

for the cause to let the separation come." Even kindly old John Morgan declared to his bosom friend, Mark Hopkins: "With all my heart I wish there may be a complete separation from the slave power which has incalculably demoralized the whole nation and will do it worse still if the shadow of a concession is made to it." Early in February the citizens of Oberlin held a mass meeting and adopted resolutions which were sent to the compromise convention then assembled in Washington. "As Christians," these resolutions read in part, "as citizens of the Commonwealth, as a part of our common country, in the name of our common humanity, and in the love and fear of God, we solemnly *protest against any concession to Slavery or to the demands made by its abettors in any form whatever,* and especially against making such concessions at the behest of traitors in arms against the Union."[2]

On Friday, April 12, 1861, a telegram was read at the regular session of the Ohio State Senate announcing that Fort Sumter had been fired upon. The news was greeted with silence by the members, including Finney's two sons-in-law, James Monroe and Jacob Dolson Cox, and their close friend, James A. Garfield, but Abby Kelley Foster, the radical abolitionist, screamed out from the visitors' gallery, "Glory to God!"[3] Oberlinites had never had much in common with Abby Kelley but most of them, like her, now seemed to welcome the catastrophe and little more was heard about "moral suasion."

On Saturday, April 13, Sumter was surrendered and the Monday morning papers contained the proclamation by President Lincoln calling for 75,000 volunteer troops to put down the rebellion. Four days after the call was received two Ohio regiments left for Washington. At Oberlin the faculty immediately moved to repeal the prohibition against student participation in military companies.[4] Mayor Hendry issued a

[2]*Lorain County News,* Nov. 21, 1860; Plumb to Monroe, Mar. 12, 1861 (Monroe MSS); John Morgan to Mark Hopkins, Mar. 27, 1861 (Morgan-Hopkins MSS), and *Oberlin Evangelist,* Feb. 13, 1861.

[3]J. D. Cox, *Military Reminiscences of the Civil War* (N. Y.—1900). For Ohio in the war see Eugene H. Roseboom and Francis P. Weisenberger, *History of Ohio,* (N. Y.—1934), 266–292, and Whitelaw Reid, *Ohio in the War,* 2 vols. (Cincinnati—1868).

[4]There are three useful secondary summaries of Oberlin's participation in the war: Fairchild, *Oberlin, the Colony and the College,* 154–172; J. M. Ellis, *Oberlin and the American Conflict* (an address delivered before the alumni of Oberlin College at their reunion, Wednesday, Aug. 23, 1865), and Wilbur

proclamation denouncing the "foul conspiracy" against the Government, "liberty and the hope of man," and calling a mass meeting of the citizenry. The great Union rally was held in the old meeting house on Wednesday evening, April 17. Among the temporary officers were Peter Pindar Pease, John M. Langston, the Negro lawyer, and A. B. Nettleton, the last an undergraduate who was soon to distinguish himself as a soldier. Speeches were given by Professors Peck and Fairchild and by Fitch, Plumb, and Langston, all of whom expressed satisfaction that the hour of decision had arrived. A vigilance committee was appointed "to take such action as circumstances may demand"; the Musical Union sang the "spirit-stirring" Marseillaise and the Star Spangled Banner. No effort, however, was made to secure enlistments, the village fathers counselling delay.[5]

The students of the College, however, were not to be put off. With the consent of the faculty they held a meeting on Friday evening and made plans for the enlistment of a company. The next morning a participant wrote to his brother: "It is in the midst of the most intense and alarming excitement that I address you these lines. WAR! and volunteers are the only topics of conversation or thought. The lessons today have been a mere form. I cannot study. I cannot sleep, I cannot work, and I don't know as I can write."[6] Professor and State Senator Monroe arrived from Columbus on Saturday and called for enlistments at a meeting held that night. Forty-eight young men came forward and entered their names on the rolls of Oberlin's first company. Over four thousand dollars was raised to outfit them. The revival technique was being effectively used again. The excitement did not abate on the Sabbath: more names were added; Father Keep rose during the giving out of the notices in church and asked if any more war news had been received; Professor Morgan preached a war sermon in the afternoon. At a meeting held on Monday evening the enlistments had reached one hundred and fifty. The Citizens' Brass Band offered to go as a unit to furnish martial music; one dear lady wrote the Governor, volunteering to nurse "those of our boys who may need

Greeley Burroughs, "Oberlin's Part in the Slavery Conflict," *Ohio Archaeological and Historical Quarterly,* XX, 269–334 (Apr.–July, 1911).

[5]*Lorain County News,* Apr. 17, 24, 1861.

[6]Lucien Warner, *Story of My Life* (New York—1914), 39–40.

such services." On Tuesday two companies began drilling on Tappan Square.

But the faculty insisted that those under age should not go without the consent of their parents and that the weak and sickly should be weeded out, so the number was cut down to exactly one hundred organized in one company, which appropriately took the name of the Monroe Rifles in honor of the Oberlin politician-professor. Giles W. Shurtleff, a theological student and Latin tutor, was elected captain. The women of the town and the young ladies of the College turned to, to prepare such a military outfit as the time and circumstances permitted. Some began to scrape lint. On Thursday, April 25, cheered on by most of the residents and students assembled at the station, the Monroe Rifles took the cars for Cleveland where they joined the Sprague Cadets, the Cleveland Light Guards, and the National Guards of Cleveland, the Painesville Union Guards, the Hudson Infantry, the Franklin Rifles, the Tyler Guards of Ravenna, the Union Guards of Youngstown, and Company A of Warren to form the Seventh Regiment, Ohio Volunteer Infantry. They were quartered at the fair grounds of the Cuyahoga Agricultural Society—renamed for the occasion Camp Taylor. On April 29, 1861, the Oberlin company, now known as Company C, was regularly mustered in for three months' service.[7]

A few excerpts from the diary of one of the boys, Sergeant E. B. Stiles, will take us closer to the thoughts and emotions of those crowded hours:

"April 25th

"There are many changes & vicisitudes in life and among them is that of changing a student's for a soldier's life, laying aside the especial study of the gospel of peace and taking up the instruments of death. It is a strange step to take, and especially so for one who is so great a coward as myself, as little addicted to placing himself in positions of peril and yet all of this has

[7]Sources on the Monroe Rifles (Co. C, 7th Ohio Volunteer Infantry) are found in Theodore Wilder, *The History of Company C, Seventh Regiment, O. V. I.* (Oberlin—1866); Lawrence Wilson, Ed., *Itinerary of the Seventh Ohio Volunteer Infantry, 1861–1864* (N. Y.—1907); *Official Roster of the Soldiers of the State of Ohio in the War of the Rebellion, 1861–1866* (Cincinnati—1886), II, 209–213. The MS Rosters of the company are in the O. C. Lib. Misc. MSS. For a romantic description of Camp Taylor see Albion W. Tourgee, *The Story of a Thousand* (Buffalo—1896), pages 1 *et seq.* The author has made much use of the MS Diary of Sergeant E. B. Stiles.

taken place to day with myself. I enlisted several days since—to day came on to the camp ground. The last few days have been filled with excitement in the usually quiet village of Oberlin. The drum has been beating to arms—great crowds assembling to listen to exciting speeches & enrol companies—two have been formed at O. . . . Started from O.[berlin] 2 P.M. Oberlin turned out *en masse* to bid us farewell. It was hard to leave those fine experiences & dear—marched through the streets at Cleveland eliciting the applause of multitudes—took supper on the camp grounds & found it better than I had expected, our quarters are not the best but we can endure it I hope.

"26th

"Did not sleep much last night, the boys laughed & joked so much that there was little chance for sleeping. This is queer business for me, we have drilled some, hope to be able to endure that part of it very well. . . .

"27th

"I should have slept some last night but it rained hard—our barrack leaked—many of us became quite wet & cold & hence were not in very good position for sleeping—was on guard 3 hours consecutive this P.M. but as I have escaped being out at night I could well afford to do it. . . .

"28th

"It has been a queer Sabbath—our company has not drilled any but others have & there has been nearly as much noise and confusion as on other days—had some services this afternoon, they were short but good. Prof. Ellis talked to our company some—we sung and had quite an interesting time. The Co. all marched down town to hear Mr. White preach. . . .

"29th

"We are not drilling near as much as the company expected hence some dissatisfaction—not very serious—we elected new officers—the result creates some dissatisfaction—it is feared a serious rupture will take place in the company tho I trust not. . . . Were mustered into service—all admitted the examination was very slight. The discipline will be more strict now.

"30th

"There are all sorts of rumors about the time of our departure & destination. I begin to realize that a soldier is nothing but a machine and is supposed to know nothing, or care nothing.

"May 1

"I had little thought when this month commenced that I should be a soldier in the U. S. service when it closed but such it seems is the fact.—Where I may be a month hence it is hard to guess—perhaps ere another 30 days shall have passed my earthly pilgrimage will have been closed. The fortunes of war are strange and unexpected—we must joyfully take them as they come, hoping for the best."

On May 5 the regiment was started from Cleveland for Camp Dennison near Cincinnati. That night was spent in Columbus. No barracks were as yet available, so the Sprague Cadets and the Monroe Rifles took over the State House, the Oberlin unit, appropriately enough, occupying the Senate Chamber. "Have each a fine sofa to rest upon to night," wrote one youngster on official Senate paper from the desk of Senator Monroe.[8] The next day, Monday, they reached the muddy, half-finished camp in the midst of a soaking rain. On Tuesday, much to the sorrow of the Oberlin boys, E. B. Tyler was elected colonel of the regiment over James Abram Garfield, their choice. But at least they had the satisfaction of knowing that the entire camp was in command of Oberlin's own newly-appointed general, Jacob Dolson Cox. The lane on which the six hastily-constructed huts assigned to the company were located was labelled College Street. The juniors and seniors called their quarters Tappan Hall; another unit was labelled in large letters LADIES' HALL. On the first week-end in Camp Dennison Professor Peck came to them from Oberlin with an offering of sweets, letters, etc. He preached to them on Sunday and found that they had already earned a unique reputation. "Them Oberlin fellows," said an outspoken sentry, "ain't worth a damn; they won't steal nor swear."[9] They were the "praying company."

[8]*Lorain County News*, May 8, 1861.

[9]Cox and Garfield had been studying military science and the campaigns of Napoleon together and were anxious to be associated on the field of battle as they had been in the legislative chamber. Garfield charged that Tyler secured his election by the use of "bargains and brandy." See J. D. Cox, *Military Reminis-*

It had become apparent to all in places of responsibility that the rebellion was not likely to be put down in the three months' period for which the first volunteers had enlisted. Therefore, on May 3, President Lincoln called for men to serve for three years. General Cox and James Monroe addressed the men of Company C on May 23, urging them to re-enlist for the longer term of service. It was argued that the moral influence of a group of men like those who composed the Oberlin company was greatly needed in the army. "Ministers of the Gospel, college alumni, and seniors, serving their country as privates, must speak eloquently for the righteous cause they had espoused." On June 1 Professor Peck again appeared in camp to add his influence to that of Cox and Monroe. ". . . Some are ashamed to turn back after putting their hand to the plough," wrote Sergeant Stiles in his diary. "Others think the demand is not urgent enough to call them away from their previous occupations—causing them to sacrifice their course of study and all their plans & bright prospects for the future . . ." About two-thirds re-enlisted. "It is hard," wrote Stiles, who was one of them, "for me to give up my studies, plans etc. but it would be harder still to remain at my desk in this hour of my country's peril." The three-years men were immediately granted a furlough, during which most of them visited Oberlin and their homes. There they received "a perfect ovation"—"old and young —grave & gay all left their usual occupations to greet & make happy the Monroe Rifle boys." At the same time the ranks were again filled to the maximum by new volunteers, also mostly Oberlin students.

The furlough enabled a majority of Company C to escape part of the uncomfortable and sickly days in the mirey camp. The supply of drinking water was secured at first from the Little Miami River not far below the point where a slaughter house drained into the stream. Probably a majority of the men were not immune to the ordinary childhood diseases. Many, like (the later Professor) George Frederick Wright, were not constitutionally hardy enough for the long stints of guard duty. The cooking arrangements were exceedingly bad and much poorly-prepared

cences, I, 29, and Theodore Clarke Smith, *Life and Letters of James Abram Garfield* (New Haven—1925), I, 161–165. Garfield soon after entered the service as lieutenant colonel of the 42nd O. V. I.

and half-cooked food was eaten. As a result there was a great deal of illness, and the barn which was appropriated for an emergency hospital was soon full of cases of measles, pneumonia, dysentery, and typhoid.

The men who kept their health or were not on leave drilled steadily, marching and countermarching in single file, in column of fours and in double ranks. When rifles arrived the manual of arms became the order of the day. Hardie's *Tactics* was studied by all who could obtain copies; an abridged edition was specially prepared for others. General Cox continued his reading of military history in English and French, setting an example of diligence for his subordinates. These first volunteers were evidently generally above the average, however, in physical stamina, moral character and education. General Cox speaks of three or four companies of college men being in the camp. President Lorin Andrews of Kenyon College was colonel of the Fourth Ohio.[10] When the men were sent into action the last of June they were probably no rawer than troops must necessarily be when but two months out of civil life.

On June 27, 1861, the Seventh Ohio was moved in a train of twenty-five cars, running in sections, by way of Columbus, to Bellair on the Ohio River. In the afternoon of the same day they crossed over into rebel territory. "Were I 30 or 40 feet lower I might be said to be on secession soil," Stiles wrote in his diary that night, "but now I am on the top of a house which has its foundations in a secession state. . . . This war business seems more & more like a reality. . . . I do not hesitate to go forward. My trust & hope is in an all divine one who will wisely direct my ways."

The western part of Virginia was debatable ground. Many of the mountaineers of this region were thoroughly loyal to the Union and quite unsympathetic with the Richmond government. In April and May part of the citizenry (perhaps a majority) had repudiated the seceded state administration and formed an independent loyal government. Two years later they were to secure recognition as the State of West Virginia. These Virginia Unionists demanded Federal military protection. The Baltimore and Ohio Railroad, a chief line of communication between

[10]J. D. Cox, *Military Reminiscences of the Civil War,* I, 21–39, and G. Frederick Wright, *Story of My Life and Work* (Oberlin—1916), 96–100.

the loyal East and the loyal West, was endangered in this region and must also be defended.

On May 23 a small detachment of Confederate troops actually reached the railway at the junction at Grafton, but were driven back by Ohio and Indiana troops led by General George Brinton McClellan and defeated in an engagement near Philippi, called the "first land battle of the Civil War." McClellan then cleared the Confederate troops from the northern portion of western Virginia.

Attention was, in the meantime, directed to the Kanawha valley further south where Union sentiment was less strong. General J. D. Cox was sent with a small force up the Kanawha, and General M. S. Rosecrans was ordered to march south from the Baltimore and Ohio to join forces with Cox at or near Gauley Bridge, the point where the New River and the Gauley unite to form the Kanawha. General H. A. Wise (Governor of Virginia in John Brown's day) commanded the Confederate forces in this region, where he was soon joined by General J. B. Floyd (formerly Secretary of War under Buchanan). It was fortunate for the Union cause that neither of these political generals would take orders from the other and that counsel in the Confederate camp was, therefore, divided. On July 21 came the battle of Bull Run. The Northern general McDowell was discredited and McClellan was called East to take his place. Robert E. Lee, temporarily put in the shade by Beauregard and Joseph E. Johnston, was shunted off to the mountains to take command and try to make Floyd and Wise cooperate.[11]

Cox reached Gauley Bridge on July 29 without serious opposition. Gauley Bridge is situated among rugged mountains covered then as now with a blanket of forest and laurel. The road to the Bridge passed through a narrow defile with a craggy precipice on the one side and the foaming and unfordable river, already hastening to the Falls of the Kanawha a mile below, on the other. It was a natural stronghold which could easily be held by a small force against superior numbers.

The Seventh was under the command of Rosecrans, at first, and was used by him for the most strenuous service. They were carried from the Ohio River on the Baltimore and Ohio to Graf-

[11]See Douglas S. Freeman, *R. E. Lee* (New York—1934), I, 527–541, and Cox, *Op. Cit.*, I, 59–79.

ton and then to Clarksburg; from that point they furnished their own transportation. On the night of June 29 and 30 the regiment undertook a forced march to Weston, some twenty-five miles to the south, where a considerable sum of Virginia State funds was known to be deposited. The objective was reached at five o'clock in the morning and the money was secured —and the men properly initiated into the life of the soldier. Another punishing and, this time, fruitless march to Glenville, twenty-eight miles, was made on July 8. Three companies started, but Company C was the only one to arrive before nightfall.

The regiment was reunited on July 23, and during the next month was moved on further south to Summersville and then to Kesler's Cross Lanes. Their duty at the latter point was to guard the communications between Cox at Gauley Bridge and Rosecrans, whose main force was held at Clarksburg to the north, and especially to keep an eye on Carnifex Ferry nearby, where it was feared that the Confederates might attempt to cross the Gauley. Cross Lanes was well located for this purpose, being at the intersection between a road from Gauley Bridge to Summersville and one which led to the ferry about four miles to the south.

General Floyd made a feint at attacking Cox directly at the Bridge and the latter, thereupon, ordered Colonel Tyler to march to his support with the Seventh. On August 20 and 21, therefore, the regiment made another all-night march, covering the twenty miles to Gauley Bridge before dawn. Carnifex Ferry thus being uncovered, Floyd crossed and advanced in the direction of Cross Lanes. On Saturday and Sunday, August 24 and 25, the Seventh marched back again to face him.

That Sunday night Company C was quartered in and about the Vaughan store and farmhouse at the crossroads; A and K were nearby. After a supper of salt meat, hardtack, and green corn from neighboring fields washed down with water from the Vaughan well, the men lay down in the road or stretched out on the platform before the store. They were wet through with sweat from the strenuous march and the cool night air chilled them to the bone. "I tried to sleep on the stoop," wrote Sergeant Stiles, the diarist, "no go—snuggled by the fire with the chaplain & surgeon and procured a little rest."

Here, while the men were at breakfast the next morning, they

KESLER'S CROSS LANES AS IT APPEARED IN AUGUST, 1936—
SEVENTY-FIVE YEARS AFTER THE BATTLE

The present store and post office at the "cross lanes" is on the site of the store occupied by part of Company C and destroyed at the time of the battle.

THE VAUGHAN HOUSE AT KESLER'S CROSS LANES—1936

Note the well-house. There has apparently been no reconstruction since the time of the battle. On this porch some of the wounded were cared for after the engagement.

(Photographs by the author)

GILES WALDO SHURTLEFF
(From the 1859 Class Album)

were surprised by the Confederates, who poured over the hills from the south and east in greatly superior numbers. "More crackers & meat for breakfast," continued Stiles. "While we were eating crack! crack! went the guns of our pickets. We were nearly surrounded & attacked by Floyd's brigade of from 3500 to 4000 men with cavalry & artillery—made some resistance—fled—had hard times in the woods—were again surprised & taken prisoners by Col. Tompkin[s] & Capt. Barber, others escaped—were led back through the old camp of the enemies and our imprisonment began. They have treated us very kindly so far."

Company C played in tough luck, being surprised and surrounded by a superior force in its first engagement. Apparently Colonel Tyler had not made proper disposal of his men to guard against such an attack and the regiment was caught completely unprepared. Only Companies K, A and C made any show of resistance, rallying on the hill behind the Vaughan house. For this, Company C paid dearly, being cut off from their fleeing comrades, and thirty-four, including Captain Shurtleff, captured. The others scattered through the woods, hiding in the laurel whenever enemy troops approached, and, after various adventures, found their way through the enemy lines and back to the regiment at Gauley Bridge. General Floyd reported to Lee: "Tyler's command is said to be of their best troops. They were certainly brave men."[12] Two college boys, Joseph Collins and Burford Jeakins (one of the captives), died of their wounds. Though it was an isolated affair and though Company C fought in many other more famous and victorious battles, the affair at Kesler's Cross Lanes should always be remembered as the Oberlin boys' first baptism of fire and, therefore, for them, and for Oberlin, "one of the most memorable fights of the war."[13]

Twenty-nine of the men of Company C who were captured at Cross Lanes were to experience life in several Southern prisons

[12]Floyd to Lee, Aug. 26, 1861, in Wilson, *Itinerary of the Seventh Ohio,* 72.

[13]Wilder, *Op. Cit.,* 13–14. The best accounts of the battle of [Kesler's] Cross Lanes are in Wilson, *Op. Cit.,* 60–101, especially that by the regimental chaplain on pages 72–79. See also J. D. Cox, *Op. Cit.,* I, 94–97, and *Official Records of the War of the Rebellion,* series I, vol. LI, Part I, 444–462. There is a good brief statement of the experience of one Oberlin boy in the MS Diary of Selden Bingham Kingsbury. The author cleared up a number of points by a visit to the spot in August, 1936. He is indebted to Mrs. Gladys Vaughan Amick of Kesler's Cross Lanes for hospitality and for her account of the battle in the *Fayette Tribune* (Fayette, W. Va.), Aug. 27, 1936.

and endure hardships as great as those of the battlefield and more demoralizing.

From the banks of the Gauley they were marched overland, the private soldiers tied together with a rope in the manner of a slave coffle. Captain Shurtleff and another officer were granted temporary parole and were, therefore, enabled to do something for the comfort of their comrades. There was not much that they could do, however, and the march was unpleasant enough: the men were lightly clad; the food was poor and inadequately cooked; on at least one night the prisoners camped in the open in a cold, drenching rain. The route was that of the present U. S. Highway 60 east through White Sulphur Springs and Lewisburg over the mountains to Jackson Station and Jackson River where they were loaded onto freight cars to be taken to Staunton.[14]

From Staunton, the next day, they were taken by train to Richmond where the officers were separated from the enlisted men, the former being placed in Liggon's tobacco warehouse, the latter in a similar building owned by John Wilder Atkinson. Selden B. Kingsbury, a freshman, here made a little notebook from material in the old office of the tobacco company in which he recorded his prison experiences:

"Sept. 4, 1861.

"Bread and meat for breakfast, I believe that I am home sick. I know I am sick. We have food twice a day. A little food and plenty of guards. When will I see home. My heart aches.

"Thursday—Sept. 5, 61.

"Our bed is the bare floor. We have no blankets. Six men were wanted to wash some clothes for wounded prisioners. I volunteer and feel better for haveing something to do.

"Fryday—6, 1861.

"How long the day is! How hard it is to have nothing to do! I almost envy the Slaves that I see pass to and fro before my bared

[14]MS Stiles Diary and Shurtleff letter in *Lorain County News,* June 4, 1862. See also Shurtleff's reminiscences in Lawrence Wilson, *Op. Cit.,* 316–329, and "My First Week of Captivity" in W. H. Jeffrey, *Richmond Prisons, 1861–1862* (St. Johnsbury, [Vt.—c. 1893]), 105–109.

windo. I am resolved to try and find something to busy myself with. I wish I had a Greek Testament."[15]

The Oberlin boys had little more in common with their irreligious fellow-prisoners than with their Confederate captors. "I do wish that Co. C could be by themselves," wrote Stiles, "then we would have some peace—anything but this cloud of smoke, spittle & horrid oaths." He continued: "September 7th Sat.—Have read some Paradise Lost. I must have me a Bible. How can I live without one? My health continues good—begin to feel the need of exercise. It is so different from the past 4 or 5 months. Shall have to practice Stewart." (The co-founder's doctrine of abstemiousness was evidently not wholly forgotten.) The next day was Sunday. "Oh, what a Sabbath! As much smoking, playing of cards, etc as ever—no church—No prayer meeting—or anything to distinguish the day."

Captain Shurtleff, in the meantime, was in somewhat pleasanter company, being associated with the officers and one Congressman (!) who had been captured at Bull Run. He was able to spend his time profitably reading Thier's *Consulate and Empire,* two novels of Thackeray, and Livy and Virgil, which books he purchased by the sale of his watch to one of the Confederate officers. On September 10 he was allowed to visit his men and say farewell to them, as the authorities had decided to remove part of the prisoners to Charleston. In company with some thirty other officers, including Colonel Corcoran of the 69th New York, and a considerable number of enlisted men, he was taken to the home of secession. At Charleston they were paraded through the streets behind a brass band to the great satisfaction of the populace who had not seen any Yankee prisoners before.[16]

Shurtleff's prison experience included the two prisons in Charleston, the one at Columbia, South Carolina, "Libby" at Richmond, and Salisbury, North Carolina. At Charleston the prisoners were kept in Castle Pinckney and the jail—most of

[15]The MS Kingsbury Diary contains entries previous to the time the book was made—evidently from memory—Aug. 25, 1861, to Feb. 29, 1862. These men were not in "Libby." Libby prison was not established until the summer of 1862. See Jeffrey, *Op. Cit.,* 89.

[16]See the *Journal of Alfred Ely, a Prisoner of War in Richmond* (New York—1862), and *The Captivity of General Corcoran etc.* (Philadelphia—1864). The latter is highly colored and melodramatic.

the time in the city jail. On December 1 Shurtleff wrote to a fellow-tutor at Oberlin:

"Well, here we are, huddled together, 30 officers and 120 men, in the most filthy, uncomfortable jail in the world. Officers 7 and 8 in a room 10 by 15; men 15 in a room the same size. I, and most others, are destitute of money and nearly destitute of clothing. The privates are many of them almost naked. Their rations are three hard crackers per day, about 3 ozs. meat, coffee and sugar for one meal. Ours is the same."[17]

"I think often of Oberlin and its dear people," he continued, "I fear for the interests of the Institution there during this crisis. I hope no course will be taken which shall weaken its power for good. I never before estimated the value of a thorough Christian education as I do now. I confess that my desire to get safely through this struggle and devote my life with all its energies to the dissemination of Christian education is most intense. I tell you, Merrell, the position you now occupy is one of the greatest responsibility and the greatest usefulness. I am glad you occupy it. Please remember me to my old pupils who may enquire about me."

On the first day of 1862 Shurtleff and others were moved to Columbia. The next day he wrote to James Monroe requesting that money, clothing and books (Herodotus and a Lexicon) be sent him. The captain always described the treatment received in Columbia in most favorable terms. ". . . Have seen more humanity and courtesy manifested here during the last 18 hours than during all our previous experience in the south," he declared to Monroe.[18] The comfort of the prisoners was added to by the articles which they purchased with Confederate paper money counterfeited by them in the jail!

Then came the joyous news that they were to be returned to Richmond for exchange! But the negotiations between the two governments relative to the terms dragged while they spent two months in the notorious Libby prison.[19] Here Shurtleff and a few companions, encouraged by the sound of the guns of McClellan's army, which was then approaching Richmond from the Peninsula, concocted an elaborate scheme for escape. They secured

17Printed in the *Lorain County News,* May 14, 1862.
18Shurtleff to Monroe, Jan. 2, 1862 (Monroe MSS).
19*Lorain County News,* June 8, 1862.

civilian clothes, cut iron bars with a saw made from a watch spring, made a hole through a floor of two-inch oak planks with a pocket knife and then tunneled through a brick wall! But their plan was foiled—and they were sent back south to the prison in Salisbury, North Carolina, early in May of 1862.

At Salisbury, though the private soldiers suffered considerably at first from close confinement and unsanitary surroundings, the officers were well housed and allowed considerable freedom for outdoor exercise in the yard of the prison. They seized the opportunity to organize baseball teams and played almost every day. On July 4, 1862, a special game was played for the entertainment of visitors from the town—this besides a greased pig race, a sack race and a wheelbarrow race. But the Oberlin captain, though taking an active part in all these games, was depressed by the irreligious atmosphere. In May he wrote a letter on thin paper which was compressed so that it would go into a brass button of an exchanged soldier's uniform and thus be carried through the lines. "Profanity & obscenity are ringing in my ears constantly," he wrote. "Oh for a breath of the precious atmosphere of our village. It seems to me now that I shall want to spend my life with you after the war is over, absorbing and enjoying the social and religious influence prominent among you."[20]

It was late in the following month that Captain Shurtleff was finally exchanged. "It was just at sunset of a bright Sabbath day in August," he wrote later, "that we stepped from rebel soil upon the flag of truce boat on the James River and saw the Stars and Stripes waving over our heads. We gathered beneath that flag, reverently uncovered our heads, and sang 'Praise God from whom all blessings flow.' "[21]

Oberlinites were following the careers of Company C in prison and on the battlefield with anxious pride, and the return of the captain and tutor was properly celebrated. Of course, the students and residents gathered to greet him at the meeting house. "And a more glad, hearty, emphatic welcome, stranger or citizen never received at Oberlin before," reported the *News*. "Applause on applause swelled and filled the church as the Cap-

[20]Shurtleff to Peck, May 21, 1862 (O. C. Lib. Misc. MSS).

[21]Lawrence Wilson, *Op. Cit.*, 326–329. Shurtleff's exchange was not officially dated until Sept. 21, 1862—*Official Records of the War of the Rebellion,* series II, Vol. IV, 583.

tain, thin and pale from his long confinement, ascended the stand. . . . A brief welcome speech from the Chairman, Mr. Fitch, was followed by an interesting recital by Capt. S. of incidents connected with his year's imprisonment. . . . The hearty hand-shakings that followed the close of the meeting must have assured the Captain that the welcome extended him was not one of mere ceremony. He has a furlough of thirty days in which to recruit health and strength, when he will again take the field."[22] But when he did "again take the field" it was not with the old company, but as commander of a regiment of Negro soldiers.

The rank and file of the Oberlin prisoners remained in Richmond eleven more days after Shurtleff's removal to Charleston, keeping themselves mentally fit by studying French, German and Latin, though occasionally disturbed by the firing into the windows by drunken guards. Of the thirty-four prisoners taken at Cross Lanes, one died of wounds soon after, four were recaptured—the remaining twenty-nine were sent to Richmond. Shurtleff, as we have seen, was separated from his command. Private Lucius V. Tuttle was sent to the prison at Tuscaloosa, Alabama. The remaining twenty-seven were removed to New Orleans.[23]

In New Orleans the prisoners were placed in the old Parish Prison (the city jail), a massive and gloomy stone structure built back in the days of French occupation. Here they were not only associated with criminals, but actually placed under the supervision of "trusties," much to their disgust. The men were badly overcrowded in their cells. The space in some cells was indeed so limited that all must lie on the same side at night "spoon fashion," like slaves on the middle passage, and all turn over at once—if at all. For several weeks no blankets were issued, but the men suffered more from heat and lack of air than from cold. A few hours every day they were granted some relief by being allowed to visit the yard, an area in the center of the building "about 3 by 6 rods in size—paved—with a water tank in one

[22] *Lorain County News,* Aug. 27, 1862.

[23] See Theodore Wilder, *History of Company C,* 44–82; Lawrence Wilson, *Itinerary of the Seventh Ohio,* 549–561; *Official Roster of the Soldiers of the State of Ohio . . . 1861–1866,* II, 209–213; and William H. Jeffrey, *Richmond Prisons, 1861–1862,* page 240. Jeffrey's list is taken from the Confederate prison records. It contains many errors; many of the names are misspelled and Christian names are often entirely erroneous.

corner." From one side the scaffold cast its menacing shadow on the flagstones; no green thing was visible. The semi-tropic sun kept the bricks and stones at a baking temperature. At night and when any of the prison rules had been disobeyed they were again returned to the stifling stench of the overcrowded cells.[24]

There is little wonder that most of them sickened—the victims of the heat, the unsanitary conditions, lack of exercise and air and poor rations. Several were infected with typhoid. Private Biggs, a country boy from near Elyria, and the brave Sergeant Parmenter, a senior in Oberlin College when he enlisted, succumbed.

But the mental and spiritual suffering of sensitive minds must have been worse than any physical disease or hardship. To combat monotony and morbid despair the men turned to carving bone, making rings, pendants, stilettoes, penholders—all sorts of "bone jewelry." Some of the cleverer ones became exceedingly skillful and sold enough of these articles to visitors and guards to purchase much-needed additions to their prison fare, especially molasses, fruit and fresh vegetables. Saws, files and other tools officially forbidden were smuggled in by interested guards.

Of the twenty-seven prisoners from Company C in New Orleans exactly twenty were Oberlin students, and they, true to their training, initiated various intellectual activities. Latin grammars were in great demand among them and several spent much time reading Livy, Caesar and Virgil. There was probably even more interest in modern languages. Sergeant Stiles found a real French tutor among his fellows, whom he was glad to discover to be a "bad Catholic!" At the end of his diary he listed "Books read while a prisoner." These included Mary J. Holmes' *Lena Rivers,* Susan Warner's *The Hills of Shatemuc, Tom Brown at Rugby,* Dickens' *Bleak House, Nicholas Nickelby,* and *Pickwick,* Hawthorne's *House of the Seven Gables* and Milton's *Paradise Lost,* Pope's *Poetical Works* and Shakespeare, as well as such religious works as *Pilgrim's Progress,* Richard Baxter's *Saint's Everlasting Rest,* Jonathan Edwards' *Religious Affection, The Life of Captain Vicars* (the pious autobiography of an

[24]Stiles MS Diary, Sept. 30, 1861, *et seq.:* Kingsbury MS Diary, and Morey, in L. Wilson. *Op. Cit.,* 336 and 337. Kingsbury wrote (Oct. 10), "We are almost sufficated every morning and evening when we are shut in our cells with closed doors."

English officer in the Crimean War), and two publications of the American Tract Society: William Allen Hallock's *Memoir of Harlan Page: or The Power of Prayer* and John Angell James' *The Anxious Enquirer after Salvation.*

The Oberlin boys, several of them Phi Delts and Phi Kaps, also led in the formation of a debating society, the *Union* Lyceum.[25] They met once a week and elected officers and listened to orations and debates and the reading of the manuscript paper called "The Stars and Stripes." Exactly half of the first officers were Oberlinites. W. H. Scott, the vice-president, was an *absentia* graduate of Oberlin in the Class of 1861; both members of the debate committee were from Oberlin; Leroy Warren (A. B., 1858, Sem. 1861) and Edwin P. Smith, a freshman in 1861; Alexander Parker, on the declamation committee, was a classmate of Warren's. The main feature on the program of the first regular meeting held on November 28, 1861, was a debate on the question "*Resolved,*—That the present war will be ended by the Spring of 1862" conducted entirely by Oberlin boys: Scott, Warren, Parker, Stiles and Smith.

But probably the reading of "The Stars and Stripes" attracted more interest than any other portion of these programs. A variety of headings was used:

THE STARS AND STRIPES.
A Weekly Publication, Devoted to Literature,
Science, The Arts, and General

INTELLIGENCE.

Published every Thursday in the Parish Prison, N. O.

Price: Attention.
Editor, J. W. Dickens.
Vol. 1 December 12, 1861. No. 3.

And—

THE STARS AND STRIPES.

Floating at Parish Prison, New Orleans.

Published in Cell No. 9, Third Floor, by the Union Lyceum.

Motto: "Liberty and Union, now and forever, one and inseparable."
Editor, Wm. C. Bates.
Vol.II. January, 1862. No. 1.

[25]"This lyceum was supported mainly by students from Oberlin College . . . ," wrote "a Member of Company B, 2nd New Hampshire Regiment Volunteers," who was also a prisoner.—Jeffrey, *Richmond Prisons,* 147.

When the Oberlin theolog, Leroy Warren, was editor, the motto was *Philippians IV, 8*: "Finally, brethren, whatsoever things are true, whatsoever things are honest, whatsoever things are just, whatsoever things are pure, whatsoever things are lovely, whatsoever things are of good report; if there be any virtue, and if there be any praise, think on these things." An excellent motto for pious young men exposed to so many temptations.[26]

"The Stars and Stripes" contained essays, poems, letters to the editor, news (mostly "local intelligence") and notices, all with a sprinkling of soldier humor. There were even market reports:

"Bread. – Readily taken in small quantities.
Bone. – Sales small, owing to change of guard.
Soup. – Considerable decrease, owing to abundance of water.
Rice. – None in market.
Meat. – Heavy.
Woollens – Very abundant in the form of rags."

Of course, there were many jokes about food and clothing:

"We notice a growing disposition among the prisoners to break out,–particularly in the pants!"

"The boys in No. 4 who were so frightened by finding a few grains of rice in their soup on Tuesday are recovering. Joe Mullaly [a criminal who served as cook] assures us it was a mistake."

"Notice to Prisoners.

"All prisoners of war leaving for the North during the month of December are cautioned that the weather there is generally cooler at this season than here, and it would be well to get accustomed to the wearing of pants or jackets before leaving their present quarters; otherwise their awkardness may attract attention in Washington and at home."

A sober note was not wanting, however, as in the letter from "In Earnest" decrying the "twin demons," "the very common vices of vulgarity and profanity."–"In many of our cells the last words you will hear at night, and the first in the morning will be either vulgar or profane." The letter is anonymous but the reader is morally certain that the author of it had sat at the feet of Finney.

[26]Portions were later published as *The Stars and Stripes in Rebeldom, a Series of Papers Written by Federal Prisoners (Privates) in Richmond, Tuscaloosa, New Orleans, and Salisbury, N. C.* (Boston–1862).

The Oberlin boys were sorely troubled by the vicious and irreligious character of many of their associates. "I wonder how much virtue there is in the Northern army?" mused Stiles. "Judging by the portion visible at present it is a very small quantity. Oh that the soldiers were all good virtuous God-fearing men! Then could they trust in an arm stronger than man's. Then would God lead them on to victory & success till truth & righteousness prevailed."

Often Sabbaths passed much like any other day to the great distress of the active Christians. Occasionally ministers came among them to preach, but even then the results were not all good, as when one man prayed for "Thy servant, Jefferson Davis, President of the Confederate States!" There was much longing for the pious atmosphere of Oberlin. "How I would like to have been there as on former Fri[days]! Blessed seasons were those spent in the chapel or Soc.[iety] rooms—wonder if I shall enjoy the like again," Stiles wrote in his diary. Again on a Monday evening: "How I would like to be at the Young People's Meeting this eve. . . . Wonder if we are remembered in their prayers. Without doubt." The Oberlin boys did all they could to bring Oberlin atmosphere into the morbid and vicious life of the prison. They conducted Bible classes every Sunday and prayer meetings twice a week, regularly announced in "The Stars and Stripes."

But with all their efforts to occupy the time, their life was often, of course, depressingly dull. For nearly a week Selden Kingsbury did not write at all in his diary. "Our prison life is so monotonous," he explained, "that one gets tired of writing the same things over every night." On another day he spent most "of the time walking, eating and wishing." But there were red-letter days like the one when the men were surprised "by an order for Co. C, 7th Reg. to fall into a line down in the yard. After thus formed letters were distributed to most of us. I received one from Theod Wilder and together with other class mates here one from our Class mate, Mr. Adams. How pleasant it is for a prisoner of war to receive those most strong proofs of friendship." —Then there was that day when it was announced that they were to be removed from the prison!

It was the first day of February, 1862. "Never did mortal feel happier than did our prisoners this P.M. when the General came in and told us that we should start from Parish Prison next Mon. Tues. or Wednes.—The boys could hardly contain themselves but performed all manner of antics."[27] The prisoners were merely being taken to another prison as it turned out, because of the threatening approach of Admiral Farragut and General Butler toward New Orleans—but, anyway, it was a change! They partially retraced the route by which they had come south—by train through Jackson to Mobile, up the river from Mobile to Montgomery and from Montgomery again by rail east through Georgia into North Carolina where they were placed in a former cotton factory building at Salisbury,the same prison depot where their own Captain Shurtleff was held.

On May 21 the parole of honor was signed and on the 30th and 31st they travelled in box cars to Tarboro where they spent Sunday, June 1, the ringing of the church bells reminding the boys of Company C of "dear old Oberlin and its precious Sabbath." From Tarboro they were sent down the Tar River to Little Washington, "the well on a couple of scows, the sick in the miserable old cabin of the boat." On June 3 they were released to officers of Burnside's command. "O most blessed of all happy days! Greeting—farewell!!!—farewell bondage—farewell hunger, thirst, & all manner of ills. About 7 o'clock we were cheered by the sight of the star spangled banner & soon we passed forever, I hope, from the hands of southern rebels." They were placed on board a comfortable little steamer and landed at New York on June 10, 1862.[28] Part of the men were mustered out because of physical disabilities resulting from their prison experience; others returned to Company C or followed Captain Shurtleff into the colored regiment which he commanded.

* * *

The remnants of the Seventh who escaped capture reassembled at Gauley Bridge under the immediate eye of General Cox, spending some weeks of a fine autumn there in complete inaction, enjoying the swimming and boating on the Kanawha, gathering paw-paws and persimmons. There at Gauley they were visited by Professor Peck who presented the regiment with a fine silk flag. He reported that the men were in excellent spirits despite

[27]Stiles MS Diary.
[28]*Ibid.*, Feb. 15 to June 10, 1862; *Stars and Stripes in Rebeldom*, 125–127.

their recent misadventure. The latter part of October the boys were removed to Charleston where the members of Company C were given a library by a local citizen in recognition of their character as student soldiers. This library was later carried east with the quartermaster's stores. At Charleston also an escaped slave who came to camp was turned over by Colonel Tyler to the "abolitionist" company and sent north by them to Oberlin for education.[29]

In mid-winter they were moved east to the Valley of Virginia where, during the next six months, they were to learn something of the art of war from that master teacher, "Stonewall" Jackson. At the battle of Kernstown Corporal A. C. Danforth, a sophomore, and three other members of Company C were killed. Danforth's body was brought back to Oberlin and impressive funeral services were held for him in the church. "I remember seeing the bullet hole in his overcoat," wrote an Oberlin boy nearly seventy years later.[30] Sergeant Day was "mentioned in the despatches" for capturing a lieutenant from Jackson's personal staff. The company lost three more killed at Port Republic.

In the summer of 1862 Company C was camped at Alexandria, from which point the Oberlin boys undertook patriotic tours of Washington and Mt. Vernon. Here the brigade celebrated Independence Day. There was a display of fireworks; Sergeant Charles P. Bowler, a College junior and Phi Delt, read the Declaration before the brigade. On the next day the men received Springfield rifles to take the place of their flintlock muskets. In August they were in the army which attacked Jackson at Cedar Mountain. In this engagement the Seventh Ohio lost nearly 60% killed and wounded, the greatest punishment endured by any Ohio unit in any single battle. Of Company C only four passed through unhurt; five were killed, including the elocutionist of July 4, Sergeant Bowler. The survivors fought also at Antietam.[31]

The autumn was spent in camp on the heights across the river from Harper's Ferry. Here the company's sadly depleted

[29]Wilson, *Op. Cit.*, 104–105, and Wilder, *Op. Cit.*, 17–18.

[30]Edward S. Steele to the author, June 3, 1931. Henry Cowles Smith (A. B. 1862) also remembered the event. Smith to the author, Dec., 1930.

[31]Lawrence Wilson, *Itinerary of the Seventh Ohio*, 421–422; William F. Fox, *Regimental Losses in the American Civil War* (Albany—1889), page 36, and *Report* of the Ohio Antietam Battlefield Commission (Springfield—c. 1904), 39.

strength was partially re-established by the addition of thirty-one new recruits. Here, also, Captain Shurtleff found them upon his return from Southern prisons, but did not resume command.

They camped in the Virginia mud during the winter of 1862–63, fought at Chancellorsville in May and at Round Top and Culp's Hill at Gettysburg in July. In the fall they were moved by train to join Grant in eastern Tennessee, where he was assembling an army to take revenge on Bragg for the battle of Chickamauga.

There they followed Hooker up Lookout Mountain into the famous "Battle Above the Clouds," though they suffered comparatively light losses, the enemies' guns being fired chiefly over their heads. Members of Company C never forgot the eclipse of the moon which they saw that night from their picket posts on the mountainside overlooking the Moccasin Bend of the Tennessee. Later many of them climbed to the highest crags hunting mementoes. Sergeant Cole "got some *laurel* and some rocks from the dizzy heights."

The original volunteers had now nearly finished their three years' period of service and, therefore, an effort was made to secure their re-enlistment, but most of them, including all of Company C, felt that they had done their share. The veterans of the Seventh reached Cleveland June 26, 1864, and encamped on Cleveland Heights to be mustered out. Only sixteen of the original Monroe Rifles returned to Oberlin at the time. Sergeant O. C. Trembley, who had fought through three years without being wounded, fell off the boat and was drowned in the Ohio River when a short distance below Cincinnati. This was in many ways the most tragic event in the history of the company. The official date of the muster-out was July 6, 1864.

The Seventh Ohio had a great record and a sad history. Fox, in his *Regimental Losses in the American Civil War,* calls it "one of the finest regiments in the service. . . . composed of exceptionally good material." The Seventh stood second in battle losses among Ohio's 198 infantry regiments in the war, and, as we have seen, it sustained the severest punishment suffered by any Ohio regiment in any one battle—at Cedar Mountain. Company C's losses were greater than those of any other single company in the regiment. Out of 151 enrolled 28 were killed or died of wounds; five died from other causes; 68 were wounded; 40 were taken prisoner—34 at Cross Lanes. Company C was the only company in the regiment to report no deserters.[32]

[32]Fox, *Op. Cit.*, 312, and Wilson, *Op. Cit.*, 628. M. M. Andrews, in the *Roster of the Survivors of Company C, 7th Ohio Volunteer Infantry* (n.p.—1909), page 15, gives the total three years' enrollment as 151, killed in battle 30, died of disease, 7, and drowned, 1. Perhaps his list of casualties includes some three-months men.

CHAPTER L

FIGHT FOR FREEDOM

BUT Company C was only one of several units of Oberlin soldiers. In the early autumn of 1861 a company made up chiefly of farmers from the neighboring district was recruited with the aid of Professor Peck and James Monroe. Fifty-two men were secured and organized as the Lorain Guards, choosing Alonzo H. Pease, the painter and nephew of Peter Pindar Pease, captain, and John W. Steele, son of a local doctor, first lieutenant. They were mustered in at Cleveland September 17, 1861, and became Company H of the 41st Ohio Volunteer Infantry. The regiment played a part in many decisive engagements, among them Shiloh, Chickamauga, Chattanooga, Resaca and the siege of Atlanta. Pease resigned because the colonel insisted on returning escaped slaves to their masters. Steele rose to the rank of major.[1]

At about the same time nine Oberlin boys (later joined by a tenth) enlisted in the 2nd Ohio Cavalry, the first cavalry unit to be raised in the northern part of the state. Among this group were Alvred Bayard Nettleton, a college junior and popular student leader, Charles Grandison Fairchild, Luman Tenney, who had just completed his prep course, John Devlin and William P. Bushnell, also preps. Fairchild's most intimate friend, William N. Hudson, son of the late beloved Professor Timothy B. Hudson, now left behind in Oberlin, could not forbear writing him a note on the very next day:

"Oberlin, Sept. 17, 1861

"My dear Charlie:

* * *

"You had just time, in the midst of the crowd and discomfort,

[1]Robert L. Kimberly and Ephraim S. Halloway, *The Forty-First Ohio Volunteer Infantry in the War of the Rebellion 1861–1865* (Cleveland—1897), 227 *et seq.* and *passim;* and *Official Roster of . . . Ohio,* IV, 197–200. For a sketch of Steele see Wilbur H. Phillips, *Oberlin Colony, the Story of a Century* (Oberlin—1933), 221–224.

to catch my hand for a moment, and to touch the extended fingertips of the two Dulcinias. Libbie had borrowed my handkerchief to wave her farewells to you and Luman, and they were crazy to see you both. I searched for you—alas unsuccessfully—with might and main. Didn't get a glance at Luman. Bid John Devlin good-bye and got a glimpse of Willie Bushnell as he stood on the rear car and shook hands with Dan. Childs, who for that privilege ran frantically after the train. I was very sorry not to see Luman & not to talk longer with you, but consoled myself and walked home with the Dulcinias aforesaid.

"I have been thinking about you dear boys in camp to-night under the cold drizzling storm. Your situation is different enough from mine. I sit here in my little room with my lamp burning before me and the brighter light of pleasant memories and ambitious hope. The snugness of the room is enhanced by the drizzle outside. Across the darkness comes the sweet voice of Phebe Haynes. Here am I with my loved books and loved friends around me—there you perhaps on guard in the dreary night. Dear, dear boys, God bless & keep you! God send that you may come again speedily and uninjured.

"Love, much love to dear Luman. Love, much love to your dear self. Remember me to Nettleton, Willie Bushnell and any other friends with you. You may rest assured that wherever you are, you are followed by anxious eyes & loving hearts—Goodbye for now.

Will."[2]

The Second Ohio Cavalry had a long, brilliant service, fighting with and against the Indians in the southwest, chasing Quantrell and Morgan, raiding into Tennessee, under Mead and Grant in the Wilderness, in Custer's division under Sheridan in the Valley of Virginia and at Five Forks. They marched and fought 22,000 miles through twelve states and one territory, watering their horses in twenty-two rivers from the Arkansas to the Appomattox. Tenney rose to the rank of major and Nettleton commanded the regiment on the last charge at Five Forks and was brevetted brigadier general for gallantry.[3] The

[2]In Oberlin College Library.

[3]The best source on the 2nd Ohio is the charming *War Diary of Luman Harris Tenney, 1861–1865* (Cleveland—1914). See also Whitelaw Reid, *Ohio in the War,* II, 757 *et seq.,* and the published reports of the reunions in 1903, 1904, 1905, 1906, 1907, 1911, and 1915. There is a sketch of Nettleton in the *D. A. B.*

A STUDENT SOLDIER OF THE SIXTIES—
COLONEL ALVRED BAYARD NETTLETON
(From the *War Diary of Luman Harris Tenney,* 1861–1865 [Cleveland—1914], page 139)

Second suffered the heaviest battle losses of any of Ohio's thirteen cavalry regiments. ". . . In my entire division, numbering twelve regiments from different states," General Custer wrote to the Governor of Ohio in February of 1865, "I have none in which I repose greater confidence than the 2nd Ohio."[4]

In May of 1862 when Stonewall Jackson, driving his troops to superhuman efforts, thrust aside all opposition in the Shenandoah Valley, captured Winchester and threatened Maryland, he gave Washington a great fright. The War Department thereupon sent out a hurry call for troops to defend the capital. Governor Tod of Ohio immediately issued a proclamation asking for three months' volunteers to meet the emergency. The response was prompt: twenty-seven out of the thirty-three students in the Cleveland Law School joined up; some twenty-odd came from Western Reserve College. Forty Oberlin boys, including a considerable percentage of students, organized the "Chase Cadets" and were mustered into service at Columbus on June 10, 1862. The Oberlin men were scattered, but most of them went into the 87th Ohio Volunteer Infantry which served at Baltimore and Harper's Ferry, where it was needlessly surrendered by Colonel Miles. Their term of service being out before the surrender, however, they were paroled, sent home and mustered out at Columbus on September 20, 1862.[5]

In the meantime, in August, another three years' company was raised in Oberlin and vicinity and became Company F of the 103rd Ohio Volunteer Infantry. Philip C. Hayes, a theological student who had graduated from the College in 1860, was captain. At the end of the war he rose to the colonelcy of the regiment and was brevetted a brigadier general.[6]

In September Cincinnati was all a-jitter because the Confederate General Kirby Smith was raiding up through Kentucky. Governor Tod seems to have shared the panic of most of his fellow Ohioans. All newly recruited Ohio troops such as the

[4]William F. Fox, *Regimental Losses in the American Civil War,* 491, and Tenney, *Op. Cit.,* 145.

[5]*Lorain County News,* June 11, 1862, and Reid, *Op. Cit.,* II, 490. See the *General Catalogue of Oberlin College* (1908) for their regimental positions. The *News* gives a list of names.

[6]*Official Roster;* Reid,*Op. Cit.,* II, 556 *et seq;* G. F. Wright *History of Lorain County,* I, 263–267, and Philip C. Hayes, *Journal-History of the Hundred and Third Ohio Volunteer Infantry* (Bryan, Ohio—1872).

103rd were ordered to the defense of the Queen City. Lew Wallace took charge of the troops and began throwing up entrenchments. The Governor issued a dramatic call for men: "Our southern border is threatened with invasion. I have therefore to recommend that all loyal men . . . form . . . into military companies and regiments to beat back the enemy at any and all points. . . . Gather up all arms in the country, and furnish yourselves with ammunition for the same. . . . The soil of Ohio must not be invaded." The order was literally obeyed by tens of thousands of Ohioans. The proclamation was received in Oberlin on September 4, and on the following day a mass meeting of all citizens and students was held on the square. Committees were appointed to enroll volunteers, collect muskets, rifles and supplies and drill guards to protect the home town. Some eighty Oberlin boys, mostly from the college and preparatory classes volunteered to go to the defense of Cincinnati. Approximately sixty others from neighboring towns joined them at the railroad station. Without uniforms, of course, and armed with whatever rusty old firearms could be dug up, one cannot help but wonder whether they were a military asset or not when they reached the city. They were, nevertheless, welcomed by the frightened citizens "with open arms and free lunches." Part of the group was sent home within a few days, but the majority organized a company under William M. Ampt, a college senior, as captain and remained on guard duty for a month until all danger of attack had clearly passed. None was ever regularly mustered into the military service, but they were given free passes on the railways and honorable discharges from the service of the "Squirrel Hunters of Ohio."[7]

At first the United States Government had refused to accept Negro recruits, and Governor Tod of Ohio was particularly averse to any such recognition of the citizenship of the colored man. In 1862, however, General David Hunter organized a regiment among the fugitive slaves in North Carolina and his example was followed in Louisiana and elsewhere. The first

[7]Reid, I, 83–98; *Oberlin Evangelist,* Sept. 10, 1862; *Lorain County News,* Sept. 10, 1862; Lucien Warner *Story of My Life,* 44 (Warner's dates are wrong and he has confused Smith and Morgan); N. E. Jones, *The Squirrel Hunters of Ohio* (Cincinnati—1898), pages 335 *et seq.* There is a reproduction of a Squirrel Hunter's discharge on page 344 of Jones. Discharges were received in Oberlin in June, 1863 (*Lorain County News,* June 10, 1863).

Negro regiment to be recruited by a Northern state was the famous 54th Massachusetts. This regiment was sponsored by prominent anti-slavery Republicans such as George L. Stearns, Amos A. Lawrence, Ralph Waldo Emerson, Professor Louis Agassiz, Samuel J. May, Gerrit Smith, John G. Palfrey and Wendell Phillips. Negro recruits were drawn from all over the North. As recruiting officer in the West, James Mercer Langston, the Negro lawyer of Oberlin (A.B., 1849), was selected. He was assisted by O. S. B. Wall, a Negro shoemaker also of Oberlin.[8] Langston's success in securing recruits is evidenced by the large number of soldiers in the regiment from Ohio, Indiana and Illinois. Among these were twenty-one from Oberlin.[9] This was the regiment which gained such martial laurels at Fort Wagner, South Carolina, under Colonel Robert Gould Shaw, the regiment immortalized by Augustus St. Gaudens' beautiful memorial on Boston Common. Henry N. Peal, another shoemaker from Oberlin, one of the color-bearers, was among four Negroes specially mentioned for gallantry. While carrying his flag in another engagement he was mortally

[8]John M. Langston, *From the Virginia Plantation to the National Capitol* (Hartford—1894), 198 *et seq.*, and Luis F. Emilio, *History of the Fifty Fourth Regiment of the Massachusetts Volunteer Infantry, 1863–1865* (Boston—1894), pages 1–16, 328–389. References to Langston in *Ibid.*, 14, and in William Schouler, *A History of Massachusetts in the Civil War* (Boston—1868), I, 482, along with items in the *Lorain County News* (Apr. 15, May 13, May 20 and July 22, 1863), substantiate Langston's own story. Of particular interest are Governor Tod's letter to Langston in *Ibid.*, May 20, 1863, and Secretary Seward's letter to Langston in *Ibid.*, July 22, 1863. On O. S. B. Wall see Emilio, *Op. Cit.*, 12; *Lorain County News*, May 27, 1863, and C. S. Williams, *Medina, Elyria and Oberlin Directory . . .*, 106 and 108.

[9]Emilio (*Op. Cit.*) gives only fourteen names from Oberlin: *Company F:* Joseph Asberry, James E. Brown, William Mitchell, Henry T. (N) Peal, Henry J. (S) Patterson, Oliver B. Ridgeway, Edward Williams and Isaiah Wilson. *Company G:* John L. Barker, William Rutledge, Harrison Nichols, Albert Wall and John Wall (both former prep students). *Company I:* Benjamin Green. There is reason to suppose, however, that seven others from Oberlin were with the regiment. The *Lorain County News* (Apr. 15, 1863) gives the following names: Falding Brown, Leander Howard, H. N. Rankin, Samuel Smith and Simpson Younger. The Fielding Brown listed by Emilio as from Lebanon, Ohio, may be the man from Oberlin. It seems quite evident that Leander Howard listed by Emilio from *Oakland*, O. is the man by the same name from *Oberlin*, O. There are two Samuel Smiths on the regimental roster, one, whose address is given as Boston and one supposedly from Missouri. Simpson Younger, a mulatto from Missouri, was sent to Oberlin at the expense of his natural father. (See letter from Mrs. Elisha Gray to George N. Jones, Nov. 21, 1907, in the Alumni Records Office, filed under Kate F. Younger.) There is evidence that Howard Howe and J. W. Bradley of Oberlin were also members of the regiment (*Lorain County News*, Aug. 12, and Sept. 2, 1863). For Peal's record see Emilio, *Op. Cit.*, 90 and 164–166.

wounded. For a while both of the regimental flags were carried by colored boys from Oberlin. Langston also secured recruits for the 55th Massachusetts, but there is no record of any Oberlin boys entering this regiment.

To Langston also belongs the credit for the organization of the first Negro regiment from Ohio. Governor David Tod finally agreed to call a Negro regiment in the summer of 1863, and gave Langston his full support from then on. Oberlin men practically created this regiment, though apparently there was not a single Oberlin Negro in the ranks. Langston was assisted by J. A. R. Rogers (A.B., 1851; Sem., 1855), one of the first teachers of Berea, in enlisting recruits in the southern part of the state. J. B. T. Marsh (A.B., 1862), a student in the Theological Department and assistant on the staff of the *Lorain County News,* was recruiting quartermaster. Captain Giles W. Shurtleff resigned from Company C to become lieutenant colonel and then colonel of the regiment, bringing three other "C" men to aid him as commissioned officers. James L. Patton (A.B., 1859; Sem., 1862) became chaplain. All, of course, were white, as it was at first the uniform practice to officer black regiments with white men, but, being Oberlin-trained, they must have been unusually sympathetic officers. The regiment was first known as the 127th O. V. I. but later was numbered Fifth United States Colored Troops (5th U.S.C.T.).[10] It established its military record in the fighting around the "Crater" at Petersburg and at New Market Heights. Shurtleff was brevetted brigadier-general at the end of the war. His statue on South Professor Street is familiar to all visitors to Oberlin. Several Oberlinites became officers in other Negro regiments.[11] Orindatus S. B. Wall of Oberlin was commissioned a captain early in 1865, one of the first Negroes ever to be commissioned in the United States Army. He was engaged in recruiting among the freedmen when the war ended.[12]

Following the crushing defeat of the Army of the Potomac at Chancellorsville in May, Lee started the invasion which led to

[10]Langston, *Op. Cit.,* 205 *et seq.;* Reid, *Op. Cit.,* II, 915–917, and *Lorain County News,* Aug. 19, Nov. 4, and Dec. 2, 1863. *Official Roster of the Soldiers of the State of Ohio,* I, 591–624. See Honor Roll in *Ibid.,* I, 760–767.

[11]From Company C: A. H. Robbins, Elias W. Morey, and John S. Cooper. See Wilder, *Op. Cit., passim.*

[12]*Lorain County News,* Mar. 15, 22, July 19, 1865.

Gettysburg. In mid-June Governor Tod issued another emergency call for troops, but little progress was made in recruiting these six-months men in Oberlin, the alarm not being taken very seriously. A second proclamation was received, however, on June 29, when Confederate troops had already entered Pennsylvania—and this time Oberlin acted. All stores were closed at three o'clock when a war meeting was held on the corner, and plans were made to enroll a company of militia. This company then enlisted was made up almost entirely of students and became Company A of the 57th Battalion, Ohio National Guard. The only other company in the battalion was from Elyria.[13] Before this unit had been organized, however, the battle of Gettysburg had been fought. It, therefore, was not called to the colors, though it maintained its organization and engaged in occasional drills. What with the Morgan Raid, the Vallandigham excitements, etc., however, there were enough alarms in Ohio in 1863 to keep the boys constantly on tenter hooks. A *News* reporter thought he heard disloyal sentiments expressed by some of the loafers at Wack's Tavern on South Main Street. The Plumbs, Fitch, Langston, E. H. Fairchild and others led in the organization of an Oberlin branch of the Loyal League to combat local "copperheadism." Nearly three hundred persons took the league's pledge of loyalty at a meeting in the church. "Plots thicken," wrote Mary Dascomb to James Monroe, then consul in Rio de Janeiro. "Our volunteer company have just received commissions, and *hope* to be ordered soon."[14] But the National Guard saw no active service until 1864.

John Brough, Tod's successor as governor of the state, had a great idea in the spring of 1864. Why should not the states of the Middle West, no longer seriously threatened by invasion due to the success of the Western campaign, send their militia to do guard duty along the Potomac, especially at Washington, so that seasoned veterans might all go to the front to help Grant smash Lee? Brough united in April with the executives of Indiana, Illinois, Iowa, and Wisconsin in offering men for that purpose, eighty-five thousand in all—thirty thousand to be

[13]*Lorain County News,* June 17, 24, July 1, 22, and Nov. 4, 1863. On the National Guard see Reid, *Op. Cit.,* I, 130–133.

[14]*Lorain County News,* June 10, 17, July 22, 1863, and Mary Dascomb [and Louisa Fitch] to James Monroe, Nov. 12, 16, 1863 (Monroe MSS).

furnished by Ohio. The offer was immediately accepted, and mobilization of the Ohio National Guard for service for a hundred days was immediately begun.

On Sunday, May 1, 1864, a great farewell meeting was held in the Oberlin meeting house, Company A being present to hear Professor Peck's timely address. On Monday the men rode in wagons over the muddy road to Elyria in a storm of sleet and snow. For a week they drilled in Elyria, being quartered about in private houses. On Monday, May 9, after a Sunday furlough which gave them a chance to hear another Finney sermon, they took the train for Cleveland, where they were mustered in as Company K of the 150th Ohio Volunteer Infantry.[15] "The departure of Company A's [later K] one hundred boys has decimated the College and Theological departments," reported the *Lorain County News,* "and very sensibly diminished the number of Preparatory students. An uncomfortable sense of loneliness rests upon those who remain. A 'goneness' is apparent everywhere. Our chapel prayers, recitations, society meetings, prayer meetings, lectures, all show it. The Musical Union has lost its tenors and basses, the societies their Anniversary representatives, the preparatory classes their teachers, the Monthly rhetorical its speakers. Several annual exhibitions have already been given up or postponed, and others no doubt, will share the same fate."[16]

Albert Allen Safford, A.B., 1861, a theological student was captain of this company. Henry L. Turner, a college senior, was first lieutenant. George W. Phinney, A.B., 1861, left his theological course and the janitorship of the meeting house to become second lieutenant. James H. Laird, the orderly sergeant, had graduated from the College in 1860 and was also studying theology. The company had actually on the muster roll eighty-six names. All but twelve were at the time students in some department of Oberlin College and three of these twelve had been at some previous date.[17] Among the rank and file were

[15]Reid, *Op. Cit.,* I, 208–220, II, 681, and James C. Cannon, *Record of Service of Company K, 150th O. V. I., 1864* ([n.p.]—1903).

[16]*Lorain County News,* May 18, 1864, and George T. Fairchild to James Monroe, May 2, 1864 (Monroe MSS).

[17]The author has checked Cannon, *Op. Cit.,* 26–39, and the *Official Roster . . . of the State of Ohio,* IX, 139–154 with the *General Catalogue of Oberlin College, 1833–1908.*

FORT STEVENS

Where Oberlin students defended Washington. This is a wartime photograph. The soldiers shown are not identified. They may or may not include the Oberlin company.

(United States Signal Corps photograph)

Albert Allen Wright, later for many years Professor of Geology and Zoology, Lucien Calvin Warner, who became a corset manufacturer and donor of buildings to Oberlin, and George K. Nash, governor of Ohio from 1900 to 1904. Members of a company in the same regiment but recruited in Cleveland were Robert R. Rhodes, a brother of James Ford Rhodes the historian, and Marcus Alonzo Hanna. Perhaps this was the beginning of the association of Nash and Hanna.

Company K participated in no bloody charges; it lost but one man in action, but it did have the fortune to be located for a few very critical days at the exact center of the military stage. The whole regiment was sent to garrison the defenses about Washington; K was moved from one fort to another until finally on July 4 they were placed in Fort Stevens. This fortification was in the northern suburbs of the city on Seventh Street not far from the Soldier's Home where President Lincoln had his summer residence. At intervals during artillery drill, for this was the men's chief duty, they were able to get away to see the sights of the Capital and often saw the "tall, gaunt form" of the great President in "his long, yellowish linen coat" with "his strong, kindly face."

The Confederate General Jubal A. Early, who had succeeded to the role of the dead "Stonewall" Jackson, defeated the Union forces under General Lew Wallace in the Shenandoah valley and, with Grant far away in the Wilderness, struck north through Maryland, and, in the first week of July, threatened Washington itself. Early marched his men toward the Seventh Street entrance, and on July 11 was before Fort Stevens, then garrisoned only by Oberlin's Company K, the Thirteenth Michigan Battery and fifty-two convalescents. This tiny force made a show of resistance; Early drove in their pickets, but did not assault the fort. The next day a reenforcement of veterans came to their assistance—and Washington was saved! The company was returned to Cleveland and mustered out after 113 days of service. The College authorities excused the men from all of the work in classes missed during their period of service.[18]

[18]Cannon, *Op. Cit.*, 13–19; Lucien C. Warner, *The Story of My Life*, 45–52; James Ford Rhodes, *History of the United States* (1928), IV, 496–503, particularly note 3 on page 502; MS Reminiscences of James H. Laird, A. B., 1860. One boy, W. E. Leach of Pittsfield, was killed and four died of disease.—*Lorain County News*, July 27, Aug. 17, 1864.

The units mentioned by no means include all the men who went from Oberlin. No complete check of the number of Oberlin students and alumni who went into the army has ever been made but guesses have been usually 750 or 850. The *Catalogues* dated 1861–62 and 1862–63 list the names of 77 undergraduates in the Collegiate Department who left school for the army, almost exactly one-third of the total enrollment of men in those two academic years. It is likely that this list is incomplete; the *Lorain County News* reported on April 1, 1863, that 188 had enlisted from the whole institution; 9 from the Theological Department, exactly one hundred from the College proper, and 79 from the Preparatory Course. By June it was reported that 295 students and townsmen had entered the army from the community.[19] Alumni, of course, usually joined regiments raised near their homes; students often did.

Probably no Oberlin men were actually conscripted; only five men were thus obtained from the entire county during the war. The system provided that if the prescribed number of volunteers could be secured by payments of bounties or otherwise there would be no actual conscription. In February of 1864 over seven thousand dollars was raised by subscription in Oberlin for the payment of such bounties. In the following summer an equal amount was secured by taxation in Russia Township.[20] In general, we may conclude that Oberlin College and town made a decidedly patriotic showing.

It is surprising that in such an idealistic community there was so little doubt expressed about the desirability of the sacrifice of embryo preachers, missionaries and teachers in this brutal, bloody work. It is clear enough, however, that there was some question in the minds of many. Captain Shurtleff must have troubled some spirits when he publicly expressed his uncertainty about the wisdom of the enlistment of such men as those who made up Company C. "God grant," he wrote to a fellow tutor in the summer of 1862, "that I have not been instrumental in causing such tremendous sacrifices without good and even glorious results! . . . I tremble lest all this

[19]*Lorain County News,* Apr. 1 and June 24, 1863. E. A. Beecher, A. B., 1854, served in the Confederate army!—*Ibid.,* Mar. 4, 1863.

[20]James H. Fairchild to Monroe, Feb. 26, 1864 (Monroe MSS); MS Records of Russia Township, May 2, 1864, and Reid, *Op. Cit.,* I, 201.

horrible carnage degenerate into a mere political struggle without any great moral results. Oberlin can do more by her prayers and influence at home, if she takes the right ground (and who can doubt it?) than a thousand regiments in the field. Let there be no further action which shall weaken the home influence of the place, or cripple the energies of the Institution. 'Tis religion our country wants and educated Christians.' " Henry Cowles commented editorially on this letter in the *Evangelist,* calling attention to the continued need for Oberlin men in " the war with spiritual arms"—men now being sacrificed in the "warfare with carnal weapons." "The work of elevating that long crushed race is but just begun. Whichever way the war works—to cripple slavery or to reestablish it, the demand for Christian anti-slavery labor and influence will be augmented fifty fold; and such Christian young men as these we let go to the camp and field of blood cannot be spared from the greater work. . . . Hence we looked with heavy heart upon these noble young men going from us to the field of war. . . . We hope better counsels will prevail henceforward."[21]

These doubts were, of course, to a considerable extent, due to Oberlin's impatience with the President's conservative policy with regard to slavery. Oberlinites said that they put righteousness before political expediency; Lincoln seemed to them to be doing the reverse. Topics discussed in the Oberlin men's literary societies in 1861 give an idea of the trend of Oberlin thought: "Resolved that dissolution without Slavery is preferable to union with Slavery," "Resolved that the government should take steps toward the immediate and unconditional emancipation of the slaves," and "Resolved that the government of the U.S. ought to declare the immediate abolition of Slavery in the Seceded States as a war policy." One student who had been among the "Rescuers," W. E. Lincoln, wrote to Gerrit Smith despairingly: "I regard the present aspect of the era as a fight for a blood-stained, oppressing Union." He was desperately searching for something practical that could be done for the slave. He continued: "Would an armed diversion a la Garibaldi be of use?—I am ready to fight at any time in this way. To fight for this Union wh. will rivit the chains of the bond

[21]*Oberlin Evangelist,* June 18, 1862.

man tighter, I never will nor can.—Oh for our hero John Brown now; has not God a successor? The Lord open the way.—Surely now we could recruit to one or 2 thousand for such a diversion. —The Lord guide—Oberlin does not sympathize with me in these ideas but holds me rather a crazy loon."[22] Evidently Smith was no more ready than the Oberlin fathers to support such radical measures, but all the old abolitionist group were dissatisfied with the situation as it was.

During the 1861 Commencement a series of special meetings were held to discuss the question whether the war power ought to be exercised to abolish slavery. Besides Oberlin faculty, townsmen, students and alumni, the discussion was participated in by guests, including Congressman Ashley from Toledo, Dr. Edward Beecher, formerly president of Illinois College, and, probably, James A. Garfield. Resolutions were unanimously adopted declaring it to be "the duty of the American people to demand of the Government immediately to abolish Slavery in the seceded States by the exercise of the war-power." In September the news of Fremont's freeing of the slaves in Missouri by proclamation was joyously received and Lincoln's reversal of that order further undermined Oberlin's confidence in him. "Fremont had taken the true ground—a noble position," declared the *Evangelist*. "But now a cold chill comes over our enthusiasm. The President's countermand . . . summons the arms of the nation once more to stand guard over the slaves of rebels, and to be very careful how they damage this 'peculiar institution.' "[23]

On July 29, 1862, a mass meeting was held at the chapel to call for definite government action against slavery. In a formal resolution the President was called upon "to proclaim universal emancipation, and to enforce the same to the full extent of his executive ability." There were speeches by President Finney, John Keep and Principal E. H. Fairchild, and J. M. Langston "stirred the blood of all by his eloquent appeals." Of course, Oberlin enthusiastically approved the Presidential Proclamation when it did come, tardy though it seemed to them. On September 24, 1862, the *News* made a feeble attempt at a headline:

[22]Phi Kappa Pi, MS Minutes, June 25, July 16, 1861; Phi Delta, Oct. 9, 1861, and W. E. Lincoln to Smith, 20/4'61 [*sic*] (Gerrit Smith MSS).

[23]*Oberlin Evangelist,* Sept. 11, and 25, 1861.

"GOOD NEWS. The President has issued a Proclamation ABOLISHING SLAVERY . . . *Laus Deo.*" On January 1, 1863, a general mass meeting was held in the chapel to hear the "words of freedom" read. "Our venerable Father Keep," reported the *News,* "gracefully assumed the chair and—not at all intrusively—took charge of the meeting. At his request the Proclamation was read by J. M. Langston, Esq., the audience seated. Then all rose to their feet, and in the ringing tones of Mr. L., it was again read. After this, his voice trembling with emotion, Prof. Cowles led in most appropriate words of thanksgiving and prayer. Then without speech or comment, Father Keep declared the meeting adjourned."[24]

Generals Fremont and Benjamin F. Butler were always popular with Oberlin and Oberlin's friends because of their aggressive stand on emancipation. In December of 1862 and January of 1863 former President Asa Mahan went to Washington, taking with him a plan for the conduct of the war which involved the appointment of Fremont as commander-in-chief. He was cordially received by Secretary Chase, Secretary Stanton and Senators Wilson and Wade, and had several long interviews with President Lincoln.[25]

President Finney allied himself definitely with the radicals and against Lincoln and his cautious policy on the slavery issue. In 1862 we note one of the young ladies' literary societies debating the question: "Resolved that Pres. Lincoln is not so bad a man as Pres. Finney thinks he is." In January of 1864 Finney wrote to Gerrit Smith expressing the hope that the Republican party would nominate for President "a less conservative man than Mr. Lincoln." "We need a more radical man to finish up this war. I hope the radicals in & out of congress, will make their influence so felt in respect to the coming nomination that Mr. L. will see that there is no hope of his renomination & election unless he takes & keeps more radical ground. The people are prepared to elect the most radical abolitionist that is if he can get a nomination." He continued: "I think he is honest, but he is

[24]*Oberlin Evangelist,* Oct. 8, 1862, and *Lorain County News,* Aug. 6, Sept. 24, 1862; Jan. 7, 1863.

[25]E. L. Stevens to J. H. Fairchild, Jan. 12, 1862 (Treas. Off. File P), and Asa Mahan, *A Critical History of the Late American War* (New York—1877), 231–243. The story that Leonard tells (*The Story of Oberlin,* note on pages 224 and 225) is probably apocryphal.

conservative constitutionally, & is by marriage interlocked with Southern interest so far as to embolden Kentucky to hold out against emancipation. If Butler were Pres. I do not think Kentucky would hold out a month. I also believe the rebellion would perish in three months. The fact is the South dont fear Mr. Lincoln. There is no man in the land they would so much fear as Gen. Butler. And they would have good reason to fear him. He would not only end the war but would reorganize the South I believe in 6 months. It seems to me that this can be done & that Butler would do it."[26]

The second Oberlin student mock convention held under the auspices of the Phi Delta society nominated Chase for President. The Phi Kappa Pi, however, debated Lincoln's renomination and the judges voted unanimously in favor of the affirmative.[27]

After Lincoln had been nominated, Oberlinites, of course, had no choice but to support him. In September John Keep wrote to Gerrit Smith: "I heartily join you in your purpose to sustain the President, as the only course, which, apparently, can save the Nation. . . . as we are now situated, it would seem to me that a vote cast against Lincoln is practically treason." On October 12 General Garfield addressed a Lincoln rally in the church. The *Lorain County News* reported that on the day of the election "the venerable FATHER KEEP appeared at the polls leaning on the arm of a friend, and with trembling limbs and voice, remarked, . . . that his first vote was given in 1800, and that this was doubtless the last vote it would ever be his privilege to give for President. He then handed up a written sentiment, which he requested might be read to the throng surrounding the polls, as follows:

" 'Palsied be the *tongue* which now wags for treason, and the *hand* which would cut the jugular vein of our Christian Commonwealth.

'John Keep, age 83.

'Oberlin, Nov. 1864.

Endorsed—"A Freeman's Vote, 1864, for Abraham Lincoln." '

[26]Aelioian Society, MS Minutes, Sept. 25, 1862, and Finney to Smith, Jan. 29, 1864 (Gerrit Smith MSS). On the other hand, Prof. Morgan wrote in Dec.: "But there is a relief in our honest president and in Chase who is a truly noble man, and in the nobleness of Burnside—God only can say, Fiat lux." (Morgan-Hopkins MSS, Dec. 24, 1862.)

[27]Allen Bailey, MS "History of the Oberlin Mock Convention" (O. C. Lib.), and Phi Kappa Pi, MS Minutes, Mar. 1, 1864.

OBERLIN STUDENTS OF THE CLASS OF 1862

J. R. Shipherd, Rescuer and nephew of the Founder, is at the upper right.

(From photographs in the Oberlin College Library)

"Late in the afternoon, Col. Giles W. Shurtleff, of the 5th U. S. Colored Regiment, who had just arrived on the cars, came up, limping from the effect of his yet unhealed wounds, and tendered his vote for Lincoln and the Union."[28]

"Joint education of the sexes" was the salvation of Oberlin College. There were enough young ladies to keep the institution running more or less as usual despite the large number of young men absent in the ranks. There were times, of course, when it was hard to keep one's mind on declensions, chemical formulae and equations. The women of Oberlin were actively engaged in the appropriate wartime activities. "At the time of the first enlistments," reported Mrs. Dascomb, "our fears were excited for the good order of our Dept. For two weeks all was excitement —Studies & study hours were trespassed on, the girls went wildly about with knitting in hand and petitions on their tongues to attend soldier's meetings, and we feared a season of disorder was about to be inaugurated. . . . But quiet returned, duties seemed duties again."[29]

When Company C was enlisted, five hundred Oberlin ladies immediately formed a "Florence Nightingale Association" and went to work immediately "preparing woolen hose and underclothing for the volunteers." In the fall the Young Ladies' Literary Society even debated whether the "ladies should organize themselves into Military Companies and drill." But it was left to an Oberlin town girl actually to join the army. She wore a uniform for several weeks before her sergeant sent her home! Probably the "Florence Nightingale Association" was identical with the "Oberlin Soldiers' Aid Society" of the later years of the war. This organization held forty-six meetings in the year ending April 8, 1864, and prepared and forwarded quantities of hospital stores to the headquarters in Cleveland: shirts, underwear, socks, sheets, quilts, pillows, napkins, besides canned tomatoes, fruit, butter, eggs, and hundreds of pounds of dried fruit. At the end of the war Oberlin needles were kept running in behalf of the Freedman's Aid Society.[30]

[28]Keep to Smith, Sept. 19, 1864 (Gerrit Smith MSS), and *Lorain County News,* Oct. 12; Nov. 9, 1864.

[29]M. P. Dascomb, MS Report to the Trustees, Aug. 25, 1862 (Misc. Archives).

[30]Y. L. L. S., MS Minutes, Sept. 18, 1861; *Lorain County News,* Aug. 24, 1861; May 4, 1864; Sept. 20, 1865, and *Cleveland Leader,* Jan. 19, 1862, in *Annals of Cleveland.*

Several Oberlin *men* engaged in volunteer nursing. Samuel Plumb went to Virginia to care for the wounded Oberlin boys after the battle at Cross Lanes. In 1864 Rev. Minor W. Fairfield, Dr. Homer Johnson and D. P. Reamer, a local business man, nursed for the United States Christian Commission. Professor Henry Peck was Oberlin's most indefatigable war-worker, spending many months altogether on good-will missions to "the boys."[31]

The news of the fall of Richmond reached Oberlin on Monday, April 3, 1865. "The old six-pounder was brought out on Tappan Square, and belched forth, a large bonfire blazed up, rockets shot towards the heavens, a balloon ascension was greeted by a score of voices singing 'John Brown's body,' drums beat, and speeches by the citizens and students occupied the time till a late hour of the night." This was the notice from the town paper. An undergraduate, John G. Fraser, wrote in his diary: "Went to Young People's Meeting in the evening. Had a pleasant time. . . . After meeting I went to celebrating the fall of Richmond. They had a big bonfire, lots of fire crackers, a little good speaking and a great deal that was rather soft." Just a week later came the news of Appomattox. "I went to Rhetorical. Heard that Lee's army had surrendered," wrote Fraser. "Glory Hallelujah! Praise God from whom all blessings flow." The following Friday was set aside as a special day of Thanksgiving by proclamation of the governor of Ohio. A salute was fired on the square at six in the morning. All classes were dismissed for the day. At ten-thirty a religious service was held in the First Church at which Professor James Fairchild, Principal E. H. Fairchild and Professor Morgan spoke "quite jubilantly." In the afternoon, prayer meetings were held in both churches. The evening was marked by a great bonfire and a general illumination, a parade with "transparencies," patriotic speeches, fireworks and balloon ascensions.[32]

That very night Lincoln was assassinated in Ford's theater; the next morning he died. The next morning, too, jubilation gave way to mourning, suspicion and hate in Oberlin and everywhere. "The news was brought to our class at the close of a reci-

[31]*Cleveland Leader,* Aug. 30, 1861, in *Annals of Cleveland,* and *Lorain County News,* June 29, 1864.

[32]J. D. Fraser, MS Diary, Apr. 5, 14, 1865, and *Lorain County News,* Apr. 6, 19, 1865.

tation," wrote Lucien Warner, who had often seen Lincoln when stationed at Fort Stevens the year before. "For nearly five minutes we sat motionless, forgetting that the class had been dismissed. I have loved other public men, but the death of no one could have affected me like that of President Lincoln. Ever since I looked upon his honest genial countenance I have loved him like an intimate friend. . . . Further study was out of the question."[33] "I can hardly think or write of anything tonight but the assassination of Mr. Lincoln & Mr. Seward," wrote young Fraser. "It seems as if it must be some lurid dream, some frightful nightmare, and still I know it must be true. . . . It seems as though it must have been a fiend from the bottomless pit who could take in cold blood the life of such a man. . . . I feel more like enlisting today than ever I did before. What fate *don't* such wretches deserve? . . . The bell has tolled all day and almost all the students have put on crepe."

It was inevitable that the late rebels should be blamed. On Sunday (it was Easter) President Finney preached two sermons, morning and afternoon, calling for the vengeance of the Lord and the Nation on the South. He declared that the Government had "already shown a dangerous amount of forbearance." "We must show the world," he insisted, "that rebellion is a fearful, terrible thing. The President was an amiable man, tender, kind-hearted, but perhaps he stood in God's way of dealing with the Rebels just as they ought to be dealt with for the good of the nation, and for the good of humanity." The South's sufferings during the war had not been punishment, he held, but only the inevitable consequences of resistance to God and the Nation's laws. Now the Rebels must be chastised; as many of the leaders as could be captured should be tried for treason and hanged![34]

Some went to Cleveland when the funeral train passed through. Among these was young Fraser. "It was a sad, sad sight," he told his diary. "The crowd was the largest I ever saw and by far the most quiet and orderly. The very skies seemed to be weeping for the good man's fall. I looked upon his face three times. It has a quiet, peaceful look upon it, as though he were

[33]Warner, *Story of My Life.*

[34]There are notes on these sermons in Theodore Wilder's MS "Index Rerum," 236–238, and John G. Fraser's MS Diary, Book 1. Fraser also refers to it in the course of the Diary, Apr. 16, 1865.

at peace with his God, himself and all the world. How could an assassin have the heart to kill such a man? . . . The crowd on the trains was very great. I am not any sorry that I went although I got pretty much wet."[35]

The next week, when the Phi Kappa Pi debated the question, "Resolved that the military leaders of the Rebellion, who will take the oath of allegiance, ought to be allowed to remain in this country unmolested," the judges' decision was unanimously in favor of the negative. Early in June the same society held a mock trial of Jefferson Davis at which the jury turned in a verdict of "guilty of High Treason."[36]

The 1865 commencement exercises were climactic. Never before had there been such a large number of returning alumni present. "Tidal currents of alumni surged up and down the walks, eddied into the bookstores, and around the corners. Handshakings alternated with reminiscences of the old days." There was more than the usual tendency to look backward as even the least discerning could see that 1865 put a period to an epoch in the history of the nation and of Oberlin. The aging Theodore Weld returned to join in a reunion of Lane Rebels and, under the auspices of the men's literary societies, to deliver a "Grand Oration . . . to thousands of delighted hearers, on Wednesday Evening which, though nearly two hours long, held the audience spell-bound."[37] President Edmund Burke Fairfield of Hillsdale College (A.B., 1842) discussed political and public issues in his *Concio ad Clerum* before the theological graduates. The College graduating class was the largest in Oberlin history (twenty-three gentlemen and thirteen ladies). Each one of these delivered an oration or read an essay—usually referring to the war or the issues associated with it. John Brewer spoke on "Illinois and the War," Cassius M. Clark on "The Patriots' Duty," and Fanny M. Jackson, a colored girl, read a poem entitled "The Grandeur of our Triumph."

The alumni collation was held in the New Ladies' Hall: "cold chicken and tongue, light biscuit, hot coffee, flaky pastry, and peaches and cream"—none of the "traditional bran bread."

[35]MS Diary, Apr. 28, 1865.
[36]MS Minutes, May 2, June 6, 13, 1865.
[37]*Lorain County News,* Aug. 30, 1865, and James A. Thome to Sarah Weld, Aug. 28, 1865 (Weld MSS).

Among the speakers were J. M. Fitch and Major-General Jacob Dolson Cox. Cox urged that the soldier dead should not be forgotten. Subscriptions for more than $500.00 were taken up for a soldiers' monument.

On Wednesday Professor Ellis, who had taken such an active interest in the student soldiers, delivered his address on *Oberlin and the American Conflict:*

"Out of the darkness and tempest, we are sailing into the quiet harbor of peace. . . . [¶] It is fit that the circumstances of the hour should give color to our meeting, and engage out thoughts and words today. [¶] We celebrate not merely the achievement of our aims for the four years past, but no less the victory of the moral conflict which for a half century preceded and culminated in the conflict of arms."

He called attention to the changed position which Oberlin had come to occupy in the public mind due to the fact that the principles which had once made Oberlin a "hissing and a by-word" had finally triumphed. He reviewed Oberlin's part in the preparation for the final conflict: on the public platform, in the mission fields, in the pulpit, in politics, in the "Kansas Crusade," on the "Underground Pathway," in propagandizing through the classroom. "It is safe to say that ten thousand advocates for the oppressed against the oppressor have gone forth from these Halls. . . . As teachers, lawyers, men of business, farmers, and in every sphere of activity they have made their influence felt."

Finally, he reviewed Oberlin's contribution in the war: major generals, brigadier generals, colonels and privates, Company C, the "Squirrel Hunters" and the "Hundred-Days men." "Let us not fail to enshrine their memory in our deepest hearts and teach it to our children."

". . . And so, taking courage from the strange past, rejoicing in the grand triumphs of the present, and trusting in God for the issues of the future, let us gird ourselves for the new conflicts, and move on to still more glorious victories."

CHAPTER LI

FULFILLMENT AND CONFORMITY

THE founding of Oberlin occupied the years 1832 to 1835. Then followed fifteen years of struggle, of aggressive and positive action. The institution was constantly on the verge of bankruptcy; the teachers were seldom paid the meager salaries promised them; the school and colony were ringed around by opposition and suspicion. But these were the years when Oberlin's reputation was established at home and abroad among the friends of social reform and revivalism as the capital of Finney evangelism, the light-house of the slave, an institution friendly to peace, to "physiological" and moral reform and to every good cause. To others it was known as the cyclone-center of trouble making: the school where Negroes, white girls and white boys were educated together, the fount of the dangerous heresy of perfectionism, and of wild fanaticism in reformed diet and other "fads." These were the years of "peculiar" Oberlin and the general public was so much impressed, positively and negatively, that in certain sections and walks of life it is supposed that there has been no change since.

But the transition from the early radicalism began early. The period after 1850 was marked by a combination of fulfillment and conformity which really by the end of the war had translated Oberlin from its unique status. In some fields, notably anti-slavery, Oberlin had triumphed and the rest of the North now applauded where it had once condemned. On other questions, such as dietetic reform and pacifism, Oberlin had retreated from its radical position.

The opening of this period of change was marked by significant events: the resignation of Mahan, the change of the official name, the establishment of the endowment and the choice of Finney for the presidency. All of these developments were of some significance.

After Shipherd, Asa Mahan was the No. 1 irreconcilable Oberlinite. He was the recognized sponsor of "Sanctification." He was the head and forefront of the war on the "heathen classics." He and Professor Thome were willing and anxious to go much farther in granting equal privileges to the young ladies in the Oberlin plan of "joint education of the sexes." No other Oberlin man, except perhaps Dresser or Walker, was so publicly identified with the peace movement; and, after Mahan's departure, of all the workers for peace in Oberlin there remained only Henry Cowles and Hamilton Hill—neither of them possessing great abilities for personal leadership. Mahan and the fallen Horace Taylor had been the outstanding male proponents of moral reform. The women leaders, Alice Welch Cowles and Lydia Andrews Finney, were dead. Mahan was not so indispensable to the anti-slavery cause, but it should be remembered that it was he who had debated the Fosters and Garrison and represented Oberlin in many anti-slavery conventions such as the Free Soil Convention at Buffalo in 1848. It was Mahan who had elaborated the whole doctrine of Christian reform in speeches at Boston in 1838 and in articles in the *Evangelist*. It was Mahan who presented the theoretical side of reformism to the students in Moral Philosophy. Finney seems to have agreed with Mahan on most of these issues but his interest in social reform, in worldly matters generally, was always secondary and subordinate to his main purpose—to save souls for Christ. The departure of Mahan, Oberlin's leading professional reformer, could not fail to have a considerable influence on the spirit of Oberlin in general.

The change of the official designation of the institution from Oberlin Collegiate Institute to Oberlin College was effected by an amendment to the Charter of 1834 approved by the Ohio State legislature on March 21, 1850. Perhaps this superficial change was significant; certainly it was symbolic. At first the peculiarity of the title had been a source of pride as was the uniqueness of the school; the change to the more regular form implied a new and greater consideration for general opinion, a conscious desire to conform. Some thought it was a most desirable change, making it clear to all that work of full college grade was done at Oberlin and that it was not just a preparatory school.[1] Others parted with the old name reluctantly because

[1]Willard Sears, Dec. 1849 (Treas. Off., File O).

endeared to so many by long association and because it seemed more logical as covering all departments. It appeared to some then, as to many today, rather odd that a "college" should include a "college" along with other departments. Besides, what was the use, asked Michael E. Strieby, "its juvenile pranks have for so many years delighted its friends, and vexed its enemies . . . that I doubt whether a new name would enable either friend or foe to know, love or hate it more or less than they do now."[2] Though the evidence is not explicit, it is fairly clear that the change was a gesture toward respectability, a bid for recognition as a not too "peculiar" educational institution, in a sense a mild apology for "juvenile pranks" of earlier years. This interpretation is further justified by the fact that the new name was adopted as a preliminary to the first endowment "drive."

It is not easy to conclude whether or not the endowment campaign made Oberlin less willing to disturb conservative sensibilities and vested interests than in the previous days of hand-to-mouth finance, though the writer is inclined to believe that it did have that effect. But certainly the achievement of the endowment as a result of the sale of scholarship certificates was a very great influence to conservatism. Complacency seems always to be the product of security, and the relative financial security of Oberlin after the endowment was established apparently produced a relative complacency in the faculty and student outlook. Though the College continued to be necessitous, it was no longer perennially on the verge of bankruptcy. Further, the investment of the funds, secured in various types of mortgages, gave Oberlin a greater interest in the maintenance of the *status quo*. Most important of all the result of the scholarship sale was the bringing in of a tidal wave of students. Oberlin became one of the largest educational institutions in the country—apparently the largest—in the early sixties. This very size militated against the old radical solidarity. And, besides, in addition to those youths who came to Oberlin because of Finney, because of their enthusiasm for anti-slavery and other reform causes, there now appeared a great number who came because some relative or friend provided them free tuition through a scholarship. Many of these, naturally, originally had no particular enthusiasm for "Oberlinism" and,

[2]M. E. Strieby to H. Hill, Dec. 24, 1849 (Treas. Off., File P).

though undoubtedly some were converted, there was certainly a greatly increased proportion of the student body who had no especial zeal for the principles of the founders.

There is every evidence that student life in the fifties became steadily more "worldly," that student thought was less and less exclusively of the soul's salvation and the social evils which it was their duty to remove and more and more of this life, and its pleasanter side at that. As has been noted elsewhere, parties and picnics, almost unheard of before, became numerous in the late fifties and sixties. Evening lectures, outdoor sports, "collations," strawberry festivals were so popular that Finney was moved to make vigorous protest against such "diverting influences"—"diverting" from the main end, religious thought and activity. Oberlin students were becoming less morally purposeful and, by-and-large, less aggressively and vocally pious.

Though Oberlin was much more than Finney, Finney was an essential part of Oberlin. The spiritual and moral heat generated by Finney's revivals had produced Oberlin. The faculty wrote to him late in 1850, ". . . You are our natural head & leader."[3] It is significant that today many persons, including Oberlin graduates, students and, occasionally, faculty members, are under the impression that Finney was President from the beginning. It is unlikely that Mahan's prestige or reputation in Oberlin or out, great though it was, ever equalled that of Finney. Finney and Oberlin were inseparable; Oberlin without Finney certainly seemed unthinkable. It was, therefore, very appropriate that Finney should be made President. Finney returned from his first evangelistic campaign in England in the spring of 1851 and at the regular commencement meeting of the trustees on August 26, 1851, he was appointed President, accepted, and immediately assumed office.[4]

Finney's address to the graduating class delivered two days before his election was really his inaugural—a powerful statement of the evangelical purpose of the founders and a rousing appeal to the students not to prove recreant to that purpose. He took his text from *I Kings 2: 2-4: "Be thou strong therefore, and show thyself a man,"* etc. Show yourselves to be men, he implored,

[3]John Morgan *et al.* to Finney, Dec. 10, 1850 (Finney MSS). A similar expression of Finney's significance to Oberlin is found in the Leonard-Fairchild MS., I, 11.

[4]T. M., Aug. 26, 1851.

above the beast in that you recognize a higher moral law, responsible to Christ because redeemed by his blood, owing more to society than most men because educated by society, and especially obligated to high Christian endeavor because educated in Oberlin—"God's College," consecrated to Christ by the founders. His words were not without special application to the great issue of the hour. "Finally, show yourselves to be men of principle in these trying times when the question is gravely raised whether the law of God is above the law of man, whether human institutions and laws are to set aside the authority of God." He closed with an appeal for Christian missions: "You need not be afraid to go among the Indians of the forest, to the Islands of the great sea, among the slaves of the South, or the African tribes on their own soil: the Lord will lead you and give his angels charge over you to keep you in all your ways." Such was the ringing challenge with which Finney began his presidency.[5]

Appropriate and inevitable as Finney's election appears, it was, nevertheless, in some ways unfortunate. Finney's attachment to Oberlin always came second to his devotion to the saving of souls, and when evangelistic labors called him to New York or to England Oberlin suffered from his absence. When he had been away longer than usual the rumor would begin to spread that he was not coming back at all, and dissatisfaction would immediately appear among the students, dissatisfaction among the theologs particularly that they should be deprived of his guidance in Pastoral and Systematic Theology, among the college seniors that they should miss his lectures on Mental and Moral Philosophy, and among the students generally that from the pulpit of the meeting house they heard each Sabbath not the dramatic and awakening appeals of Finney but the labored didacticism of Morgan or the uninspired scholarship of Henry Cowles. There seemed to be a general feeling among the students that if they came to Oberlin and Finney wasn't there they were somehow being cheated. It was, after all, a perfectly understandable feeling. Wasn't Finney listed in the *Catalogue* as President and Professor of Mental and Moral Philosophy and Theology? They had been attracted to Oberlin, forsooth, under false pretenses. The faculty and trustees felt more or less at a loss in their leader's

[5]*Oberlin Evangelist,* Sept. 10, 1851.

PRESIDENT FINNEY, IN THE LATE FIFTIES
(From the 1859 Class Album)

absence and were subject to considerable pressure from the students. As a result, when Finney was away any length of time he was the recipient of repeated letters begging him to come back and certainly not to resign.

Nor were the rumors of Finney's resignation entirely unfounded in fact. Within a few months after his entrance upon the duties of the presidency he was considering withdrawal in order that he might devote more of his time to revivals. John Keep wrote to him early in March of 1852 begging him not to take the step. The Theological Department, he insisted, could not possibly continue without Finney. Would he willingly and consciously destroy it and thus injure the whole cause of Christianity in the West? Finney, he declared, must not overlook or "undervalue the *moral power* you now have in & through the Oberlin school." What would friends and enemies think? "Finney, turning his back upon Oberlin, & leaving his own child of promise to die. Finney, the Evangelist, the Reformer, whom God has used to make a deep & widely extended *mark* upon Christendom, abandoning the very strongest agency within his reach to carry on & secure a triumph to his toils when he is dead." "What!" asked Keep, "Is this sagacity[?] Is it wisdom[?] Is it generalship[?] Is it common sense[?] Is it Christian prudence[?] Is it in accordance with God's method[?] Is it benevolence[?]"[6] Professor Morgan supported Keep, pleading with Finney to limit his evangelistic work to four or five months in the year and spend the remainder in writing and teaching at Oberlin. Besides, was not the Oberlin audience worth preaching to? "There is here now the greatest congregation I have even seen in Oberlin, the galleries of the noble church crowded with masses of young people twice as numerous as usual and on Thursday the Chapel is crowded to a jam, orchestra included. If you have anywhere else a more important assembly to address, it must be an exceedingly interesting one. As I have aimed my feeble pocket-pistol at the vast assembly from Sabbath to Sabbath, I have earnestly wished you were here to pour in your heaviest shot in the name of the Lord." Morgan's appeal must have been almost irresistible, for Finney loved a good audience, and in May he was back again in the Oberlin meeting house preaching from the text: "Verily I say unto you, Except

[6]Keep to Finney, Mar. 12, 1852 (Finney MSS).

ye be converted, and become as little children, ye shall not enter into the kingdom of heaven."[7]

In the spring of 1855 again when Finney was in Brooklyn rumors of impending resignation so disturbed the faculty that a special committee was chosen to communicate with him on the subject. The hope was expressed that there were no grounds for the persistent rumors and that Finney would soon return. ". . . We exceedingly desire your presence. . . . We have every reason to feel that the great mass of the community, the whole body of students, and the entire Faculty most sincerely, earnestly, and affectionately desire your early return, and desire it too with the hope that your last days may be spent at Oberlin." A year later while the president was in Oberlin and preaching regularly (one sermon on "The Destruction of the Wicked") he was seriously considering resignation, but Professor Morgan again begged him to hold on, emphasizing the danger of jealousy and dissension in the faculty over the selection of a successor. "May God have mercy on us and never suffer Satan to triumph over us." Again in 1860, when Finney had been in England over a year, the faculty and trustees felt called upon to make official protestations of their confidence in him and need of his leadership because of, at least implied, threats of resignation. "We cannot think of the closing of such labors among us without sorrow. We trust they will not close but with your life."[8] One is led to conclude that President Finney had something of the temperament of the *prima donna* and that, as a result, Oberlin's peaceful, Sabbath calm was rather artificially maintained during the first decade of his presidency.

It is not surprising to find that dissatisfaction was expressed on both sides. Finney found the piety of Oberlin declining (as perhaps it was); he objected to the more "worldly" spirit among the students, to the increased number of evening lectures, the parties and picnics and other recreations engaged in. James A. Thome, on the other hand, a Lane Rebel and trustee, hoped the President would resign. "I am inclined to believe," he wrote to Henry Cowles, "that a *change* in the Presidency & Theo. [logical] Headship is indispensable, & *awaits* us in the gracious provisions of

[7]Morgan (unsigned) to Finney, Mar. 15, 1852 (Finney MSS), and *Oberlin Evangelist,* May 26, 1852.

[8]T. B. Hudson and E. H. Fairchild to Finney, Apr. 21, 1855; Morgan to Finney, Apr. 21, 1856, and John Keep *et al.* to Finney, July 21, 1860 (Finney MSS).

Him whose ways & whose times are wiser than ours. Bro Finney is *not the man for the work . . .*" Lewis Tappan agreed with Thome that Finney was not fitted for the presidency but reminded him that Finney had said so when elected, but the position had been forced upon him. James H. Fairchild, in later years, ratified this opinion: Finney, he concluded, had none of the qualities of a good administrator; he did not try to exercise the powers of an administrator; he was never more than nominally president, only a figurehead.[9] One cannot refrain from commenting that he was a very impressive figurehead and that his moral and spiritual leadership was of more significance than any merely administrative activity could ever have been.

Finney's very weakness as an administrator plus his continued absence from Oberlin were of positive advantage to the faculty, for they were left to run their own affairs to a large extent. Even when present and presiding over trustees' or faculty meetings Finney never attempted to dictate. Though his opinions, of course, bore great weight, they were often questioned, argued against and voted down. Repeatedly he was forced to yield and did so graciously. There was a marked contrast between his position as arbitrator and chairman and the dictatorial and dogmatic procedure of Mahan. Therefore, the tradition and precedent of faculty independence, first established by Finney's insistence in 1835, were further strengthened by his neglect and tolerance while President.[10]

As has been noted before,[11] the sales of scholarships in the fifties did not furnish a permanent solution of the financial problems of the College. Approximately fourteen hundred certificates providing for tuition for six or eighteen years or perpetually had been distributed and, as a result, the attendance pushed above the thousand mark in 1851-52, passed thirteen hundred in 1852-53 and 1859-60 and never dropped below a thousand again except in the war years 1861-62, 1862-63 and 1863-64. All scholarships were transferable, and, until the six-year certificates had been retired, the College had no income from tuition, all students being invariably provided with scholarships. Even when those were out

[9]Thome to Cowles, Aug. 31, 1854 (Cowles-Little MSS), L. Tappan to Thome, June 21, 1855 (Tappan Letter Books, L. C.), and Leonard-Fairchild MS, I, 8–9.

[10]*Idem,* and G. F. Wright, *Charles Grandison Finney,* 161.

[11]See above pages 501-502.

of the way the College's obligations to the holders of perpetual and eighteen-year certificates were so great that receipts from tuition were only nominal. In 1862-63, for example, the expense of instruction was almost all met from the seven thousand dollars in interest received from investments; tuition payments were reported at $27.05![12] Not until the seventies were the eighteen-year scholarships retired and, though every effort was made to buy up or beg the four hundred perpetuals, a number were still outstanding at the time of the fiftieth anniversary in 1883.

The teaching burden was greatly increased by this doubling of the number of students in the institution. The College could not possibly afford to hire more teachers, and so the faculty had to teach more and larger classes and more of the work was turned over to student teachers. (The expenditure for the payment of student teachers advanced from $1,451.74 in 1853-54 to over $2,000.00 in 1859-60.) Besides, almost immediately after the College had undertaken this heavy instructional obligation the general price level advanced greatly, and the professors found increasing difficulty in making ends meet with their meager salaries of six hundred dollars a year. Professor Morgan found himself in desperate straits in 1855. In a pitiful report presented to the trustees in that year he estimated his personal debts (for "current expenses," piano, "garden ditching," and "Subscription for Theo. [logical] Lib. [rary]") at nearly eight hundred dollars, his available assets ("Due from boarders—½ perhaps good," "Due on salary," a pair of steers, a heifer, "wood chopped in the woods" and three pigs) at less than six hundred dollars. "I have not mentioned hens & cows because they cannot well be spared to pay debts"—"P.S. We have no provisions of any value on hand except our garden."[13] Salaries could not be increased without new income; there was an annual deficit each year even with six-hundred-dollar salaries. Tuition charges could not be increased to balance the general inflation of prices and provide the additional income

[12]"Instruction fund acc't, 1862/63" (Trustees' MSS., Misc. Archives). There is a good brief sketch of finances in this period in J. H. Fairchild, *Oberlin, the Colony and College,* 211–216. The cost of the plant (repair of buildings, scientific apparatus, and insurance), office expenses, and "contingencies" was met from rentals, special donations, the sale of diplomas and "incidental" charges. See "General acco't current, 1862/63" (Trustees' MSS., Misc. Archives).

[13]John Morgan—"Statement respecting my debts" (Trustees' MSS., 1855, Misc. Archives).

required—because practically no tuition was ever paid. What to do?

The only solution was to solicit more contributions—a difficult thing to do successfully when Oberlin had just announced the completion of its endowment campaign. Pleas for donations went out through the *Evangelist* in 1855, and an attempt was initiated to endow a Finney Professorship of Systematic Theology. Just before the war it was decided to attempt to secure an endowment for the Theological Department. The general endowment did not properly provide for that department, the scholarships not being necessary for theological students who never paid any tuition. Henry Cowles, editor of the *Evangelist* and former professor and financial agent, undertook the task of collecting the funds needed in the years 1858 to 1863. He had a hard time of it due to the financial disorders following the panics of 1857 and 1861. The Finney endowment he was entirely unable to secure—and the effort was abandoned for the time being. But, with the aid of his wife, who travelled with him some of the time, and a letter of recommendation from Governor Salmon P. Chase, he collected about ten thousand dollars for the theological endowment (largely in promissory notes and partly in old scholarship certificates and odd sums of money and donations of clothing to relieve the distress of the faculty).[14] As a result it was possible to make a slight general increase in salaries in 1860, the unrestricted donations being distributed equally between the individual professors, the Treasurer and the Principal of the Preparatory Department.[15]

Additional funds came from other sources. Hamilton Hill, the British treasurer, returned to his native land in the winter of 1862-63 to try to duplicate the achievement of Keep and Dawes over twenty years before. He collected about two thousand dollars, over a quarter of it from the Sturges, old friends of Oberlin, and £10 from the Ladies' Anti-Slavery Society of Edinburgh. The

[14]Henry Cowles' copies of agency reports for 1858–59, 1859–60 and 1862–63 (Cowles' MSS), and Henry Cowles to Finney, Sept. 9, 1859 (Finney MSS). See also annual reports of Theological Endowment Fund in Trustees' MSS (Misc. Archives).

[15]T. M., Aug. 19, 21, 1859. Receipts signed by the members of the faculty for the increases received and dated June (or Jan.) 20, 1860, are in the Misc. Archives. The Trustees' MSS, also in the Misc. Archives, contain much material on financial matters.

mission produced a net amount of a little over a thousand dollars —nothing remarkable, but a help.[16]

Back in 1843 the "Society for the Promotion of Collegiate and Theological Education at the West" had been organized to direct financial support away from Oberlin to Oberlin's more orthodox and conservative rivals. Now during the war Oberlin had become "respectable" enough to ask, through the person of Michael Strieby, financial agent following Cowles, to be added to the list of beneficiary institutions. At the annual meeting of the Society in 1862, after "a full hearing of the case" and discussion, the request was acceded to and Oberlin received the official endorsement of the organization. In the ensuing year fifteen hundred dollars was appropriated specifically for the use of the Theological Department. Additional amounts were obtained by Strieby and other agents under the auspices of this society in later years— $3,634.00 in 1863-64; $4,350.00 in 1864-65, and about $3,500.00 in 1866-67.[17]

Large gifts from W. C. Chapin, formerly of Providence but then of Lawrence, Massachusetts, Dr. Charles Avery of Pittsburgh and I. P. Williston of Northampton were of very substantial assistance. Chapin had long been an important benefactor of Oberlin, in many years paying Finney's entire salary. He had considerable investments in cotton mills and made enough profits even during the war to contribute considerable sums from time to time. On January 1, 1864, he made his largest gratuity: $10,000 in personal notes and thirty shares in "Saunders' Cotton Mills—Lawrence, Mass. at $500 per Share" totalling $15,000. Dr. Avery, a well-to-do Pittsburgh abolitionist, contributed important sums for the education of colored students at Oberlin and, in 1866, $25,000 was set aside from his estate by his executors, the income to be used for the aid of worthy Negroes studying in Oberlin College. J. P. Williston gave considerable sums. In May, 1862,

[16]T. M., Aug. 25, 1862, and Feb. 11, 1863, and "Report of Agency to England by H. Hill"—1862–63 (Trustees' MSS). The Oberlin College Library possesses a copy of the circular used by Hill, entitled *To the Friends of the African Race. . . .*

[17]Donald G. Tewkesbury, *The Founding of American Colleges and Universities Before the Civil War* (New York—1932), pages 10–13; T. M., Aug. 26, 1862, and Aug. 26, 1863; Theron Baldwin to George N. Allen, Feb. 18, 1863, and Dec. 9, 1864 (Treas. Off., File V); *Reports* of the society for 1861–62, page 35; 1862–63, pages 6 and 51; 1863–64, page 40; 1864–65, page 42, and 1866–67, pages 26 and 54, and page 436 above.

he wrote a surprise letter to Treasurer Hill enclosing a check for a thousand dollars. "I have unexpectedly made considerable profits," he wrote, "in manufacturing free labor cotton from India & I wish to give a portion of it to your College that has always taught . . . that we should love our Neighbor as ourselves." During the next three years he gave several thousand more, most of which was used to raise the professors' salaries.[18]

Salary increases were made possible by these various additions to income, and when Professor Monroe went to Rio de Janeiro as consul no substitute was hired to take his place, but the rest of the faculty divided his salary among them—one hundred dollars additional for each and two hundred to those who did extra work on account of Professor Monroe's absence. In 1865, after Monroe's return, all professors' salaries were advanced to a thousand dollars and the next year the salary of the Principal of the Ladies' Department was increased to $650.00. John Morgan reported a comparatively munificent income in 1867; a thousand dollars from the College and eight hundred for his services as co-pastor of the church.[19]

The income tax returns for 1865 under the war revenue act give us an unusually accurate picture of the financial status of Oberlin professors and residents. President Finney reported $2,235; Dr. Dascomb, $1,775; Professor James H. Fairchild, $1,440; Professor Morgan, $1,226; George Allen only $801, and Professor Churchill less than $800; Professor Peck less than $700. Faculty incomes were still considerably lower than those of most town merchants and professional men: Max Straus reported net profits of over five thousand dollars from his dry-goods store; store-keeper Isaac M. Johnson over three thousand. Banker Samuel Plumb was listed for $2,572, over three hundred more than the President of the College. James M. Fitch, bookseller and printer, Sunday-school superintendent and Rescuer, gave his income as $2,257, a few dollars more than President Finney. The

[18]W. C. Chapin to Hamilton Hill, Dec. 20, 1861, W. C. C. to M. E. Strieby, Dec. 16, 1863 (Treas. Off., File R); T. M., Jan. 30, 1864; Report of "Theological Endowment Fund," Trustees' MSS, 1864 (Misc. Archives); Cowles' report, 1859; John Keep to Gerrit Smith, June 16, 1866 (Gerrit Smith MSS); P. C. M., May 23, 1862, June 10, 1863, Aug. 29, 1864; W. C. Chapin to Strieby, Dec. 16, 1863 (Treas. Off., File R); "Report of Committee on Treasurer's Annual Report, 1864" (Trustees' MSS, 1864); T. M., Aug. 18, 1865, and Fairchild, *Op. Cit.*, 212.

[19]T. M., Aug. 26, 1863; Aug. 22, 1865; June 26, 1866, and John Morgan to Mark Hopkins, Jan. 9, 1867 (Morgan-Hopkins MSS).

income of S. S. Calkins of the business college was $1,942. Even John M. Langston, Negro attorney, had an income larger than that of most professors. It is evident that, considering the high commodity prices at the time, the Oberlin professors were quite clearly not yet on Easy Street, but their status must have seemed fortunate if they looked back to any of the three preceding decades.[20]

Never since coming to Oberlin had Finney's health been really robust, and as he reached the sixties fears of a general breakdown increased among his friends and associates. Oberlinites were already lamenting the great and imminent loss to Oberlin in the first weeks of 1861. But when the second Mrs. Finney died in the winter of 1863-64 he bore up well under the loss and the next year married Mrs. Rebecca Rayl, the Assistant Principal of the Ladies' Department. Soon after, however, being seventy-three years of age, he determined to resign the presidency. "Our college," he wrote to the trustees, "needs a President who can give more attention to the details of its duties than I can give. My duties as Pastor & as Professor of Theology demand the use of all my remaining strength. . . . Last year I was quite overdone by the labor & excitement connected with the commencement & the meeting of the Board of Trust. . . . I now feel quite clear that I should sustain this responsibility no longer. . . . I have given you my views of the man we need as President & must leave the responsibility of the appointment upon the Board of Trust, praying earnestly that you may be Divinely directed, & that God will give us a man who has the requisite qualifications & whose whole heart & strength will be given to the realization of the great end for which Oberlin College was founded." The trustees accepted the resignation, paying just and appropriate tribute to their great leader as "the main earthly source of [Oberlin's] popular power and spiritual influence." "You came to it in the day of small things," they reminded him. "You have stood by it in the days of trial and adversity. You have lived to see it prospered, honored and useful." They recognized that his leadership was not dependent on the title of President. "You have always been, and always will be while you live, its recognized head. To you the nominal Presidency is of little significance. It was only by great urgency

[20]Income tax reports for 1865 printed in *Lorain County News,* July 25, 1866.

that you were induced to accept it. It, and not you, was honored by that acceptance: and now that you resign it, you only lay aside a name, and not your real power either in the College or in the estimation of the public."[21]

Finney dropped his responsibilities at Oberlin one at a time: he had discontinued his teaching of Systematic Theology in 1858; he left the presidency in 1865; he discontinued his church pastorate in 1872, but he continued to give his lectures on Pastoral Theology to the theological students down to the very year of his death in 1875.[22]

First Michael Strieby and then James Monroe, perhaps the most logical candidate, were invited to accept the presidency, but both declined; and at a meeting of June 22, 1866, James Harris Fairchild was appointed, his service beginning immediately.[23] Fairchild had been associated with Oberlin from 1834 either as student, as teacher, or as administrator, for under Finney much of the routine work of the presidential office had been performed by him. He was, therefore, already thoroughly acquainted with the administrative duties involved. "The new appointment to the Presidency meets but one response from all the great army of Oberlin students and alumni—that of hearty approval," commented the local paper editorially. "The man whom all admire and esteem, one who has been identified with the Institution from the outset, one who has done not less than any other to give it its present character all welcome to its Presidency." The evening after his appointment became known, a crowd of the young men marched to his house and stood in his flower beds while he made a modest speech from his porch in reply to their vociferous congratulations.[24]

James H. Fairchild was formally inducted into the presidency by Father Keep and delivered his inaugural address on the afternoon of August 22, 1866, during commencement week. The title of his discourse was "Educational Arrangements and College

[21]William Johnson to James Monroe, Jan. 16, 1861, and Hamilton Hill to James Monroe, Feb. 2, 3, 1864 (Monroe MSS); Finney to the Trustees, Aug. 19, 1865 (Misc. Archives); T. M., Aug. 19, 1865, and Keep *et al.* to Finney, Aug. 21, 1865 (Finney MSS).

[22]Fairchild, *Op. Cit.*, 280.

[23]On the offer to Monroe see the rumor in the *Lorain County News,* Oct. 4, 1865, and verification in a letter from J. H. Fairchild to Monroe, Sept. 17, 1866 (Monroe MSS), and in A. T. Swing, *James Harris Fairchild,* 194.

[24]*Lorain County News,* Aug. 22, 1866, and Swing, *Op. Cit.* 195.

Life at Oberlin."[25] It is an important historical document. President Fairchild had, years before, assumed the role of Oberlin historian, had shown himself historically minded and objective, seeing more clearly than most others the essentials of the Oberlin spirit and the true significance of the Oberlin contribution. His inaugural, like so much of his writing, is essentially historical, a kind of stock-taking of Oberlin at the shifting of administrations. This is perhaps what inaugurals always are at their best. Coming from a man like Fairchild, however, whose associations with Oberlin lay as much in the past as in the future, there is more of the retrospective than usual, and one feels that it is not so much Fairchild as Oberlin, itself, speaking.

With just pride he called his hearers' attention to the achievements of the past third-of-a-century: achievements in the field of Western education and contributions "to the solution of some special problems, educational, social, political, ecclesiastical and theological." Oberlin had expanded physically beyond the most sanguine dreams of its decidedly sanguine founders. Oberlin had become a hotbed of radicalism. "No doctrine was accepted because it was old, or rejected because it was new. Possibly the presumption was held to be in favor of the new, but the old never yielded without a vigorous struggle." From this "magazine of living energy" had gone out a disturbing but vitalizing influence through all the Northwest and all the nation. Fairchild recalled these days, climaxed by the further excitement of the war, with satisfaction, but accepted their passing without any apparent great regret. Such extreme pressure, he felt, could not be permanently maintained. "Earnest sympathy with every good work" should be continuously maintained, of course, but he saw in the future a period of less aggressive action, a period of relaxation from the fury of the fight, and he clearly welcomed it.

He advanced seven great factors as essential to Oberlin's success in the past and in the future: (1) the sympathy and support of an interested and Christian community; (2) the joint education of the sexes, an elevating and stimulating influence on both sexes; (3) the Preparatory Department, a recruiting ground for college students and laboratory for students who planned to be-

[25] James H. Fairchild, *Educational Arrangements and College Life at Oberlin: Inaugural Address of President J. H. Fairchild, Delivered at the Commencement of Oberlin College, August 22, 1866* (New York—1866).

come teachers; (4) the practice of students going out as country-school teachers in the winter vacations, thus bringing them "a knowledge of the world and a sympathy with its needs"; (5) the Theological Department, contributing a moral and religious tone to the whole institution; (6) the welcome to colored students, a blessing to the Negroes and to the white students who were "so educated as to take naturally a right position on the great question of our country and our time"; and (7) the deep, prevailing Christian piety.

But the central theme was the "somewhat unusual style of college life" which prevailed at Oberlin. Here he grasped at a unique and significant feature of the Oberlin of that day: "Each student belongs still to the world, not isolated from sympathies and obligations and activities. The ends he pursues are such as appeal to men in general, the reputation he desires is the same that will serve him in the work of life, and the motives to excellence are the natural motives which operate on men at large." This situation he saw as inseparably associated with joint education, the absence of grades and prizes, the prohibition of secret societies, and freedom of discussion of current political and economic issues, and producing unusually good order, assiduity and real and practical interest in studies. His own opinions, as here expressed, may be taken as those of Oberlin down at least to 1866. "Study will be effective in proportion to the motives which induce it, and he who lives in sympathy with the movements of the world and feels its claims, is most likely to give himself earnestly to a preparation for his work. . . . The college is a place for education, not merely for the acquisition of learning . . . the great object is such a discipline as is qualified for service in the world." These were strange words in the academic world of 1866.

The man who thus came to the presidency, though of the very stuff of Oberlin, was a conservative compared to the leaders who had preceded him. He was no aspiring prophet-dreamer like Shipherd; he had too much "common sense" to be a dietetic reformer like Stewart; he was too essentially temperate to fight as fanatically for universal reform as Mahan did; he was too bashful and self-distrustful to deliver the thrilling, scorching sermons of a Finney. He was never an extremist: he had opposed certain students' hastily-made plan to go to Kansas in the summer of 1855; he severely criticized Calvin Fairbank for his attempt to kidnap slaves in the border states; he went against the majority opinion at Oberlin on the issue of the ethics of the Harper's Ferry raid; his participation in the "Rescue" was limited to harboring the fugitive—at the request of the Rescuers. Those who knew him best, attempting to characterize him, constantly used such words as "moderation," "gentleness," "balance," "quiet trust in the ruling of Providence," "a most judicial mind," "quiet dignity," "solidity," "serenity," "steadiness," "sanity," "perfect control." In a sense he represented a reaction against the zealous reformism and heresy of the early days. At the time of Fairchild's death in 1902, a graduate, who had in later life accumulated considerable wealth, commented on his influence: "Oberlin was radical in its early days, and radicalism easily becomes rant. It is but a step from the reformer to the crank. That Oberlin escaped this danger was largely owing to the clear vision of President Fairchild:"[26] So the personal character of the man who understood the essence of Oberlin's primitive aggressiveness better than any other was an added force in the trend toward conformity.

As Finney's preoccupation with more central and exciting interests had strengthened faculty self-government, Fairchild's modesty, diffidence and temperance served to preserve that tradition. Fairchild simply did not have the makings of a dictator, and he never pretended to be the "executive" of Oberlin College. One spoke of him as not so much the President as "the *regulator* or *balance wheel* keeping the parts of our educational machinery . . . in harmonious relation and movement." When he passed from office in 1890 he wrote a statement of the traditional position of the President in Oberlin as it had come to be recognized at that time. "The President of the College," he wrote in part, "is chairman of the faculty and also of the trustees, but his personal authority is limited to special cases of emergency." The presidential status was clearly partly the expression of his own unassuming personality.[27]

In the sixties and seventies there are numerous other evidences of change besides the succession of Fairchild to the presidency. There were a number of important additions to the teaching staff:

[26]Swing, 371, and *passim,* and C. F. Thwing, *Guides, Philosophers and Friends* (New York—1927), 178–194.

[27]J. G. W. Cowles, "President Fairchild as an Administrator" (O. C. Lib. Misc. MSS).

JAMES HARRIS FAIRCHILD
(From the 1859 Class Album in the Oberlin College Library)

TAPPAN SQUARE IN THE SEVENTIES

The Chapel, Tappan and Council halls. Note the posts on the sidewalk which keep the cattle off the square.

(From a photograph in the Oberlin College Library)

Giles Shurtleff in 1865; Judson Smith in 1866; in 1869, Hiram Mead in Theology and Fenelon B. Rice in Music; in 1870 and 1871, Madam A. A. F. Johnston, Principal of the Ladies' Department, W. H. Ryder in Greek, E. P. Barrows, and James R. Severance, later Secretary and Treasurer. Henry Matson came as the first full-time librarian in 1874. Treasurer Hamilton Hill resigned in 1864 and retired to his native England in the following year. Henry E. Peck resigned in 1865; Mrs. Dascomb retired in 1870; Father Keep, dean of trustees, died in the same year; George Allen retired in 1871; Dr. Dascomb in 1878. James M. Fitch's relations to the College were not official, but his activities as printer, editor, bookseller, abolitionist-politician and superintendent of the Sunday School had given him a status at least equal to that of a faculty member. He sold his bookstore in the spring of 1867 and, on a Sabbath early in June, sent his death-bed blessing to the Sunday School.[28] Professor Morgan's service ended in 1880 and Henry Cowles died the next year. The services of four men of the older Oberlin continued through the ninth decade of the century and beyond and helped to keep alive old traditions and old memories. They were James Monroe, who returned to teach in 1883, Charles H. Churchill, J. M. Ellis, and President Fairchild, himself. But at the end of the century James H. Fairchild, then retired, was the last surviving protagonist of the old Oberlin.

And there were physical changes. The first Ladies' Hall was torn down in 1865 when the second Ladies' Hall, on the present site of Talcott, was ready for occupancy. New recitation buildings, French and Society halls, were constructed in 1866-68. Colonial Hall was removed and in 1870 the soldiers' monument was erected on its site.[29] Council Hall was begun in 1871 (the cornerstone laid at the Oberlin meeting of the National Council of Congregational Churches) and completed in 1874. Two years later

[28]*Lorain County News,* Apr. 17, 1867, and Mary Wright to A. A. Wright, June 9, 1867 (Wright MSS).

[29]On September 17, 1866, President Fairchild wrote to James Monroe: "We are laying the foundations of two new lecture room buildings—cottage structures—One in the rear of the chapel [French Hall]—the other [Society Hall] where the 'gymnasium' stood. We hope to get them enclosed this fall. The old Colonial Hall has its foundations taken out, & stands on blocks preparatory to a removal. It will probably not take a start until spring.—The old Ladies' Hall has entirely disappeared & a street is opened across the site.—So we change. It makes me feel bad some times to see the old landmarks disappear, but if one can get better ones we ought to accept them." (Monroe MSS.)

the College Chapel was enlarged and its original simple beauty destroyed. Flagstone walks were constructed; the trees on the square grew tall enough to cast an appreciable shade.

In the sixties the Theological Department was threatened with extinction, but by a supreme effort, which involved the collection of considerable funds from Oberlin townsmen, it was saved and its faculty increased. With the passing of Finney, however, that department lost its chief attraction. The rapid growth and firm establishment of the Conservatory of Music and the Business College caused or reflected a greater interest in secular things. There was a fairly steady increase in the proportion of young lady students; since 1881 they have always been more numerous than the men students. The vivid personality and prestige of Madam Johnston and her insistence on the admission of the lady students to most of the privileges open to the young men further emphasized the feminine trend. Perhaps there was some relationship between this trend and the swing from aggressive radicalism toward mid-Victorian conservatism.

The system of "joint education of the sexes," which had made Oberlin more peculiar and bizarre in the early years, now, in the sixties and seventies, under the name of coeducation, made it prominent, as the higher education of women became a matter of increasing general concern. Considerable expansion of the practice of collegiate "joint education" had taken place quietly in the first third of a century after its adoption at Oberlin, particularly through its introduction at small religious colleges in the West which looked to Oberlin for inspiration and leadership. These included Olivet, Hillsdale and Adrian in Michigan, Iowa College (later Grinnell), Drury, Tabor, and Cornell College in Iowa, Knox and Wheaton in Illinois, Beloit, Lawrence, and Ripon in Wisconsin, Wilberforce, the Ohio Negro college, Northfield College (later Carleton) in Minnesota, Berea in Kentucky, Washburn College in Kansas and Pacific University in Oregon.[30] In most instances the introduction of coeducation in these schools was directly traceable to the Oberlin influence.

In the late sixties the eyes of the educational world began to be turned on Oberlin's plan of associating the sexes in the same college. In 1865, Sophia Louisa Jex-Blake, the English feminist

[30]See R. S. Fletcher, "Oberlin and Co-education," *Ohio State Archaeological and Historical Quarterly*, XLVII, 1–19 (Jan., 1938).

and first English woman physician, came to Oberlin to observe the workings of coeducation on the campus.[31] The Rev. Thomas Markby in an article on "Joint Education" published in the *Contemporary Review* of London in 1868 quoted some of the material on Oberlin presented by Miss Jex-Blake.[32] About the same time M. Célestine Hippeau, a leading French educational reformer, was sent by the French Government to study the practice at Oberlin and other American coeducational institutions. He gave a favorable impression in his *L'Instruction publique aux Etats Unis,* published in Paris in 1869. In 1867 Lord and Lady Amberley, the liberal-minded parents of the liberal-minded Bertrand Russell, included Oberlin in a tour of experimental American institutions. The Honorable Dudley Campbell (M. A. Cant.), a distinguished London barrister, came to Oberlin in 1871 and, in an article on "Mixed Education of Boys and Girls in England and America," first published in the *Contemporary Review* in 1872 and later as a separate pamphlet by Rivingtons, described coeducation as he found it.[33] "At Oberlin College in the State of Ohio," he wrote, "where the pupils number a thousand, half of them women, the ages vary from seventeen to seven-and-twenty; and there the system has been in successful operation for more than five-and-thirty years. The testimony of the Professors is unanimous to the effect that the general tone of the students, not only as to conduct, but also as to industry, is far superior to what is usual in colleges managed on the separate principle. Cases of ungentlemanly behavior are almost unknown." He reported a conversation with one of the faculty members in which the professor said in part, "The system answers very well with us. . . . We find that the presence of the girls has a good effect upon the men and that of the men upon the girls. We think that the girls if kept away from young men will be dreaming about them, and it is better that they should see them. Nothing acts as a better antidote for romance than young men and women doing geometry together at eight o'clock every morning." "After spend-

[31]Sophia Jex-Blake, *A Visit to Some American Schools and Colleges* (London—1867). There is a sketch of Miss Jex-Blake in the *D. N. B.*, 1912–1921 Supplement.

[32]"On the Education of Women," *Contemporary Review* (London), VII, 242–261 (Feb., 1868).

[33]*Ibid.*, XXII, 257–265 (July, 1873), and pamphlet published in 1874. Further data on Hippeau is in the *Enciclopedia Universal Ilustrada Europeo-Americana* (Bilbao, Madrid, Barcelona—192? +). On the Amberleys see *The Amberley Papers,* edited by Bertrand and Elizabeth Russell, 2 vol. (New York—1937).

ing some days in visiting the different classes," continued Campbell, "I became convinced that the words above cited were free from the slightest exaggeration. Whether they were being instructed by a gentleman or a lady, the attention of the pupils was above criticism. And the women seemed to have no difficulty in holding their own with the other students."

An American woman, Miss Mary E. Beedy, delivered a lecture in 1873 before the "London Sunday Lecture Society" on the subject of "joint education" as practiced in the United States. The lecture was published in pamphlet form. Despite the fact that this Miss Beedy was an Antioch graduate she drew her illustrations largely from Oberlin and quoted Fairchild's 1867 address on coeducation extensively. She explained the spread of coeducation in America in the following words: "Oberlin sent out staunch men and women. Wherever these men and women went it was observed that they worked with a will and with effect. The eminent success of Oberlin led many parents in different parts of the country to desire its advantages for their sons and daughters. But Oberlin was a long way off from New England and from many other parts of the country; besides some thought it an uncomfortably religious place; negroes were admitted, and it was altogether very democratic, much more so than many people liked. So parents began to say, Why can't we have other colleges that shall provide all the advantages of Oberlin and omit the peculiarities we dislike?"[34] The European interest in Oberlin and its plan for the higher education of women should, of course, be seen against the background of developments going on there: the founding of Girton College for women at Cambridge in 1872 and the opening to women students of continental universities such as Zurich in 1868, Copenhagen in 1875, and all Swedish universities in 1870.

Probably the most important document in the history of college coeducation is President Fairchild's address before a meeting of college presidents at Springfield, Illinois, on July 10, 1867. It was entitled "Coeducation of the Sexes," and was a description of the Oberlin experience and a defense of the practice. It was published in full in Barnard's *American Journal of Education* in

[34]Mary E. Beedy, *The Joint Education of Young Men and Women in American Schools and Colleges; Being a Lecture Delivered Before the Sunday Lecture Society, on 27th of April, 1873* (London, 1873).

January, 1868, in the *Report* of the [United States] Commissioner of Education for 1867–68, and in James Orton's *The Liberal Education of Women: the Demand and the Method, Current Thoughts in America and England,* published in 1873. In the generation which followed it was easily the article most quoted by proponents of the cause of coeducation. Thus Oberlin's primacy came to have a more than accidental significance. Oberlin became, as Anna Tolman Smith has put it in a later *Report* of the Commissioner of Education, "a model and exemplar for all colleges that proposed the open door for women."[35]

A great impetus was given to the collegiate coeducational movement as a result of its adoption in the late sixties and early seventies by Bates and Boston University in New England, Swarthmore in Pennsylvania, and Cornell and Syracuse in New York. The possibilities were thoroughly canvassed by specially appointed committees at Williams, Dartmouth, Amherst and Harvard, and those institutions were the target of considerable criticism because they decided in the negative.[36] All of the Western state universities established under the Morrill Act became coeducational: Iowa, Michigan, Wisconsin, Indiana, Ohio State. Michigan became the favorite example of coeducation in a state university, and President Angell, an enthusiastic protagonist of the practice.

The 70's was the period of the great debate on coeducation. Dr. Edward H. Clarke, a physician of Boston, issued in October, 1873, a book entitled *Sex in Education*[37] in which he warned that coeducation threatened the physical well-being of the whole mass of American women. The book was widely quoted in the press and is now most important for the flood of matter in defense of coeducation which it called out. In this literature, Oberlin, as the

[35]"Coeducation in the Schools and Colleges of the United States," United States Commissioner of Education, *Report,* 1903, I, 1055.

[36]James Orton, *The Liberal Education of Women* (New York and Chicago—1873). On Dartmouth see Leon Barr Richardson, *History of Dartmouth College* (Hanover—1932), II, 552. Samuel Eliot Morison makes the statement (*Three Centuries of Harvard, 1636–1936* [Cambridge, 1936], 393) that "no proposition to make Harvard College coeducational has ever been seriously entertained." In a letter to the author (August 7, 1937) Morison explains that Clarke's report was not "seriously entertained" because it was a report to a committee only and did not reach the Board of Overseers. It seemed significant, however, that anyone like Clarke, who served as an overseer for seventeen years, should have taken such a stand.

[37]*Sex in Education; or, a Fair Chance for the Girls* (Boston—1873).

college where coeducation had been longest established, was often called to witness as an example of practical success and Fairchild's address of 1867 was cited. President Edward H. Magill of Swarthmore delivered *An Address upon the Co-education of the Sexes* in the same year, giving Oberlin "where coeducation has been well tested for more than thirty years," Antioch, and Michigan as proofs of the safety and advantages of coeducation.[38] Dean George F. Comfort of Syracuse wrote a book in reply to Dr. Clarke which was published in 1874 under the title of *Woman's Education, and Woman's Health.*[39] He recognized Oberlin's pioneer position as the place where "the movement for opening colleges and universities to women was inaugurated." The most complete collection of opinion on the question of woman's education at this time is that entitled *The Liberal Education of Women,* edited by James Orton of Vassar College.[40] In this volume President Fairchild's address is reprinted as also the reports favoring coeducation for Williams, Cornell and Harvard. President Andrew D. White of Cornell presented the statistics of Oberlin as the most effective reply to Dr. Clarke. James Freeman Clarke in his report to a committee of the Harvard Board of Overseers recommended coeducation for that institution on the basis of the experience at Michigan and Oberlin. "I believe the system is good in itself," he concluded, "that it is in accordance with the ideas of modern society—that in practice it has worked very well, wherever tried, and that the sooner it can be introduced at Cambridge the better it will be for our excellent University." Also included is a paper read by Thomas Wentworth Higginson at a "Social Science Convention" in 1873 favoring the plan and also citing President Fairchild and Oberlin. President Eliot, however, demurred. Admitting that Oberlin was "altogether the most favorable example of an institution for the coeducation of the sexes in this country, and therefore in the world," he insisted that he had evidence that it was not wholly successful even there and therefore still on trial. Whichever side they took few omitted some reference to the Oberlin experience.

Meanwhile coeducation was so widely adopted in American

38 (Philadelphia—1873.)

39 (Syracuse—1874.)

40 *The Liberal Education of Women: the Demand and the Methods, Current Thoughts in America and England* (New York and Chicago—1873).

colleges and universities that interest in the debate declined. Even the conservative South was invaded in 1882 when the University of Mississippi admitted women. It was something of a moral triumph for Oberlin when her ancient rival Western Reserve accepted women students and President Carroll Cutler presented a statement to the Western Reserve Board of Trustees in praise of the once-despised Oberlinism of "joint education."[41] Already in 1873 there were nearly a hundred coeducational colleges in the United States. In 1890 there were 282 and in 1902, 330, about half of them still in the Middle West, the region of Oberlin's greatest influence. Coeducation, once an Oberlin "peculiarity," thus became a typical Americanism.[42]

The admission of women and Negroes had been, perhaps, the two most notorious features of the old Oberlin College. With the triumph of emancipation the Negro came to be recognized in the North as educable, and the nation, suddenly interested in the cultural and intellectual elevation of the freedmen, turned to Oberlin as the institution most prominently identified with Negro education. As Oberlin testified to a listening world that women really had minds, so Oberlin also testified that the Negro was a human being and produced examples of colored persons who had made notable progress in scholarship. "There is no essential difference," reported Principal E. H. Fairchild, "other things being equal, between their standing and that of the white students."[43]

Berea College in Kentucky, closed after the John Brown raid by vigilantes because of its abolitionist taint, was reopened in 1865 on the full Oberlin pattern—coeducational and coracial. Several members of the staff, as in pre-war years, were Oberlin graduates, and Principal E. H. Fairchild was secured in 1869 to become President. He visited the commencement exercises in 1868 "held in the grove, on the college grounds, under a bower prepared with considerable expenditure of labor, and quite artistic," in which fourteen white and twelve colored students participated. "The spirit and tone of the place" reminded him forci-

[41]Carroll Cutler, *Shall Women Now be Excluded From Adelbert College of Western Reserve University?* (Cleveland [1884]).

[42]"Coeducation in the Schools and Colleges of the United States," *Loc. Cit.*, 1903, I, 1064.

[43]J. W. Alvord, *Tenth Semi-Annual Report on Schools for Freedmen, July 1, 1870* (Washington—1870), 50.

bly of the early days of Oberlin.[44] Of course, there was opposition in a border state like Kentucky. The Ku Klux often threatened the town. A visitor from the North was startled in the night to hear shouts of "Hurrah for Jeff Davis" and "Jeff Davis was a white man"; horsemen often galloped wildly through the streets firing revolvers in every direction. But there was no actual bloodshed, and by the mid-eighties Fairchild, speaking at an educational conference in New Orleans, dared to proclaim the system of "coeducation of the sexes and the races" practiced at Berea. "They room in the same buildings, board at the same tables, recite in the same classes, sit promiscuously in all assemblies, work at the same wood-piles or in the same dining-hall, play on the same grounds at the same games. No distinction whatever is made on account of color."[45]

In 1870, Richard Theodore Greener, a Negro prepared at Oberlin, graduated from Harvard College and received the A.B. degree, reputedly the first colored man to finish the course at America's leading scholarly institution. By that date most first-class Northern colleges admitted properly qualified colored students.[46] Another Oberlin peculiarity had thus ceased to be peculiar.

As Union troops conquered parts of the slave states Oberlinites beheld the opening of the great opportunity to do something constructive for the "contraband"—after January 1, 1863, freedmen. Former and present Oberlin students gave active support to the various "Freedmen's Aid" societies and especially to the American Missionary Association. Rev. Jacob R. Shipherd (Oberlin, A.B., 1862), Rescuer and nephew of the Founder, was

[44]American Missionary Association, *Twenty-Second Annual Report* (New York—1868), pages 5–53. On the history of Berea see [E. H. Fairchild] *Berea College, Kentucky* (Cincinnati—1883); J. A. R. Rogers, *Birth of Berea College* (Philadelphia—1903); John G. Fee, *Autobiography* (Chicago—1891); and Lloyd V. Hennings, "The American Missionary Association, a Christian Anti-Slavery Society" (MS Master's thesis in Oberlin College Library).

[45]J. W. Alvord, *Letters from the South . . .* (Washington, D. C.—1870), 37–38, and E. H. Fairchild, "Berea College, Kentucky," United States Commissioner of Education, *Special Report, Educational Exhibits and Conventions at the World's Industrial and Cotton Centennial Exposition, New Orleans, 1884–85* (Washington—1886), Part I, 230–232. Kentucky law later forced the exclusion of Negroes from Berea.

[46]Oberlin College, *General Catalogue, 1833—1908;* Mary Church Terrell, "History of the High School for Negroes in Washington," *Journal of Negro History,* II, 252–266 (July, 1917), and Alvord, *Tenth Semi-Annual Report on Schools for Freedmen,* July 1, 1870, page 50.

the first corresponding secretary and leading full-time worker of the Northwestern Freedmen's Aid Commission with headquarters at Chicago. When, in 1865, all the freedmen's societies were federated in the American Freedmen's Union Commission, Shipherd went to Washington as one of the national secretaries in association with Frederick Law Olmsted and others.[47]

The sixteenth annual meeting of the American Missionary Association, from the beginning an Oberlin anti-slavery enterprise, was held at Oberlin in October of 1862. A resolution was adopted expressing gratitude for the Emancipation Proclamation which, it was declared, "inspires the hope that under God the freedom of large masses of the enslaved is near at hand." Within a few weeks after the adjournment of this meeting five Oberlin students had left to work among the "contraband" at Fortress Monroe or in South Carolina, including among their number the Negro Thomas D. Tucker, brought over from Africa by George Thompson to be educated at Oberlin. "We are thankful," commented the editor of the *Evangelist,* "that at last a new direction is given to the enlistments from Oberlin College."[48] In April of 1863 the Commandant of the Contraband Camp at Washington spoke before the Students' Missionary Society. The crowd in attendance was so large that an adjournment to the First Church was necessary. Students were beginning to go off in troops to become preachers and teachers among the former slaves. Ten left in one band in September of 1864, seven young ladies at another time in the following year. Early in 1866 Professor Cowles contributed an admittedly incomplete list of between thirty and forty students engaged in this work among the freedmen with the American Missionary Association.[49] By 1866 the association had 353 persons under its supervision working among the Southern Negroes—264 of them being women teachers. For the next few years this was the main field of effort, and in it Oberlin students and former students played, as would be expected, a very large part. In 1868 not only were both of

[47]Cf. *The Freedmen's Bulletin* (Chicago), 1864–65, *passim;* the *Western Freedmen's Bulletin* (Cincinnati), Jan., 1866, and *Lorain County News,* Sept. 6, 1865.

[48]American Missionary Association, *Sixteenth Annual Report* (New York—1862); 5, and *Oberlin Evangelist,* Dec. 3, 1862.

[49]Oberlin Students' Missionary Society, MS Records, Apr. 5, 1863, and the *Lorain County News,* Sept. 28, 1864; Dec. 6, 1865; Jan. 24, 1866. See letter from S. G. Wright in *Ibid.,* Apr. 18, 1866.

the executive secretaries in New York Oberlin men (George Whipple and Michael Strieby), but in the two subordinate departments, the Middle-West Department (Kentucky, Tennessee, Georgia, and part of Alabama) and the Western Department (Kansas, Illinois, Missouri, Arkansas, Mississippi, part of Alabama and Texas), Oberlin men were in charge as field secretaries. Jacob R. Shipherd was at the head of the Western Department, and E. M. Cravath, a graduate of the College of 1857 and of the Theological Department in 1860, headed the Middle-West Department. The general field agent with headquarters in New York, the Rev. Edward P. Smith, had been a student in the Preparatory Department for two years.[50]

Oberlin's work in the Negro schools of Washington was important from the beginning. Fugitives naturally flooded into the capital city in large numbers and there was a great demand for social, educational, and religious workers among them. Rev. Danforth B. Nichols (A.B., Oberlin, 1839) had been a city missionary in the Chicago slums in the fifties; he was one of the pioneer group of missionaries who went from Boston in the spring of 1862 to teach and preach among the fugitives in the occupied area along the South Carolina coast. The next year he returned from that field to become Civil Superintendent of the fugitives in Washington and environs. He taught schools in Duff Green's Row on Capitol Hill, in McClellan Barracks and, later, at Freedman's Village, Arlington Heights, where "the first thoroughly systematic and genuine contraband school was established within the sight of the national Capitol." John Watson Alvord, Lane Rebel and graduate of the Oberlin Theological Department in the famous class of 1836, came to Washington at about the same time to distribute the schoolbooks and religious books especially compiled by the American Tract Society of Boston for the use of Negro fugitives.[51] In 1868 George F. T. Cook, a student in Oberlin from 1853 to 1860, was made superintendent of colored schools for the District of Columbia, a position which he held to the end of the century. In 1871, Mary

50American Missionary Association, *20th Annual Report* (New York—1866), 13, and *22nd Annual Report* (New York—1868), 7, 50 and 67.

51D. B. Nichols, MS Autobiography (in the possession of G. G. Wenzlaff, Los Angeles, Calif.); B. L. Pierce, *History of Chicago*, II, 369; F. B. Simkins and R. H. Woody, *South Carolina During Reconstruction* (Chapel Hill, N. C.—1932), 426 *et seq.*, and *Lorain County News*, Apr. 8, Dec. 9, 1863.

Jane Patterson, first colored woman to earn a bachelor's degree (Oberlin, A.B., 1862), became principal of the colored high school. Miss Patterson continued as assistant principal after Richard T. Greener, of Oberlin and Harvard, took charge in 1872.[52]

In 1865 the United States Congress established the Bureau of Refugees, Freedmen and Abandoned Lands to furnish relief and educational opportunities for the Negroes, and President Johnson, following Lincoln's known intention, appointed General Oliver Otis Howard as its executive head. Howard was a benevolent but, perhaps, rather inefficient and gullible administrator, who was also, more important to our story, a Congregationalist.[53] He made the Oberlinite Alvord general superintendent of the schools for freedmen which were established and administered by the Bureau. John Mercer Langston, Negro lawyer and graduate of the Collegiate and Theological Departments at Oberlin, became general inspector. Alvord was also head of the ill-starred Freedmen's Bank, and Langston was associated on the Board of Trustees with Frederick Douglass and others. The chief clerk of the Bureau from 1867 to 1872 was an Oberlin Negro graduate in the Class of 1864 (John H. Cook), and Capt. Orindatus S. B. Wall, the colored Oberlin business man, was appointed "Employment Agent." In 1867 President Johnson, having broken with General Howard, offered the commissionership to Langston, but the latter suspected a disruptive purpose on Johnson's part and refused the offer.[54]

Howard, Alvord and Langston were naturally partial to Oberlin men and women and to the Oberlin-affiliated American Missionary Association. Bureau funds to the extent of nearly a quarter-of-a-million were turned over to the association for the extension of its educational program. Money was even allocated to Oberlin to help build college buildings, because it trained so many white and Negro teachers for the South.[55] In 1868, nearly

[52]G. Smith Wormley, "Educators of the First Half Century of Public Schools of the District of Columbia," *Journal of Negro History*, XVII, 124–140 (April, 1932), and Mary Church Terrell, "History of the High School for Negroes in Washington," *Loc. Cit.*, II, 252–266 (July, 1917).

[53]*D. A. B.*, and *Autobiography of Oliver Otis Howard* (New York—1907).

[54]Oberlin College, *Semi Centennial Register*, 1883, page 106; *Lorain County News*, Jan. 30, 1867; *Cleveland Leader*, Aug. 30, 1867, in *Annals of Cleveland*, 2273, and J. M. Langston, *From the Virginia Plantation to the National Capital* (Hartford—1894), 275–6.

[55]"Minority Report on Charges Against General Howard," House Doc., 41st Cong., 2 sess., *Report No. 125*, page 7, and letter from Henry M. Whittelsey of

a quarter (532) of all the teachers under Alvord's supervision (2,300) were supplied by the Oberlin-dominated A. M. A.[56] Oberlinites—Alvord, Langston, Whipple, Strieby, Shipherd, Cravath and Smith—were not only the leaders in this educational work among the Negroes, but many of the rank and file of the teachers, certainly scores, probably hundreds, were Oberlin graduates, undergraduates or former students. Lovejoy Johnson (Oberlin, A.B., 1861) was superintendent of colored schools at Helena, Arkansas; Joseph H. Barnum (A.B., 1854), formerly superintendent of Oberlin schools, was superintendent of Negro schools in Memphis from 1866 to 1875. After a tour through the South in the winter of 1866–67 a Cleveland pastor wrote: "At every place, from Lexington, Ky., to Charleston, S. C., I found some representatives of Oberlin connected with the schools."[57]

The agents and teachers of the American Missionary Association and the Freedmen's Bureau were not, it may be imagined, enthusiastically welcomed by the Southern whites. The name Oberlin was a red flag south of Mason's and Dixon's Line and it is not surprising that Oberlin teachers, especially if they were black, were occasionally visited by the K K K. At Mayfield, Kentucky, Alvord reported in 1869, the night-riders "proceeded to the boarding place of the teacher, a young colored lady educated at Oberlin, and drove her from the town."[58] When Rev. John P. Bardwell (Sem., 1844) was in Grenada, Mississippi, attempting to organize Negro schools "he was assailed by a former slaveholder—backed up and encouraged by a mob—dragged out of his chair, beaten with a heavy cane and his life directly threatened." In Memphis where the teachers of the Negro schools came mainly from Oberlin, a mob burned the schoolhouses and attempted to frighten the teachers away. Rev. George W. Andrews (A.B., 1858), preaching and teaching among the colored people at Marion, Alabama, wrote to James Monroe that he was ostracized by all Southern ministers and forced to carry firearms on all occasions to protect himself and his congregation and pupils

the Freedmen's Bureau to George Kinney, Treasurer of Oberlin College, Feb. 19, 1870 (Treas. Off.), acknowledging the receipt of "bills for material and labor in constructing buildings at Oberlin College" and stating that the Commissioner would "appropriate $5,000 towards the payment of the same."

56John W. Alvord, *Sixth Semi-Annual Report on Schools for Freedmen, July 1, 1868* (Washington—1868), page 4.

57*Cleveland Leader*, Feb. 25, 1867, in the *Annals of Cleveland*, 3522.

58*Seventh Semi-Annual Report* (Washington—1869), page 45.

from the Ku Klux Klan.[59] It is quite possible that Oberlin-educated teachers were overly enthusiastic and tactless in their dealings with the extremely delicate race situation. Southern whites and some modern historians charge them with being "political emissaries among the Negroes, organizing them into 'loyal leagues,' and impressing upon them the duty of voting the Republican ticket."[60] Langston was frank about his activities in behalf of the Republican party and was notorious among white Democrats for his political work.[61] The whole question as to whether the carpetbag teacher did more good or evil is still one to arouse passionate recriminations. Most hundred-percent Southerners still can see nothing but evil in their story. But some recent Southern students of reconstruction are willing to admit that they "did much to lift the pall of illiteracy which had been imposed upon the Negroes while slaves."[62] The chief difference between the Oberlinites and the Southern whites was, quite definitely, not how but whether the Negroes should be educated.

Howard University was founded in Washington to be the cap-stone of the system of Negro education. The idea originated with a group of members of the Washington Congregational Church, particularly three ministers: C. B. Boynton, pastor and founder of the church and Chaplain of the House of Representatives, Benjamin F. Morris, and Danforth B. Nichols, the Oberlin graduate. Nichols was one of the first trustees and a member of the first faculty and was responsible for the adoption of the name of the Commissioner of the Freedmen's Bureau by the new institution. A charter was granted by Congress, and "Howard Uni-

59*Lorain County News,* May 9, 1865; "Special Committee . . . charged with investigation into . . . the riots at Memphis . . . ," 39 Cong., 1 sess., House *Report,* No. 101, and G. W. Andrews to James Monroe, Mar. 16, 1871 (Monroe MSS).

60James Wilford Garner, *Reconstruction in Mississippi* (New York—1901), page 359.

61Langston wrote in his third-person autobiography (*From the Virginia Plantation to the National Capitol* [Hartford—1894], page 263): "That Mr. Langston's position with respect to the Republican party and the advocacy of its principles, measures and men at the great meetings which he addressed may be properly understood, it should be stated that from the time he entered upon his duties as general inspector of the Bureau he acted by special engagement as the representative and duly accredited advocate of that party. Nowhere, therefore, as he traveled and spoke, did he fail to present and defend in moderate, wise manner, its claims upon the support of the newly emancipated classes and their friends."

62Simkins and Woody, *Op. Cit.,* 429 *et seq.*

versity" was established without "restriction based on race, sex, creed or color." Other Oberlinites played an important part in its early years: Amzi Lorenzo Barber (A.B., Oberlin, 1867) was Principal of the important preparatory division for some time; John M. Langston founded the Law School and was acting President for one year.[63]

The American Missionary Association was responsible for the establishment of a whole chain of consolidated elementary and advanced schools for Negroes in the South. It had taken the initiative in the reopening of Berea in 1865. In 1866 Fisk University was founded in Tennessee by Erastus Milo Cravath and E. P. Smith (A.M.A. agents and Oberlinites) associated with General Clinton B. Fisk and Professor John Ogden. Cravath (A.B., Oberlin, 1857; Sem., 1860) served first as Secretary and then as President. At Talladega, which dates from 1867, most of the early teachers, including H. E. Brown, the first Principal, were former Oberlin students.[64] Oberlin men and women played an important part in the other colored schools founded by the A. M. A., and Oberlin principles and the Oberlin tradition inspired them all. No other American college was so well suited to serve as a pattern. Oberlin's racial tolerance was of primary significance but hardly less important were the Oberlin musical tradition, Oberlin's practice of mixing "learning and labor," and coeducation of the sexes.[65]

There was a close connection between educational and religious missionary work in the South and economic and political carpetbaggism. New England had "civilized" the Middle West

[63]Dwight O. W. Holmes, "Fifty Years of Howard University," *Journal of Negro History*, III, 128–138, and United States Commissioner of Education, *Special Report . . . on the Condition and Improvement of Public Schools in the District of Columbia . . .* (Washington—1871), pages 245–252. George Whipple, Lane Rebel and Oberlinite, was president-elect of Howard University when he died.—Oliver Johnson, *William Lloyd Garrison and His Times* (Boston—1881), 175.

[64]Dwight O. W. Holmes, *The Evolution of the Negro College* (New York—1934); *Fisk University, Nashville, Tenn.* (a pamphlet n.p.—n.d.); J. B. T. Marsh, *The Story of the Jubilee Singers* (Boston—n.d.), and *Oberlin College Review*, July 8, 1874; Feb. 19, Mar. 19, Apr. 30, 1889.

[65]It is interesting to note that when the African Methodist Episcopal Church established a Methodist college for Negroes at Xenia, Ohio (1863)—Wilberforce University—they turned to Oberlin for a large number of their teachers. At least ten members of the faculty in the period 1863–76 were Oberlin-educated. Daniel A. Payne, "Historical Sketch of Wilberforce University," Ohio Centennial Education Committee, *Historical Sketches of the Higher Educational Institutions and Also of Benevolent and Reformatory Institutions of the State of Ohio* (n.p.—1876), no page numbers.

through missionary work and colonization. Oberlin was a notable example of what could be done. Yankee missionaries and emigrants had "saved" Kansas. Colonization in the South would, many believed, be necessary to support activities of ministers and teachers. "Now the South must be converted and puritanized," declared the Oberlin *Lorain County News* in January, 1864. "It must be settled by men who at heart hate slavery and oppression in every form, and who will labor not more for pecuniary reward, than for the social and moral elevation of the people, both black and white."[66]

Some Oberlinites joined the migration. Late in 1865 the *News* reported that Samuel Plumb, Capt. L. H. Tenney, C. T. Marks and several others had gone South with an eye to business. Joseph H. Barnum engaged in cotton planting before he turned to school administration at Memphis; John Lynch (Oberlin, A.B., 1851) became a planter in Louisiana. Horace C. Taylor went into business at Corpus Christi, Texas, and was appointed postmaster. James H. Piles, a Negro graduate in 1866, became a member of the Louisiana legislature and Assistant Secretary of State. Benjamin Franklin Randolph, a former Oberlin student, was murdered in South Carolina while campaigning for the Black Republicans.[67]

Stephen W. Dorsey, a runaway boy from Vermont, was befriended by Samuel Plumb when he wandered into Oberlin just before the war. He married Helen Mary Wack, daughter of Chauncey Wack, Oberlin Democrat and proprietor of the Russia House (or Railroad House), and served in the Union army as an artillery officer, surviving charges of cowardice at Murfreesboro. After the end of the war he acquired two cotton plantations and a store at Demopolis, Alabama. He was also appointed postmaster but was forced out and, after a visit to Ohio, went to Helena, Arkansas. In Arkansas he was the leading representative of the corrupt railroad interests which were closely allied with the Republican state machine. He was chairman of the Republican state committee for several years, United States Senator for one term, and secretary of the Republican National Committee in 1880, in which capacity he managed Garfield's successful cam-

[66]*Lorain County News,* Jan. 20, 1864.

[67]*Ibid.,* Dec. 27, 1865; Oberlin College, *Semi-Centennial Register,* 1883, and *Cleveland Leader,* Oct. 21, 1868, in *Annals of Cleveland,* 4674.

paign for the Presidency. His involvement in the "Star Route" post office frauds led to his retirement from public life. The fortuitous association of this adventurer with Oberlin cast a dark shadow on what was otherwise an unselfish and benevolent program.[68]

John M. Langston (A.B., 1849) and another Oberlin colored man, William H. Day (A.B., 1847), worked for two decades for Negro suffrage. In 1848–50 they had organized Ohio Negroes into a Negro suffrage society. In 1853 they called a national convention to meet at Rochester and in 1853–54 Day published the *Aliened American* at Cleveland as the organ of the campaign. Langston looked upon the enlistment of Negro troops in which he was so active as a step toward Negro citizenship and suffrage. In 1864 the National Equal Rights League was founded at a convention of Negroes at Syracuse, a prominent part being played by Frederick Douglass, Charles B. Ray, George B. Vashon (Oberlin's first Negro graduate), and Langston. Langston was elected president and re-elected in the following year. As president of this organization he lectured throughout the North in behalf of Negro suffrage—at the Cooper Union in New York City, at the Chapel in Oberlin and in various towns further west. Apparently most Oberlinites followed Langston rather than Gov. J. D. Cox (A.B., 1851) who, in a much publicized letter to Oberlin friends in the summer of 1865, declared his opposition to the general extension of the suffrage to Negroes. Though the adoption of the Fifteenth Amendment was chiefly the result of political considerations, Langston's campaign helped to get the idealists' wing of the Radical Republican group in line.[69]

In Northern and national politics Oberlin was no longer outcast. Oberlin had been abolitionist when that meant treason; Oberlin had been "Free Soil" when that was heresy; Oberlin had been Republican in the fifties when to be Republican was to be dangerously radical. Oberlin was also Republican in the sixties and seventies when only Republicans were patriotic and "respectable." Oberlinites who had once defied and flouted the

[68]*Dictionary of American Biography,* and *Lorain County News,* Feb. 20, 1861; Jan. 7, 14, Feb. 4, 11, 1863; Aug. 29, 1866.

[69]*Cleveland Daily True Democrat,* Dec. 24, 1849; Jan. 21—Feb. 14, 1850; June 13, 1853, in the *Annals of Cleveland; Semi-Centennial Register,* 1883; *Oberlin Evangelist,* Apr. 20, 1853; *Lorain County News,* Oct. 10, 1864; Mar. 8, July 26, Aug. 9, 23, Oct. 4, 1865; Feb. 21, 1866, and Jan. 16, 1867.

national law were now making and administering it and labelling traitors those who disobeyed or criticized the law thus made. Jacob Dolson Cox became Governor of Ohio and Secretary of the Interior. James Monroe was Consul in Rio and, after 1870, Member of Congress, passing out the post offices to the friends of Oberlin and other loyal supporters of the G.O.P. and hobnobbing with his old friend, later President, James A. Garfield. Prof. Henry E. Peck was appointed Minister to Haiti in 1865 and died of yellow fever in 1867. Langston followed him in the same position from 1877 to 1885. Isaac Stone (A.B., 1852) was consul at Singapore from 1864 to 1869, and Almond A. Thompson (A.B., 1854) held the consulship at Goderich, Canada, in the seventies. An anonymous writer to the *Lorain County News* in 1863[70] reported Oberlin people numerous at the capital: "I meet them at every turn and hear of more than I see." Many held minor clerkships, but William M. Ampt (A.B., 1863) was Chief Clerk of the Quartermaster's Department, Edward G. Chambers (A.B., 1848) was clerk to the Joint Committee on the Conduct of the War, Newell C. Brooks (A.B., 1858) was Chief Clerk of the Army Medical Department, and Charles C. Darwin (A.B., 1868) became Assistant Librarian of Congress in the seventies.[71]

Other educational ideas of early Oberlin were also being widely adopted. More colleges, especially in the West where Oberlin's influence was strongest, had music departments, and there was a slowly increasing number of independent conservatories or conservatories associated with colleges. Great strides were made in higher practical education, agricultural and mechanical especially, as a result of the establishment of the land grant colleges, but Oberlin had given up its work in this field with the decline of manual labor. At the same time there came a new era of experimentation with manual labor for college students. In Berea and in some of the Negro colleges the system used was directly influenced by the early experiences of Oberlin, and Berea preserves today a practice based on the old Oberlin plan of the thirties and forties, a practice which seems to function most successfully in an agricultural and self-sufficing society. The

[70]Dec. 16, 1863. On Peck and Langston see James A. Padgett, "Diplomats to Haiti and Their Diplomacy," *Journal of Negro History,* XXV, 265–330 (July, 1940).

[71]*Semi-Centennial Register.*

influence of Oberlin is less clearly evident in the experiment with manual labor in the land grant institutions such as Cornell.[72] There was considerable expansion, too, in the late nineteenth century in the teaching of domestic science and in business training, but Oberlin had dropped these also, though the Oberlin Business College was, for several years, closely associated with the College proper. In the 70's there was an hiatus in the emphasis on practical physical education at Oberlin, but the later distinguished work of Dr. Frederick Eugene Leonard and Dr. Delphine Hannah in that field must have been inspired by some surviving vestiges of the early theories of "physiological reform." In general the Oberlin curriculum had subsided to the normal, classics and all, and the territory so suddenly seized in the thirties and then evacuated was only slowly reconquered in later years in the wake of many other institutions. In general there was an increasing tendency for Oberlin to cease to experiment and to adopt innovations only after Eastern institutions had tested them and given to them their stamp of approval. Oberlin did hold stubbornly to her ban on grades and honors and yielded to the advance of Phi Beta Kappa belatedly at the end of the century.

Oberlin was received also into the full fellowship of the orthodox Congregational Church. Oberlin's ultraisms had long since been given up. Dietetic reform and the memory of Graham were a laughingstock even at Ladies' Hall. Pacifism had been tramped down under the feet of blue-coated Oberlin soldiers fighting a holy war for human rights. Sanctification was seldom mentioned, and then apologetically. Oberlin was too successful and too respectable now to be heretical. The final love-feast came in 1871 when the first regular National Council of the Congregational Churches of the United States of America was held *at Oberlin*.[73] That good Congregationalist soldier and friend of the black man, Oliver Otis Howard, was assistant moderator. Finney prayed and preached repeatedly before the assembled ministers and pious laymen. The cornerstone of a new Oberlin theological

[72]Earle D. Ross, "The Manual Labor Experiment in the Land Grant College," *Mississippi Valley Historical Review,* XXI, 513–528 (Mar., 1935).

[73]It is interesting to note that A. Hastings Ross, a graduate of Oberlin College, was chiefly instrumental in the reorganization of Congregational Church government at this time and was responsible for the beginning of the series of biennial or triennial national councils. See Williston Walker, *A History of the Congregational Churches in the United States* (New York—1894), 392 *et seq.*

building—Council Hall—was laid.[74] It was a brave day for Oberlin—now triumphant.

A great change in public sentiment toward Oberlin had been going on since the later fifties and was generally completed, in the North, when it became apparent that now Oberlin was generally very much the same as many other colleges: coeducational as most Western colleges were, admitting Negroes as all did, and pious in a Victorian and quiet sort of way. Oberlin's financial agents found gratifying evidences of this change. In 1859 Henry Cowles came back from a tour through Michigan reporting that: "Oberlin's students are no longer despised among the Michigan churches. The day of their exclusion from Christian confidence & fellowship seems to have passed away." Four years later he reasserted this opinion at the end of a similar mission. "In general," he wrote, "the unfavorable opinions of Oberlin held by many in its early years, have largely passed away. Intelligent people generally admit that the college has done good:—usually they say, *great good.*" The decision of the Society for Promoting Collegiate and Theological Education at the West to aid Oberlin, reached after long years of opposition, is further evidence of this change. Henry Cowles' observations were mostly made in the West but, in 1866, Charles H. Churchill reported a similar change of opinion even in New England.[75]

It was recognized by some, however, that this more respectable reputation and status was gained at a certain cost. "Oberlin now is not what Oberlin was," lamented the ladies of the Maternal Association at a meeting in 1865. They proudly recognized that this was partly the result of the spread of Oberlin principles "all over the land," but some suspected a "degeneracy from true Christian principles."[76] Many of the old leaders were much troubled by what they conceived of as a grave declension of aggressive, single-minded, Christian devotion in the Oberlin school and community. Henry Cowles, in resigning his agency in 1863, gave expression to his troubled thoughts on this question. He

[74]William E. Barton, *The Law of Congregational Usage* (Chicago—1910), 399–403, and National Council of the Congregational Churches, *Minutes . . . at the First Session, Held in Oberlin, Ohio, November 15–21, 1871* (Boston—1872).

[75]Henry Cowles to Finney, Sept. 9, 1859 (Finney MSS); "Annual Report of Henry Cowles, Agent of Oberlin College, for the year ending Aug. 26/63" (Cowles MSS), and *Lorain County News,* Mar. 7, 1866.

[76]Oberlin Maternal Association, MS Minutes, Nov. 1, 1865.

wrote: "The Oberlin that was, I loved, approved, & was never weary of defending & commending. The Oberlin that *is,* I am often afraid I do not fully understand. I am in perpetual danger of presenting the Oberlin of old as the Oberlin that now is, & am not unfrequently startled by some new development that seems to indicate a wide departure from the old paths, ways & spirit. . . . I am sometimes greatly distressed by these indications of degeneracy." Finney had agonized over what he believed was the decay of vital Christianity in Oberlin since the fifties. "The fact is," he wrote in 1868, "our students, especially of late years, I mean the mass of them, lack the power of the Holy Ghost." Young ministers going out from Oberlin, he feared, were too much like other ministers to attract any special attention.[77] The cost in terms of the reform spirit was not so often counted, but was an even higher price.

The day of Oberlin as a cyclone center of reform, as an "experimental college," a great disturbing, driving force in American social, religious and educational life was over. Oberlin had spent its initial dynamic energy. A little leaven had leavened the whole mass, as Shipherd had dreamed, and now was absorbed and overwhelmed in that mass. Oberlin had lost its uniqueness, but had contributed thereby to the character of American society.

77"Annual Report of Henry Cowles . . . Aug. 26/63" (Cowles MSS), and Finney to Keep, Aug. 3, 1868 (Cowles-Little MSS).

"The history of Oberlin has been very romantic. If it were written, it would prove that 'facts are sometimes stranger than fiction.' I have lived to see more accomplished than I ever expected. And now, when I walk the streets & see our throngs of students and our fine buildings going up, & recall the dangers overcome, and the obstacles removed, in our early history, it reminds me of the saying 'A little one shall chase a thousand,' and I am ready to put my hand upon my mouth, before the Lord, and be still."

CHARLES G. FINNEY

at the Dedication of Council Hall, August 1, 1874.

A PARTIAL LIST OF SOURCES

A PARTIAL LIST OF SOURCES

I. MANUSCRIPTS

The author has depended to a very large extent upon manuscript material: personal letters and diaries, the archives of various organizations and unpublished narratives.

1. Personal Papers

The letters and memoranda of Professor George N. Allen and Mrs. Caroline Rudd Allen are partly in the *Oberlin College Library* (Allen MSS) and partly in the possession of *Mary Cochran of Cincinnati.*

A letter from Daniel Babst (Prep., 1865–68), Oberlin, September 9, 1867. (*Mrs. Daniel Babst and Mrs. Don. C. Minick, Toledo, Ohio*)

Letters of Julius O. Beardslee (Coll., 1834–37) written in 1835 and 1837. (*Mrs. L. M. Houser, Amherst, Ohio*)

A letter from M. A. Broadner to Julia Clark, October 4, 1846, written in Oberlin by one who was apparently a student, though her name is not in the *General Catalogue.* (*Herbert Clough, Kirksville, Mo.*)

A framed letter from Levi Burnell to William Dawes, Oberlin, June 26, 1840. (*Oberlin College Library*)

Compositions written by Ann-Elisa Chaney while a student in Oberlin, 1836. (*Oberlin College Library*)

A letter from Thomas A. Cheney (Prep., 1849–50) written (however) from Oberlin in October, 1848. (*Mrs. Charles E. Lansing, Albany, New York*)

A letter of Mrs. C. H. Churchill from Oberlin, January 27, 1850. The story of Emily Pillsbury Burke. (*Mrs. Azariel Smith, Whittier, California*)

The war diary of Stephen M. Cole (Prep., 1853–61) from February, 1863, to January, 1864. (*Mrs. A. C. Shattuck, Cincinnati, Ohio*)

Letters written from Oberlin in 1851 and 1852 by Frances A. Collister, a young lady student. (*Oberlin College Library*)

The journal of Elam J. Comings (Coll., 1835–36, 1837–38; Sem., 1839–41), which contains interesting data on travel conditions on the way to Oberlin in the thirties. (*Eliza J. Comings, Kingsville, Ohio*)

Letters of Zephaniah Congden (Prep., 1853–54) written in 1853. (*Eulala Smith, Exeter, Nebraska*)

The Cowles manuscripts include some 130 items (1834 to 1863) from the papers of Henry and Alice Welch Cowles selected by Professor Clayton S. Ellsworth from the collection of Alice and Elizabeth Little, granddaughters of Henry Cowles. This collection contains the letters from Harriet Beecher Stowe relative to the Edmondson girls. President J. H. Fairchild's sketch of Professor Cowles delivered at his funeral in 1881 is also included. There are letters from Giddings, Weld, Edward Wade and Elizur Wright. A calendar, prepared by Mrs. J. G. H. Hubbard under the author's direction, is in the library. The great mass of the Cowles papers are still in the possession of the Misses Little. (*Oberlin College Library*)

By far the most important private collection in Oberlin is that of the Cowles papers owned by the Misses Little. It includes manuscripts in the handwriting of Henry Cowles, Alice Welch Cowles, John P. Cowles, Henry Cowles' children and the Penfields, as well as thousands of letters written to them. The Cowles MSS in the library are merely a few items selected from this mass—and by no means the most important ones. This larger collection is referred to as the Cowles-Little MSS to distinguish it from the collection in the library. The significance of these papers arises from the fact that the Rev. Henry Cowles joined the Oberlin faculty in 1835 and was soon after joined by his brother John P. Cowles. Henry Cowles was long editor of the *Oberlin Evangelist*. His first wife, Alice Welch Cowles, was Principal of the Female Department from 1836 to 1840. His second wife, Minerva Dayton Penfield Cowles, widow of an early settler, was active on the Ladies' Board and in the temperance cause. The Cowles and Penfield children attended various departments of the Institute and College. Various members of the faculty, Board of Trustees and friends of Oberlin wrote letters to Professor Henry Cowles—many of which, of great value, are preserved in this collection. Mrs. Alice Welch Cowles' notes for her talks to the young lady students are useful sources on the beginnings of collegiate female education. The diaries of Mary Louisa Cowles as a student in the fifties are most revealing. There is matter of interest also in Henry Cowles' "Day Book" for 1835–43 and Mrs. Alice Welch Cowles' diary of 1830 to 1840. Unique are several compositions written by little Helen Cowles in the forties describing Oberlin scenes and events. (*The Misses Alice and Elizabeth Little, Oberlin, Ohio*)

A note from Kenyon Cox (Prep., 1846–49), brother of J. D. Cox and uncle of the well-known artist of the same name. (*A. A. Drew, Chicago, Illinois*)

James Dascomb's Notebook, 1833–46, containing records of births and deaths in Oberlin, physician's accounts of services performed and charges and some class notes. (*Oberlin College Library*)

Between 150 and 200 letters mostly written by James Harris Fairchild, the majority dated from 1838 to 1842, are referred to in the footnotes as the Fairchild MSS. Parts of some of these letters have been published in the *Oberlin Alumni Magazine*. (*James Thome Fairchild, Bethlehem, Pennsylvania*)

A letter written by James Harris Fairchild and E. H. Fairchild to J. B. Clark from Oberlin, Apr., 2, 1835. (*Edith M. Clark, Oberlin*)

Letters from Mary P. Fairchild (Prep., 1833–35, 1841, 1842; Ladies' Course, 1842–44) written in 1843–44. (*Dr. C. G. Baldwin, Palo Alto, California*)

Letters written by Delia Fenn from Oberlin in 1835 while she was a student here. (*Oberlin College Library*)

The papers of Charles Grandison Finney, evangelist, professor, President and dominant personality of early Oberlin, consist primarily of about 2500 letters mostly addressed to Finney and Mrs. Finney. These letters cover the period 1824 to 1875 and contain material on practically all angles of the story of Oberlin. The collection includes letters from the Tappans, from John Keep, from Theodore Weld, from Shipherd, from Mahan, from the Lane Rebels, from many alumni, teachers and friends of Oberlin. The letters in the twenties and early thirties relate chiefly to his revival activities, especially in New York. Included also are letters from his English converts and friends, written during and after his visits to England in 1850 and 1859. The bulk of the later correspondence from 1868 to 1875 relates to anti-masonry. A calendar and index have been prepared, under the direction of the author, by Mrs. J. G. H. Hubbard, Walter Rogers, Le Roy Graf and others. Besides the letters the collection includes a number of manuscripts in Finney's own hand: the original draft of his "Memoirs," which contains much matter never published, hundreds of sermon skeletons, three personal account books, and manuscripts of several articles such as the one on "Innocent Amusements." Some of these manuscripts are catalogued separately; others are kept with the other Finney papers. (*Oberlin College Library*)

Charles G. Finney, Lecture Notes on Pastoral Theology, 1848[?], 1872, 1875. (*Oberlin College Library*)

Letters of Mr. and Mrs. Charles G. Finney to the Barlows, English friends, 1862–65. (*Oberlin College Library*)

Fanny Fletcher, Class Notes, 1835. (*Eliza J. Comings, Kingsville, Ohio*)

Robert S. Fletcher. The author's working file in the Oberlin Room of the library contains many photostatic and typescript copies of manuscript letters, records and minutes. The most important photostats are of the Shipherd MSS, part of the Prudden MSS, letters from the Lewis Tappan Letter Books, letters from the Gerrit Smith MSS, and certain unique college records, the originals of which are in the Administration Building. All of these are referred to elsewhere. The file also includes many letters from historians, archivists, descendants of students and faculty members, etc., relating to Oberlin history. (*Oberlin College Library*)

The diary and notebooks of Benjamin Foltz, Lane Rebel. (*Oberlin College Library*)

The J. D. Fowler family papers contain much on Oberlin town in the later period. (*Miss Mary Fowler, Milwaukee, Wisconsin*)

The journal, compositions, and critiques of John Gaius Fraser, A. B., 1867. (*Mrs. Grace F. Waugh, Mentor, Ohio*)

Journal and essays of Mary Minerva Gilbert (Ladies' Course, 1853–55), dated 1853. (*Gladys Sperling, Pulaski, New York*)

Letters from Mary Gorham (Ladies' Course, 1853–1855). (*Esther A. Close, Oberlin*)

Letters from Elizabeth Hanmer (Ladics' Course, 1852–54). (*Mildred Durbin, Columbus, Ohio*)

Account book of Frances M. Hubbard (Prep., 1853–54; Ladies' Course, 1854–55, 1856–57). (*Fred P. Bemis, Santa Monica, California*)

Letters from Professor and Mrs. Timothy B. Hudson, 1844. (*Myra Cowles, Austinburg, Ohio*)

A letter from William N. Hudson ["Will"] to Charles Fairchild, Oberlin, September 17, 1861. (*Oberlin College Library*)

Letters of Nehemiah A. Hunt (Prep., 1833–35), 1834 and 1881. (*E. F. Hunt, Riverside, California*)

Letters from Sarah Ingersoll, 1838 to 1840. (*Mrs. Friedrich Lehman, Oberlin*)

The Keep MSS contains letters written by John Keep in England in 1839 and 1840 and other material relating to the English mission as well as some miscellaneous items, Keep's brief MS autobiography among them. (*Mrs. George M. Clark, Evanston, Illinois*)

A letter from L. D. Kingsbury (a student) written in Oberlin, May 10, 1852. (*Oberlin College Library*)

War diary of Selden B. Kingsbury (Prep., 1857–60; Coll., 1860–64) covering the period from August, 1861, to February, 1862. (*Fred C. Kingsbury, Los Angeles, California*)

Delevan L. Leonard, "Notes on Talks with Pres. Fairchild from December 20, '94 ——." (*Oberlin College Library*)

A letter from Maud M. Little [later Macy], a student from 1860 to 1864, written from Oberlin on May 29, 1862. (*Oberlin College Library*)

The Elizabeth Russell Lord papers. (*Mrs. John W. Lumbard, White Plains, New York*)

Some papers of the family of Asa Mahan. (*Mrs. Edward Gage, Winter Park, Florida*)

A volume of Asa Mahan's sermon and lecture notes. (*Office of the President of Adrian College, Adrian, Michigan*)

Letters from Elizabeth Maxwell (Monroe), first wife of Professor James Monroe and Oberlin student (Ladies' Course, 1842–46). (*Mrs. Charles N. (Emma Monroe) Fitch, Staten Island, New York*)

There are over five thousand letters in the James Monroe papers addressed to him over the period 1841 to 1898. A number of the comparatively small proportion dating from the forties and fifties deal with the anti-slavery movement. There are several invaluable items relating to the Rescue Case. The major portion of the correspondence is political, relating to Monroe's service in the Ohio state legislature, as U. S. Consul at Rio de Janeiro and as Congressman. Scattered throughout, however, is much which reflects life and conditions at Oberlin. The letters are filed chronologically in boxes in the Oberlin Room of the library. An index of these letters has been prepared by Mrs. J. G. H. Hubbard, R. N. Current, Lucille Dorn and Phyllis Olson under the direction of the author. Besides the letters there are a brief autobiographical summary of Monroe's life, evidently based on a diary now destroyed, 39 manuscripts of addresses delivered from 1846 up to a few years before his death, and several MS subscription books. (*Oberlin College Library*)

The Morgan-Hopkins MSS consist of ninety-five letters written by Professor John Morgan to Mark Hopkins of Williams from 1830 to 1883. Most of them were written from Oberlin. They contain some pertinent comments on Oberlin and the contemporary scene but are overburdened with abstruse disquisitions on theological matters. Besides the letters from Morgan, there are several from other persons—two from Finney. A calendar of these letters prepared by the author of this history is in the library. (*Oberlin College Library*)

Papers relating to John P. Morgan, co-founder of the Oberlin Conservatory. (*Mrs. F. T. Morgan-Stephens, Atlanta, Georgia*)

Smith Norton, Notes on President Finney's Sermons, 1853, etc. (*Oberlin College Library*)

The Oberlin College Library Miscellaneous Manuscript Collection contains between five and six hundred items. A list of these manuscripts was prepared by the author with the assistance of two of his students and is now available at the library. It is an extremely miscellaneous assortment, but includes much material of great value to the student of Oberlin history. In the collection, for example, are several of the most significant letters written by Shipherd, the Founder, a number of letters from Lane Rebels, the letter from the Oberlin colonists to Shipherd written in June, 1833, and the student questionnaire on the admission of Negroes in 1834.

Letters of Brewster and Thirza Pelton written from Oberlin, January, 1835. (*Jeannette Kinney, Willoughby, Ohio*)

A letter from Aaron Penfield written in Oberlin, Mar. 4, 1837. (*Office of the President of Oberlin College*)

One of the most interesting groups of student letters is the Prudden manuscripts. These are eighteen letters written by George, Davis and Nancy Prudden in 1836, 1837 and one in 1838. Eleven were given to the College by Miss Harriet E. Prudden of Medina, New York, and are now in the library. Seven, all written in 1836, were lent by *Mrs. Lee Allen of Niagara Falls, New York,* and returned to her. Photostats were made, however, and are in the library. These letters contain much data on manual labor, diet, student routine, etc., in 1836–37.

Letters of Henry Prudden (Prep., 1859–61) written in 1859 from Oberlin. (*Lillian E. Prudden, New Haven, Connecticut*)

Diary of William Henry Scott (Prep., 1865–66; Coll., 1866–69) from August through December, 1865. (*William J. Scott, Rochester, N. Y.*)

A letter from John H. Scovill, Oberlin, Dec. 17, 1833. Oberlin's first teacher describes the opening of the Institute. (*Mrs. Wells L. Griswold, Youngstown, Ohio*)

A letter from John H. Scovill, Oberlin, Jan. 2, 1834. (*Louise M. Edwards, Youngstown, Ohio*)

Forty-three letters written by John Jay Shipherd from 1819 to 1836 to his brother Fayette Shipherd. These letters of the Founder together constitute the most important single source on the founding of Oberlin. All of the letters were photostated, and the photostats are in the library, as noted above. In the footnotes these letters are referred to as Shipherd MSS. Included also is an interesting MS autobiography of Fayette Shipherd, parts of which were kindly copied for the use of the author. (*May Bragdon, Rochester, New York*)

The above collection is supplemented by thirteen other letters written by John Jay Shipherd from 1818 to 1842 and cited in the notes as the Shipherd-Randolph MSS. (*Walter Shipherd, Randolph, New York*)

Letters from Egbert, George W., and Pamela R. Smith (students), 1854–57. (*Warren J. Wightman, Buffalo, New York*)

The very extensive collection of papers of Gerrit Smith, the New York State reformer-philanthropist, were made accessible to the author through the kindness of Professor William E. Mosher, Professor Ralph V. Harlow and Librarian Wharton Miller of Syracuse University. Photostats of the letters of most interest in relation to Oberlin have been made and are in the author's working file. These include a letter from Anthony Burns when at Oberlin, several letters from John Keep, letters from C. G. Finney, and letters from Antoinette Brown (Blackwell). (*Library of Syracuse University*)

The war diary of Edmund Root Stiles (Prep., Coll. and Sem., 1852–54, 1856–61) covering the period April, 1861, to June, 1862. This is one of the best sources on the prison experiences of the men of Company C. (*Mrs. M. B. Fisher, Berkeley, California*)

Letters and compositions written by Lucy Stone (Blackwell) (Coll., 1843–47). (*Alice Stone Blackwell, Boston, Massachusetts*)

A letter from Lucy Stone, July 9, 1842. (*W. C. MacLaurin, Ware, Massachusetts*)

Lewis Tappan's letter books. Photostats of approximately a hundred letters from Tappan to prominent Oberlinites have been made from these and are in the author's working file in the library. There are letters to Finney, Mahan, Keep, Cowles, etc. (*Library of Congress*)

Letters of Jane B. Trew (Coll., 1841–45), written from Oberlin in 1841 and 1843. (*Mary Ewalt, Lakewood, Ohio*)

The diary of [Jonathan] Sprague Upton (Prep., 1858–59, Coll., 1859–61, Hon. A. M., 1900), kept in Oberlin in 1857. (*Prof. W. T. Upton, Oberlin and Washington, D.C.*)

Letters from Warren W. Warner and his sister Hannah Maria Warner and friends from Oberlin, 1841–45. (*Oberlin College Library*)

The valuable papers of Theodore D. Weld, only partially published by Gilbert H. Barnes and D. M. Dumond. (*Dr. L. D. H. Weld, New York City*)

William A. Westervelt, Notes on Political Economy (Prof. Amasa Walker), Chemistry, Pastoral Theology, 1842–43. (*Oberlin College Library*)

Letters of Adelia A. Whipple (Prep., 1858–60) written from Oberlin in 1858. (*Jessie Wright, Wellington, Ohio*)

Letters from David George Wilder (Prep., and Coll., 1866–71) and others, dated 1865 to 1868. (*Glenn Wilder, Chardon, Ohio*)

Theodore Wilder, "Index Rerum," 1860–65, containing miscellaneous class notes and notes on Finney sermons. (*Oberlin College Library*)

Letters of Sarah Minerva Winegar (Ladies' Course, 1864–65) from Oberlin. (*Mrs. Robert W. Allen, Pasadena, California* and *Mrs. H. N. Roberts, Wichita, Kansas*)

A diary of James L. Wright at Yale which throws much light on the "Conic Sections Rebellion" and the two letters written by Benjamin D. Wright, Mary Wright, and their brothers, "Cap'n" and William W. Wright, from Oberlin in 1846 and 1847 to their family in Tallmadge. (*The late Mrs. H. H. Carter, Oberlin*)

The papers of W. W. Wright and his son (later Professor) A. A. Wright and their family are of great interest for the later period. (*Norman H. Wright, Cranbury, New Jersey*)

2. Oberlin College Archival Material

The Alumni Records consist of three files of personal data on (1) graduates, (2) former students, and (3) officers not students. (*Alumni Records Office*)

The Archives Card Index prepared by Mrs. J. Geraldine H. Hubbard and Miss Gertrude Ransom is not yet complete. (*Secretary's Office*)

The Board of Trustees Minutes are complete from the first official meeting on March 10, 1834. (*Secretary's Office*)

The Board of Trustees Minutes, 1834–66, typescript copy. (*Oberlin College Library*)

The Boarding House Book, 1840. (*Treasurer's Office*)

Conservatory of Music, charter, deed of sale, 1872, and F. B. Rice's sworn statement, 1900. (*Office of the Director*)

The Faculty Minutes are preserved from 1834 to 1846. The loss of the minutes for the last twenty years covered by this study created the largest gap in the sources. But faculty minutes were concerned chiefly with discipline and those extant plus the minutes of the Ladies' Board give what is apparently a pretty complete picture of that subject. When the old Chapel was burned in 1901 the college archives were hastily removed from the building. It seems probable that the missing portion of the minutes was lost at that time. (*Secretary's Office*)

The Keep-Dawes Mission to England, 1839–40, two credential and subscription books. (*Oberlin College Library*)

The Ladies' Board of Managers, Minutes, 1851–62. (*Oberlin College Library*)

The Library's first Catalogue and records of books drawn. (*Oberlin College Library*)

The Library's list of books brought from England by Keep and Dawes in 1839–40. (*Oberlin College Library*)

Manual Labor Records

1. "An Account of Manual Labor Furnished to Students, 1835 [–1843]." This volume includes also records of the "Oberlin Board of Education," established in 1839 to secure aid for indigent students attending Oberlin Institute. (*Oberlin College Library*)

2. "An Account of Manual Labor furnished to Students [of Oberlin College] by those who occupy the college lands & who hold leases from the college, etc., etc." (*Oberlin College Library*)

The Miscellaneous Archives contain many invaluable items. Among these are the first "By Laws," adopted in October 1834, various papers of the Oberlin Peace Society, hundreds of student's manual labor reports, and student bills, the important letter of Shipherd to the trustees urging their reconsideration of the question of the admission of Negro students, papers relating to Stewart's stove, the earliest records of the Oberlin Colony, reports of Mrs. Dascomb on the administration of the Ladies' Department, N. P. Fletcher's "Critical Letters," and many papers presented at meetings of the trustees in early years. These papers have been filed and calendared under the direction of the author. When first unearthed at the suggestion of Secretary Jones they were packed in wooden boxes just as they had been removed from the Chapel at the time of the fire—burned bits of wood and plaster among them. The edges of many bundles of papers had been charred. (*Administration Building*)

The Official Correspondence of the Oberlin Collegiate Institute and the later Oberlin College includes thousands of letters from the early years. Among them are letters from Stewart, from Shipherd, from Lewis Tappan, hundreds from students and would-be students and other hundreds from financial agents. This collection has been drawn upon heavily by the author for material for this work. The letter file boxes in which it is preserved are labelled by letters and numbers and are cited in footnotes as "Treas. Off., File B," "Treas. Off., File K," etc. (*Treasurer's Office*)

The President's Annual Reports begin with 1866–67. (*Secretary's Office*)

The Prudential Committee Minutes are complete from 1835. They are much more detailed than the trustees' minutes and throw much light on the week-to-week story of the Institute and College. (*Secretary's Office*)

Student Confessions, 1834–50. (*Oberlin College Library*)

Students, Negro, card index. (*Secretary's Office*)

Student Roll Books. (*Secretary's Office*)

The Treasurer's Day Books and Ledgers are apparently complete from 1833. Not only are the regular routine entries of salary payments, boarding-hall expenses, receipts from students, etc., valuable as historical sources—but occasionally the Treasurer or a clerk wrote personal comments among the debits and credits. (*Treasurer's Office*)

3. Other Minutes and Archives

The American Home Missionary Society Manuscripts include tens of thousands of reports from Yankee home missionaries, John Jay Shipherd among them. (*Hammond Library, Chicago Theological Seminary*)

The Domestic Missionary Society of the Western Reserve, Minutes, 1826–62, in one volume. Became the "Western Reserve Agency of the American Home Missionary Society" in 1846. (*Oberlin College Library*)

The Elyria Female Moral Reform Society, Minutes, 1837–40. (*Elyria Public Library*)

The Elyria First Presbyterian Society, Minutes. (*First Congregational Church of Elyria*)

The Lane Seminary Manuscripts constitute the most important source on the founding of this institution and the "Rebellion." These are several thousand items, well arranged and properly filed. (*Virginia Library, Presbyterian Theological Seminary, Chicago*)

The Lane Seminary Board of Trustees and Executive Committee, Minutes. (*Office of the Treasurer of the Presbyterian Theological Seminary, Chicago*)

The Lorain County Congregational Association, Minutes, 1837–54 (one volume). (*Oberlin College Library*)

New York, The Synod of, Minutes, Book II, 1823–36. (*Library of Auburn Theological Seminary*)

The Oberlin Agricultural and Historical Society Manuscripts. These are among the best contemporary sources on Oberlin village. They include the reports of occasional amateur censuses of manufactures, agricultural production, and livestock and also the papers of the agricultural fairs and reports of committees on gardens, ornamental trees, and "hogs running at large." (*Oberlin College Library*)

The Oberlin Bible Society, Minutes, 1849–75 (one volume). (*Oberlin College Library*)

The Oberlin Choir. See Oberlin Musical Association.

Oberlin Christ Episcopal Church Manuscripts. (*In the possession of the Rector*)

The Oberlin [College] Alumni Association, Minutes, 1839– (*Oberlin College Library*)

The [Oberlin College] Aelioian Society.
See the [Oberlin College] Young Ladies Lyceum.

The [Oberlin College] Dialectic Society changed its name to the Young Men's Lyceum, and then to Phi Kappa Pi. Its minutes are in volumes dated: 1839–43, 1843–49, 1849–56, 1856–65, and 1865–76. (*Oberlin College Library*)

The [Oberlin College] L.L.S.
See the Oberlin [College] Young Ladies' Association.

The [Oberlin College] Ladies Societys' [*sic*] Library Association, Minutes, 1859–74. (*Oberlin College Library*)

The [Oberlin College] Phi Delta Society.
See the [Oberlin College] Philomathesian Society.

The [Oberlin College] Phi Kappa Pi Society.
See the [Oberlin College] Dialectic Society.

The [Oberlin College] Philomathesian Society became the Union Society and later the Phi Delta. Its minutes are in volumes dated 1841–50, 1850–55, 1855–60, and 1860–69. There is supplementary material in the Phi Delta, Constitution, By Laws & Record of Members, 1839–82. (*Oberlin College Library*)

The [Oberlin] College Societies Library Association, Account Book, 1855–1869, and a second volume containing the constitution and lists of members. (*Oberlin College Library*)

The Oberlin College Students' Missionary Society, Minutes, 1852–64. (*Oberlin College Library*)

The [Oberlin College] Theological Literary Society and Theological Society Minutes are in volumes dated: 1844–51, 1854–65 (this volume contains also minutes of the Theological Library Association) and 1865–1875. (*Oberlin College Library*)

The [Oberlin College] Union Society.
See the [Oberlin College] Philomathesian Society.

The Oberlin [College] Young Ladies' Association changed its name to the [Oberlin College] Young Ladies' Literary Society and later to "L.L.S." Its minutes are in volumes dated 1846–51, 1851–54, 1855–59, 1859–63, and 1863–70. (*Oberlin College Library*)

The [Oberlin College] Young Ladies' Lyceum later changed its name to Aelioian. Its minutes are in two volumes dated 1856–60 and 1860–75. (*Oberlin College Library*)

The [Oberlin College] Young Men's Anti-Slavery Society, Minutes, 1851–53. (*Oberlin College Library*)

The [Oberlin College] Young Men's Lyceum.
See the [Oberlin College] Dialectic Society.

The Oberlin Colony, Covenant and Minutes. This volume includes minutes of the colonists' meetings from July 4, 1837, to August 20, 1837, and a note on subsequent meetings. The draft of the covenant in this volume differs somewhat in wording from that published in Fairchild, *Oberlin, the Colony and College* and elsewhere. It is signed by the colonists. (*Oberlin College Library*)

The [Oberlin] Empire Hook and Ladder Company, Minutes, 1865–74. (*Oberlin College Library*)

The Oberlin Female Moral Reform Society, Minutes, 1835–57. (*Oberlin College Library*)

The Oberlin [First] Congregational Church Manuscripts contain several hundred items dating from 1836 through 1870. The papers relate chiefly to finances, church property, and especially to church trials—for stealing, immorality, dishonesty, lying, blasphemy, and heresy. (*Oberlin College Library*)

The Oberlin [First] Congregational Church, Minutes, 1834–91, are in three volumes. (*Oberlin College Library*)

The Oberlin [First Congregational Church] Society, Minutes, 1841–75 (2 volumes). These records relate to the building and maintenance of the meeting house and the care of church property and church finances in general after the society ceased to be also the governing body of the village. (*Oberlin College Library*)

Oberlin, The First National Bank of, Director's Minutes, 1863–82. (*Oberlin College Library*)

The Oberlin Maternal Association, Minutes, 1835–66. These are preserved in volumes dated: 1835–38, 1838–51 (incorrectly labelled "1st Vol." on binding, and 1851–66. (*Oberlin College Library*)

The Oberlin Musical Association was founded in 1837; changed its name in 1856 to the Oberlin Choir and in 1860 to the Oberlin Musical Union. Its very valuable minutes are in volumes dated: 1837–47, 1847–65, 1865–95, etc. They constitute the most important single source on Oberlin's early musical history. (*Oberlin College Library*)

The Oberlin School District, Minutes, 1834–51. Originally known as District 5 and later District 3 of Russia Township. (*Oberlin College Library*)

The Oberlin Second Congregational Church, Minutes, 1860–1918. (*Oberlin College Library*)

The Oberlin Society, Constitution and Minutes. "Incorporated by an Act of the Legislature of the State of Ohio Togather [*sic*] with all the Societies Record from March 10, A.D. 1834." Minutes go through March 25, 1841. These are records of the government of the Oberlin Colony. After 1841 the society became merely the fiscal organization of the church. These later minutes are cited above as Oberlin [First Congregational Church] Society Minutes. (*Oberlin College Library*)

The Oberlin Temperance League, Minutes, 1870–74. (*Oberlin College Library*)

The Oneida Presbytery, Minutes. (*Rev. George Frost, Utica, New York*)

The Rochester (New York) Moral Reform Society, Minutes, 1836–37. (*Rochester Public Library*)

The Russian Township Trustees' Minutes, 1855–69. The volume contains an introduction on the early settlement and history of the township. (*Oberlin College Library*)

Russian Township Justice's Court Docket, 1838–57. (*Oberlin College Library*)

Russian Township Board of Education, Records, 1842–71. (*Oberlin College Library*)

The Stockbridge (Mass.) Congregational Church, Records. Excerpts were kindly furnished by the *Rev. A. R. Brown.* (*Congregational Church, Stockbridge, Massachusetts*)

The Strongsville (Ohio) First Congregational Church, Minutes, 1817–47. (*Oberlin College Library*)

Western Reserve, The General Association [of Congregational Churches] of the, Minutes, 1836–50. (*Oberlin College Library*)

The Western Reserve College Church, Minutes, 1831–34. (*Western Reserve University Library*)

The Western Reserve College Faculty Minutes, 1835–36. (*Western Reserve University Library*)

4. Manuscript Narratives

Bailey, Allen Metcalf, "Mock Conventions in Oberlin, 1860–1932," an honors thesis in History. (*Oberlin College Library*)

Block, Muriel Louise, "Beriah Green, The Reformer," a master's thesis, 1935. (*Syracuse University Library*)

Ellsworth, Clayton S., "Oberlin and the Anti-Slavery Movement up to the Civil War," a doctoral dissertation of great value in this history. (*Cornell University Library*)

Gates, Charles N., "The Red Lakes Mission," a mimeographed radio talk delivered over KSTP Minneapolis, January 2, 1935. (*Oberlin College Library*)

Hennings, Lloyd V., "The American Missionary Association, A Christian Anti-Slavery Society," a master's thesis in History. (*Oberlin College Library*)

Hightower, Raymond L., "Joshua L. Wilson: Frontier Controversialist," a doctoral dissertation, 1933. (*University of Chicago Library*)

Holtz, Maude E., "Cleveland University, a Forgotten Chapter in Cleveland's History," a master's thesis. (*Western Reserve University Library*)

Gilson, Mrs. Claude U., "Antoinette Brown Blackwell, the First Woman Minister." (*Mrs. S. T. Jones, Montclair, New Jersey*)

Hubbard, Mrs. J. Geraldine H., "Garrison's Abolitionism vs. Oberlin Anti-Slavery," an honors thesis in History. (*Oberlin College Library*)

Keep, W. J., "The History of the Stove." (*Library of the Business Historical Society, Boston*)

Laird, Dr. Arthur T., "Reminiscences of Student Days and the Civil War." (*The author, Nopeming, Minnesota*)

Rice, Helen M., "Musical Reminiscences of Oberlin," written in 1908. (*Office of the Director of the Conservatory*)

Robinson, Thomas H., "Reminiscences of the [Oberlin] Class of Eighteen Hunred and Fifty," 1900. (*Oberlin College Library*)

Rogers, Walter P., "A College Education a Hundred Years Ago," a master's thesis in History, 1932. (*Oberlin College Library*)

Shipherd, Esther Raymond, "A Sketch of the Life and Labors of John J. Shipherd." This is largely autobiographical. (*Oberlin College Library*)

Steele, Samuel F., "Sketch of James Steele's Life." (*Oberlin College Library*)

II. PRINTED MATTER

1. Newspapers and Periodicals

The Advocate of Moral Reform (New York).
See *McDowall's Journal*

The Advocate and Family Guardian (New York).
See *McDowall's Journal*

The American Almanac (Boston), 1830–61.

The American Annals of Education (Boston), 1830–33. Edited by William C. Woodbridge, educational reformer.

The American Journal of Education (Boston), 1830.
Predecessor of the *Annals of Education.*

The American Missionary (New York), 1846–.
Organ of the American Missionary Association. Continuing the *Union Missionary.*

The American Quarterly Register (*Quarterly Register and Journal of the American Education Society,* published at Andover, Mass.), 1828–41.
One of the most important sources on college and church history in the United States.

The American Sunday School Magazine (Philadelphia), 1828.

The Annals of Cleveland, 1818–1935, A Digest and Index of the Newspaper Record of Events and Opinions (Cleveland—1936 and later). A very useful WPA production.

The Anti-Slavery Bugle (Salem and New Lisbon, Ohio), 1845–50.
A pro-Garrison journal, friendly to the Fosters, unfriendly to Oberlin.

The Boston Medical Intelligencer, 1826.

Burritt's Christian Citizen (Worcester, Mass.), 1849–50. The organ of Elihu Burritt, leader of the League of Universal Brotherhood.

The Cincinnati Journal, October 10, 1834.

The Cleveland Liberalist, 1836–38.
Dr. Samuel Underhill, Editor. There is a file of this anti-ecclesiastical periodical in the library of the Western Reserve Historical Society in Cleveland.

The Cleveland Plain Dealer (daily), 1850.
Valuable material on Cleveland University was found in the *Plain Dealer* for this year.

The Cleveland Observer.
See *Observer & Telegraph.*

The Cleveland Whig, 1846–54.

The Elyria Courier, 1846–53.
The name was changed to *Elyria Weekly Courier* in 1849. There is a broken file in the library of the Western Reserve Historical Society.

The Emancipator (New York), 1834–38.
The title varies—always including the word *"Emancipator."* It was the official publication of the American Anti-Slavery Society. It contains valuable data on the activities of Oberlin anti-slavery agents.

The Friend of Man (Utica, New York), 1836.

The Gem (Rochester, New York), 1830.

The Graham Journal of Health aand Longevity (Boston), 1837–39.
The chief organ of the physiological reform movement, edited by David Cambell, later of Oberlin.

The Home Missionary and American Pastor's Journal (New York), 1828–1836.
Official organ of the American Home Missionary Society, edited by Rev. Absalom Peters.

The Independent (New York), 1848–61.
Edited by Leonard Bacon, J. P. Thompson, R. S. Storrs, and Joshua Leavitt.

The Independent Treasury (Elyria, Ohio), 1842.

The Journal of Health (Philadelphia), 1829–30.

The Liberator (Boston), 1833.

The Library of Health (Boston), 1841.
Edited by Dr. William A. Alcott.

The Lorain County News (Oberlin), 1860–66.
The excellent local newspaper of Oberlin during the war period. Full of valuable material on those years.

McDowall's Journal, 1833–65.
Became the *Advocate of Moral Reform* in 1835 and the organ of the New York Female Moral Reform Society. Name changed to *Advocate of Moral Reform and Family Guardian* in 1848, and to *Advocate and Family Guardian* in 1855. The author has consulted a complete file (except for 1840 and 1847) made up from several different libraries.

The Moral Reformer (Boston), 1836.
Edited by Dr. William A. Alcott.

The New York Evangelist, 1830–44.
Edited by Joshua Leavitt to July 1837, founded as the organ of "Finneyism."

The New York Observer, 1834.

The Oasis (Boston), 1834.

The Oberlin Alumni Magazine, 1904– .
Articles separately cited below.

The Oberlin Evangelist, 1838–62.
Most important of all periodical sources. See text, pages 418–422.

The Oberlin Quarterly Review, 1845–49.

The Oberlin Review, 1874–
The student paper in recent years. Contains valuable data in obituaries and other retrospective articles.

The Oberlin Students' Monthly, 1858–61.
See text, pages 764–765.

The Observer & Telegraph (Hudson, Ohio), 1830–45.
Changed name to *Ohio Observer,* September 28, 1833. September 28, 1837, it was moved to Cleveland and became the *Cleveland Observer.* Returned to Hudson on April 16, 1840, and resumed the title of *Ohio Observer.*

The Ohio Atlas and Elyria Advertiser (Elyria, Ohio), 1832–41.
First published as the *Ohio Atlas and Lorain County Gazette.*

The Ohio Cultivator (Columbus, Ohio), 1846–47, 1849, 1851–54, 1859.
The editor, M. B. Bateham, married Josephine Penfield Cushman, step-daughter of Professor Henry Cowles.

The Ohio Observer (Hudson)
See *The Observer & Telegraph.*

The Ohio State Journal and Columbus Gazette, 1834–35.

The Owl (Oberlin), 1898.
The issue of April 29, 1898, contains a letter from A. H. Redington quoting Shipherd's original contract with Street and Hughes.

The People's Press (Oberlin), October, 1845.

The Philanthropist (Cincinnati, Ohio), 1838–41.
Scattered numbers in the Oberlin College Library.

The Radical Abolitionist (New York), 1855–58.
Edited by William Goodell.

The Religious Intelligencer [and New Haven Journal] (New Haven, Conn.), 1824 and 1836.

The Rescuer (Cleveland), July 4, 1859.

The Rights of Man (Rochester, N. Y.), 1834.
Published by the Rochester Anti-Slavery Society. There are seven scattered numbers in the Rochester Public Library.

The Rochester Daily Advertiser, 1833.

The Rochester Daily Democrat, 1834 and 1836.

The Rochester Observer, 1827–31.
The most important periodical source on the Finney group in Rochester.

The Silk Culturist and Farmer's Manual (Hartford), 1835–39.
This paper was the national organ of the silk culture "craze."

The Times (London), March 27, 1840.

The Union Missionary (New York), 1844–46.
Organ of the Union Missionary Society. Continued after September, 1846, as the *American Missionary.*

The University Quarterly (New Haven, Conn.), 1860–61.
Sub-title: "Conducted by an Association of Collegiate and Professional Students, in the United States and Europe."

The Vermont Chronicle (Bellows Falls and Windsor, Vermont), 1826–1835.

The Western Recorder (Utica, New York), 1825–28, 1832.
An organ of the Finney Revivals, edited by Thomas Hastings.

The Youth's Herald and Sabbath School Magazine (Middlebury, Vermont), 1829–30.
A partial file of this little magazine, edited by John J. Shipherd, is in the library of the American Antiquarian Society at Worcester, Mass.

2. Special Articles

Alilunas, Leo, "Fugitive Slave Cases in Ohio Prior to 1850," *Ohio State Archaeological and Historical Quarterly,* XLIX, 182-184 (Apr.-June, 1940).

Anderson, L. F., "The Manual Labor School Movement," *Educational Review,* XLVI, 369-386 (Nov., 1913).

Ashley, Franklin P., "Whitestown Seminary," *Town Topics of the Mohawk Valley,* IV, No. 9, pages 12, 25, 32 (Oct., 1929).

Ball, G. L., "Liberty and Slavery," *Freewill Baptist Quarterly,* IX, 146-172 (Apr., 1861).

Barton, William E., "History of the First Congregational Church of Wellington, Ohio." Ohio Church History Society, *Papers,* II, 21-55 (Oberlin—1892).

Bosworth, L. A. M., "Civil War Days in Oberlin," *Oberlin Alumni Magazine,* XV, 65-69 (Dec. 1918).

Bosworth, Mrs. L. A. M., "A Stormy Epoch," Ohio Church History Society, *Papers,* VI, 1-22 (Oberlin—1895).

Brand, James, "History of the Congregational Association of Ohio," *Ibid.,* VII, 56-75 (Oberlin—1896).

Brewster, H. Pomeroy, "The Magic of a Voice, Rochester Revivals of Rev. Charles G. Finney," Rochester Historical Society, *Publications,* IV (1925), 281.

Bridges, Flora, "Antoinette Brown Blackwell," *Oberlin Alumni Magazine,* V, 203-211 (March, 1909).

Brown, J. H., Gengembre, P. W., and Davis, W. V., "Report on the Co-Education of the Sexes to the Members of the Pennsylvania State Teachers' Association," *Pennsylvania School Journal,* III, 211-215 (Jan., 1855).

Burroughs, Wilbur Greeley, "Oberlin's Part in the Slavery Conflict," *Ohio State Archeological and Historical Quarterly,* XX, 269-334 (April—July, 1911).

Chapin, W. C., "Dr. Dascomb's Old Laboratory and the Beginnings of the Chemistry Department," *Oberlin Alumni Magazine,* XXVI, 205 (Apr., 1930).

Cochran, William C., "Charles Grandison Finney," *Ibid.,* IV, 375-400 July, 1908). Reprinted as a separate book in Philadelphia in 1908. Cited below under books and pamphlets.

"When Oberlin College Was Peculiar," *Ibid.,* XXII, No. 2, pages 8-10 (Nov., 1925).

"College Magazines," *Yale Literary Magazine,* XXIV, 333-340 (July, 1859).

Comings, Mrs. Emilie Royce, and Hosford, Frances J., "The Story of L.L.S., the First Woman's Club in America," *Oberlin Alumni Magazine,* XXIII, No. 6, pages 10-13 (Mar., 1927).

Combs, John P., "Mrs. F. P. Grant—Mrs. William B. Banister," Barnard's *American Journal of Education,* XXX (n. s., V), 612-624 (Sept., 1880).

Commager, H. S., "The Blasphemy of Abner Kneeland," *New England Quarterly,* VIII, 29-41 (Mar., 1935).

"The Congregational Convention," *New Englander,* XI, 72-92 (Feb., 1853).

Dickinson, Cornelius E., "The Come-Outer Movement," Ohio Church History Society, *Papers,* IX, 57-67 (Oberlin—1898).

"History of Congregationalism in Ohio before 1852," *Ibid.* VII, 31-55 (Oberlin—1896).

Dumond, Dwight, L., "Race Prejudice and Abolition," *Michigan Alumni Quarterly Review,* XLI, 377-385 (Apr., 1935).

Ellsworth, Clayton Sumner, "Ohio's Legislative Attack Upon Abolition Schools [Oberlin]," *Mississippi Valley Historical Review,* XXI, 379-386 (Dec., 1934).

Fairchild, James Harris, "The Coeducation of the Sexes," Barnard's *American Journal of Education,* XVII, 385-400 (Jan., 1868). Reprinted in James Orton, ed., *Liberal Education of Women* (New York and Chicago—1873), 238-256.

"The Doctrine of Sanctification at Oberlin," *Congregational Quarterly,* N. S., VIII, 237-260 (Apr., 1876).

"Grandfather's Story," *Oberlin Alumni Magazine,* IV, 1-7 (Oct., 1907), 41-46 (Nov., 1907), 87-92 (Dec., 1907), 139-142 (Jan., 1908), 176-181 (Feb., 1908), 226-231 (Mar., 1908), 269-272 (Apr., 1908), 301-310 (May, 1908). A few reprints of the entire narrative were published in pamphlet form. There is one copy in the Oberlin College Library, cited below under "books and pamphlets." A charming and extremely valuable narrative—containing a classic description of pioneer life.

"John Keep," *Congregational Quarterly,* XIII, 209-224 (Apr., 1871).

"The Joint Education of the Sexes," *The Ohio Journal of Education,* I, 353-369 (Dec., 1852). Also published separately as *The Joint Education of the Sexes: A Report Presented at a Meeting of the Ohio State Teachers' Association, Sandusky City, July 8th* (Oberlin—1852).

"Letters," *Oberlin Alumni Magazine,* I, 31-33 (Nov., 1904), 59-62 (Dec., 1904), 92-94 (Jan., 1905), 122-124 (Feb., 1905), 151-153 (Mar., 1905), 179-182 (Apr., 1905), 247-249 (June, 1905), 302-305 (July, 1905). These letters constitute part of the Fairchild MSS owned by James Thome Fairchild and cited above.

"The Story of Congregationalism on the Western Reserve," Ohio Church History Society, *Papers,* V, 1-27 (Oberlin—1894).

"The Underground Railroad," Western Reserve Historical Society, *Tracts,* IV, no. 87 (Cleveland—1895).

Fletcher, Robert Samuel, "Bread and Doctrine at Oberlin," *Ohio State Archaeological and Historical Quarterly,* XLIX, 58-67 (Jan.—Mar.—1940).

"The Centennial of the Musical Union," *Oberlin Alumni Magazine,* XXXIII, no. 5, pages 12-13 (Mar., 1937).

"Distaff and Gavel, Women's Organizations in Early Oberlin," *Ibid.,* XXXVI, no. 6, pages 4-5 and 19 (Apr., 1940).

"The First Coeds," *American Scholar,* VII, 78-93 (Winter, 1938); reprinted in Harrison G. Platt, Jr., and Porter G. Perrin, *Current Expressions of Fact and Opinion* (Chicago—c. 1941).

"The Government of the Oberlin Colony," *Mississippi Valley Historical Review,* XX, 179-190 (Sept., 1933).

"John Brown and Oberlin," *Oberlin Alumni Magazine,* XXVIII, 135-141 (Feb., 1932).

"Oberlin and Co-education," *Ohio State Archaeological and Historical Quarterly,* XLVII, 1-19 (Jan., 1938).

"Oberlin in the Fifties as Recorded by Twelve-year-old Mary Louisa Cowles," *Oberlin Alumni Magazine,* XXVII, 233-237 (May, 1931).

"Oneida and Oberlin," *Town Topics of the Mohawk Valley,* Utica (Oct., 1931).

"The Pastoral Theology of Charles G. Finney," Ohio Presbyterian Historical Society, *Proceedings,* III, 28-33 (June, 1941).

"Ransom's John Brown Painting," *Kansas Historical Quarterly,* IX, 343-346 (Nov., 1940).

Foster, Frank H., "The Oberlin Ojibway Mission," Ohio Church History Society, *Papers,* II, 1-25 (Oberlin—1892).

Fraser, John G., "A Century of Congregationalism in Cleveland," *Ibid.,* VIII, 1-44, (Oberlin—1897).

Fuller, Mrs. A. O., "Early Annals of the Austinburg Church," *Ibid.* X, 63-79 (Oberlin—1899).

Hall, James, "Education and Slavery," *Western Monthly Magazine,* II, 266-273 (May, 1834).

Harlow, Ralph, V., "Rise and Fall of the Kansas Aid Movement," *American Historical Review,* XLI, 1-25 (Oct., 1935).

Harring, H. A., "The Ohio Observer and Western Reserve College," Western Reserve University, *Bulletin,* XI, 3-74, 151-202 (May-Nov., 1908).

Henderson, Gavin B., "The Pacifists of the Fifties," *Journal of Modern History,* IX, 314-341 (Sept., 1937).

Hightower, Raymond L., "Joshua L. Wilson; Frontier Controversialist," *Church History,* III, 300-316 (Dec., 1934).

Hosford, Frances J., "The Pioneer Women of Oberlin College," *Oberlin Alumni Magazine,* XIII, No. 2 (Nov., 1926), pages 16-18, No. 4 (Jan., 1927), pages 7-10, No. 5 (Feb., 1927), pages 7-10, No. 6 (Mar., 1927), pages 10-13 (cited above as *16*), No. 7 (Apr., 1927), pages 10-13 and No. 8 (May, 1927), pages 7-9.

James, Edward J., "Commercial Education," N. M. Butler, ed., *Monographs on Education in the United States,* 2 vols. (Albany—1900).

Jameson, George C., "Historical Sketch of Medicine in Oberlin," reprinted from "The Historians Notebook," *Ohio State Medical Journal,* XXXIII, No. 3 (Mar., 1937).

Jewett, Frank Fanning, and Jewett, Frances Gulick, "The Chemical Department of Oberlin College from 1833 to 1912," *Oberlin Alumni Magazine,* XVIII, No. 10—Supplement (July, 1922).

Johnston, A. A. F., "Significant Events and Noted People," *Ibid.* VI, 51-63, (Nov., 1909).

Kauffman, Albert W., "Early Years of Adrian College," *Michigan History Magazine,* XIII, 79-90, (Jan., 1929).

Knight, Edgar W., "Manual Labor Schools in the South," *South Atlantic Quarterly,* XVI (July, 1917).

Laine, William R., "Some Civil War Memories," *Oberlin Alumni Magazine,* XV, 11-12, (Oct., 1918) and 123-124 (Feb., 1919).

Landon, Fred, "Anthony Burns in Canada," reprinted from the Ontaria Historical Society, *Papers and Records,* XXII, (1925).

Leonard, D. L., "Early Annals of the Oberlin Church," Ohio Church History Society, *Papers,* VIII, 80-109 (Oberlin—1897).

McKelvey, Blake, "The Flower City, Center of Nurseries and Fruit Orchards, Rochester Historical Society, *Publications,* XVIII (1940), 128.

Marvin, N. L., "Address of ——— at Unveiling of Shurtleff Monument," *Oberlin Alumni Magazine,* VII, 305-325 (June, 1911).

Mathews [Rosenbery], Lois Kimball, "The Mayflower Compact and Its Descendants," Mississippi Valley Historical Association, *Proceedings,* for the year 1912-1913 (Cedar Rapids, Iowa—1913), VI, 79-106.

Metcalf, Maynard M., "Oberlin as a Model of College Administration," *School and Society,* III, 635-638 (Apr., 29, 1916).

Munger, Asahel, "Diary of Asahel Munger and Wife," Oregon Historical Society, *Quarterly,* VIII, 387-405 (Dec., 1907).

Nichols, R. H., "The Plan of Union in New York," *Church History,* V, 29-52 (Mar., 1936).

Oliphant, J. Orin, "The American Missionary Spirit, 1828–1835," *Ibid.,* VII, 125-137 (June, 1938).

Padgett, James A., "Diplomats to Haiti and Their Diplomacy," *Journal of Negro History,* XXV, 265-330 (July, 1940). —On Henry E. Peck and John M. Langston.

Painter, John H., "The Fugitives of the Pearl," *Ibid.,* I, 243-264 (July, 1916).

Pond, Chauncey N., "Ohio Sunday-School History," Ohio Church History Society, *Papers,* III, 1-20 (Oberlin—1892).

Power, R. L., "A Crusade to Extend Yankee Culture," *New England Quarterly,* XIII, 638-653 (Dec., 1940).

Price, Robert, "Further Notes on Granville's Anti-abolition Disturbance in 1836," *Ohio State Archeological and Historical Quarterly,* XLV, 365-368 (Oct., 1936).

"Morus Multicaulis, or Silk Worms Must Eat," *Ibid.,* XLV, 265-272 (July, 1936).

"The Ohio Anti-Abolition Disturbances in 1836," *Ibid.,* XIV, 173-188 (Apr., 1936).

Rodabaugh, James H., "Miami University, Calvinism, and the Anti-Slavery Movement," *Ohio State Archaeological and Historical Quarterly,* XLVIII, 66-73 (Jan., 1939).

Root, Azariah S., "Old Houses in Oberlin," *Oberlin Alumni Magazine,* XXI, No. 4, pages 14-15 (Jan., 1925).

Ross, Earle D., "The Manual Labor Experiment in the Land Grant College," *Mississippi Valley Historical Review,* XXI, 513-528 (Mar., 1935).

Rowe, Mrs. L. E., "History of the First Baptist Church, Oberlin," Lorain County Baptist Association, *Minutes,* 1903, 21-24.

Schmidt, G. P., "Cross Currents in American Colleges," *American Historical Review,* XLII, 46-67 (Oct., 1936).

Shryock, Richard H., "Public Relations of the Medical Profession in Great Britain and the United States, 1600–1870," *Annals of Medical History,* II, (n. s.), 308-309 (May, 1930).

"Sylvester Graham and the Popular Health Movement, 1830–1870," *Mississippi Valley Historical Review,* XVIII, 172-189 (Sept., 1931).

Sloane, Rush P., "The Underground Railroad in the Firelands," *Magazine of Western History,* VIII (1888).

Smith, Clifford Hayes, "Philo Penfield Stewart," *The Vermonter* (White River Junction, Vermont), XL, 12-15 (Jan., 1935).

Snow, Leroi C., "Who Was Professor Joshua Seixas?" *The Improvement Era* (Salt Lake City), XXXIX, No. 2 (Feb., 1936).

Southall, E. P., "Arthur Tappan and the Anti-Slavery Movement," *Journal of Negro History,* XV, 162-197 (Apr., 1930).

Stearns, Bertha-Monica, "Reform Periodicals and Female Reformers, 1830–1860," *American Historical Review,* XXXVII, 678-697 (July, 1932).

Stiven, Frederic B., "Sketch of the Oberlin Conservatory of Music," *Oberlin Alumni Magazine,* XI, 271-278 (Apr., 1915).

Stoddard, John F., and Brown, J. H., "Debates at the Pottsville Meeting of the State Teacher's Association, Remarks on the Co-Education of the Sexes," *Pennsylvania School Journal,* III, 119-122 (Oct., 1854).

Terrell, Mary Church, "History of the High School for Negroes in Washington," *Journal of Negro History,* II, 252-266 (July, 1917).

Thalheimer, M. E., "History of the Vine Street Congregational Church in Cincinnati," Ohio Church History Society, *Papers,* IX, 41-56 (Oberlin—1898).

Walton, Perry, "The Mysterious Case of the Long, Low Black Schooner," *New England Quarterly,* VI, 353-361 (June, 1933).
The story of the *Amistad.*

Whipple, Henry E., "The General Conference of the Freewill Baptist Connexion," *Freewill Baptist Quarterly,* VIII, 198-207 (Apr., 1860).

Whitlock, Frank, "History of Central North Conference," *Ohio* Church History Society, *Papers,* VI, 23-42 (Oberlin—1895).

Wickersham, J. P., and Thompson, James, "On the Co-Education of the Sexes," *Pennsylvania School Journal,* III, 87-92 (Sept., 1854).

Wilcox, F. C., "Piety and Profit in College Building," *Journal of Higher Education,* VIII, 147-149 (Mar., 1937).
Discussing Shipherd's first college ventures in Michigan.

Williams, Samuel R., "A History of Physics in Oberlin College," *Oberlin Alumni Magazine,* XI, 50-56 (Nov., 1914).

Williams, Walcott B., "Two Early Efforts to Found Colleges in Michigan at Delta and at Marshall," *Historical Collections of the Michigan Pioneer and Historical Society,* XXX, 524 *et seq.* (Lansing—1906).

Wright, Etta, "A Bibliography of Oberlin," *Oberlin Alumni Magazine,* XXVIII, 199-204 (Apr., 1932).

Wright, George Frederick, "Company C," *Ibid.,* VII, 326-333 (June, 1911).
"The Oberlin I First Knew and Oberlin Today," *Ibid.,* XVII, 148-151 (Apr., 1921).

Wright, W. E. C., "Oberlin's Contribution to Ethics," *Bibliotheca Sacra,* LVII, 429-444 (July, 1900).

Zorbaugh, Charles L., "The Plan of Union in Ohio," *Church History,* VI, 145-164 (June—1937).

3. College and School Documents

Andover Theological Seminary, *General Catalogue of the Theological Seminary, Andover, Mass., 1880* (Andover—1883).

Auburn Theological Seminary, *General Biographical Catalogue, 1818–1918* (Auburn, N. Y.—1918).

Calkins, Griffins, & Co's. Union Business Institute (Oberlin, O.), *Circulars, 1865 and 1866.* See also Oberlin Business Institute, and Spencerian . . . Institute.

Hamilton College, *Complete Alumni Register* (1922).

Lane Theological Seminary, *Fifth Annual Report . . . Together with the Laws of the Institution, and a Catalogue of the Officers and Students. November, 1834* (Cincinnati—1834).
General Catalogue, 1828–1881 (Cincinnati—1881).
History of the Foundation and Endowment . . . of the Lane Theological Seminary (Cincinnati—1848).

Michigan, University of, *Records of the University of Michigan, 1817–1837* (Ann Arbor—1935). Data on John Monteith.

Middlebury College, *Catalogue of the Officers and Students of Middlebury College* (Middlebury, Vermont—1901).

Oberlin Business Institute, *Catalogue and Circular of the Oberlin Business Institute and College Writing Department, Oberlin, Ohio, 1882–1883.* (See also Calkins, Griffins & Co. and Spencerian . . . Institute.)

Oberlin Collegiate Institute (College after 1850), *Alumni Catalogue of 1926* (Oberlin—1928). Limited to officers, teachers, and graduates.

An Appeal on Behalf of the Oberlin Institute, in Aid of the Abolition of Slavery in the United States of America (Broadside, 1838).

Catalogues, 1835–. *The First Annual Report, 1834,* listed students and served the purposes of a catalogue. (See below.) There was some irregularity in the publication of the *Catalogue.* The one published in 1835 lists students in all departments for the academic year 1835–36; the *Catalogue* published in 1836 lists students for the academic year 1836–37. None was published in 1837, however, and the *Catalogue* issued June, *1838,* lists students for the academic year 1837–38. Beginning with the *Catalogue* published in September, 1839, students in the Preparatory Department were listed for the preceding academic year and students in other departments for the current year. Thus the 1840 *Catalogue* lists "Prep" students for 1839–40 but students in the Collegiate and Theological departments for 1840–41.

Circular, Oberlin Collegiate Institute, March 8, 1834. A broadside announcing the work in the Oberlin Collegiate Institute. There are two copies in the Oberlin College Library.

Circular Presenting the Claims of the Cabinet of Natural History in Oberlin College, by George N. Allen. (n.p.—n.d.).

[Circular, 1842] "Dearly Beloved in the Lord: Peace be to you and to your household. . . ." There is a copy in a letter from Charles Smith, January 24, 1842, in File I in the Official Correspondence, Treasurer's Office.

[Circular, 1862] "To the friends of the African race. . . ." Printed in connection with Hamilton Hill's mission to England.

Commencement Programs (usually labelled *Order of Exercises*).

Collegiate Department, 1837–40, 1845–46, 1848, 1850–66 [2 editions for 1851].

Theological Department, 1838–41, 1845–46, 1848, 1850–65.

Ladies' Department, 1845–48, 1850–66.

Preparatory Department [Exercises in Exhibition of Senior Preparatory Class], 1850, 1852, 1859–63, 1865–66.

The First Annual Report of the Oberlin Collegiate Institute, November, 1834 (Elyria). Really the first catalogue.

General Catalogue of Oberlin College (Oberlin—1908). Lists alphabetically all persons connected with the institution in the first seventy-five years. A list of omissions and corrections is kept in the Secretary's Office.

Junior Exhibition Programs, 1860–63, 1865–67.

Laws and Regulations, First Edition (Oberlin: Printed by James Steele—1840); Second Edition (Oberlin: Printed by F. Cowdery—1842); Fourth Edition (Oberlin: J. M. Fitch—1847); Fifth Edition (Oberlin: James M. Fitch—1849); Seventh Edition (Oberlin: James M. Fitch—1853); Ninth Edition (Oberlin: James M. Fitch—1856) ; Eleventh Edition (Oberlin: Shankland and Harmon—1859); Twelfth Edition (Oberlin: Shankland and Harmon—1860) ; Unnumbered Edition (Oberlin: J. B. T. Marsh—1867).

Also see Oberlin College—Ladies' Department.

Monthly Rhetorical Programs, August 23, 1861; August 19, 1864; May 22, 1865; August 18, 1865.

Necrology, 1887/1888 ["Deceased alumni"], 1892/1893–1898/1899, 1900/1901–1907/1908, 1920/1921–1924/1925, 1925/1930, 1930/-1931.

Schedules of Examination[s], August, 1846; August, 1850; August, 1855; August, 1856; August, 1858; August, 1859; August, 1860; May, 1861; August, 1863; August, 1864; May, 1866.

Semi-Centennial Register of Officers and Alumni of Oberlin College (Chicago—1883).

Gives more biographical detail regarding early graduates than the biographical catalogues of 1908 and 1926.

Oberlin College—Choir. (See Oberlin College, Musical Union.)

Oberlin College—Conservatory of Music, *Announcements,* 1866–70 and 1872.

Oberlin College—Female Department. (See Ladies' Department.)

Oberlin College—French Class, *Programs of Annual Exhibitions: French Exercises,* 1863; *French Anniversary,* 1864; *Diplomes conférés à la classe française de 1865.*

Oberlin College—Ladies' Department, *Laws and Regulations of the Female Department* (Oberlin: Fitch's Power Press—1852); (Oberlin, O.: Shankland and Harmon, Printers—1859) ; (Oberlin: J. F. Harmon, Printer—1865); *Laws and Regulations of the Ladies' Department* (Cleveland—1874).—See also Oberlin College, Commencement Programs.

Oberlin College—Literary Societies, *Anniversary Programs:* Aelioian, 1861–67; Ladies' Literary Society, 1854–67 (The official title of the society is not always used on the programs.) ; Phi Delta, 1855–66; Phi Kappa Pi, 1859–66; Theological Society, 1855; Union Exhibition of Phi Delta and Phi Kappa Pi, 1862–63, 1865–66; Union Literary Society, 1845–46, 1848–52, 1854 (became Phi Delta); Young Ladies' Literary Society, 1848–52 (The official title of the society is not always used on the programs); Young Ladies' Lyceum, 1857–60 (became Aelioian) ; Young Men's Lyceum, 1846, 1849, 1851, 1854–56, 1858 (became Phi Kappa Pi). Programs are also pasted in the MS society minutes.

Oberlin College–Musical Association (1837–56), Choir (1856–60), Musical Union (1860–70), *Programs,* August 24-25, 1852; July 1, 1853; August 24, 1853; August 26, 1857; August 25 [1858]; February 9, 1860; August 24, 1861; August 28, 1861; August 27 [1862]; August 24, 1864; August 28, 1867; July 31 and August 5, 1868. Other programs are pasted in the MS minutes of the society. The official title is not always used on the printed programs.

Oberlin College–Musical Convention, *Invitation,* July 20, 1855, and *Program,* August 22, 1855.

Oberlin College–Preparatory Department. (See Oberlin College–Commencement Programs.)

Oberlin College–Theological Department. (See Oberlin College–Commencement Programs and Oberlin College–Literary Societies.)

Oberlin College–Winter School, *Announcement,* 1857; *Catalogue,* 1864/1865.

Ohio Agricultural College, Oberlin, Lorain Co., O., *Prospectus,* 1854.

Olivet College (Olivet, Michigan), *Catalogues,* 1846 and 1846/7. The catalogue dated 1846 was the first published and contains a brief history of the founding.

Oneida Institute of Science and Industry (Whitesboro, New York), *First Report of the Trustees of Oneida Academy* (Utica–1828) ; *Third Report of the Trustees of the Oneida Institute of Science and Industry* (Utica–1831).

Sketch of the Conditions and Prospects of the Oneida Institute (Utica–1834).

Princeton Theological Seminary, *Biographical Catalogue* (Trenton, N. J.–1919).

Spencerian Commercial and Chirographic Institute, Oberlin, O., *Circular and Catalogue,* 1862. (See also Calkins, Griffins & Co., and Oberlin Business Institute.)

Teachers' Seminary, Andover, Mass., *Catalogue,* 1836.

Western Reserve College (Hudson, O.), *Centennial Catalogue of Graduates and Former Students of Western Reserve College and of Adelbert College, 1826–1926,* published as a *Bulletin* of Western Reserve University, XXIX, No. 8 (Aug., 1926).

Catalogues, 1835/1836, 1836/1837, 1837/1838, etc.

Laws, 1833, 1838, 1845.

Williams College, *Williams Biographical Annals,* by Calvin Durfee (Boston—1871).

Yale College, *Biographical Memoranda Respecting All Who Ever Were Members of the Class of 1832 in Yale College,* compiled by Edward E. Salisbury (New Haven—1880).

Biographical Sketch of the Class of 1824 (Norwalk, Conn.—1855).

Catalogues, passim.

Report on the Course of Instruction of Yale College . . . (New Haven—1828).

Yale Divinity School, *Eighth General Catalogue of the Yale Divinity School, Centennial Issue, 1822–1922* (New Haven—1922).

4. Printed Records of Religious and Reform Organizations

American and Foreign Anti-Slavery Society, *Annual Reports,* seventh to thirteenth (New York), 1847–53.

American Anti-Slavery Society, *Annual Reports,* first to sixth; twenty-second to twenty-eighth (New York), 1834–39, 1855–61.

American Education Society, *Quarterly Register and Journal.* See the *American Quarterly Register.*

American Home Missionary Society, *Sixth Report* (New York), 1832.

American Missionary Association, *Annual Reports,* fourth and later (New York), 1850–.

American Physiological Society, *Publications* (Boston), 1837 and 1838.

Second Annual Report (Boston), 1838.

American Sunday School Union, *Sixth Annual Report* (Philadelphia), 1830.

American Tract Society (Boston), *Address of the Executive Committee of the American Tract Society, Boston to the Friends of the Society; etc.* [1858], by John W. Alvord.

Annual Reports, 1853–55, 1860, 1862, 1863, 1865–68.

General Series of Tracts (Boston, n.d.).

American Vegetarian Society, *Circular,* July 9, 1850.

Anti-Slavery Convention . . . Held in London, . . . 1840, *Proceedings* (London—1840).

Anti-Slavery Convention . . . Held in London, . . . 1843, *Proceedings* (London—1843).

Canada Mission, *Seventh Annual Report* (Rochester—1844).

Christian Anti-Slavery Convention—1850, *Minutes* (Cincinnati—1850).

Christian Anti-Slavery Convention—1851, *Minutes* (Chicago—1851).

Church Anti-Slavery Society, *Proceedings* (New York—1859).

Congregational Convention, *Proceedings of the General Convention of Congregational Ministers and Delegates in the United States, Held at Albany, N. Y., on the 5th, 6th, 7th and 8th of October, 1852, etc.* (New York—1852).

Glasgow Emancipation Society, *Report* (Glasgow—1840).

Oberlin Non-Resistance Society, *Constitution . . . June 18, 1840* (n.p.-n.d.).

Ohio Anti-Slavery Convention . . . at Putnam . . . 1835, *Proceedings* (n.p.-n.d.).

Ohio Anti-Slavery Society, *Proceedings,* 1835 [Same as above], 1836, 1837, 1838, 1839, and 1840.

Ohio Congregational Convention Held at Mansfield . . . 1852, *Proceedings* (Cleveland—1852).

Ohio State Christian Anti-Slavery Convention, *Proceedings,* 1859.

Peace Congresses at Brussels, Paris, Frankfort, London, and Edinburgh, *Reports,* 1848, 1849, 1850, 1851, and 1853 (London—1861). (There is a copy in the Ginn Library, Goddard Hall, Tufts College.)

Peace Convention Held in London . . . 1843, *Proceedings* (London—1843).

Society for Promoting Manual Labor in Literary Institutions, *First Annual Report* (New York—1833). The work of Theodore D. Weld.

5. Official Documents

CITY OF LONDON, ENGLAND

London Court of Common Council, *Minutes of the Court of Common Council of the Corporation of London,* 1839 (Thomas Henry Coe, Cheapside, London, Printer).

VILLAGE OF OBERLIN

Charter and Ordinances of the Town of Oberlin, 1848, 1856, and 1861.

Oberlin Union School, *Manual* [1867].

STATE OF OHIO

Acts of the State of Ohio, *Local,* XXXIII (1834).

Commissioner of Public Schools, *Sixteenth and Seventeenth Annual Reports,* 1859 and 1860 (Columbus–1860 and 1861).

General Assembly, *Reports, Including Messages and Other Communications, Made to the Thirty-Fifth General Assembly of the State of Ohio* (Columbus–1836).

House *Journal,* 1835.

Official Roster of the Soldiers of the State of Ohio in the War of the Rebellion, 1861-1866, 12 vols. (Akron, O.–1886–95).

[Ohio Centennial Committee], *Historical Sketches of the Higher Educational Institutions and Also of Benevolent and Reformatory Institutions of the State of Ohio* (n.p.–1876).

Historical Sketches of Public Schools . . . of Ohio (Columbus–1876). Contains a "History of Oberlin Public Schools."

A History of Education in the State of Ohio, Published by Authority of the General Assembly (Columbus–1876).

Senate *Journal,* 1834, 1837, 1840.

UNITED STATES

"Allowances to [Mail] Contractors," March 19, 1840, 26 Cong., 1 sess., *House Document 149.*

Boykin, James C., "Physical Training," Commissioner of Education, *Report,* 1891–1892 (Washington–1894), 491–594.

Bureau of Refugees, Freedmen and Abandoned Lands: *First Semi-Annual Report on Schools and Finances of Freedmen,* January 1, 1866 (Washington–1868) ; *Second,* July 1, 1866 (Washington–1868); *Third Semi-Annual Report on Schools for Freedmen,* January 1, 1867 (Washington–1868); *Fourth,* July 1, 1867 (Washington –1868); *Fifth,* January 1, 1868 (Washington–1868); *Sixth,* July 1, 1868 (Washington–1868); *Seventh,* January 1, 1869 (Washington–1869) ; *Eighth,* July 1, 1869 (Washington–1869); *Tenth,* July 1, 1870 (Washington–1870).

Cajori, Florian, *The Teaching and History of Mathematics in the United States,* Commission of Education, *Circular of Information,* No. 3 (Washington–1890).

Census *Reports: Sixth,* 1840; *Seventh,* 1850; *Eighth,* 1860, and *Ninth.* 1870.

Commissioner of Education, *Annual Reports* (Washington—1868 and later).

Special Report, Educational Exhibits and Conventions at the World's Industrial and Cotton Centennial Exposition, New Orleans, 1884–85 (Washington—1886).

Special Report . . . on the Condition and Improvement of Public Schools in the District of Columbia (Washington—1871).

[De Hazzi], *A Treatise on the Culture of Silk in Germany, and Especially in Bavaria; or Complete Instruction for the Plantation and the Management of Mulberry Trees, and the Rearing of Silk-Worms, by the Councillor of State De Hazzi,* 20 Cong., 1 sess., *House Document 226* (Washington—1828).

House of Representatives, *Journal,* 31 Cong., 1 sess. and 32 Cong., 1 sess. (Washington—1849 and 1850).

Howard, L. C., "The United States Department of Agriculture and Silk Culture," Department of Agriculture, *Yearbook,* 1903 (Washington—1904).

Knight, George W., and Commons, John R., *The History of Higher Education in Ohio,* Commissioner of Education, *Circular of Information, No. 5* (Washington—1891).

"Memorial of sundry inhabitants of the counties of Windham and Tolland, State of Connecticut, praying for aid of Government in the cultivation of the mulberry tree and of silk," 20 Cong., 1 sess., *House Document 159* (Washington—1828).

"Minority Report on Charges Against General Howard," 41 Cong., 2 sess., *House Report 125.*

"Offers for Carrying the United States Mail," January 5, 1851, 26 Cong., 2 sess., *House Document 44.*

Postmaster General, *Annual Reports* (Washington—1834–44).

"Select Committee of the Senate appointed to inquire into the late invasion and seizure of the public property at Harper's Ferry"—Testimony, 36 Cong., 1 sess., *Senate Report 278.*

Smith, Anna Tolman, "Coeducation in the Schools and Colleges of the United States," Commissioner of Education, *Report, 1903* (Washington—1905), I, 1047–1078.

"Special Committee . . . charged with investigation into . . . the riots at Memphis . . ." 39 Cong., 1 sess., *House Report 101.*

Wold, Ansel, *Biographical Directory of the American Congress, 1774–1927,* 69 Cong., 2 sess., *House Document,* vol. 16 (Washington—1928).

6. Maps, Gazetteers, Guides and Directories

Camp's Directory of Oberlin, 1873–1874 (Oberlin—1873).
Contains valuable data on the earlier history of the village.

Cincinnati Directory for the Year 1834 (Cincinnati—1834).

Directory of 1829—Cincinnati (Cincinnati—1829).

Geil, John T., *Map of Lorain Co., Ohio, from Actual Surveys in 1857*. A large wall map.

Gordon, Thomas F., *Gazetteer of the State of New York . . .* (Philadelphia—1836).

Jenkins, Warren, *The Ohio Gazetteer and Traveler's Guide* (Columbus—1837).

MacCabe, Julian P. Bolivar, *Directory—Cleveland and Ohio City, for the Years 1837–38* (Cleveland—1837).
Reprinted in 1908 by the Guardian Savings and Trust Company, Cleveland.

Mitchell, S. Augustus, *An Accompaniment to Mitchell's Reference and Distance Map of the United States . . .* (Philadelphia—1834).
Mitchell's New Traveller's Guide Through the United States and the Canadas . . . (Philadelphia—1856).
Mitchell's Traveller's Guide Through the United States . . . (Philadelphia—1836).
The Tourist's Pocket Map of the State of Ohio (Philadelphia—1834).

Moss, C. D., *Map of Oberlin, Ohio, Surveyed and Drawn by C. D. Moss* (Philadelphia—1870). Wall map.

Peet, Elijah, *Peet's General Business Directory of the City of Cleveland, for the Years 1846–7 . . .* (Cleveland—1846).

A Reference & Statistical Map of Oberlin, Lorain Co., O. (Cleveland—1851).
The first known printed map of Oberlin.

Robinson, Lewis, *Map of the Connecticut Reserve, Compiled from the Latest Authorities* (Akron—1837).
At first glance a very interesting map, but extremely inaccurate.

Rochester (New York) *Directory,* 1834.

Sheffer, David H., *Cincinnati Directory for 1840* (Cincinnati—1840).

View of the Valley of the Mississippi: or the Emigrant's and Traveller's Guide to the West (Philadelphia—1832).

The Western Reserve Register for 1852 (Hudson, Ohio—1852).

Williams, C. S., *Williams' Medina, Elyria & Oberlin City Directory, City Guide, and Business Mirror.* (n.p.—1859).

7. Biographical Books and Pamphlets

Beecher, Charles, *Autobiography, Correspondence, etc., of Lyman Beecher, D.D.*, 2 vols. (New York—1874).

Benham, Welcome E., *Life and Writings of ——, by Himself* (Meridan, Conn.—1882).

Blackwell, Alice Stone, *Lucy Stone* (Boston—1930).

Contains an interesting chapter on the life of a "coed" in early Oberlin.

Bowen, Clarence Winthrop, *Arthur and Lewis Tappan* (n.p.—n.d.).

Bristol, Sherlock, *The Pioneer Preacher, Incidents of Interest and Experiences in the Author's Life* (New York—c. 1887 and 1898).

The autobiography of a graduate of the Class of 1838. The latest edition is most useful.

Chadwick, John White, *A Life for Liberty, Anti-Slavery and Other Letters of Sallie Holley* (New York and London—1899).

Sallie (or Sally) Holley attended Oberlin from 1847 to 1851, graduating from the Ladies' Course in the latter year.

Cochran, William C., *Charles Grandison Finney* (Philadelphia—1908).

A reprint of the sketch which appeared in the *Oberlin Alumni Magazine* in the same year.

Coffin, Levi, *Reminiscences of Levi Coffin, the Reputed President of the Underground Railroad* (Cincinnati—c. 1876).

Tells part of the story of the Cage sisters.

Commager, Henry S., *Theodore Parker* (New York—1936).

Cowles, Helen, *Grace Victorious* (Oberlin—1856).

Selections from the journal of Helen Cowles, daughter of Professor Henry Cowles and a member of the Preparatory Department and Ladies' Department from 1848 to her death in 1851.

Dictionary of American Biography (New York—1928–36), edited by Allen Johnson and Dumas Malone. Sketches of:

William Andrus Alcott
Frederic DeForest Allen
Zilpah Polly Grant Banister
Amzi Lorenzo Barber
Catharine Beecher
Lyman Beecher
May Ann Ball Bickerdyke
(Said to have attended Oberlin but Oberlin records do not mention her.)
William Hilliard Bidwell
Antoinette Louisa Brown Blackwell
Jacob Brinkerhoff
Blanche K. Bruce
(This colored United States Senator is said to have attended Oberlin but Oberlin records do not mention him.)
Stevenson Burke
Anthony Burns
Elihu Burritt
Levi Coffin
Lorenzo S. Coffin
Jacob Dolson Cox
Erastus Milo Cravath
James Brooks Dill

Dan Parmelee Eells
Joseph Emerson
Calvin Fairbank
George Thompson Fairchild
James Harris Fairchild
Edward Burke Fairfield
John Gregg Fee
John Comfort Fillmore
Charles Grandison Finney
Abigail Kelley Foster
Stephen Symonds Foster
George Washington Gale
Sylvester Graham
Beriah Green
Samuel Read Hall
Thomas Hastings
Ferdinand Vandiveer Hayden
Myron Holley
Henry Howe
Byron Bancroft Johnson
Robert Clark Kedzie
John Mercer Langston
Asa Dearborn Lord
Asa Mahan
Sarah Towne Smith Martyn
Lowell Mason
Emily Clark Huntington Miller
Nathan Jackson Morrison
Alvred Bayard Nettleton
Asahel Nettleton
Edward N. Nettleton
Almira Hart Lincoln Phelps
Parker Pillsbury
William Bramwell Powell
John Wesley Powell
Fenelon Bird Rice
John Almanza Rowley Rogers
Abel Hastings Ross
Edward James Roye
Helen Almira Shafer
John Jay Shipherd
Gerrit Smith
Judson Smith
Denton Jaques Snider
Lorenzo Snow
Oliver Lyman Spaulding
Platt Rogers Spencer
Henry Brewster Stanton
Philo Penfield Stewart
Lucy Stone
Arthur Tappan
Lewis Tappan
James Milton Turner
Emory Upton
Amasa Walker
Theodore Dwight Weld
William Channing Woodbridge
Isaac Baker Woodbury
Elizur Wright
George Frederick Wright
—and others

See the index under "Oberlin College."

Dictionary of National Biography (London—1885–1921).
Sketches of Ebenezer Henderson, Joseph Sturge, Sophia Jex-Blake, Sir Thomas Fowell Buxton and others.

Dobbs, Caroline D., *Men of Champoeg* (Portland, Oregon—1932).
Contains a good sketch of John Smith Griffin, a graduate of the Theological Department in the Class of 1838.

Dodge, D., *Memorials of William E. Dodge* (New York—c. 1887).

Dresser, Amos, *Narrative of the Arrest, Lynch Law Trial, and Scourging of Amos Dresser, at Nashville, Tennessee, August, 1835* (Oberlin—1849).

Fairbank, Calvin, *During Slavery Times* (Chicago—1890).

Fairchild, James Harris, *Grandfather's Story, an Autobiography of James Harris Fairchild* (Oberlin—c. 1906).
Reprinted from the *Oberlin Alumni Magazine.*

Finney, Charles Grandison, *Memoirs of Rev. Charles G. Finney* (New York—1826).
Edited from the original MS by James Harris Fairchild.

Finney, Reminiscences of Rev. Charles G., (Oberlin—1876).
Anecdotes recorded by former students and associates.

Garrison, Wendell Phillips, *William Lloyd Garrison, 1805–1879; the Story of His Life Told by His Children,* 4 vols. (New York–1885–1889).

Guilford, L. T., *The Use of a Life; Memorials of Mrs. Z. P. Grant Banister* (New York [1885?]).

Mrs. Banister was the head of the Ipswich Female Seminary and friend and relative of Professor and Mrs. Henry Cowles.

Hallowell, Anna D., *James and Lucretia Mott, Life and Letters* (Boston–1884).

Harlow, Ralph Volney, *Gerrit Smith, Philanthropist and Reformer* (New York–1939).

Hopkins, Mark, *Early Letters of Mark Hopkins* (New York–c. 1929).

Contains early letters from Brownhelm.

Howard, Oliver Otis, *Autobiography,* 2 vols. (New York–1907).

Professor, T. B. Hudson, the Casualty, Biographical Sketch, the Funeral, the Coroner's Inquest, etc. (n.p.–n.d.).

Huntington, E. B., *Eminent Women of the Age* (Hartford–1868).

Contains a sketch of "Mrs. Marianne P. Dascomb."

Keeler, Harriet L., *The Life of Adelia A. Field Johnston* (Cleveland –1912).

Mrs. Johnston was a graduate from the Ladies' Course in the Class of 1856 and for many years Dean of Women.

Kemper, Andrew Carr, *A Memorial of the Rev. James Kemper for the Centennial for the Synod of Kentucky* (n.p. [1899]).

Langston, John Mercer, *From the Virginia Plantation to the National Capitol . . .* (Hartford–1894).

The autobiography of a prominent colored graduate of Oberlin College in the Class of 1849.

Mahan, Asa, *Autobiography, Intellectual, Moral, and Spiritual* (London–1882).

Of scant biographical value.

Out of Darkness Into Light (Boston and New York–c. 1876).

More spiritual autobiography.

[Marks, Mrs. M.], *Memoir of the Life of David Marks* (Dover, N. H.–1846).

Martyn, Carlos, *William E. Dodge, The Christian Merchant* (New York–1890).

Memorial Record of the County of Cuyahoga and City of Cleveland, Ohio (Chicago–1894).

Some material on the Jennings family.

Miall, Charles S., *Henry Richard* (London–1889).
Useful on the peace congresses.

National Cyclopaedia of American Biography (New York, 1898–).

Parker, Robert A., *A Yankee Saint, John Humphrey Noyes and the Oneida Community* (New York–1935).

Pease, David, *Genealogical and Historical Record of the Descendants of John Pease of Enfield, Conn.* (Springfield, Mass.–1869).
Some material on Peter Pindar Pease.

Rogers, Cameron, *Colonel Bob Ingersoll* (New York–1927).
The account of the Ingersolls' experience in Oberlin seems absurd. There is no evidence that this narrative is based on original records.

Sherwood, Elisha B., *Fifty Years on the Skirmish Line* (New York–c. 1893).
The life of a graduate of the Theological Department in the Class of 1836.

Smith, Eliza R. Snow, *Biography and Family Record of Lorenzo Snow* (Salt Lake City–1884).

Snider, Denton J., *A Writer of Books in His Genesis* (St. Louis, Mo.–n.d.).
The autobiography of a graduate in the Class of 1862.

Stanton, Henry B., *Random Recollections* (New York–1887).
Stanton was a Lane Rebel.

Stevens, Charles Emery, *Anthony Burns, a History* (Boston–1856).
The story of the famous fugitive who became an Oberlin student.

[Stewart, Mrs. E. C.], *P. P. Stewart, . . . a Life Sketch* (New York–1873).
A brief biography of the co-founder by his wife.

Swing, Albert Temple, *James Harris Fairchild, or Sixty-Eight Years With a Christian College* (New York–c. 1907).
A rather inadequate biography, which, nevertheless, contains useful material.

[Tappan, Lewis], *The Life of Arthur Tappan* (New York–1870).
Inadequate, dull.

Tenney, Luman Harris, *War Diary of ——, 1861–1865* (Cleveland–1914).

Thwing, Charles Franklin, *Guides, Philosophers and Friends, Studies of College Men* (New York–1927).
Contains a sketch of James H. Fairchild.

Walker, Amasa, *Memoir of Rev. Amos Dresser* (Reprinted from Cushman genealogy n.p.–n.d.).

Ware, John, *Memoir of the Life of Henry Ware, Jr.* (Boston—1876).

Warner, Lucien Calvin, *The Story of My Life* (New York—1914).
Warner graduated from Oberlin College in the Class of 1865. He later became a trustee and great benefactor of the institution.

Weed, Edward, *Faith and Works: or the Life of Edward Weed, Minister of the Gospel* (New York—1853).
Weed was a Lane Rebel who married Zeruiah Porter, the first graduate of the Ladies' Course.

Wenzlaff, Gustav Gottlieb, *Danforth Goes to College* (Mitchell, S.D.—c. 1929).
Based largely on a MS autobiography of Danforth B. Nichols, a graduate of Oberlin College in the Class of 1838.

Willard, Frances E., and Norton, Minerva Brace, *A Great Mother, Sketches of Madam Willard* (Chicago—1894).

Wright, Arthur D., and Gardner, George E., *Hall's Lectures on School-Keeping* (Hanover, N. H.—1929).
The biography of Samuel Read Hall in the introduction has been useful.

Wright, Elizabeth, and Wright, Philip Green, *Elizur Wright, Father of Life Insurance* (Chicago—1937).

Wright, George Frederick, *Charles Grandison Finney* (Boston and New York—1893).
An excellent brief biography.

Wright, George Frederick, *Story of My Life and Work* (Oberlin—1916).

8. Books and Pamphlets on Education

Barber, Edgar M., *A Contribution to the History of Commercial Education* (Brooklyn—1903).

Campbell, Dudley, *Mixed Education of Boys and Girls* (London—1874).

Beecher, Lyman, *An Address, Delivered at the Tenth Anniversary Celebration of the Union Literary Society of Miami University, September 29, 1835* (Cincinnati—1835).

Bennett, C. A., *History of Manual and Industrial Education up to 1860* (Peoria, Ill. [1926]).

Curti, Merle E., *The Social Ideas of American Educators* (New York—c. 1935).

Hall, Samuel Read, *Lectures to Female Teachers on School-Keeping* (Boston—1832).
Lectures on School-Keeping (Boston—1829).

Mason, Lowell, *Manual of the Boston Academy of Music for Instruction in the Elements of Vocal Music, on the System of Pestalozzi* (Boston—1836).

Monroe, Will S., *History of the Pestalozzian Movement in the United States* (Syracuse, N.Y.—1907).

Orton, James, Ed., *The Liberal Education of Women: the Demand and the Method, Current Thought in America and England* (New York and Chicago—1873).

True, A. C., *A History of Agricultural Education in the United States, 1785–1925* (Washington, D. C.—1929).

Woody, Thomas, *History of Women's Education in the United States,* 2 vols. (New York—1929).

9. Books and Pamphlets on College History

[Adrian College], *Semi-Centennial Souvenir, Adrian College, 1859–1909* (n.p.—n.d.).

Coulter, Ellis Merton, *College Life in the Old South* (New York—1928).

A history of early days at the University of Georgia.

Cutler, Carroll, *A History of Western Reserve College* (Cleveland—1876).

Davis, Henry, *A Narrative of the Embarrassments and Decline of Hamilton College* [Clinton, N. Y.—1833].

Garst, Henry, *Otterbein University,* 1847–1907 (Dayton, Ohio [1907?]).

Green, F. M., *Hiram College and the Western Reserve Eclectic Institute, Fifty Years of History, 1850–1900* (Cleveland—1901).

Holmes, Dwight O. W., *The Evolution of the Negro College* (New York—1934).

Kirkpatrick, John Ervin, *Academic Organization and Control* (Yellow Springs, Ohio—1931).

[Lane Theological Seminary], *History of the Foundation and Endowment . . . of the ———* (Cincinnati—1848).

Mendenhall, Thomas C., Ed., *History of the Ohio State University,* 4 vols. (Columbus, 1920–1935).

Morison, Samuel Eliot, *Three Centuries of Harvard, 1636–1936* (Cambridge—1936).

Osborne, James Insley, and Gronert, Theodore G., *Wabash College* (Crawfordsville, Ind.—1932).

[Pacific Coast Congregational Alliance for the Promotion of Education], *Christian Education by Congregationalists in the Seven Pacific Coast States* . . . ([San Francisco?] 1893).

Rammelkamp, C. H., *Illinois College, a Centennial History, 1829–1929* (New Haven–1928).

Rogers, J. A. R., *Birth of Berea College* (Philadelphia–1903).

Schmidt, George P., *The Old Time College President* (New York–1930).

One of the most useful studies of the nineteenth-century college.

Shepardson, Francis W., *Denison University, 1831–1931, a Centennial History* (Granville, Ohio–1931).

Starret, A. L., *Through One Hundred and Fifty Years, the University of Pittsburgh* (Pittsburgh–1937).

Stephens, L. V., *The Story of the Founding of Lane; Address Delivered at the Centennial of Lane Theological Seminary, June 25, 1929.*

Taylor, James Monroe, *Before Vassar Opened* (Boston–1914).

Tewksbury, Donald G., *The Founding of American Colleges and Universities Before the Civil War* (New York–1932).

Thwing, Charles F., *American Colleges: Their Students and Work* (New York–1879).

Williams, Wolcott B., *History of Olivet College* (Olivet–1901).

Wills, Elbert Vaughan, *The Growth of American Higher Education, Liberal, Professional and Technical* (Philadelphia–c. 1936).

A brief, but suggestive, recent outline survey.

10. Books and Pamphlets on the Reform Movement

Allen, Devere, *The Fight for Peace* (New York–1931).

Barnes, Gilbert H., *The Antislavery Impulse* (New York–1933).

A revisionist treatment placing great emphasis on Theodore Weld and the Lane Seminary rebellion. A valuable background for Oberlin history.

Barnes, Gilbert H., and Dumond, Dwight L., *Letters of Theodore Dwight Weld, Angelina Grimke Weld and Sarah Grimke, 1822–1844*, 2 vols. (New York–c. 1934).

The valuable Weld papers which the author used in manuscript. The editors' notes are of great value, though not accurate in every instance.

Blanchard, Jonathan, *A Perfect State of Society* (Oberlin–1839).

Clarke, Lewis and Milton, *Narratives of the Sufferings of ——*, . . . (Boston–1846).

The narrative of fugitive slaves.

Cochran, William C., *The Western Reserve and the Fugitive Slave Law,* The Western Reserve Historical Society, *Collections,* No. 101 (Cleveland—1920).

Coleman, J. W., *Slavery Times in Kentucky* (Chapel Hill, N.C.—1941).

Curti, Merle E., *The American Peace Crusade, 1815–1860* (Durham, N. C.—1929).

The best background for the peace movement at Oberlin.

Peace or War, the American Struggle, 1636–1936 (New York—c. 1936).

Dresser, Amos, *The Bible Against War* (Oberlin—1849).

Dumond, Dwight L., Ed., *Letters of James Gillespie Birney, 1831–1857,* 2 vols. (New York—c. 1938).

Fairchild, James Harris, *Woman's Rights and Duties* (Oberlin—1849).

Woman's Right to the Ballot (Oberlin—1870).

Fitch, Charles, *Slaveholding Weighed in the Balance of Truth and its Comparative Guilt Illustrated* (Boston—1837).

Galpin, William F., *Pioneering for Peace, a Study of American Peace Efforts to 1846* (Syracuse, N. Y.—1933).

Graham, Sylvester, *Lectures on the Science of Human Life,* 2 vols. (Boston—1839).

The key to Grahamism.

Nature's Own Book (New York—1835).

Rules for the Grahamite, recipes, etc.

Green, Beriah, *Four Sermons Preached in the Chapel of the Western Reserve College, On Lord's Days, November 18th and 25th, and December 2nd and 9th, 1832* (Cleveland—1833).

Hitchcock, Edward, *Dyspepsy Forestalled & Resisted: or Lectures on Diet, Regimen, & Employment: Delivered to the Students of Amherst College: Spring Term, 1830* (Amherst—1830).

Ingraham, S. R., *Walks of Usefulness, or, Reminiscences of Mrs. Margaret Prior* (New York—1844).

A publication of the American Female Moral Reform Society by the secretary.

James, Henry Field, *Abolitionism Unveiled; or its Origin, Progress, and Pernicious Tendency Fully Developed* (Cincinnati—1856).

Includes gossip with regard to Oberlin.

Jennings, Isaac, *The Philosophy of Human Life* (Cleveland—1852).

A Treatise on Man's Physical Being and Disorders, Embracing an

Outline of a Theory of Human Life and a Theory of Disease—Its Nature, Cause, and Remedy (Oberlin—1847).

The Tree of Life; or Human Degeneracy; Its Nature and Remedy, as Based on the Elevating Principle of Orthopathy (New York—1867).

Krout, John A., *The Origins of Prohibition* (New York—1925).
The best source on the early nineteenth century temperance movement.

Lloyd, Arthur Young, *The Slavery Controversy, 1831–1860* (Chapel Hill, N. C.—1939).
From the point of view of the "unreconstructed rebel."

Martineau, Harriet, *Martyr Age of the United States of America* (New Castle-upon-Tyne-1840).
Propaganda for the cause of Oberlin in England by the distinguished English woman traveller, author, and liberal.

[Oberlin Village], *An Expression of the Public Sentiment of the Inhabitants of Oberlin in Reference to the Commencement of the Sale of Intoxicating Drinks in the Village* (Oberlin—1852).

Phelps, Amos A., *Lectures on Slavery and Its Remedy* (Boston—1834).
Evidence of John Jay Shipherd's early abolitionism.

Phelps, Christina, *The Anglo-American Peace Movement in the Mid-Nineteenth Century* (New York—1930).

Rankin, John, *A Review of the Statement of the Faculty of Lane Seminary in Relation to the Recent Difficulties in That Institution* (Ripley, Ohio—1835).

Shipherd, Jacob R., *History of the Oberlin-Wellington Rescue* (Boston—1859).
The most complete collection of material on the rescue and trial.

[Shipherd, John J.], *An Appeal to Patriots, Philanthropists and Christians, in Behalf of Our Endangered Republic, and Its Suffering Members* (Elyria—1832).

Siebert, William H., *The Underground Railroad from Slavery to Freedom* (New York—1898).

Smith, T. C., *The Liberty and Free Soil Parties in the Northwest* (New York—1897).

Stanton, Henry B., *Sketches of Reforms and Reformers of Great Britain and Ireland* (New York—1850).
By a Lane Rebel. Useful for the situation in Great Britain.

Stowe, Harriet Beecher, *The Edmondson Family and the Capture of the Schooner Pearl* (Cincinnati—1856).
Reprinted from the *Key to Uncle Tom's Cabin.*

Tanser, H. A., *The Settlement of Negroes in Kent County, Ontario, and a Study of the Mental Capacity of Their Descendants* (London, Ont.?—c. 1939).

Webster, Delia A., *Kentucky Jurisprudence, A History of the Trial of Miss Delia A. Webster* . . . (Vergennes, Vt.—1845).

[Weld, Theodore D., etc.], *A Statement of the Reasons Which Induced the Students of Lane Seminary to Dissolve Their Connection with that Institution* (Cincinnati—1830).

Woodson, Carter G., *The Mind of the Negro as Reflected in Letters Written During the Crisis, 1800, 1860* (Washington—c. 1926).

11. Books and Pamphlets on State and Local History

Ambler, C. H., *A History of West Virginia* (New York—1933).

Armstrong, Robert Grenville, *Amherst's* (Amherst, Ohio) *Story* (n.p.—1914).

Boynton, Washington Wallace, *The Early History of Lorain County,* . . . (Elyria, O.—1876).

Burkett, Charles W., *History of Ohio Agriculture* (Concord, N. H.—1900).

Fairchild, James Harris, *Early Settlement and History of Brownhelm* (Oberlin—1867).

Flick, A. C., *History of the State of New York,* 10 vols. (New York—1933–37).

Galbreath, C. B., *History of Ohio,* 5 vols. (Chicago—1925).

Greve, Charles Theodore, *The Centennial History of Cincinnati,* 2 vols., (Chicago—1904).

Himes, George H., *Souvenir of the Eighty-Second Anniversary of the Organization of the First American Civil Government West of the Rocky Mountains* . . . (Portland, Oregon—1925).

History of Cincinnati and Hamilton County (Cincinnati—1894).

Howe, Henry, *Historical Collections of Ohio* (Cincinnati—1848 and later editions).

Orcutt, Samuel, and Beardsley, Ambrose, *The History of the Old Town of Derby, Connecticut, 1642–1880* (Springfield, Mass.—1880).

O'Reilly, Henry, *Sketches of Rochester, with Incidental Notices of Western New York* . . . (Rochester—1838).

Peck, W. F., *Semi-Centennial History of Rochester* (Syracuse—1884).

Pierce, Bessie L., *History of Chicago,* 2 vols., (New York—1937 and 1939).

Randall, Emilius O., and Ryan, David J., *History of Ohio,* 4 vols. (New York—1912).

Roseboom, Eugene H., and Weisenburger, Francis P., *History of Ohio* (New York—1934).

Stone, L. G., and Haynes, T. E., *History of Strongsville, Ohio* (Berea, O.—1901).

Thompson, Zadock, *History of Vermont, Natural, Civil and Statistical* . . . (Burlington—1842).

Townshend, Norton Strange, *The Agriculture of Lorain County* (Columbus—1867).

Wager, Daniel E., *Our Country and its People, a Descriptive Work on Oneida County, New York* (Boston—1896).

Webber, A. R., *Early History of Elyria and Her People* (Elyria—1930).

Weisenburger, Francis P., *The Passing of the Frontier, 1825–1850* (Columbus—1941), vol. III of Carl Wittke, *History of the State of Ohio.*

Wright, George Frederick, *Standard History of Lorain County, Ohio* (Chicago and New York—1916).

12. Books and Pamphlets on Churches and Religion

[Andover Theological Seminary], *Religious Condition of Colleges, February 18, 1857* (n.p.—n.d.).

Barton, William E., *The Law of Congregational Usage* (Chicago—1916).

Beard, Augustus F., *A Crusade of Brotherhood, a History of the American Missionary Association* (New York—c. 1909).

Boynton, C. B., and others, *Semi-Centennial Celebration of the Vine St. Congregational Church, Cincinnati, Ohio, Sunday, April 10, 1881* (n.p.—n.d.).

Bradley, D. B., *Letters to American Churches* (Oberlin—1848).

Cady, George L., *The American Missionary Association and the Churches of the Midwest before 1861* [New York—1936?].

Canfield, S. B., *et al., An Exposition of the Peculiarities, Difficulties and Tendencies of Oberlin Perfectionism* (Cleveland—1841).
An unfriendly statement.

Cowles, Henry, *A Defense of Ohio Congregationalism and of Oberlin College* [Oberlin–1856?].

Holiness of Christians in the Present Life (Oberlin–1840).

Tracts on the Holiness Practicable to Christians in the Present Life, No. 1, Rochester Convention, July, 1841 (Oberlin–1841).

Douglas, Truman O., *The Pilgrims of Iowa* (Boston–c. 1911).

Fairchild, James Harris, *History of the Congregational Church of Brownhelm* (Oberlin–1895).

Finney, Charles Grandison, *The Character, Claims and Practical Workings of Freemasonry* (Cincinnati–c. 1869).

Guide to the Savior (Oberlin–1848).

Lectures on Revivals of Religion (New York–1835).

Lectures on Systematic Theology (Oberlin–1847).

Letters on Revivals (Oswego, N. Y.–1845).

Foster, Frank Hugh, *A Genetic History of New England Theology* (Chicago–1907).

Fowler, P. H., *Historical Sketch of Presbyterianism within the Bounds of the Synod of Central New York* (Utica, N. Y.–1877).

This is the most valuable published source on the personalities associated with Finney in this region.

Freewill Baptists, *Centennial Record of –, 1780–1880* (Dover, N. H.–1881).

Frost, John, *et al., A Narrative of the Revival of Religion in the County of Oneida . . . in the Year 1826* (Utica–1826).

Gillett, E. H., *History of the Presbyterian Church in the United States*, 2 vols. (Philadelphia–1864).

Hallock, G. B. F., and Motley, Maude, *A Living Church, The First Hundred Years of the Brick Church in Rochester* (Rochester–1925).

Hart, Jeannette, *et al., Pilgrim Church, History and Directory, 1859–1929* (Cleveland–n.d.).

Hastings, Walter E., *et al.*, Editors, *A Century with Central Church* [Rochester, N. Y.], *1836–1936* (Rochester–1936).

Hotchkin, James H., *History of the Purchase and Settlement of Western New York and of the Rise, Progress, and Present State of the Presbyterian Church in That Section* (New York–1848).

Keep, John, *Congregationalism and Church Action: with the Principles of Christian Union, etc.* (New York–1845).

Nature and Operations of Christian Benevolence, a Sermon Delivered October 21, 1818 before the Directors of the Domestic Mis-

sionary Society of Massachusetts Proper at Northampton (Northampton—1818).

Narrative of the Origin and Progress of the Congregational Church in Homer, Cortland County, N. Y. (Homer—1833).

Keller, Charles R., *The Second Great Awakening in Connecticut* (New Haven, Conn.—1942).

Kennedy, William S., *The Plan of Union, or a History of the Presbyterian and Congregational Churches of the Western Reserve . . .* (Hudson, Ohio—1856).

Primarily an attack on Oberlin.

Leonard, Delavan L., *A Century of Congregationalism in Ohio* (Oberlin—1896).

A Hundred Years of Missions (New York and London—1903).

Ludlow, Arthur C., *The Old Stone Church, the Story of a Hundred Years, 1820–1920* (Cleveland—1920).

Mahan, Asa, *Scripture Doctrine of Christian Perfection* (Boston—1839).

The Doctrine of the Will (New York—1845).

Michigan Congregational Association, *The Congregational Churches of Michigan for the First Fifty Years of Their Organization into a State Association* (n.p. [1892]).

Mode, Peter G., *The Frontier Spirit in American Christianity* (New York—1928).

Mostly from the Baptist point of view.

Moore, R. Braden, *History of Huron Presbytery* (Philadelphia—1892).

Morgan, John, *The Holiness Acceptable to God* (Oberlin—1846).

Nichols, L. Nelson, *History of the Broadway Tabernacle of New York City* (New Haven, Conn.—1940).

North, Earl R., *et al., One Hundred and Fifty Years of Presbyterianism in the Ohio Valley, 1790–1940* (Cincinnati—1941).

Parsons, Levi, *History of Rochester Presbytery* (Rochester—1889).

Robinson, Charles Mulford, *First Church Chronicles, 1815–1915, Centennial History of the First Presbyterian Church, Rochester, New York* (Rochester—1915).

Schell, James Perry, *In the Ojibway Country* (Walhalla, North Dakota—1911).

An account of the Congregational missions in Minnesota and Dakota.

Sears, Clara M., *Days of Delusion, a Strange Bit of History* (Boston–1924).
A history of the Millerites.

Shipherd, John Jay, *The Sabbath School Guide; or, a Selection of Interesting and Profitable Scripture Lessons, Illustrated and Applied, by Questions and Answers. Designed as a Permanent System of Sabbath School Instruction, No. 1* (Burlington, Vermont–1828).

Sweet, William Warren, *Religion on the American Frontier, 1783–1850:* vol. II, *The Presbyterians* (New York–1936), vol. III, *The Congregationalist* (Chicago–c. 1939).

Tappan, Lewis, *History of the American Missionary Association* (New York–1855).

Thompson, George, *Letters to Sabbath School Children on Africa,* 3 vols. (Cincinnati–1855 and 1858).
The Palm Land (Cincinnati–1859).
Thompson in Africa (New York–1852).

Walker, Williston, *The Creeds and Platforms of Congregationalism* (New York–1893).

Ward, F. DeW., *Churches of Rochester, Ecclesiastical History of Rochester, N. Y. . . .* (Rochester–1871).

Ward, Susan H., *The History of the Broadway Tabernacle Church from its Organization in 1840 to the Close of 1900, Including Factors Influencing Its Formation* (New York–1901).

Warfield, Benjamin B., *Perfectionism,* 2 vols. (New York–1931)
The Calvinist-Princeton viewpoint.

Weeks, William R., *Pastoral Letter of the Oneida Association, to the Churches under their Care, on the Subject of Revivals of Religion* (Utica–1827).

Woods, Leonard, *Examination of the Doctrine of Perfection as Held by Rev. Asa Mahan . . . Rev. Charles Fitch and Others Agreeing with Them* (Rochester–1841).

13. Books and Pamphlets—Travel and Travellers

Albion, Richard G., *The Rise of New York Port, 1815–1860* (N. Y.–1939).
Square-Riggers on Schedule (Princeton–1938).

Burke, Mrs. Emily Pillsbury, *Reminiscences of Georgia . . .* (J. M. Fitch [Oberlin]–1850).

Burns, Jabez, *Notes of a Tour in the United States and Canada in the Summer and Autumn of 1847* (London–1848).

Dunbar, Seymour, *A History of Travel in America,* 4 vols. (Indianapolis [1915]).

Farnham, Thomas J., "Travels in the Great Western Prairies" in Thwaites, Reuben Gold, *Early Western Travels,* XXVIII (Cleveland—1906).

Fletcher, Robert S., *Going West to College in the Thirties,* Oberlin College Library, *Bulletin,* II, no. 1 (Oberlin—1930).

Jex-Blake, Sophia, *A Visit to Some American Schools and Colleges* (London—1867).

Reed, Andrew, and Matheson, James, *A Narrative of the Visit to the American Churches by the Deputation from the Congregational Union of England and Wales,* 2 vols. (New York—1835).

14. Books and Pamphlets on the Civil War and Reconstruction

Cannon, James C., *Record of Service of Company K, 150th O[hio] V[olunteer] I[nfantry], 1864* (n.p.—1903).

[Company C], *Roster of the Survivors of Company C, 7th Ohio Volunteer Infantry* (n.p.—1907).

Cox, Jacob Dolson, *Military Reminiscences of the Civil War* (New York—1900), 2 vols.

Valuable material on the western Virginia campaign by a distinguished Oberlin graduate.

Ellis, John Millott, *Oberlin and the American Conflict* (n.p.—n.d.).

Ely, Alfred, *Journal of Alfred Ely, a Prisoner of War in Richmond* (New York—1862).

Emilio, Luis F., *History of the Fifty-fourth Regiment of the Massachusetts Volunteer Infantry, 1863–1865* (Boston—1894).

The best source on the famous Negro regiment in which Oberlin men were enlisted.

Fox, William F., *Regimental Losses in the American Civil War* (Albany—1889).

Freeman, Douglas Southall, *R. E. Lee, a Biography* (N. Y.—1934–1935), 4 vols.

Contains an account of Lee's venture in western Virginia.

Hayes, Philip C., *Journal-History of the Hundred and Third Ohio Volunteer Infantry* (Bryan, Ohio—1872).

Henderson, George Francis Robert, *Stonewall Jackson and the American Civil War* (London—1899), 2 vols.

The best source on the "valley campaigns."

Hesseltine, William Best, *Civil War Prisons, a Study in War Psychology* (Columbus, Ohio—1930).

Jeffrey, W. H., *Richmond Prisons, 1861–1862* (St. Johnsbury [Vermont—c. 1893]).

Kimberly, Robert L., and Holloway, Ephraim S., *The Forty-first Ohio Volunteer Infantry in the War of the Rebellion, 1861–1865* (Cleveland—1897).

Mahan, Asa, *A Critical History of the Late American War* (New York—1877).

Pierce, Paul S., *The Freedman's Bureau* (Iowa City—1904).

Reid, Whitelaw, *Ohio in the War*, 2 vols. (Cincinnati—1868).

Simkins, F. B., and Woody, R. H., *South Carolina During Reconstruction* (Chapel Hill, N. C.—1932).

The Stars and Stripes in Rebeldom, a Series of Papers Written by Federal Prisoners (Privates) in Richmond, Tuscaloosa, New Orleans, and Salisbury, N. C. (Boston—1862).

The reprint of the prison paper issued by Oberlin boys and others.

Swint, Henry Lee, *The Northern Teacher in the South, 1862–1870* (Nashville, Tenn.—1941).

Tourgee, Albion W., *The Story of a Thousand* (Buffalo—1896).

Wilder, Theodore, *The History of Company C, Seventh Regiment, O[hio] V[olunteer] I[nfantry]* (Oberlin—1866).

An interesting, useful and accurate narrative.

Wilson, Lawrence, Editor, *Itinerary of the Seventh Ohio Volunteer Infantry, 1861–1864* (New York—1907).

This book contains the best material on Oberlin's Company C.

Wood, George L., *The Seventh Regiment: a Record* (New York—1865).

15. A Few Books and Pamphlets on Early Oberlin

Ballantine, William Gay, Editor, *The Oberlin Jubilee 1833–1883* (Oberlin—c. 1883).

Fairchild, Edward Henry, *Historical Sketch of Oberlin College* (Springfield—1868).

Fairchild, James Harris, *Oberlin: its Origin, Progress and Results, An Address, Prepared for the Alumni of Oberlin College, Assembled August 22, 1860* (Oberlin—1860).

Oberlin: the Colony and the College, 1833–1883 (Oberlin—1883).

The classic reminiscences of a student, teacher and president.

Fletcher, Robert S., and Wilkins, Ernest H., *The Beginning of College Education for Women and of Coeducation on the College Level,* Oberlin College, *Bulletin,* Mar. 20, 1937.

Fletcher, Robert S., *The Story of the* [Oberlin College] *Libe* (Oberlin —June, 1941).

Hosford, Frances Juliette, *Father Shipherd's Magna Charta, a Century of Coeducation in Oberlin College* (Boston—1937).

A Living Stone, the Story of the First Church in Oberlin [Oberlin (?)—1933].

Leonard, Delavan L., *The Story of Oberlin* (Boston and Chicago—1898).

The most useful general history.

Phillips, Wilbur H., *Oberlin Colony, the Story of a Century* (Oberlin—1933).

Reproduces the interesting colony map of 1836.

Shumway, A. L., and Brower, C. De W., *Oberliniana* (Cleveland [1883]).

Traditions as collected by two students.

Smith, Delazon, *A History of Oberlin or New Lights of the West* (Cleveland—1837). Cover title: *Oberlin Unmasked.*

Malicious scandal and unpleasant truth.

Strieby, Michael E., *Oberlin and the American Missionary Association* (Oberlin—1891).

16. Miscellaneous Books and Pamphlets

[Browne, Charles F.], *The Complete Works of Artemus Ward* (London—1900).

Cobb, J. H., *A Manual Containing Information Respecting the Growth of the Mulberry Tree, with Suitable Directions for the Culture of Silk. In Three Parts.* (Boston—1833).

Demaree, A. L., *The American Agricultural Press, 1819–1860* (N. Y. —1941).

Howard, John Tasker, *Our American Music* (New York—c. 1930 and 1931).

[Locke, David Ross] Petroleum V. Nasby, *The Struggles (Social, Financial and Political) of Petroleum V. Nasby* (Boston—c. 1872), 44–46.

Monroe, James, *Oberlin Thursday Lectures* (Oberlin—1897).

INDEX

INDEX